THE
Hinge
of Fate

★★★★

The Second World War

★ ★ ★ ★

THE Hinge of Fate

Winston S. Churchill

HOUGHTON MIFFLIN COMPANY BOSTON

The Riverside Press Cambridge

1950

PRINTED IN THE UNITED STATES OF AMERICA BY KINGSPORT PRESS, INC., KINGSPORT, TENNESSEE

★

PREFACE

IN *The Gathering Storm, Their Finest Hour,* and *The Grand Alliance* I have described as I saw them the events leading to the Second World War, the conquest of Europe by Nazi Germany, the unflinching resistance of Britain alone until the German attack on Russia and the Japanese assault brought the Soviet Union and the United States to our side.

In Washington, at the turn of the year, President Roosevelt and I, supported by our Chief Military and Naval Advisers, proclaimed *The Grand Alliance,* and prescribed the main strategy for the future conduct of the war. We had now to face the onslaught of Japan.

Such was the scene when on January 17, 1942, I landed at Plymouth; and here the tale of this volume begins.

Again it is told from the standpoint of the British Prime Minister, with special responsibility, as Minister of Defence, for military affairs. Again I rely upon the series of my directives, telegrams, and minutes, which owe their importance and interest to the moment in which they were written, and which I could not write in better words now. These original documents were dictated by me as events broke upon us. As they are my own composition, written at the time, it is by these that I prefer to be judged. It would be easier to produce a series of afterthoughts when the answers to all the riddles were known, but I must leave this to the historians who will in due course be able to pronounce their considered judgments.

I have called this volume *The Hinge of Fate* because in it we turn from almost uninterrupted disaster to almost unbroken success. For the first six months of this story all went ill; for the last six months everything went well. And this agreeable change continued to the end of the struggle.

WINSTON S. CHURCHILL

Chartwell,
Westerham,
Kent
September 1, 1950

★

ACKNOWLEDGMENTS

I MUST AGAIN ACKNOWLEDGE the assistance of those who helped me with the previous volumes, namely, Lieutenant-General Sir Henry Pownall, Commodore G. R. G. Allen, Colonel F. W. Deakin, and Sir Edward Marsh, Mr. Denis Kelly, and Mr. C. C. Wood. I have also to thank the very large number of others who have kindly read these pages and commented upon them.

Lord Ismay has continued to give me his aid, as have my other friends.

I record my obligation to His Majesty's Government for permission to reproduce the text of certain official documents of which the Crown Copyright is legally vested in the Controller of His Majesty's Stationery Office. At the request of His Majesty's Government, on security grounds I have paraphrased some of the telegrams published in this volume. These changes have not altered in any way the sense or substance of the telegrams.

I wish to acknowledge my debt to Captain Samuel Eliot Morison, U.S.N.R., whose books on naval operations give a clear presentation of the actions of the United States Fleet.

I am indebted to the Roosevelt Trust for the use they have permitted of the President's telegrams quoted here, and also to others who have allowed their private letters to be published.

★

MORAL OF THE WORK

In War: Resolution
In Defeat: Defiance
In Victory: Magnanimity
In Peace: Good Will

★

THEME OF THE VOLUME

How the power of the
Grand Alliance
became preponderant

CONTENTS

Book One

THE ONSLAUGHT OF JAPAN

Book Two
AFRICA REDEEMED

MAPS AND DIAGRAMS

★

Book One

THE ONSLAUGHT OF JAPAN

1

Australasian Anxieties

The New Shape of the War — Assurance of Final Victory — Anglo-American Nakedness in the Pacific — Potential Impact of Japan upon Australia and New Zealand — My Correspondence with Mr. Curtin — His Appeal to President Roosevelt — Mr. Bowden's Reports of the Peril of Singapore — Mr. Curtin's Article in the "Melbourne Herald" — I Accept Full Responsibility for the Distribution of Our Resources — My Reply to Mr. Curtin of January 3 — And of January 14 — Safe Arrival of the First Convoy at Singapore — Explanations to New Zealand — Mr. Curtin's Cable of January 18, and My Answer — A General Survey — The Australian Case — The Pacific War Councils in London and Washington Begin to Function.

THIS NEW YEAR of the Second World War, 1942, opened upon us in an entirely different shape for Britain. We were no longer alone. At our side stood two mighty Allies. Russia and the United States were, though for different reasons, irrevocably engaged to fight to the death in the closest concert with the British Empire. This combination made final victory certain unless it broke in pieces under the strain, or unless some entirely new instrument of war appeared in German hands. There was indeed a new instrument of war for which both sides were avidly groping. As it turned out it was into our already stronger hands that the secret of the atomic bomb was destined to fall. A fearful and bloody struggle lay before us and we could not foresee its course, but the end was sure.

The Grand Alliance had now to face the onslaught of Japan.

3

This had been long prepared, and fell upon the British and American fronts — if such they could be called — with cruel severity. At no moment could it be conceived that Japan would overcome the United States, but heavy forfeits had to be paid by them, in the Philippines and other islands, and by the British and the hapless Dutch in Southeast Asia and the Pacific Ocean. Russia, in mortal grip with the main German Army, suffered only from the Japanese assault by the diversion of Anglo-American energies and supplies which would have aided her. Britain and the United States had a long period of torturing defeats before them which could not affect the final issue but were hard for their peoples to endure. Britain was naked because our strength was absorbed elsewhere, and the Americans had scarcely begun to gather their almost limitless resources. To us in the British Isles it seemed that everything was growing worse, although on reflection we knew that the war was won.

In spite of the heavy new burdens which fell upon us, there was no addition to our dangers at home. Australia and New Zealand, on the other hand, felt suddenly plunged into the forefront of the battle. They saw themselves exposed to the possibility of direct invasion. No longer did the war mean sending aid across the oceans to the Mother Country in her distress and peril. The new foe could strike straight at Australian homes. The enormous coast-lines of their continent could never be defended. All their great cities were on the seaboard. Their only four well-trained divisions of volunteers and the New Zealand Division, all their best officers, were far away across the oceans. The naval command of the Pacific had passed in a flash and for an indefinite period to Japan. Australasian air-power hardly existed. Can we wonder that deep alarm swept Australia or that the thoughts of their Cabinet were centred upon their own affairs?

It will always be deemed remarkable that in this deadly crisis, when, as it seemed to them and their professional advisers, destruction was at the very throat of the Australian Commonwealth, they did not all join together in a common effort. But such was their party phlegm and rigidity that local politics ruled unshaken. The Labour Government, with its majority of two, monopolised the whole executive power, and conscription even for home defence was banned. These partisan decisions did less than justice to the spirit of the Australian nation, and made more difficult our task in providing, so far as possible, for their security while observing a true sense of proportion in world strategy.

The sombre pages of this volume must open with my correspondence with the Australian Prime Minister, Mr. Curtin. Our discussions about the relief of the Australian troops in Tobruk had not been agreeable. Later in the war, in easier times, when he came over to England and we all got to know him well, there was general respect and liking for this eminent and striking Australian personality, and I personally formed with him a friendship which, alas, was cut short by his untimely death. At this moment however, when pressures from all sides were so fierce, I was too conscious of the depth and number of the differences in outlook that divided us, and I regret any traces of impatience which my telegrams may bear.

While in Washington I received a series of messages from Mr. Curtin and Dr. Evatt, Australian Minister for External Affairs, through their representative in Washington, Mr. Casey. Mr. Curtin also sent the following telegram to President Roosevelt.

26 Dec. 41

At this time of great crisis I desire to address you both while you are conferring for the purpose of advancing our common cause.

2. I have already addressed a communication to Mr. Churchill on the question of Russia, which I regard as of great importance in relation to the war with Japan, and which I hope will receive the consideration of you both during the conference.

3. I refer now to a matter of more pressing importance.

4. From all reports it is very evident that in North Malaya the Japanese have assumed control of air and sea. The small British army there includes one Australian division, and we have sent three air squadrons to Malaya and two to the Netherlands East Indies. The army must be provided with air support, otherwise there will

be a repetition of Greece and Crete, and Singapore will be grievously threatened.

5. The fall of Singapore would mean the isolation of the Philippines, the fall of the Netherlands East Indies, and an attempt to smother all other bases. This would also sever our communications between the Indian and Pacific Oceans in this region.

6. The setback would be as serious to the United States' interests as to our own.

7. Reinforcements earmarked by the United Kingdom for dispatch to Malaya seem to us to be utterly inadequate, especially in relation to aircraft, and more particularly fighting aircraft. . . . Small reinforcements are of little avail. In truth, the amount of resistance to the Japanese in Malaya will depend directly on the amount of resistance provided by the Governments of the United Kingdom and the United States.

8. Our men have fought and will fight valiantly. But they must be adequately supported. We have three divisions in the Middle East. Our airmen are fighting in Britain and the Middle East and are training in Canada. We have sent great quantities of supplies to Britain, to the Middle East, and to India. Our resources here are very limited indeed.

9. It is in your power to meet the situation. Should the Government of the United States desire, we would gladly accept an American commander in the Pacific area. The President has said that Australia will be a base of increasing importance, but, in order that it shall remain a base, Singapore must be reinforced.

10. In spite of our great difficulties, we are sending further reinforcements to Malaya.

11. I would be glad if this matter could be regarded as of the greatest urgency.

The reports which Dr. Evatt received from Mr. Bowden, the Commonwealth Commissioner in Singapore, were also transmitted to me. They were grave and proved true.

26 Dec. 41

Reports read today indicate air situation deteriorating daily. Eight British fighters lost yesterday against three or four Japanese. Kuala Lumpur and Port Swettenham are now our advance landing-grounds for air reconnaissance, but difficult even to carry out air reconnaissance in face of Japanese superiority in machines. Greater part of our fighters now withdrawn to Singapore for defence of island and base. Nevertheless, Air Officer Commanding stated that to provide effective fighter escort for naval convoys approaching with sorely needed reinforcements, men, and material, he would have to leave Singapore unguarded.

And further:

I feel I must emphasise that deterioration of war position in Malayan defence is assuming [the aspect of a] landslide collapse of whole defence system. Expected arrival of modern fighter planes in boxes, requiring weeks of assembly, under danger of destruction by bombing, cannot save the position. The renewal of military reinforcements expected will be absorbed in relief of tired front-line troops and will create little difference. British defence policy now concentrates greater part of fighter and anti-aircraft defence of Malaya on Singapore Island to protect naval base, starving forward troops of such defence, including the Australian Imperial Force.

Present measures for reinforcement of Malayan defences can from the practical viewpoint be little more than gestures. In my belief, [the] only thing that might save Singapore would be the immediate dispatch from the Middle East by air of powerful reinforcements, large numbers of the latest fighter aircraft, with ample operationally trained personnel. Reinforcements should be not in brigades but in divisions, and to be of use they must arrive urgently. Anything that is not powerful, modern, and immediate is futile. As things stand at present, the fall of Singapore is to my mind only [a] matter of weeks. If Singapore and A.I.F. in Malaya are to be saved there must be very radical and effective action immediately.

[I] Doubt whether visit of an Australian Minister can now have any effect, as the plain fact is that without immediate air reinforcement Singapore must fall. Need for decision and action is matter of hours, not days.

Dr. Evatt added that in his judgment Bowden's summary set out the position correctly. "If it cannot be met in the way he suggests, the worst can be expected."

* * * * *

On December 27 Mr. Curtin wrote a signed article in the *Melbourne Herald* which was flaunted round the world by our enemies. Among other things he said:

We refuse to accept the dictum that the Pacific struggle must be treated as a subordinate segment of the general conflict. By that it is not meant that any one of the other theatres of war is of less importance than the Pacific, but that Australia asks for a concerted plan evoking the greatest strength at the Democracies' disposal, determined upon hurling Japan back.

The Australian Government therefore regards the Pacific struggle as primarily one in which the United States and Australia must have the fullest say in the direction of the Democracies' fighting plan.

Without any inhibitions of any kind, I make it quite clear that Australia looks to America, free of any pangs as to our traditional links with the United Kingdom.

We know the problems that the United Kingdom faces. We know the constant threat of invasion. We know the dangers of dispersal of strength. But we know too that Australia can go, and Britain can still hold on.

We are therefore determined that Australia shall not go, and we shall exert all our energies toward the shaping of a plan, with the United States as its keystone, which will give to our country some confidence of being able to hold out until the tide of battle swings against the enemy.

Summed up, Australian external policy will be shaped toward obtaining Russian aid, and working out, with the United States, as the major factor, a plan of Pacific strategy, along with British, Chinese, and Dutch forces.

This produced the worst impression both in high American circles and in Canada. I was sure that these outpourings of anxiety, however understandable, did not represent Australian feeling. Mr. W. M. Hughes, Australian Prime Minister in the First World War and leader of the Federal United Australia Party (the famous "Billy Hughes"), immediately said that it would be "suicidal and a false and dangerous policy for Australia to regard Britain's support as being less important than that of other great associated countries." There was a keen controversy in Australia. I cabled from Washington to Mr. Attlee: "I hope there will be no pandering to this, while at the same time we do all in human power to come to their aid. . . ." I weighed painfully in my mind the idea of making a broadcast direct to the Australian people. At the same time I fully accepted the responsibility which fell on me. "I hope you will endeavour to let all issues stand over until I return, so that I may face any opposition myself. . . . If the Malay peninsula has been starved for the sake of Libya and Russia, no one is more responsible than I, and I would do exactly the same again. Should any questions be asked in Parliament I should be glad if it could be stated that I particularly desire to answer them myself on my return."

I replied at once to Mr. Curtin on the military position:

Prime Minister to Mr. Curtin   3 Jan. 42

General Wavell's command area is limited to the fighting zone where active operations are now proceeding. Henceforward it does not include Australia, New Zealand, and communications between the United States and Australia, or indeed any other ocean communications. This does not of course mean that these vital regions and communications are to be left without protection so far as our resources admit. In our view, the American Navy should assume the responsibility for the communications, including the islands right up to the Australian or New Zealand coast. This is what we are pressing for. Admiral King has only just been given full powers over the whole of the American Navy, and he has not yet accepted our views. Obviously, if I cannot persuade the Americans to take over, we shall have to fill the gap as best we can, but I still hope our views will be accepted, in which case of course any vessels we or you have in that area will come under United States direction while operating there. There never has been any intention to make the main Allied concentration in the newly defined Southwest Pacific theatre, and I do not know where you got this from. . . .

Night and day I am labouring here to make the best arrangements possible in your interests and for your safety, having regard to the other theatres and the other dangers which have to be met from our limited resources. It is only a little while ago that you

were most strongly urging the highest state of equipment for the
Australian Army in the Middle East. The battle there is still not
finished, though the prospects are good. It would have been folly
to spoil Auchinleck's battle by diverting aircraft, tanks, etc., to the
Malay peninsula at a time when there was no certainty that Japan
would enter the war. The ease-up of the Caucasian danger through
the Russian victories and the Auchinleck successes have made possible the considerable reinforcements, at the temporary expense of
the Middle East, of which you have been advised, and which are
also justified because Malaya has now become a war theatre. . . .

Continuous interchanges took place between me and
Mr. Curtin.

Prime Minister of Australia to Prime Minister   11 Jan. 42

It is naturally disturbing to learn that the Japanese have been
able to overrun so easily the whole of Malaya except Johore and
that the Commander-in-Chief considers that certain risks have to
be accepted even now in carrying on his plan for the defence of
this limited area.

It is observed that the 8th Australian Division is to be given
the task of fighting the decisive battle. The Government has no
doubt that it will acquit itself in accordance with the highest traditions of the Australian Imperial Force. However, I urge on you
that nothing be left undone to reinforce Malaya to the greatest
degree possible in accordance with my earlier representations and
your intentions. I am particularly concerned in regard to air
strength, as a repetition of the Greece and Crete campaigns would
evoke a violent public reaction, and such a happening should be
placed outside the bounds of possibility.

You will be aware of our agreement to the dispatch of the 6th
and 7th Australian Divisions together with Corps troops and maintenance and base organisations from the Middle East to the Netherlands East Indies.

I continued to reassure the Australian Government and
explain more fully our motives in the policy of the united
command of the Southeast Asia theatre. On the eve of my
departure from Washington I summed up our position.

Prime Minister to Prime Minister of Australia 14 Jan. 42

I do not see how any one could expect Malaya to be defended once the Japanese obtained the command of the sea and while we are fighting for our lives against Germany and Italy. The only vital point is Singapore Fortress and its essential hinterland. Personally, my anxiety has been lest in fighting rearguard actions down the peninsula to gain time, we should dissipate the force required for the prolonged defence of Singapore. Out of the equivalent of four divisions available for that purpose, one has been lost and another mauled to gain a month or six weeks' time. Some may think it would have been better to have come back quicker with less loss.

2. It is clearly our duty to give all support to decisions of the Supreme Commander. *We* cannot judge from our distant post whether it is better to fight on the northwestern side of the peninsula at some risk to Mersing, or whether all troops should now withdraw into the island fortress. Personally, I believe Wavell is right, and that view is supported by the Chiefs of Staff. I feel sure that you will agree to most of this.

3. I have great confidence that your troops will acquit themselves in the highest fashion in the impending battles. Everything is being done to reinforce Singapore and the hinterland. Two convoys bearing the 4th Indian Brigade Group and its transports have got through, and a very critical convoy containing the leading brigade of the British 18th Division is timed to arrive on 13th. I am naturally anxious about these 4500 men going through the Straits of Sunda in a single ship. I hope however they will arrive in time to take their stand with their Australian brothers. I send you the full details of what we have on the move towards this important battlefield, with the dates of arrival. There is justification in this for Wavell's hope that a counter-stroke will be possible in the latter part of February.

4. You are aware, no doubt, that I have proposed your withdrawal of two Australian divisions from Palestine to the new theatre of so much direct interest to Australia. The only limiting factor on their movement will be the shipping. We shall have to do our best to replace them from home.

5. I do not accept any censure about Crete and Greece. We are doing our utmost in the Mother Country to meet living perils and onslaughts. We have sunk all party differences and have imposed

universal compulsory service, not only upon men, but women. We
have suffered the agonising loss of two of our finest ships which we
sent to sustain the Far Eastern war. We are organising from reduced forces the utmost further naval aid. In the battle of Libya,
British and Empire losses to January 7 are reported at 1200 officers
and 16,000 men, out of the comparatively small force it is possible
to maintain forward in the Desert. A heavy battle around Agheila
seems to be impending. We have successfully disengaged Tobruk,
after previously relieving all your men who so gallantly held it for
so long. I hope therefore you will be considerate in the judgment
which you pass upon those to whom Australian lives and fortunes
are so dear.

Here at least was good news:

Prime Minister to Mr. Curtin   14 Jan. 42
    The vital convoy, including the American transport *Mount
Vernon,* carrying fifty Hurricanes, one anti-tank regiment, fifty
guns; one heavy anti-aircraft regiment, fifty guns; one light anti-
aircraft regiment, fifty guns; and the 54th British Infantry Brigade
Group, total about 9000, reached Singapore safely and punctually
yesterday.

Mr. Fraser also expressed his anxieties, and I replied:

Prime Minister to Prime Minister of New Zealand   17 Jan. 42
    I welcome, as always, the frank expression of your views, with
which, in the main, I am much in sympathy, and the well-balanced
reasoning with which you have presented them to me.
    2. The Government and people of New Zealand have always
adopted a helpful and realist attitude to this war, which, beginning in the narrow confines of Europe, has gradually spread over
almost the entire world and is now at the doorstep of New Zealand.
    3. If you have thought us unmindful of your necessities in the
past, although indeed we have never been so, I can assure you that
the vast distance in miles which separates London from Wellington
will not cause us to be unmindful of you or leave you comfortless
in your hour of peril.
    4. You will, I am sure, forgive me if in the time at my disposal
I do not take up each of your points in detail. From the telegram

which you have now received, since sending your telegram to me, you will know of the army and air reinforcements which we and America are sending to you. The establishment of a new Anzac naval area will, I hope, also be agreeable to you.

Moreover, the United States contemplate the dispatch at an early date of considerable land and air forces to the Far East area.

5. Nevertheless, you would not expect me to make promises of support which cannot be fulfilled, or of the early redress of a situation in the Far East which must take time to rectify, as rectified it will be.

6. I sense your [reproach at our] having been misled by a too complacent expression of military opinion in the past on probable dangers in the Pacific area in general and to New Zealand in particular. But who could have foretold the serious opening setback which the United States Fleet suffered on December 7, with all that this and subsequent losses of our two fine ships entail?

The events of this war have been consistently unpredictable, and not all to our disadvantage. I am not sure that the German General Staff have always forecast events with unerring accuracy. For example, the Battle of Britain, the Battle of the Atlantic, and the Russian resistance must have shaken Hitler's faith in careful calculation of military appreciations.

*   *   *   *   *

In due course Mr. Curtin replied to my telegram of the 14th.

Prime Minister of Australia to Prime Minister   18 Jan. 42

I do not understand how you can read into my telegram any expression of opinion that we expected the whole of Malaya to be defended without superiority of sea-power.

2. On the contrary, if you refer to the Australian Government's cable of December 1, 1941, on the report of the first Singapore Conference you will read the following, which unfortunately has proved rather too true a forecast:

"The general conclusion reached by the delegation was that in the absence of a main fleet in the Far East the forces and equipment at present available in this area for the defence of Malaya are totally inadequate to meet a major attack by Japan."

3. The United Kingdom Chiefs of Staff laid down the strengths of:

   (i) Land forces considered necessary for the defence of Malaya.
  (ii) The total quantity of equipment to be provided for the
       forces in (i).
 (iii) The air forces required "to give a fair degree of security"
       to Malaya.

4. We have contributed what we could in land and air forces
and material to this region and consistently pressed for the strengthening of the defences, but there have been suggestions of com-
placency with the position which have not been justified by the
speedy progress of the Japanese. That is why I said in my telegram [of December 5] these events were disturbing. . . .

6. As far back as 1937 the Commonwealth Government received
assurances that it was the aim of the United Kingdom Government
to make Singapore impregnable. When the defence of Singapore
was under survey by the Committee of Imperial Defence in 1933
the [Australian] High Commissioner pointed out the grave effects
that would flow from the loss of Singapore or the denial of its use
to the main fleet. He stated that in the last resort the whole internal defence system of Australia was based on the integrity of
Singapore and the presence of a capital fleet there. He added that,
if this was not a reasonable possibility, Australia, in balancing a
doubtful naval security against invasion, would have to provide
for greater land and air forces as a deterrent against such risk. I
repeat these earlier facts to make quite clear the conception of the
Empire and local defence in which we have been brought to believe. It has also influenced our decision on co-operation in other
theatres from the relatively small resources we possess in relation
to our commitments in a Pacific war.

7. My observations on Crete and Greece imply no censure on
you, nor am I passing judgment on anyone, but there is no denying
the fact that air support was not on the scale promised. . . . I have
stated this position frankly to the Australian people because I believe it is better that they should know the facts than assume that
all is well and later be disillusioned by the truth.

8. No one has a greater admiration for the magnificent efforts
of the people of the United Kingdom than their kinsfolk in Australia. Nevertheless, we make no apologies for our effort, or even
for what you argue we are not doing. The various parts of the
Empire, as you know, are differently situated, possess various resources, and have their own peculiar problems.

It was my duty to make the fullest allowance for the alarm which racked the Commonwealth Government and the dangers which beset them. I could not however forbear a reference to the strong support which Australian political parties, particularly the Labour Party, had given before the war both to the neglect of our defences and to the policy of appeasement. As this telegram sums up the position I felt myself entitled to take, it should be printed here.

Prime Minister to Mr. Curtin   19 Jan. 42

I thank you for your frank expression of views. I have no responsibility for the neglect of our defences and policy of appeasement which preceded the outbreak of the war. I had been for eleven years out of office, and had given ceaseless warnings for six years before the war began. On the other hand, I accept the fullest responsibility for the main priorities and general distribution of our resources since I became Prime Minister in May, 1940. The eastward flow of reinforcements and aircraft from this Island has been maintained from that date forward to the utmost limit of our shipping capacity and other means of moving aircraft and tanks. I deemed the Middle East a more urgent theatre than the new-christened A.B.D.A. area. We had also to keep our promises to Russia of munitions deliveries. No one could tell what Japan would do, but I was sure that if she attacked us and you the United States would enter the war and that the safety of Australia and ultimate victory would be assured.

2. It must be remembered that only three months ago we faced in the Middle East, where the Australian Imperial Force lay, the threat of a double attack by Rommel from the west and the overrunning of the Caucasus, Persia, Syria, and Iraq from the north. In such a plight all the teachings of war show that everything should be concentrated on destroying one of the attacking forces. I thought it best to make a job of Rommel while forming with the rest of our resources the best Levant-Caspian front possible. This latter was largely beyond our resources. Since then two-thirds of Rommel's army has been destroyed, and Cyrenaica cleared, but only by a very narrow margin. In fact, it hung in the balance at the moment when Auchinleck superseded Cunningham.

3. Although I cannot promise total destruction of Rommel, we

have at least gained a very substantial success, which has already
rid us of one serious danger and liberated important forces. At
the same time the tremendous, unexpected resistance of Russia has
given a considerable breathing-space, and it may be more, on the
Levant-Caspian front. Thus we are able to move the 17th Indian
Division and soon several other Indian infantry divisions previously
assigned to the Levant-Caspian front, together with the 18th British and the 6th and 7th Australian Divisions, with substantial aircraft and some armoured forces, from the Middle to the Far Eastern
theatre. This we are doing with all speed. You may judge how
melancholy our position would have been if we had been beaten
by Rommel, and if the Caucasus, the Baku oil-wells, and Persia
had been overrun by the enemy. I am sure it would have been
wrong to send forces needed to beat Rommel to reinforce the Malay
peninsula while Japan was still at peace. To try to be safe everywhere is to be strong nowhere.

4. We have to be thankful, first, for the Russian victories, secondly, for our good success against Rommel, and, thirdly, that the
United States was attacked by Japan at the same time as ourselves.
The blame for the frightful risks we have had to run, and will
have to run, rests with all those who, in or out of office, failed to
discern the Nazi menace and to crush it while it was weak.

5. No one could foresee the series of major naval disasters which
befell us and the United States around the turn of the year 1941–
42. In an hour the American naval superiority in the Pacific was
for the time being swept away. In another hour the *Prince of
Wales* and *Repulse* were sunk. Thus the Japanese gained the temporary command of Pacific waters, and no doubt we have further
grievous punishment to face in the Far East. In this new crisis
affecting you I should have approved the sending of the three fast
Mediterranean battleships to form, with the four "Rs" and the
Warspite, just repaired, a new fleet in the Indian Ocean, to move
to your protection as might be most helpful.

6. I have already told you of the *Barham* being sunk. I must
now inform you that the *Queen Elizabeth* and *Valiant* have both
sustained underwater damage from a "human torpedo," which put
them out of action, one for three and the other for six months.
As the enemy do not yet know about these three last-mentioned
ships, you will see that we have no need to enlighten them, and I
must ask you to keep this last deadly secret to yourself alone.

7. However, these evil conditions will pass. By May the United States will have a superior fleet at Hawaii. We have encouraged them to take their two new battleships out of the Atlantic if they need them, thus taking more burden upon ourselves. We are sending two, and possibly three, out of our four modern air-craft-carriers to the Indian Ocean. *Warspite* will soon be there, and thereafter *Valiant*. Thus the balance of sea-power in the Indian and Pacific Oceans will, in the absence of further misfortunes, turn decisively in our favour, and all Japanese overseas operations will be deprived of their present assurance. Meanwhile we are try-ing to make up by air-power in the Mediterranean our lack of a battle fleet, and the impending arrival of *Anson* [our latest battle-ship] and complete working up of *Duke of York* enable us to face large reductions in American strength in the Atlantic for the sake of the Pacific.

8. We must not be dismayed or get into recrimination, but re-main united in true comradeship. Do not doubt my loyalty to Australia and New Zealand. I cannot offer any guarantees for the future, and I am sure great ordeals lie before us, but I feel hopeful as never before that we shall emerge safely, and also gloriously, from the dark valley.

The following answer was received:

Prime Minister of Australia to Prime Minister   22 Jan. 42

I appreciate your full reply and reciprocate your sentiments on the unity of our efforts.

2. Just as you foresaw events in Europe, so we feel that we saw the trend of the Pacific situation more clearly than was realised in London.

3. Events have unfortunately justified our views regarding Malaya, and I am very disturbed by reports from Gordon Bennett as to the seriousness of the position.

4. The long-distance programme you outline is encouraging, but the great need is in the immediate future. The Japanese are going to take a lot of repelling, and in the meantime may do very vital damage to our capacity to eject them from the areas they are capturing.

The Australians' claim that they had understood and fore-

seen the dangers in the Far East and from Japan better than I
had done in London can only be judged in relation to the war
as a whole. It was their duty to study their own position with
concentrated attention. We had to try to think for all.

*   *   *   *   *

I reported to the Prime Ministers of Australia and New
Zealand on the final form of the machinery that it was proposed
to set up in London for securing full and continuous association of the Australian, New Zealand, and Netherlands Governments in the whole conduct of the war against Japan.

19 Jan. 42

A Far Eastern Council [should] be established on the Ministerial
plane. I would preside, and other members would be Lord Privy
Seal (who is my Deputy on the Defence Committee), Duff Cooper,
and representatives of Australia, New Zealand, and the Netherlands. Australian member would presumably be Earle Page, and
New Zealand representative might be the High Commissioner to
begin with. There would also be a Dutch Cabinet Minister. Council would be assisted by a staff group of Dominions Liaison Officers
in consultation with United Kingdom Joint Planners. Duties of
Council [would] be to focus and formulate views of represented
Powers to the President, whose views [would] also be brought before the Council. This [would] not of course interfere with Earle
Page's attending Cabinet as at present when Australian affairs are
affected. Do you agree? Am also consulting Fraser and Netherlands
Government.

The first meeting of the Pacific War Council was held on
February 10. I presided, and others present were the Lord
Privy Seal, the Secretary of State for Foreign Affairs, the Prime
Minister of the Netherlands (Dr. P. S. Gerbrandy), the Nether-
lands Minister (Jonkheer E. Michiels Van Verduynen), Sir
Earle Page (representing Australia), Mr. W. J. Jordan (repre-
senting New Zealand), Mr. Amery (representing India and
Burma), and the Chiefs of Staff. At subsequent meetings China
was also represented. The main function of the Council was

"to review the broad fundamental policies to be followed in the war against Japan throughout the Pacific area."

A Pacific War Council was also set up in Washington, under President Roosevelt, and the two Councils kept in close touch with each other. The last meeting of the Council in London was held in August, 1943. The war continued to be run by the old machinery, but meetings of the Pacific War Councils enabled those countries which were not represented in this permanent machinery to be consulted about what was going on.

All this was soon to be swept away by disastrous events.

2

The Setback in the Desert

*Rommel Effects His Retreat to Agheila — Shortage of Transport
— A Fateful January — My Correspondence with General Auchinleck from Washington — Auchinleck's Confidence Unshaken
— His Intention to Attack in Mid-February — His Telegram of
January 15 — Surrender of Bardia and Halfaya with 14,000
Prisoners to Our XXXth Corps — I Return to London — And Prepare My Statement for Parliament — Rommel Launches a Reconnaissance in Force — Unfavourable News — A Shock: Benghazi!
— Auchinleck Flies to the Advanced Headquarters — His Telegram of January 26 — Rommel Pursues His Advantage — Evacuation of Benghazi — Auchinleck's Reports of January 29 and
January 31 — We Retreat Nearly Three Hundred Miles — An
Extraordinary Turn of Fortune — Numbers and Quality of British Armour — The Case of the 1st Armoured Division — A
Far-Reaching Reverse.*

THE PREVIOUS VOLUME has described General Auchinleck's long-prepared victory in the Western Desert and the relief of Tobruk. I had felt able, during my visit to Washington, to speak with confidence about his future operations. Rommel however contrived to withdraw his forces in good order to a position running south from Gazala. Here he was attacked by the XIIIth Corps under General Godwin-Austen, and on December 16, after a three-day action, forced to retreat. Our mobile forces tried by moving round the Desert Flank to block his withdrawal along the coast roads leading to Benghazi. Bad weather, rough going, and above all maintenance diffi-

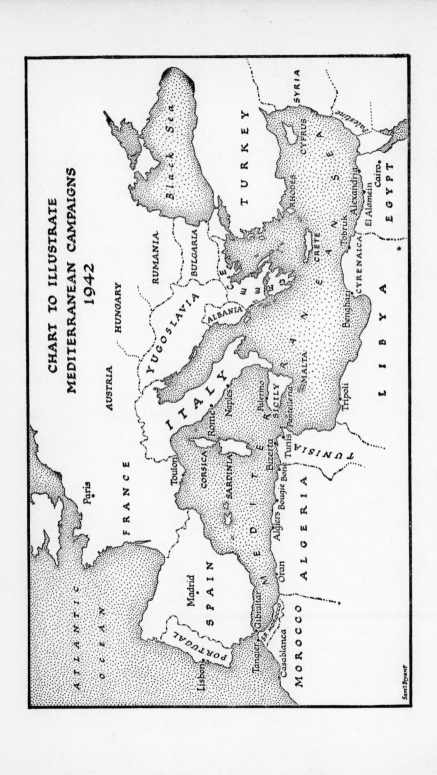

CHART TO ILLUSTRATE
MEDITERRANEAN CAMPAIGNS
1942

culties caused this attempt to fail, and the enemy columns, though hard pressed, reached Benghazi, pursued by the 4th British-Indian Division. The enemy's armour withdrew by the desert route through Mechili, followed by the 7th Armoured Division, reinforced later by the Guards Brigade.

It was hoped to repeat the success achieved a year before, when the Italian retreat southward from Benghazi had been cut off by a swift advance to Antelat and a great haul of prisoners taken. It was found impossible however to supply in time a strong enough force, and the enemy were fully aware of their danger of being caught a second time. When therefore our leading troops reached Antelat, they found it firmly held and could make no headway. Behind this shield Rommel withdrew all his forces to Agedabia, which he held against our attacks while preparing the strong Agheila position to which he withdrew unmolested on January 7.

The XIIIth Corps were now at the extreme end of their administrative tether. There was an unfortunate delay, ascribed to bad weather and enemy air interference, in bringing the port of Benghazi into working order. Supplies for the forward troops had therefore to be brought by road from Tobruk, and not much was accumulated. Consequently the 4th Indian Division could not be brought south from Benghazi, and our forces facing the enemy at Agheila consisted only of the Guards Brigade and the 7th Armoured Division, which in mid-January was relieved by the 1st Armoured Division, newly arrived from home. For some time these troops were neither rendered strong enough to attack nor occupied in preparing a defensive system against a counter-stroke.

The military disaster which, for the second time, at this same fatal corner and one year later, was to ruin the whole British campaign in the Desert for 1942 requires a precise account of what actually happened in this fateful month of January.

* * * * *

On January 9 General Auchinleck, after describing his dispositions, cabled to me at Washington as follows:

Following is forecast of possible enemy action. Stand on line Agheila-Marada. Xth Italian Corps, with Brescia and Pavia Divisions, to hold Agheila area, stiffened by elements German 90th Light Division. Italian Mobile Corps, with Trento and Trieste Divisions and elements German 90th Light Division, at Marada to prevent envelopment Agheila by us from south. German 15th and 21st Armoured Divisions and possibly Ariete Armoured Division in reserve for counter-attack purposes.

And the next day:

Yesterday Guards Brigade Group (two battalions) still held up by enemy in position twelve miles southwest of Agedabia.

It was not difficult for me, with my map room at the White House functioning, to see what these innocent-looking telegrams meant.

Prime Minister to General Auchinleck   11 Jan. 42

I fear this means that the bulk of seven and a half enemy divisions have got away round the corner, and will now be retreating directly along their communications. I note also that nine merchant ships of 10,000 tons are reported to have reached Tripoli safely. It was understood that you believed your advance down the El Abd track would certainly cut off Rommel's Italian infantry, but now it appears they are out of the net. How does this all affect "Acrobat" [the advance into Tripoli]? I am sure you and your armies did all in human power, but we must face the facts as they are, which greatly influence both "Gymnast" and "Super-Gymnast."

Here must be noted once more the dominating influence of the war at sea on the fortunes of the Eighth Army. The disaster to Force K (the Malta squadron), involving the loss of the cruiser *Neptune* in the minefield off Tripoli on December 19, had enabled the enemy convoy with its vital supplies to get through and replenish Rommel's armies at a critical moment.

"Gymnast," it will be remembered, was our plan to send aid to General Weygand in French North Africa, if he would accept it. For this we held one armoured and three field divisions in readiness to embark at short notice from England, and a considerable air contingent. Neither Weygand nor Vichy had responded favourably to our overtures, but we had always hoped that the decisive defeat of Rommel and an advance into Tripoli on the long road to Tunis might encourage one or both to take the plunge. "Super-Gymnast" was the far larger scheme of British and American intervention in French North Africa, to which I had already found President Roosevelt most responsive, and which I had set forth in my paper of December 16 as the main Anglo-American amphibious operation in the West for the campaign of 1942. The enemy's firm stand at Agedabia and his orderly withdrawal to Agheila was therefore of far greater significance to me and to all my thought than the mere arrest of our westward movement in the Desert. In fact, it was an adverse point in my whole theme of discussion with the President. However, it seemed from General Auchinleck's next telegrams that all was still going well and that the decisive action impended.

General Auchinleck to Prime Minister   12 Jan. 42

I do not think it can be said that bulk of enemy divisions have evaded us. It is true that he still speaks in terms of divisions, but they are divisions only in name. For instance, we know that strength of 90th German Light Division, originally 9000, is now 3500, and it has only one field gun left.

2. I estimate that not more than one-third of original German-Italian forces got away round the corner, totalling 17,000 Germans and 18,000 Italians. These are much disorganised, short of senior officers, short of material, and due to our continuous pressure are tired and certainly not as strong as their total strength, 35,000, might be thought to indicate.

3. I have reason to believe six ships recently reached Tripoli, averaging 7200 tons.

4. I am convinced that we should press forward with "Acrobat," for many reasons, not the least in order that Germany may continue to be attacked on two fronts, Russia and Libya. I promise you I will not be led into any rash adventure, nor will General Ritchie, but in view of heartening news from Russian front I feel that we should do all we can to maintain the pressure in Libya. . . . I am convinced the enemy is hard-pressed more than we dared to think.

General Auchinleck to Prime Minister   12 Jan. 42

Enemy appears to have completed his withdrawal to the Mersa-El Brega-Maatex-Giofen-Agheila area, and our troops are in touch with him on his eastern and southern fronts. From our knowledge of his dispositions it seems that his formations and units are numerically weak and that he is eking out his scant resources in German troops to stiffen the remnants of the Italian divisions.

2. Benghazi is developing well as a ground base, but the unloading and shipping are hampered by bad weather, which continues unabating, including atrocious sandstorms, which reduce visibility to nil.

3. General Ritchie is going ahead with his plans, and I hope we shall soon have stronger forces concentrated forward. Evidence as to enemy weakness and disorganisation is growing daily.

Prime Minister to General Auchinleck   13 Jan. 42

Very pleased with your message of 12th. I am showing it to the President today. I am sure you are quite right to push on and bid highly for decision in battle on Agheila-Marada front. Will support you whatever the result.

From January 12 to January 21 Rommel's army remained motionless in the Agheila position, holding the gap of about fifty miles from the Mediterranean to what was called the "Libyan Sand Sea" to the southward. The salt pans, sand dunes, and little cliffs of this front were highly favourable for defence, and every precaution had been taken by the enemy to strengthen them by minefields and wire entanglements. General Auchinleck did not feel he could assault this position before the middle of February. In the meanwhile he maintained contact with Rommel's forces by the two leading battalions of the Guards Brigade and the Support Group of the 1st Armoured Division. Behind these, at Antelat, nearly ninety miles away, lay the remainder of the British 1st Armoured Division, commanded by General Messervy. These, together with the 4th British-Indian Division at and to the east of Benghazi, composed the XIIIth Army Corps, under General Godwin-Austen. This wide dispersal of the corps, through administrative difficulties, left the front weak and reinforcements distant. No arrangements were made to defend the British front by mines or other obstructions. The plan was that if Rommel counter-attacked, our forward troops were to withdraw. General Auchinleck did not however believe that Rommel would be able to attack, and thought he himself had plenty of time to build up his forces and supplies.

General Auchinleck to C.I.G.S. 15 Jan. 42

Enemy apparently is now stabilising position round Agheila. . . . Total enemy strength in forward area, estimated: German, 17,000 men, 50 field guns, 70 anti-tank guns, 42 medium and 20 light tanks; Italian, 18,000 men, 130 field guns, 60 anti-tank guns, 50 M.13 tanks, about one-third original strength.

2. Our forward troops, comprising the Guards Brigade Group, the Support Groups of 1st and 7th Armoured Divisions,[1] four armoured-car regiments, the 2d Armoured Brigade, are in touch with enemy on his whole front, and patrols have reached Agheila-Marada track.

3. Enemy is not aggressive except in air, where his activity has increased recently, probably owing to improvements in his fuel situation caused by ships reaching Tripoli. Our Air Force continues to be very active against enemy targets and in covering our ports as well as our forward troops. Enemy bombing attacks against our ports and road communications eastward from Benghazi continue, but no serious damage done.

4. Development of Benghazi port proceeds satisfactorily, and supplies are being landed in spite of delay due to bad weather and rough seas.

* * * * *

The news soon arrived of the surrender of Bardia, Sollum, and Halfaya to our XXXth Corps with 14,000 prisoners and much war material at a cost of less than 500 casualties. Eleven hundred of our own men were also liberated at this time.

* * * * *

Nothing more of importance reached me before I flew back

---

[1] The Support Group of the 7th Armoured Division was withdrawn for reorganisation on January 19, two days before the enemy attack.

from Bermuda, and I certainly parted from the President with the feeling, which afterwards proved fully justified, that our thought about a large North African venture was moving forward on the same lines. The news still continued good after I had reached London, though there would evidently be a longer pause than we had hoped before the new battle.

Immediately on my arrival, amid a surge of business, I was forced to prepare myself for a full-dress Parliamentary debate. The immense world events which had happened since I last addressed the House of Commons at length had now to be presented to the nation. From what I could see of the newspapers, to the reading of which I gave at least an hour a day, there was a rising swell of discontent and apprehension about our evident unreadiness to meet the Japanese onfall in the East and Far East. To the public the Desert battle seemed to be going well, and I was glad to lay the facts before Parliament. I asked my colleagues to give me reasonable time.

* * * * *

Unfortunately, General Auchinleck had underestimated his enemy's power of recuperation. The Royal Air Force in Malta, which, under the determined leadership of Air Vice-Marshal Lloyd, had contributed to the land victory by its autumn attacks on Italian ports and shipping, had been set upon in December by a powerful concentration of German air squadrons in Sicily and subdued. Our recent misfortunes at sea had so weakened Admiral Cunningham's fleet that for a time it could not intervene effectively on the sea route to Tripoli. Supplies were now reaching Rommel freely. On January 21 he launched a reconnaissance in force, consisting of three columns each of about a thousand motorised infantry supported by tanks. These rapidly found their way through the gaps between our contact troops, who had no tanks working with them. General Goodwin-Austen thereupon ordered withdrawal, first to Agedabia and thereafter to block the enemy's way from Antelat to Msus.

On the 23d news of an unfavourable character arrived.

General Auchinleck to Prime Minister 23 Jan. 42

It seems clear that Rommel's eastward move on January 21 was made in anticipation [of an] expected attack by us. Finding only light forces confronting him, he evidently decided to push on with the intention of disturbing our main L. of C., which he appears to believe rests on Benghazi. During withdrawal on January 21 in difficult sand-dune country southwest of Agedabia, columns of the Support Group, 1st Armoured Division, reported to have lost nine guns and a hundred mechanical transport; also a number of casualties, details as yet unknown.

2. If Rommel persists in his advance, particularly on the Benghazi axis, he is likely to expose his eastward flank to attack by our armour, which in that area now amounts to about 150 cruiser and American tanks. The small enemy column which penetrated almost into Antelat last night is presumed to be a commando.

3. I realise the public at home may be upset by enemy reoccupying Agedabia, but it may well be that Rommel may be drawn on into a situation unfavourable to him. Rommel's move has held up reconnaissances and other preparations for our planned offensive against Agheila, but, as you know, prime retarding factor was and still is need for building up adequate reserve in and forward of Benghazi. . . . Am confident that General Ritchie is watching for opportunity to force encounter battle in conditions which may be more favourable to us than those obtaining round Agheila, with its swamps and bad going. . . .

I accepted this view at the time, not having the slightest idea of what had happened on the 21st, or of the general and rapid retreat of all our advanced forces now in progress. Up to this point no reason had ever been suggested to me to expect misfortune. On the contrary, I had been told of an impending British offensive. Our turn of the corner into Tripolitania might have been delayed, but Auchinleck seemed confident for the future. But now on this same 24th came news of different import.

General Auchinleck to Prime Minister 24 Jan. 42, 3 P.M.

. . . . Enemy has been able to maintain unexpected strength forward apparently, and his initial advance seems to have disconcerted temporarily at any rate our forward troops. These, as you know, were weak and were pushed aside from main road. . . . Once again Rommel has made a bold stroke. . . . His unexpected initial success probably encouraged him, as happened last year, to go farther than he originally intended. But his supply position this time is in no way comparable with last year, when he also had fresh troops. The situation has not developed quite as I should have liked, but I hope to turn it to our ultimate advantage.

Here however was the shock. A Service message arrived late on the 24th:

Naval Liaison Officer Eighth Army to C.-in-C. Mediterranean
24 Jan. 42

Preparations to evacuate Benghazi are being made as a precautionary measure only. Demolition work is not being ordered yet. Non-fighting personnel in the circumstances are being moved eastward as far as possible by night. . . . Should Benghazi fall, Derna will follow.

This led me to send the following to General Auchinleck, from whom I had as yet heard nothing of the sort:

Prime Minister to General Auchinleck   25 Jan. 42

I am much disturbed by the report from the Eighth Army, which speaks of evacuation of Benghazi and Derna. I had certainly never been led to suppose that such a situation could arise. All this movement of non-fighting personnel eastward, and statement that demolition work at Benghazi has not been ordered *yet,* places the campaign on different level from any we had considered. Have you really had a heavy defeat in the Antelat area? Has our fresh armour been unable to compete with the resuscitated German tanks? It seems to me this is a serious crisis, and one to me quite unexpected. Why should they all be off so quickly? Why should not the 4th [British-]Indian Division hold out at Benghazi, like the Huns at Halfaya? The kind of retirement now evidently envisaged by subordinate officers implies the failure of "Crusader" and the ruin of "Acrobat." [2]

Auchinleck rightly hastened to General Ritchie's advanced headquarters.

[2] Our offensive in Libya and advance into Tripoli.

General Auchinleck to Prime Minister   26 Jan. 42

I flew here from Cairo yesterday. Position is not satisfactory owing to apparent inability of 1st Armoured Division and Guards Brigade Group [to] stabilise situation in spite of hard fighting. Enemy yesterday pushed our troops back to Msus and beyond, though yesterday evening retiring columns still east of this place were apparently engaged with enemy.[3] . . .

4. Heavy installations and base establishments have been moved from Benghazi as precautionary measure with my approval. General Ritchie has taken 4th Indian Division under his direct control, and ordered it to strike south from Benghazi as strongly as possible, using mixed columns against enemy communications and flank about Antelat. 1st Armoured Division is to do everything possible to hold enemy south [of] Charruba and west of Mechili and protect flank of 4th Indian Division.

5. Enemy formations identified as having been engaged are 15th and 21st Panzer Divisions, Ariete Division, and 90th Light Division.

Rommel, having established his main force at Msus, had the option of striking northwest to Benghazi or northeast towards Mechili. He did both. His intention was to capture Benghazi, but he also sent a force northeast as a feint against our communications. The feint was highly successful. Our projected counter-attack southward by a part of the 4th Indian Division from Benghazi, the Armoured Division, and the Guards Brigade from Charruba was hurriedly cancelled, Benghazi was evacuated, and the whole XIIIth Corps fell back to the line Gazala-Bir Hacheim.

*   *   *   *   *

The loss of Benghazi soon emerged as the outstanding fact.

General Auchinleck (Advanced Headquarters) to Prime Minister
27 Jan. 42

I also was much disturbed by reports of premature action at Benghazi. Have inquired, and there was apparently some misunderstanding, possibly due to overprecipitate action by subordinate commander, who ordered evacuation of all naval personnel,

3 For detailed disposition see map, page 32.

and who before leaving destroyed some lighters and also bollards on quays. Major destruction of port, which is responsibility of Army, has not been carried out, nor have any demolitions been carried out except destruction of some enemy stores. R.A.F. apparently destroyed some petrol, also through misunderstanding. These avoidable mistakes are regrettable, but not disastrous. I am inquiring as to responsibility for them.

After describing the military movement at length, General Auchinleck summarized the story as follows:

. . . There is no doubt, I fear, that our armoured forces failed to compete with enemy satisfactorily and that they have had heavy losses without prospect [of being] able to inflict comparable damage on enemy. Cause of this not yet clear, but probably that our troops, being dispersed widely, were unable to concentrate for concerted action against enemy compact mass. This is probably only one reason of several. 1st Armoured Division, or what remains of it, is now concentrated and covered by armoured-car screen, and I hope it may be fit for offensive action at once, but I await report from its commander. Other aspect of the operations demands inquiry, which will be made. Meanwhile object is to regain initiative, close in on enemy, destroy him if we can, otherwise push him back. Am confident General Ritchie is fully determined to effect this object. Tedder and I staying here for the present.

And the next day:

Enemy has divided his forces, apparently in attempt to secure both Mechili and Benghazi. This is a bold move typical of Rommel, and may indicate an underestimate of our power to resist an attack. Likely that majority of his tanks [are] with eastern thrust. His movements, except perhaps that towards Benghazi, have not dislocated plans made previously by General Ritchie for counter-offensive.

* * * * *

It was quite clear to me at this point that General Auchinleck had not hitherto understood what had happened in the Desert. None of his telegrams cast any light upon the fate of the 1st Armoured Division, or indeed of the XIIIth Corps. I hoped that now he was at General Ritchie's headquarters he would find out the truth. Meanwhile I also remained in the dark.

Prime Minister to General Auchinleck   28 Jan. 42

I have complete confidence in you, and am glad you are staying up.

2. You have no doubt seen the information about Rommel's presumed intentions, namely, clearing up the triangle Benghazi-Msus-Mechili, and then withdrawing to waiting line about Agheila. This seems to reinforce the importance of our holding on.

3. I am most anxious to hear further from you about defeat of our armour by inferior enemy numbers. This cuts very deep.

No explanation except complaints about the quality of our tanks was offered for the disaster that had taken place, and worse news now arrived.

General Auchinleck to Prime Minister   29 Jan. 42

Situation has deteriorated, and I fear we shall have to evacuate Benghazi temporarily at any rate. Early today 7th Indian Infantry Brigade were forced back by two enemy columns of all arms in superior strength. Each enemy column had at least twenty-five tanks.

Simultaneously strong column containing at least 1500 mechanised vehicles advanced from south on El Abiar. Threatened with envelopment, commander 4th Indian Division decided if possible to break off action south of Benghazi. . . . In the circumstances I consider he acted rightly. Benghazi demolitions were ordered to be carried out. We have little of value there.

It must be admitted that enemy has succeeded beyond his expectations and mine, and that his tactics have been skilful and bold. Much will depend now on extent to which he may have to thin out his Panzer units round Msus to maintain the large force used to attack Benghazi. Rommel has taken considerable risks, and so have we. So far he is justified by results, but General Ritchie and I are seeking every possible means to turn the tables on him. Losses of 1st Armoured Division in tanks and guns are heavy, and the fighting value of this key formation may be temporarily impaired, though I hope not.

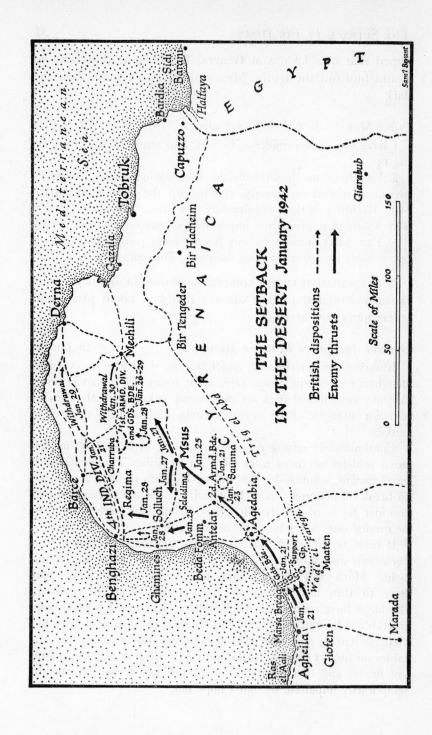

THE SETBACK
IN THE DESERT January 1942

British dispositions - - - - ▶
Enemy thrusts ━━━▶

Scale of Miles
0   50   100   150

Sam'l Bryant

There is no disorganisation or confusion, nor any loss of morale as far as I can see.

General Auchinleck to Prime Minister   31 Jan. 42

Thank you for your message of January 28, received yesterday afternoon. Very sorry we had to let Benghazi go, but loss is only temporary.

2. Regarding action 1st Armoured Division: Am not certain that enemy tanks were appreciably less in number than ours actually in running order on any one day, though it is likely that our strength in tanks in battle area was superior to theirs. I have given you some reasons for defeat of our armoured force, and I think these still hold good. Other and at present irremediable causes which I have already mentioned are short range and inferior performance of our two-pounder gun compared with German gun, and mechanical unreliability of our cruiser tanks compared with German tanks. In addition, I am not satisfied that tactical leadership of our armoured units is of sufficiently high standard to offset German material advantages. This is in hand, but cannot be improved in a day, unfortunately.

3. I am reluctantly compelled to conclusion that to meet German armoured forces with any reasonable hope of decisive success our armoured forces, as at present equipped, organised, and led, must have at least two to one superiority. Even then they must rely for success on working in very closest co-operation with infantry and artillery, which, except perhaps for their weakness in anti-tank guns, are fully competent to take on their German opposite numbers. These principles are being worked to here as closely as circumstances will permit, but I am afraid there are signs that personnel of Royal Armoured Corps are in some instances losing confidence in their equipment. Everything possible will be done to rectify this.

4. General Ritchie and I are fully alive to Rommel's probable intentions, but whatever these may be he will certainly try to exploit success by use of even smallest columns until he meets resistance. Plans are in train to counter such action. . . .

Rommel had again proved himself a master of Desert tactics, and, outwitting our commanders, regained the greater part of Cyrenaica. This retreat of nearly three hundred miles ruined

our hopes and lost us Benghazi and all the stores General
Auchinleck had been gathering for his hoped-for offensive in
the middle of February. Rommel must have been astounded
by the overwhelming success of the three small columns with
which he started the attack, and he supported them with whatever troops he could muster. General Ritchie reassembled the
crippled XIIIth Corps and other forces which had been sent
forward in the neighbourhood of Gazala and Tobruk. Here
pursuers and pursued gasped and glared at each other until the
end of May, when Rommel was able to strike again.

This extraordinary reversal of fortune and the severe military disaster arose from the basic facts that the enemy had
gained virtually free passage across the Mediterranean to
reinforce and nourish his armour, and had brought a large part
of his Air Force back from Russia. But the tactical events on
the spot have never been explained. The decisive day was
January 25, when the enemy broke through to Msus. Thereafter confusion and changes of plan left the initiative to
Rommel. The Guards Brigade could not understand why they
were not allowed to make a stand, but the orders to retreat
were reiterated and imperative. The 4th British-Indian Division was given no useful part to play.

Only recently has it come to light from enemy records that
the enemy tank strength was superior to ours. The Afrika
Corps had 120 tanks in action and the Italians 80 or more
against the 150 of the 1st Armoured Division. Nevertheless, the
ineffective use made of the division remains unexplained. We
are told in Auchinleck's dispatch, "being newly arrived from
the United Kingdom, it was inexperienced in Desert fighting,"
and as a general comment, "not only were all our tanks out-
gunned by the German tanks, but our cruiser tanks were
mechanically inferior under battle conditions. The inferior
armament and mechanical unreliability of our tanks was
aggravated by the great shortage of anti-tank weapons, compared with the Germans'."

All these statements require careful scrutiny. The 1st
Armoured Division was one of the finest we had. It consisted

largely of men who had more than two years' training and
represented as high a standard of efficiency as any to be found
in our Regular forces. They had landed in Egypt in November.
Before they left England every effort had been made, in accordance with all the latest information and experience, to make
their vehicles Desert-worthy. After the usual overhaul in the
Cairo workshops, this division moved across the Desert to
Antelat, which it reached on January 6. In order to preserve
the tracks, its tanks were carried on special transporters across
the whole Desert, and arrived at Antelat unworn and in good
order. Yet, without having been deeply committed into action,
this fine division lost over a hundred of its tanks. The very
considerable petrol supplies which had been brought forward
were abandoned in its precipitate retreat, and many of its tanks
were left behind because they ran out of fuel.

The Guards Brigade, withdrawing under orders, found
large petrol supplies which they had to destroy, as the enemy
were near. As however they found numbers of our tanks
abandoned in the Desert, they brought on as much petrol as
they could and manned these tanks themselves. One company
of the Coldstream alone collected six, which they drove to
safety, and other units collected more. In fact, some companies
emerged actually stronger than they had set out, having
acquired a few tanks to work with their motorised infantry in
the German fashion. When we remember the cost, time, and
labour the creation of an entity like an armoured division, with
all its experts and trained men, involves, the effort required
to transport it round the Cape, the many preparations made to
bring it into battle, it is indeed grievous to see the result
squandered through such mismanagement. Still more are these
reflections painful when our failure is contrasted with what
the Germans accomplished, although over four hundred miles
from their base at Tripoli. Nor should the British nation, in
probing these matters, be misled into thinking that the technical inferiority of our tanks was the only reason for this considerable and far-reaching reverse.

3

Penalties in Malaya

Severe Fighting in the Malay Peninsula — Continued Japanese Advance — The Battle of Segamat-Muar — Our Retreat to Singapore Island — An Arguable Question of Strategy — Dissipation of the Singapore Defending Army — General Pownall's Memorandum — My Complaint of the West Coast Naval Defence — The First Sea Lord's Reply — General Wavell's Doubts About Prolonged Defence of Singapore — My Telegram of January 15 — Wavell's Reply of January 16 — No Permanent Landward Fortifications — Or Field Defences — My Minute to the Chiefs of Staff, January 19 — The Chiefs of Staff's Instructions to General Wavell of January 20 — My Telegram to Wavell of January 20 — Emphasis on the Keeping Open of the Burma Road — Wavell's Pessimistic Reports — The Dilemma of the Chiefs of Staff — Intervention of Sir Earle Page — Mr. Curtin's Message of January 24 — "An Inexcusable Betrayal" — We Pursue the Policy of Fighting to the End in Singapore.

THE EVENTS in Malaya up to the end of December, 1941, have been described in a previous volume. When the New Year opened, our IIId Corps, consisting of the 9th and 11th British-Indian Divisions, commanded by Lieutenant-General Heath, was under strong attack on both east and west coasts.[1] The enemy had moved south from Kota Bharu by the coast road, and were now in close contact with a brigade group of our 9th Division at Kuantan. On the west the 11th Indian Division held a strong hill position at Kampar, with a

[1] See map, page 37.

brigade on its left watching the river Perak. The two brigades
of the 8th Australian Division were retained in Johore State,
one of them guarding the beaches at Mersing, where an enemy
landing, always a possibility, would have cut in behind our
forward troops. The Japanese had by now deployed at least
three full divisions against us, and an assembly of shipping at
Singora indicated the possible arrival of another. On our side
too the eagerly awaited reinforcements were approaching. The
45th Indian Brigade, the leading brigade of the 18th British
Division, and fifty Hurricane fighters arrived safely by mid-
January. By the end of the month the whole of the 18th
Division and another brigade from India were expected.

The protection of these convoys in the narrow waters south
of Singapore demanded the use of all our available naval
forces except small craft, and nearly all our remaining fighter
aircraft. In consequence the Japanese Air Force could strike
freely against our troops and communications. The Dutch, in

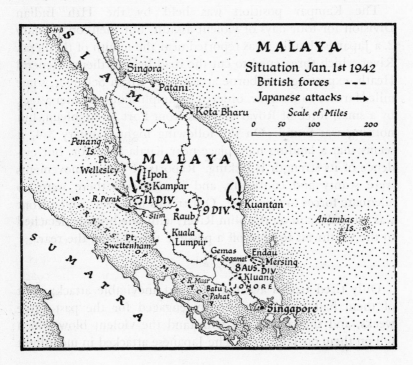

loyal fulfilment of their agreements with us, had sent four
squadrons to join in the defence of Singapore, but these, like
our own squadrons, were a wasting asset. What few bombers
still remained lacked fighter escort and could do little. The
task of our fighting troops was to gain time till the reinforcements arrived, by holding the enemy in successive positions as
far north as possible without being committed so deeply as to
destroy all prospect of defending Singapore Island.

Towards the end of December an attempt had been made to
organise a small amphibious force to strike along the west coast
behind the enemy's lines. A successful raid was carried out on
December 27, but the enemy, having almost complete mastery
of the air, was soon able to immobilise our puny naval force
operating from Port Swettenham. On January 1 a new flotilla
of six fast landing-craft just arrived from America was
destroyed. Thereafter only attempts to parry any Japanese
thrust by sea were found possible.

The Kampar position was held by the 11th Indian
Division for four days of violent assault, but then, on January
2, a Japanese landing was reported near the mouth of the Perak
River which threatened to cut the road behind them. General
Heath, expecting a seaborne attack near Kuala Selangor, some
miles farther to the rear, ordered an amphibious counter-attack
by a small force of Royal Marines from Port Swettenham, but
nothing was found. On the following night, January 3/4, it
seems that a landing took place near Kuala Selangor, but evidence of its strength is lacking. Reports of enemy movements
were scanty and confusing, and in any case there were no
adequate forces to intervene. Our troops withdrew, and a front
was formed again on the Slim River, with one brigade detached
to the southwest to hold off a possible thrust from the rear.

*   *   *   *   *

Only tired troops awaited the next inevitable attack; most
of them had been continuously engaged for the past three
weeks, and they could not withstand the violent blow which
fell on them on January 7. The Japanese attacked in moonlight

with tanks straight down the main road, and broke the line. Both brigades were thrown into confusion, and extricated themselves only after heavy loss. This severe reverse imperilled the whole plan of delaying the enemy until our reinforcements arrived. Moreover, on the east coast the 9th Division was severely affected. Its brigade at Kuantan had been withdrawn after inflicting two thousand casualties on the Japanese, and the division was concentrated near Raub. Any further withdrawal on the west coast would expose its flank.

At this moment General Wavell, who had arrived in Singapore on his way to take up the A.B.D.A. Command, visited the front. He ordered a deep withdrawal to get well clear of the Japanese, and thus give a breathing-space to our exhausted men behind whatever fresh, or comparatively fresh, troops could be gathered. The position selected was a hundred and fifty miles farther back, along the river Muar, with its right near Segamat. Major-General Gordon Bennett, of the Australian Division, was placed in command, with one of his own brigades (the 27th), the 9th British-Indian Division, withdrawn from the east coast, and the newly arrived 45th Indian Infantry Brigade. The 11th British-Indian Division, on whom hitherto the brunt had fallen, was to rest and refit behind this front. The retreat began on January 10. The enemy was shaken off after some stiff rearguard fighting, and four days later the new front was formed. At the same time our base on the sea at Port Swettenham was abandoned and the remnants of our light naval craft retired to Batu Pahat. Here on January 16 a small Japanese force landed from the sea. Only two craft were available to intercept, and these failed to find the enemy.

The all-important convoy with the leading brigade (the 53d) of the 18th Division and the consignment of fifty Hurricanes was now unloading at Singapore. They had been safely escorted by the Navy and the Air Force through the perils of the sea approach, within easy striking distance of the enemy's air. The value of these reinforcements was less than their numbers suggest. The 45th Indian Brigade was young, only partly trained, and not trained at all in jungle warfare. The 18th British Division, which, after three months on board ship, needed time to get on their tactical feet, had to be thrown into the losing battle as soon as they were landed.

Great hopes were pinned on the Hurricane fighters. Here at last were aircraft of quality to match the Japanese. They were assembled with all speed and took the air. For a few days indeed they did much damage, but the conditions were strange to the newly arrived pilots, and before long the Japanese superiority in numbers began increasingly to take its toll. They dwindled fast.

*   *   *   *   *

The Battle of Segamat-Muar was fiercely contested for a week. General Gordon Bennett posted the bulk of his force to block the approaches to Segamat, with the 45th Indian Brigade and one Australian battalion, joined later by a second, to defend the lower reaches of the Muar River. A highly successful ambush in front of Segamat cost the Japanese several hundred men, and although later fighting was intense the enemy was firmly held. At Muar however the four defending battalions were assailed on January 15 by the whole of the Imperial Guards Division both frontally and by a series of flank landings from the sea. For some days they were surrounded as they fought their way south. In the end they were forced to abandon their transport and break out in small parties. Of the 4000 men of this force only about 800 returned. Brigadier Duncan and all the battalion commanders and the seconds-in-command of the 45th Brigade were killed. This small force, by dogged resistance against an enemy greatly superior in numbers and master of the air, had held off the threat to the flank and rear of the defenders of Segamat, who were thus enabled to withdraw, though only just in time. To safeguard this retreat, two British battalions of the 53d Brigade were drawn into the fight, and part of the 11th British-Indian Division, refitting behind the front, was posted to deal with landings, or the threat of them, on the coast at Batu Pahat and farther south.

Our forces now stood on a ninety-mile front across the southern tip of the Malayan peninsula from Mersing to Batu Pahat. The enemy followed closely. At Mersing and Kluang there were sharp encounters, but again the decisive attack came on the west coast, where the two British battalions held Batu Pahat for five days. By then all direct exit was blocked, and the troops made their twenty miles retreat down the coast where two thousand men were taken off by the Navy on successive nights.

Meanwhile strong reinforcements reached the Japanese. On January 15 a large convoy discharged two fresh divisions at Singora, whence they marched south upon Kluang, the centre of our line. The enemy now had a full five divisions in Malaya. On January 26 our courageous if scanty air reconnaissance reported two cruisers, eleven destroyers, two transports, and many small craft off Endau. All the twenty-three aircraft that could be mustered for an air-strike went against them in two attacks. The convoys were protected by Japanese fighters, and our losses, especially of the obsolete Wildebeestes, were heavy. But the attacks were pressed home, both transports were hit, and at least thirteen enemy aircraft were destroyed. This gallant sortie was the expiring effort of our air striking force. The following night two destroyers from Singapore tried to attack, but they were intercepted and one of them was sunk. The landed Japanese came rapidly down the coast from Endau to attack the 22d Australian Brigade at Mersing. Thus, on January 27 there was close action on the right of our line at Mersing, in the centre at Kluang, and on our exposed left. General Percival decided to retire to Singapore Island. Every man and vehicle had in the final stage to pass over the causeway thither. The greater part of one brigade was lost in the early stages, but on the morning of January 31 the rest of the force had crossed and the causeway was blown up behind them.

*   *   *   *   *

It is at least arguable whether it would not have been better to concentrate all our strength on defending Singapore Island, merely containing the Japanese advance down the Malayan

peninsula with light mobile forces. The decision of the commanders on the spot, which I approved, was to fight the battle
for Singapore in Johore, but to delay the enemy's approach
thereto as much as possible. The defence of the mainland consisted of a continuous retreat, with heavy rearguard actions and
stubborn props. The fighting reflects high credit on the troops
and commanders engaged. It drew in to itself however nearly
all the reinforcements piecemeal as they arrived. Every advantage lay with the enemy. There had been minute pre-war
study of the ground and conditions. Careful large-scale plans
and secret infiltration of agents, including even hidden reserves
of bicycles for Japanese cyclists, had been made. Superior
strength and large reserves, some of which were not needed,
had been assembled. All the Japanese divisions were adept in
jungle warfare.

The Japanese mastery of the air, arising, as has been described, from our bitter needs elsewhere, and for which the
local commanders were in no way responsible, was another
deadly fact. In the result the main fighting strength of such an
army as we had assigned to the defence of Singapore, and
almost all the reinforcements sent after the Japanese declaration of war, were used up in gallant fighting on the peninsula,
and when these had crossed the causeway to what should have
been their supreme battleground their punch was gone. Here
they rejoined the local garrison and the masses of base details
which swelled our numbers though not our strength. There remained the two fresh brigades of the 18th British Division, newly
landed from their ships in strange and unimagined surroundings after their long voyage. The army which could fight the
decisive struggle for Singapore and had been provided for that
supreme objective in this theatre was dissipated before the
Japanese attack began. It might be a hundred thousand men;
but it was an army no more.

*   *   *   *   *

The reader will find among the Appendices [2] a memorandum,

2 See Appendix D, Book One, pages 871–74.

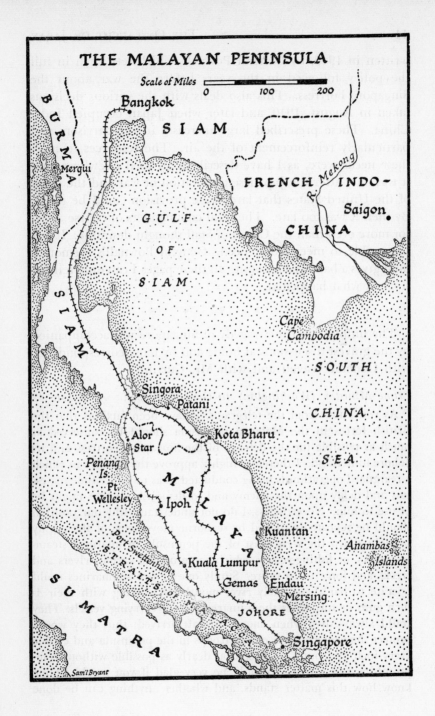

THE MALAYAN PENINSULA

Scale of Miles

0   100   200

Bangkok

S I A M

BURMA

Mergui

FRENCH INDO-

R. Mekong

Saigon

G U L F

O F

S I A M

CHINA

Cape
Cambodia

S O U T H

Singora
Patani

C H I N A

Alor
Star

Kota Bharu

S E A

Penang
Is.

Pt.
Wellesley

Ipoh

M A L A Y A

Kuantan

Anambas
Islands

Port Swettenham

S T R A I T S

Kuala Lumpur

Gemas

Endau

Mersing

O F   M A L A C C A

JOHORE

S U M A T R A

Singapore

Sam'l Bryant

written in 1949, by General Pownall, which sets forth in full
the policy followed in the years before the war about the
Singapore Fortress. This also deals with the various decisions
taken in August, 1940, and later when Japan occupied Indo-
China. These prescribed large increases in the garrison, and
particularly reinforcement of the air. The resources to meet
these needs were, as I have described, all used elsewhere, and
it was only after the Japanese declaration of war and the entry
of the United States that large-scale provision could be made.
By then it was too late. The local commanders of course asked
for more even than the Chiefs of Staff thought desirable. It was
impossible to meet either need. General Pownall's memorandum gives a balanced account. In these pages I can only tell the
story of what happened.

*   *   *   *   *

The unfolding of the tragedy of Singapore was accompanied
by the gravest discussions at home and by tense correspondence
with General Wavell and with Mr. Curtin.

Prime Minister (Washington) to General Wavell   9 Jan. 42
     As you know from the telegrams, I have been anxious that the
British forces in the Malayan peninsula should be conserved as
much as possible for the defence of the Singapore Fortress and its
Johore hinterland. I therefore highly approve the manner in which
a rearguard operation is being conducted so as to inflict the greatest
loss and delay upon the enemy and to demolish all that might be
of use to him. Nevertheless, I do not understand why our position
should be repeatedly turned by seaborne movements of the enemy
brought down the west coast of the peninsula in unarmed steamers, junks, or fishing-vessels, which come up the various rivers and
creeks and force us to retire. Surely one or two submarines could
operate to bar these likely river mouths by sinking with their 4-
inch guns or torpedoes these unarmed troop-carrying vessels. They
could always dive when enemy aircraft arrived; thus they would
protect the western flank of our troops in the peninsula and enable
every inch of ground to be sold as dearly as possible without com-
promising our forces. I should be very glad if you would let me
know how this matter stands, and whether anything can be done

about it, so that I may explain it to the President, with whom I am constantly discussing all aspects of the war.

To the critical questions I had put about the Japanese amphibious activities on the west coast of Malaya, General Wavell replied:

General Wavell to Prime Minister 10 Jan. 42

You will have seen my telegram to the Chiefs of Staff on general situation in Malaya. Naval action against threat to western flank has been under attention since this was first apparent. Patrol boats were tried at beginning, but were shot up by air attacks during the day. Destroyer *Scout* has been operating last three nights from base in Sumatra. Only three Dutch submarines are now operating in Malaya, and arrangements have already been made for first one returned from other operations to operate off west coast between Penang and Selangor, commencing January 12.

I could not feel satisfied with this, or a fuller explanation which reached us later.

Prime Minister to First Sea Lord 22 Jan. 42

This is really not good enough. Here we have been absolutely outmanoeuvred and apparently outfought on the west coast of Malaya by an enemy who has no warship in the neighbourhood. Consequently our forces are made to retire from successive positions, precious time is gained by the enemy, and a general state of insecurity engendered in our fighting troops. The shortcomings are only too evident. Why were the enemy allowed to obtain all these craft? We apparently have none or very few, although these were waters we, until recently, controlled. Secondly, when mention is made of heavy machine-gun fire from the banks, how is it the enemy hold these banks? They cannot be manning with machine-guns points commanding every part of the sea [coast] down which these barges must come.

You should surely call for much more precise reports. This command of the western shores of Malaya by the Japanese without the possession of a single ship of war must be reckoned as one of the most astonishing British lapses recorded in naval history. I am sorry to be disagreeable, but I look for a further report of a far more searching inquiry.

Admiral Pound sent a full reply.

First Sea Lord to Prime Minister   24 Jan. 42

In your minute of January 22 you have treated the operation on the west coast of Malaya purely from the naval point of view, whereas we have learnt from bitter experience that wherever small craft have to work close inshore where the enemy have air superiority the problem is both a naval and an air one.

2. Had this infiltration down the coast taken place in 1914, I think it could fairly have been said that the Navy had failed to play its part. In 1942 the conditions are entirely different. . . .

4. With the knowledge now in our possession it appears that the sequence of events was as follows: (*a*) According to the Governor's telegram to the Secretary of State for the Colonies, arrangements had been made before the war that the denial of small craft to the enemy should be achieved by sending all craft well up the rivers, and this was apparently done when the military authorities were advised that the locality had become threatened. This move on our part was partly defeated by the infiltration by the enemy through the jungle paths by which they reached positions where our craft were hidden up the rivers. We know however that all power boats and the majority of other craft were destroyed. (*b*) The rot appears to have started at Penang, where the arrangements to put into force the "scorched-earth" policy appear to have completely broken down. The enemy thus had a considerable number of small craft with which to commence working down the coast. At that end we had nothing. Nor could we have maintained anything owing to the enemy's air superiority. (*c*) To counter the enemy movements from Penang, which is 340 miles from Singapore, we had a small number of small craft at the latter place mounting light guns which were improvised on the outbreak of war. Owing to the enemy control of air it was practically impossible for these craft to move by day, and those which had attempted to do so were sunk. (*d*) The enemy have transported motor landing-craft overland from Singora and are using these.

5. The situation at the present time is that the Rear-Admiral in Malaya is making every effort to supplement the patrol craft, and General Wavell has been asked if the Dutch can help, and the Government of India has been asked if the Royal Indian Navy can assist. The Air Force are also co-operating with limited resources.

It must be recognised that our effective fighting ships were barely enough to escort our reinforcing convoys and to keep open the sea approaches to Singapore. For coastal work there was nothing beyond a few weakly armed small craft and some converted coasters equipped with inferior weapons. Our few feeble craft persevered against overwhelming air power. Their spirit was not lacking, but they had not the means to win success.

*   *   *   *   *

It soon became clear that General Wavell had already doubts of our ability to maintain a prolonged defence of Singapore. The reader will have seen how much I had counted upon the island and fortress standing a siege requiring heavy artillery to be landed, transported, and mounted by the Japanese. Before I left Washington I still contemplated a resistance of at least two months. I watched with misgivings but without effective intervention the consumption of our forces in their retreat through the Malay peninsula. On the other hand, there was the gain of precious time.

General Wavell to Chiefs of Staff   14 Jan. 42

Flew [to] Singapore yesterday, January 13, and motored [to] Segamat to meet Heath and Gordon Bennett. Plan is being carried out, but 9th and 11th Divisions have been further weakened both in numbers and morale by the fighting north of Kuala Lumpur, and enemy's advance has been more rapid than I had hoped. Battle for Singapore will be a close-run thing, and we shall need luck in getting in convoys safely and up to time. Continuous heavy rain all yesterday sheltered important convoy in final approach and may help to delay enemy. Gordon Bennett and Australians in good heart and will handle enemy roughly, I am sure.

*   *   *   *   *

In order to make sure about the landward defences, which hitherto I had taken for granted, and the preparation for standing a siege, I sent the following telegram:

Prime Minister (Washington) to General Wavell   15 Jan. 42

Please let me know your idea of what would happen in event of your being forced to withdraw into the island.

How many troops would be needed to defend this area? What means are there of stopping landings as were made in Hong Kong? What are defences and obstructions on landward side? Are you sure you can dominate with fortress cannon any attempt to plant siege batteries? Is everything being prepared, and what has been done about the useless mouths? It has always seemed to me that the vital need is to prolong the defence of the island to last possible minute, but of course I hope it will not come to this. . . .

3. Everyone here is very pleased with the telegrams you have sent, which give us all the feeling how buoyantly and spaciously you are grappling with your tremendous task. All the Americans seem to have the same confidence in you as have your British friends.

Wavell's reply to this message did not reach me till after my return to London.

General Wavell to Prime Minister   16 Jan. 42

I discussed the defence of island when recently at Singapore, and have asked for detailed plans. Until quite recently all plans were based on repulsing seaborne attacks on island and holding land attack in Johore or farther north, and little or nothing was done to construct defences on north side of island to prevent crossing Johore Straits, though arrangements have been made to blow up causeway. The fortress cannon of heaviest nature have all-round traverse, but their flat trajectory makes them unsuitable for counter-battery work. Could certainly not guarantee to dominate enemy siege batteries with them. Supply situation satisfactory. Have already authorised removal of certain Air Force establishments and stores to Sumatra and Java to prevent congestion. Will cable further when I receive detailed plans. Much will depend on air situation.

It was with feelings of painful surprise that I read this message on the morning of the 19th. So there were no permanent fortifications covering the landward side of the naval base and of the city! Moreover, even more astounding, no measures worth speaking of had been taken by any of the commanders since the war began, and more especially since the Japanese had established themselves in Indo-China, to construct field defences. They had not even mentioned the fact that they did not exist.

All that I had seen or read of war had led me to the conviction that, having regard to modern fire-power, a few weeks will suffice to create strong field defences, and also to limit and canalise the enemy's front of attack by minefields and other obstructions. Moreover, it had never entered into my head that no circle of detached forts of a permanent character protected the rear of the famous fortress. I cannot understand how it was I did not know this. But none of the officers on the spot and none of my professional advisers at home seem to have realised this awful need. At any rate, none of them pointed it out to me — not even those who saw my telegrams based upon the false assumption that a regular siege would be required. I had read of Plevna in 1877, where, before the era of machine-guns, defences had been improvised by the Turks in the actual teeth of the Russian assault; and I had examined Verdun in 1917, where a field army lying in and among detached forts had a year earlier made so glorious a record. I had put my faith in the enemy being compelled to use artillery on a very large scale in order to pulverise our strong points at Singapore, and in the almost prohibitive difficulties and long delays which would impede such an artillery concentration and the gathering of ammunition along Malayan communications. Now, suddenly, all this vanished away and I saw before me the hideous spectacle of the almost naked island and of the wearied, if not exhausted, troops retreating upon it.

I do not write this in any way to excuse myself. I ought to have known. My advisers ought to have known and I ought to have been told, and I ought to have asked. The reason I had not asked about this matter, amid the thousands of questions I put, was that the possibility of Singapore having no landward defences no more entered into my mind than that of a battleship being launched without a bottom. I am aware of the various reasons that have been given for this failure: the pre-occupation of the troops in training and in building defence works in Northern Malaya; the shortage of civilian labour;

pre-war financial limitations and centralised War Office control; the fact that the Army's rôle was to protect the naval base, situated on the north shore of the island, and that it was therefore their duty to fight in front of that shore and not along it. I do not consider these reasons valid. Defences should have been built.

My immediate reaction was to repair the neglect so far as time allowed. I at once dictated the following minute:

Prime Minister to General Ismay, for C.O.S. Committee 19 Jan. 42

I must confess to being staggered by Wavell's telegram of the 16th and other telegrams on the same subject. It never occurred to me for a moment, nor to Sir John Dill, with whom I discussed the matter on the outward voyage, that the gorge of the fortress of Singapore, with its splendid moat half a mile to a mile wide, was not entirely fortified against an attack from the northward. What is the use of having an island for a fortress if it is not to be made into a citadel? To construct a line of detached works with searchlights and cross-fire combined with immense wiring and obstruction of the swamp areas, and to provide the proper ammunition to enable the fortress guns to dominate enemy batteries planted in Johore, was an elementary peace-time provision which it is incredible did not exist in a fortress which has been twenty years building. If this was so, how much more should the necessary field works have been constructed during the two and a half years of the present war? How is it that not one of you pointed this out to me at any time when these matters have been under discussion? More especially should this have been done because in my various minutes extending over the last two years I have repeatedly shown that I relied upon this defence of Singapore Island against a formal siege, and have never relied upon the Kra Isthmus plan. In England at the present time we have found it necessary to protect the gorges of all our forts against a landing raid from the rear, and the Portsdown Hill forts at Portsmouth show the principles which have long prevailed. . . .

3. Seaward batteries and a naval base do not constitute a fortress, which is a *completely encircled* strong place. Merely to have seaward batteries and no forts or fixed defences to protect their rear is not to be excused on any ground. By such neglect the whole

security of the fortress has been at the mercy of ten thousand men breaking across the straits in small boats. I warn you this will be one of the greatest scandals that could possibly be exposed.

4. Let a plan be made at once to do the best possible while the battle in Johore is going forward. This plan should comprise: (*a*) An attempt to use the fortress guns on the northern front by firing reduced charges and by running in a certain quantity of high explosive if none exists. (*b*) By mining and obstructing the landing-places where any considerable force could gather. (*c*) By wiring and laying booby-traps in mangrove swamps and other places. (*d*) By constructing field works and strong points, with field artillery and machine-gun cross-fire. (*e*) By collecting and taking under our control every conceivable small boat that is found in the Johore Straits or anywhere else within reach. (*f*) By planting field batteries at each end of the straits, carefully masked and with searchlights, so as to destroy any enemy boat that may seek to enter the straits. (*g*) By forming the nuclei of three or four mobile counter-attack reserve columns upon which the troops when driven out of Johore can be formed. (*h*) The entire male population should be employed upon constructing defence works. The most rigorous compulsion is to be used, up to the limit where picks and shovels are available. (*i*) Not only must the defence of Singapore Island be maintained by every means, but the whole island must be fought for until every single unit and every single strong point has been separately destroyed. (*j*) Finally, the city of Singapore must be converted into a citadel and defended to the death. No surrender can be contemplated. . . .

On this the Chiefs of Staff sent the following instructions:

Chiefs of Staff to General Wavell   20 Jan. 42

The eventuality of the Battle of Johore going against you should be taken into account, and all preparations should be made for the utmost possible defence of the island. Following are some particular points:

1. Full preparations should be made to use fortress guns against landward attack and effective fire-control should be organised. Report most urgent requirements high explosives, when possibility of provision will be examined.

2. Land approaches from the straits and landing-places and exits

therefrom in the island should be obstructed with wire, mines, booby-traps, or any other means possible.

3. A proportion of beach defence guns and M.G.s should be diverted from the south sectors to the north and west of the island.

4. All boats or small craft in the straits or outside them within reach of the island should be collected under our control or destroyed.

5. Defence must be based on system of localities for all ground defence sited to cover most dangerous avenues of approach. In view of the difficulty of siting beach defences in the swamps, a good system of mobile reserves ready to deliver rapid counter-attack should be built up. A system of switch lines should also be developed in the interior to prevent exploitation of successful landings. Full use should be made of all available civilian and military labour for this, and generally for defence works of all kinds.

6. All possible measures should be taken to guard against attempted night landings succeeding by surprise. In this connection, unlikely landing-places should again be reconnoitred in the light of Japanese tactics and mobility.

7. Adequate measures should be made for defence of aerodromes and other possible landing-grounds in Johore and Singapore against Japanese airborne forces reported under preparation in Indo-China. Full use must be made of R.A.F. personnel.

8. Effective measures should be worked out to disperse and control the civil population and to suppress fifth column activity.

9. Personnel for fixed defences should be armed and assigned tasks in the local defence scheme.

10. The best possible signal communications should be developed throughout the island, and also to aerodromes in Sumatra, on which close support aircraft may be based.

11. [We] realise that action will already have been taken on many of these points, in which case we shall be grateful for an early report. Action on the remainder should be initiated without delay and all possible steps taken to prepare for protracted defence.

Meanwhile I had telegraphed to General Wavell:

20 Jan. 42

Now that you have become Supreme Commander of the A.B.D.A. nations in the Southwestern Pacific, I cannot of course

send you any direct instructions. All your operative orders, which
I hope will be as few as possible, will come through the combined
C.O.S. Committee from the President at Washington. Nevertheless,
I propose to continue our correspondence whenever I have suggestions to make or questions to ask. This will be especially the
case where the local defence of a fortress like Singapore is involved.
It is in this light that you must view the telegram sent you today
by the C.O.S. Committee about the landward defences of Singapore
Island. I was greatly distressed by your telegrams, and I want to
make it absolutely clear that I expect every inch of ground to be
defended, every scrap of material or defences to be blown to pieces
to prevent capture by the enemy, and no question of surrender to
be entertained until after protracted fighting among the ruins of
Singapore City.

I also minuted to the Chiefs of Staff:

Prime Minister to General Ismay, for C.O.S. Committee 20 Jan. 42

This [the reinforcement of Burma] is surely a matter for the
Supreme Commander, but an opinion should be expressed by the
Chiefs of Staff. Obviously nothing should distract us from the Battle of Singapore, but should Singapore fall, quick transference
of forces to Burma might be possible. As a strategic object, I regard keeping the Burma Road open as more important than the
retention of Singapore.

Chiefs of Staff to General Percival (Singapore)   21 Jan. 42

War Cabinet discussed recent developments in Malaya.

2. They were disturbed by the reports of continued Japanese
landings behind our lines on the west coast of Malaya. It had been
hoped that local naval forces could have been improvised to deal
effectively with these incursions by presumably unarmed enemy
vessels. Please report fully what has been done and what you hope
to do in this matter.

3. Another question which came under discussion was the water
supply in Singapore Island. Bearing in mind that Hong Kong
had to surrender through shortage of water, are you satisfied that
Singapore could carry on, even if cut off from the mainland?

4. The Governor was instructed over a month ago to evacuate
as many *bouches inutiles* as possible from Singapore. Please telegraph numbers already evacuated and future plans.

*   *   *   *   *

When I awoke on the morning of the 21st, the following most pessimistic telegram from General Wavell about the prospects of holding Singapore lay at the top of my box:

General Wavell to Prime Minister   19 Jan. 42

Officer whom I had sent to Singapore for plans of defence of island has now returned. Schemes are now being prepared for defence of northern part of island. *Number of troops required to hold island effectively probably are [as] great or greater than number required to defend Johore.*[3] I have ordered Percival to fight out the battle in Johore, but to work out plans to prolong resistance on island as long as possible should he lose Johore battle. I must warn you however that I doubt whether island can be held for long once Johore is lost. The fortress guns are sited for use against ships, and have mostly ammunition for that purpose only; many can only fire seaward.[4] Part of garrison has already been sent into Johore, and many troops remaining are [of] doubtful value. I am sorry to give you depressing picture, but I do not want you to have false picture of island fortress. Singapore defences were constructed entirely to meet seaward attack. I still hope Johore may be held till next convoy arrives.

And also later the following arrived:

General Pownall to Prime Minister   20 Jan. 42

Wavell has flown [to] Singapore at short notice, as situation appears to be worsening.

Situation Muar front confused, but 45th Brigade and 2d Australian Battalion withdrawing Bakri area to link up with 53d Infantry Brigade, which is to secure Payong Hill, eight miles north of Batu Pahat. Right flank now withdrawn behind river Segamat and to Labis tonight.

Wavell will telegraph on return.

General Wavell to Chiefs of Staff   20 Jan. 42

Flew [to] Singapore today and saw Percival, Heath, and Simmons.

Situation in Malaya greatly deteriorated. Whole of 45th Indian Infantry Brigade and two Australian battalions cut off about

---

[3] My italics — Author.
[4] This is inaccurate. The majority of the guns could fire landward also.

Bakri, east of Muar, and have apparently failed to make good their withdrawal. 53d Brigade at Payong, 20 miles east of Bakri, also being heavily attacked.

2. This situation in south will necessitate withdrawal of troops in Segamat-Labis area, and may necessitate general withdrawal towards Johore Bahru, and eventually to island.

3. Preparatory measures for defence of island being made with limited resources available. Success of defence will depend on numbers and state of troops withdrawn from Johore, arrival of reinforcements, and ability of Air Force to maintain fighters on island. If all goes well, hope prolonged defence possible.

4. Singapore was bombed twice this morning by about fifty planes each time. Military damage at present unknown.

General Wavell also replied to my telegram of the 20th, but this reached me in the evening.

General Wavell to Prime Minister   21 Jan. 42

Am glad that you will continue to let me know your mind.

2. I am anxious that you should not have false impression of defences of Singapore Island. I did not realise myself until lately how entirely defences were planned against seaward attack only. Points in C.O.S. telegram have all been considered, and are in hand as far as possible.

3. I hope to get Indian Brigade and remainder of 18th Division into Singapore. After allowing for losses, this should give equivalent of approximately three divisions for defence of island, if we are driven into it. Subsequent reinforcements will probably have to be used for defence of Java and Sumatra, which are both weakly held. We are concocting plans with Dutch for this.

*   *   *   *   *

I pondered over Wavell's telegram of the 19th for a long time. So far I had thought only of animating, and as far as possible compelling, the desperate defence of the island, the fortress, and the city, and this in any case was the attitude which should be maintained unless any decisive change of policy was ordered. But now I began to think more of Burma and of the reinforcements on the way to Singapore. These could be doomed or diverted. There was still ample time to turn their prows northward to Rangoon. I therefore prepared the following minute to the Chiefs of Staff, and gave it to General Ismay in time for their meeting at 11.30 A.M. on the 21st. I confess freely however that my mind was not made up. I leaned upon my friends and counsellors. We all suffered extremely at this time.

Prime Minister to General Ismay, for C.O.S. Committee 21 Jan. 42

In view of this very bad telegram from General Wavell, we must reconsider the whole position at a Defence Committee meeting tonight.

We have already committed exactly the error which I feared when I sent my "Beware" telegram from the ship on the way out. Forces which might have made a solid front in Johore, or at any rate along the Singapore waterfront, have been broken up piecemeal. No defensive line has been constructed on the landward side. No defence has been made by the Navy to the enemy's turning movements on the west coast of the peninsula. General Wavell has expressed the opinion that it will take more troops to defend Singapore Island than to win the battle in Johore. The battle in Johore is almost certainly lost.

His message gives little hope for prolonged defence. It is evident that such defence would be only at the cost of all the reinforcements now on the way. If General Wavell is doubtful whether more than a few weeks' delay can be obtained, the question arises whether we should not at once blow the docks and batteries and workshops to pieces and concentrate everything on the defence of Burma and keeping open the Burma Road.

2. It appears to me that this question should be squarely faced now and put bluntly to General Wavell. What is the value of Singapore [to the enemy] above the many harbours in the Southwest Pacific if all naval and military demolitions are thoroughly carried out? On the other hand, the loss of Burma would be very grievous. It would cut us off from the Chinese, whose troops have been the most successful of those yet engaged against the Japanese. We may, by muddling things and hesitating to take an ugly decision, lose both Singapore and the Burma Road. Obviously the decision depends upon how long the defence of Singapore Island can be maintained. If it is only for a few weeks, it is certainly not worth losing all our reinforcements and aircraft.

3. Moreover, one must consider that the fall of Singapore, accompanied as it will be by the fall of Corregidor, will be a tremendous shock to India, which only the arrival of powerful forces and successful action on the Burma front can sustain.

Pray let all this be considered this morning.

* * * * *

The Chiefs of Staff reached no definite conclusion, and when we met in the evening at the Defence Committee a similar hesitation to commit ourselves to so grave a step prevailed. The direct initial responsibility lay with General Wavell as Allied Supreme Commander. Personally I found the issue so difficult that I did not press my new view, which I should have done if I had been resolved. We could none of us foresee the collapse of the defence which was to occur in little more than three weeks. A day or two could at least be spared for further thought.

Sir Earle Page, the Australian representative, did not of course attend the Chiefs of Staff Committee, nor did I invite him to the Defence Committee. By some means or other he was shown a copy of my minute to the Chiefs of Staff. He immediately telegraphed to his Government, and on January 24 we received a message from Mr. Curtin, which contained a severe reproach:

Mr. Curtin to Prime Minister 23 Jan. 42

I am communicating the following message as the result of an emergency meeting of the War Cabinet summoned today to consider reports on the situation in Malaya:

. . . Page has reported that the Defence Committee has been considering the evacuation of Malaya and Singapore. After all the assurances we have been given, the evacuation of Singapore would be regarded here and elsewhere as an inexcusable betrayal. Singapore is a central fortress in the system of the Empire and local defence. As stated in my telegram, we understood that it was to be made impregnable, and in any event it was to be capable of holding out for a prolonged period until the arrival of the main fleet.

Even in an emergency diversion of reinforcements should be
to the Netherlands East Indies and not Burma. Anything else
would be deeply resented, and might force the Netherlands East
Indies to make a separate peace.

On the faith of the proposed flow of reinforcements, we have
acted and carried out our part of the bargain. We expect you not
to frustrate the whole purpose by evacuation.

The trend of the situation in Malaya and the attack on Rabaul
are giving rise to a public feeling of grave uneasiness at Allied
impotence to do anything to stem the Japanese advance. The
Government, in realising its responsibility to prepare the public for
the possibility of resisting an aggressor, also has a duty and obligation to explain why it may not have been possible to prevent
the enemy reaching our shores. It is therefore in duty bound to
exhaust all the possibilities of the situation, the more so since the
Australian people, having volunteered for service overseas in large
numbers, find it difficult to understand why they must wait so long
for an improvement in the situation when irreparable damage
may have been done to their power to resist, the prestige of Empire,
and the solidarity of the Allied cause.

Mr. Curtin's telegram was both serious and unusual. The
expression "inexcusable betrayal" was not in accordance with
the truth or with military facts. A frightful disaster was approaching. Could we avoid it? How did the balance of loss
and gain stand? At this time the destination of important forces
still rested in our control. There is no "betrayal" in examining
such issues with a realistic eye. Moreover, the Australian War
Committee could not measure the whole situation. Otherwise
they would not have urged the complete neglect of Burma,
which was proved by events to be the only place we still had
the means to save.

It is not true to say that Mr. Curtin's message decided the
issue. If we had all been agreed upon the policy, we should,
as I had suggested, certainly have put the case "bluntly" to
Wavell. I was conscious however of a hardening of opinion
against the abandonment of this renowned key point in the
Far East. The effect that would be produced all over the
world, especially in the United States, of a British "scuttle"

while the Americans fought on so stubbornly at Corregidor was terrible to imagine. There is no doubt what a purely military decision should have been.

By general agreement or acquiescence however all efforts were made to reinforce Singapore and to sustain its defence. The 18th Division, part of which had already landed, went forward on its way.

4

A Vote of Confidence

The Political Atmosphere — Need to Warn Parliament of Impending Misfortunes — Desire for a Ministry of Production — Sir Stafford Cripps Returns from Russia — I Offer Him the Ministry of Supply — The House of Commons and the Broadcasting of My Statement — I Ask for a Vote of Confidence — Importance of a Division — An Account of the Desert Battle — My Tribute to Rommel — Our Nakedness in the Far East — The Limits of Our Resources — I Accept Full Responsibility — Hard Times Ahead — Friendly Tone of the Debate — Four Hundred and Sixty-Four to One — American and Allied Relief — Six Liberal Abstentions out of Twenty — Sir Stafford Cripps Declines the Ministry of Supply — My Letter to Him of January 31.

I WAS EXPECTED to make a full statement to Parliament about
my mission to Washington and all that had happened in the
five weeks I had been away. Two facts stood out in my mind.
The first was that the Grand Alliance was bound to win the
war in the long run. The second was that a vast, measureless
array of disasters approached us in the onslaught of Japan.
Everyone could see with intense relief that our life as a nation
and Empire was no longer at stake. On the other hand, the fact
that the sense of mortal danger was largely removed set every
critic, friendly or malevolent, free to point out the many errors
which had been made. Moreover, many felt it their duty to
improve our methods of conducting the war and thus shorten
the fearful tale. I was myself profoundly disturbed by the

defeats which had already fallen upon us, and no one knew
better than I that these were but the beginnings of the deluge.
The demeanour of the Australian Government, the well-in-
formed and airily detached criticism of the newspapers, the
shrewd and constant girding of twenty or thirty able Members
of Parliament, the atmosphere of the lobbies, gave me the
sense of an embarrassed, unhappy, baffled public opinion,
albeit superficial, swelling and mounting about me on every
side.

On the other hand, I was well aware of the strength of my
position. I could count on the good will of the people for
the share I had had in their survival in 1940. I did not underrate the broad, deep tide of national fidelity that bore me
forward. The War Cabinet and the Chiefs of Staff showed me
the highest loyalty. I was sure of myself. I made it clear, as
occasion required, to those about me that I would not consent
to the slightest curtailment of my personal authority and
responsibility. The press was full of suggestions that I should
remain Prime Minister and make the speeches, but cede the
actual control of the war to someone else. I resolved to yield
nothing to any quarter, to take the prime and direct personal
responsibility upon myself, and to demand a Vote of Confidence from the House of Commons. I also remembered that
wise French saying, *"On ne règne sur les âmes que par le
calme."*

It was necessary above all to warn the House and the country
of the misfortunes which impended upon us. There is no
worse mistake in public leadership than to hold out false
hopes soon to be swept away. The British people can face peril
or misfortune with fortitude and buoyancy, but they bitterly
resent being deceived or finding that those responsible for
their affairs are themselves dwelling in a fool's paradise. I felt
it vital, not only to my own position but to the whole conduct
of the war, to discount future calamities by describing the
immediate outlook in the darkest terms. It was also possible
to do so at this juncture without prejudicing the military situation or disturbing that underlying confidence in ultimate

victory which all were now entitled to feel. In spite of the
shocks and stresses which each day brought, I did not grudge
the twelve or fourteen hours of concentrated thought which
ten thousand words of original composition on a vast, many-
sided subject demanded, and while the flames of adverse war
in the Desert licked my feet, I succeeded in preparing my statement and appreciation of our case.

*   *   *   *   *

At this time there was a widely expressed wish for the setting
up of a Ministry of Production, with its chief in the War
Cabinet. In July, 1941, before starting on my voyage to meet
President Roosevelt, I had argued at length in the House that
this was not at that time necessary. But the current of opinion
still flowed, and was strengthened, not only by events, but by
the positions of the men and offices involved. The President,
for instance, had appointed Mr. Donald Nelson to supervise
the whole field of production. Ought he not to have an opposite number? All centred upon Lord Beaverbrook, whose
success at Washington has already been described, and who
exerted powerful influence upon the highest American circles
concerned. In the Ministry of Munitions in 1917 and 1918,
I had presided over the spheres now covered by the Ministry
of Supply and the Ministry of Aircraft Production. These departments were so closely interwoven in the fields of raw
materials and skilled labour that a single directing authority
would have great advantages. As everything became more
gigantic, this applied with increasing force. Beaverbrook had
the confidence both of the Russians and of the Americans, and
no one seemed more fitted to head so great a combination as he.

Since he had left the Ministry of Aircraft Production for that
of Supply there had been much friction, some of it inevitable,
on the frontiers of these two departments, and I hoped not
only to restore harmony but to improve results by joining these
two great branches of our armament production under a
Minister of Production of War Cabinet rank, which he already
held. In Colonel Moore-Brabazon, Minister of Aircraft Pro-

duction, and in Sir Andrew Duncan, who I considered would
be admirable as Minister of Supply, I thought he would have
two subordinates each with his own wide sphere of initiative
and judgment. While all this was still revolving in my mind,
a new figure appeared upon the scene.

*   *   *   *   *

Sir Stafford Cripps had long wished to end his mission
in Russia. The post of Ambassador to the Soviets has been
found extremely unattractive by all British and Americans
who had been called upon to fill it, both during and after the
war. During the period before Hitler's attack ranged Russia
with us, our envoy had been almost entirely ignored in
Moscow. He had hardly ever had access to Stalin, and Molotov
held him and all other Allied Ambassadors at a frigid arm's-
length. The shift of the Soviet diplomatic capital from Moscow
to Kuibyshev in the crisis of December had only repro-
duced the unpleasant and unfruitful conditions of Moscow
in an aggravated form. When so much was being done by
direct communication between me and Stalin and now between
President Roosevelt and Stalin, the functions of an Ambassador
became increasingly separated from the scene of decisive business. Sir Stafford had already, when at home at the time of the
German invasion, expressed to me his wish to be relieved, but he
accepted and shared my view that this should not take place at
the first shock of Russia's agony. Nearly eight months had
passed since then, and there was certainly nothing inappropriate
in a political personage of his quality seeking to return to the
House of Commons, at the centre of our political life. I therefore agreed early in January to his relief by Sir Archibald
Clark-Kerr.

On January 23 Cripps arrived home from Russia. He was at
this time an important political figure adrift from the Labour
Party, by whom he had been expelled for extremism some
years earlier. His reputation was enhanced by the enthusiasm
felt throughout Britain for the valiant Russian resistance with
which his position as Ambassador was associated. The Leftists

and their press in Britain had built up the story that he more
than any living man had been responsible for bringing Russia
into the war on the side of solitary, hard-pressed Britain. There
were some on the extreme Left who appeared to regard him
as worth running as an alternative Prime Minister, and in these
circles it was said that he would lead the new group of critics of
the Government, which it was hoped to organise into an effective Parliamentary force. Knowing his abilities and liking him
personally, I was anxious to bring him into the Government,
where we needed all the help we could get. As his former
colleagues in the Labour Party raised no objection, I looked
about for an opportunity.

Although I was kept well informed about the Left Wing
ideas I acted wholly on the merits of the case. In the first
World War, while I was Minister of Munitions, Cripps had
been assistant superintendent of the largest explosive factory
in the British Empire, and had filled the post with remarkable
efficiency. This practical administrative experience was combined with his outstanding intellectual gifts. It seemed to me
that his appointment to the Ministry of Supply would be in
best accord with the public interest, and might form a part of
the major design for creating a Ministry of Production. Sir
Stafford and Lady Cripps came to luncheon at Chequers on
January 25, and he and I had a long and agreeable talk in the
afternoon. When I made him a definite proposal and explained
the position which the office in question would have in the
general sphere of war production, he said he would reflect
upon it and let me know.

*   *   *   *   *

On January 27 the debate began, and I laid our case before
the House. I could see they were in a querulous temper, because when I had asked as soon as I got home that my forthcoming statement might be electrically recorded so that it could
be used for broadcasting to the Empire and the United States,
objection was taken on various grounds which had no relation
to the needs of the hour. I therefore withdrew my request,

although it would not have been denied in any other Parliament in the world. It was in such an atmosphere that I rose to speak.

Since my return to this country I have come to the conclusion that I must ask to be sustained by a Vote of Confidence from the House of Commons. This is a thoroughly normal, constitutional, democratic procedure. A debate on the war has been asked for. I have arranged it in the fullest and freest manner for three whole days. Any Member will be free to say anything he thinks fit about or against the Administration or against the composition or personalities of the Government, to his heart's content, subject only to the reservation which the House is always so careful to observe about military secrets. Could you have anything freer than that? Could you have any higher expression of democracy than that? Very few other countries have institutions strong enough to sustain such a thing while they are fighting for their lives.

I owe it to the House to explain to them what has led me to ask for their exceptional support at this time. It has been suggested that we should have a three days' debate of this kind, in which the Government would no doubt be lustily belaboured by some of those who have lighter burdens to carry, and that at the end we should separate without a division. In this case sections of the press which are hostile — and there are some whose hostility is pronounced — could declare that the Government's credit was broken, and it might even be hinted, after all that has passed and all the discussion there has been, that it had been privately intimated to me that I should be very reckless if I asked for a Vote of Confidence from Parliament. . . .

We have had a great deal of bad news lately from the Far East, and I think it highly probable, for reasons which I shall presently explain, that we shall have a great deal more. Wrapped up in this bad news will be many tales of blunders and shortcomings, both in foresight and action. No one will pretend for a moment that disasters like these occur without there having been faults and shortcomings. I see all this rolling towards us like the waves in a storm, and that is another reason why I require a formal, solemn Vote of Confidence from the House of Commons, which hitherto in this struggle has never flinched. The House would fail in its duty if it did not insist upon two things: first, freedom of debate, and, secondly, a clear, honest, blunt vote thereafter. Then we shall all know where we are, and all those with whom we have to deal, at home and abroad, friend or foe, will know where we are and where they are. It is because we are to have a free debate, in which perhaps twenty to thirty Members can take part, that I demand an expression of opinion from the four or five hundred Members who will have to sit silent.

It is because things have gone badly and worse is to come that I demand a Vote of Confidence. If a Member has helpful criticisms to make, or even severe corrections to administer, that may be perfectly consistent with thinking that in respect of the Administration, such as it is, he might go farther and fare worse. But if an honourable gentleman dislikes the Government very much and feels it in the public interest that it should be broken up, he ought to have the manhood to testify his convictions in the lobby. There is no objection to anything being said in plain English, or even plainer, and the Government will do their utmost to conform to any standard which may be set in the course of the debate. But no one need be mealy-mouthed in debate, and no one should be chicken-hearted in voting. I have voted against Governments I have been elected to support, and, looking back, I have sometimes felt very glad that I did so. Everyone in these rough times must do what he thinks is his duty.

*   *   *   *   *

I gave them some account of the Desert battle.

General Auchinleck had demanded five months' preparation for his campaign, but on November 18 he fell upon the enemy. For more than two months in the Desert the most fierce, continuous battle has raged between scattered bands of men, armed with the latest weapons, seeking each other dawn after dawn, fighting to the death throughout the day and then often long into the night. Here was a battle which turned out very differentl' from what was foreseen. All was dispersed and confused. Much depended on the individual soldier and the junior officer. Much, but not all; because this battle would have been lost on November 24 if General Auchinleck had not intervened himself, changed the command, and ordered the ruthless pressure of the attack to be maintained without regard to risks or consequences. But for this robust decision we should now be back on the old line from which we had started, or perhaps farther back. Tobruk would possibly have fallen, and Rommel might be marching towards the Nile. Since then the battle has declared itself. Cyrenaica has been regained. It has still to be held. We have not succeeded in destroying Rommel's army, but nearly two-thirds of it are wounded, prisoners, or dead.[1]

The House did not of course appreciate the significance of Rommel's successful counter-stroke, for they could be given no inkling of the larger plans that would be opened by a swift British conquest of Tripolitania. The loss of Benghazi and Agedabia, which had already become public, seemed to be a part of the sudden ebbs and flows of Desert warfare. Moreover, as the telegrams here printed have shown, I had no precise information as to what had happened, and why.

I could not resist paying my tribute to Rommel.

I cannot tell what the position at the present moment is on the western front in Cyrenaica. We have a very daring and skilful opponent against us, and, may I say across the havoc of war, a great general. He has certainly received reinforcements. Another battle is even now in progress, and I make it a rule never to try to prophesy beforehand how battles will turn out. I always rejoice that I have made that rule. Naturally, one does not say that we have not a chance. . . .

My reference to Rommel passed off quite well at the moment. Later on I heard that some people had been offended. They could not feel that any virtue should be recognised in an enemy leader. This churlishness is a well-known streak in human nature, but contrary to the spirit in which a war is won or a lasting peace established.

* * * * *

I presently came to the larger issue of our nakedness in the Far East.

[1] Corrected figures, with post-war information of enemy casualties, are given in Volume III, Book Two, Chapter X. Total British casualties were 17,704, enemy casualties about 33,000.

I have told the House the story of these few months, and honourable Members will see from it how narrowly our resources have
been strained and by what a small margin and by what strokes of
fortune — for which we claim no credit — we have survived — so
far. Where should we have been, I wonder, if we had yielded to
the clamour which was so loud three or four months ago that
we should invade France or the Low Countries? We can still see
on the walls the inscription "Second Front Now." Who did not
feel the appeal of that? But imagine what our position would
have been if we had yielded to this vehement temptation. Every
ton of our shipping, every flotilla, every aeroplane, the whole
strength of our Army would be committed, and would be fighting
for life on the French shores or on the shores of the Low Countries.
All these troubles of the Far East and the Middle East might have
sunk to insignificance compared with the question of another and
far worse Dunkirk. . . .

I suppose there are some of those who were vocal and voluble,
and even clamant, for a second front to be opened in France who
are now going to come up bland and smiling and ask why it is
that we have not ample forces in Malaya, Burma, Borneo, and
Celebes.

In two and a half years of fighting we have only just managed
to keep our heads above water. . . . We are beginning to see our
way through. It looks as if we were in for a very bad time; but
provided we all stand together, and provided we throw in the last
spasm of our strength, it also looks, more than it ever did before,
as if we were going to win.

*   *   *   *   *

While facing Germany and Italy here and in the Nile Valley, we
have never had any power to provide effectively for the defence of
the Far East. . . . It may be that this or that might have been done
which was not done, but we have never been able to provide
effectively for the defence of the Far East against an attack by
Japan. It has been the policy of the Cabinet at almost all costs
to avoid embroilment with Japan until we were sure that the
United States would also be engaged. We even had to stoop, as
the House will remember, when we were at our very weakest
point, to close the Burma Road for some months. I remember
that some of our present critics were very angry about it, but we

had to do it. There never has been a moment, there never could have been a moment, when Great Britain or the British Empire, single-handed, could fight Germany and Italy, could wage the Battle of Britain, the Battle of the Atlantic, and the Battle of the Middle East, and at the same time stand thoroughly prepared in Burma, the Malay peninsula, and generally in the Far East, against the impact of a vast military empire like Japan, with more than seventy mobile divisions, the third Navy in the world, a great Air Force, and the thrust of eighty or ninety millions of hardy, warlike Asiatics. If we had started to scatter our forces over these immense areas in the Far East, we should have been ruined. If we had moved large armies of troops urgently needed on the war fronts to regions which were not at war and might never be at war, we should have been altogether wrong. We should have cast away the chance, which has now become something more than a chance, of all of us emerging safely from the terrible plight in which we have been plunged. . . .

The decision was taken to make our contribution to Russia, to try to beat Rommel, and to form a stronger front from the Levant to the Caspian. It followed from that decision that it was in our power only to make a moderate and partial provision in the Far East against the hypothetical danger of a Japanese onslaught. Sixty thousand men, indeed, were concentrated at Singapore, but priority in modern aircraft, in tanks, and in anti-aircraft and anti-tank artillery was accorded to the Nile Valley.

For this decision in its broad strategic aspects, and also for the diplomatic policy in regard to Russia, I take the fullest personal responsibility. If we have handled our resources wrongly, no one is so much to blame as me. If we have not got large modern air forces and tanks in Burma and Malaya tonight, no one is more accountable than I am. Why then should I be called upon to pick out scapegoats, to throw the blame on generals or airmen or sailors? Why then should I be called upon to drive away loyal and trusted colleagues and friends to appease the clamour of certain sections of the British and Australian press, or in order to take the edge off our reverses in Malaya and the Far East, and the punishment which we have yet to take there?

I had to burden the House for nearly two hours. They took what they got without enthusiasm. But I had the impression that they were not unconvinced by the argument. In view of what I saw coming towards us I thought it well to end by putting things at their worst, and making no promises while not excluding hope.

Although I feel the broadening swell of victory and liberation bearing us and all the tortured peoples onwards safely to the final goal, I must confess to feeling the weight of the war upon me even more than in the tremendous summer days of 1940. There are so many fronts which are open, so many vulnerable points to defend, so many inevitable misfortunes, so many shrill voices raised to take advantage, now that we can breathe more freely, of all the turns and twists of war. Therefore, I feel entitled to come to the House of Commons, whose servant I am, and ask them not to press me to act against my conscience and better judgment and make scapegoats in order to improve my own position, not to press me to do the things which may be clamoured for at the moment but which will not help in our war effort, but, on the contrary, to give me their encouragement and to give me their aid. I have never ventured to predict the future. I stand by my original programme, blood, toil, tears, and sweat, which is all I have ever offered, to which I added, five months later, "many shortcomings, mistakes, and disappointments." But it is because I see the light gleaming behind the clouds and broadening on our path that I make so bold now as to demand a declaration of confidence from the House of Commons as an additional weapon in the armoury of the United Nations.

*   *   *   *   *

The debate then ran on for three days. But the tone was to me unexpectedly friendly. There was no doubt what the House would do. My colleagues in the War Cabinet, headed by Mr. Attlee, sustained the Government case with vigour and even fierceness. I had to wind up on the 29th. At this time I feared that there would be no division. I tried by taunts to urge our critics into the lobby against us without at the same time offending the now thoroughly reconciled assembly. But nothing that I dared say could spur any of the disaffected figures in the Conservative, Labour, and Liberal Parties into voting.

Luckily, when the division was called, the Vote of Confidence was challenged by the Independent Labour Party, who numbered three. Two were required as tellers, and the result was four hundred and sixty-four to one. I was grateful to James Maxton, the leader of the minority, for bringing the matter to a head. Such a fuss had been made by the press that telegrams of relief and congratulation flowed in from all over the Allied world. The warmest were from my American friends at the White House. I had sent congratulations to the President on his sixtieth birthday. "It is fun," he cabled, "to be in the same decade with you." The naggers in the press were not however without resource. They spun round with the alacrity of squirrels. How unnecessary it had been to ask for a Vote of Confidence! Who had ever dreamed of challenging the National Government? These "shrill voices," as I called them, were but the unknowing heralds of approaching catastrophe.

Prime Minister to Chief Whip   31 Jan. 42

I congratulate you on the splendid Conservative vote and on the steady increase in it over nearly two years.

I am writing to the Leader of the Liberal Party about their vote. Perhaps you will check the enclosed letter, and, if you do not disagree with it, seal and send on.

Mr. Churchill to Sir Archibald Sinclair   31 Jan. 42

I must draw your attention to the voting of the Liberal Party in the House on the Vote of Confidence. Out of a total of twenty, six abstained or were absent, leaving fourteen to represent the party. Of these fourteen three were Ministers, viz., yourself, Johnstone, and Foot. You also have an Under-Secretaryship in the Lords. This is a lot of sail to carry on so small a hull, and I fear that the Conservative Party, which in the three divisions during the life of the present Government has voted 252, 281, and 309 respectively, will become critical of the lack of support given to the Government.

At the same time, the *News Chronicle* has become one of the most critical and often hostile newspapers, and fallen sadly below the splendid but instructed independence of the *Manchester Guardian*.

I suggest to you that these matters require your very earnest attention. As you know, I have never measured the strength of the Liberal Party by its Parliamentary representation. Nevertheless, when its numbers are so small it seems to me all the more necessary to have unity of action on occasions of confidence in the Government, which the party has formally and officially decided to join and support.

*   *   *   *   *

Sir Stafford Cripps had not spoken in the course of the debate, but during its progress he wrote me a friendly letter declining my proposal that he should become Minister of Supply under the conditions I had suggested. The least that was necessary, he said, to get the increased production looked for was that the Minister of Supply should be complete master in his own department, a member of the War Cabinet, and responsible for allocations and priorities. "From this you will see that I should not feel myself justified in taking on the task under the conditions suggested, as I do not feel I could make a success of the post, and I should only disappoint both you and the public. I am sorry that I feel myself compelled, after the most careful and anxious consideration, to come to this negative conclusion, as I had hoped that I might be able to give you some small help with the heavy burden you are bearing."

I replied:

31 Jan. 42

I am sorry that you do not feel able to help us by taking over the vast business of the Ministry of Supply, except under conditions which it is not in my power to meet.

That the Minister of Supply should be a member of the War Cabinet would vitiate the policy, upon which Parliament has lately shown itself so strongly set, of having a Minister of Production with general supervisory duties over the whole field of war supply. It would also still further depart from the principle of a small War Cabinet, upon which so much stress was laid by public opinion at the time and after the formation of the present Government. We have already increased our numbers from five to eight, and if you count the Minister of State in Cairo we should be nine. If the Minister of Supply were added [*ex officio* 2] it would be impossible to exclude the Minister for Aircraft Production. If the heads of these two supply departments were in the War Cabinet, it would be necessary to include the Ministerial heads of the fighting departments whom they serve. Thus, the two principles of a [small] War Cabinet and a Minister of Production would both be frustrated. I am sure neither the House of Commons nor the public would approve of this.

It will be a pleasure for me to see you from time to time as you suggest. I shall always be ready to receive your friendly advice, though what I had wanted was your active help. Perhaps I may be able to obtain this some day.

There matters rested — but only for the moment.

2 The words *ex officio* were added in my letter to Sir Stafford Cripps dated February 9. See Chapter 5, page 79.

5

Cabinet Changes

THE VOTE OF CONFIDENCE gave but a passing relief. I had at least given full warning of the disasters ahead. Now during February they came. Meanwhile I could feel the tension in political circles growing. There was a demand that the Government should be "strengthened." "New blood," it was said, should be added. The most noticeable new blood available was of course Sir Stafford Cripps. I disliked very much making changes under external pressure, and had used some bold words about it in the Confidence debate. But it seemed necessary, as the days of February passed, that the changes, which the formation of a Ministry of Production would in any case require, should be of a character amounting to a Ministerial reconstruction. The Ministry of Information agents in many parts of the world reported that England's domestic political wranglings were doing infinite harm. It was evident that decision on the difficult and painful personal questions involved must be taken soon. On the other hand, the creation of the Ministry of Production would be better achieved by agreeable processes than rough ones, though these might well be necessary.

As my plans for the Ministry of Production approached completion, I observed with pain that Lord Beaverbrook's physical health was rapidly breaking down. He began to suffer acutely from asthma, which often deprived him of sleep, that healer of all. One night after my return from Washington, when we were in conference at the Annexe, I was vexed by a persistent noise, and said abruptly, "Let someone go out and stop that cat mewing." A silence fell upon the company, and I realised that this was the asthma of my poor friend. I expressed my regrets and the incident ended, but I recount it because it shows the strain of those exhausting times and it is one of the keys to Beaverbrook's actions. Indeed, he seriously contemplated flying for three or four hours at night above ten thousand feet in order to obtain the relief from asthma which comes from altitude.

This physical affliction was a source of what I can only call a nervous breakdown in Beaverbrook. I had already brushed aside an impulsive resignation during our visit to Washington. But he now developed an unaffected and profound weariness and distaste for office, and, while in one mood demanding ever wider and more untrammelled powers, sought in his heart that relief from burdens and anxieties which many others of my colleagues also desired.

People who did not know the services he had rendered during his tenure of office or his force, driving power, and judgment as I did, often wondered why his influence with me stood so high. They overlooked our long association in the events of the First World War and its aftermath. Apart from Lord Simon, the Lord Chancellor, with whom, though I greatly respected him, I had never been intimate, Beaverbrook was the only colleague I had who had lived through the shocks and strains of the previous struggle with me. We belonged to an

older political generation. Often we had been on different
sides in the crises and quarrels of those former days; sometimes we had even been fiercely opposed; yet on the whole a
relationship had been maintained which was a part of the continuity of my public life, and this was cemented by warm
personal friendship, which had subsisted through all the vicis-
situdes of the past. It was often a comfort to me in these new
years of storm to talk over their troubles and problems, and
to compare them with what we had surmounted or undergone
already, with one who had been throughout in a station, if not
of official, often of commanding power. All my other colleagues had been unknown figures, and most of them young
lieutenants on the battlefields of those bygone but still living
days.

I had completed the preparations to give Beaverbrook a new
tremendous sphere, where his gifts would have their full scope
and where the irritation which any kind of obstruction raised
in him would be at its minimum. On February 4 the creation
of a Ministry of Production and the appointment of Lord
Beaverbrook to this office and of Sir Andrew Duncan to succeed
him had been announced to Parliament. But some important
details had still to be settled behind the scenes. At Beaverbrook's desire, and with Lord Leathers' full consent, I had
added to the proposed Ministry of Production the control of
War Transport. This had not been in my original conception,
but as Leathers wished to work with and under Beaverbrook,
and they got on famously together, I recognised the advantages
of the more extended merger. Every point of detail in dividing
the various responsibilities had however to be fought for as in
a battle. At last I reached the end of my patience, which may
be deemed considerable.

Mr. Churchill to Lord Beaverbrook   10 Feb. 42

I send you a proof of the White Paper which I have undertaken
to give to Parliament in a few hours from now. So far as I am
concerned, it is in its final form. I have lavished my time and
strength during the last week in trying to make arrangements
which are satisfactory to you and to the public interest and to

allay the anxieties of the departments with whom you will be brought in contact. I can do no more.

I am sure it is your duty to undertake this work and try your best to make a success of it, and that you have ample powers for the purpose. I think there is great force in Leathers' argument about the Ministry of War Transport having an effective say in the types of merchant vessels, as they are the only authorities on the subject and have the knowledge. If, after all else has been settled, you break on this point, or indeed on any other in connection with the great office I have shaped for you, I feel bound to say that you will be harshly judged by the nation and in the United States, having regard to the extreme emergency in which we stand and the immense scale of the interests which are involved. I therefore hope that you will not fall below the high level of events and strike so wounding a blow at your country, at your friend, and above all at your reputation.

In this case I shall proceed as arranged and lay the White Paper this morning. If, on the other hand, you have decided to sever our relations, I shall ask Parliament to let me defer my statement till Thursday. Pray let me know by Bridges, who is bringing you this letter himself.

Lord Beaverbrook accepted this decision, and the White Paper exactly defining the Ministry of Production was presented by me to Parliament on February 10. I read to the House the four opening and dominating paragraphs:

The Minister of Production is the War Cabinet Minister charged with prime responsibility for all the business of war production in accordance with the policy of the Minister of Defence and the War Cabinet. He will carry out all the duties hitherto exercised by the Production Executive, excepting only those relating to man-power and labour.

2. These duties include the allocation of available resources of productive capacity and raw materials (including arrangements for their import), the settlement of priorities of production where necessary, and the supervision and guidance of the various departments and branches of departments concerned.

3. Notwithstanding anything in this paper, the responsibilities to Parliament of the Ministers in charge of departments concerned with production for the administration of their departments re-

main unaltered, and any Ministerial head of a department has the right to appeal either to the Minister of Defence or to the War Cabinet in respect of the proper discharge of such responsibilities.

4. The Minister of Production will also be the Minister responsible for handling, on behalf of the War Cabinet, discussions on the combined bodies set up here and in the United States to deal with munitions assignments and raw materials as between the Allies.

At this point I was interrupted by Mr. Hore-Belisha, who asked why questions of man-power and labour were excluded from this proposal. This of course trenched upon the very strong personal antagonisms which had developed between Lord Beaverbrook and Mr. Ernest Bevin. I therefore read three other paragraphs, as follows:

8. The Minister of Labour and National Service is the War Cabinet Minister who will in future, under the general authority of the War Cabinet, discharge the functions hitherto performed by the Production Executive in regard to man-power and labour. These functions include the allocation of man-power resources to the armed forces and civil defence, to war production, and to civil industry, as well as general labour questions in the field of production.

9. As part of his function in dealing with demands for and allocating man-power, the Minister of Labour and National Service has the duty of bringing to notice any direction in which he thinks that greater economy in the use of man-power could be effected, and for this purpose his officers will have such facilities as they require for obtaining information about the utilisation of labour.

10. All labour questions between the production departments and the Ministry of Labour will be settled between the Minister of Labour and the Minister of Production, or such officers as they may appoint. The three supply departments will retain their existing separate labour organisations.

Finally I asked that the White Paper should be carefully studied and that the scheme should be given a fair trial, and I offered all facilities for a debate, if it was desired.

*   *   *   *   *

While all this was in progress the position and attitude of Sir Stafford Cripps became increasingly more important. He bore himself as though he had a message to deliver. Encouraged by the reception of his broadcast delivered on his return from Moscow, he pressed the Minister of Information for further opportunities to speak on the radio. I wrote to him on February 9 as follows:

I see that you replied to a question at Bristol about your joining the Government, "You had better ask Mr. Churchill," or words to that effect. In these circumstances would it not be well to publish your letter of January 29 and my reply of the 31st?

I find that I omitted on page 2 to insert *"ex officio"* after the words "If the Minister of Supply were added." Lord Beaverbrook did not of course sit in the War Cabinet in virtue of his being Minister of Supply, but was appointed in the autumn of 1940 when Minister of Aircraft Production for reasons of a general character. I should propose therefore to add these words, which do no more than make my original meaning plain.

At his wish I did not publish the correspondence, but it was evident to me that his accession to the War Cabinet would be widely welcomed. It was not easy to meet this need and at the same time to comply with equally strong desires expressed in many influential quarters that the War Cabinet should be actually reduced in numbers, and that its members should be free so far as possible from departmental responsibilities. I therefore bethought me of a new expedient.

When the Government was formed in May, 1940, I had added to my other offices the post of Leader of the House of Commons. Mr. Attlee had done all the daily work, and I had only attended on matters of consequence, which would have been necessary in any case. It seemed to me that Sir Stafford had every quality for leading the House. He was a Parliament man and one of its best debaters. Such an appointment, carrying with it membership of the War Cabinet, whose exponent he would be, would give him the wide and general scope which he sought and now tacitly demanded. I discussed the project with Mr. Attlee, whose simple, steadfast loyalty amid such strains was invaluable. I proposed to him that he should hand over the Privy Seal and the Leadership of the House of Commons to Cripps, and that he himself should take the Dominions Office and should be styled, though no constitutional change would be made, Deputy Prime Minister. Here again was a change in form rather than in fact.

Mr. Attlee agreed, and I therefore had to ask Lord Cranborne to move to the Colonial from the Dominions Office. I coupled this with the leadership in the House of Lords. Both these offices were held by Lord Moyne, a man and a friend for whom I had the highest regard. His omission from the Government was of course a heavy blow to him, which it distressed me to inflict. In the long sequence of events it was to cost him his life at the hands of an Israelite assassin in Cairo.

My dear Walter,   19 Feb. 42

It is with very deep regret on every ground, personal and public, that I find myself compelled to make a change in the Colonial Office. The considerable reconstruction of the Government which events and opinion alike require makes it necessary for me to give Attlee the Dominions Office, which many have pressed should be held by a member of the War Cabinet. That being so, I am anxious that Cranborne should take your place, and I feel sure from all I know of you and from your previous conduct in this war that you will be willing to fall in with my wishes and needs.

It has been a great pleasure to me to work with you during this stormy period, and I thank you most earnestly for all the help and friendship you have always shown me, as well as for the high competence with which you have discharged your functions, both as Colonial Secretary and Leader of the House of Lords.

Moyne accepted his dismissal from the Cabinet circles with his customary dignity and good humour. "I need hardly say," he wrote, "that I well understand your necessity to reconstruct the Government, and I only add that I shall always be grateful to you for having given me the opportunity of serving for a year in such an interesting office and for the unvarying consideration and kindness which you have shown me."

*   *   *   *   *

While all this was in flux in the centre of our hard-pressed Government machine, the crash of external disaster fell upon us. Singapore, as will be related in the next chapter, surrendered on February 15, and a hundred thousand British and Imperial troops, as we then estimated them, became Japanese prisoners of war. But even before this, on February 12, an episode of minor importance, as I judged it, but arousing even greater wrath and distress among the public, had occurred. The battle-cruisers *Scharnhorst* and *Gneisenau*, with the cruiser *Prinz Eugen*, had escaped from Brest and made their way up the Channel, running the gantlet of the batteries of Dover and of all our air and sea forces unscathed, so far as the public knew or could be told. We shall return to this in due course. It was certainly not strange that public confidence in the Administration and its conduct of the war should have quavered.

* * * * *

The changes inside the Government arising out of the formation of the Ministry of Production and the need to accommodate Sir Stafford Cripps, who had new strength to bring, already amounted to considerable reconstruction. I resolved to make certain other changes at the same time. Captain Margesson, who had served so well, ceased to be Secretary of State for War, and I advised the appointment in his stead of his Permanent Under-Secretary, Sir James Grigg. Grigg was a civil servant of the highest reputation for efficiency and will power. He had not only been reared in the Treasury, where he had for nearly five years been my principal private secretary when I was Chancellor of the Exchequer, but he had served in India as financial member of the Viceroy's Council, and had left his mark behind him there. He had the whole business of the War Office at his fingers' ends, and commanded the confidence of all the generals and officials. He did not wish to go to the House of Lords; he had no experience of the House of Commons; he had to find, and if necessary fight, a constituency and to adapt himself to the wider and more varied sphere and more flexible methods imposed on a political chief. His force of character, his disinterestedness, his courage, and I must add his obstinacy, were all remarkable. In advancing him to a Ministerial position I certainly lost one of the finest of our civil servants.

I also made a change at the Ministry of Aircraft Production, substituting Colonel Llewellin, who had done extremely well in the United States, with which all our air production was now so closely integrated, for Colonel Moore-Brabazon, who had accepted a peerage with deep regret.

My dear Moore-Brabazon,   21 Feb. 42

It is with very great regret that I write to tell you that the reconstruction of the Government in which I have been involved through pressure of events and opinion makes it necessary for me to have the Ministry of Aircraft Production at my disposal.

I know how hard you have worked there, and I am deeply grateful to you for all your invariable kindness to me. You know what my difficulties are in the midst of this hard and adverse war, and I earnestly hope that an official severance will not affect a friendship which I value so much.

His answer shows his quality:

Dear Prime Minister,   21 Feb. 42

I quite understand. There are one or two points on policy I would like to have spoken to you on, as I consider them of paramount importance, but never mind now.

I enjoyed it all so. It was kind of you to have given me your trust. The Ministry and the work is better than when I came. Best of luck.   BRAB.

In order to reduce the numbers of the War Cabinet I had to ask the Chancellor of the Exchequer to cease to be formally a member.

Mr. Churchill to Sir Kingsley Wood   19 Feb. 42

I send you the enclosed composition of the new War Cabinet which I have found it necessary to form. You will see that I have not been able to include the Chancellor of the Exchequer in it, and have thus reverted to our original plan when the present Government was formed.

I am very sorry about this, but in all the circumstances there is
no choice. Of course you will always have to come when your
affairs are involved.

Lastly among the important changes at this time, Mr.
Greenwood retired from the War Cabinet to facilitate its reduction in numbers, and thereafter behaved with the utmost
patriotism and selflessness.

* * * * *

During the process of Cabinet remaking Lord Beaverbrook
had given much good advice. He was able to take a coolly
detached view of everyone's affairs except his own. For
instance:

Dear Prime Minister,   17 Feb. 42
  Here is the letter which I mentioned on the telephone.
  The people have lost confidence in themselves, and they turn
to the Government, looking for a restoration of that confidence.
It is the task of the Government to supply it.
  What can be done, by means of changes in the structure of the
Administration, to give the people what they want?
  1. The addition of Sir Stafford Cripps to the Government? But
the desire of the public for Cripps is a fleeting passion. Already
it is on the wane.
  2. The appointment of a Minister of Defence, or perhaps a
Deputy Minister of Defence? But no one can be found for this
post who will at once give satisfaction to the public and to you,
under whom he would serve.
  It might be possible to appoint someone who, like Cripps, would
satisfy the public in its present mood. But Cripps would not be
satisfactory to you.
  3. The setting-up of a War Cabinet composed of a few Ministers,
each of whom would preside over groups of departments and
would be free from departmental duties? This plan should be
adopted.
  The War Cabinet should consist of Bevin, the strongest man in
the present Cabinet; Eden, the most popular member of the
Cabinet; and Attlee, the leader of the Socialist Party.

The other members of the Cabinet should be wiped out. They are valiant men, more honourable than the thirty, but they attain not to the first three.

4. Lastly, some members of the Government are looked on by the public as unsatisfactory Ministers. Their names are well known to you.

One at any rate of the Defence [Service] Ministers is in trouble with the public. Maybe two of them.

This is of course a personal letter, with no intention on my part to help or give countenance to any public agitation.

Yours ever

MAX

He also sent me, undated, the following quotation from Thucydides, which he had perhaps tried in vain upon himself:

Open no more negotiations with Sparta. Show them plainly that you are not crushed by your present afflictions. They who face calamity without wincing, and who offer the most energetic resistance, these, be they States or individuals, are the truest heroes.

*   *   *   *   *

But now that all appeared settled, Lord Beaverbrook resigned. His health had completely broken down, and he did not feel he could face the new and great responsibilities he had assumed. I did my utmost to dissuade him, but the long and harassing discussions which took place in my presence between him and other principal Ministers convinced me that it was better to press him no further. I therefore agreed to his quitting the War Cabinet and going on some vaguely defined mission to the United States, where he could exert his influence in the Presidential circle in a helpful sense, and also find in a West Indian island the rest and peace which he sorely needed. Many who did not appreciate his qualities or know of his contribution to our war effort, and some with whom he had quarrelled, were well content. But I felt his loss acutely.

His final letter, written a few days later, shows the terms on which we parted:

My dear Winston,   26 Feb. 42

I am leaving this office today and going to the place I came
from. And now I must tell you about twenty-one months of high
adventure, the like of which has never been known.

All the time everything that has been done by me has been due
to your holding me up.

You took a great chance in putting me in, and you stood to be
shot at by a section of Members for keeping me here.

It was little enough I gave you compared with what you gave
me. I owe my reputation to you. The confidence of the public
really comes from you. And my courage was sustained by you.
These benefits give me a right to a place in your list of lieutenants
who served you when you brought salvation to our people in the
hour of disaster.

In leaving, then, I send this letter of gratitude and devotion
to the leader of the nation, the saviour of our people, and the
symbol of resistance in the free world.

Yours affectionately

MAX

I always meant to have him back when he was restored to
health and poise, but this intention I did not impart to my
colleagues at this time.

*   *   *   *   *

The Ministry of Production, with all the consequences
attached to it, was now again vacant. I found no difficulty in
choosing a successor. In Oliver Lyttelton I had a man of wide
business experience and great personal energy, which have
proved themselves in the test of time. I had known him from
childhood in his father's house, and in 1940 brought him into
office as President of the Board of Trade, and into Parliament,
from private life. He had won the confidence of all parties at
the Board of Trade, and as Minister of State in Cairo for the
best part of a year he had faced the brunt of military misfortunes in the Middle East and had initiated or carried through
many great improvements in the administrative and railway
services behind the front. These had brought him into the
closest contact with Mr. Averell Harriman, and he was very

well esteemed at Washington. I had still to find someone to replace him as Minister of State in Cairo. Mr. R. G. Casey, the Australian representative in Washington, was appointed to succeed him on March 18.

The reconstruction of the War Cabinet was announced on February 19. Although it now embraced two new personalities, it was reduced from eight to seven. The reader will notice that, in direct contrariety to a strong current of opinion, I had now given full effect to my view that War Cabinet members should also be the holders of responsible offices and not mere advisers at large with nothing to do but think and talk and take decisions by compromise or majority.

Old

Prime Minister	MR. CHURCHILL
Lord Privy Seal	MR. ATTLEE
Lord President of the Council	SIR JOHN ANDERSON
Foreign Secretary	MR. EDEN
Minister without Portfolio	MR. GREENWOOD
Minister of Supply	LORD BEAVERBROOK
Chancellor of the Exchequer	SIR KINGSLEY WOOD
Minister of Labour	MR. BEVIN

New

Prime Minister	MR. CHURCHILL
Deputy Prime Minister and Secretary of State for Dominion Affairs	MR. ATTLEE
Lord Privy Seal and Leader of the House of Commons	SIR STAFFORD CRIPPS
Lord President of the Council	SIR JOHN ANDERSON
Foreign Secretary	MR. EDEN
Minister of Production	MR. OLIVER LYTTELTON
Minister of Labour	MR. BEVIN

There were of course various consequential problems. Lord Cranborne felt that as Leader of the House of Lords he should be a member of the War Cabinet, or at least be always present at its meetings. He was also anxious to improve the debating power of the Government in the Lords, where, according to usage — though it was not constitutionally imperative — there should be at least two Secretaries of State. At this time I thought Sir James Grigg would do his new work as a peer.

Mr. Churchill to Lord Cranborne   20 Feb. 42

I do not think it will be possible to concede to whoever leads the House of Lords the "absolute right always to be present when the War Cabinet meets," because the argument for a small body is so strongly pressed. The only previous link between the Lords and the War Cabinet was Beaverbrook, who hardly ever attended, and then only on his own topics.

Neither could I guarantee that the second Secretary of State who must be appointed in the Lords will necessarily be a man of Parliamentary experience and standing. I have to think of efficiency in the great departments. On the other hand, I must certainly see that adequate debating power is available. Perhaps Duff Cooper, who holds the Duchy of Lancaster, might be willing to go aloft, though I have not mentioned it to him.

I do not propose however to make any final arrangements for the next two or three days. Meanwhile I am treating the appointment which I proposed for you as in suspense. It might be possible, for instance, to divide the task and have one Minister to lead the House of Lords and another to take charge of the Colonial Office.

Thank you so much for writing frankly. I quite see the difficulty, and will endeavour to meet it.

And a few days later:

Sir James Grigg having desired most strongly to remain in the House of Commons, and this being evidently the wish of the House, I shall be unable to give you his help in the Lords. The constitutional requirements are fully maintained. If however you require further help I could ask Duff Cooper to take the Duchy upstairs. Perhaps you will see how you get on for a few weeks.

Several other changes were made in the minor offices. In this I was much helped. No fewer than nine of the principal Under-Secretaries of State voluntarily placed their offices at my disposal, in order to smooth the painful path. The final list of changes, some of which were not made effective for several weeks, was as follows:

February 22, 1942

Secretary of State for the Colonies	LORD CRANBORNE, in succession to Lord Moyne
Minister of Aircraft Production	COLONEL LLEWELLIN, in succession to Colonel Moore-Brabazon
President of the Board of Trade	MR. DALTON, in succession to Colonel Llewellin
Minister of Economic Warfare	LORD SELBORNE, in succession to Mr. Dalton
Secretary of State for War	SIR JAMES GRIGG, in succession to Captain Margesson (resigned)
Minister of Works	LORD PORTAL, in succession to Lord Reith (resigned)

March 4, 1942

Paymaster-General	SIR WILLIAM JOWITT, in succession to Lord Hankey
Solicitor-General	MAJOR MAXWELL FYFE, in succession to Sir William Jowitt

I solved the problem of representation of the Upper House in the War Cabinet by the device, already introduced, of having several Ministers who, though not formally members, were actually in practice "constant attenders." Before the end of the month I was able to resume our regular routine.

Prime Minister to Sir Edward Bridges   27 Feb. 42

The Cabinet arrangements for the next week should be as follows:

Monday, 5.30 P.M. at No. 10. General parade with the constant attenders, the Chiefs of Staff, and the Dominions and Indian representatives. Business: the general war situation, without reference

to special secret matters such as forthcoming operations; and any
other appropriate topics.

2. *Tuesday,* 6 P.M. at No. 10. Pacific Council.

3. *Wednesday,* 12 noon at House of Commons. War Cabinet
only, with yourself. We summon anyone we need for particular
points.

4. *Thursday,* 12 noon at House of Commons. War Cabinet.
(On both Wednesday and Thursday, if the business requires it,
another meeting will be held at 6 P.M.)

5. *Wednesday,* 10 P.M. Defence Committee. This will consist
of the Chiefs of Staff, Service Ministers, India and Dominions if
and as required, myself, the Deputy Prime Minister and the
Foreign Secretary, and probably Mr. Oliver Lyttelton.

Let us see how this works.

On the whole the main reconstruction was well received by
the press and public. After so great a Ministerial upheaval,
Parliament also felt the need of stability, and thus we gained
a breathing-space in which to endure the further misfortunes
that were coming upon us.

*   *   *   *   *

My own position had not seemed to be affected in all this
period of political tension and change at home and disaster
abroad. I was too much occupied with hourly business to have
much time for brooding upon it. My personal authority even
seemed to be enhanced by the uncertainties affecting several of
my colleagues or would-be colleagues. I did not suffer from
any desire to be relieved of my responsibilities. All I wanted
was compliance with my wishes after reasonable discussion.
Misfortunes only brought me and the Chiefs of Staff closer
together, and this unity was felt through all the circles of the
Government. There was no whisper of intrigue or dissidence,
either in the War Cabinet or in the much larger number of
Ministers of Cabinet rank. From outside however there was
continuous pressure to change my method of conducting the
war, with a view to obtaining better results than were now
coming in. "We are all with the Prime Minister, but he has

too much to do. He should be relieved of some of the burdens that fall upon him." This was the persistent view, and many theories were pressed. I was very glad to receive from Sir Frederick Maurice [1] the following letter:

My dear Prime Minister,   14 Feb. 42

I gather from conversations which I have had with certain Members of Parliament that you are to be pressed to revert to the system adopted by Mr. Lloyd George in 1916–18 for the co-ordination of policy and strategy, to abolish the post of Minister of National Defence, and to bring the Chiefs of Staff in direct relation with a small War Cabinet composed of Ministers without Portfolio.

Having had two and a half years of Mr. Lloyd George's system, I am convinced that, with one exception, your system is much the better of the two. I advocated it for years, both at the Imperial Defence College and at the Staff Colleges. I am convinced that there should be a Minister of Defence, in direct personal touch with the Chiefs of Staff, and that the only possible Minister of Defence in time of war is the Prime Minister. You, to pass from principles to particularities, have the enormous advantage, rare amongst politicians, of being able to talk the same language as sailors, soldiers, and airmen. The method of having the Chiefs of Staff in attendance at War Cabinet meetings involved great waste of the time of the Chiefs of Staff, and they were rarely as ready to speak their minds at War Cabinet meetings as they would be to a Prime Minister with whom they were in close association.

The one defect in the present system, as I view it from outside, is the Joint Planning Committee. My experience is that the members of this committee are, *ex officio,* too much occupied with the affairs of their own Services to give their minds to joint planning, and that when they meet they are disposed rather to find difficulties in, and objections to, proposals for action than to initiate

[1] Sir Frederick Maurice had been Director of Military Operations in 1918 during the First World War. In a letter to the *Times* he attacked the Prime Minister, Mr. Lloyd George, on the subject of the use of the available manpower in the Army. He was dismissed from his post, and a formidable debate, followed by a division, took place in the House of Commons. Whether Liberals voted for Mr. Asquith or Mr. Lloyd George on this occasion was afterwards made the test in the post-war election. General Maurice became President of the British Legion in 1932.

such proposals. I believe that the only way to get effective action is to choose the man who is to execute the plan, to give him such help as he needs for planning, and then get him to submit his plan for approval to you and the Chiefs of Staff. It will then be for you and the Chiefs of Staff to decide whether the plan is good and whether what is required for its execution is available.

With all my sympathy and good wishes for you in these grave times,

Yours sincerely
F. MAURICE

In thanking Sir Frederick for this I added (February 24, 1942): "I am coming to the conclusion that when a 'task' is proposed an officer from one of the three Services should definitely be put over the others in accordance with the nature of the task."

I was entirely resolved to keep my full power of war-direction. This could only be exercised by combining the offices of Prime Minister and Minister of Defence. More difficulty and toil are often incurred in overcoming opposition and adjusting divergent and conflicting views than by having the right to give decisions oneself. It is most important that at the summit there should be one mind playing over the whole field, faithfully aided and corrected, but not divided in its integrity. I should not of course have remained Prime Minister for an hour if I had been deprived of the office of Minister of Defence. The fact that this was widely known repelled all challenges, even under the most unfavourable conditions, and many well-meant suggestions of committees and other forms of impersonal machinery consequently fell to the ground. I must record my gratitude to all who helped me succeed.

6

The Fall of Singapore

No Inquiry Has Been Held upon Singapore — General Percival's Dispositions — A Weakened Garrison — No Illusions in Whitehall — Importance of Demolitions — General Policy in A.B.D.A. Area — My Minute to the Chiefs of Staff of February 2 — Air Weakness at Singapore — The Japanese Cross the Strait, February 8 — They Establish Themselves in the Island — My Telegram to General Wavell of February 10 — Wavell's Unhopeful Reply, February 11 — Heavy Fighting on the Whole Front During the 12th — The Japanese Checked — The Ill-Fated Evacuation Party — Grave Conditions in Singapore City — Wavell Orders the Defence to Hold On — His Telegram to Me of February 14 — The Chief of the Imperial General Staff and I Give Wavell Discretion to Surrender — His Last Orders to General Percival — Capitulation — A Message from President Roosevelt.

I JUDGED it impossible to hold an inquiry by Royal Commission into the circumstances of the fall of Singapore while the war was raging. We could not spare the men, the time, or the energy. Parliament accepted this view; but I certainly thought that in justice to the officers and men concerned there should be an inquiry into all the circumstances as soon as the fighting stopped. This however has not been instituted by the Government of the day. Eight years have passed, and many of the witnesses are dead. It may well be that we shall never have a formal pronouncement by a competent court upon the worst disaster and largest capitulation of British history. In these pages I do not attempt to set myself up in the place of such a court or pronounce an opinion on the conduct of individuals. I confine myself to recording the salient facts as I believe them, and to documents written at the time. From these the reader must form his own opinion.

In this military narrative, for which I take responsibility, I have been greatly aided by General Pownall. He had actually taken up his appointment as Commander-in-Chief in the Far East, with his headquarters at Singapore, when the decision to create the A.B.D.A. command was reached at Washington. Thereupon he became General Wavell's Chief of Staff. But for this he would have been called upon to bear the terrible load which fell upon the shoulders of General Percival.

General Percival's dispositions for the defence of Singapore Island are shown on the map. The IIId Corps (General Heath) was now composed of the 18th British Division (Major-General Beckwith-Smith), the main body of which had arrived on January 29, and the 11th British-Indian Division (Major-General Key), which had absorbed what remained of the 9th

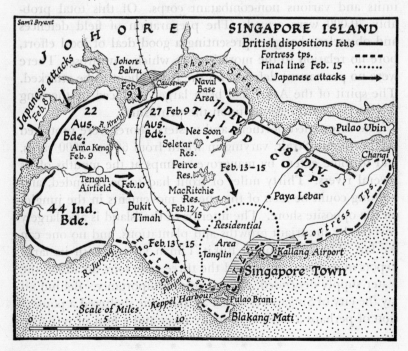

Division. The area of responsibility of the corps extended along the northern shore of the island up to but excluding the causeway. Thence the line was taken up by the 8th Australian Division (Major-General Gordon Bennett), with the 44th Indian Brigade under command. This brigade had arrived only a few days before, and, like the 45th, was composed of young and partly trained troops. The southern shore was defended by the fortress troops, with two Malayan infantry brigades and the volunteer force, the whole under Major-General Simmons.

Those of the heavy guns of the coast defences which could fire northward were not much use, with their limited ammunition, against the thick country in which the enemy was gathering. Only one squadron of fighter aircraft remained on the island, and only a single aerodrome was now usable. Losses and wastage had reduced the numbers of the garrison, now finally concentrated, from the 106,000 estimated by the War Office to about 85,000 men, including base and administrative units and various non-combatant corps. Of this total probably 70,000 were armed. The preparation of field defences and obstacles, though representing a good deal of local effort, bore no relation to the mortal needs which now arose. There were no permanent defences on the front about to be attacked. The spirit of the Army had been largely reduced by the long retreat and hard fighting upon the peninsula.

The threatened northern and western shores were protected by the Johore Strait, varying in width from 600 to 2000 yards, and to some extent by mangrove swamps at the mouths of its several rivers. Thirty miles of front had to be defended, and nothing could be seen of the enemy movements in the jungles on the opposite shore. The interior of the island is also largely covered by luxuriant growths and plantations, and no one can see far. The area around Bukit Timah village, with its large depots of military stores, and the three reservoirs on which the water supply depended, were of prime importance. Behind all lay the city of Singapore, which at that time sheltered a population of perhaps a million of many races and a host of refugees.

*   *   *   *   *

At home we no longer nursed illusions about the protracted defence of Singapore. The only question was how long. The Chiefs of Staff had as early as January 21 been concerned about demolitions, and had cabled General Percival to make sure that there should be no failure in Singapore "should the worst come to the worst." "You should," they said, "ensure that nothing which could possibly be of any use to the enemy is omitted from the general scorched-earth scheme." They also spoke of destroying ammunition. I commented on this correspondence on January 31 that "the obvious method is to fire the ammunition at the enemy. Should evacuation become inevitable, which is by no means admitted, there will be two or three days to do this. . . . Firing away the ammunition at the enemy is the natural and long-prescribed course when the fall of a fortress is imminent. There ought to be plenty of time to make good arrangements. If the fortress is properly defended, we are more likely to have a shortage of ammunition towards the end than be left with large dumps."

And again two days later:

Prime Minister to General Ismay, for C.O.S. Committee   2 Feb. 42

What is indispensable is: first, the naval base should be completely wrecked so that the docks and workshops are rendered utterly useless for at least eighteen months; and, secondly, the fortress guns should all be destroyed and rendered unusable for a similar period. Thus, Singapore will lose its value to the enemy as an effective naval base. The preparation for the above demolitions ought not to cause alarm, because they are all in military areas, from which the public is rigorously excluded, and also the actual work of putting in the explosive charges could be done by the engineers.

2. Plans should also be made for the destruction of other valuable property, but preparations for this should not be allowed to weaken the defence, which, as the General rightly says, must be prolonged to the last possible hour. Every day gained is vital.

*   *   *   *   *

On the general situation in the Indian Ocean I had long conferences with the Staff, and posed various questions to them.

Prime Minister to General Ismay   2 Feb. 42

I should like to have a Staff meeting at 10 P.M. tonight with the Chiefs of Staff, in order to discuss further reinforcements of Malaya and Burma and the defence of the Indian Ocean.

The following points occur to me:

Singapore. How is it that we were only told last week that two out of the three aerodromes on the island are commanded by artillery from the mainland? Why were no others constructed? What progress has been made on the northern shore defences? What has been done about interior communications, radial roads, etc.? I presume the causeway, which has been partly breached, is specially covered by artillery and machine-gun fire. What plans are in hand for counter-attacks from the sea upon the Japanese communications to Malaya, observing that they seem to be able to do everything, and we nothing, in the matter of landings?

2. What plans are being made for the relief of Singapore by running convoys in of reinforcements, troops, aircraft, and food? What arrangements have been made to give relief by attacking the Japanese aerodromes with heavy bombers from Sumatra and Java? Have any plans been made to establish new air bases on the subsidiary islands? What has been done about enforcing compulsory labour on the male population remaining in Singapore Island? A further effort must be made to reduce the useless mouths. Many of these matters are within General Wavell's province, but we must have full knowledge of the position and make sure that no point is overlooked.

3. *Indian Ocean Bases.* What is being done to make sure of these? For instance, Trincomalee: what is its garrison? What are its guns? Has anything been done to protect its gorge? What aerodromes are available in the neighbourhood? The Navy is responsible for the defence of the Indian Ocean. What is the programme of reinforcements? When will the three aircraft-carriers be at work? What are the proposed future movements of *Warspite*? How are the repairs of *Valiant* getting on? I observed that a U-boat sank a merchant ship by *gunfire* in the Bay of Bengal. Are merchant ships in those areas armed? Have they proper gunners on board? What measures are being taken to secure local command of the Bay of Bengal? At present we seem to have no naval forces, light or heavy, that can operate. What destroyers, corvettes, and cruisers is it proposed to assign to Indian waters? Let me have the

proposed time-table month by month, for the next four months, of reinforcements.

4. After the two Australian divisions have been moved into the A.B.D.A. area, what other reinforcements are proposed? It would seem that at least four divisions should be sent from this country agreeably with the arrival of the Americans under "Magnet" [in Northern Ireland] and the retardation of the date of probable invasion due to Russia and other causes. Whether these divisions should go to Egypt, to the Levant-Caspian front, to India, or to the A.B.D.A. area must be considered later. The great thing is to get them on the move. We must be prepared for substantial reductions in rations and in imports in order to carry out larger troop movements. The movements of troops by the smaller type of merchant ships must be considered. What about the West African Brigade from Freetown? We must have more men east of Suez. The whole field must be surveyed.

5. The reinforcement of India has become most urgent. I am deeply concerned with the reactions from Japanese victories throughout Asia. It will be necessary to have an additional number of British troops in India. These need not be fully formed divisions, as they are for internal security against revolt. In this connection beach divisions should be considered, and also separate battalions.

6. On other papers I have already mentioned the possibility of the Americans coming into the Persian Gulf area and forming an army on the Levant-Caspian front.

Let me have proposals, with time-tables, for giving effect to the above, and pray add to these queries as you think best.

* * * * *

The air position at Singapore grew worse.

Prime Minister to General Wavell 2 Feb. 42

I observe that you have ordered the Hurricanes which had just reached Singapore to Palembang. Should be grateful for some explanation of this new decision, which appears at first sight to indicate despair of defending Singapore.

General Wavell to Prime Minister 3 Feb. 42

Decision to withdraw majority fighters to Sumatra was taken

during my visit to Singapore with Peirse on January 29. Withdrawal of troops into Singapore exposes three out of four of
island's aerodromes to artillery fire. Increased scale air attacks on
aerodromes had already necessitated withdrawal [of] bombers to
more secure bases in Sumatra. Loss of Malaya emphasises vital
importance of holding Southern Sumatra, and maintenance of
aerodromes there for offensive operations to reduce scale of attacks
on Singapore. Fighter defence of these aerodromes essential.

To leave fighters on exposed aerodromes in Singapore would
be to invite their destruction in [a] few days. Meanwhile every
effort [is] being made to maintain fighter defence by keeping equivalent of one squadron on Kallang aerodrome and by using other
aerodromes as circumstances permit for refuelling fighters operating
from Sumatra.

Consider these dispositions offer best prospects of air defence of
Singapore, which there is every intention and hope of holding.

Prime Minister to General Wavell   4 Feb. 42

I am relieved to learn that you intend to maintain fighter defence of Singapore by refuelling Hurricanes operating from
Sumatra.

2. Nevertheless, it is a grievous disadvantage that the bulk of
your fighter force should be unable to intercept from their base
and should have to waste so much flying time between Sumatra
and Singapore.

3. Although I realise the risks to which aeroplanes based on
Singapore would be exposed, I am not clear that the need for
fighter defence at the Sumatra bases will be strongly felt so long
as the Japanese are engaged with Singapore. Moreover, we hope
to send you about ninety more Hurricanes by *Athene* and *Indomitable* before the end of February. I therefore hope that all proper
risks will be taken in supporting Singapore with fighters.

4. It is difficult to see why half of the fighters left in the island
should be Buffaloes. If numbers must be limited, surely they
should be of the highest quality available.

*   *   *   *   *

On the morning of February 8, patrols reported that the
enemy were massing in the plantations northwest of the island,
and our positions were heavily shelled. At 10.45 P.M., the 22d

Australian Infantry Brigade, west of the river Kranji, were attacked by the 5th and 18th Japanese Divisions. The leading waves of assault were carried across the Johore Strait in armoured landing-craft brought, as the result of long and careful planning, to the launching-sites by road. There was very heavy fighting and many craft were sunk, but the Australians were thin on the ground and enemy parties got ashore at many points. By the time the brigade had been reorganised, the enemy had taken Ama Keng village, where roads and tracks of the neighborhood met. At 8 A.M. next morning they were attacking Tengah aerodrome. The obvious place to organise a stop line was the comparatively narrow neck of land between the headwaters of the Kranji and Jurong rivers.[1] The 22d Australian and the 44th Indian Brigades were ordered back to this position, and reinforced by two battalions from the Command reserve.

The military report was as follows:

General Percival to General Wavell   9 Feb. 42

Enemy landed in force on west coast last night and has penetrated about five miles. Tengah aerodrome is in his hands. Australian Brigade, holding this sector, has had heavy casualties. Advance stopped temporarily by use of Command reserve, but situation is undoubtedly serious in view of the very extended coastline which we have to watch. Have made plan for concentrating forces to cover Singapore if this becomes necessary.

*　　*　　*　　*　　*

On the evening of the 9th a new and similar attack developed on the front of the 27th Australian Brigade between the causeway and the river Kranji, and again the enemy succeeded in gaining a footing, so that a gap developed between this brigade and the Kranji-Jurong line. Nor was this all, for the two brigades withdrawing from the west to this line, on which there were no prepared defences, overshot the mark, and before they could be redirected the enemy had passed it. A brigade from

[1] See map, page 93.

the 11th Indian Division and a group of three battalions
from the 18th British Division were sent up in succession to
restore the position on Gordon Bennett's front, but by the
evening of the 10th the Japanese were close upon Bukit Timah
village, and during that night, supported by tanks, made
further headway.

On this news reaching us:

Prime Minister to General Wavell   10 Feb. 42

I think you ought to realise the way we view the situation in
Singapore. It was reported to the Cabinet by the C.I.G.S. that
Percival has over 100,000 men, of whom 33,000 are British and
17,000 Australian. It is doubtful whether the Japanese have as
many in the whole Malay peninsula, namely, five divisions forward
and a sixth coming up. In these circumstances the defenders must
greatly outnumber Japanese forces who have crossed the straits,
and in a well-contested battle they should destroy them. There
must at this stage be no thought of saving the troops or sparing
the population. The battle must be fought to the bitter end at
all costs. The 18th Division has a chance to make its name in history. Commanders and senior officers should die with their troops.
The honour of the British Empire and of the British Army is at
stake. I rely on you to show no mercy to weakness in any form.
With the Russians fighting as they are and the Americans so stubborn at Luzon, the whole reputation of our country and our race
is involved. It is expected that every unit will be brought into close
contact with the enemy and fight it out. I feel sure these words
express your own feeling, and only send them to you in order to
share your burdens.

Wavell reported on his visit in unhopeful terms.

General Wavell to Prime Minister   11 Feb. 42

I returned today from twenty-four hours in Singapore. I received your telegram just before I left. I had seen all divisional
commanders and the Governor, and had already spoken to them
on the lines of your telegram. I left with Percival [a] written
message to [the] same effect.

2. Battle for Singapore is not going well. Japanese, with usual

infiltration tactics, are getting on much more rapidly than they should in west of island. I ordered Percival to stage counter-attack with all troops possible on that front. Morale of some troops is not good, and none is as high as I should like to see. Conditions of ground are difficult for defence, where wide frontages have to be held in very enclosed country. The chief troubles are lack of sufficient training in some of reinforcing troops and inferiority complex which bold and skilful Japanese tactics and their command of the air have caused.

3. Everything possible is being done to produce [a] more offensive spirit and optimistic outlook, but I cannot pretend that these efforts have been entirely successful up to date. I have given the most categorical orders that there is to be no thought of surrender and that all troops are to continue fighting to the end.

4. I do not think that Percival has the number of troops at his disposal that you mention. I do not think that he has more than sixty to seventy thousand at the most. He should however have quite enough to deal with enemy who have landed if the troops can be made to act with sufficient vigour and determination.

5. One of three northern aerodromes [is] now in hands of enemy, and [the] other two under shell-fire and out of use. Remaining aerodrome in south of island has been reduced by constant bombing to extremely limited use.

6. While returning from Singapore I fell from quay in dark and have broken two small bones in back. Damage not serious, but I shall be in hospital for [a] few days and somewhat crippled for two or three weeks probably.

*   *   *   *   *

February 11 was a day of confused fighting on the whole front. A composite force from the reserve was sent to fill a gap between the MacRitchie reservoir and the Bukit Timah road. The causeway had been breached towards the enemy's end, and they were able to repair it rapidly as soon as our covering troops withdrew. The Japanese Imperial Guards advanced across it that night and approached Nee Soon village. The next day, the 12th, the IIId Corps was ordered to withdraw to a perimeter running from the Bukit Timah road to the two reservoirs held by the 53d Division, and

thence extending to Paya Lebar village and Kallang. Fortress
troops from the Changi promontory were drawn in behind this
line. South of the Bukit Timah road there was heavy fighting
all the 12th. The 22d Australian Brigade was still holding its
ground south of Bukit Timah village, whence the enemy had
been for forty-eight hours unable to dislodge them. They were
now isolated, and withdrawn under orders to Tanglin, where
the 44th Indian and 1st Malaya Brigades continued the line
southward.

The Japanese made little ground during the 13th. The
Malay regiment holding the Pasir Panjang ridge stubbornly
repulsed the Japanese 18th Division, who attacked after a
heavy two-hour bombardment.

*   *   *   *   *

On the 13th, the prepared scheme for evacuating to Java by
sea some three thousand nominated individuals was put into
effect. Those ordered to go included key men, technicians,
surplus staff officers, nurses and others whose services would
be of special value for the prosecution of the war. With them
went Air Vice-Marshal Pulford and Rear-Admiral Spooner,
who had commanded air and naval forces in the fortress. It
was their last voyage. A Japanese naval force escorting the
expedition against Sumatra fell upon them. Of about eighty
little ships of all kinds which set out from Singapore on this
and the following day, almost all were lost or captured by the
enemy. It was only after the war that the fate of Pulford and
Spooner became known. On February 15, their vessel was attacked by enemy destroyers and driven ashore on a small island.
They and about forty-five others who had embarked with them
succeeded in landing without interference. One of their number, a young New Zealand officer, then set off in a native boat,
and after many adventures reached Batavia in safety on
February 27. By this time Java itself was in a turmoil, but
arrangements were made to send an aircraft to rescue the survivors. By mischance this effort failed. On the island itself the
forlorn and now fever-stricken party lingered on with fading

hope, but unmolested by the enemy. Before the end of March, Pulford and thirteen others had died; Spooner and three more died in April. On May 14, the senior surviving officer, Wing-Commander Atkins, knew that the end was in sight. With seven others he sailed to Sumatra in a native boat and surrendered to the Japanese who thereupon sent to the island and took off the remaining survivors, to languish later in a Singapore prison camp.

*   *   *   *   *

The principal fighting on the 14th was in the southern sector, on each side of the Bukit Timah road, where our troops were forced back to what proved to be their final line. Conditions in the city of Singapore were now shocking. Civil labour had collapsed, failure of the water supply seemed imminent, and reserves of food and ammunition for the troops had been seriously depleted by the loss of depots now in enemy hands. By this time the programme of organised demolitions had been put in hand. The guns of the fixed defences and nearly all field and anti-aircraft guns were destroyed, together with secret equipment and documents. All aviation petrol and aircraft bombs were burned or blown up. Some confusion arose concerning demolitions in the naval base. The orders were issued, the floating dock was sunk and the caisson and pumping machinery of the graving dock destroyed, but much else in the full plan was left incomplete.

On this day the Governor of the Straits Settlement reported to the Colonial Office:

14 Feb. 42

General Officer Commanding informs me that Singapore City now closely invested. There are now one million people within radius of three miles. Water supplies very badly damaged and unlikely to last more than twenty-four hours. Many dead lying in the streets and burial impossible. We are faced with total deprivation of water, which must result in pestilence. I have felt that it is my duty to bring this to notice of General Officer Commanding.

*   *   *   *   *

The following telegrams passed between Generals Wavell and Percival, though these were not received in London till I asked for them some weeks later.

General Wavell to General Percival   13 Feb. 42

You must all fight it out to the end as you are doing. But when everything humanly possible has been done, some bold and determined personnel may be able to escape by small craft and find their way south to Sumatra through the islands. Any such small craft with sandbag protection and mounting an automatic or small gun such as two-pounder would be valuable also in defending Sumatra rivers.

General Percival to General Wavell   13 Feb. 42

Enemy now within 5000 yards of sea-front, which brings whole of Singapore town within field artillery range. We are also in danger of being driven off water and food supplies. In opinion of commanders troops already committed are too exhausted either to withstand strong attack or to launch counter-attack. We would all earnestly welcome the chance of initiating an offensive, even though this would only amount to a gesture, but even this is not possible, as there are no troops who could carry out this attack. In these conditions it is unlikely that resistance can last more than a day or two. My subordinate commanders are unanimously of the opinion that the gain of time will not compensate for extensive damage and heavy casualties which will occur in Singapore town. As Empire overseas is interested, I feel bound to represent their views. There must come a stage when in the interests of the troops and civil population further bloodshed will serve no useful purpose. Your instructions of February 10 are being carried out, but in above circumstances would you consider giving me wider discretionary powers?

General Wavell to General Percival   14 Feb. 42

You must continue to inflict maximum damage on enemy for as long as possible by house-to-house fighting if necessary. Your action in tying down enemy and inflicting casualties may have vital influence in other theatres. Fully appreciate your situation, but continued action essential.

Wavell now sent me the following message, which seemed conclusive:

General Wavell to Prime Minister   14 Feb. 42

Have received telegram from Percival that enemy are close to town and that his troops are incapable of further counter-attack. Have ordered him to continue [to] inflict maximum damage to enemy by house-to-house fighting if necessary. Fear however that resistance [is] not likely to be very prolonged.

*   *   *   *   *

The reader will recall my minute to the Chiefs of Staff of January 21 about abandoning the defence of Singapore and diverting reinforcements to Rangoon, and how I did not press this point of view. When all our hearts hardened on fighting it out at Singapore, the only chance of success, and indeed of gaining time, which was all we could hope for, was to give imperative orders to fight in desperation to the end. These orders were accepted and endorsed by General Wavell, who, as the telegrams show, put the utmost pressure on General Percival. It is always right that whatever may be the doubts at the summit of war direction, the general on the spot should have no knowledge of them and should receive instructions which are simple and plain. But now when it was certain that all was lost at Singapore I was sure it would be wrong to enforce needless slaughter, and without hope of victory to inflict the horrors of street fighting on the vast city, with its teeming, helpless, and now panic-stricken population. I told General Brooke where I stood, and found that he also felt that we should put no more pressure from home upon General Wavell, and should authorise him to take the inevitable decision, for which, by this telegram, we should share the responsibility.

Prime Minister to General Wavell   14 Feb. 42

You are of course sole judge of the moment when no further result can be gained at Singapore, and should instruct Percival accordingly. C.I.G.S. concurs.

The Commander-in-Chief thereupon issued the orders to General Percival contained in this telegram to me:

General Wavell to Prime Minister   15 Feb. 42

Have had two telegrams from Percival in last forty-eight hours indicating that due to shortage of water in the town and other difficulties his powers of resistance are now much diminished. On both occasions have ordered him to fight on to the last. I have now sent him [the] following:

General Wavell to General Percival   15 Feb. 42

So long as you are in position to inflict losses and damage to enemy and your troops are physically capable of doing so, you must fight on. Time gained and damage to enemy are of vital importance at this crisis. When you are fully satisfied that this is no longer possible, I give you discretion to cease resistance. Before doing so all arms, equipment, and transport of value to enemy must of course be rendered useless. Also just before final cessation of fighting, opportunity should be given to any determined bodies of men or individuals to try and effect escape by any means possible. They must be armed. Inform me of [your] intentions. Whatever happens I thank you and all troops for your gallant efforts of [the] last few days.

Sunday, February 15, was the day of the capitulation. There were only a few days of military food reserves, gun ammunition was very short, and there was practically no petrol left for vehicles. Worst of all, the water supply was expected to last only another twenty-four hours. General Percival was advised by his senior commanders that of the two alternatives, counter-attack or surrender, the first was beyond the capacity of the exhausted troops. He decided upon capitulation and sent his last tragic telegram to General Wavell:

15 Feb. 42

Owing to losses from enemy action, water, petrol, food, and ammunition practically finished. Unable therefore to continue the fight any longer. All ranks have done their best and are grateful for your help.

The Japanese demanded and received unconditional surrender. Hostilities closed at 8.30 P.M.

*   *   *   *   *

In this dark moment it was a comfort to receive the following message from our greatest Ally:

President Roosevelt to Former Naval Person   19 Feb. 42

I realise how the fall of Singapore has affected you and the British people. It gives the well-known back-seat driver a field day, but no matter how serious our setbacks have been — and I do not for a moment underrate them — we must constantly look forward to the next moves that need to be made to hit the enemy. I hope you will be of good heart in these trying weeks, because I am very sure that you have the great confidence of the masses of the British people. I want you to know that I think of you often, and I know you will not hesitate to ask me if there is anything you think I can do. . . . Do let me hear from you.

7

The U-Boat Paradise

*Formidable Expansion of the U-Boat Fleet — The Attack on Ship-
ping in American Coastal Waters — Grievous Losses of February,
1942 — Hitler's Fatal Concentration of the German Fleet at
Home — The "Tirpitz" Sent to Trondheim — Hitler Decides
to Withdraw the "Scharnhorst" and "Gneisenau" from Brest —
The Escape is Made, February 11–12 — Wrath in Britain — A
Manoeuvre Highly Advantageous to Us — President Roosevelt's
View — My Defence of the Admiralty in Secret Session in April
— U-boat Havoc Along the Atlantic Coast of the United States
— Britain Sends Anti-Submarine Craft to America — My Telegram of March 12 to Harry Hopkins — President Roosevelt's Re-
quest for Air Attacks on U-Boat Bases — I Explain Our Position
to Him — Brilliant Exploit at St. Nazaire — Introduction of
the Convoy System by the United States Navy, April 1 — Admiral Doenitz Shifts His Attack — Hitler's Mistake in Not Concentrating upon the U-Boat War — Table of Allied Losses from
January to July — The Autumn Fighting — Need of Very
Long-Range Aircraft and Escort Carriers — "Support Groups"
of Surface Forces — I Convene a New Anti-U-Boat Committee,
November 4 — I Ask Mr. Mackenzie King for Help — The Winter Weather Brings Relief.*

WE HAD GREETED THE ENTRY of the United States into the
war with relief and an uprising of spirit. Henceforth
our load would be shared by a partner of almost unlimited
resources and we might hope that in the war at sea the U-boats
would soon be brought under control. With American help
our Atlantic life-line would become secure, although losses

must be expected until the full power of our Ally was engaged. Thus preserved, we could prosecute the war against Hitler in Europe and in the Middle East. The Far East would for the time be the darkest scene.

But the year 1942 was to provide many rude shocks and prove in the Atlantic the toughest of the whole war. By the end of 1941 the U-boat fleet had grown to nearly two hundred and fifty, of which Admiral Doenitz could report nearly a hundred operational, with a monthly addition of fifteen. At first our joint defences, although much stronger than when we stood alone, proved unequal to the new assault upon what had now become a much larger target. For six or seven months the U-boats ravaged American waters almost uncontrolled, and in fact almost brought us to the disaster of an indefinite prolongation of the war. Had we been forced to suspend, or even seriously to restrict for a time, the movement of shipping in the Atlantic, all our joint plans would have been arrested.

On December 12 at a conference with the Fuehrer it was resolved to carry the U-boat war into American coastal waters. As many U-boats and several of the best German commanders had been transferred to the Mediterranean, and as by Hitler's order Doenitz was also compelled to maintain a strong group in Norwegian and Arctic waters, only six U-boats of the larger 740-ton type were at first dispatched. These left the Biscay ports between December 18 and 30, with orders to penetrate the northern end of the coastal route between Newfoundland and New York, near the assembly ports of the homeward-bound convoys. Their success was immediate. By the end of January thirty-one ships, of nearly 200,000 tons, had been sunk off the United States and Canadian coast. Soon the attack spread southward off Hampton Roads and Cape Hatteras, and thence to the coast of Florida. This great sea highway teemed with defenceless American and Allied shipping. Along it the precious tanker fleet moved in unbroken procession to and from the oil ports of Venezuela and Mexico. The interruption of this traffic would affect our whole war economy and all fighting plans.

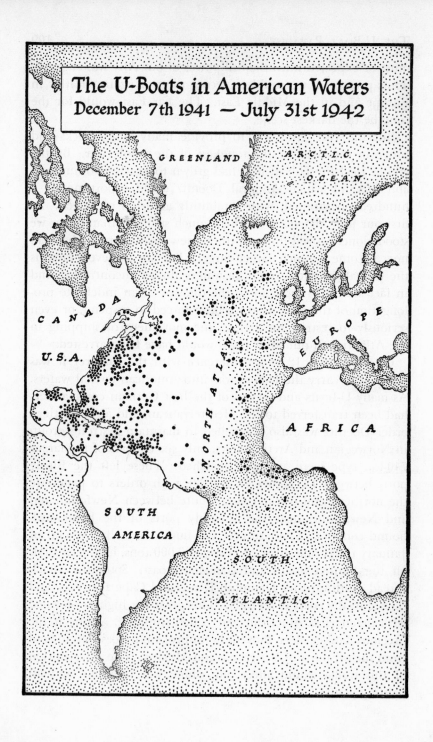

The U-Boats in American Waters
December 7th 1941 — July 31st 1942

In the Caribbean Sea, amid a wealth of targets, the U-boats chose to prey chiefly on the tankers. Neutrals of all kind were assailed equally with Allied ships. Week by week the scale of this massacre grew. In February the U-boat losses in the Atlantic rose to seventy-one ships, of 384,000 tons, all but two of which were sunk in the American zone. This was the highest rate of loss which we had so far suffered throughout the war. It was soon to be surpassed.

* * * * *

All this destruction, far exceeding anything known in this war, though not reaching the catastrophic figures of the worst period of 1917, was caused by no more than twelve to fifteen boats working in the area at one time. The protection afforded by the United States Navy was for several months hopelessly inadequate. It is surprising indeed that during two years of the advance of total war towards the American continent more provision had not been made against this deadly onslaught. Under the President's policy of "all aid to Britain short of war" much had been done for us. We had acquired the fifty old destroyers and the ten American revenue cutters. In exchange we had given the invaluable West Indian bases. But the vessels were now sadly missed by our Ally. After Pearl Harbour the Pacific pressed heavily on the United States Navy. Still, with all the information they had about the protective measures we had adopted, both before and during the struggle, it is remarkable that no plans had been made for coastal convoys and for multiplying small craft.

Neither had the Coastal Air Defence been developed. The American Army Air Force, which controlled almost all military shore-based aircraft, had no training in anti-submarine warfare, whereas the Navy, equipped with float-planes and amphibians, had not the means to carry it out. Thus it happened that in these crucial months an effective American defence system was only achieved with painful, halting steps. Meanwhile the United States and all the Allied nations suffered grievous losses in ships, cargoes, and lives. These losses might have been far greater had the Germans sent their heavy surface ships raiding into the Atlantic. Hitler was however obsessed with the idea that we intended to invade Northern Norway at an early date. With his powerful one-track mind he sacrificed the glittering chances in the Atlantic, and concentrated every available surface ship and many a precious U-boat in Norwegian waters. "Norway," he said, "is the zone of destiny in this war." It was indeed, as the reader is aware, most important, but at this time the German opportunity lay in the Atlantic. In vain the admirals argued for a naval offensive. Their Fuehrer remained adamant, and his strategic decision was strengthened by the shortage of oil fuel.

Already in January he had sent the *Tirpitz*, his only battleship, but the strongest in the world, to Trondheim.

Prime Minister to General Ismay, for C.O.S. Committee   25 Jan. 42

The presence of *Tirpitz* at Trondheim has now been known for three days. The destruction or even the crippling of this ship is the greatest event at sea at the present time. No other target is comparable to it. She cannot have ack-ack protection comparable to Brest or the German home ports. If she were even only crippled, it would be difficult to take her back to Germany. No doubt it is better to wait for moonlight for a night attack, but moonlight attacks are not comparable with day attacks. The entire naval situation throughout the world would be altered, and the naval command in the Pacific would be regained.

2. There must be no lack of co-operation between Bomber Command and the Fleet Air Arm and aircraft-carriers. A plan should be made to attack both with carrier-borne torpedo aircraft and with heavy bombers by daylight or at dawn. The whole strategy of the war turns at this period on this ship, which is holding four times the number of British capital ships paralysed, to say nothing of the two new American battleships retained in the Atlantic. I regard the matter as of the highest urgency and importance. I shall mention it in Cabinet tomorrow, and it must be considered in detail at the Defence Committee on Tuesday night.

*   *   *   *   *

As part of his defensive policy, Hitler had determined to

recall to their home ports the battle-cruisers *Scharnhorst* and *Gneisenau,* which had been blockaded in Brest for nearly a year, and were, at the same time, a serious menace to our ocean convoys. There was a special conference on the question in Berlin on January 12, when the German naval authorities discussed their plan for carrying out the Fuehrer's wishes. Hitler spoke as follows:

The naval force at Brest has above all the welcome effect of tying up enemy air forces and diverting them from making attacks upon the German homeland. This advantage will last exactly as long as the enemy considers himself compelled to attack because the ships are undamaged. With our ships at Brest, enemy sea forces are tied up to no greater extent than would be the case if the ships were stationed in Norway. If I could see any chance that the ships might remain undamaged for four or five months, and thereafter be employed in operations in the Atlantic, in consequence of a changed over-all situation, I might be more inclined to consider leaving them at Brest. Since in my opinion such a development is not to be expected however, I am determined to withdraw the ships from Brest, in order to avoid exposing them to chance hits day after day.

This decision led to an incident which caused, at the time, so much commotion and outcry in England that it requires a digression here.

*   *   *   *   *

On the night of February 11 the two battle-cruisers, with the cruiser *Prinz Eugen,* escaped from Brest and successfully made the passage of the English Channel to regain the shelter of their home ports.

Owing to the very serious losses we had suffered in the Mediterranean during the winter and the temporary disablement of our whole Eastern Fleet, we had been forced, as I have stated in the previous volume, to send almost all our torpedo-carrying aircraft to protect Egypt against potential overseas invasion. But all possible preparations were made to watch Brest and to attack any sortie with bomb and torpedo by air and sea. Mines were also laid along the presumed route both in the Channel and near the Dutch coast. The Admiralty expected that the passage of the Dover Strait would be attempted by night; but the German admiral preferred to use darkness to elude our patrols when leaving Brest and run the Dover batteries in daylight. He sailed from Brest before midnight on the 11th.

The morning of the 12th was misty, and when the enemy ships were spotted, the radar of our patrolling aircraft broke down. Our shore radar also failed to detect them. At the time we thought this an unlucky accident. We have learnt since the war that General Martini, the chief of the German radar, had made a careful plan. The German jamming, which had previously been fairly ineffective, was invigorated by the addition of much new equipment, but in order that nothing should be suspicious on the vital day the new jammers were brought into operation gradually, so that the jamming should appear only a little more vicious each day. Our operators therefore did not complain unduly, and nobody suspected anything unusual. By February 12 however the jamming had grown so strong that our sea-watching radar was in fact useless. It was not until 11.25 A.M. that the Admiralty received the news. By then the escaping cruisers and their powerful air and destroyer escort were within twenty miles of Boulogne. Soon after noon the Dover batteries opened fire with their heavy guns, and the first striking force of five M.T.B.s immediately put to sea and attacked. Six torpedo-carrying Swordfish aircraft from Manston, in Kent, led by Lieutenant-Commander Esmonde (who had led the first attack on the *Bismarck*), set off without waiting for more than ten Spitfires in support. The Swordfish, fiercely attacked by enemy fighters, discharged their torpedoes against the enemy, but at a heavy cost. None returned, and only five survivors were rescued. Esmonde was awarded a posthumous V.C.

Successive waves of bombers and torpedo-bombers assailed the enemy till nightfall. There was much bitter and confused fighting with the German fighters, in which we suffered more severe losses than the enemy with his superior numbers. When

the German cruisers were off the Dutch coast at about 3.30 P.M.
five destroyers from Harwich pressed home an attack, firing
their torpedoes at about three thousand yards under tremendous fire. Nevertheless, unscathed either by the Dover batteries
or the torpedo attacks, the German squadron held its course,
and by the morning of the 13th all the German ships had
reached home. The news astonished the British public, who
could not understand what appeared to them, not unnaturally,
to be a proof of the German mastery of the English Channel.
Very soon however we found out, by our Secret Service, that
both the *Scharnhorst* and the *Gneisenau* had fallen victims to
our air-laid mines. It was six months before the *Scharnhorst*
was capable of service, and the *Gneisenau* never appeared again
in the war. This however could not be made public and
national wrath was vehement.

To allay complaints an official inquiry was held, which
reported the publishable facts. Viewed in the after-light and in
its larger aspects the episode was highly advantageous to us.
"When I speak on the radio next Monday evening," cabled
President Roosevelt, "I shall say a word about those people who
treat the episode in the Channel as a defeat. I am more and
more convinced that the location of all the German ships in
Germany makes our joint North Atlantic naval problem more
simple." But it looked very bad at the time to everyone in the
Grand Alliance outside our most secret circles.

I took the same view as Mr. Roosevelt:

Prime Minister to President Roosevelt   17 Feb. 42

The naval position in home waters and the Atlantic has been
definitely eased by the retreat of the German naval forces from
Brest. From there they threatened all our Eastbound convoys,
enforcing two battleship escorts. Their squadron could also move
either on to the Atlantic trade routes or into the Mediterranean.
We would far rather have it where it is than where it was. Our
bomber effort, instead of being dispersed, can now be concentrated
on Germany. Lastly, as you may have learnt, *Prinz Eugen* was
damaged and both *Scharnhorst* and *Gneisenau* were mined, the
former twice. This will keep them out of mischief for at least six

months, during which both our Navies will receive important accessions of strength. Naturally, we were very sorry we did not sink them, and an inquiry is being held as to why we did not know at daylight they were out.

*   *   *'   *   *

It was not until more than two months later that the Secret Session of April 23 enabled me to tell the salient facts to the House of Commons.

I have been impressed by the shock which the passage of these two ships through the Channel gave to the loyal masses of the British nation. . . . Our torpedo-carrying aircraft were depleted by the needs of Egypt. As to the Navy, we do not, for obvious reasons, keep capital ships in the Narrow Seas. Attention has however also been drawn to the fact that there were only six destroyers capable of attacking the German battle-cruisers. Where, it is asked, were all the rest of our flotillas? The answer is that they were and are out on the approaches from the Atlantic convoying the food and munitions from the United States without which we cannot live. . . . Most people thought the passage of these ships through the Channel very astonishing and very alarming. They could have broken south and perhaps got into the Mediterranean. They could have gone out into the Atlantic as commerce raiders. They could have gone northabout and tried to reach their own home waters by the Norwegian fiords. But the one way which seemed impossible to the general public was that they could come up the Channel and through the Straits of Dover. I will therefore read an extract from the Admiralty appreciation which was written on February 2, ten days before the cruisers broke out, and when their exercises and steam trials and the arrival of escorting German destroyers showed what they had in mind:

At first sight this passage up the Channel appears hazardous for the Germans. It is probable however that as their heavy ships are not fully efficient they would prefer such passage, relying for their security on their destroyers and aircraft, which are efficient, and knowing full well that we have no heavy ships with which to oppose them in the Channel. We might well therefore find the two battle-cruisers and the eight-inch cruiser, with five large and five small destroyers, also say twenty fighters constantly overhead (with reinforcements within call), proceeding up-Channel.

Taking all factors into consideration, it appears that the German ships can pass east up the Channel with much less risk than they will incur if they attempt an ocean passage to Norway, and as it is considered the Germans will evade danger until they are fully worked up, the Channel passage appears to be their most probable direction if and when they leave Brest.

This quotation of what the Naval Staff had written *before* the event made, as I expected, an impression upon the House which no subsequent explanations could ever have done.

* * * * *

Meanwhile havoc continued to reign along the Atlantic coast of the United States. A U-boat commander reported to Doenitz that ten times as many U-boats could find ample targets. Resting on the bottom during daylight, the U-boats used their high surface speed at night to select the richest prey. Nearly every torpedo they carried claimed its victim, and when torpedoes were expended the gun was almost equally effective. The towns of the Atlantic shore, where for a while the waterfronts remained fully lighted, heard nightly the sounds of battle near the coast, saw the burning, sinking ships offshore, and rescued the survivors and wounded. There was bitter anger against the Administration, which was much embarrassed. It is however easier to infuriate Americans than to cow them.

In London we had marked these misfortunes with anxiety and grief. As early as February 6, I sent a private warning to Hopkins:

It would be well to make sure that the President's attention has been drawn to the very heavy sinkings by U-boats in the Western North Atlantic. Since January 12, confirmed losses are 158,208, and probable losses 83,740 and possible losses 17,363, a total of 259,311 tons.

On February 10 we offered, unasked, twenty-four of our best-equipped anti-submarine trawlers and ten corvettes with their

trained crews to the American Navy. These were welcomed
by our Ally, and the first arrived in New York early in March.
It was little enough, but the utmost we could spare. " 'Twas
all she gave, 'Twas all she had to give." Coastal convoys could
not begin until the necessary organisation had been built up
and the essential minimum escorts gathered. The available
fighting ships and aircraft were at first used only to patrol
threatened areas. The enemy, easily evading the patrols,
pursued their defenceless prey elsewhere. On February 16 a
U-boat appeared off the great oil port of Aruba, in the Dutch
West Indies, and, after sinking one small tanker and damaging
another, shelled the installations ashore from outside the
harbour without causing serious damage. An attempt to
torpedo a large tanker lying alongside also failed. The same
day other U-boats sank three more tankers at sea in the same
area. Soon afterwards another U-boat entered the British
harbour of Trinidad, sank two ships at anchor, and withdrew
unharmed. This latter incident forced us to divert the liners
transporting troops to the Far East, which frequently refuelled
there. By good fortune neither the *Queen Mary* nor any other
of these great ships was attacked in this area.

In March the main stress fell in the area between Charleston
and New York, while single U-boats prowled over all the
Caribbean and the Gulf of Mexico, with a freedom and inso-
lence which was hard to bear. During this month the sinkings
were nearly half a million tons, of which three-quarters were
sunk within three hundred miles of the American coast, and
nearly half was in tanker tonnage. Against this could only be
set the loss of two U-boats in American waters sunk by American aircraft on ocean convoy escort off Newfoundland in March.
The first kill off the American coast here by a surface vessel
was not made until April 14, by the United States destroyer
Roper.

*   *   *   *   *

In March I recurred to what had by then become a major
feature of the war.

Prime Minister to Mr. Harry Hopkins 12 Mar. 42

I am most deeply concerned at the immense sinkings of tankers west of the 40th meridian and in the Caribbean Sea. In January 18 ships, totalling 221,000 dead-weight tons, were sunk or damaged; in February, the number rose to 34, totalling 364,941 dead-weight tons; in the first eleven days of March, seven vessels, totalling 88,449 dead-weight tons, have been sunk. Yesterday alone 30,000 tons were reported as sunk or damaged. Thus, in little over two months, in these waters alone, about 60 tankers have been sunk or damaged, totalling some 675,000 dead-weight tons. In addition to this several tankers are overdue.

2. By rearrangement of Atlantic convoy duties a considerable number of American destroyers have been released from escort duties on the cross-Atlantic routes for other services. We have handed over 24 anti-submarine trawlers, of which 23 have now reached you.

3. The situation is so serious that drastic action of some kind is necessary, and we very much hope that you will be able to provide additional escort forces to organise immediate convoys in the West Indies-Bermuda area by withdrawing a few of your destroyer strength in the Pacific, until the ten corvettes we are handing over to you come into service.

4. The only other alternatives are either to stop temporarily the sailing of tankers, which would gravely jeopardise our operational supplies, or to open out the cycle of Halifax-United Kingdom convoys [i.e., lessen the traffic], thus for a period releasing sufficient escort vessels to make up the West Indies convoys. It must be realised however that not only will this further reduce our imports by about 30,000 tons a month, but it will also take some little time to become effective.

5. I should like these alternatives to be discussed on the highest naval level at once.

If through opening out the convoy cycle we were forced to reduce our imports for a time, this would have to be taken into consideration by you in helping us out with new tonnage in the last half of the year. Please let me know whether you think it well to bring all this before the President straightaway.

6. I am enormously relieved by the splendid telegrams I have had from the President on the largest issues. It is most comforting to feel we are in such complete agreement of war outlook. Please con-

vey my personal greetings to King [and] Marshall, and say, "Happy days will come again."

*   *   *   *   *

The President, after anxious consultations with his admirals upon this and the whole naval position, replied at length to my cable. He welcomed the arrival of the trawlers and the corvettes. He proposed various economies in the trans-Atlantic escorts involving opening the cycle of convoys till July 1, by which time the mounting production of small escort vessels and planes in America would come fully into play. He gave me the reassurance which I needed about our import pro-gramme in the second half of the year.

A few days later he added, with what I felt was a touch of strain:

President Roosevelt to Former Naval Person   20 Mar. 42

Your interest in steps to be taken to combat the Atlantic sub-marine menace as indicated by your recent message to Mr. Hopkins on this subject impels me to request your particular consideration of heavy attacks on submarine bases and building and repair yards, thus checking submarine activities at their source and where sub-marines perforce congregate.

I replied, after making inquiries and plans:

Former Naval Person to President Roosevelt   29 Mar. 42

In order to cope with future U-boat hatchings, we are empha-sising bombing attacks on U-boat nests, and last night went to Lübeck with 250 bombers, including 43 heavy. Results are said to be the best ever. This is in accordance with your wishes.

2. Admiralty and Coastal Command, R.A.F., have evolved a plan for a day-and-night patrol over the debouches from the Bay of Biscay. Biscay ports are the shortest and best departure points for U-boats operating on Caribbean and American coasts. German present practice is to proceed submerged by day and make speed on the surface at night. We hope that night attacks and menace by aircraft will hamper their night passage and force increasing ex-posure by day. Essential therefore to menace both by day and

night, thus increasing length of voyage and diminishing operational spell on your side. This advantage would be additional to any killings or maimings, some of which might be hoped for each month, since there are never less than six U-boats going or coming through the area to be patrolled.

3. In view of the very heavy sinkings still occurring on your side, to which convoy, when organised, can only be partial remedy, Admiralty are pressing to allocate four and later on six bomber squadrons to this new Biscay patrol. On merits I am most anxious to meet their wish.

4. On the other hand, the need to bomb Germany is great. Our new method of finding targets is yielding most remarkable results. However, our bombing force has not expanded as we hoped. We have had a heavy disappointment in a structural defect with the wing-tips of the Lancasters which requires laying up four squadrons of our latest and best for several months. Just at the time when the weather is improving, when Germans are drawing away flak from their cities for their offensive against Russia, when you are keen about our bombing U-boat nests, when the oil targets are especially attractive, I find it very hard to take away these extra six squadrons from Bomber Command, in which Harris is doing so well.

*   *   *   *   *

March closed for us with the brilliant and heroic exploit of St. Nazaire. This was the only place along all the Atlantic coast where the *Tirpitz* could be docked for repair if she were damaged. If the dock, one of the largest in the world, could be destroyed, a sortie of the *Tirpitz* from Trondheim into the Atlantic would become far more dangerous and might not be deemed worth making. Our Commandos were eager for the fray, and here was a deed of glory intimately involved in high strategy. Led by Commander Ryder of the Royal Navy, with Colonel Newman of the Essex Regiment, an expedition of destroyers and light coastal craft sailed from Falmouth on the afternoon of March 26, carrying about two hundred and fifty Commando troops. They had four hundred miles to traverse through waters under constant enemy patrol, and five miles up the estuary of the Loire.

The goal was the destruction of the gates of the great lock. The *Campbeltown,* one of the fifty old American destroyers, carrying three tons of high explosive in her bows, drove into the lock gates, in the teeth of a close and murderous fire. Here she was scuttled, and the fuses of her main demolition charges set to explode later. Lieutenant-Commander Beattie had led her here. From her decks Major Copeland, with a landing party, leaped ashore to destroy the dock machinery. The Germans met them in overwhelming strength, and furious fighting began. All but five of the landing-party were killed or captured. Commander Ryder's craft, although fired on from all sides, miraculously remained afloat during his break for the open sea with the remnants of his force, and got safely home. But the great explosion was still to come. Something had gone wrong with the fuze. It was not till the next day, when a large party of German officers and technicians were inspecting the wreck of the *Campbeltown,* jammed in the lock gates, that the ship blew up, with devastating force, killing hundreds of Germans and shattering the great lock for the rest of the war. The Germans treated the prisoners, four of whom received the Victoria Cross, with respect, but severe punishment was inflicted on the brave Frenchmen who on the spur of the moment rushed from every quarter to the aid of what they hoped was the vanguard of liberation.

*　　*　　*　　*　　*

At last on April 1 it became possible for the United States Navy to make a start with a partial coastal convoy system. At first this could be no more than daylight hops of about a hundred and twenty miles between protected anchorages by groups of ships under escort, and all shipping was brought to a standstill at night. On any one day there were upwards of a hundred and twenty ships requiring protection between Florida and New York. The consequent delays were misfortune in another form. It was not until May 14 that the first fully organised convoy sailed from Hampton Roads for Key West. Thereafter the system was quickly extended northward to New

York and Halifax, and by the end of the month the chain along
the east coast from Key West northward was at last complete.
Relief was immediate, and although the U-boats continued to
avoid destruction the shipping losses fell.

Admiral Doenitz forthwith changed his point of attack to the
Caribbean and the Gulf of Mexico, where convoys were not yet
working. Here the loss of tanker tonnage rose steeply. Ranging
farther, the U-boats also began to appear off the coast of Brazil
and in the St. Lawrence River. It was not until the end of the
year that a complete interlocking convoy system covering all
these immense areas became fully effective. But June saw an
improvement, and the last days of July may be taken as closing
the terrible massacre of shipping along the American coast.
From the diagram on page 125 the reader will see that in this
period of seven months the Allied losses in the Atlantic from
U-boats alone amounted to over three million tons, including
181 British ships of 1,130,000 tons. Less than one-tenth of all
these losses occurred in convoys. All this cost the enemy up to
July no more than fourteen U-boats sunk throughout the
Atlantic and Arctic Oceans, and of these kills only six were in
North American waters. Thereafter we regained the initiative
in this area. In July alone five U-boats were destroyed off the
Atlantic coast, besides six more German and three Italian
elsewhere. This total of fourteen for the month, half by convoy
escorts, gave us encouragement. It was the best figure so far
achieved, but even so the number of new boats coming into
service each month still exceeded the rate of our kills.

Moreover, wherever Allied counter-measures began to take
effect Admiral Doenitz shifted his U-boats. With the oceans
to play in he could always gain a short period of immunity in a new area before we overtook him there. Already in May the comparative freedom which trans-Atlantic
shipping had enjoyed was broken by an attack on a convoy
about seven hundred miles west of Ireland, in which seven
ships were lost. This was followed by an attack in the Gibraltar
area and the reappearance of U-boats near Freetown. Once
more Hitler came to our aid by insisting that a group of U-boats

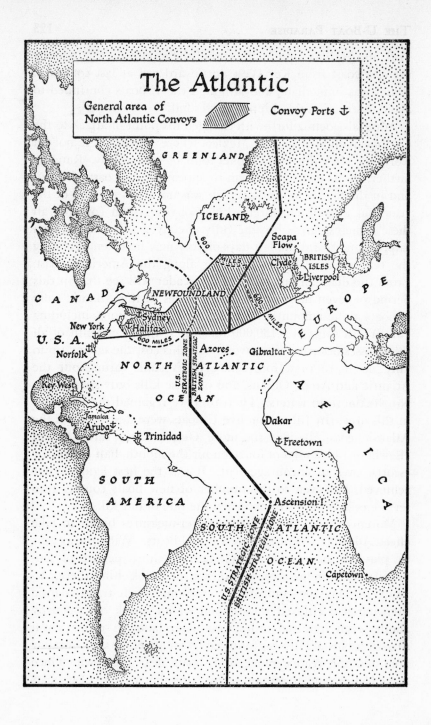

The Atlantic

General area of
North Atlantic Convoys   Convoy Ports ⚓

GREENLAND

ICELAND

Scapa
Flow

600

MILES

Clyde

BRITISH
ISLES

Liverpool

CANADA

NEWFOUNDLAND

600

MILES

Sydney

New York

Halifax

U. S. A.

Norfolk

600 MILES

U.S. STRATEGIC ZONE

BRITISH STRATEGIC ZONE

Azores

Gibraltar

NORTH   ATLANTIC

EUROPE

Key West

OCEAN

AFRICA

Jamaica

Aruba

Trinidad

Dakar

Freetown

SOUTH

AMERICA

Ascension I.

SOUTH   ATLANTIC

OCEAN

U.S. STRATEGIC ZONE

BRITISH STRATEGIC ZONE

Capetown

Saml Bryant

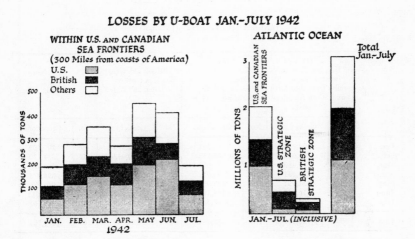

LOSSES BY U-BOAT JAN.-JULY 1942

should be held ready to ward off an Allied attempt to occupy the Azores or Madeira. His thought in this direction was, as the reader knows, not altogether misplaced, but it is unlikely that U-boats alone could have made any decisive intervention had we resolved upon such a stroke. Doenitz regretted this fresh demand on his cherished U-boats, coinciding as it did with the end of the halcyon days on the American coast, and when he was collecting his strength for a renewed attack on the main convoy routes.

The U-boat attack was our worst evil. It would have been wise for the Germans to stake all upon it. I remember hearing my father say, "In politics when you have got hold of a good thing, stick to it." This is also a strategic principle of importance. Just as Goering repeatedly shifted his air targets in the Battle of Britain in 1940, so now the U-boat warfare was to some extent weakened for the sake of competing attractions. Nevertheless, it constituted a terrible event in a very bad time.

The table which follows should be studied.

MERCHANT SHIP LOSSES BY U-BOAT
IN THE ATLANTIC OCEAN

JANUARY–JULY, 1942 (INCLUSIVE)

Month	(1) U.S. Sea Frontiers (west of a line 300 miles from the North and South American coasts)		(2) U.S. Strategic Area (west of Long. 26° W. exclusive of (1))		(3) British Strategic Area (east of Long. 26° W.)		(4) Totals	
	No.	Gross tons	No.	Gross tons	No.	Gross tons	No.	Gross tons
Jan.	31	196,243	9	68,284	6	32,575	46	297,102
Feb.	50	286,613	19	86,555	2	10,942	71	384,110
Mar.	61	354,489	13	70,058	7	35,638	81	460,185
Apr.	48	276,131	13	88,917	6	30,975	67	396,023
May	91	451,991	26	133,951	3	15,567	120	**601,509**
June	80	416,843	25	164,186	9	45,982	114	**627,011**
July	45	192,851	8	46,383	16	111,529	69	350,763
Totals	406	2,175,161	113	658,334	49	283,208	568	3,116,703

Of the total of 568 ships, of 3,116,703 gross tons, only 53 ships, of 284,000 gross tons, were sailing in convoy.

* * * * *

It will be well here to record the course of events elsewhere and to trace briefly the progress of the Atlantic battle up to the end of 1942.

In August the U-boats turned their attention to the area around Trinidad and the north coast of Brazil, where the ships carrying bauxite to the United States for the aircraft industry and the stream of outward-bound ships with supplies for the Middle East offered the most attractive targets. Other roving U-boats were at work near Freetown; some ranged as far south as the Cape of Good Hope, and a few even penetrated into the Indian Ocean. For a time the South Atlantic caused us anxiety. Here in September and October five large homeward-bound liners sailing independently were sunk, but all our troop transports outward-bound for the Middle East in convoy came through unscathed. Among the big ships lost was the *Laconia,* of nearly 20,000 tons, carrying two thousand Italian prisoners of war to England. Many were drowned.

The main battle was by now once more joined along the great convoy routes in the North Atlantic. The U-boats had already learned to respect the power of the air, and in their new assault they worked almost entirely in the central section, beyond the reach of aircraft based on Iceland and Newfoundland. Two convoys were severely mauled in August, one of them losing eleven ships, and during this month U-boats sank 108 ships, amounting to over half a million tons. In September and October the Germans reverted to the earlier practice of submerged attack by day. With the larger numbers now working in the "wolf packs," and with our limited resources, serious losses in convoy could not be prevented. It was now that we felt most acutely the lack of sufficient numbers of very long-range (V.L.R.) aircraft in the Coastal Command. Air cover still ranged no more than about six hundred miles from our shore bases, and the accompanying chart of the Atlantic Ocean, on which these zones are shown, discloses the large unguarded gap in the centre where the sorely tried surface escorts could gain no help from the air.[1]

*   *   *   *   *

In the early months of 1942 our Coastal Command had been passing through an unhappy period. The overwhelming demands for reinforcements in the Far East and the Mediterranean had made great inroads into its resources in aircraft and trained crews, which melted away to meet the harsh needs elsewhere. Moreover, the expansion of the Command with new long-range squadrons, which had been eagerly expected, had perforce been temporarily arrested. Against this distressing background our airmen did their utmost.

Naval escorts alone, although providing reasonable protection against attacks launched in the traditional manner by submerged U-boats in daylight, could never range widely from the convoys and break up the heavy concentrations on the flanks. Thus, when the "wolf packs" struck they could deliver a combined blow in numbers sufficient to saturate the defence. We realised that the remedy lay in surrounding each convoy, not

1 See map on page 124.

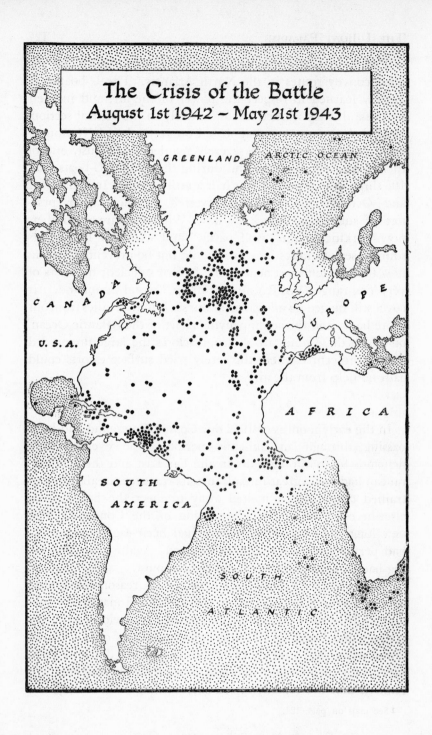

The Crisis of the Battle
August 1st 1942 – May 21st 1943

only with surface escorts, but also with a screen of aircraft
sufficient to find and force any U-boats nearby to dive, thus
providing a lane through which the convoy might move unmolested. This purely defensive measure was not in itself
enough. To overcome the U-boats we must seek out and
attack them vigorously wherever we could find them, both by
sea and air. The aircraft, the trained air crews, and the air
weapons needed were not yet numerous enough to have a
decisive influence, but we now made a start by forming a "Support Group" of surface forces.

This tactical idea had long been advocated, but the
means were lacking. The first of these Support Groups,
which later became a most potent factor in the U-boat
war, consisted of two sloops, four of the new frigates
now coming out of the builders' yards, and four destroyers. Manned by highly trained and experienced crews and
provided with the latest weapons, they were intended to work
independently of the convoy escorts, and, untrammelled by
other responsibilities, to seek, hunt, and destroy the U-boat
packs wherever they threatened. Co-operation between the
support groups and aircraft was an essential feature in the
success of these plans, and in 1943 it became a common occurrence for an aircraft sighting a U-boat to guide a Support Group
to its prey. Moreover, there was always the likelihood that the
pursuit of one U-boat would disclose others, and thus the
original sighting might lead to a pack.

Meanwhile the need of seaborne air support with the convoys had been receiving close attention. The reader will recall
from an earlier volume the successes attending the brief, vivid
career of our first escort carrier, *Audacity*, which perished in
December, 1941. By the end of 1942 six of these ships were in
service. Eventually many were built in America, besides others
in Great Britain, and the first of them, the *Avenger*, sailed
with a North Russian convoy in September. They made their
first effective appearance against the U-boats with the "Torch"
convoys late in October. Equipped with naval Swordfish aircraft, they met the need — namely, all-round reconnaissance in

depth, independent of land bases, and in intimate collaboration with the surface escorts. Thus by the utmost exertions and ingenuity our anti-U-boat measures were markedly improving; but the power of the enemy was growing too and we still had many severe setbacks to face.

Between January and October, 1942, the number of operational U-boats had risen from 90 to 196 in spite of losses. Moreover, by the autumn about half this number were again active in the North Atlantic, where our convoys were subjected to fierce attacks by larger groups of U-boats than ever before. At the same time all our escorts had to be cut to the bone for the sake of our main operations in Africa. In November the Allied losses at sea were the heaviest of the whole war, including 117 ships, of over 700,000 tons, by U-boats alone, and another 100,000 tons lost from other causes.

*   *   *   *   *

So menacing were the conditions in the outer waters beyond the range of air cover that on November 4 I personally convened a new Anti-U-boat Committee to deal specially with this aspect. The power of this body to take far-reaching decisions played no small part in the conflict. In a great effort to lengthen the range of our radar-carrying Liberator aircraft, we decided to withdraw them from action for the time needed to make the necessary improvements. As part of this policy President Roosevelt at my request sent all suitable American aircraft fitted with the latest type of radar, to work from the United Kingdom. Thus we were presently able to resume operations in the Bay of Biscay in greater strength and with far better equipment. This decision, and other measures taken in November, 1942, were to reap their reward in 1943.

Prime Minister to Mr. Mackenzie King   23 Nov. 42

I am seriously concerned at recent heavy losses from convoys in the centre of the trans-Atlantic route. Experience has shown the great protection given by air escorts, which can keep U-boats down by day and so make the gathering of packs extremely difficult.

2. Until auxiliary aircraft-carriers can be made available we must rely on long-range shore-based aircraft. All available auxiliary carriers are now being used for combined operations, and in any case there will not be sufficient for all convoys for many months. We intend to increase petrol tankage of some Liberator aircraft to give an operational range of 2300 sea-miles, but to reach all convoys these very long-range aircraft would have to operate from airfields on your side of the Atlantic as well as from Iceland (C) and Northern Ireland.

3. We are therefore most anxious to make use of Goose Airfield, in Labrador, for these long-range aircraft on anti-submarine operations, and request that the necessary refuelling and servicing facilities should be made available as early as possible. We would require similar facilities at Gander, and ask that the same steps be taken there. We might later wish to send a Coastal Command squadron to operate from these bases. In the meantime any extension of the range at which Canadian aircraft can go to the assistance of threatened convoys would be of great value in reducing losses.

*   *   *   *   *

The Canadians gave us their fullest co-operation, and under the lash of our defence the attacks began to lose their vigour and audacity. Sixteen U-boats were destroyed in October, the highest monthly figure so far attained in the war. However, in the closing days of 1942 a pack of about twenty U-boats fell upon an outward-bound convoy near the Azores. In three days fifteen ships, twelve of them British, were lost.

The story of the decisive battle in 1943, when the U-boats, at their fullest strength, were effectively challenged and mastered, is reserved for the next volume.

The winter weather brought a welcome relief.

8

The Loss of the Dutch East Indies

SCORES OF THOUSANDS OF WORDS in the surest codes had been telegraphed between the British, United States, Dutch, Australian, New Zealand, Indian, and Chinese Governments to create the A.B.D.A. Command under its Supreme Commander. It was staffed in strict proportion to the claims of the different Powers, and all in triplicate for the Army, Navy, and Air. There were elaborate arguments about whether as a compromise a Dutch admiral might command the naval forces; how all was to be arranged with the Americans and the British; where the Australians came in, and so forth. Hardly had all this been agreed for the five Powers and the three Services when the whole vast area concerned was conquered by the Japanese, and the combined fleet of the Allies was sunk in the forlorn battle of the Java Sea.

*   *   *   *   *

At the outset a misunderstanding arose with **Chiang Kai-shek**, which, though it did not affect the course of events, involved high politics. At Washington I had found the extraordinary significance of China in American minds, even at the top, strangely out of proportion. I was conscious of a standard of values which accorded China almost an equal fighting power with the British Empire, and rated the Chinese armies as a factor to be mentioned in the same breath as the armies of Russia. I told the President how much I felt American opinion overestimated the contribution which China could make to the general war. He differed strongly. There were five hundred million people in China. What would happen if this enormous population developed in the same way as Japan had done in the last century and got hold of modern weapons? I replied I was speaking of the present war, which was quite enough to go on with for the time being. I said I would of course always be helpful and polite to the Chinese, whom I admired and liked as a race and pitied for their endless misgovernment, but that he must not expect me to adopt what I felt was a wholly unreal standard of values.

While still Commander-in-Chief in India, General Wavell flew over the Himalayas to see Generalissimo Chiang Kai-shek at Chungking. This was in harmony with American ideas. The results of the interview were however disappointing, and Chiang Kai-shek complained to President Roosevelt of the British commander's apparent lack of enthusiasm about any contribution China could make to his own problem. I sought to put this right.

Prime Minister to General Wavell   23 Jan. 42

I am still puzzled about your reasons for refusing Chinese help in the defence of Burma and the Burma Road. You have, I un-

derstand, now accepted 49th and 93d Chinese Divisions, but the
Chinese Fifth Army and the rest of the Sixth Army are available
just beyond the frontier. Burma seems in grave danger of being
overrun. When we remember how long the Chinese have stood up
alone and ill-armed against the Japanese, and when we see what
a very rough time we are having at Japanese hands, I cannot understand why we do not welcome their aid.

2. I must enlighten you upon the American view. China bulks
as large in the minds of many of them as Great Britain. The President, who is a great admirer of yours, seemed a bit dunched at
Chiang Kai-shek's discouragement after your interview with him.
The American Chiefs of Staff insisted upon Burma being in your
command for the sole reason that they considered your giving your
left hand to China and the opening of the Burma Road indispensable to world victory. And never forget that behind all looms
the shadow of Asiatic solidarity, which the numerous disasters and
defeats through which we have to plough our way may make more
menacing.

3. If I can epitomise in one word the lesson I learned in the
United States, it was "China."

General Wavell to Prime Minister

I did not refuse Chinese help. You say I have "now" accepted
49th and 93d Divisions. I accepted both these divisions when I was
at Chungking on December 23d, and any delay in moving them
down has been purely Chinese. These two divisions constitute
Fifth Chinese Army, I understand, except for one other division
of very doubtful quality. All I asked was that Sixth Army should
not be moved to Burmese frontier, as it would be difficult to feed.
. . . British troops due for Burma from India and Africa should
have been sufficient if all went well, and as many as communications could support. . . . I am aware of American sentiment about
the Chinese, but democracies are apt to think with their hearts
rather than with their heads, and a general's business is, or should
be, to use his head for planning. I consider my judgment in accepting the Chinese help I did (two divisions of Fifth Army) and
asking that Sixth Army should be held in reserve in Kunming area
was quite correct, and I am sorry that my action seems to have
been so misunderstood. I hope you will correct [the] President's
impression if you get opportunity. I agree British prestige in China

is low, and can hardly be otherwise till we have had some success. It will not be increased by admission that we cannot hold Burma without Chinese help.

Prime Minister to General Wavell   28 Jan. 42

Thank you. I am glad we are in agreement. I will not lose any chance of explaining to President.

*   *   *   *   *

General Wavell had arrived in Batavia on January 10, and established his headquarters near Bandoeng, the centre of the Dutch Army Command. With but a small nucleus of officers, separated by great distances from sources of reinforcement, and with active operations in progress at many points on his five-thousand-mile front, he applied himself to the intricate and urgent business of setting up the first of the several inter-Allied commands of the war.

The Japanese conquests already threatened the chain of islands that form the southern fringe of the Malay barrier, of which the largest are Sumatra and Java. To the east General MacArthur, without hope of rescue, continued his spirited resistance on the Bataan peninsula in the Philippines. On the west British Malaya had for the most part been overrun. Singapore was in peril. Between these two flanking but threatened pillars of Allied resistance other Japanese forces were pressing southward through the maze of Dutch islands. Sarawak and Brunei, the Dutch oil ports in Borneo and the Celebes, had already been lost. At each step the enemy consolidated his gains by establishing air bases from which he could also strike against the next chosen victim. Never did his forces pass beyond the reach of his powerful shore-based air cover or of his aircraft-carriers at sea. Here was the fulfilment in full strategic surprise of the long cherished and profound plans of a military nation.

For Wavell all turned on the arrival of reinforcements. Nothing could be done to save the small Dutch garrisons at the key points of the central islands, and we have seen what happened at Singapore. The Dutch, with their homeland in bondage, had no further resources on which to call. Their full effort had been engaged from the outset, and was now waning. The two Australian divisions from the Middle East and an armoured brigade were on their way. Three anti-aircraft regiments were hurried to the naked airfields of Java. The *Indomitable* flew forty-eight Hurricanes off her deck; two more squadrons of bombers flew from Egypt via India to Sumatra. Eight of these aircraft eventually reached Java. Everything that we could lay our hands upon was sent. The United States Asiatic Fleet, withdrawn from the Philippines, had already been sent to join the British and Dutch naval forces. Every effort was made by the Americans to send aircraft by air or sea to the Allied command; but the distances were immense, and the Japanese machine was working with speed and precision.

The end of January saw the loss of Kendari, in the Celebes, and of the great petroleum port of Balikpapan, in Eastern Borneo. The island of Ambon, with its important airfield, was captured by greatly superior forces. Farther east and beyond the A.B.D.A. area the Japanese took Rabaul in New Britain, and Bougainville in the Solomon Islands. This was the first step in a serious attempt to sever Australia's life-line with the United States. Early in February the first Japanese troops landed at Finschaven, in New Guinea, but for the moment the scale of events elsewhere prevented them from extending their grip in these remote regions. At the other extremity, in Burma, the invasion was progressing.

*   *   *   *   *

It is of interest to see what the Germans thought at this time. On February 13 Admiral Raeder reported to the Fuehrer:

Rangoon, Singapore, and, most likely, also Port Darwin, will be in Japanese hands within a few weeks. Only weak resistance is expected on Sumatra, while Java will be able to hold out longer. Japan plans to protect this front in the Indian Ocean by capturing

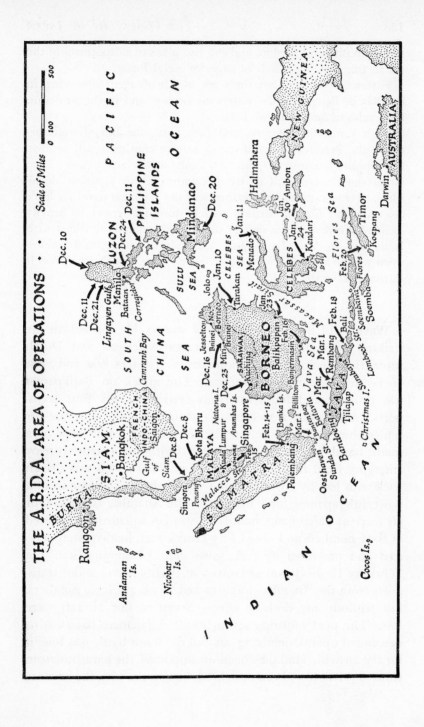

THE A.B.D.A. AREA OF OPERATIONS · ·

Scale of Miles

0   100   500

BURMA

Rangoon.

Andaman
Is.

Nicobar
Is.

SIAM

Bangkok.

FRENCH
INDO-CHINA

Saigon.

Gulf
of
Siam   Dec.8

Dec.8

SOUTH

CHINA

SEA

Dec.11
Dec.21

Lingayen Gulf
Camranh Bay

Dec.10

LUZON
Manila
Bataan
Corregidor

Dec.11
Dec.24

PACIFIC

PHILIPPINE
ISLANDS

Mindanao

Dec.20

OCEAN

SULU
SEA

Jolo

MALAYA

Singora

Penang
Kota Bharu

Kuala Lumpur
Natoena I.
Anambas Is.

Singapore
Johore

Feb.14-15

Malacca Str.

Dec.16 Jesselton
Brunei
Miri   Borneo
Brunei
Dec.23
SARAWAK
Kuching

No.

Jan.10

CELEBES

Tarakan

Menado

Jan.11

Jan.
23

CELEBES

Kendari

Jan.
24

Halmahera

Jan.
30 Ambon

NEW GUINEA

BORNEO

Balikpapan
Feb.16

Banjermasin

Banka Is.
Billiton

Palembang

Batavia

Banten Bay
Mar.1

Oosthaven

Sunda Str.
Bandoeng

Christmas I.

Java Sea

Macassar Strait

Rembang Feb.18
Mar.1

Mar.
1

JAVA

Tjilajap

Bali

Lombock Str.(Sumb)

Soembawa

Flores

Flores
Feb.20

Flores Sea

Timor

Koepang

Darwin

AUSTRALIA

SUMATRA

Cocos Is.

INDIAN   OCEAN

the key position of Ceylon, and she also plans to gain control of the sea in that area by means of superior naval forces.

Fifteen Japanese submarines are at the moment operating in the Bay of Bengal, in the waters off Ceylon, and in the straits on both sides of Sumatra and Java.

With Rangoon, Sumatra, and Java gone, the last oil-wells between the Persian Gulf and the American continent will be lost. Oil supplies for Australia and New Zealand will have to come from either the Persian Gulf or from America. Once Japanese battle-ships, aircraft-carriers, submarines, and the Japanese naval air force are based on Ceylon, Britain will be forced to resort to heavily escorted convoys if she desires to maintain communications with India and the Near East. Only Alexandria, Durban, and Simons-town will be available as repair bases for large British naval vessels in that part of the world.

*   *   *   *   *

Wavell did his best to face the storm. He formed an air striking force at Palembang. At sea American and Dutch submarines harried the various invasion forces east and west of Borneo, not without success. The attack on Balikpapan was resisted, and four American destroyers sank four transports. A fifth fell a victim to a Dutch aircraft. But the air replenishments had barely replaced wastage. An attempt by a small naval squadron to interfere with an enemy convoy emerging from the Macassar Strait on February 4 was driven back with loss by air attack, and reports began to come in of a powerful Japanese force massing at the Anambas Islands. Our air force at Palembang, mainly Australian squadrons, consisted of sixty bombers and about fifty Hurricanes, inadequately serviced and protected by A.A. guns short of ammunition. On February 13 the Japanese convoy of twenty-five or more transports from the Anambas was attacked by all available bombers, but without any decisive effect. Seven of our aircraft were lost. The next morning seven hundred Japanese parachutists descended upon Palembang, and all day a hot battle was fought for the airfield. Had they been unsupported, the parachutists in time could all have been destroyed, but on the 15th the advance echelon of the powerful invasion force arrived on the scene, equipped with landing-craft that carried them up the river approaches. Every available aircraft was used against the ships and landing-craft, great losses were inflicted, and the attack was stayed — only to be resumed as our air effort inevitably declined. Our strength at Palembang was now but a score of Hurricanes and forty bombers, many of them unserviceable, all based upon an as yet undected airfield. By nightfall it was obvious that our scanty forces must withdraw and that all Southern Sumatra would fall into Japanese hands. That day also saw the fall of Singapore.

On the eve of this disaster General Wavell sent us a full warning of the probable course of events, which I repeated to the two Dominions Premiers directly concerned.

General Wavell to Prime Minister   13 Feb. 42

. . . The unexpectedly rapid advance of enemy on Singapore and approach of an escorted enemy convoy toward Southern Sumatra necessitate review of our plans for the defence of the Netherlands East Indies, in which Southern Sumatra plays a most important part. With more time and the arrival of 7th Australian Division, earmarked for Southern Sumatra, strong defence could be built up. But ground not yet fully prepared.

The leading infantry brigade of the 7th Australian Division will not be operative until about March 8, nor the whole division before March 21.

If Southern Sumatra is lost prolonged defence of Java becomes unlikely. Garrison is weak for size of island. 6th Australian Division at present planned to reinforce Java, but not effective before end of March. 7th Australian Division, if diverted from Southern Sumatra, would be available for Java.

From air aspect defence of Java is a hard matter; without Southern Sumatra it is formidable. Even with air reinforcements in view it is likely that our air forces will waste more quickly than they can be replaced.

Our limited air force is not engaged merely in a straight deal with enemy air force. It has also to attack enemy shipping, and is unable to protect our own.

It is clear that retention of Southern Sumatra is essential for successful defence of Java. The situation does not at present demand change in plans, but it may be forced on us. If that were so the destination of the Australian Corps would be first consideration, for it contains great majority of fully trained and equipped Australian troops.

We must reinforce Sumatra until it is clearly useless to do so. Subsequent reinforcement of Java would probably be unprofitable.

*   *   *   *   *

On the morrow of the fall of Singapore the Supreme Commander again surveyed the situation in his command, and his businesslike account gives a clear and comprehensive picture of the scene.

General Wavell to Prime Minister   16 Feb. 42

As you will gather, recent events at Singapore and in Southern Sumatra have faced us with extremely grave and urgent problem of strategy and policy.

2. *Geographical.* Java is 500 miles [long] — i.e., approximately distance from London to Inverness — and practically whole northern coast affords easy landing facilities.

3. *Enemy scale of attack and probable action.* With shipping and escorts available enemy can probably engage four divisions against Java within next ten to fourteen days, and reinforce with two or more divisions within month. Maximum scale of air attack possibly 400 to 500 fighters (including carrier-borne) and 300 to 400 bombers.

Our resources to meet enemy attack on Java are as follows:

(*a*) *Naval.* Maximum of three to four cruisers and about ten destroyers as striking force. If this is divided between two threatened ends of island it is too weak at either. If kept concentrated it is difficult, owing to distance involved, to reach vital point in time. Wherever it is, it is liable to heavy air attack.

(*b*) *Land forces.* At present three weak Dutch divisions. British Imperial troops: One squadron 3d Hussars, complete with light tanks, and about 3000 Australians in various units. There are several thousand R.A.F. ground personnel available, but proportion unarmed. American: One field artillery regiment, but without full equipment.

(c) Air Forces. At present about fifty fighters, sixty-five medium or dive bombers, twenty heavy bombers.

Landings on Java in near future can only be prevented by local naval and air superiority. Facts given show that it is most unlikely that this superiority can be obtained. Once enemy has effected landing, there is at present little to prevent his rapidly occupying main naval and air bases on island.

First flight of Australian Corps does not reach Java till about end of month. It cannot become operative till March 8, and whole division will not be unloaded and operative till March 21. The remaining division of corps could not be unloaded before middle of April.

To sum up. Burma and Australia are absolutely vital for war against Japan. Loss of Java, though severe blow from every point of view, would not be fatal. Efforts should not therefore be made to reinforce Java, which might compromise defence of Burma or Australia.

Immediate problem is destination of Australian Corps. If there seemed good chance of establishing corps in island and fighting Japanese on favourable terms, I should unhesitatingly recommend risks should be taken, as I did in matter of aid to Greece year ago. I thought then that we had good fighting chance of checking German invasion, and in spite of results still consider risk was justifiable. In present instance I must recommend that I consider risk unjustifiable from tactical and strategical point of view. I fully recognise political considerations involved. . . .

On this I minuted:

Prime Minister to General Ismay, for C.O.S. Committee 17 Feb. 42

I am sure it would be impossible to act contrary to General Wavell's main opinion. Personally, I agree with him. The best course would seem to be: *(a)* To divert the leading Australian division to Burma, if the Australian Government will allow it. *(b)* To send the 70th Division next, via Bombay, in the ships hitherto marked for the 2d Australian Division, dropping one brigade at Ceylon. *(c)* To send the remaining two Australian divisions as fast as possible to Australia as shipping becomes available. *(d)* To make absolutely sure of Trincomalee by A.A. reinforcements from Convoy W.S. 17, and send the rest of this convoy to Rangoon.

I am not clear as to how General Wavell proposes to use the existing forces in Java. Are they to be used to fight it out with the Dutch, so as to delay the occupation, or is any attempt to be made to get them away? It seems to me this is a more arguable question than the other.

To President Roosevelt I said:

You will have seen Wavell's telegrams about new situation created by fall of Singapore and Japanese strong landings in Sumatra. We are considering our position tonight on the Defence Committee and tomorrow on the Pacific Council, and will send you our recommendations. Unless there is good prospect of effective resistance in Sumatra and Java the issue arises whether all reinforcements should not be diverted to Rangoon and Australia. The Australian Government seem inclined to press for the return of their two divisions to Australia. I could not resist them for long, and probably their 3d Division, now in Palestine, will follow. It seems to me that the most vital point at the moment is Rangoon, alone assuring contact with China. As you see, Wavell has very rightly already diverted our Armoured Brigade, which should reach there on the 20th instant. The Chiefs of Staff will send you the result of our discussions tomorrow through the military channel.

2. A battle is impending in Libya, in which Rommel will probably take the offensive. We hope to give a good account of ourselves. Preliminary air fighting yesterday was very good.

General Wavell had forecast that the invasion of Java, our last stronghold, would begin before the end of February, and that with what he had, or was likely to get, there was little hope of success. He therefore recommended that all the Australian troops in transit should be sent to Burma. On the 18th the beautiful island of Bali, next to Java on the east, fell, and in the next few days Timor, our only remaining air link with Australia, was occupied. At this moment Admiral Nagumo's fast carrier group of Pearl Harbour fame, now consisting of four large carriers with battleship and cruiser support, appeared in the Timor Sea, and on the 19th delivered a devastating air attack on the crowded shipping in Port Darwin, causing much loss of life. For the remainder of this brief campaign Darwin ceased to be of value as a base.

As we now know, the Japanese D-Day for the invasion of Java was February 28. On the 18th the Western Attack Group, comprising fifty-six transports, with a powerful escort, left Camranh Bay, in French Indo-China. On the 19th the Eastern Attack Group of forty-one transports sailed from Jolo, in the Sulu Sea, to Balikpapan, where they arrived on the 23d. On the 21st our Combined Chiefs of Staff told General Wavell that Java was to be defended to the last by the troops already in the island, but that no more reinforcements would be sent. He was also ordered to withdraw his headquarters from Java. Wavell replied that he considered that the A.B.D.A. Command should be dissolved and not withdrawn, and this was agreed.

* * * * *

As events took their full course I saw that the end was near.

Prime Minister to General Wavell   20 Feb. 42

Obviously the whole plan for defence [of] A.B.D.A. area is affected by the rapid progress of enemy in all directions. It has been decided to fight to the utmost for Java with existing forces and some that were *en route,* and to divert main reinforcements to Burma and India. The President's mind is turning to United States looking after the Australian flank and we concentrating everything on defending or regaining Burma and Burma Road, of course after everything possible has been done to prolong the resistance in Java. He also realises vital importance of Ceylon, which is our only key of naval re-entry.

2. I surmise that it is not unlikely that General MacArthur, if extricated [from Corregidor], will look after the Australian side. I have not heard from you where you would move your headquarters if forced to leave Java.

3. My own idea is that you should become again C.-in-C. in India, letting Hartley [1] go back to his Northern Command. From this centre you would be able to animate the whole war against Japan from our side.

[1] General Sir Alan Hartley had been appointed Commander-in-Chief India when General Wavell left to take over the Command of A.B.D.A.

On February 21 I received a sombre answer from General Wavell.

I am afraid that the defence of A.B.D.A. area has broken down and that defence of Java cannot now last long. It always hinged on the air battle. . . . Anything put into Java now can do little to prolong struggle; it is more [a] question of what you will choose to save. . . . I see little further usefulness for this H.Q. . . .

Last about myself. I am, as ever, entirely willing to do my best where you think best to send me. I have failed you and [the] President here, where a better man might perhaps have succeeded. . . . If you fancy I can best serve by returning to India I will of course do so, but you should first consult Viceroy both whether my prestige and influence, which count for much in East, will survive this failure, and also as to hardship to Hartley and his successor in Northern Command.

I hate the idea of leaving these stout-hearted Dutchmen, and will remain here and fight it out with them as long as possible if you consider this would help at all.

Good wishes. I am afraid you are having very difficult period, but I know your courage will shine through it.

I always followed, so far as I could see, the principle that military commanders should not be judged by results, but by the quality of their effort. I had never had illusions about A.B.D.A., and now sought only to save Burma and India. I admired the composure and firmness of mind with which Wavell had faced the cataract of disaster which had been assigned to him with so much formality and precision. Some men would have found reasons for declining, or asked for impossible conditions before accepting a task so baffling and hopeless, failure in which could not but damage their reputation with the public. Wavell's conduct had conformed to the best traditions of the Army. I therefore replied:

Prime Minister to General Wavell   22 Feb. 42
When you cease to command the A.B.D.A. area you should proceed yourself to India, where we require you to resume your position as Commander-in-Chief to carry on the war against Japan from this main base.

It may be you will need a deputy Commander-in-Chief to take routine matters off your hands; but this can be settled when you get to Delhi. All other considerations are subsidiary.

I hope you realise how highly I and all your friends here, as well as the President and the Combined Staffs in Washington, rate your admirable conduct of A.B.D.A. operations in the teeth of adverse fortune and overwhelming odds.

Wavell replied:

We are planning provisionally to leave on February 25. I am most grateful for your very generous message and confidence in again entrusting me with command in India. If Hartley can remain as deputy it would be most helpful.

And on the 25th:

I am leaving tonight with Peirse for Colombo. From there I shall fly [to] Rangoon or Delhi, according to answer to telegram I have sent Hartley.

Wavell and Peirse left Bandoeng by air. The American pilot of the aeroplane for the Supreme Commander said to someone who came into his cockpit, "Say, I have only this railway map, but it's all right, as I am told we are to go to a place called Saylon, which is marked." And they flew off nearly two thousand miles to "Saylon." Wavell had an extraordinary record in the air. He was in danger of fatal accident at least six or seven times, but he never got hurt. He was thought to be a Jonah in an aeroplane; but Jonah always survived, and so did the aeroplane. On this occasion the plane caught fire in the air, but after a struggle the crew extinguished the flames without waking the Commander-in-Chief.

At Ceylon he found the following:

Prime Minister to General Wavell   26 Feb. 42

Pray consider whether key situation Ceylon does not require a first-rate soldier in supreme command of all local services, including civil government, and whether Pownall is not the man. We do not want to have another Singapore.

General Pownall assumed command of the garrison on
March 6.

*   *   *   *   *

To those who were left in Java to fight to the end with the
Dutch I sent this message:

Prime Minister to Air Vice-Marshal Maltby   26 Feb. 42

I send you and all ranks of the British forces who have stayed
behind in Java my best wishes for success and honour in the great
fight that confronts you. Every day gained is precious, and I know
that you will do everything humanly possible to prolong the battle.

The Dutch Admiral Helfrich now took command of the
dwindling Allied naval forces. This resolute Dutchman never
abandoned hope, and continued to attack the enemy vigorously
regardless of cost or the overwhelming strength opposed to
him. He was a worthy successor to the famous Dutch seamen
of the past. To meet the attack on Java, for which large convoys were at sea, he formed two striking forces, the Eastern at
Surabaya, under Admiral Doorman, and the Western, of
British ships, at Tanjong Priok, the port of Batavia. On the
28th the Western striking force, comprising the cruisers *Hobart*
(Australian), *Danae,* and *Dragon,* with the destroyers *Scout* and
Tenedos, having made various attempts to find the enemy, were
ordered to retire through the Sunda Straits to Colombo, which
they reached safely a few days later. Scarcity of fuel and the
continuous air attack on Tanjong Priok were the reasons why
the Western striking force was dismissed at this juncture. Had
they joined Admiral Doorman's Eastern force they could only
have shared its fate.

Meanwhile at 6.30 P.M. on the 26th, Doorman sailed from
Surabaya in the *De Ruyter,* with the heavy cruisers *Exeter*
(British) and *Houston* (American), whose after turret was
out of action, the light cruisers *Java* (Dutch) and *Perth*
(Australian), and nine destroyers, of which three were British,
four American, and two Dutch. Admiral Helfrich's orders
to Doorman were, "You must continue attacks till the

enemy is destroyed." This is a sound principle, and the Japanese invasion convoys were a tremendous prize, but in this case it ignored the crushing superiority of the enemy, his complete mastery of the air, and the fact that the Western striking force had been sent away. Admiral Doorman also lacked a common code of tactical signals. His orders had to be translated on the *De Ruyter's* bridge by an American liaison officer before transmission. His urgent plea for protection by the few fighters remaining at Surabaya met with no response. During the night of the 26th he sought the enemy in vain, and in the morning he returned to Surabaya to fuel his destroyers. As he was entering the harbour, peremptory orders reached him from Admiral Helfrich to attack an enemy force located west of Baween.

Doorman turned his tired forces again to seaward, and an hour later, soon after 4 P.M., the battle was joined. At first the forces were not unevenly balanced. A gun duel at long range caused no damage to either side, and a series of torpedo attacks by Japanese destroyers were equally ineffective. One enemy ship was hit and set on fire after half an hour's fighting, but a little later the *Exeter* was struck in a boiler room; her speed dropped and she turned away to port. The ships astern of her conformed to her movements. About the same time the Dutch destroyer *Kortenaer* was torpedoed and sunk. Admiral Doorman then retired southeast and the general action was broken off, except that the destroyer *Electra,* trying to deliver a torpedo attack through the Japanese smoke-screen, was intercepted by three Japanese destroyers and sunk.

The *Exeter,* after being stopped for a while, was able to steam at fifteen knots, and was ordered back to Surabaya, escorted by the remaining Dutch destroyer.

Admiral Doorman re-formed his scattered and shrunken squadron and led them round the enemy's flank, hoping to strike the convoy of transports. Intermittent confused fighting continued. The enemy, who had now been reinforced, were fully informed of all his movements from the air. The American destroyers had discharged all their torpedoes and were sent back to Surabaya. The British destroyer *Jupiter* struck a mine, laid by the Dutch that very day, and sank immediately, with heavy loss of life. Some time after 10.30, Admiral Doorman, steaming forward, encountered two Japanese cruisers, and after a fierce action both the Dutch cruisers were torpedoed and sunk, carrying with them the brave Dutch admiral, who had fought so well against such heavy odds. The *Perth* and *Houston*, having successfully disengaged, steered for Batavia, which they reached the following afternoon.

*   *   *   *   *

We must follow the story to its bitter end. After refuelling, the Australian and American cruisers left Batavia again the same night, seeking to pass through the Sunda Straits. By chance they fell amidst the main Japanese Western Attack Force just as its transports were disembarking troops in Banten Bay, at the extreme western end of Java. They took their vengeance before they perished, sinking two transports while they were unloading their troops. Three hundred and seven officers and men of the *Perth* and three hundred and sixty-eight from the *Houston* survived to face the Japanese prison camps. Both the Australian and American captains went down with their ships.

Meanwhile the wounded *Exeter* and the only surviving British destroyer, *Encounter,* had returned to Surabaya, which was rapidly becoming untenable. Although every escape route seemed likely to be held by the enemy in strength, they put to sea. The four American destroyers which had fought in the battle the previous day had used all their torpedoes. Nevertheless, they sailed on the night of February 28, and slipped through the narrow Bali Strait, encountering only a single enemy patrol, which they brushed aside. By daylight they were clear away to the southward, and reached Australia. This route was not possible for the larger *Exeter,* and on the evening of the 28th she sailed with the *Encounter* and the United States destroyer *Pope,* hoping to pass the Sunda Straits and reach Ceylon. Next morning this little group was discovered, and soon four prowling Japanese cruisers, supported by destroyers and aircraft, closed in on the prey. Smothered by overwhelming gunfire, the *Exeter,* famous from the Plate battle in 1939, was soon reduced to impotence, and received her death-blow from a torpedo before noon.

Both the *Encounter* and the *Pope* were sunk. Fifty officers and seven hundred and fifty ratings from the two British ships were picked up by the Japanese, together with the survivors from the *Pope.*

*　　*　　*　　*　　*

Our naval forces were thus destroyed, and Java was closely invested on three sides by the Japanese. A last forlorn attempt to replenish the rapidly wasting air strength was made by two American ships carrying between them fifty-nine fighters. One, the old aircraft-tender *Langley,* was sunk by air attack when approaching; the other arrived safely, but by then there was no longer the means even to land the crated aircraft. After the Supreme Headquarters had been dispersed, all the Allied forces passed to the command of the Dutch for the defence of the island. General ter Poorten commanded the 25,000 regular troops of the Dutch garrison, who were joined by the British contingent under Major-General Sitwell, comprising three Australian battalions, a light tank squadron of the 3d Hussars, and an improvised unit of armed men from administrative units, including 450 men of the R.A.F., together with a number of American artillerymen. The Dutch had about ten air squadrons, but many of their aircraft were now unserviceable. The R.A.F. after the withdrawal from Sumatra was formed into five squadrons, of which only about forty machines were fit. There remained a score of American fighters and bombers.

To this scanty force fell the duty of defending the island, whose northern shore was eight hundred miles long, with countless landing beaches. The Japanese convoys from the east and west discharged four or five divisions. The end could not be long delayed. Many thousands of British and Americans, including five thousand airmen, with their fine commander,

Maltby, and over eight thousand British and Australian troops, were surrendered by Dutch decision on March 8.

It had been decided to fight to the end with the Dutch in Java. Although no hopes remained of victory, at least considerable enemy expeditions were delayed in their quest for new prizes. The Japanese conquest of the Dutch East Indies was complete.

9

The Invasion of Burma

Japanese Air Attacks upon Rangoon — Their Advance from Siam into Burma, January 16 — The 17th British-Indian Division Defeated at the River Salween — The Crossing of the Sittang — Our Retreat to the Pegu River — A Painful Difference with the Australian Government — The Australian Point of View — My Telegram to Mr. Curtin of February 20 — And to President Roosevelt — The President's Messages to Mr. Curtin — Importance of United States Aid to Australasia — Mr. Curtin's Reply, February 22 — I Divert the Australian Convoy Towards Rangoon — Adverse Reaction of the Australian Government — We Comply with Their Request, February 23 — President Roosevelt's Further Efforts — No Australian Troops for Burma — General Alexander Sent to Take Command — He Cuts His Way Out of Rangoon — Successful Retreat to Prome — Complications of Command in the Theatre — Extrication of the Remnants of Our Army — The Road to India Barred.

THERE WAS A GENERAL BELIEF that the Japanese would not start a major campaign against Burma until at least their operations in Malaya had been successfully concluded. But this was not to be. Japanese air raids on Rangoon had begun before the end of December. Our defending air force then amounted only to one British and one United States fighter squadron of the American Volunteer Group, formed before the war, to support the Chinese. I appealed to President Roosevelt to leave this gallant unit at Rangoon.

151

Prime Minister to President Roosevelt   31 Jan. 42

I am informed that there is a danger that the fighter squadrons of the American Volunteer Group now helping so effectively in the defence of Rangoon may be withdrawn by Chiang Kai-shek to China after January 31. Clearly the security of Rangoon is as important to Chiang as to us, and withdrawal of these squadrons before arrival of Hurricanes, due 15th to 20th February, might be disastrous. I understand that General Magruder has instructions to represent this to the Generalissimo, but I think the matter is sufficiently serious for you to know about it personally.

The President granted my request. With these slender forces very heavy casualties were inflicted on the Japanese raiders. Military damage was small, but the bombing caused havoc and many casualties occurred in the crowded city. Great numbers of native workers and subordinate staffs, both military and civilian, quitted their posts, seriously affecting though not preventing the working of the port. All through January and February the Japanese air attack was held in check and paid its price for every raid.

The Japanese advance from Siam into Burma began on January 16 with an attack on Tavoy, which they captured with little difficulty, and our small garrison farther south at Mergui was consequently withdrawn by sea. On January 20 a Japanese division advanced on Moulmein from the east, after overcoming the resistance of the Indian Brigade at Kawkareik. They captured Moulmein a few days later.

The Governor of Burma, Sir Reginald Dorman-Smith, had shown qualities of firmness and courage during the anxious weeks that had passed since the Japanese advance into Burma had begun. I thought the morrow of the fall of Singapore a suitable moment to compliment him, and warn him of the crisis that impended.

Prime Minister to Governor of Burma   16 Feb. 42

I have not hitherto troubled you with a message, but I want to tell you how much I and my colleagues have admired your firm, robust attitude under conditions of increasing difficulty and danger.

Now that Singapore has fallen more weight will assuredly be put into the attack upon you. The substantial reinforcements, including the Armoured Brigade and two additional squadrons of Hurricanes, should reach you soon. We are meeting tonight to discuss further possibilities. I regard Burma and contact with China as the most important feature in the whole [Eastern] theatre of war. All good wishes.

*   *   *   *   *

After a fortnight of fighting against superior and growing Japanese forces the three British-Indian brigades who formed the 17th Division were all forced back to the line of the river Salween, and here a fierce battle of attacks and counter-attacks was fought at heavy odds around Bilin. By February 20 it was obvious that a further retreat to the Sittang River was imperative if the whole force was not to be lost. Over this swift-flowing river, five hundred yards wide, there was only one bridge. Before the main body of the 17th Division could reach it, the bridgehead was attacked by a strong Japanese force, while the marching columns retiring upon it were themselves beset by a fresh enemy division, newly arrived, which caught them in flank. Under the impression that our three retiring brigades were greatly weakened, scattered, and beaten, and were in fact trapped, the order was given by the commander of the bridgehead, with the permission of the divisional commander, to blow up the bridge. When the division successfully fought its way back to the riverbank, it found the bridge destroyed and the broad flood before it. Even so, thirty-three hundred men contrived to cross this formidable obstacle, but with only fourteen hundred rifles and a few machine-guns. Every other weapon and all equipment were lost. This was a major disaster.

There was now only the defence line of the Pegu River between the Japanese and Rangoon. Here the remnants of the 17th Division reorganised themselves, and were joined by three British battalions from India and by the 7th British Armoured Brigade, newly arrived from the Middle East on the way to Java and diverted to Burma by General Wavell. This brigade played an invaluable part in all the later fighting.

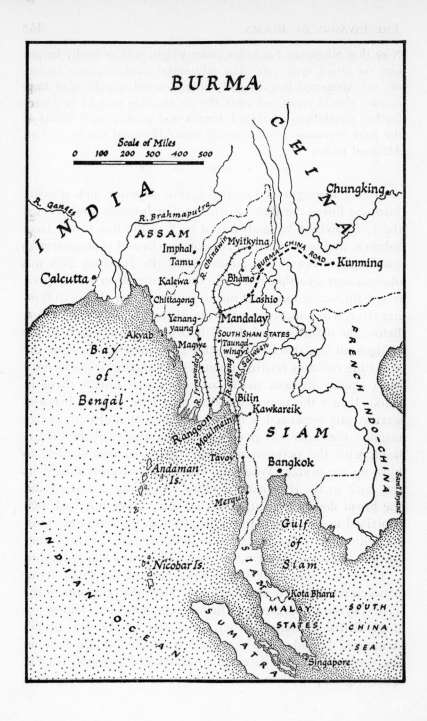

BURMA

Farther north the 1st Burma Division, after relief in the South
Shan States by the Chinese Sixth Army, had moved to the
south of Toungoo, where it guarded the main northward route
to Mandalay.

*   *   *   *   *

I have now to record a painful episode in our relations with
the Australian Government and their refusal of our requests
for aid. I could wish that it had not fallen to me to tell the
facts, but the story of the Burma campaign requires it. They
are already known in an imperfect manner to many people at
home and in Australia. It is better that both sides should be
fully stated, so that a fair judgment can be formed, and the
necessary lessons drawn as a guide to the future.

Amid the stresses of the time bitter feelings swept our circle,
military and political, in London, and there was only one
opinion in the War Cabinet and among the Chiefs of Staff.
It must however be remembered that the Australian Government had an entirely different point of view. Their predecessors under Mr. Menzies had raised the Australian Imperial
Force and had sent no less than four divisions, composed of the
flower of their military manhood, across the world to aid the
Mother Country in the war, with the making of which and in
the want of preparations for which they had no share. From
the days of Bardia, Australian troops and the New Zealand
Division had played a foremost part in the Desert war for the
defence of Egypt. They had shone in the van of its victories
and shared in its many grievous reverses. The 9th Australian
Division had yet to strike what history may well proclaim as
the decisive blow in the Battle of Alamein, still eight months
away. They had risked all and suffered much in Greece. An
Australian division, after fighting extremely well in Johore,
had been destroyed or captured at Singapore, in circumstances
which had never been explained and for which the British war
direction was responsible. The disaster at the Sittang River
seemed to settle the fate of Burma, where again the resources
and arrangements of the Imperial Government were shown to

be woefully inadequate. No one among those who knew the facts could doubt that the Japanese onslaught, with its vast superiority of men, with the general mastery of the air, with the command of the sea and the free choice of points of attack, would in the next few months dominate and control all the enormous regions comprised in General Wavell's A.B.D.A. command.

All Australian military thought had regarded Singapore as the key to the whole defence of the outposts and forward positions upon which Australia relied for gaining the time necessary for the recovery by the United States of the command of the Pacific, for the arrival of American armed aid in Australia, and for the concentration and reorganisation of Australian forces for the defence of their own homeland. Naturally they regarded a Japanese invasion of Australia as a probable and imminent peril which would expose the people of Australia, men, women, and children alike, to the horrors of Japanese conquest. To them as to us Burma was only a feature in the world war, but whereas the advance of Japan made no difference to the safety of the British Isles, it confronted Australia with a mortal danger. In the remorseless tide of defeat and ruin which dominated our fortunes at this time the Australian Government could feel very little confidence in the British conduct of the war or in our judgment at home. The time had come, they thought, to give all the strength they could gather to the life-and-death peril which menaced their cities and people.

On the other hand, we could not help feeling that when in 1940 we had been exposed to the same fearful danger in a far closer and more probable form we had not lost our sense of proportion or hesitated to add to our risks for the sake of other vital needs. We therefore felt entitled to ask from them a decision of the same kind as we took when, in August, 1940, to maintain the Desert we had sent half our scanty armour to the defence of Egypt. And this had not been in vain. A similar act of devotion by Australia in this emergency might also have been attended by good results.

For my part I did not believe that Japan, with all the rich, long-coveted prizes of the Dutch East Indies in their grasp, would be likely to send an army of a hundred and fifty thousand — less would have been futile — across the equator four thousand miles to the south to begin a major struggle with the Australian nation, whose men had proved their fighting quality on every occasion when they had been engaged. Nevertheless, I was the first to propose that two of the best Australian divisions in the Middle East should return to Australia, and had announced this fact to Parliament without being asked by the Australian Ministers to do so. Furthermore, I had at Washington in January procured from President Roosevelt his promise to accept responsibility and use the United States Fleet for the ocean defence of Australia, and to send upwards of ninety thousand American soldiers there; and these measures were being rapidly fulfilled. Now a battle crisis of decisive intensity had arisen in Burma, and with the cordial support of the War Cabinet and Chiefs of Staff I addressed myself to Mr. Curtin.

Prime Minister to Mr. Curtin   20 Feb. 42

I suppose you realise that your leading division, the head of which is sailing south of Colombo to Netherlands East Indies at this moment in our scanty British and American shipping (*Mount Vernon*), is the only force that can reach Rangoon in time to prevent its loss and the severance of communication with China. It can begin to disembark at Rangoon about the 26th or 27th. There is nothing else in the world that can fill the gap.

2. We are all entirely in favour of all Australian troops returning home to defend their native soil, and we shall help their transportation in every way. But a vital war emergency cannot be ignored, and troops *en route* to other destinations must be ready to turn aside and take part in a battle. Every effort would be made to relieve this division at the earliest moment and send them on to Australia. I do not endorse the United States request that you should send your other two divisions to Burma. They will return home as fast as possible. But this one is needed now, and is the only one that can possibly save the situation.

3. Pray read again your message of January 23, in which you said that the evacuation of Singapore would be "an inexcusable betrayal." Agreeably with your point of view, we therefore put the 18th Division and other important reinforcements into Singapore instead of diverting them to Burma, and ordered them to fight it out to the end. They were lost at Singapore and did not save it, whereas they could almost certainly have saved Rangoon. I take full responsibility with my colleagues on the Defence Committee for this decision; but you also bear a heavy share on account of your telegram.

4. Your greatest support in this hour of peril must be drawn from the United States. They alone can bring into Australia the necessary troops and air forces, and they appear ready to do so. As you know, the President attaches supreme importance to keeping open the connection with China, without which his bombing offensive against Japan cannot be started, and also most grievous results may follow in Asia if China is cut off from all Allied help.

5. I am quite sure that if you refuse to allow your troops which are actually passing to stop this gap, and if, in consequence, the above evils, affecting the whole course of the war, follow, a very grave effect will be produced upon the President and the Washington circle, on whom you are so largely dependent. See especially the inclination of the United States to move major naval forces from Hawaii into the Anzac area.

6. We must have an answer immediately, as the leading ships of the convoy will soon be steaming in the opposite direction from Rangoon and every day is a day lost. I trust therefore that for the sake of all interests, and above all your own interests, you will give most careful consideration to the case I have set before you.

I also cabled to President Roosevelt, who not only took a special interest in the Burma Road to China, but had the strongest claims upon Australian consideration.

Former Naval Person to President Roosevelt   20 Feb. 42

The only troops who can reach Rangoon in time to stop the enemy and enable other reinforcements to arrive are the leading Australian division. These can begin to arrive there by the 26th or 27th. We have asked Australian Government to allow this diversion for the needs of battle, and promised to relieve them at earliest. All other Australian troops are going home at earliest. Australian Government have refused point-blank. I have appealed to them again in the interests of the vital importance of keeping open Burma Road and maintaining contact with Chiang.

2. In view of your offer of American troops to help defend Australia and possible naval movements, I feel you have a right to press for this movement of Allied forces. Please therefore send me a message which I can add to the very strong cable I have just sent off. Our Chiefs of Staff here are most insistent, and I have no doubt our Combined Chiefs of Staff Committee in Washington feel the same way. There is no reason why you should not also talk to Casey.

President Roosevelt sent two messages forthwith. To me he replied on February 21:

I hope you can persuade Australian Government to allow proposed temporary diversion of their leading Australian division to Burma. I think this is of utmost importance. Tell them I am speeding additional troops as well as planes to Australia, and that my estimate of the situation there is highly optimistic and by no means dark.

To Mr. Curtin he telegraphed:

President Roosevelt to Prime Minister of Australia   20 Feb. 42

I fully appreciate how grave are your responsibilities in reaching a decision in the present serious circumstances as to the disposition of the first Australian division returning from the Middle East.

I assume you know now of our determination to send, in addition to all troops and forces now *en route,* another force of over twenty-seven thousand men to Australia. This force will be fully equipped in every respect. We must fight to the limit for our two flanks — one based on Australia and the other on Burma, India, and China. Because of our geographical position we Americans can better handle the reinforcement of Australia and the right flank.

I say this to you so that you may have every confidence that we are going to reinforce your position with all possible speed. More-

over, the operations which the United States Navy have begun and
have in view will in a measure constitute a protection to the coast
of Australia and New Zealand. On the other hand, the left flank
simply must be held. If Burma goes it seems to me our whole
position, including that of Australia, will be in extreme peril.
Your Australian division is the only force that is available for immediate reinforcement. It could get into the fight at once, and
would, I believe, have the strength to save what now seems to be a
very dangerous situation.

While I realise the Japs are moving rapidly, I cannot believe
that, in view of your geographical position and the forces on their
way to you or operating in your neighbourhood, your vital centres
are in immediate danger.

While I realise that your men have been fighting all over the
world, and are still, and while I know full well of the great sacrifices which Australia has made, I nevertheless want to ask you in
the interests of our whole war effort in the Far East if you will
reconsider your decision and order the division now *en route* to
Australia to move with all speed to support the British forces
fighting in Burma.

You may be sure we will fight by your side with all our force
until victory.

General Wavell, who was responsible for the whole defence
of the A.B.D.A. area, and had been so accepted by the Curtin
Government, had made quite independently a similar request
a few days earlier. He had indeed asked that the whole
Australian Army Corps should be so transferred.

There was general surprise at the response.

Field-Marshal Dill to Prime Minister   22 Feb. 42

Hopkins has just told me that Curtin has refused President's
appeal to let first Australian division go to Burma.

Prime Minister of Australia to Prime Minister   22 Feb. 42

I have received your rather strongly worded request at this late
stage, though our wishes in regard to the disposition of the A.I.F.
in the Pacific theatre have long been known to you, and carried
even further by your statement in the House of Commons. Fur-

thermore, Page was furnished with lengthy statements on our viewpoint on February 15.

2. The proposal for additional military assistance for Burma comes from the Supreme Commander of the A.B.D.A. area. Malaya, Singapore, and Timor have been lost, and the whole of the Netherland East Indies will apparently be occupied shortly by the Japanese. The enemy, with superior sea- and air-power, has commenced raiding our territory in the northwest, and also in the northeast from Rabaul. The Government made the maximum contribution of which it was capable in reinforcement of the A.B.D.A. area. It originally sent a division less a brigade to Malaya, with certain ancillary troops. A machine-gun battalion and substantial reinforcements were later dispatched. It also dispatched forces to Ambon, Java, and Dutch and Portuguese Timor. Six squadrons of the Air Force were also sent to this area, together with two cruisers from the Royal Australian Navy.

3. It was suggested by you that two Australian divisions be transferred to the Pacific theatre, and this suggestion was later publicly expanded by you with the statement that no obstacle would be placed in the way of the A.I.F. returning to defend their homeland. We agreed to the two divisions being located in Sumatra and Java, and it was pointed out to Page in the cablegram of February 15 that should fortune still favour the Japanese this disposition would give a line of withdrawal to Australia for our forces.

4. With the situation having deteriorated to such an extent in the theatre of the A.B.D.A. area, with which we are closely associated, and the Japanese also making a southward advance in the Anzac area, the Government, in the light of the advice of its Chiefs of Staff as to the forces necessary to repel an attack on Australia, finds it most difficult to understand that it should be called upon to make a further contribution of forces to be located in the most distant part of the A.B.D.A. area. Notwithstanding your statement that you do not agree with the request to send the other two divisions of the A.I.F. Corps to Burma, our advisers are concerned with Wavell's request for the Corps and Dill's statement that the destination of the 6th and 9th Australian Divisions should be left open, as more troops might be badly needed in Burma. Once one division became engaged it could not be left unsupported, and the indications are that the whole of the Corps might become com-

mitted to this region, or there might be a recurrence of the
experiences of the Greek and Malayan campaigns. Finally, in view
of superior Japanese sea-power and air-power, it would appear to
be a matter of some doubt as to whether this division can be
landed in Burma, and a matter for greater doubt whether it can
be brought out as promised. With the fall of Singapore, Penang,
and Martaban, the Bay of Bengal is now vulnerable to what must
be considered the superior sea- and air-power of Japan in that
area. The movement of our forces to this theatre therefore is not
considered a reasonable hazard of war, having regard to what has
gone before, and its adverse results would have the gravest consequences on the morale of the Australian people. The Government therefore must adhere to its decision.

5. In regard to your statement that the 18th Division was
diverted from Burma to Singapore because of our message, it
is pointed out that the date of the latter was January 23, whereas
in your telegram of January 14 you informed me that one brigade
of this division was due on January 13 and the remainder on
January 27.

6. We feel therefore, in view of the foregoing and the services
the A.I.F. have rendered in the Middle East, that we have every
right to expect them to be returned as soon as possible, with
adequate escorts to ensure their safe arrival.

7. We assure you, and desire you to so inform the President,
who knows fully what we have done to help the common cause,
that if it were possible to divert our troops to Burma and India
without imperilling our security in the judgment of our advisers
we should be pleased to agree to the diversion.

I had carefully phrased my statement to which paragraph 5
was a rejoinder so as to avoid saying that we had been influenced in our judgment *because* of Mr. Curtin's protest. In
fact one brigade of the 18th Division had landed before his
message; but this could have been transferred, and the two
other brigades and other important reinforcements were still
uncommitted. The decision was taken on our responsibility, as
I have always stated, but it was not for Mr. Curtin, after taking
so strong a part in the discussion, to feel that he had no more
share in it.

Meanwhile, assuming a favourable response, I had diverted the Australian convoy to Rangoon. This at least gave time for further reflection by the Australian Government.

Prime Minister to Prime Minister of Australia   22 Feb. 42

We could not contemplate that you would refuse our request, and that of the President of the United States, for the diversion of the leading Australian division to save the situation in Burma. We knew that if our ships proceeded on their course to Australia while we were waiting for your formal approval they would either arrive too late at Rangoon or even be without enough fuel to go there at all. We therefore decided that the convoy should be temporarily diverted to the northward. The convoy is now too far north for some of the ships in it to reach Australia without refuel-ling. These physical considerations give a few days for the situa-tion to develop, and for you to review the position should you wish to do so. Otherwise the leading Australian division will be returned to Australia as quickly as possible in accordance with your wishes.

Prime Minister to General Wavell   22 Feb. 42

The Australian Government have refused to allow their leading division to take a hand at Rangoon. However, yesterday we turned the convoy northward, being sure Australian Government would not fail to rise to the occasion. Convoy has now got so far north that it will have to refuel before going to Australia. So what about it? This gives three or four days for the Australian Government, with its majority of one, to think matters over in the light of the President's reiterated appeals, and it also enables us to see how the Hutton situation develops on the Burma front.

Many thanks for your kind wishes. I believe the nation is solid behind me here, and this would be a good thing considering the troubles we have to face.

The reaction of the Australian Government was adverse.

Prime Minister of Australia to the Prime Minister   23 Feb. 42

In your telegram of February 20 it was clearly implied that the convoy was not proceeding to the northward. From your telegram of February 22 it appears that you have diverted the convoy towards Rangoon and had treated our approval to this vital diversion as merely a matter of form. By doing so you have established a physical situation which adds to the dangers of the convoy, and the responsibility of the consequences of such diversions rests upon you.

2. We have already informed the President of the reasons for our decision, and, having regard to the terms of his communications to me, we are quite satisfied from his sympathetic reply that he fully understands and appreciates the reasons for our decision.

3. Wavell's message considered by Pacific War Council on Saturday reveals that Java faces imminent invasion. Australia's outer defences are now quickly vanishing and our vulnerability is completely exposed.

4. With A.I.F. troops we sought to save Malaya and Singapore, falling back on Netherlands East Indies. All these northern defences are gone or going. Now you contemplate using the A.I.F. to save Burma. All this has been done, as in Greece, without adequate air support.

5. We feel a primary obligation to save Australia, not only for itself, but to preserve it as a base for the development of the war against Japan. In the circumstances it is quite impossible to reverse a decision which we made with the utmost care, and which we have affirmed and reaffirmed.

6. Our Chief of the General Staff advises that although your telegram of February 20 refers to the leading division only, the fact is that owing to the loading of the flights it is impossible at the present time to separate the two divisions, and the destination of all the flights will be governed by that of the first flight. This fact reinforces us in our decision.

I replied:

Prime Minister to Prime Minister of Australia   23 Feb. 42

Your telegram of February 23.

Your convoy is now proceeding to refuel at Colombo. It will then proceed to Australia in accordance with your wishes.

2. My decision to move it northward during the few hours required to receive your final answer was necessary because otherwise your help, if given, might not have arrived in time.

3. As soon as the convoy was turned north arrangements were

made to increase its escort, and this increased escort will be maintained during its voyage to Colombo, and on leaving Colombo again for as long as practicable.

4. Of course I take full responsibility for my action.

All that was possible had now been done.

President Roosevelt to Prime Minister 23 Feb. 42

In view of Curtin's final answer in the negative to our strong request I have sent him the following dispatch in the hope that we can get the next contingent to help hold the Burma line:

2. *"For Curtin.* Thank you for yours of the 20th. I fully understand your position, in spite of the fact that I cannot wholly agree as to the immediate need of the first returning division in Australia. I think that today the principal threat against the main bases of Australia and Burma, both of which must be held at all costs, is against the Burma or left flank, and that we can safely hold the Australian or right flank. Additional American fully equipped reinforcements are getting ready to leave for your area. In view of all this, and depending of course on developments in the next few weeks, I hope you will consider the possibility of diverting the second returning division to some place in India or Burma to help hold that line so that it can become a fixed defence. Under any circumstances you can depend upon our fullest support. Roosevelt."

3. I am working on additional plans to make control of islands in Anzac area more secure, and further to disrupt Japanese advances.

Prime Minister to Prime Minister of Australia 26 Feb. 42

Telegram from Governor of Burma dispatched from Rangoon at 18.30 hours on February 24: "No important change, but if we can get Australians here we might effect radical change for the better. Obviously it will be anxious business getting them [in], but I feel it is a risk well worth taking, as otherwise Burma is wide open for Japanese. . . ."

2. Telegram from Governor of Burma dispatched from Rangoon at 23.20 hours on February 25: "It is infinitely important to us to know whether Australian division will arrive. Please say yes or no."

3. I have of course informed the Governor of your decision.

Prime Minister to Governor of Burma   25 Feb. 42

We have made every appeal, reinforced by President, but Australian Government absolutely refuses. Fight on.

Prime Minister to General Ismay, for C.O.S. Committee 27 Feb. 42

Let me have a short statement of what forces we can direct to the Rangoon front and what are *en route*. Let me also have a statement of the forces available in India to resist raids or invasion. Finally, let me have the exact state of the garrison of Ceylon, naval, air, and military, and the dates of air and military reinforcements.

Prime Minister to Brigadier Hollis, for C.O.S. Committee

28 Feb. 42

It is a question whether, in view of the evacuation of Rangoon and the consequent restriction of the new communications, the 2d Brigade of the 70th Division should not go to Ceylon. How soon could it get there?

2. Let me have a report about the radar installation and any proposed improvements, with dates.

3. I am relying upon the Admiralty to keep sufficient heavy ships at Trincomalee to ward off a seaborne expedition in the anxious fortnight or three weeks which must elapse before we are reinforced.

4. It will, I feel sure, be necessary for the *Indomitable* squadrons to be off-loaded in Ceylon.

5. Let me have a list and time-table of the naval reinforcements and the building-up of our fleet in the Indian Ocean during March, April, and May.

*   *   *   *   *

No troops in our control could reach Rangoon in time to save it. But if we could not send an army we could at any rate send a man. While the correspondence which darkens these pages was proceeding, it was resolved to send General Alexander by air to the doomed capital. To save time he was to fly direct over large stretches of enemy territory. After he had been made fully acquainted with all the facts of the situation by the Chiefs of Staff and by the War Office, and a few hours before his departure, he dined at the Annexe with me and my wife. I

remember the evening well, for never have I taken the responsibility for sending a general on a more forlorn hope. Alexander
was, as usual, calm and good-humoured. He said he was delighted to go. In the First Great War, in years of fighting as a
regimental officer with the Guards Division, he was reputed to
bear a charmed life, and under any heavy fire men were glad
to follow exactly in his footsteps. Confidence spread around
him, whether as a lieutenant or in supreme command. He was
the last British commander at Dunkirk. Nothing ever disturbed or rattled him, and duty was a full satisfaction in itself,
especially if it seemed perilous and hard. But all this was combined with so gay and easy a manner that the pleasure and
honour of his friendship was prized by all those who enjoyed it,
among whom I could count myself. For this reason I must
admit that at our dinner I found it difficult to emulate his composure.

On March 5 General Alexander took command, with instructions to hold Rangoon if possible, and failing that to withdraw
northward to defend Upper Burma, while keeping contact with
the Chinese forces on his left. It was soon clear to him that
Rangoon was doomed to fall. The Japanese were attacking
heavily at Pegu, and moving round the northern flank to cut
the road from Rangoon to Prome, thus barring the last land
exit from the city. Wavell, now Commander-in-Chief in India,
had the supreme direction of the Burma campaign.

General Wavell to C.I.G.S. and Prime Minister   7 Mar. 42

Communication with Burma has been subject to long delays in
last two days; wireless seems to have broken down altogether and
I am without any message from Alexander. I gather from naval
message received this morning that decision was suddenly taken
about midnight last night to abandon Rangoon, turn back convoys *en route*, and carry out demolitions. Wired Alexander at once
to inquire situation, but have had no reply. Will inform you as
soon as I have official news.

Alexander had in fact given orders for the destruction of the
great oil refineries at Rangoon and many other demolitions,

and for the whole force to cut its way out northward along the road to Prome. The Japanese had intended to attack the city from the west. In order to protect their encircling division they placed a strong force astride the road. The first attempts by our troops to break out were repulsed, and it was necessary to gather all available reinforcements. Hard fighting continued for twenty-four hours, but the Japanese commander adhered rigidly to his instructions, and having made sure that the encircling division had reached its positions for the attack from the west, he conceived that his task as a blocking force was finished. He therefore opened the road to Prome and marched on to join the main Japanese attack on the city. At the same time Alexander with his whole force pressed forward and escaped from Rangoon in good order, and with his transport and artillery. The Japanese did not press our northward retreat, as they needed to reorganise after the severe fighting and many casualties they had sustained and the long marches they had made. The Burma Division fought a steady delaying action back to Toungoo, while the 17th Division and the Armoured Brigade moved by easy stages to Prome.

* * * * *

A long and painful struggle was required to extricate the army from Upper Burma. Wavell did not underrate the difficulties.

General Wavell to Prime Minister 19 Mar. 42

I do not think we can count on holding Upper Burma for long if Japanese put in a determined attack. Many troops [are] still short of equipment and shaken by experiences in Lower Burma, and remaining battalions of Burma Rifles of doubtful value. There is little artillery. Reinforcements in any strength impossible at present. Chinese co-operation not easy. They are distrustful of our fighting ability and inclined to hang back. Not certain that they will compete with Japanese jungle tactics any more successfully than we have. Alexander can however be relied on to put up good fight and Japanese difficulties must be great.

The difficulties about the command as between Alexander, Chiang Kai-shek, and the American General Stilwell were a complication. General Stilwell had arrived from China to take command of the Fifth and Sixth Chinese Armies, comprising six divisions,[1] who were now in Burma. Generalissimo Chiang Kai-shek accepted our claim that Alexander should have supreme command over all forces actually in Burma. But President Roosevelt thought it better to preserve the duality between Alexander and Stilwell. I did not press the point at this difficult moment.

President Roosevelt to Former Naval Person   20 Mar. 42

Reference your message concerning command in Burma, I have recently requested the Generalissimo to continue reinforcing the Burma front and to permit Stilwell to make co-operative arrangements relative command according to the principles laid down in his original directive approved by the Combined Chiefs of Staff. Recent messages from Stilwell indicate that he and Alexander can continue to work effectively together, but that the urgent need is for additional Chinese troops. The Generalissimo has placed Stilwell in command of the Fifth and Sixth Chinese Armies, but unfortunately will not permit completion of their transfer to Burma pending clarification of the command situation. Stilwell has not only urgently requested the Generalissimo to recede from this position, but has actually ordered additional units southward in the hope that the Generalissimo will approve. Despite command complications Stilwell provides a means of assuring complete co-operation, whereas a Chinese commander might make the situation impossible for General Alexander. Stilwell is not only an immensely capable and resourceful individual, but is thoroughly acquainted with the Chinese people, speaks their language fluently, and is distinctly not a self-seeker. His latest telegram states, "Have arranged with General Alexander for co-operation, and matter of command need not affect conduct of operations. Have asked Generalissimo to start another three divisions toward Burma." Under the circumstances I suggest we should leave the command status at that for the present. I feel that Generals Alexander and Stilwell

[1] A Chinese division was about one-third the strength of a British or Indian division.

will co-operate admirably. Strange that these two, who were originally intended to meet at "Super-Gymnast" [i.e., in French North
Africa], should in fact meet at Maymyo.

*   *   *   *   *

The loss of Rangoon meant the loss of Burma, and the rest
of the campaign was a grim race between the Japanese and the
approaching rains. There was no hope of reinforcements for
Alexander, because we had no port at which to land them.
Our small air force, which had covered the evacuation and
held at bay the much more numerous enemy planes, had to
move from its well-established base at Rangoon to landing-
grounds where there was no warning system, and before the
end of March it was virtually destroyed, mostly on the ground.
Aircraft based on India managed to drop stores and medical
supplies and to evacuate 8600 persons, including 2600
wounded, but for the rest of our troops and the mass of civilians
there was no way out but a six-hundred-mile march through
the jungles and mountains.

On March 24 the enemy resumed their offensive by attacking the Chinese division at Toungoo, and captured the town
after a week of sharp fighting. Four days later they advanced
on both banks of the Irrawaddy against Prome. At the end of
April the enemy stood before Mandalay, and the hope of keeping touch with the Chinese forces and holding the Burma Road
was gone. Part of the Chinese forces withdrew into China; the
rest followed General Stilwell up the Irrawaddy and struck
across the mountain ranges to India. Alexander, with the
British, marched northwest to Kalewa. Only thus could they
guard the eastern frontier of India, which was already threatened by a Japanese column moving up the Chindwin, and disturbed from within by the Hindu Congress. The routes were
little more than jungle paths. Thousands of refugees encumbered them, many of them wounded and sick and all of them
hungry. By an administrative feat of General Alexander's
army and the civil Government of Burma, in which the Governor and his wife played their part, and aided by helping

hands stretched out from India, notably by the planters of Northern Assam, this mass of humanity was brought to safety; and on May 17, only two days after the rains were expected, Alexander was able to report that his force had won through and was concentrated at Imphal, albeit with the loss of all its transport and its few surviving tanks. In this his first experience of independent command, though it ended in stark defeat, he showed all those qualities of military skill, imperturbability, and wise judgment that brought him later into the first rank of Allied war leaders. The road to India was barred.

10

Ceylon and the Bay of Bengal

Japanese Successes — Ceylon the Key Point — "Port T" — Forma-
tion of the British Eastern Fleet — Reinforcement of the Indian
Theatre — Extravagant Estimates of Japanese Naval Construction
— China Their Likely Objective — Defence of Colombo More
Secure — Crisis in the Indian Ocean — Incursion of the Japanese
Fleet — Our Fortunate Withdrawal — Air Attack upon Colombo
— Fate of the "Dorsetshire" and "Cornwall" — Havoc in the Bay
of Bengal — My Telegram to President Roosevelt of April 7 —
Decision to Withdraw the Eastern Fleet to East Africa — Vital
Need to Hold Ceylon — Further Representations to President
Roosevelt of April 15 — His Reply, April 17 — My Reassurances
to Wavell — The Japanese Inroad Ceases — A Vacuum in Indian
Waters — We Adhere to Our Main Objectives.

J APANESE EXPEDITIONS, borne and sustained by overwhelming sea- and air-power, had engulfed the whole island barrier
of the Dutch East Indies, together with Siam and all British
Malaya. They had occupied Southern Burma and the Andaman Islands, and now menaced India itself. The coasts of
India and Ceylon, and, farther west, the vital sea route by
which alone we sustained the armies in the Middle East, lay
open to raids on the largest scale. Madagascar, where it seemed
the Vichy French would certainly yield as they had done earlier
in Indo-China, was already a cause of deep anxiety.

It became our first duty to reinforce India with a considerable army and to secure the naval command of the Indian
Ocean and particularly of the Bay of Bengal. The only really

good base for the Eastern Fleet which we were forming was Ceylon, with its harbours of Colombo and Trincomalee. Energetic and almost frantic efforts were made by us to procure a sufficient force of fighter aircraft for the island before the expected Japanese attack. The carrier *Indomitable*, instead of being used at this juncture as a fighting ship, was made simply to go to and fro at full speed ferrying aircraft and their equipment. The Australian Government agreed to allow two of their brigade groups, returning to their country from the Desert, to break their voyage and help to garrison Ceylon during the crisis till British forces could arrive. This was a welcome stop-gap.

Secret and secluded anchorages in the Indian Ocean for our Fleet during a war with Japan had been long studied by the Admiralty. Addu Atoll, a ring of coral islands surrounding a deep-water lagoon at the southern end of the Maldive Islands, about six hundred miles southwest of Ceylon, was a makeshift alternative to Colombo. Here, remote from all the main shipping routes, and approachable by an enemy only after a long ocean passage, our Fleet could find shelter, fuel, and stores within striking range of Colombo. The lagoon is as big as Scapa Flow, and is entered through four deep channels in the barrier reef. Batteries and searchlights were erected on the surrounding jungle-clad islands. Store ships and hospital ships were gathered within. An airfield and a flying-boat base were being provided. All this remained for some time unknown to the enemy. This harbour, which we called Port T, played a helpful part in the strategy of the Indian Ocean.

Since the beginning of the year our naval effort had been to build up in the Indian Ocean a force capable of defending our interests there. Admiral Somerville, who had acquitted himself so well in command of the famous Force H at Gibraltar, had been selected to command in succession to the ill-fated Tom Phillips. On March 24 he arrived at Colombo in the carrier *Formidable*. On assuming command he had at his disposal the battleship *Warspite*, which had just arrived from America via Australia after completing repairs to damage inflicted in the battle of Crete ten months before, the four old battleships of the "R" class, three aircraft-carriers, including the light carrier *Hermes,* seven cruisers, including the Dutch *Heemskerck,* and sixteen destroyers.

There had been no time for this force, gathered from afar, to train together as a co-ordinated fleet. It was at first divided into two parts, one at Colombo and the other at Port T. Reiterated orders were also given to hurry on the completion of the air bases along the east coast of the Bay of Bengal, where some aircraft were already arriving. But in India everything goes very slowly. I made sure that all these measures were concerted and pressed with extreme urgency.

Prime Minister to General Ismay, for C.O.S. Committee   4 Mar. 42

Let me again set out the reinforcement story for the Indian theatre. The leading brigade of the 70th Division must reach Ceylon at the earliest moment (? when). Also the big convoy of anti-aircraft and anti-tank. Then come the two brigade groups, 16th and 17th, of the Australian 6th Division. These ought to stay seven or eight weeks, and the shipping should be handled so as to make this convenient and almost inevitable. Wavell will then be free to bring the remaining two brigades of the 70th Division into India and use them on the Burma front, additional to all other reinforcements on the way. The knowledge [that] they are coming should make him freer to use the British Internal Security Battalion on the Burma front.

2. The *Indomitable's* two [air] squadrons should reach Ceylon 6th instant, and this, with the existing air elements, should give good protection both to the two Australian brigade groups (when they come) and to the two "R" class battleships in the harbour, having regard to the fact that enemy air attack can only be from a carrier. Before the end of the month *Indomitable* should be armed for war and *Warspite* not far away. Some cruisers and a considerable flotilla, nearly twenty, will be gathered. Thereafter the situation improves steadily, as *Formidable* will arrive and *Valiant* may not be many weeks away.

3. Pray let me know if we are all agreed about this, as cross purposes and misunderstanding on points of detail add greatly to our burdens.

*   *   *   *   *

The most serious views were naturally taken of the Japanese strength. It was important that this should not be exaggerated.

Prime Minister to First Lord and First Sea Lord   10 Mar. 42

Is it credible that the Japanese have at present nine capital ships and two large aircraft-carriers all building simultaneously? If so the future is indeed serious. On what evidence does this statement rest? What would be the amount of armour-plate, steel, and modern fittings of all kinds required for the completion of such an enormous fleet within two years from now? What yards are available for the simultaneous construction of so many ships? When is it supposed they were laid down? What is known of the ordnance industry of Japan? There may be other questions which should be asked. Pray let me have a considered reply.

We must on no account underrate the Japanese. Facts however are what is needed.

2. While not at present being completely convinced by the above assumptions, I cordially approve the development of shore-based torpedo aircraft.

Prime Minister to First Lord   19 Mar. 42

The assumption is that all these ships are completed punctually. *Kuro,* laid down in 1937, should have been finished in 1941. She is only now thought to have joined the fleet, a year later. Five years are assigned for *Sasebo,* but *Maizuru* is given only four years. How does this compare with the five ships of the *King George V* class or the contemporary American vessels? Again, can they construct 27,000-ton aircraft-carriers in four years? Can they really complete from date of launch in one year? Pray let me have parallel figures of British and American construction.

One cannot always provide against the worst assumptions, and to try to do so prevents the best disposition of limited resources. The Admiralty Intelligence Staff were right to be on the safe side, but in my position many risks of being proved wrong had to be run. In fact, as we now know, the Japanese naval construction, like our own, lagged far behind their paper programme.

The distribution of the Japanese divisions set forth by our Intelligence reports was in some respects reassuring.

Prime Minister to Chiefs of Staff Committee   13 Mar. 42

On this layout of Japanese forces it seems very unlikely that an immediate full-scale invasion of Australia could take place. You are now making an appreciation for Australia of her position, and this disposition of Japanese forces might well be the starting-point.

2. It seems to me that if the Japanese encounter difficulties in moving through Assam, and if the Ceylon situation becomes solid for us, they will be more likely to turn northward upon China.

Prime Minister to Prime Minister of Australia   20 Mar. 42

We note the opinions you have expressed and fully understand your point of view. It would not be possible for us, as you suggest, to uncover the whole of our sea communications with the Middle East, on which the life of the considerable armies fighting there depends. Neither would it be possible for us to neglect the security of Ceylon so far as it is in our power to preserve it, or to deprive ourselves of the means of reinforcing or defending India. The dispatch to the Pacific of three out of four of our fast armoured aircraft-carriers would, as you perceive, leave any battleships we have placed or may place in the Indian Ocean entirely unprotected from air attack, and consequently unable to operate. This would expose all our convoys to the Middle East and India, averaging nearly fifty thousand men a month, to destruction at the hands of two or three fast Japanese cruisers or battle-cruisers, supported by, perhaps, a single aircraft-carrier. While admiring the offensive spirit of your memorandum and sharing your desire for an early acquisition of the initiative, we do not feel that we should be justified in disregarding all other risks and duties in the manner you suggest.

These matters will, however, no doubt form part of the discussions which will take place in Washington when agreement has been reached upon the new organisation proposed by President Roosevelt, upon which I have sent you the views which His Majesty's Government in the United Kingdom have transmitted to the President.

I was by now convinced that the Japanese would not invade Australia, provided all possible preparations were made to deter, or, if need be, resist them. It seemed to me that their best policy was to finish up China.

Prime Minister to General Ismay, for C.O.S. Committee 25 Mar. 42

The right move for the Japanese is to advance northward towards Chungking, where they can get a *decision* which might elude them in India, especially now that we are more comfortable at Ceylon. It is important however, if we are going to throw in our lot thus intimately with the Chinese, that we should reach a good understanding with the Generalissimo, and, if possible, make him ask us to do what on the merits is strategically right.

Prime Minister to General Ismay, for C.O.S. Committee 27 Mar. 42

Let us be clear about Ceylon. What we want there is the integrity of the defences of the naval base [at Colombo]. This is because we want the Fleet to operate from there into the Bay of Bengal, and not have to go six hundred miles away to Port T. Nothing must be taken from Ceylon which endangers the naval base or deters the Fleet from using it.

2. One had hoped that *Warspite* and two armoured carriers would be able to play an important part in the Bay of Bengal. It seems a great loss to have to send one of these fast carriers to Port T to guard the fairly useless "R" class. If they are no use and only an encumbrance, why don't they get out of the way, say to Aden or cruising, and give the aircraft-carriers their chance? Two [aircraft-carriers] together are much more than twice one, and three together more than twice two.

By the end of March the position at Colombo was decidedly more secure. After all our efforts, we had gathered about sixty serviceable fighters and a small short-range striking force of bombers under Air Vice-Marshal Dalbiac. This at least made sure that a Japanese air attack would be sharply resisted.

* * * * *

Breath-taking events were now to take place in the Bay of Bengal and in the Indian Ocean. On March 28 Admiral Somerville received information of an impending attack on Ceylon by powerful Japanese forces, including carriers, about April 1. He concentrated his fleet on March 31 to the southward of Ceylon, where he would be well placed to intervene, and sent air patrols to a distance of 120 miles from Colombo.

Only six Catalina flying-boats were available for extended reconnaissance. Admiral Layton, the capable Commander-in-Chief in Ceylon, brought all his forces to instant readiness and dispersed the merchant shipping from the ports. The refit of the cruiser *Dorsetshire* was abruptly stopped, and she sailed with the *Cornwall* to join Admiral Somerville's concentration.

From March 31 to April 2 extreme expectancy prevailed. The Fleet continued to cruise in its chosen waiting position, but nothing happened except that Japanese submarine patrols were reported to the southeastward of Ceylon. By the evening of the 2d the "R" class battleships were running short of water, and Admiral Somerville judged that either the enemy were waiting until he was forced to withdraw for want of fuel, or that his intelligence about the impending attack had been wrong. Reluctantly, but fortunately, he decided to return to Port T, six hundred miles away.

Scarcely had the Fleet reached Addu Atoll on April 4 when

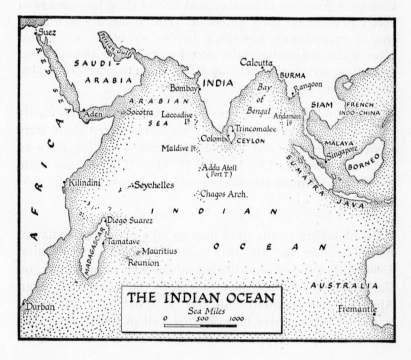

THE INDIAN OCEAN

Sea Miles
0   500   1000

a Catalina aircraft on patrol sighted large enemy forces approaching Ceylon. Before she could report their strength the Catalina was shot down. The original warning had thus proved correct, except in the matter of timing, and there could be no doubt that Ceylon would be heavily attacked the next day. The Admiral left Addu Atoll that night with the *Warspite,* the carriers *Indomitable* and *Formidable,* two cruisers, and six destroyers, ordering Admiral Willis to follow when ready with the "Rs" and the rest.

The *Dorsetshire* and *Cornwall* again sailed from Colombo to join the Fleet.

During the night of the 4th, reports of the enemy's approach continued to reach Admiral Layton from his air patrols, and just before eight o'clock on Easter Sunday morning, April 5, the expected attack, delivered by about eighty Japanese dive-bombers, struck Colombo. All was ready. Twenty-one of the attacking aircraft were destroyed at the cost of nineteen of our own fighters and six Swordfish of the Fleet Air Arm, in tense air combat. By 9.30 A.M. the action ceased. Thanks to the timely dispersal of shipping from the harbour, losses were not severe, but some damage was done to port installations. The destroyer *Tenedos* and the armed merchant cruiser *Hector* were sunk, but only one merchant ship was hit.

Meanwhile the *Dorsetshire* and *Cornwall* were on their way to join Admiral Somerville. The day was calm and clear. Captain Agar, in the *Dorsetshire,* knew how close were the enemy, and was proceeding at his best speed. At 11 A.M. a single Japanese aircraft was sighted. About 1.40 P.M. the attack burst upon the two ships in a crescendo of violence. Waves of dive-bombers followed each other in formations of three at intervals of a few seconds. In little more than fifteen minutes both our cruisers were sunk. The survivors clung to the floating wreckage and faced with fortitude the ordeal of waiting for rescue which all knew must be long. Eleven hundred and twenty-two officers and men from the two ships, many of them wounded, were saved the following evening by the *Enterprise* and two destroyers after enduring thirty hours under a tropical sun in shark-infested waters. Twenty-nine officers and 395 men perished.

Admiral Somerville had learned by now that the Japanese Fleet was far superior to his own in strength. We now know that Admiral Nagumo, who had conducted the raid against Pearl Harbour, was in command of five aircraft-carriers and four fast battleships, besides cruisers and destroyers, accompanied by tankers. This was the antagonist for whom our Fleet had waited so eagerly up till April 2. We had narrowly escaped a disastrous fleet action. Somerville, after rescuing the survivors, retired to the westward, reaching Port T on the morning of April 8.

*   *   *   *   *

The next day more misfortunes came upon us in Ceylon. Early in the morning a heavy air raid smote Trincomalee. Fifty-four Japanese bombers, escorted by fighters, damaged the dockyard, workshops, and airfield. They were met by our aircraft, which shot down fifteen of the enemy for the loss of eleven. Our handful of light bombers also made an heroic but forlorn attack against overwhelming odds upon the Japanese carriers. Less than half returned. The small aircraft-carrier *Hermes* and the destroyer *Vampire*, which had left Trincomalee for safety the night before, were both sunk by the Japanese planes with the loss of over three hundred lives.

Meanwhile in the Bay of Bengal a second Japanese striking force comprising a light carrier and six heavy cruisers was attacking our defenceless shipping. On March 31, the same day as emergency measures were taken in Colombo, it was decided to clear the port of Calcutta. Our naval forces in all this area were negligible, and it was decided to sail the ships in small groups. This questionable policy was reversed five days later when a ship was sunk south of Calcutta by air attack, and thereafter sailings were stopped. In the next few days the Japanese, ranging freely by sea and air, sank 93,000 tons of shipping. Adding the damage inflicted by Nagumo's force at the same time, our losses in this period amounted to nearly 116,000 tons.

*　　*　　*　　*　　*

The heavy concentration of Japanese naval power upon us made me anxious for a diversion by the United States Fleet.

Former Naval Person to President Roosevelt　　　　　　．" Apr. 42

According to our information, five, and possibly six, Japanese battleships, probably including two of sixteen-inch guns, and certainly five aircraft-carriers, are operating in the Indian Ocean. We cannot of course make head against this force, especially if it is concentrated. You know the composition of our fleet. The four "R" class battleships were good enough, in combination with the others, to meet the three *Kongos,* which were all we believed were over on our side. They cannot of course cope with modernised Japanese ships. Even after the heavy losses inflicted on the enemy's aircraft in their attack on Colombo, we cannot feel sure that our two carriers would beat the four Japanese carriers concentrated south of Ceylon. The situation is therefore one of grave anxiety.

2. It is not yet certain whether the enemy is making a mere demonstration in the Indian Ocean or whether these movements are the prelude to an invasion in force of Ceylon. In existing circumstances our naval forces are not strong enough to oppose this.

3. As you must now be decidedly superior to the enemy forces in the Pacific, the situation would seem to offer an immediate opportunity to the United States Pacific Fleet, which might be of such a nature as to compel Japanese naval forces in the Indian Ocean to return to the Pacific, thus relinquishing or leaving unsupported any invasion enterprise which they have in mind or to which they are committed. I cannot too urgently impress the importance of this upon you.

*　　*　　*　　*　　*

The experiences of the last few days had left no doubt in anyone's mind that for the time being Admiral Somerville had not the strength to fight a general action. Japanese success and power in naval air warfare were formidable. In the Gulf of Siam two of our first-class capital ships had been sunk in a few minutes by torpedo aircraft. Now two important cruisers had also perished by a totally different method of air attack — the dive-bomber. Nothing like this had been seen in the Mediterranean in all our conflicts with the German and Italian Air Forces. For the Eastern Fleet to remain near Ceylon would be courting a major disaster. The Japanese had gained control of the Bay of Bengal, and at their selected moment could obtain local command of the waters around Ceylon. The British aircraft available were far outnumbered by the enemy. The battle fleet, slow, outranged, and of short endurance, except for the *Warspite,* was itself at this moment a liability, and the available carrier-borne air protection would be ineffective against repeated attacks on the scale of those which had destroyed the *Dorsetshire* and *Cornwall.* There was but little security against large-scale air or surface attacks at the Ceylon bases, and still less at Addu Atoll.

On one point we were all agreed. The "Rs" should get out of danger at the earliest moment. When I put this to the First Sea Lord there was no need for argument. Orders were sent accordingly, and the Admiralty authorised Admiral Somerville to withdraw his fleet two thousand miles westward to East Africa. Here it could at least provide cover for the vital shipping routes to the Middle East. He himself, with the *Warspite* and his two carriers, would continue to operate in Indian waters in defence of our sea communications with India and with the Persian Gulf. For this purpose, he intended to base himself on Bombay. His actions were promptly approved by the Admiralty, whose thoughts in the grave events of the past few days had followed almost identical lines. These new dispositions were brought into effect forthwith.

There now arose one of those waves of alarm which sometimes spread through High Commands. The vital point was to keep Ceylon. I thought it premature that the *Warspite* and her two aircraft-carriers should quit Bombay, where for the moment they seemed safe.

Prime Minister to General Ismay, for C.O.S. Committee 14 Apr. 42

We must make every effort and run great risks to hold Ceylon.

Admiral Somerville is well posted for the time being at Bombay. Why should it be assumed that Ceylon and Southern India are going to be lost in so short a time that Bombay will soon become unsafe? This is going to extremes with a vengeance. He should surely be told not on any account to propose evacuation of any staff from Ceylon.

The Chiefs of Staff agreed that Ceylon was to be built up to provide a main fleet base, and that meanwhile the fast portion of the Eastern Fleet should be based at Kilindini, on the British East African coast. Admiral Somerville left for Kilindini a fortnight later. We had now for the time being completely abandoned the Indian Ocean, except for the coast of Africa.

*   *   *   *   *

I renewed my representations to President Roosevelt, who had not yet replied to my message of the 7th.

Former Naval Person to President Roosevelt   15 Apr. 42

I must revert to the grave situation in the Indian Ocean arising from the fact that the Japanese have felt able to detach nearly a third of their battle fleet and half their carriers, which force we are unable to match for several months. The consequences of this may easily be: (*a*) The loss of Ceylon. (*b*) Invasion of Eastern India, with incalculable internal consequences to our whole war plan, including the loss of Calcutta and of all contact with the Chinese through Burma. But this is only the beginning. Until we are able to fight a fleet action there is no reason why the Japanese should not become the dominating factor in the Western Indian Ocean. This would result in the collapse of our whole position in the Middle East, not only because of the interruption to our convoys to the Middle East and India, but also because of the interruptions to the oil supplies from Abadan, without which we cannot maintain our position either at sea or on land in the Indian Ocean area. Supplies to Russia via the Persian Gulf would also be cut. With so much of the weight of Japan thrown upon us we have more than we can bear.

2. We had hoped that by the end of April the American Pacific Fleet would be strong enough to reoccupy Pearl Harbour and offer some menace to the Japanese, which they would have to consider

seriously. At present there seems to be no adequate restraint upon Japanese movements to the west. We are not sure however whether, owing to the great distances, even the reoccupation of Pearl Harbour in force by the United States battle fleet would necessarily exercise compulsive pressure upon the Japanese High Naval Command. We are deeply conscious of the difficulties of your problem in the Pacific area.

3. If you do not feel able to take speedy action which will force Japan to concentrate in the Pacific, the only way out of the immense perils which confront us would seem to be to build up as quickly as possible an ample force of modern capital ships and carriers in the Indian Ocean.

I also asked for help in the air.

6. It is also most important to have some American heavy bombers in India. There are at present about fourteen, and fifty more are authorised. But none of these was able to attack the Japanese naval forces last week. We have taken everything from Libya which is possible without ruining all prospects of a renewed offensive. We are sending every suitable aircraft to the East which can be efficiently serviced out there, but without your aid this will not be sufficient. Might I press you, Mr. President, to procure the necessary decisions?

As I had expected, the President preferred to work through the air.

President Roosevelt to Prime Minister   17 Apr. 42

We have been [making] and are continuing studies of immediate needs. I hope you will read our Air Force suggestions sent to Marshall for your consideration. This would be much the quickest way of getting planes to India, though they would be land-based planes, and for the time being would compel you to keep your fleet under their coverage. On the other hand, this plan would do the most good to prevent Japanese landing at Ceylon, Madras, or Calcutta. In other words, they would definitely improve the general military situation in India area. These planes however involve [the] use of *Ranger* as a ferry-boat and prevent her use as [a] carrier with her own planes. The *Ranger* is of course best suited for ferrying, as we are not proud of her compartmentation and her structural strength. Measures now in hand by Pacific Fleet have not been conveyed to you in detail because of secrecy requirements, but we hope you will find them effective when they can be made known to you shortly. I fully appreciate the present lack of naval butter to cover the bread, but I hope you will agree with me that because of operational differences between the two Services there is a grave question as to whether a main fleet concentration should be made in Ceylon area with mixed forces. Partly because of this and partly because of my feeling that for the next few weeks it is more important to prevent [the] Japanese landing anywhere in India or Ceylon, we are inclined to give greater consideration to temporary replacement of your Home Fleet units rather than mixing units in Indian Ocean.

It is my personal thought that your fleet in Indian Ocean can well be safeguarded during next few weeks without fighting major engagement, in the meantime building up land-based plane units to stop Japanese transports. I hope you will let me know your thought in regard to the Air Force measures indicated above. We could put them into effect at once.

I gave Wavell all the reassurances I could.

Prime Minister to General Wavell   18 Apr. 42

We are endeavouring to build up a fleet in the Indian Ocean sufficiently strong to cause the Japanese to make a larger detachment from their main fleet than they would wish. I have therefore asked President Roosevelt to send the *North Carolina* to join the *Washington* at Scapa Flow; these are the two latest American battleships. The *Duke of York* will then be released for the Indian Ocean, and be accompanied by *Renown*. As *Illustrious* should be with Admiral Somerville in May and *Valiant* should be ready in June, we shall quite soon have three fast capital ships and three of our largest armoured carriers in the Indian Ocean. We are taking steps to make the carriers as prolific in aircraft as possible. Thus, in eight to ten weeks Somerville's fleet, growing continually stronger, should become powerful. Especially is this so as there is reason to believe that the United States' main fleet will become more active and a greater preoccupation to the Japanese than in the past.

But if in the meantime Ceylon, particularly Colombo, is lost, all this gathering of a naval force will be futile. Therefore the defence of Colombo by flak and aircraft must be considered as an object more urgent and not less important than the defence of Calcutta. As to the long Indian coast-line between Ceylon and Calcutta, it is impossible in the near future to provide air forces either to repel landings or to give an air umbrella for naval movements. But do you really think it likely that Japan would consider it worth while to send four or five divisions roaming about the Madras Presidency? What could be achieved comparable to the results obtainable by taking Ceylon or by pushing north into China and finishing off Chiang Kai-shek? Only in China can the Japanese obtain a major decision this year. Therefore my thought is that you must be selective in your treatment of the problem. The naval base at Colombo and the link with China through Calcutta have pre-eminence.

I must point out that at least fifteen and perhaps twenty Japanese divisions would be freed by the collapse of China. Thereafter a major invasion of India would indeed be possible.

*   *   *   *   *

The grievous anxieties which we felt at having to lose even for a spell the naval command of the Bay of Bengal and the Indian Ocean were removed by the course of events. We were in fact at the end of the Japanese advance towards the west. Their naval incursion was outside the main orbit of Japanese expansionist policy. They were making a raid and a demonstration. They had no serious plan for an overseas invasion of Southern India or of Ceylon. If of course they had found Colombo unprepared and devoid of air defence, they might have converted their reconnaissance in force into a major operation. They might have encountered the British Fleet and inflicted, as was not impossible, a severe defeat upon it. If this had happened, no one could set limits to their potential action. Such a trial of strength was avoided by good fortune and prompt decision. The stubborn resistance encountered at Colombo convinced the Japanese that further prizes would be dearly bought. The losses they had suffered in aircraft convinced them that they had come in con1act with bone. The renascent sea-power of the United States in the Pacific was the dominating factor. Apart from isolated activities by a few U-boats and disguised raiders, the Japanese Navy never appeared again in Indian waters. It vanished as suddenly as it had come, leaving behind a vacuum from which both antagonists had now withdrawn.

We could not of course know that the danger to all our communications in the Indian Ocean was in fact over. We had still to reckon upon the enemy, with his command of the sea, sending an invading army to the mainland of India. Our responsibilities, anxieties, and preparations continued. These expressed themselves in many demands for air reinforcement for the East upon a scale which would seriously have deranged the main strategy of the war in Europe.

On April 12, in a message to the Chiefs of Staff, General Wavell had said:

Unless a serious effort is made to supply our essential needs, which I have not overstated, I must warn you that we shall never regain control of the Indian Ocean and Bay of Bengal, and run the risk of losing India. It certainly gives us furiously to think when, after trying with less than twenty light bombers to meet attack which has cost us three important warships and several others and nearly 100,000 tons of merchant shipping, we see that over two hundred heavy bombers attacked one town in Germany.

These opinions naturally found support in some Dominions circles.

Prime Minister to Dominions Secretary   16 Apr. 42

These views are certainly fashionable at the moment. Everybody would like to send Bomber Command to India and the Middle East. However, it is not possible to make any decisive change. All that is possible is being done. I should be very glad if you would see C.A.S. and hear what he has to say. The question is one of precise detail. It is no use flying out squadrons which sit helpless and useless when they arrive. We have built up a great plant here for bombing Germany, which is the only way in our power of helping Russia. From every side people want to break it up. One has to be sure that we do not ruin our punch here without getting any proportionate advantage elsewhere.

We were in no way drawn from our main purposes, and were not deterred, as will be seen later, from new and vigorous offensive action. It had been a harassing episode, but it was over. From this time forward we began to grow stronger.

*   *   *   *   *

The air fighting in Ceylon had important strategical results which at the time we could not foresee. Admiral Nagumo's now celebrated carrier force, which had ranged almost unmolested for four months with devastating success, had on this occasion suffered such losses in the air that three of his ships had to be withdrawn to Japan for refit and re-equipment. Thus, when a month later Japan launched her attack against Port Moresby, in New Guinea, only two of these carriers were able to take part. Their appearance at full strength then in the Coral Sea might well have turned the scale against the Americans in that important encounter.

11

The Shipping Stranglehold

Need of a Mobile Reserve in the East — I Ask President Roosevelt for Transport for Two More Divisions — And for Cargo Shipping — My General Survey of the War, March 5 — The Japanese Theatre — President Roosevelt's Reply — My Request for Transport Granted — Important Conditions — American Troop-Carrying Resources and Prospects — Distribution of the United States Air Force — Our Close Accord on Policy — The President's Personal Views on Simplification of Strategic Spheres — His First Hint of a European Front in 1942 — The Rising Tide of United States Shipbuilding — The President's Letter to Me of March 18 — My Reply, April 1.

GRAVE CONDITIONS arising from the U-boat war overhung our minds, but did not distract them from other great combinations. Early in March I addressed myself to President Roosevelt on the strategic employment of our shipping resources in relation to our import budget. I earnestly sought from him the loan of American shipping sufficient to carry an additional two British divisions to the East. No one could tell what would happen in this vast area, with its many theatres of war or potential war. I had a great desire to have something in hand. If I could have two divisions rounding the Cape in May or June, it would give me the priceless advantage of a mobile reserve which could be sent to Egypt, Persia, India, or Australia, as events decreed.

Former Naval Person to President Roosevelt   4 Mar. 42

Since my return to this country I have been giving much atten-

189

tion to the shipping situation, which is likely to impose severe
limitations upon our efforts throughout 1942. There are two main
aspects. First, military movements. You know we are moving very
large numbers, including an Australian corps of three divisions
and the 70th British Division, from the Middle East across the
Indian Ocean. To make good the depletion of the Middle East
and to send large reinforcements, both land and air, to India and
Ceylon, we should like to ship from the United Kingdom 295,000
men in the months February, March, April, and May. A convoy
of 45,000 men sailed in February. Another convoy of 50,000, including the 5th Division and seven squadrons of aircraft, will sail
in March. Two further convoys, totalling 85,000 men, will sail in
April and May. To achieve this we are scraping together every ton
of man-lift shipping we can lay our hands on and adopting every
expedient to hasten the turn-round and increase the carrying
capacity of the shipping. Even so, we shall fall short of our aim
by 115,000 men.

This is the situation in which I turn to you for help.

I think we must agree to recognise that "Gymnast" [the varying
forms of intervention in French North Africa by Britain from the
east and by the United States across the Atlantic] is out of the
question for several months. Taking this factor into account, can
you lend us the shipping to convoy to the Indian Ocean during
the next critical four months a further two complete divisions (say
40,000 men), including the necessary accompanying M.T., guns, and
equipment? This would mean that we would like the shipping to
load in [the] United Kingdom during April and the first half of
May. The combat loading ships now allocated to "Magnet" [the
transportation of American troops to Northern Ireland] might
provide for 10,000 of this total, and these and any other ships you
are able to find could bring such a substantial proportion of
"Magnet" on their way to the United Kingdom that we could
defer the balance of that movement.

Further, the cargo shipping at our disposal has not only to maintain the flow of essential imports to the United Kingdom, but also
to keep up supplies to Russia and to meet increasing demands for
the supply and maintenance of our troops in the East. Ships are
having to be withdrawn from importing service to carry supplies
to the East, not only from this country, but also from [the] United
States, as many of the American ships that have been helping with

the latter task are being diverted to other urgent duties. These developments, with other consequences of the Far Eastern war, are having a very serious effect on our importing capacity. During the first four months of this year we expect imports of only 7,250,000 tons, and recently sinkings have greatly increased.

This will mean a serious running down of stocks during the first part of the year, which cannot be continued, and which must be made good by a substantial improvement in the rate of importation in the later months. We have made a careful analysis of the imports which we must secure during 1942, in order to maintain our full effort and to make sure that our stocks shall not be run down below the danger line by the end of the year, and are satisfied that it is not reasonable to aim at anything less than 26,000,000 tons of non-tanker imports. This will certainly not be realised without very substantial additions to our shipping resources. It would therefore be a great help to us in connection with all our plans if you could let me know to what extent we can expect assistance for our imports and for carriage of our equipment from [the] United States to the Middle East to be made available from your shipbuilding programme month by month as vessels come increasingly into service.

And the next day:

Former Naval Person to President Roosevelt   5 Mar. 42

When I reflect how I have longed and prayed for the entry of the United States into the war, I find it difficult to realise how gravely our British affairs have deteriorated by what has happened since December 7. We have suffered the greatest disaster in our history at Singapore, and other misfortunes will come thick and fast upon us. Your great power will only become effective gradually because of the vast distances and the shortage of ships. It is not easy to assign limits to the Japanese aggression. All can be retrieved in 1943 and 1944, but meanwhile there are very hard forfeits to pay. The whole of the Levant-Caspian front now depends entirely upon the success of the Russian armies. The attack which the Germans will deliver upon Russia in the spring will, I fear, be most formidable. The danger to Malta grows constantly, and large reinforcements are reaching Rommel in Tripoli *en route* for Cyrenaica.

2. Since we last talked I have not been able to form a full picture of the United States plans by sea, air, and land against Japan. I am hoping that by May your naval superiority in the Pacific will be restored, and that this will be a continuing preoccupation to the enemy. We expect by the middle of March, in addition to the four renovated *Ramillies* class battleships, to have two of our latest aircraft-carriers working with *Warspite* in the Indian Ocean, and that these will be reinforced by a third carrier during April and by *Valiant* during May. This force will have available four modern cruisers and a number of older ones and about twenty destroyers. Based upon Ceylon, which we regard as the vital point now that Singapore is gone, it should be possible to prevent oversea invasion of India unless the greater part of the Japanese Fleet is brought across from your side of the theatre, and this again I hope the action and growing strength of the United States Navy will prevent.

We hope that a considerable number of Dutch submarines will have escaped to Ceylon, and these, together with the only two submarines we have been able to spare from the Mediterranean, should be able to watch the Malacca Straits. As we understand your submarines from the A.B.D.A. area will be based on Fremantle for the purpose of patrolling the Sunda Straits and other exits through the Dutch islands, we should not only get notice of, but be able to take a toll of, any Japanese forces breaking out into the Indian Ocean. The next fortnight will be the most critical for Ceylon, and by the end of March we ought to be solidly established there, though by no means entirely secure.

3. With the *Tirpitz* and *Scheer* at Trondheim our Northern Force has not only to watch the northern passages, but also to guard the Russian convoys. The tension is however temporarily eased by the disabling of the *Scharnhorst, Gneisenau,* and *Eugen,* the latter severely, we believe, and we are taking the opportunity of refitting *Rodney. Rodney* and *Nelson* should be ready for service in May, but *Anson* will not be in fighting trim until August.

4. I should be glad to have from you a short statement of the dispositions and plans of the American Air Force. We have both suffered heavy casualties on the ground in Java, and I was most grieved to see the untoward sinking of the *Langley,* with her invaluable consignment. Particularly I shall be glad to know to what point your plans for operating from China or the Aleutian Islands have advanced. We also hope that United States bombers

based in Northeast India may operate in force against enemy bases in Siam and Indo-China.

5. You will realise what has happened to the army we had hoped to gather on the Levant-Caspian front, and how it has nearly all been drawn off to India and Australia, and you will see at once what our plight will be should the Russian defence of the Caucasus be beaten down. It would certainly be a great help if you could offer New Zealand the support of an American division as an alternative to their recalling their own New Zealand division, now stationed in Palestine. This also applies to the last Australian division in the Middle East. One sympathises with the natural anxiety of Australia and New Zealand when their best troops are out of the country, but shipping will be saved and safety gained by the American reinforcement of Australia and New Zealand rather than by a move across the oceans of these divisions from the Middle East. I am quite ready to accept a considerable delay in "Magnet" to facilitate your additional help to Australasia. Finally, it seems of the utmost importance that the United States main naval forces should give increasing protection in the Anzac area, because this alone can meet the legitimate anxieties of the Governments there and ensure the maintenance of our vital bases of re-entry.

6. Everything however turns upon shipping. I have sent you a separate telegram about the import programme into Great Britain in the current calendar year, 1942. It will certainly require a considerable allocation of the new American tonnage in the third and fourth quarters of the year. The immediate and decisive concern however is the provision of troop-carrying tonnage. I am advised that we have at the present time a total man-lift of 280,000 men, but of course at least half of this will be returning empty of troops from very long voyages. You have a comparable man-lifting power of 90,000 men, and what has most alarmed me has been the statement that even by the summer of 1943 the American man-lift will only be increased by another 90,000. If this cannot be remedied there may well be no question of restoring the situation until 1944, with all the many dangers that would follow from such a prolongation of the war. Surely it is possible, by giving orders now, to double or treble the American man-lift by the summer of 1943? We can do little more beyond our 280,000, and losses have been very heavy lately in this class of vessel. I should be most grateful

if you would relieve my anxieties on this score. I am entirely with you about the need for "Gymnast," but the check which Auchinleck has received and the shipping stringency seem to impose obstinate and long delays.

7. We are sending from 40,000 to 50,000 men in each of our monthly convoys to the East. The needs of maintaining the Army and of building up the air and anti-aircraft forces in the Indian theatre will at present prevent us from sending more than three divisions from here in the March, April, and May convoys, these arriving two months later in each case. It seems to me that all these troops may be needed for the defence of India, and I cannot make any provision other than that suggested in paragraph 5 for the Trans-Caspian front and all that that means.

8. Permit me to refer to the theme I opened to you when we were together. Japan is spreading itself over a very large number of vulnerable points and trying to link them together by air and sea protection. The enemy are becoming ever more widely spread, and we know this is causing anxiety in Tokyo. Nothing can be done on a large scale except by long preparation of the technical and tactical apparatus. When you told me about your intention to form Commando forces on a large scale on the Californian shore I felt you had the key. Once several good outfits are prepared, any one of which can attack a Japanese-held base or island and beat the life out of the garrison, all their islands will become hostages to fortune. Even this year, 1942, some severe examples might be made, causing great perturbation and drawing further upon Japanese resources to strengthen other points.

9. But surely if plans were set on foot now for the preparation of the ships, landing-craft, aircraft, expeditionary divisions, etc., all along the Californian shore for a serious attack upon the Japanese in 1943, this would be a solid policy for us to follow. Moreover, the strength of the United States is such that the whole of this Western party could be developed on your Pacific coast without prejudice to the plans against Hitler across the Atlantic we have talked of together. For a long time to come it seems your difficulty will be to bring your forces into action, and that the shipping shortage will be the stranglehold.

I received a full reply from the President on the 8th, which was clearly the result of prolonged Staff studies.

"We have been in constant conference," he said, "since the receipt of your message of March 4. We recognise fully the magnitude of the problems confronting you in the Indian Ocean, and are equally concerned over those which confront us in the Pacific, particularly since we have assumed responsibility for the defence of Australia and New Zealand." The United States, he pointed out, was using a large part of the Pacific Fleet in the Anzac region and in the A.B.D.A. area. Japan was extending herself by a skillfully executed deployment. The energy of the Japanese attack was still very powerful. The Pacific situation was now grave. The loan of transports to the British for further troop movements to India would reduce the possibilities of American offensive action in other regions. Nevertheless, if the two Australian and New Zealand divisions were left by their Governments in the Middle East and available for India, the United States was prepared to send two divisions, one to Australia and one to New Zealand, in addition to the two already under orders for Australia and New Caledonia, making a total of ninety thousand American troops in Australasia. This would entail a temporary reduction in the transport of Lend-Lease material through the Red Sea to China. All was dependent upon leaving the two Anzac divisions in the Middle East. In no other way could the shipping be put to the highest use.

Besides this the President agreed to meet my main request in the manner I had suggested. He would furnish the ships to move our two divisions with their equipment from Britain round the Cape. The first convoy could sail about April 26, and the remainder about May 6. We shall see later on how helpful the precaution proved. Certain very important conditions must however rule. "The supplying of these ships," said the President, "is contingent upon acceptance of the following during the period they are so used: (a) 'Gymnast' [intervention in French North Africa] cannot be undertaken. (b) Movements of United States troops to the British Isles will be limited to those which these ships can take from the United States. (c) Direct movements to Iceland (C) cannot be made. (d)

Eleven cargo ships must be withdrawn from sailings for Burma
and Red Sea during April and May. These ships are engaged
in transportation of Lend-Lease material to China and the Middle East. (*e*) American contribution to an air offensive against
Germany in 1942 would be somewhat curtailed and any American contribution to land operations on the Continent of
Europe in 1942 will be materially reduced. It is considered
essential that United States ships used for the movement of the
two British divisions be returned to us upon completion of the
movement."

I was well content with this. One of my fundamental ideas
has always been the importance of keeping as many options as
possible open to serve the main purpose, especially in time of
war. The President's loan of the additional transport which
enabled me *for a second time* to have a couple of divisions on
the move round the Cape is an illustration of this principle.

About our joint resources in troop-lifting capacity the
President and his advisers gave some figures which should be
borne in mind as this account proceeds. The present shipbuilding programme, he said, seemed to be about the maximum
that could be attained, and any increases would not be available until after June, 1944.

We now have under construction troopships that will carry
225,250 men. It is understood that the British do not plan to increase their total of troop-carrying ships. Shipping now available
under the U.S. flag will lift a total of about 130,000 men. Increases
from conversions during 1942 are estimated at least 35,000 men.
By June, 1943, new construction will give an additional 40,000, by
December, 1943, an additional 100,000, and by June, 1944, an additional 95,000. Thus, neglecting losses, the total troop-carrying
capacity of U.S. vessels by June, 1944, will be 400,000 men.

These facts governed the course of Anglo-American
strategy.

The tentative distribution of the whole American Air Force
aimed at by the end of 1942 was then given in detail.

The President added that as much as possible of this force

was essential in the United Kingdom if a concerted offensive against German military strength and resources was to be made in 1942. It included forces previously set up for "Gymnast" and "Magnet." He ended:

> In confiding thus fully and personally to you the details of our military arrangements I do not mean that they should be held from your close military advisers. I request however that further circulation be drastically reduced.
>
> I am sending you a personal suggestion on Sunday in regard to simplification of area responsibilities.
>
> This may be a critical period, but remember always it is not as bad as some you have so well survived before.

I was in full accord with all this, and replied:

Former Naval Person to President Roosevelt   9 Mar. 42

> Am most deeply grateful for your prompt and generous response to my suggestions. New position is being examined by our Staffs, and I will cable you shortly.

The President now added a personal message of his own, which raised complicated questions of command and spheres of responsibility, eventually solved in a satisfactory manner. "I telegraphed you Saturday night," he said, "in accordance with the general recommendations of Combined Staffs, as you doubtless recognised from the context. I want to send you this purely personal view so that you may know how my thoughts are developing." He went on:

> Ever since our January meetings the excellent arrangements of that period have largely become obsolescent in relation to the whole Southwest Pacific area.
>
> I wish therefore that you would consider the following operational simplification:
>
> The whole of the operation[al] responsibility for the Pacific area will rest on the United States. The Army, Navy, and Air operating decisions for the area as a whole will be made in Washington by the United States Chiefs of Staff, and there will be in Washington an Advisory Council on operational matters, with members

from Australia, New Zealand, Netherlands East Indies, and China, with an American presiding. Canada could be added. The Pacific Council now sitting in London might well be moved here; at any rate, the operational part of its functions, including supply, should operate from here. You may think it best to have a Pacific Council in London considering political questions. The Supreme Command in this area will be American. Local operating command on the continent of Australia will be in charge of an Australian. Local operating command in New Zealand will be under a New Zealander. Local operating command in China will be under the Generalissimo. Local operating command in Dutch East Indies would be given to a Dutchman, if later on an offensive can regain that area from the Japanese.

Under such an arrangement decisions for immediate operating strategy would be determined in Washington and by an American Supreme Commander for [the] whole Pacific area under supervision of United States Chiefs of Staff. The methods of regaining the offensive would be similarly decided. This would include, for example, offensives in northwesterly direction from the main southern bases and attacks on Japan proper from Chinese or Aleutian or Siberian bases. There would be definite responsibility on our part, thus relieving British from any tasks in this area other than supplementing our efforts with material where possible.

2. The middle area, extending from Singapore to and including India and the Indian Ocean, Persian Gulf, Red Sea, Libya, and the Mediterranean, would fall directly under British responsibility. All operating matters in this area would be decided by you; but always with understanding that as much assistance would be given to India or Near East by Australia and New Zealand as could be worked out with their Governments. We would continue to allocate to it all possible munitions and vessel assignments. It is understood that this presupposes the temporary shelving of "Gymnast."

There was a third sphere of the utmost importance.

I am becoming more and more interested in the establishment of a new front this summer on the European continent, certainly for air and raids. From the point of view of shipping and supplies it is infinitely easier for us to participate in because of a maximum distance of about three thousand miles. And even though losses will doubtless be great, such losses will be compensated by at least equal German losses and by compelling Germans to divert large forces of all kinds from Russian fronts.

Furthermore, under this plan Iceland and "Magnet" [the transportation of American troops to Northern Ireland] become of less importance because of offensive conducted against enemy on European soil itself. It is intended of course to carry through all possible aid to Russia.

Shipping was at once the stranglehold and sole foundation of our war strategy. With the entry of Japan into the war the strength of the Anglo-American military effort depended almost directly upon the replacement of our shipping losses by new production. During the first six months of 1942 the sinkings of British and American vessels were nearly as heavy as for the whole of 1941, and exceeded the whole Allied shipbuilding programme by nearly three million tons. At the same time the demands of the American Army and Navy increased enormously. But already in March the United States building programme for the following year was raised to twelve million tons. By May, 1942, the Americans balanced their current losses with new ships. It was only late in August that this goal was achieved by the Allies as a whole. Another year elapsed before we could replace all our earlier losses. In spite of increasing American commitments, we were allowed to retain in our service nearly three million tons of American cargo and tanker shipping. Even this generous decision on the part of the United States did not make up for the mounting casualties in the British and Allied vessels.

* * * * *

As the story progresses it will be seen how new possibilities unfolded; how additional tasks were laid upon the two mighty navies of the English-speaking world, and with what varying fortunes they were discharged. The whole scene was soon to receive a brighter light from the first American naval victories over Japan in the Pacific, and all sea problems were eventually to be solved by the stupendous United States construction of merchant vessels. The intimacy of our collaboration during these anxious weeks is shown by the following interchange between President Roosevelt and myself:

Dear Winston,

I am sure you know that I have been thinking a lot about your troubles during the past month. We might as well admit the difficult military side of the problems; and you have the additional burdens which your delightful unwritten Constitution puts your form of government into in wartime just as much as in peacetime. Seriously, the American written Constitution, with its four-year term, saves the unfortunate person at the top a vast number of headaches.

Next in order is that delightful god, which we worship in common, called "the freedom of the press." Neither one of us is much plagued by the news stories, which, on the whole, are not so bad. But literally we are both menaced by the so-called interpretative comment by a handful or two of gentlemen who cannot get politics out of their heads in the worst crisis, who have little background and less knowledge, and who undertake to lead public opinion on that basis.

My own press — the worst of it — are persistently magnifying relatively unimportant domestic matters and subtly suggesting that the American rôle is to defend Hawaii; our east and west coasts do the turtle act and wait until somebody attacks our home shores. Curiously enough, these survivors of isolationism are not attacking me personally, except to reiterate that I am dreadfully overburdened, or that I am my own strategist, operating without benefit of military or naval advice. It is the same old story. You are familiar with it.

Here is a thought from this amateur strategist. There is no use giving a single further thought to Singapore or the Dutch Indies. They are gone. Australia must be held, and, as I telegraphed you, we are willing to undertake that. India must be held, and you must do that; but, frankly, I do not worry so much about that problem as many others do. The Japanese may land on the seacoast west of Burma. They may bombard Calcutta. But I do not visualise that they can get enough troops to make more than a few dents on the borders — and I think you can hold Ceylon. I hope you can get more submarines out there — more valuable than an inferior surface fleet. I hope you will definitely reinforce the Near East more greatly than at present. You must hold Egypt, the Canal, Syria, Iran, and the route to the Caucasus.

Finally, I expect to send you in a few days a more definite plan for a joint attack in Europe itself.

By the time you get this you will have been advised of my talk with Litvinov, and I expect a reply from Stalin shortly. I know you will not mind my being brutally frank when I tell you that I think I can personally handle Stalin better than either your Foreign Office or my State Department. Stalin hates the guts of all your top people. He thinks he likes me better, and I hope he will continue to do so.

My Navy has been definitely slack in preparing for this submarine war off our coast. As I need not tell you, most naval officers have declined in the past to think in terms of any vessel of less than two thousand tons. You learned the lesson two years ago. We still have to learn it. By May 1 I expect to get a pretty good coastal patrol working from Newfoundland to Florida and through the West Indies. I have begged, borrowed, and stolen every vessel of every description over eighty feet long — and I have made this a separate command with the responsibility in Admiral Andrews.

I know you will keep up your optimism and your grand driving force, but I know you will not mind if I tell you that you ought to take a leaf out of my notebook. Once a month I go to Hyde Park for four days, crawl into a hole, and pull the hole in after me. I am called on the telephone only if something of really great importance occurs. I wish you would try it, and I wish you would lay a few bricks or paint another picture.

Give my warm regards to Mrs. Churchill. I wish much that my wife and I could see her.

As ever yours

FRANKLIN D. ROOSEVELT

P.S. Winant is here. I think he is really a most understanding person.

I replied in similar strain.

Former Naval Person to President Roosevelt   1 Apr. 42

Delighted by your letter of March 18, just received. I am so grateful for all your thoughts about my affairs, and personal kind-

ness. Our position here has always been quite solid, but naturally
with nothing but disaster to show for all one's work people were
restive in Parliament and the press. I find it very difficult to get
over Singapore, but I hope we shall redeem it ere long.

2. Dickie's show at St. Nazaire, though small in scale, was very
bracing. For your personal and secret eye, I made him Vice-Admiral, Lieutenant-General, and Air Marshal some few weeks ago,
and have put him on the Chiefs of Staff Committee as Chief of
Combined Operations. He is an equal member, attending whenever either his own affairs or the general conduct of the war are
under consideration. He will be in the centre of what you mention
about the joint attack on Europe. I am looking forward to receiving your plan. We are working very hard here, not only at plans
but at preparations.

3. Speaking as one amateur to another, my feeling is that the
wisest stroke for Japan would be to press on through Burma northward into China and try to make a job of that. They may disturb
India, but I doubt its serious invasion. We are sending forty to
fifty thousand men each month to the East. As they round the
Cape we can divert them to Suez, Basra, Bombay, Ceylon, or
Australia. I have told Curtin that if he is seriously invaded — by
which I mean six or eight enemy divisions — Britain will come to
his aid. But of course this could only be at the expense of the most
urgent needs in the other theatres. I hope you will continue to
give Australia all possible reinforcement, and thus enable me to
defend Egypt, the Levant, and India successfully. It will be a hard
task.

4. We cannot send any more submarines from the Mediterranean
to the Indian Ocean and have only two British and four Dutch
there. We are much stronger now at Ceylon, and are fairly well
equipped with garrisons, Hurricanes, some torpedo planes, and
radar, together with pretty stiff flak. Admiral Somerville's fleet is
growing to respectable proportions, and it may be an opportunity
of fighting an action will occur. Meanwhile Operation "Ironclad"
[Madagascar] is going ahead. This also concerns Dickie a good
deal. Altogether I hope we shall be better off in the Indian Ocean
in a little while, and that the Japanese will have missed their
opportunity there.

5. It seems important to make the Japanese anxious for their
numerous conquests and prevent them scraping together troops for

further large excursions. I should be very glad to know how your plans for Californian Commandos are progressing. I see some hints that Donovan is working at them.

6. All now depends upon the vast Russo-German struggle. It looks as if the heavy German offensive may not break till after the middle of May, or even the beginning of June. We are doing all we can to help, and also to take the weight off. We shall have to fight every convoy through to Murmansk. Stalin is pleased with our deliveries. They are due to go up fifty per cent after June, and it will be very difficult to do this in view of the new war, and also of shipping. Only the weather is holding us back from continuous, heavy bombing attack on Germany. Our new methods are most successful. Essen, Cologne, and above all Lübeck, were all on the Coventry scale. I am sure it is most important to keep this up all through the summer, blasting Hitler from behind while he is grappling with the Bear. Everything that you can send to weight our attack will be of the utmost value. At Malta also we are containing, with much hard fighting, nearly six hundred German and Italian planes. I am wondering whether these will move to the South Russian front in the near future. There are however many rumours of an airborne attack on Malta, possibly this month.

7. Having heard from Stalin that he was expecting the Germans would use gas on him, I have assured him that we shall treat any such outrage as if directed upon us, and will retaliate without limit. This we are in a good position to do. I propose, at his desire, to announce this towards the end of the present month, and we are using the interval to work up our own precautions. Please let all the above be absolutely between ourselves.

I am personally extremely well, though I have felt the weight of the war rather more since I got back than before. My wife and I both send our kindest regards to you and Mrs. Roosevelt. Perhaps when the weather gets better I may propose myself for a week-end with you and flip over. We have so much to settle that would go easily in talk.

12

India — The Cripps Mission

British Loyalty to India — Our Heavy Bill Incurred for Defending the Indian Peoples — Loyalty and Valour of the Indian Army — Two and a Half Million Indian Volunteers — Effects of the Westward Advance of Japan — Congress Party Defeatism — Chiang Kai-shek's Visit — My Message to Him of February 12 — The Offer of Dominion Status after the War — My Own Conception of a Constituent Assembly — A Ministerial Committee on Indian Affairs — United States Interest — I Send President Roosevelt Full Statements from Indian Sources — Views of the Governor of the Punjab — President Roosevelt's Private Views — British Draft Declaration — Sir Stafford Cripps' Mission — Congress Rejects Our Proposals — My Letter to Sir Stafford of April 11 — The President Dismayed at the Breakdown — A United Cabinet — My Reply to the President, April 12 — Sir Stafford's Return.

N O GREAT PORTION of the world population was so effectively protected from the horrors and perils of the World War as were the peoples of Hindustan. They were carried through the struggle on the shoulders of our small Island. British Government officials in India were wont to consider it a point of honour to champion the particular interests of India against those of Great Britain whenever a divergence occurred. Arrangements made when the war was expected to be fought out in Europe were invoked to charge us for goods and services needed entirely for the defence of India. Contracts were fixed in India at extravagant rates, and debts incurred in inflated rupees were converted into so-called "sterling balances" at the pre-war rate of exchange. Thus enormous so-called "sterling balances" — in other words, British debts to India — were piled up. Without sufficient scrutiny or account we were being charged nearly a million pounds a day for defending India from the miseries of invasion which so many other lands endured. We finished the war, from all the worst severities of which they were spared, owing them a debt almost as large as that on which we defaulted to the United States after the previous struggle. I declared that these questions must remain open for revision, and that we reserved the right to set off against this so-called debt a counterclaim for the defence of India, and I so informed the Viceroy.

But all this is only the background upon which the glorious heroism and martial qualities of the Indian troops who fought in the Middle East, who defended Egypt, who liberated Abyssinia, who played a grand part in Italy, and who, side by side with their British comrades, expelled the Japanese from Burma, stand forth in brilliant light. The loyalty of the Indian Army to the King-Emperor, the proud fidelity to their treaties of the Indian Princes, the unsurpassed bravery of Indian soldiers and officers, both Moslem and Hindu, shine for ever in the annals of war. The British Government in India busied itself in raising an enormous Indian Army. The two great Indian political parties, the Congress and the Moslem League, were either actively hostile or gave no help. Nevertheless, upwards of two and a half million Indians *volunteered* to serve in the forces, and by 1942 an Indian Army of one million was in being, and volunteers were coming in at the monthly rate of fifty thousand. Although this policy of a swollen Indian Army was mistaken in relation to the world conflict, the response of the Indian peoples, no less than the conduct of their soldiers, makes a glorious final page in the story of our Indian Empire.

* * * * *

The atmosphere in India deteriorated in a disturbing manner with the westward advance of Japan into Asia. The

news of Pearl Harbour was a staggering blow. Our prestige
suffered with the loss of Hong Kong. The security of the
Indian sub-continent was now directly endangered. The
Japanese Navy was, it seemed, free to enter, almost unchal-
lenged, the Bay of Bengal. India was threatened for the first
time under British rule with large-scale foreign invasion by an
Asiatic Power. The stresses latent in Indian politics grew. Although only a small extremist section, led by men such as
Subhas Bose, were directly subversive and hoped for an Axis
victory, the powerful body of articulate opinion which supported Gandhi ardently believed that India should remain
passive and neutral in the world conflict. As the Japanese advanced this defeatism spread. If India, it was suggested, could
somehow throw off British connections, perhaps there would
be no motive for a Japanese invasion. The peril to India might
possibly only consist in her link with the British Empire. If
this link could be snapped surely India could adopt the position of Eire. So, not without force, the argument ran.

The attitude of the Congress Party worsened with the Japanese menace. This became very clear when, in February, 1942,
Generalissimo Chiang Kai-shek and his wife visited India. The
object of their journey was to rally Indian opinion against
Japan and to emphasise the importance for Asia as a whole,
and for India and China in particular, of Japanese defeat. The
Indian party leaders used the occasion to bring pressure upon
the British Government through the Generalissimo to yield
to the demands of Congress.

The War Cabinet could not agree to the head of a foreign
state intervening as a kind of impartial arbiter between representatives of the King-Emperor and Messrs. Gandhi and Nehru.
I therefore wrote to the Generalissimo:

12 Feb. 42

We think here in the Cabinet that your suggested visit to Mr.
Gandhi at Wardha might impede the desire we have for rallying
all India to the war effort against Japan. It might well have the
unintended effect of emphasising communal differences at a moment when unity is imperative, and I venture to hope that Your

Excellency will be so very kind as not to press the matter contrary to the wishes of the Viceroy or the King-Emperor. I look forward most hopefully to the increasing co-operation of the British, Indian, and other Imperial forces with the valiant Chinese armies, who have so long withstood the brunt of Japanese aggression.

In the event the Generalissimo deferred to my wishes, and, helped by the tact of the Viceroy, the ill-timed visit passed off without doing any harm.

*   *   *   *   *

On February 15 Singapore surrendered. Indian politics and the press echoed the rising discords between the Hindu and Moslem communities. In the hope of creating some common front, proposals had been put forward by certain of the Congress leaders for the recognition of India's sovereign status and for the formation of an all-Indian National Government. These issues were carefully considered by the Cabinet, and the usual voluminous correspondence passed between the India Office and the Viceroy. I sent him a personal telegram which expresses the view I had formed about Indian self-government, to which I was of course committed. It was felt by almost all my colleagues that an offer of Dominion status after the war must be made in the most impressive manner to the peoples of India.

Prime Minister to Viceroy of India   16 Feb. 42

My own idea was to ask the different communities of India — Hindus, Moslems, Sikhs, Untouchables, etc. — to give us their best and leading men for such a body as has been outlined. However, the electoral basis proposed, which was the best we could think of here, may have the effect of throwing the whole Council into the hands of the Congress caucus. This is far from my wish.

This conception of a Constituent Assembly for which each great community and race would pick its foremost leaders was the method I should have followed, at this time and later. It would have avoided dealing only with party politicians.

On February 25 I formed a group of Ministers to study the course of Indian affairs from day to day and advise the War Cabinet. Every member had direct personal knowledge of India gained on the spot. Mr. Attlee, who presided, and the Lord Chancellor, Lord Simon, had both been members of the "Simon" Commission in 1930. Sir Stafford Cripps was deeply versed in Indian politics and had close relations with Mr. Gandhi and Mr. Nehru. The Lord President of the Council, Sir John Anderson, had been for five years Governor of Bengal. Sir James Grigg, Secretary of State for War, had been the Finance Member of the Viceroy's Council. The Secretary of State for India, Mr. Amery, was the only member of the Conservative Party on the Committee. All the others were Labour, Liberal, or non-party. I reserved my right to attend if I thought it necessary. In practice however the views of the Committee were so much in accordance with my own convictions that I never found occasion to do so. The War Cabinet had complete confidence in the Committee, and was largely guided by its advice. We were thus well situated to take difficult decisions. Nevertheless, I also consulted the members of Cabinet rank outside the War Cabinet.

Prime Minister to Sir Edward Bridges   28 Feb. 42

The India business will be brought before the War Cabinet at noon on Tuesday. Thereafter, in consequence of the gravity of the decision, it will be necessary to consult certainly all the Ministers of Cabinet rank, and probably all the Under-Secretaries. Moreover, the King's assent must be obtained at an early date, as the rights of the Imperial Crown are plainly affected. You should bring this to the notice of the India Committee forthwith.

I am favourably impressed by the draft, but we must not run the risk of a schism, and I must see the reaction upon a larger body than our present small group.

*   *   *   *   *

The United States had shown an increasingly direct interest in Indian affairs as the Japanese advance into Asia spread westward. The concern of the Americans with the strategy of a world war was bringing them into touch with political issues on which they had strong opinions and little experience. Before Pearl Harbour, India had been regarded as a lamentable example of British imperialism, but as an exclusive British responsibility. Now that the Japanese were advancing towards its frontiers the United States Government began to express views and offer counsel on Indian affairs. In countries where there is only one race, broad and lofty views are taken of the colour question. Similarly, states which have no overseas colonies or possessions are capable of rising to moods of great elevation and detachment about the affairs of those who have.

The President had first discussed the Indian problem with me, on the usual American lines, during my visit to Washington in December, 1941. I reacted so strongly and at such length that he never raised it verbally again. Later, at the end of February, 1942, he instructed Averell Harriman to sound me on the possibilities of a settlement between the British Government and the Indian political leaders. I told Harriman that I was about to cable the President, and did so on March 4.

Former Naval Person to President Roosevelt   4 Mar. 42

We are earnestly considering whether a declaration of Dominion status after the war, carrying with it, if desired, the right to secede, should be made at this critical juncture. We must not on any account break with the Moslems, who represent a hundred million people, and the main army elements on which we must rely for the immediate fighting. We have also to consider our duty towards thirty to forty million Untouchables, and our treaties with the Princes' states of India, perhaps eighty millions. Naturally we do not want to throw India into chaos on the eve of invasion.

The Americans were familiar with the Hindu attitude. I thought it right to let them see the Moslem side of the picture. Accordingly, on the same day I sent the President full statements of the Indian position from Indian sources. Of these the following extracts give the pith. The first note was from Mr. Jinnah, President of the Moslem League.

The Sapru Conference [1] of a few individuals, with no following, and acting as exploring and patrol agents for the Congress, have put forward plausible, subtle, and consequently more treacherous proposals. If the British Government is stampeded into the trap laid for them, Moslem India would be sacrificed, with most disastrous consequences, especially in regard to the war effort. The Sapru proposals virtually transfer all power immediately to a Hindu all-Indian Government, thus practically deciding at once far-reaching constitutional issues in breach of the pledges given to the Moslems and other minorities in the British Government's Declaration of August 8, 1940, which promised no constitutional change, interim or final, without Moslem agreement, and that Moslems would not be coerced to submit to an unacceptable system of government. The Sapru proposals would introduce major changes on the basis of India's becoming a single national unit, thereby torpedoing the Moslem claim for Pakistan, which is their article of faith. Moslems entertain grave apprehensions and the situation is tense. They call upon the British Government, in the event of any major constitutional move being intended, to declare their acceptance of the Pakistan scheme if His Majesty's Government wish to have free and equal partnership of Moslems.

"Pakistan" meant a separate domain and government for the Moslems, and the consequent partition of India. This vast evolution has now at length been accomplished, but only at the cost of nearly half a million lives and the transmigration of tens of millions of people. It was impossible to carry out such changes in wartime, with invasion already looming upon the scene.

The second paper was from Sir Firoz Khan Noon, a Moslem member of the Viceroy's Executive Council. He repeated in cogent terms the objections to a Hindu solution which Mr. Jinnah had urged. He concluded:

I consider it my duty to draw His Majesty's Government's attention to the great danger which will face India if they yield to

---

[1] Proposals for an interim Government had been put forward by Sir Tej Bahadur Sapru on behalf of a body called the Non-Party Conference. The idea of two nations — Hindu and Moslem — was completely ignored by these spokesmen. They were thus immediately repudiated by the Moslem League.

browbeating by anti-British elements in India and against their former pledges. It will be a betrayal of the trust which Great Britain claims she has always held on behalf of all the peoples of India and not on behalf of Congress only. I hope His Majesty's Government will stand firmly by their duty to protect the best interests of the Indian peoples as a whole, irrespective of pressure from outside quarters which regard the British Commonwealth from a different angle.

The third note was from the Military Adviser to the Secretary of State for India, and contained the following information about the Indian Army:

The classes from which the Indian Army is drawn cannot be geographically divided by provinces. The bulk of Mohammedans come from the Northwest Frontier Province and the Punjab, but Rajputana, Central India, the United Provinces, Bihar, and Madras all contribute. Large numbers of martial class Hindus (Dogras, Jats, etc.), as well as Sikhs, come from the Punjab. Gurkhas from Nepal, which is foreign territory, are a large and separate element. Particular reactions of any one class cannot be gauged till general reception of a declaration is known, but the immediate general effect on Army can be forecast.

Indian soldiers are voluntary mercenaries [he might have said volunteers]. They fight for their pay and to support their families, also in the hope of rewards, of gratuities, pensions, and possibly grants of land, but above all, being drawn from classes with long martial traditions, they take pride in their profession, in which a leading element is personal loyalty to their British officers and general loyalty to the British Raj. Any indication of a fundamental change in the conditions or the authority under which they have accepted service, whether as affecting their material prospects or their creed as soldiers of the British Crown, cannot fail to have at once an unsettling effect.

On March 7 I again telegraphed to President Roosevelt:

Former Naval Person to President Roosevelt   7 Mar. 42

In pursuance of my plan of keeping you informed about our Indian policy, I now send you a telegram from the Governor of the Punjab. These are not, of course, the only opinions on these matters, but they are very serious when the enemy is battering at the gate and when the Punjab supplies half of all the fighting troops which can take part in the defence of India. We are still persevering to find some conciliatory and inspiring process, but I have to be careful that we do not disturb British politics at a moment when things are increasingly a-quiver.

The Governor wrote:

The following are my views on the effect on the Punjab of an immediate declaration that India will at some future date be given the right to secede from the Empire. Responsible section of Moslems, who are the majority, hold an unshakable view that until constitution for Moslem India is devised Britain must continue to hold the ropes. They will certainly be worried that a constitution on the lines contemplated would place power in the hands of Hindus, whom they already suspect of pro-Japanese tendencies. They will therefore be diverted from working for the defence of India as a whole and seek to align themselves elsewhere. Unprecedented intensification of bitterness between Sikhs and Moslems, between whom relations are already dangerously strained, will result. All communities will wish to keep their own men at home to defend their own interests, and recruitment will as a result be very seriously affected. Disorders will be inevitable, and the present reduced scale of security troops is likely to be insufficient.

* * * * *

The President also sent me at this time his private views about India.

President Roosevelt to Former Naval Person   11 Mar. 42

I have given much thought to the problem of India, and I am grateful that you have kept me in touch with it. As you can well realise, I have felt much diffidence in making any suggestions, and it is a subject which of course all of you good people know far more about than I do. I have tried to approach the problem from the point of view of history and with a hope that the injection of a new thought to be used in India might be of assistance to you. That is why I go back to the inception of the Government of the United States. During the Revolution, from 1775 to 1783, the

British Colonies set themselves up as 13 States, each one under a different form of government, although each one assumed individual sovereignty. While the war lasted there was great confusion between these separate sovereignties, and the only two connecting links were the Continental Congress (a body of ill-defined powers and large inefficiencies), and second, the Continental Army, which was rather badly maintained by the 13 States. In 1783, at the end of the war, it was clear that the new responsibilities of the 13 sovereignties could not be welded into a Federal Union because the experiment was still in the making and any effort to arrive at a final framework would have come to naught. Therefore the 13 sovereignties joined in the Articles of Confederation, an obvious stopgap Government, to remain in effect only until such time as experience and trial and error could bring about a permanent union. The 13 sovereignties, from 1783 to 1789, proved, through lack of federal power, that they would soon fly apart into separate nations. In 1787 a Constitutional Convention was held with only 20 to 25 or 30 active participants, representing all of the States.[2] They met, not as a Parliament, but as a small group of sincere patriots, with the sole objective of establishing a Federal Government. The discussion was recorded, but the meetings were not held before an audience. The present Constitution of the United States resulted, and soon received the assent of two-thirds of the States.[2]

It is merely a thought of mine to suggest the setting up of what might be called a temporary Government in India, headed by a small representative group, covering different castes, occupations, religions and geographies — this group to be recognised as a temporary Dominion Government. It would of course represent existing Governments of the British provinces, and would also represent the Council of Princes, but my principal thought is that it would be charged with setting up a body to consider a more permanent Government for the whole country — this consideration to be extended over a period of five or six years, or at least until a year after the end of the war. I suppose that this central temporary governing group, speaking for the new Dominion, would have certain executive and administrative powers over public services, such as finances, railways, telegraphs, and other things which we call public services.

[2] Actually, Rhode Island was not represented and the Constitution became effective upon the ratification of nine states.

Perhaps the analogy of some such method to the travails and problems of the United States from 1783 to 1789 might give a new slant in India itself, and it might cause the people there to forget hard feelings, to become more loyal to the British Empire, and to stress the danger of Japanese domination, together with the advantage of peaceful evolution as against chaotic revolution.

Such a move is strictly in line with the world changes of the past half-century and with the democratic processes of all who are fighting Nazism. I hope that whatever you do the move will be made from London and that there should be no criticism in India that it is being made grudgingly or by compulsion. For the love of Heaven don't bring me into this, though I do want to be of help. It is, strictly speaking, none of my business, except in so far as it is a part and parcel of the successful fight that you and I are making.

This document is of high interest because it illustrates the difficulties of comparing situations in various centuries and scenes where almost every material fact is totally different, and the dangers of trying to apply any superficial resemblances which may be noticed to the conduct of war.

*   *   *   *   *

On March 8 the Japanese Army had entered Rangoon. If the effective defence of India was to be organised it seemed to most of my colleagues important to make every effort to break the political deadlock. Indian affairs were discussed constantly by the War Cabinet. The British Government's reactions to the British-Indian Government's proposals were embodied in a draft declaration, and it was decided to send Sir Stafford Cripps to India to conduct direct discussions on the spot with the leaders of all Indian parties and communities.

Prime Minister to Viceroy of India   10 Mar. 42

I agree with you that to fling out our declaration without knowing where we are with the Indian parties would be to court what you rightly call a flop, and start an acrimonious controversy at the worst possible moment for everybody. Yesterday, before I was shown your telegram, we decided not to publish any declaration now, but to send a War Cabinet Minister out to see whether it could be put across on the spot, because otherwise what is the use of having all the trouble? Stafford Cripps, with great public spirit, volunteered for this thankless and hazardous task. He will start almost immediately. In spite of all the differences in our [respective] lines of approach, I have entire confidence in his over-riding resolve to beat Hitler and Co. at all costs. The announce-ment of his mission will still febrile agitation, and will give time for the problem to be calmly solved, or alternately proved to be, for the time being, insoluble.

2. The document on which we have agreed represents our united policy. If that is rejected by the Indian parties, for whose benefit it has been devised, our sincerity will be proved to the world, and we shall stand together and fight on it here, should that ever be necessary.

3. I hope therefore that you will await the Lord Privy Seal's arrival and go into the whole matter with him. He is of course bound by the draft declaration, which is our utmost limit. More-over, he will give full weight to the military and executive position in which India is now placed.

4. It would be impossible, owing to unfortunate rumours and publicity and the general American outlook, to stand on a purely negative attitude, and the Cripps Mission is indispensable to prove our honesty of purpose and to gain time for the necessary con-sultations.

5. My own position is that nothing matters except the successful and unflinching defence of India as a part of the general victory, and this is also the conviction of Sir Stafford Cripps.

On the following day I made a public announcement of these decisions.

*   *   *   *   *

Sir Stafford Cripps arrived in Delhi on March 22, and upon the basis of the draft declaration approved by the British Cab-inet he conducted lengthy discussions. The essence of the Brit-ish proposal was that the British Government undertook sol-emnly to grant full independence to India if demanded by a Constituent Assembly after the war. Space does not allow a detailed account of these negotiations to be recorded here. The

result cannot be better stated than in Sir Stafford Cripps'
telegrams.

Lord Privy Seal (Delhi) to Prime Minister   11 Apr. 42

I have tonight received long letter from Congress President
stating that Congress is unable to accept proposals. Rejection on
widest grounds and not solely on Defence issue, although it indicates that while Congress would agree that Commander-in-Chief
should have freedom to control conduct of the war and connected
activities as Commander-in-Chief and War Member, proposed
Formula left functions of Defence Member unduly restricted. Main
ground of rejection is however that in the view of Congress there
should be immediately a National Government, and that without
constitutional changes there should be "definite assurances in con-
ventions which would indicate that the new Government would
function as a free Government whose members would act as members of a Cabinet in a constitutional Government." Letter also
states that picture of proposed immediate arrangements is not
essentially different from old ones. "The whole object which we
have in view — that is, to create a new psychological approach to
the people to make them feel that their own national freedom had
come, that they were defending their new-won freedom — would
be completely frustrated when they saw this old picture again,
which is such that Congress cannot fit into it."

2. There is clearly no hope of agreement, and I shall start home
on Sunday.

And further on the same day:

You will have heard of refusal of Congress upon what is almost
a new point. But difficulties cannot be explained by telegram.

We have done our best under the circumstances that exist here,
and I do not think you need worry about my visit having worsened
the situation from the point of view of morale or public feeling.
In the last few days the temper has, I think, been better. My own
view is that despite failure the atmosphere has improved quite
definitely.

Nehru has come out in a fine statement for total war against
Japanese; Jinnah has pledged me unwavering support of Moslems;
and Sikhs and other minorities will be on the whole relieved, and

I hope to some extent reassured. The real difficulty has been the
internal feelings in Congress itself; hence their long discussions and
the veering of indications of their decisions.

There is a chance, if we handle the situation wisely and without
recrimination, the All-India Congress Committee on April 21 may
give an indication of a changing spirit, as it is much more representative than [the] Working Committee.

We are not depressed, though sad at the result. Now we must
get on with the job of defending India. I will tell you as to this
on my return. All good wishes. Cheerio.

In the intensity of the struggle for life from day to day, and
with four hundred million helpless people to defend from the
horrors of Japanese conquest, I was able to bear this news,
which I had thought probable from the beginning, with phil-
osophy. I knew how bitterly Stafford Cripps would feel the
failure of his Mission, and I sought to comfort him.

Prime Minister to Lord Privy Seal   11 Apr. 42

You have done everything in human power, and your tenacity,
perseverance, and resourcefulness have proved how great was the
British desire to reach a settlement. You must not feel unduly
discouraged or disappointed by the result. The effect throughout
Britain and in the United States has been wholly beneficial. The
fact that the break comes on the broadest issues and not on
tangled formulas about defence is of great advantage. I am very
glad you are coming home at once, where a most cordial welcome
awaits you. Even though your hopes have not been fulfilled, you
have rendered a very important service to the common cause, and
the foundations have been laid for the future progress of the
peoples of India.

I at once forwarded to President Roosevelt the texts of
Cripps' first telegram of April 11 and of my reply. The President was dismayed at the breakdown, and urged me to postpone
the departure of Cripps in the hope that a final effort could be
made.

President Roosevelt to Mr. Harry Hopkins (London)   12 Apr. 42

Kindly give the following message immediately to the Former

Naval Person. Every effort must be made by us to prevent a
breakdown.

I hope most earnestly that you may be able to postpone the
departure from India of Cripps until one more effort has finally
been made to prevent a breakdown of the negotiations.

[For Former Naval Person]

I regret to say that I am unable to agree with the point of view
contained in your message to me, that public opinion in the
United States believes that negotiations have broken down on
general broad issues. Here the general impression is quite the
contrary. The feeling is held almost universally that the deadlock
has been due to the British Government's unwillingness to concede the right of self-government to the Indians notwithstanding
the willingness of the Indians to entrust to the competent British
authorities technical military and naval defence control. It is impossible for American public opinion to understand why if there
is willingness on the part of the British Government to permit the
component parts of India to secede after the war from the British
Empire it is unwilling to permit them to enjoy during the war
what is tantamount to self-government.

I feel that I am compelled to place before you this issue very
frankly, and I know you will understand my reasons for doing
this. Should the current negotiations be allowed to collapse because
of the issues as presented to the people of America, and should
India subsequently be invaded successfully by Japan, with attendant serious defeats of a military or naval character for our side,
it would be hard to overestimate the prejudicial reaction on American public opinion. Would it not be possible therefore for you to
have Cripps' departure postponed on the ground that you personally transmitted instructions to him to make a final effort to find a
common ground of understanding? According to my reading, an
agreement appeared very near last Thursday night. If you could
authorise him to say that he was personally empowered by you
to resume negotiations as at that point, with the understanding
that both sides would make minor concessions, it appears to me
that an agreement might be yet found.

As I expressed to you in an earlier message, I still feel that if
the component groups in India could be given now the opportunity to set up a Nationalist Government in essence similar to our

own form of government under the Articles of Confederation, with the understanding that following the termination of a period of trial and error they would be enabled then to determine upon their own form of constitution and to determine, as you have promised them already, their future relationship with the British Empire, probably a solution could be found. If you were to make such an effort and if Cripps were still unable then to find an agreement, at least you would on that issue have public opinion in the United States satisfied that the British Government had made a fair and real offer to the Indian people, and that the responsibility for such failure must be placed clearly, not upon the British Government, but upon the Indian people.

*   *   *   *   *

I was thankful that events had already made such an act of madness impossible. The human race cannot make progress without idealism, but idealism at other people's expense and without regard to the consequences of ruin and slaughter which fall upon millions of humble homes cannot be considered as its highest or noblest form. The President's mind was back in the American War of Independence, and he thought of the Indian problem in terms of the thirteen colonies fighting George III at the end of the eighteenth century. I, on the other hand, was responsible for preserving the peace and safety of the Indian continent, sheltering nearly a fifth of the population of the globe. Our resources were slender and strained to the full. Our armies had surrendered or were recoiling before the devastating strokes of Japan. Our Navy had been driven out of the Bay of Bengal, and indeed out of most of the Indian Ocean. We had been apparently outmatched in the air. Still, there was the hope and the chance that all could be repaired and that we should not fail in our duty to preserve from hideous and violent destruction the vast, ancient Indian society over which we had presided for nearly two hundred years. Without the integrity of executive military control and the power to govern in the war area, hope and chance alike would perish. This was no time for a constitutional experiment with a "period of trial and error" to determine the "future relationship" of India to the British Empire. Nor was the issue one upon which the satisfying of public opinion in the United States could be a determining factor. We could not desert the Indian peoples by abandoning our responsibility and leaving them to anarchy or subjugation. That was at least a policy, but a policy of shame. It was our bounden duty to send all possible aid to Indian defence, and if this were so we should have betrayed not only the Indian peoples but our own soldiers by allowing their base of operations and the gallant Indian Army fighting at their side to disintegrate into a welter of chattering politics and bloody ruin.

Happily, I had all my principal colleagues who had studied the Indian problem in agreement with me. Had this not been so, I would not have hesitated to lay down my personal burden, which at times seemed more than a man could bear. The greatest comfort on such occasions is to have no doubts. Nor, as will be seen as this account proceeds, were my convictions and those of the War Cabinet without their vindication.

I sent the following reply to the President:

Former Naval Person (Chequers) to President Roosevelt

12 Apr. 42

About 3 A.M. this morning, the 12th, when, contrary to your instructions [about Hopkins' health], Harry and I were still talking, the text of your message to me about India came through. I could not decide such a matter without convening the Cabinet, which was not physically possible till Monday. Meanwhile Cripps had already left, and all the explanations have been published by both sides. In these circumstances, Harry undertook to telephone to you explaining the position, but, owing to atmospherics, he could not get through. He is going to telephone you this afternoon, and also cable you a report.

You know the weight which I attach to everything you say to me, but I did not feel I could take responsibility for the defence of India if everything had again to be thrown into the melting-pot at this critical juncture. That, I am sure, would be the view of [the] Cabinet and of Parliament. As your telegram was addressed to Former Naval Person, I am keeping it as purely private, and I do not propose to bring it before the Cabinet officially unless you tell me you wish this done. Anything like a serious difference between you and me would break my heart, and would surely deeply injure both our countries at the height of this terrible struggle.

*   *   *   *   *

On April 12 Sir Stafford Cripps left Delhi by air for England. A fortnight later the All-India Congress Committee met, and confirmed the line adopted by the Working Committee in their negotiations with the Lord Privy Seal. They confirmed that it was impossible "for Congress to consider any schemes or proposals which retain even a partial measure of British control in India. . . . Britain must abandon her hold in India."

Pandit Nehru held, as Sir Stafford Cripps had predicted, to his resolve that the Japanese must be resisted. On the morrow of the Mission's departure he said: "We are not going to surrender to the invader. In spite of all that has happened, we are not going to embarrass the British war effort in India. . . . The problem for us is how to organise our own." He was alone, or almost alone. The majority of the Congress leaders reverted to the total pacifism of Gandhi, who wrote in his newspaper on May 10: "The presence of the British in India is an invitation to Japan to invade India. Their withdrawal would remove the bait. Assume however that it does not, Free India would be better able to cope with invasion. Unadulterated non-co-operation would then have full sway."

13

Madagascar

ALTHOUGH Madagascar is separated from Ceylon by the
breadth of the Indian Ocean, the possibility of a Japanese
descent or a Vichy betrayal was a haunting fear. We had so
much on our hands and such strained resources that it was hard
to take a decision.

On February 7, 1942, when I learnt of pending discussions
between the United States and Vichy which might imply a
recognition of Vichy continuing their control of Madagascar, I
telegraphed at once to President Roosevelt.

I hope nothing will be done to give guarantees for the non-
occupation of Madagascar and Réunion. The Japanese might

222

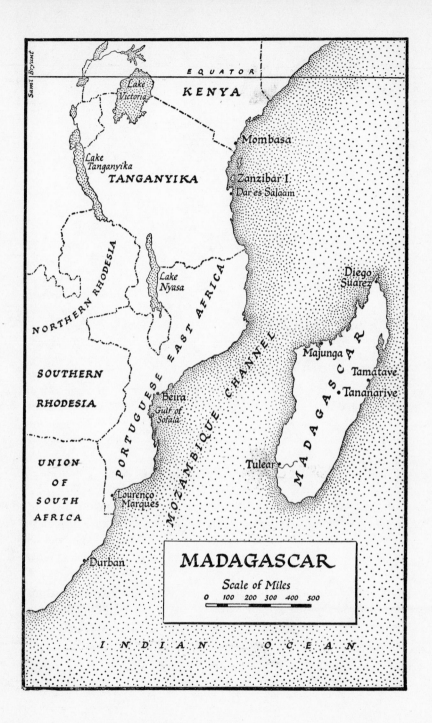

EQUATOR

KENYA

Lake Victoria

Mombasa

Lake Tanganyika

TANGANYIKA

Zanzibar I.
Dar es Salaam

NORTHERN RHODESIA

Lake Nyasa

Diego Suarez

PORTUGUESE EAST AFRICA

Majunga

MADAGASCAR

Tamatave
Tananarive

SOUTHERN

RHODESIA

Beira
Gulf of Sofala

MOZAMBIQUE CHANNEL

UNION

OF

SOUTH

AFRICA

Tulear

Lourenço Marques

Durban

MADAGASCAR

Scale of Miles

0   100   200   300   400   500

INDIAN   OCEAN

Sam'l Bryant

well turn up at the former one of these fine days, and Vichy will offer no more resistance to them there than in French Indo-China. A Japanese air, submarine, and/or cruiser base at Diego Suarez would paralyse our whole convoy route both to the Middle and to the Far East. We have therefore for some time had plans to establish ourselves at Diego Suarez by an expedition either from the Nile or from South Africa. At present action is indefinitely postponed as our hands are too full, but I do not want them tied. Of course we will let you know before any action is resolved.

I received in reply the following assurance:

You can be sure there will be no guarantees given about non-occupation of Madagascar or Réunion.

Smuts, who, like me, had been alarmed by the parleyings with Vichy about Madagascar, telegraphed on February 12 that he greatly feared "surrendering our freedom of action for a paltry trade consideration." He went on: "I look upon Madagascar as the key to the safety of the Indian Ocean, and it may play the same important part in endangering our security there that Indo-China has played in Vichy and Japanese hands. All our communications with our various war fronts and the Empire in the East may be involved."

I was able to set his mind at rest by repeating to him the telegrams I had exchanged with the President.

*   *   *   *   *

General de Gaulle had urged a Free French operation against Madagascar as early as December 16, 1941, after the entry of Japan into the war. He wrote again to me on February 19, 1942, pressing for a decision, and also submitted a plan to our Chiefs of Staff for a Free French expedition in co-operation with British air and naval support.

I had always been favourable to the idea of installing the de Gaullists in Madagascar.

Prime Minister to Foreign Secretary and C.O.S. Committee 21 Feb. 42

If there was any chance of the Free French mastering Madagascar

I should be strongly in favour of it. But what can be done to render this possible?

The Chiefs of Staff in their comments to me pointed out that if we took it ourselves the British forces necessary would be considerable, and their allotment would imperil the reinforcement of India, Ceylon, and the Indian Ocean bases.

I did not at first feel strong enough to mount the expedition, and minuted as follows:

Prime Minister to C.O.S. Committee   1 Mar. 42

I agree that Madagascar must still have a low priority.

Whatever happens, we must not have a mixed expedition. Either it must be Free French only, once they have been put ashore, or British Empire only.

I should not be in too great a hurry to reject de Gaulle's plan. Remember sixteen men took the French Cameroons.

Prime Minister to General Smuts   5 Mar. 42

We have now carefully considered General de Gaulle's proposals for the occupation of Madagascar by Free French forces. Plan is dependent on support by British naval and air forces, and we are doubtful whether the necessary Free French forces are available. We are anxious not to reject de Gaulle's plan out of hand, but we cannot afford to risk a failure, particularly in view of the present attitude of the Vichy Government.

*   *   *   *   *

In the end the threat which was developing in the Bay of Bengal, and the peril to Ceylon, resolved us to secure the control of the invaluable harbour of Diego Suarez. The rest of the enormous island was of less strategic importance, but to let the Japanese establish a submarine flotilla working from Madagascar would be a disaster. The stream of reinforcements which was flowing round the Cape to India could, it seemed, be made to do this job on their way without any great loss of time. With memories of Dakar in our mind we could not complicate the operation by admitting the Free French. The decision was taken for a purely British expedition.

Prime Minister to General Ismay, for C.O.S. Committee 12 Mar. 42

It is necessary to study Madagascar with urgent attention. For this purpose it should be assumed: (1) that Force H [the strong British squadron which guarded the Western Mediterranean] moves from Gibraltar; (2) that its place is taken by an American Task Force — I would ask the President about this tomorrow, if desired; (3) that the four thousand men and ships mentioned by the Chief of Combined Operations (Lord Mountbatten) at the same meeting should be employed; (4) that zero should be about April 30; (5) that in the event of success the Commandos should be relieved by garrison troops at the earliest moment. The Foreign Secretary has suggested that their place could be taken by Belgian troops from the Congo, which are said to be good and numerous and would readily be forthcoming. Some British or South African elements could no doubt be found. The question of allowing Free French troops to come in on strictly limited terms after the fighting is over in order to conciliate French opinion should be considered. The advantage of the Americans being stationed at Gibraltar *pro tem* is considerable in itself, and would, as First Sea Lord pointed out, probably prevent bombing reprisals for "Bonus" [1] being taken on the harbour.

All the above seems to form a harmony. Pray let me have a plan of action, or, alternatively, reasons against it. We shall need some of these Commandos in the East anyhow.

* * * * *

We were not the only people whose minds turned in this direction. There was a conference at Hitler's headquarters on the evening of this same day at which the Naval Commander-in-Chief reported to the Fuehrer as follows:

The Japanese have recognised the great strategic importance of Madagascar for naval warfare. According to reports submitted, they are planning to establish bases on Madagascar in addition to Ceylon, in order to be able to cripple sea traffic in the Indian Ocean and the Arabian Sea. From there they could likewise successfully attack shipping round the Cape. Before establishing

[1] This was the original code-word for the operation against Madagascar. It was later called "Ironclad."

these bases Japan will have to get German consent. For military reasons such consent ought to be granted. Attention is called to the fact however that this is a matter of great political significance, since it touches on the basic question of France's relation to the Tripartite Powers on the one hand and the Anglo-Saxon on the other. Such action on the part of the Japanese may have repercussions in the French homeland and the African colonies, as well as in Portuguese East Africa.

Hitler said that he did not think France would give her consent to a Japanese occupation of Madagascar.

*   *   *   *   *

So extensive were the naval movements involved and so hard was the menace of the *Tirpitz* in home waters that I had to invoke the aid of President Roosevelt in giving us a temporary reinforcement in the Atlantic. I could of course form no opinion as to how this would fit in with his own problems, but I knew he would do his utmost to help.

Former Naval Person to President Roosevelt   14 Mar. 42

We have decided to do "Bonus," and as it is quite impossible to weaken our Eastern Fleet we shall have to use the whole of Force H, now at Gibraltar. This will leave the western exit of the Mediterranean uncovered, which is most undesirable. Would it be possible for you to send, say, two battleships, an aircraft-carrier, some cruisers and destroyers from the Atlantic to take the place of Force H temporarily? Force H would have to leave Gibraltar not later than March 30, and could hardly reach Gibraltar again before the end of June. We have not planned any operation for Force H inside the Mediterranean between April 1 and the end of June. It is most unlikely that French retaliation, if any, for "Bonus" would take the form of attacking United States ships by air. Moral effect of United States ships at Gibraltar would in itself be highly beneficial on both sides of the Straits. Operation "Bonus" cannot go forward unless you are able to do this. On the other hand, there are the greatest dangers in leaving "Bonus" to become a Japanese base. We are not telling anyone about our plans, and assaulting troops mingle quite easily with our March convoy to the East. . . .

The President made a satisfactory response, though in a different form from that which the Admiralty had led me to suggest. He preferred to send his latest battleship and several other important vessels to join our Home Fleet, rather than base an American squadron upon Gibraltar.

*   *   *   *   *

In my mind there lurked the fear that even if there were no leakage of our plans the general aspect of affairs might lead to a Vichy reinforcement of Madagascar from Dakar, where leaders and forces extremely hostile to us were gathered. I therefore asked for extreme vigilance about any convoys or shipping which might pass from Dakar to the island, towards which our forces were already about to start. The naval preparations for their interception at the Cape naturally came to General Smuts' notice, and he was perplexed by them. I therefore telegraphed to him:

24 Mar. 42

We have decided to storm and occupy Diego Suarez, as arrival of Japanese there would not be effectively resisted by the Vichy French and would be disastrous to the safety of our Middle East convoys and most menacing to South Africa. Operation is, we believe, on a sufficiently large scale to be successful. Assaulting force leaves tonight, intermingled with a convoy of 50,000 men for the East.

2. Special naval escort requires movement of Gibraltar Squadron and various aircraft-carriers and tank landing-craft, all of which has been arranged. In order to facilitate this, President Roosevelt is sending his latest battleship and several other important vessels to strengthen our Home Fleet, from which Gibraltar replacements will be made.

3. We cannot allow the island in question to be reinforced by French troops from Dakar. There has been no leakage of our plans, but the strategic significance of this island harbour is obvious, and of course no one can prevent German-Vichy suggestions or British newspaper surmises. None the less, if we stop this Dakar crowd we can get there first, and an enormous advantage will be gained if the operation is successful.

4. Although our plans have been studied for many weeks, we could not take decision till President Roosevelt had given us the naval replacements we needed. This was only settled late last week, and I have been seeking an hour in which to tell you about it all. Naturally, I do not go into technical details myself, but I know that great pains have been taken, and confidence is felt by the Chiefs of Staff that the powerful forces employed will make good work of the local garrison. We have carefully considered all the reactions with Vichy. I do not think they will be so much upset as they were about the bombing of the Paris workshops, which, after all, they swallowed.

5. I must beg you therefore to favour this enterprise and facilitate our indispensable arrest of the French ships, should it be necessary to catch them at the Cape. Every possible consideration will be used, but of course they cannot go to the island in question on any account.

6. I am having a very rough time now, but look how much better things are than a year ago, when we were alone. We must not lose our faculty to dare, especially in dark days.

Smuts replied at once:

General Smuts to Prime Minister   24 Mar. 42
Your message alters whole situation. From previous correspondence I had concluded that Madagascar operation had been postponed till Ceylon situation had been stabilised. In that case, interception of Vichy convoy now might have precipitated a crisis with [the] French prematurely, with added risk of misunderstanding with America. Both these risks now disappear, and I shall give all necessary support for interception of convoy.

Your courageous attitude has my complete sympathy. I am confident you will pull through all these troubles.

Smuts was enthusiastic for the project, but immediately began to nourish plans for the occupation of the whole of the island and to gather South African forces to aid us in this indefinite extension of our plan. It must be remembered however that the capture of a naval base in Madagascar, or indeed of the whole island, however necessary in itself, was but an incidental by-product of our main policy, namely, to reinforce

India for what might well seem an impending Japanese invasion.

Prime Minister to General Ismay, for C.O.S. Committee 2 Apr. 42

Operation "Ironclad" [Madagascar, formerly called "Bonus"]. How do our plans stand for leaflets and propaganda on the Vichy garrison? It is reported that, while the French Navy is anti-British, their troops are rather anti-Vichy. We must not neglect this side. I have telegraphed to President Roosevelt, asking whether we may say it is an Anglo-American enterprise. Anyhow, we ought to let the garrison know that we shall take the place only to keep out the Japanese, and [shall] restore it to France after the Axis is defeated. Have the leaflets been written? Let me see them, if so. If not, there is still time to have them printed through General Smuts at Capetown. Let them therefore be drafted. I should be quite prepared, unless we have an absolute veto from the President, to say that the island is under the joint guarantee of Great Britain and the United States until France is liberated. The Foreign Office should be consulted.

2. Would it not be possible, while the landing operation is taking place at the back, for a launch with a white flag to steam into the harbour and offer the most tempting terms for capitulation in the face of overwhelming force? All this must be carefully studied.

Prime Minister to President Roosevelt 27 Mar. 42

We value your contacts with Vichy, and it is well worth paying a certain price for them, but please:

Nothing must interfere with Operation "Ironclad," to which we are now committed, and no assurances offered by the French about defending their Empire like they did Indo-China should be accepted by the United States in such a way as to enable them to complain of a breach of faith.

Our operation has been carefully planned. It comprises two strong and well-trained brigades, with a third in case of a check, together with tank landing-craft and two carriers, as well as a battleship and cruisers. All these are additional to our Eastern Fleet, which is now growing in size and balance. It would be a great help if we could give the impression, by dropping leaflets at the moment of attack, that the expedition was Anglo-American. Please consider whether you can let us do this or anything like it.

The President was disinclined to accept my suggestion about dropping American leaflets, because he wished to preserve his relations with Vichy for greater objects.

President Roosevelt to Prime Minister   3 Apr. 42

I feel that it would be unwise to identify the expedition in the manner indicated by your telegram. My reason for this is that we are the only nation that can intervene diplomatically with any hope of success with Vichy, and it seems to me extremely important that we are able to do this without the complications which might arise by the dropping of leaflets or other informal methods in connection with your operation. I do hope that you will agree with this.

I was convinced.

*   *   *   *   *

By April 22 the whole expedition was assembled at Durban, and now included the battleship *Ramillies,* detached from Admiral Somerville's fleet, the carrier *Illustrious,* two cruisers, and eleven destroyers, besides minesweepers, corvettes, and about fifteen assault ships and transports carrying the Army. In addition, the carrier *Indomitable* was to join later in place of the sunken *Hermes.* Strenuous days followed. Cargoes in many of the ships had to be restowed to meet assault conditions, final details of the plan had to be perfected, orders distributed, the troops exercised after the long sea voyage and rehearsed in their specific and for the most part unaccustomed tasks. This was our first large-scale amphibious assault since the Dardanelles twenty-seven years before, and the whole technique of such events had meantime been completely revolutionised. The commanders and staffs of both Services as well as the troops lacked experience in fighting this most difficult type of battle.

I was especially anxious not to be drawn too deeply into the Madagascar jungles, once the main naval harbour had been captured.

Prime Minister to General Ismay, for C.O.S. Committee 30 Apr. 42

Too much stress should not be laid on "gaining control of the whole island." It is nine hundred miles long, and all that really matters are the two or three principal centres, and above all Diego Suarez. We are not setting out to subjugate Madagascar, but rather to establish ourselves in key positions to deny it to a far-flung Japanese attack. A principal object must be to get our good troops forward to India and Ceylon at the earliest moment, replacing them with garrison battalions from East or West Africa. Getting this place is meant to be a help and not a new burden. The true defence of Madagascar will be the Eastern Fleet, when based with adequate air on Colombo and Port T.[the atoll]. I should be glad to have this point of view recognised. . . . Portsmouth could be held with the enemy in Caithness, and so Diego Suarez with hostile forces still in Antananarivo and Tamatave.

I also took pains to reassure General Wavell, who lay under the threat of a Japanese invasion of India, and who asked for more information upon the general position.

Prime Minister to General Wavell   5 May 42

Madagascar is of high importance to India, because if Japanese by-pass Ceylon and establish themselves there with French connivance as they did in Indo-China, the whole of our communications with you and the Middle East would be imperilled, if not cut. There is of course the danger of our getting hung up there and of the place becoming a burden and not a help. We hope to have minimised this risk by the use of strong forces and severe, violent action. As soon as Diego Suarez is taken everything will be pushed on to you as fast as possible. We hope to garrison Madagascar with two African brigades and one from the Belgian Congo or West Coast. The two African brigades are already under orders, and the first begins movement on June 1. They may just as well be in Madagascar as in Africa. The 5th Division moves on at once independently. . . .

I agree with you that the months of May and June must be most anxious for us in the East, but I have every hope you will get the 5th Division in May and the 2d Division in June. These at any rate are our resolves, subject to the incalculable hazards of war.

I also explained the position to General Auchinleck.

Prime Minister to General Auchinleck   5 May 42

The next two months are no doubt very dangerous in the Indian

and Pacific Oceans, as no one can predict with certainty what the
next Japanese move will be. The Australians naturally think they
are going to be invaded in great force. It certainly looks as if the
Japanese would menace or attack Port Moresby and Darwin, with
a view no doubt, *inter alia,* of making us lock up as many troops
as possible in Australia. Most significant movement is however
three Japanese divisions from the remaining ten in Japan being
sent to reinforce the twenty on the Russian-Manchurian front. It
would clearly be in Japanese interests to finish off China, and the
strong thrusts they are making northward would seem to favour
that idea.

One thing is certain — they cannot do everything at once.
They did not like what they got at Colombo and Trincomalee,
and all their carriers went back to Japan or Formosa to make good
heavy losses in aircraft. If they were going to invade Ceylon
and/or India in strength, it is odd they did not do it as early as
possible after the fall of Java, or at any rate when they made their
strong naval and air raid into the Indian Ocean in early April. We
know of no special grounds for assuming that a heavy invasion
of India is at this moment imminent or certain. . . .

We hope today to occupy Diego Suarez, for which strong
forces have been assembled. . . . The 8th British Armoured Division
rounds the Cape early in July, and will be available to go either
to India or the Middle East or to Australia, if that country were
invaded in force. . . .

We are grateful to you for your offer to denude the Middle East
further for the sake of the Indian danger, but we feel that the
greatest help you could give to the whole war at this juncture
would be to engage and defeat the enemy on your western front.
All our directions upon this subject remain unaltered in their purpose and validity, and we trust you will find it possible to give full
effect to them about the date which you mentioned to the Lord
Privy Seal.

*   *   *   *   *

The fast convoy with the assault troops had left Durban on
April 28. The slower ships carrying the army transport and
stores had already gone ahead. Admiral Syfret and General
Sturges were together in the *Ramillies,* and on May 4 the whole
expedition was within striking distance. Diego Suarez Bay cuts

so deeply into the northeast coast of Madagascar as almost to
sever the land lying to the northward from the rest of the
island.[2] The defended port of Antsirane opposite to the town
controlled the entrance. The approach from the eastward was
known to be strongly guarded, but to the west of the isthmus
are several bays which, though difficult of access, are capable
of accommodating large ships. Here the defences were not
strong; surprise might be achieved by a night approach, and
once ashore, the army would be no more than eighteen miles
from Antsirane. Courrier Bay, on the west coast, had therefore
been chosen as the initial point of attack. The transports had
to be guided in the dark through tortuous and shallow channels, which might well be mined, towards an unknown and
hostile coast. The first troops landed without loss at 4.30 A.M.
on the 5th, and quickly overran the only battery which could
fire to seaward. Half an hour later, aircraft of the Fleet Air Arm
attacked the airfields and shipping in Diego Suarez Bay. A
feint attack from the eastward was carried out by the cruiser
Hermione. The Vichy French, though completely surprised,
resisted. By the afternoon however the whole of the 29th Brigade and nearly all its equipment had been landed and was
moving forward, the Commando had reached the eastern end
of the Andraka peninsula, and the disembarkation of the 17th
Brigade was beginning.

The leading units of the 29th Brigade, supported by two
guns and a dozen tanks, after overcoming opposition on two
enemy delaying positions, were brought to a stop at the enemy
main position astride the road two miles south of Antsirane.
This was strongly defended, and well prepared with concrete
block-houses. At dawn on the 6th the 2d South Lancashire
penetrated the enemy left and established themselves behind
their front, where they created havoc all day. Before the news
of this success arrived, General Sturges asked Admiral Syfret to
land a party of Marines in the port of Antsirane itself. This
was a daring stroke. Fifty Royal Marines from the *Ramillies*
started in the destroyer *Anthony,* which, handled with great

2 See map, page 178.

skill, ran the entrance of the harbour at nightfall and succeeded in landing the Marines at the quay in the town. The
destroyer then escaped under heavy fire. Captain Price and his
fifty men groped their way into the town. They soon found
and captured what proved to be the naval depot, where they
found large supplies of rifles and machine-guns and about fifty
British prisoners. This was a brilliant diversion. Meanwhile
the 29th Brigade, now reinforced by the 17th Brigade, gained
complete success. Before daybreak on the 7th the enemy commanders had surrendered Antsirane, and the town and most of
its defences were in our possession. The forts covering the
harbour entrance remained to be dealt with, but after a brief
bombardment in the morning by the *Ramillies* these too surrendered. By 11 A.M. all fighting had ceased, and that afternoon
the British fleet entered the harbour. The total army casualties
were under 400.

Prime Minister to Admiral Syfret and General Sturges   9 May 42

I congratulate you cordially upon the swift and resolute way in
which your difficult and hazardous operation was carried through.
Pray give all ranks my best wishes and tell them that their exploit
has been of real assistance to Britain and the United Nations.

Add for 29th Brigade only: I was sure when I saw you at Inverary
nine months ago that the 29th Brigade Group would make its
mark.

* * * * *

To Admiral Syfret, who had been my Naval Secretary at the
Admiralty and was a personal friend, I sent a full explanation
of our policy.

Prime Minister to Admiral Syfret   15 May 42

I want you to see clearly our picture of the Madagascar operation. It must be a help and not a hindrance. It must be a security
and not a burden. We cannot lock up active field army troops
there for any length of time. The 13th and 17th Brigades must go
on to India almost immediately. If you could take Tamatave and
Majunga in the next few days they could help you in this, but
they have got to go on anyhow.

Since "Ironclad" was conceived and executed, the Indian Ocean situation has changed to our advantage. Time has passed. The Japanese have not yet pressed their attack upon Ceylon or India. On the contrary, these dangers look less near and likely than before. . . . One can hardly imagine the Japanese trying to take Diego Suarez with less than ten thousand men in transports, with battleships and carrier escort, involving a very large part of their limited fleet. They have to count every ship even more carefully than we do. Therefore your problem is one of holding the place with the least subtraction from our limited resources.

It may be that you will think it better to let matters simmer down and make some sort of *modus vivendi* with the French authorities. Money and trade facilities should be used.

The way you can help the war best is to get the 13th and 17th Brigades on to India at earliest, and the 29th Brigade within the next two months. Everything else is subordinate to this, except of course holding Diego Suarez, which must on no account be hazarded.

Admiral Syfret replied at once.

15 May 42

The general picture you have given is greatly helping us. . . . So far as our occupation of Diego Suarez is concerned, I think [the] French will adopt [a] policy of live and let live. But we shall never get any closer relations or extend our control unless we occupy Tamatave and Majunga. . . . I do not think this will ever be achieved except by force.

I replied that operations for the capture of Tamatave and Majunga should be abandoned for the present, and that Diego Suarez should be made secure with the minimum forces. General Smuts however still pressed for further operations, and used cogent arguments.

General Smuts to Prime Minister   28 May 42

Tamatave and Majunga, as well as other ports, have been regularly used by French submarines, and can be so used by Japanese. Madagascar authorities are violently hostile, though not the population. After capture of Diego no material resistance likely at present, but if time is given to organise resistance we may have a stiff job. Control of Madagascar is all-important for our lines of communication in [the] Indian Ocean and no risk can be run.

The Foreign Office also were anxious to go forward. But I had always Wavell's needs and the threatened Japanese invasion of India to consider.

*   *   *   *   *

So far all had gone like clockwork, but now a most disconcerting incident occurred. On May 29 an unknown aircraft appeared over the harbour and then made off. Extreme vigilance was ordered, as it seemed this might be the prelude to air or submarine attack. The following evening the *Ramillies* and a tanker nearby were struck by torpedoes. Where had they come from? What did they portend?

General Smuts to Prime Minister   1 June 42

Sincere condolences on Diego mishap. Attack must have been made by Vichy submarine or by Japanese submarine on Vichy information and advice. It all points to necessity of eliminating Vichy control completely from whole island as soon as possible. Appeasement is as dangerous in this case as it has proved in all others, and I trust we shall soon make a clean job of this whole business. My South Africa brigade group stands ready and simply awaits transport. All good wishes.

*   *   *   *   *

It is necessary to conclude the Madagascar story. After the capture of Diego Suarez an interval was allowed to the French Governor-General to amend his pro-Vichy attitude. The west coast ports were needed for the control of the Mozambique channel, where our main eastern convoys were molested by the U-boats. The Governor-General remained obdurate. Further operations therefore had to take place under the orders of General Platt, who commanded in East Africa. On September 10 the 29th British Infantry Brigade captured Majunga with little opposition. Next to land was the 22d East African Brigade, which, passing through the 29th, headed down the road for Tananarive, the capital and seat of government. Simultaneously small columns of South African troops worked their way southward along the coastal roads. The 29th Brigade was re-embarked and carried round to Tamatave, on the east coast, which they took almost unopposed on September 18, and then moved on Tananarive. The capital fell on September 23.

Our troops were welcomed by the inhabitants, but the Governor-General and some of his staff had retreated southward with his troops. He was pursued, and a very successful action on October 19 brought in seven hundred and fifty prisoners at the cost of no casualties to ourselves. This was final. On November 5 the Governor-General accepted our surrender terms. The government of the island was left in French hands. But as a result of these operations, and at the cost of little more than a hundred casualties, we had gained full military control over an island of high strategic importance to the safety of our communications with the Near and Far East. The Madagascar episode was in its secrecy of planning and precision of tactical execution a model for amphibious descents. The news arrived at a time when we sorely needed success. It was in fact for long months the only sign of good and efficient war direction of which the British public were conscious.

14

American Naval Victories*

The Coral Sea and Midway Island

Period of Japanese Triumph — Their New Forward Policy of Expansion — Admiral Nimitz's Concentration in the Coral Sea — Japanese Landing at Tulagi — The First Clash, May 7 — Admiral Fletcher's Action on May 8 — The Air Grapple — American Success — The First Air Carrier Battle in Naval History — Fate of the "Lexington" — Admiral Yamamoto's Plan — The Main Strength of the Japanese Navy Applied — Heavy Odds Against the United States — Their Preparations at Pearl Harbour — The Battle Begins, June 4 — Stroke and Counter Stroke — Brilliant Tactics of Admirals Fletcher and Spruance — Extraordinary Hazards on Both Sides — Destruction of the Four Japanese Carriers — The Turning-Point of the War in the Pacific — Yamamoto's Retreat — United States' Pursuit — A Splendid American Victory — Qualities of the Japanese Naval High Command — Triumph of American Courage and Devotion.

S TIRRING EVENTS affecting the whole course of the war now occurred in the Pacific Ocean. By the end of March the first phase of the Japanese war plan had achieved a success so complete that it surprised even its authors. Japan was master of Hong Kong, Siam, Malaya, and nearly the whole of the immense island region forming the Dutch East Indies. Japanese troops were plunging deeply into Burma. In the Philippines the Americans still fought on at Corregidor, but without hope of relief.

Japanese exultation was at its zenith. Pride in their martial triumphs and confidence in their leadership was strengthened

* See S. E. Morison, *Coral Sea, Midway and Submarine Actions.*

by the growing belief that the Western Powers had not the will to fight to the death. Already the Imperial armies stood on the frontiers, so carefully chosen in their pre-war plans as the prudent limit of their advance. Within this enormous area, comprising measureless resources and riches, they could consolidate their conquests and develop their newly won power. Their long-prepared scheme had prescribed a pause at this stage to draw breath, to resist an American counter-attack or to organise a farther advance. But now in the flush of victory it seemed to the Japanese leaders that the heaven-sent fulfilment of their destiny had come. They must not be unworthy of it. These ideas arose not only from the natural temptations to which dazzling success exposes mortals, but from serious military reasoning. Whether it was wiser to organise their new perimeter thoroughly or by surging forward to gain greater depth for its defence seemed to them a balanced strategic problem.

After deliberation in Tokyo the more ambitious course was adopted. It was decided to extend the grasp outwards to include the western Aleutians, Midway Island, Samoa, Fiji, New Caledonia, and Port Moresby in Southern New Guinea.[1] This expansion would threaten Pearl Harbour, still the main American base. It would also, if maintained, sever direct communication between the United States and Australia. It would provide Japan with suitable bases from which to launch further attacks.

The Japanese High Command had shown the utmost skill and daring in making and executing their plans. They started however upon a foundation which did not measure world forces in true proportion. They never comprehended the vast latent power of the United States. They thought still, at this stage, that Hitler's Germany would triumph in Europe. They felt in their veins the surge of leading Asia forward to measureless conquests and their own glory. Thus they were led into a gamble, which even if it had won would only have lengthened their predominance by perhaps a year, and, as they lost, cut it down by an equal period. In the actual result they exchanged a fairly strong and gripped advantage for a wide and loose

[1] See map of Pacific Theatre, page 240.

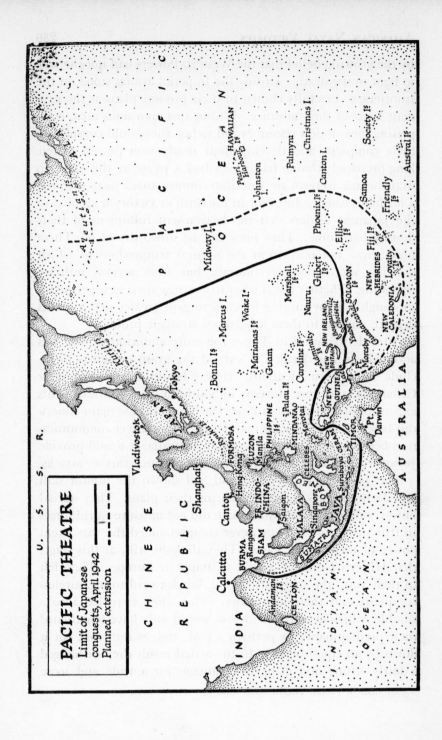

PACIFIC THEATRE

Limit of Japanese
conquests, April 1942 _____
Planned extension ------

domain, which was beyond their power to hold; and, being beaten in this outer area, they found themselves without the forces to make a coherent defence of their inner and vital zone.

Nevertheless at this moment in the world struggle no one could be sure that Germany would not break Russia, or drive her beyond the Urals, and then be able to come back and invade Britain; or as an alternative spread through the Caucasus and Persia to join hands with the Japanese vanguards in India. To put things right for the Grand Alliance there was needed a decisive naval victory by the United States, carrying with it the predominance in the Pacific, even if the full command of that ocean were not immediately established. This victory was not denied us. I had always, as has been shown, believed that the command of the Pacific would be regained by the American Navy, with any help we could give from or in the Atlantic, by May. Such hopes were based only upon a computation of American and British new construction, now maturing, of battleships, aircraft-carriers, and other vessels. We may now describe in a necessarily compressed form the brilliant and astonishing naval battles which asserted this majestic fact in an indisputable form.

* * * * *

At the end of April, 1942, the Japanese High Command began their new policy of expansion. This was to include the capture of Port Moresby and the seizure of Tulagi, in the southern Solomons, opposite the large island of Guadalcanal. The occupation of Port Moresby would complete the first stage of their domination of New Guinea and give added security to their advanced naval base at Rabaul, in New Britain. From New Guinea and from the Solomons they could begin the envelopment of Australia.

American Intelligence quickly became aware of a Japanese concentration in these waters. Forces were observed to be assembling at Rabaul from their main naval base at Truk, in the Caroline Islands, and a southward drive was clearly imminent. It was even possible to forecast May 3 as the date

when operations would begin. The American aircraft-carriers were at this time widely dispersed on various missions. These included the launching of General Doolittle's bold and spectacular air attack against Tokyo itself on April 18. This event, occurring at a crucial moment, had indeed been a factor in determining the new Japanese policy.

Conscious of the threat in the south, Admiral Nimitz at once began to assemble the strongest possible force in the Coral Sea. Rear-Admiral Fletcher was already there, with the carrier *Yorktown* and three heavy cruisers. On May 1 he was joined by the carrier *Lexington* and two more cruisers from Pearl Harbour under Rear-Admiral Fitch, and three days later by a squadron commanded by a British officer, Rear-Admiral Crace, which comprised the Australian cruisers *Australia* and *Hobart* and the American cruiser *Chicago*. The only other carriers immediately available, the *Enterprise* and *Hornet,* had been engaged in the Tokyo raid, and though they were sent south as rapidly as possible they could not join Admiral Fletcher until the middle of May. Before then the impending battle had been fought.

On May 3, while refuelling at sea about four hundred miles south of Guadalcanal, Admiral Fletcher learned that the enemy had landed at Tulagi, apparently with the immediate object of establishing there a seaplane base from which to observe the eastern approaches to the Coral Sea. In view of the obvious threat to this outpost the small Australian garrison had been withdrawn two days previously. Fletcher at once set off to attack the island with only his own task group; Fitch's group were still fuelling. Early on the following morning aircraft from the *Yorktown* struck at Tulagi in strength. The enemy covering forces had however withdrawn and only a few destroyers and small craft remained. The results were therefore disappointing.

The next two days passed without important incident, but it was evident that a major clash could not be long delayed. Fletcher's three groups, having refuelled, were now all in company, standing to the northwestward towards New Guinea. He knew that the Port Moresby invasion force had left Rabaul, and would probably pass through the Jomard Passage, in the Louisiade Archipelago, on either the 7th or 8th. He knew also that three enemy carriers were in the neighbourhood, but not their positions. The Japanese striking force, of the carriers *Zuikaku* and *Shokaku,* with two heavy cruisers in support, had come south from Truk, keeping to the eastward of the Solomons, well out of range of air reconnaissance, and had entered the Coral Sea from the east on the evening of the 5th. On the 6th they were fast closing in on Fletcher, and at one time in the evening were only seventy miles away, but neither side was aware of the presence of the other. During the night the forces drew apart, and on the morning of the 7th, Fletcher reached his chosen position south of the Louisiades, whence he intended to strike at the invasion force.[2] He now detached Crace's group to go on ahead and cover the southern exit from the Jomard Passage, where the enemy might be expected that day. Crace

2 See map of the Solomons — New Guinea.

was soon spotted, and in the afternoon was heavily attacked by successive waves of shore-based torpedo bombers, comparable in strength with those which had sunk the *Prince of Wales* and *Repulse*. By skilful handling and good fortune not a ship was hit, and he continued towards Port Moresby, until, hearing that the enemy had turned back, he withdrew to the southward.

Meanwhile the enemy carriers, of which Admiral Fletcher still had no precise news, remained his chief concern. At dawn he commenced a wide search, and at 8.15 A.M. he was rewarded by a report of two carriers and four cruisers north of the Louisiades. In fact the enemy sighted was not the carrier striking force, but the weak escort group covering the invasion transports, which included the light carrier *Shoho*. However, Fletcher struck with all his strength, and three hours later the *Shoho* was overwhelmed and sunk. This event deprived the invasion force of its air cover, and made it turn back. Thus the transports intended for Port Moresby never entered the Jomard Passage, and remained north of the Louisiades until finally ordered to withdraw.

*   *   *   *   *

Fletcher's whereabouts were now disclosed to the enemy and he was in a serious plight. An enemy attack must be expected at any time, and his own striking forces would not be rearmed and ready for further action until the afternoon. Luckily for him the weather was thick and getting worse and the enemy had no radar. The Japanese carrier force was in fact well within striking distance to the eastward. They launched an attack during the afternoon, but in the squally, murky weather the planes missed their target. Returning empty-handed to their carriers, they passed close to Fletcher's force, and were detected on the radar screen. Fighters were sent out to intercept, and in a confused *mêlée* in the gathering darkness many Japanese planes were destroyed. Few of the twenty-seven bombers which had set out regained their ships to take part in the battle next day.

Both sides, knowing how close they were together, contemplated making a night attack with surface forces. Both

judged it too risky. During the night they once more drew
apart, and on the morning of the 8th the luck of the weather
was reversed. It was now the Japanese who had the shelter of
low cloud, while Fletcher's ships were bathed in brilliant sunshine. The game of hide-and-seek began again. At 8.38 a
search plane from the *Lexington* at last located the enemy, and
about the same time an intercepted signal made it plain that
the enemy had also sighted the American carriers. A full-scale
battle between two equal and well-balanced forces was at hand.

Before 9 A.M. an American striking force of eighty-two aircraft was being launched, and by 9.25 all were on their way.
About the same time the enemy were launching a similar strike
of sixty-nine. The American attack developed about 11 A.M.,
the Japanese some twenty minutes later. By 11.40 all was over.
The American aircraft had trouble with low cloud round the
target. When they found it, one of the enemy carriers headed
for the cover of a rain-squall and the whole of the attack was
thrown against the other, the *Shokaku*. Three bomb hits were
scored and the ship was set on fire, but the damage was overestimated. Although put out of action for the time being, the
Shokaku was able to reach home for repair. The *Zuikaku*
remained unscathed.

Meanwhile in clear weather the Japanese attack went in
against the *Yorktown* and *Lexington*. By most skilful manoeuvring the *Yorktown* evaded nearly all attacks, but suffered
many near misses. One bomb hit caused severe casualties and
started a fire. This was soon mastered and the ship's fighting
efficiency was little impaired. The less handy *Lexington* was
not so fortunate, taking two torpedo hits and two or three
bombs. The end of the action found her heavily on fire and
listing to port, with three boiler rooms flooded. By gallant exertions the fires were brought under control, the list was corrected, and the ship was soon making twenty-five knots. The
aircraft losses of both sides in this fierce encounter, the first in
history between carriers, were assessed after the war: American,
33; Japanese, 43.

*   *   *   *   *

If events in the Coral Sea had ended here the balance would clearly have been in the Americans' favour. They had sunk the light carrier *Shoho*, severely damaged the *Shokaku*, and turned back the invasion force intended for Port Moresby. Their own two carriers seemed to be in fair shape, and their only loss up to this point was a fleet tanker, and her attendant destroyer, which had been sunk the day before by the Japanese carriers. But a disaster now overtook them. An hour after the battle ended, the *Lexington* was heavily shaken by an internal explosion. Fires broke out below which spread and became uncontrollable. Valiant efforts to save the ship proved of no avail, and that evening she was abandoned without further loss of life and sunk by an American torpedo. Both sides now withdrew from the Coral Sea, and both claimed the victory. The Japanese propaganda, in strident terms, declared that not only both Admiral Fletcher's carriers, but also a battleship and a heavy cruiser, had been sunk. Their own actions after the battle were inconsistent with this belief. They postponed until July their advance towards Port Moresby, although the way was now open to them. By then the whole scene had changed, and the stroke was abandoned in favour of an overland advance from the bases they had already gained in New Guinea. These days marked the limit of the Japanese drive by sea towards Australia.

On the American side the conservation of their carrier forces was the prime necessity. Admiral Nimitz was well aware that greater events were looming farther north, which would need everything he had. He was content to have arrested for the time being the Japanese move into the Coral Sea, and instantly recalled to Pearl Harbour all his carriers, including the *Enterprise* and *Hornet*, then hastening to join Fletcher. Wisely, too, the loss of the *Lexington* was concealed until after the Midway Island battle, as the Japanese were obviously uncertain about the true state of affairs and were groping for information.

This encounter had an effect out of proportion to its tactical importance. Strategically, it was a welcome American victory, the first against Japan. Nothing like it had ever been seen before. It was the first battle at sea in which surface ships never exchanged a shot. It also carried the chances and hazards of war to a new pitch. The news blazed round the world with tonic effect, bringing immense relief and encouragement to Australia and New Zealand as well as to the United States. The tactical lessons learned here at heavy cost were soon applied with outstanding success in the Battle of Midway Island, the opening moves of which were now about to begin.

* * * * *

The advance into the Coral Sea was only the opening phase in the new Japanese policy of expansion. Even while it was in progress Yamamoto, the Japanese Admiralissimo, was preparing to challenge American power in the Central Pacific by seizing Midway Island, with its airfield, from which Pearl Harbour itself, another thousand miles to the east, could be threatened and perhaps dominated. At the same time a diversionary force was to seize points of vantage in the western Aleutians. By careful timing of his movements, Yamamoto hoped first to draw the American fleet north to counter the threat to the Aleutians and leave him free to throw his main strength against Midway Island.[3] By the time the Americans could intervene here in force, he hoped to have possession of the island and to be ready to meet the counter-attack with overwhelming force. The importance to the United States of Midway, the outpost of Pearl Harbour, was such that these movements must inevitably bring about a major clash. Yamamoto felt confident that he could force a decisive battle on his own terms, and that with his great superiority, particularly in fast battleships, he would stand an excellent chance of annihilating his enemy. That was the broad plan which he imparted to his subordinate, Admiral Nagumo. All depended however on Admiral Nimitz falling into the trap, and equally on his having no counter-surprise of his own.

But the American Commander was vigilant and active. His

3 See map of Pacific Theatre, page 240.

Intelligence kept him well informed, even as to the date when the expected blow was to fall. Although he could not be quite sure whether the plan against Midway was a blind to conceal a real stroke against the Aleutian chain of islands, which might herald an advance towards the American continent, Midway was incomparably the more likely and greater danger, and he never hesitated to deploy his strength in that direction. His chief anxiety was his paucity of carriers, which at best must needs be inferior to Nagumo's experienced four, which had fought with outstanding success from Pearl Harbour to Ceylon. Two others of this group had been diverted to the Coral Sea, and one of them had been damaged; but Nimitz, on the other hand, had lost the *Lexington,* the *Yorktown* was crippled, the *Saratoga* had not yet rejoined him after making good battle damage, and the *Wasp* was still near the Mediterranean, where she had succoured Malta. Only the *Enterprise* and *Hornet,* hurrying back from the South Pacific, and the *Yorktown* if she could be repaired in time, could be made ready for the coming battle. Admiral Nimitz had no battleships nearer than San Francisco, and these were too slow to work with carriers; Yamamoto had eleven, three of them among the strongest and fastest in the world. The odds against the Americans were heavy, but Nimitz could now count on powerful shore-based air support from Midway Island itself.

*   *   *   *   *

During the last week of May the main strength of the Japanese Navy began to move from their bases. The first to go was the Aleutian diversionary force, which was to attack Dutch Harbour on June 3 and draw the American fleet in that direction. Thereafter landing forces were to seize the islands of Attu, Kiska, and Adak, farther to the westward. Nagumo with his group of four carriers would strike at Midway the following day, and on June 5 the landing force would arrive and capture the island. No serious opposition was expected. Yamamoto with his battle-fleet would meanwhile lie well back to the westward, outside the range of air search, ready to strike when the expected American counter-attack developed.

This was the second supreme moment for Pearl Harbour. The carriers *Enterprise* and *Hornet* arrived from the south on May 26. The *Yorktown* appeared next day, with damage calculated to take three months to repair, but by a decision worthy of the crisis, within forty-eight hours she was made taut and fit for battle and was rearmed with a new air group. She sailed again on the 30th to join Admiral Spruance, who had left two days before with the other two carriers. Admiral Fletcher remained in tactical command of the combined force. At Midway the airfield was crammed with bombers, and the ground forces for the defence of the island were keyed to the highest pitch of expectancy. Early information of the approach of the enemy was imperative, and continuous air search began on May 30. United States submarines kept their watch west and north of Midway. Four days passed in acute suspense. At 9 A.M. on June 3 a Catalina flying-boat on patrol more than seven hundred miles west of Midway sighted a group of eleven enemy ships. The bombing and torpedo attacks which followed were unsuccessful, except for a torpedo hit on a tanker, but the battle had begun, and all uncertainty about the enemy's intentions was dispelled. Admiral Fletcher, through his Intelligence sources, had good reason to believe that the enemy carriers would approach Midway from the northwest, and he was not put off by the reports received of the first sighting, which he correctly judged to be only a group of transports. He turned his carriers to reach his chosen position about two hundred miles north of Midway by dawn on the 4th, ready to pounce on Nagumo's flank if and when he appeared.

June 4 broke clear and bright, and at 5.34 A.M. a patrol from Midway at last broadcast the long-awaited signal reporting the approach of the Japanese aircraft-carriers. Reports began to arrive thick and fast. Many planes were seen heading for Midway, and battleships were sighted supporting the carriers. At 6.30 A.M. the Japanese attack came in hard and strong. It met fierce resistance, and probably one-third of the attackers never returned. Much damage was done and many casualties suffered, but the airfield remained serviceable. There had been time to

launch a counter-attack at Nagumo's fleet. His crushing superiority in fighters took heavy toll, and the results of this gallant
stroke, on which great hopes were set, were disappointing. The
distraction caused by their onslaught seems however to have
clouded the judgment of the Japanese commander, who was
also told by his airmen that a second strike at Midway would
be necessary. He had retained on board a sufficient number of
aircraft to deal with any American carriers which might appear,
but he was not expecting them, and his search had been under-
powered and at first fruitless. Now he decided to break up the
formations which had been held in readiness for this purpose
and to rearm them for another stroke at Midway. In any case,
it was necessary to clear his flight decks to recover the aircraft
returning from the first attack. This decision proved fatal, and
although Nagumo later heard of an American force, including
one carrier, to the eastward, it was too late. He was condemned
to receiving the full weight of the American attack with his
flight decks encumbered with useless bombers, refuelling and
rearming.

*   *   *   *   *

Admirals Fletcher and Spruance by their earlier cool judgment were well placed to intervene at this crucial moment.
They had intercepted the news streaming in during the early
morning, and at 7 A.M. the *Enterprise* and *Hornet* began to
launch a strike with all the planes they had, except for those
needed for their own defence. The *Yorktown,* whose aircraft had
been carrying out the morning search, was delayed while these
were recovered, but her striking force was in the air soon after
9 A.M., by which time the first waves from the other two
carriers were approaching their prey. The weather near the
enemy was cloudy, and the dive-bombers failed at first to find
their target. The *Hornet's* group, unaware that the enemy had
turned away, never found them and missed the battle. Owing
to this mischance, the first attacks were made by torpedo
bombers alone from all three carriers, and, although pressed
home with fierce courage, were unsuccessful in the face of the
overwhelming opposition. Of forty-one torpedo bombers which

attacked only six returned. Their devotion brought its reward. While all Japanese eyes and all available fighter strength were turned on them, the thirty-seven dive-bombers from the *Enterprise* and *Yorktown* arrived on the scene. Almost unopposed, their bombs crashed into Nagumo's flagship, the *Akagi,* and her sister the *Kaga,* and about the same time another wave of seventeen from the *Yorktown* struck the *Soryu.* In a few minutes the decks of all three ships were a shambles, littered with blazing and exploding aircraft. Tremendous fires broke out below, and it was soon clear that all three ships were doomed. Admiral Nagumo could but shift his flag to a cruiser and watch three-quarters of his fine command burn.

It was past noon by the time the Americans had recovered their aircraft. They had lost over sixty, but the prize was great. Of the enemy carriers only the *Hiryu* remained, and she at once resolved to strike a blow for the banner of the Rising Sun. As the American pilots were telling their tale on board the *Yorktown* after their return, news came that an enemy attack was approaching. The enemy, reported to be about forty strong, pressed it home with vigour, and, besides being heavily mauled by fighters and gunfire, the *Yorktown* suffered three bomb hits. Severely damaged but with her fires under control, she carried on until two hours later the *Hiryu* struck again, this time with torpedoes. This attack ultimately proved fatal. Although the ship remained afloat for two days she was sunk by a Japanese submarine.

The *Yorktown* was avenged, even while she still floated. The *Hiryu* was marked at 2.45 P.M., and within the hour twenty-four dive-bombers from the *Enterprise* were winging their way towards her. At 5 P.M. they struck, and in a few minutes she too was a flaming wreck, though she did not sink until the following morning. The last of Nagumo's four fleet carriers had been smashed, and with them were lost all their highly trained air crews. These could never be replaced. So ended the battle of June 4, rightly regarded as the turning-point of the war in the Pacific.

*   *   *   *   *

The victorious American commanders had other perils to face. The Japanese Admiralissimo with his formidable battle fleet might still assail Midway. The American air forces were sorely depleted, and there were no heavy ships capable of successfully engaging Yamamoto if he chose to continue his advance. Admiral Spruance, who now assumed command of the carrier group, decided against a pursuit to the westward, not knowing what strength the enemy might have, and having no heavy support for his own carriers. In this decision he was unquestionably right, but the action of Admiral Yamamoto in not seeking to retrieve his fortunes is less easily understood. At first he resolved to press on, and ordered four of his most powerful cruisers to bombard Midway in the early hours of June 5. At the same time another powerful Japanese force was advancing to the northeastward, and had Spruance chosen to pursue the remnants of Nagumo's group he might have been caught in a disastrous night action. During the night however the Japanese commander abruptly changed his mind, and at 2.55 A.M. on June 5 he ordered a general retirement. His reasons are by no means clear, but it is evident that the unexpected and crushing destruction of his precious carriers had deeply affected him. One more disaster was to befall him. Two of the heavy cruisers proceeding to bombard Midway came into collision while avoiding attack by an American submarine. Both were severely damaged, and were left behind when the general retirement began. On June 6 these cripples were attacked by Spruance's airmen, who then sank one and left the other apparently in a sinking condition. This much-battered ship, the *Mogami*, eventually succeeded in making her way home.

After seizing the small islands of Attu and Kiska, in the western group of the Aleutians, the Japanese withdrew as silently as they had come.

*   *   *   *   *

Reflection on Japanese leadership at this time is instructive. Twice within a month their sea and air forces had been deployed in battle with aggressive skill and determination. Each time when their air component had been roughly handled they had withdrawn from their objective, even though on each occasion it was within their grasp. The men of Midway, Admirals Yamamoto, Nagumo, and Kondo, were those who planned and carried out the bold and tremendous operations which in four months destroyed the Allied Fleets in the Far East and drove the British Eastern Fleet out of the Indian Ocean. Yamamoto withdrew at Midway because, as the entire course of the war had shown, a fleet without air cover and several thousand miles from its base could not risk remaining within range of a force accompanied by carriers with air groups largely intact. He ordered the transport force to retire because it would have been tantamount to suicide to assault, without air support, an island defended by air forces and physically so small that surprise was impossible.

The rigidity of the Japanese planning and the tendency to abandon the object when their plans did not go according to schedule is thought to have been largely due to the cumbersome and imprecise nature of their language, which rendered it extremely difficult to improvise by means of signalled communications.

One other lesson stands out. The American Intelligence system succeeded in penetrating the enemy's most closely guarded secrets well in advance of events. Thus Admiral Nimitz, albeit the weaker, was twice able to concentrate all the forces he had in sufficient strength at the right time and place. When the hour struck this proved decisive. The importance of secrecy and the consequences of leakage of information in war are here proclaimed.

*   *   *   *   *

This memorable American victory was of cardinal importance, not only to the United States, but to the whole Allied cause. The moral effect was tremendous and instantaneous. At one stroke the dominant position of Japan in the Pacific was reversed. The glaring ascendancy of the enemy, which had

frustrated our combined endeavours throughout the Far East
for six months, was gone for ever. From this moment all our
thoughts turned with sober confidence to the offensive. No
longer did we think in terms of where the enemy might strike
the next blow, but where we could best strike at him to win
back the vast territories that he had overrun in his headlong
rush. The road would be long and hard, and massive preparations were still needed to win victory in the East, but the issue
was not in doubt; nor need the demands from the Pacific bear
too heavily on the great effort the United States was preparing
to exert in Europe.

*   *   *   *   *

The annals of war at sea present no more intense, heart-
shaking shock than these two battles, in which the qualities of
the United States Navy and Air Force and the American race
shone forth in splendour. The novel and hitherto utterly un-
measured conditions which air warfare had created made the
speed of action and the twists of fortune more intense than
has ever been witnessed before. But the bravery and self-
devotion of the American airmen and sailors and the nerve
and skill of their leaders was the foundation of all. As the
Japanese Fleet withdrew to their far-off home ports their commanders knew not only that their aircraft-carrier struggle was
irretrievably broken, but that they were confronted with a will-
power and passion in the foe they had challenged worthy of
the highest traditions of their Samurai ancestors and backed
by a development of power, numbers, and science to which no
limit could be set.

15

The Arctic Convoys

1942

The Northern Route to Russia — The "Tirpitz" at Trondheim —
Our Losses in March — The Supplies Bank Up — President
Roosevelt's Pressure on Me — My Reply of May 2 — Stalin's
Request — My Reply of May 9 — The Tragedy of Convoy
P.Q.17 — The First Sea Lord's Signals — The Cruisers and
Destroyers Withdraw — The German Side of the Picture — Ter-
rible Consequences to the Convoy — Our Decision to Suspend
Arctic Convoys till Perpetual Daylight Ends — "In Defeat Defi-
ance" — My Full Explanation to Stalin of July 17 — The Persian
Alternative Route — My Request for the Polish Divisions from
Russia — The President Agrees with My Message — A Rough
and Surly Answer from Stalin — I Decide to Accept It in Silence
— Record of the Naval Conference with the Fuehrer, August 26,
1942 — General Smuts' Comprehending View — The September
Convoy Fights Its Way Through — Magnitude of the British
Effort to Aid Russia in 1941 and 1942 — A Successful Convoy
and Its Sequel — A Major Crisis in German Naval Policy.

WHEN SOVIET RUSSIA was attacked by Hitler, the only
way we and the Americans could help them was by
sending weapons and supplies. These were given on a grand
scale from United States and British production, and from
American munitions already given to Britain. The equipment
of our ravenous armies was therefore heavily smitten, and all
effective preparations against an impending attack by Japan
made virtually impossible. The Beaverbrook-Harriman Anglo-
American Mission which visited Moscow in October, 1941,

255

arranged a great series of deliveries to Russia, and their proposals were substantially endorsed by their Governments. The direct route by which these supplies could be carried to the Russian armies was by sea, around the North Cape and through Arctic waters to Murmansk and later Archangel. By the agreement the Soviet Government was responsible for receiving the supplies in their own ships at British or American ports and transporting them to Russia. However, they did not possess enough ships for the immense amounts we were willing to send, and British and American vessels soon constituted three-quarters of the traffic. For the first four or five months all went well, only one ship was lost, and it was not till March, 1942, that German aircraft, flying from northern Norway, and German U-boats began seriously to molest the convoys.

We have seen how Hitler directed the German Navy to concentrate its strength in Norway in the winter, not only to prevent a British descent, but also to obstruct the flow of supplies and munitions to Russia. He also held back a proportion of his U-boats from the attack on the Atlantic and trans-Atlantic shipping in order to guard Norway. These were, as I have already remarked, wrong decisions on Hitler's part. We and our American Allies were very glad that the pressure of major raids by the fast German warships was not added to the strain of the U-boat war in its most deadly period. Nevertheless, as the attack on our Arctic convoys developed, ever-increasing burdens fell upon the British Admiralty.

The *Tirpitz* was moved to Trondheim in January. Here, a little later, she was joined by the *Scheer,* and in March by the cruiser *Hipper.* This group of surface ships was to have been joined by the battle-cruisers *Scharnhorst* and *Gneisenau* from Brest, and by the *Prinz Eugen,* which had escaped with them. But the *Scharnhorst* and *Gneisenau* had both fallen victims to our mines and were for many months out of action. While they were being repaired they were subjected to heavy air attack. On the night of February 27 the *Gneisenau* was hit in dock at Kiel, and, although we did not know it at the time, was so heavily damaged that she never appeared again in the war at sea. There remained the *Prinz Eugen*, which was sent at the same time as the *Scheer* to join the *Tirpitz*. She was torpedoed by the British submarine *Trident*, but managed to reach Trondheim. After making temporary repairs she succeeded in returning to Germany, where she remained out of action till October. Although the naval force at Trondheim was only half as strong as Hitler had hoped, it riveted our attention.

Convoy P.Q.12 had left Iceland on March 1, and the *Tirpitz* was ordered out to attack it. She was reported by a British submarine. Admiral Tovey, who was covering the convoy with the *King George V* and the aircraft-carrier *Victorious*, at once turned to intercept and attack. The German air reconnaissance failed to find the convoy, and *Tirpitz* turned back before Admiral Tovey could get between her and home. On March 9 the aircraft from the *Victorious* found her, and a striking force of torpedo-carrying machines was at once launched. The *Tirpitz* however succeeded in avoiding all their torpedoes and regained the shelter of West Fiord. Thus the convoy P.Q.12 reached its destination safely. The April convoy, P.Q.13, was heavily attacked by aircraft and by German destroyers, and lost five ships out of nineteen. One German destroyer was sunk, but our cruiser *Trinidad* was torpedoed and eventually sank. The arrival at Scapa Flow in April of the United States Task Force, comprising the new battleship *Washington*, the carrier *Wasp*, two heavy cruisers, and six destroyers, was a very welcome addition to our strength, and had made the occupation of Madagascar possible. But the difficulties and perils of the convoys grew. Three more sailed for North Russia in April and May. The first ran into heavy pack-ice north of Iceland, and fourteen ships out of twenty-three had to return. One of the remainder was sunk, and only eight reached their destination. The second and third convoys suffered an increasing scale of attack, and between them lost ten ships. Fifty however got safely through, but in the process we lost the cruiser *Edinburgh* by U-boat action.

At the end of March, 1942, the delivery of American and

British supplies had already far outstripped the sea transport
we could spare. There was thus a heavy banking up both of
shipping and supplies, and urgent demands were made from
both Washington and Moscow that we should do more.
Hopkins cabled me about this.

Prime Minister to Mr. Harry Hopkins   26 Apr. 42

Thank you for your personal telegram about shipping accumulations for Russia.

We have been considering this question very carefully in the
light of the serious convoy situation, and Harriman was given
today full information on number of convoys we are able to send
by northern route, number of cargo ships in each convoy, and our
proposals for dealing with accumulation of shipping. I hope you
will feel able to agree. We are asking the Russians to help with
increased measures of protection for convoys.

President Roosevelt to Prime Minister   27 Apr. 42

About the shipments to Russia. I am greatly disturbed by your
cable to Harry, because I fear not only the political repercussions
in Russia, but even more the fact that our supplies will not reach
them promptly. We have made such a tremendous effort to get our
supplies going that to have them blocked except for most compelling reasons seems to me a serious mistake. I realise in talks I
have had with Pound this morning and my own naval advisers
that the matter is extremely difficult. I do hope particularly that
you can review again the size of the immediate convoys, so that
the stuff now banked up in Iceland can get through. I can and
will make some immediate adjustments at this end, but I very much
prefer that we do not seek at this time any new understanding with
Russia about the amount of our supplies in view of the impending
assault on their armies. It seems to me that any word reaching
Stalin at this time that our supplies were stopping for any reason
would have a most unfortunate effect.

President Roosevelt to Former Naval Person   30 Apr. 42

Admiral King is communicating with Pound today about the
urgent necessity of getting off one more convoy in May in order
to break the log jam of ships already loaded or being loaded for

Russia. I am very anxious that ships should not be unloaded and reloaded in England, because I believe it would leave an impossible and very disquieting impression in Russia. Our problem is to move 107 ships now loaded or being loaded in the United Kingdom and the United States prior to June 1. I hope you will agree to the proposal King is making, because I think on balance that this is the most important thing we can use our escorts for.

We would watch our loadings from here out so that the agreed-upon number leaving Iceland after June 1 would fall within the possibilities of our convoy system. I know that this is a difficult enterprise, but I think it is so important that I hope you will examine King's proposal with Pound carefully.

It was impossible to meet these requests, great as was our desire to do so.

Former Naval Person to President Roosevelt   2 May 42

With very great respect, what you suggest is beyond our power to fulfil. Admiral King has expressed opinion that our trans-Atlantic escorts are already too thin. Reduction proposed would dislocate convoy system for eight weeks, during which, if enemy switched from your east coast to mid-ocean, disastrous consequences might follow to our main life-line.

2. Moreover, difficulty of Russian convoys cannot be solved merely by anti-submarine craft. Enemy heavy ships and destroyers may at any time strike. Even on this present convoy we have been attacked by hostile destroyers, which were beaten off with damage to one of ours. *Edinburgh,* one of our best six-inch cruisers, has been badly damaged by U-boats and is being towed to Murmansk, where *Trinidad,* damaged last convoy, is still penned. Just now I have received news that *King George V* has collided with our destroyer *Punjabi, Punjabi* being sunk, and her depth-charges exploding have damaged *King George V.* Difficulty of Russian convoy escorts is therefore at least as much surface ships of high fighting quality as of anti-submarine craft. We have made desperate attacks on *Tirpitz* in Trondheim, but, alas, although near the target, have not achieved any damage.

3. I beg you not to press us beyond our judgment in this operation, which we have studied most intently, and of which we have not yet been able to measure the full strain. I can assure you, Mr.

President, we are absolutely extended, and I could not press the Admiralty further.

4. Six ships from Iceland have already arrived at the Clyde, and their reloading ought to begin forthwith. Three convoys every two months, with either thirty-five or twenty-five ships in each convoy, according to experience, represent extreme limit of what we can handle. Pound is cabling separately to Admiral King.

President Roosevelt to Former Naval Person   3 May 42

It is now essential for us to acquiesce in your views regarding Russian convoys, but I continue to hope that you will be able to keep convoys at strength of thirty-five ships. I propose to press Russians to reduce requirements to absolute essentials, on grounds that preparations for "Bolero"[1] will require all possible munitions and shipping.

Premier Stalin to Premier Churchill   6 May 42

I have a request of you. Some ninety steamers loaded with various important war materials for the U.S.S.R. are bottled up at present in Iceland or in the approaches from America to Iceland. I understand there is a danger that the sailing of these ships may be delayed for a long time because of the difficulty to organise convoy escorted by the British naval forces.

I am fully aware of the difficulties involved and of the sacrifices made by Great Britain in this matter. I feel however incumbent upon me to approach you with the request to take all possible measures in order to ensure the arrival of all the above-mentioned materials in the U.S.S.R. in the course of May, as this is extremely important for our front.

Accept my sincere greetings and best wishes for success.

Prime Minister to Premier Stalin   9 May 42

I have received your telegram of May 6, and thank you for your message and greetings. We are resolved to fight our way through to you with the maximum amount of war materials. On account of *Tirpitz* and other enemy surface ships at Trondheim the passage of every convoy has become a serious fleet operation. We shall continue to do our utmost.

1 Code-name for preparations for the main invasion of France, afterwards the foundation of "Overlord."

No doubt your naval advisers have pointed out to you the dangers to which the convoys are subjected from attack by enemy surface forces, submarines, and air from the various bases in enemy hands which flank the route of the convoy throughout its passage.

We are throwing all our available resources into the solution of this problem, have dangerously weakened our Atlantic convoy escorts for this purpose, and, as you are no doubt aware, have suffered severely.

I am sure that you will not mind my being frank and emphasising the need of increasing the assistance given by the U.S.S.R. naval and air forces in helping to get these convoys through safely.

Premier Stalin to Prime Minister   13 May 42

I have received your message, and am writing to thank you for the promise to arrange for maximum delivery of war materials to the U.S.S.R. We quite understand the difficulties which Great Britain is overcoming, and those heavy sea losses which you are suffering while accomplishing this big task.

As for your suggestion for the Air Force and Navy of the U.S.S.R. to take more effective measures for protection of transports in the area mentioned by you, you may not doubt that on our part all possible measures will be taken immediately. It is necessary however to take into consideration the fact that our naval forces are very limited, and that our air forces in their vast majority are engaged at the battle-front.

Please accept my sincere greetings.

Prime Minister to General Ismay, for C.O.S. Committee   17 May 42

Not only Premier Stalin but President Roosevelt will object very much to our desisting from running the convoys now. The Russians are in heavy action, and will expect us to run the risk and pay the price entailed by our contribution. The United States ships are queueing up. My own feeling, mingled with much anxiety, is that the convoy ought to sail on the 18th. The operation is justified if a half gets through. Failure on our part to make the attempt would weaken our influence with both our major Allies. There are always the uncertainties of weather and luck, which may aid us. I share your misgivings, but I feel it is a matter of duty.

*   *   *   *   *

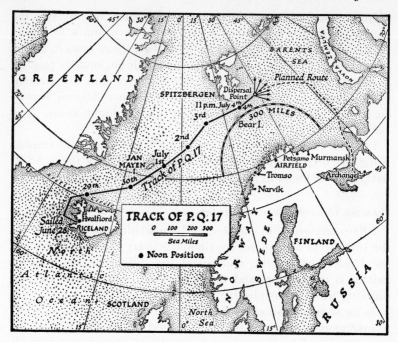

The climax of our endeavours was reached in the painful
episode involving the fate of P.Q.17. This convoy, comprising
thirty-four merchant ships, sailed from Iceland for Archangel
on June 27. Its escort consisted of six destroyers, two anti-
aircraft ships, two submarines, and eleven smaller craft. In
immediate support were two British and two American cruisers,
with three destroyers, under Rear-Admiral Hamilton. Nine
British and two Russian submarines were disposed along the
north coast of Norway to attack, if possible, the *Tirpitz* and German cruisers, or at least to give warning of their approach.
Finally, to the westward,. under the Commander-in-Chief,
Admiral Tovey, cruised our main covering force — the battleships *Duke of York* and *Washington,* with the carrier *Victorious,* three cruisers, and a flotilla of destroyers.

The convoy passed north of Bear Island, where the pack-ice
held it within three hundred miles of the German air bases.[2]

2 See map, "Track of P.Q.17."

The Admiralty instructed Admiral Hamilton that his cruiser
force was not to go east of Bear Island "unless the convoy was
threatened by a surface force which he could fight." This
clearly meant that he was not intended to fight the *Tirpitz*.
Meanwhile the Commander-in-Chief with the heavy ships remained in an area about 150 miles northwest of Bear Island,
ready to attack the *Tirpitz* should she appear, first of all with
the aircraft from the *Victorious*. The convoy was located by the
enemy on July 1, and thereafter was shadowed from the air and
frequently attacked. On the morning of July 4 the first ship
was sunk, and three more were torpedoed by aircraft that
evening, by which time the convoy was already 150 miles
beyond Bear Island. Rear-Admiral Hamilton had used his
discretionary authority to remain with the convoy. It was
known that the *Tirpitz* had left Trondheim some time before
the afternoon of the 3d, but there was no precise news of her
movements or of other German heavy ships.

In view of what followed, it is necessary to examine the
situation as it was known at the time in the Admiralty, where
the progress of the convoy was being watched with keen
anxiety. On the 4th there were strong reasons to believe that
the *Tirpitz* and her consorts, after refuelling at Altafiord, were
about to sail to intercept the convoy. The risk of this overwhelming major attack outweighed any from the air or U-
boats. Admiral Hamilton's cruisers would be of no avail against
the force the Germans could employ, and it seemed that the
only hope of saving a proportion of the convoy lay in scattering as widely as possible before the enemy arrived. They could
be on the spot ten hours after leaving harbour, and the merchant ships could only do seven or eight knots. If scattering
was to be effective there was no time to lose. That evening the
following "Immediate" signals went out to Admiral Hamilton
on the direct personal orders of the First Sea Lord, who
believed an attack to be imminent:

9.11 P.M.
Cruiser Force withdraw to the westward at high speed.

9.23 P.M.

Owing to threat from surface ships, convoy is to disperse and
proceed to Russian ports.

Convoy is to scatter.   9.36 P.M.

The decision, once taken, left no option with the cruiser
Admiral. His instructions were definite and peremptory, and
whatever his distress at having to leave his hapless charges he
could do nothing to help them. Nor was our fleet able to reach
the scene in time. Unfortunately the destroyers of the convoy
escort also withdrew, and although this decision was at the
time accepted as right in the circumstances, their presence
later on would have helped to collect the scattered ships into
little groups and would have afforded them some protection
against air and U-boat attacks during the remainder of the long
and hazardous voyage.

Admiral Pound would probably not have sent such vehement
orders if only our own British warships had been concerned.
But the idea that our first large joint Anglo-American operation under British command should involve the destruction of
the two United States cruisers as well as our own may well
have disturbed the poise with which he was accustomed to deal
with these heart-shaking decisions. This is only my surmise
from what I knew of my friend, for I never discussed the matter
with him. Indeed, so strictly was the secret of these orders
being sent on the First Sea Lord's authority guarded by the
Admiralty that it was not until after the war that I learned
the facts.

The Allied cruiser squadron was already ahead of the limit
of its mission. If no new orders had gone out from the
Admiralty the cruisers would in any case have withdrawn an
hour or so later in accordance with their original instructions.
Their earlier movement did not in fact influence the tactical
situation. In the light of later knowledge however the decision
to scatter was precipitate. The dismay felt by the merchant
ships at witnessing the headlong departure of the cruisers might
have been averted if Admiral Hamilton could have remained
in the vicinity until the dispersal of the convoy had been ac-

complished, but from the signals he had received he could only suppose that the *Tirpitz* was likely to appear over the horizon at any moment.

Now let us turn to the German side of the picture. The enemy force, comprising the *Tirpitz, Scheer,* and *Hipper,* with their attendant destroyers, which had assembled at Altafiord, did not in fact leave harbour until midday on the 5th. By this time they knew from their air reconnaissance that the convoy had scattered and that the British cruisers had withdrawn. The German ships were soon sighted, first by a Russian submarine, which attacked and incorrectly claimed two hits on the *Tirpitz,* and later by a British submarine, which reported her still steering to the northeast at high speed. The German admiral, knowing that he had been reported, feared attack from British aircraft which he believed might be within striking distance, but proposed none the less to continue his mission. However, the German High Command now took a different view of the matter, and, remembering the fate of the *Bismarck* a year before, decided on withdrawal. They also estimated, with some justice, that the scattered convoy could be more effectively dealt with by air and U-boat attack. That evening the German heavy ships were ordered back to port. The potential threat which they created had caused the scattering of the convoy. Thus their mere presence in these waters had directly contributed to a remarkable success for them.

The consequences for us were painful. The scattered, defenceless convoy now fell an easy prey to the marauding aircraft and U-boats. The dismal tale of each ship or little group of ships, some of them accompanied by one or more of the smaller escort vessels, became a saga in itself. Some took refuge along the frozen coast of Nova Zembla. Of the thirty-four ships which left Iceland twenty-three were sunk, and their crews perished in the icy sea or suffered incredible hardships and mutilation by frost-bite.[3] Two British, six American, one Panamanian, and two Russian merchant ships reached Archangel, and delivered 70,000 tons of cargo out of the 200,000

---

[3] In addition three rescue ships accompanied the convoy. One of these was sunk.

which had started from Iceland. Fourteen American ships in all were sunk. This was one of the most melancholy naval episodes in the whole of the war.

On July 15 I minuted to the First Lord and First Sea Lord, "I was not aware until this morning that it was the Admiral of the cruisers, Hamilton, who ordered the destroyers to quit the convoy. What did you think of this decision at the time? What do you think of it now?" I awaited the results of the inquiry into the conduct of those concerned. This took a considerable time, and assigned no blame to anyone. How could it do so in view of the signals made on the orders of the First Sea Lord?

In the throng of events which now fell upon me, involving my journeys to Cairo and Moscow, which future chapters will describe, I let the matter drop so far as I was concerned, and it is only now that I have to write the tale. If the *Tirpitz* and her consorts were approaching the escort cruisers and the convoy, it was right to order the cruisers to withdraw, as otherwise they would have been a useless sacrifice, and the best hope for the merchant ships lay in dispersal. The departure of the destroyers raises another problem. In his report Admiral Hamilton referred to the fuel situation, pointing out that the scattering of the convoy made it unlikely that they could find a tanker from which to replenish their limited supply. He also dwelt on the chances of a fleet action developing, in which case the destroyers would be needed with the fleet. Nevertheless, while the scattering of the convoy gave little scope for destroyer action against superior surface attack, their withdrawal was certainly a mistake. All risks should have been taken in defence of the merchant ships.

Since the war there has been criticism of this incident by American writers, and there was at once a cataract of abuse and insult from the Soviet Government. However, we learnt by our misfortunes.

* * * * *

In view of the disaster to P.Q.17 the Admiralty proposed to suspend the Arctic convoys at least till the northern ice-packs melted and receded and until perpetual daylight passed. I felt this would be a very grave decision, and was inclined not to lower but on the contrary to raise the stakes, on the principle of "In defeat defiance."

Prime Minister to First Lord and First Sea Lord   15 July 42

Let the following be examined:

Suspend the sailing of P.Q.18 as now proposed from 18th instant. See what happens to our Malta operation. If all goes well, bring *Indomitable, Victorious, Argus,* and *Eagle* north to Scapa, and collect with them at least five of the auxiliary aircraft-carriers, together with all available "Didos" and at least twenty-five destroyers. Let the two sixteen-inch battleships go right through under this air umbrella and destroyer screen, keeping southward, not hugging the ice, but seeking the clearest weather, and thus fight it out with the enemy. If we can move our armada in convoy under an umbrella of at least a hundred fighter aircraft we ought to be able to fight our way through and out again, and if a fleet action results so much the better.

I could not however persuade my Admiralty friends to take this kind of line, which of course involved engaging a vital force to us out of proportion to the actual military importance of the Arctic convoys. I had therefore to send the following telegram to Stalin, to which I obtained the approval of President Roosevelt beforehand.

Prime Minister to Premier Stalin   17 July 42

We began running small convoys to North Russia in August, 1941, and until December the Germans did not take any steps to interfere with them. From February, 1942, the size of the convoys was increased, and the Germans then moved a considerable force of U-boats and a large number of aircraft to North Norway and made determined attacks on the convoys. By giving the convoys the strongest possible escort of destroyers and anti-submarine craft the convoys got through with varying but not prohibitive losses. It is evident that the Germans were dissatisfied with the results which were being achieved by means of aircraft and U-boats alone, because they began to use their surface forces against the convoys.

Luckily for us, however, at the outset they made use of their heavy
surface forces to the westward of Bear Island and their submarines
to the eastward. The Home Fleet was thus in a position to prevent an attack by enemy surface forces. Before the May convoy
was sent off, the Admiralty warned us that the losses would be
very severe if, as was expected, the Germans employed their surface forces to the eastward of Bear Island. We decided however
to sail the convoy. An attack by surface ships did not materialise,
and the convoy got through with a loss of one-sixth, chiefly from
air attack. In the case of P.Q.17 however the Germans at last used
their forces in the manner we had always feared. They concentrated their U-boats to the westward of Bear Island and reserved
their surface forces for attack to the eastward of Bear Island. The
final story of P.Q.17 convoy is not yet clear. At the moment only
four ships have arrived at Archangel, but six others are in Nova
Zembla harbours. The latter may however be attacked from the
air at any time. At the best therefore only one-third will have
survived.

I must explain the dangers and difficulties of these convoy operations when the enemy's battle squadron takes its station in the
extreme north. We do not think it right to risk our Home Fleet
east of Bear Island or where it can be brought under the attack of
the powerful German shore-based aircraft. If one or two of our
very few most powerful battleships were to be lost or even seriously
damaged while *Tirpitz* and her consorts, soon to be joined by
Scharnhorst, remained in action, the whole command of the Atlantic would be [temporarily] lost. Besides affecting the food supplies by which we live, our war effort would be crippled; and above
all, the great convoys of American troops across the ocean, rising
presently to as many as 80,000 in a month, would be prevented and
the building up of a really strong second front in 1943 rendered
impossible.

My naval advisers tell me that if they had the handling of the
German surface, submarine, and air forces, in present circumstances, they would guarantee the complete destruction of any convoy to North Russia. They have not been able so far to hold out
any hopes that convoys attempting to make the passage in perpetual daylight would fare better than P.Q.17. It is therefore with
the greatest regret that we have reached the conclusion that to
attempt to run the next convoy, P.Q.18, would bring no benefit

to you and would only involve dead loss to the common cause. At the same time, I give you my assurance that if we can devise arrangements which give a reasonable chance of at least a fair proportion of the contents of the convoys reaching you, we will start them again at once. The crux of the problem is to make the Barents Sea as dangerous for German warships as they make it for ours. This is what we should aim at doing with our joint resources. I should like to send a senior officer of the R.A.F. to North Russia to confer with your officers and make a plan.

Meanwhile we are prepared to dispatch immediately to the Persian Gulf some of the ships which were to have sailed in the P.Q. convoy. . . .

You have referred to combined operations in the North. The obstacles to sending further convoys at the present time equally prevent our sending land forces and air forces for operations in northern Norway. But our officers should forthwith consider together what combined operations may be possible in or after October, when there is a reasonable amount of darkness. It would be better if you could send your officers here, but if this is impossible ours will come to you.

In addition to a combined operation in the North, we are studying how to help on your southern flank. If we can beat back Rommel we might be able to send powerful air forces in the autumn to operate on the left of your line. The difficulties of maintaining these forces over the trans-Persian route without reducing your supplies will clearly be considerable, but I hope to put detailed proposals before you in the near future. We must however first beat Rommel. The battle is now intense. . . .

I am sure it would be in our common interest, Premier Stalin, to have the three divisions of Poles you so kindly offered join their compatriots in Palestine, where we can arm them fully. These would play a most important part in future fighting, as well as keeping the Turks in good heart by the sense of growing numbers to the southward. I hope this project of yours, which we greatly value, will not fall to the ground on account of the Poles wanting to bring with the troops a considerable mass of their women and children, who are largely dependent on the rations of the Polish soldiers. The feeding of these dependents will be a considerable burden to us. We think it well worth while bearing that burden for the sake of forming this Polish army, which will be used faithfully for our common advantage. We are very hard up for food ourselves in the Levant area, but there is enough in India if we can bring it [from] there.

If we do not get the Poles we should have to fill their places by drawing on the preparations now going forward on a vast scale for the Anglo-American mass invasion of the Continent. These preparations have already led the Germans to withdraw two heavy-bomber groups from South Russia to France. Believe me, there is nothing that is useful and sensible that we and the Americans will not do to help you in your grand struggle. The President and I are ceaselessly searching for means to overcome the extraordinary difficulties which geography, salt water, and the enemy's air-power interpose. I have shown this telegram to the President.

I need scarcely say I got a rough and surly answer.

Premier Stalin to Premier Churchill   23 July 42

I received your message of July 17. Two conclusions could be drawn from it. First, the British Government refuses to continue the sending of war materials to the Soviet Union via the northern route. Second, in spite of the agreed communiqué concerning the urgent tasks of creating a second front in 1942 the British Government postpones this matter until 1943.

2. Our naval experts consider the reasons put forward by the British naval experts to justify the cessation of convoys to the northern ports of the U.S.S.R. wholly unconvincing. They are of the opinion that with good will and readiness to fulfil the contracted obligations these convoys could be regularly undertaken and heavy losses could be inflicted on the enemy. Our experts find it also difficult to understand and to explain the order given by the Admiralty that the escorting vessels of the P.Q.17 should return, whereas the cargo boats should disperse and try to reach the Soviet ports one by one without any protection at all. Of course I do not think that regular convoys to the Soviet northern ports could be effected without risk or losses. But in wartime no important undertaking could be effected without risk or losses. In any case, I never expected that the British Government would stop dispatch of war materials to us just at the very moment when the Soviet Union, in view of the serious situation on the Soviet-German front, requires these materials more than ever. It is obvious

that the transport *via* Persian Gulf could in no way compensate
for the cessation of convoys to the northern ports.

3. With regard to the second question, i.e., the question of
creating a second front in Europe, I am afraid it is not being
treated with the seriousness it deserves. Taking fully into account
the present position on the Soviet-German front, I must state in
the most emphatic manner that the Soviet Government cannot
acquiesce in the postponement of a second front in Europe until
1943.

I hope you will not feel offended that I [have] expressed frankly
and honestly my own opinion as well as the opinion of my colleagues on the question raised in your message.

These contentions are not well-founded. So far from breaking "contracted obligations" to deliver the war supplies at
Soviet ports, it had been particularly stipulated at the time of
making the agreement that the Russians were to be responsible
for conveying them to Russia. All that we did beyond this was
a good-will effort. As to the allegations of a breach of faith
about the second front in 1942, our *aide-mémoire* was a solid
defence. I did not however think it worth while to argue out
all this with the Soviet Government, who had been willing
until they were themselves attacked to see us totally destroyed
and share the booty with Hitler, and who even in our common
struggle could hardly spare a word of sympathy for the heavy
British and American losses incurred in trying to send them aid.
The President agreed with this view.

President Roosevelt to Former Naval Person   29 July 42

I agree with you that your reply to Stalin must be handled with
great care. We have got always to bear in mind the personality
of our Ally and the very difficult and dangerous situation that confronts him. No one can be expected to approach the war from
a world point of view whose country has been invaded. I think we
should try to put ourselves in his place. I think he should be
told, in the first place, quite specifically that we have determined
upon a course of action in 1942. I think that, without advising
him of the precise nature of our proposed operations, the fact that

they are going to be made should be told him without any qualifications.

While I think that you should not raise any false hopes in Stalin
relative to the northern convoy, nevertheless I agree with you that
we should run one if there is any possibility of success, in spite
of the great risk involved.

I am still hopeful that we can put air-power directly on the
Russian front, and I am discussing that matter here. I believe it
would be unwise to promise this air-power only on condition that
the battle in Egypt goes well. Russia's need is urgent and immediate. I have a feeling it would mean a great deal to the Russian
Army and the Russian people if they knew some of our air force
was fighting with them in a very direct manner.

While we may believe that the present and proposed use of our
combined air forces is strategically the best, nevertheless I feel that
Stalin does not agree with this. Stalin, I imagine, is in no mood to
engage in a theoretical strategical discussion, and I am sure that
other than our major operation, the enterprise that would suit him
the best is direct air support on the southern end of his front.

I therefore let Stalin's bitter message pass without any
specific rejoinder. After all, the Russian armies were suffering
fearfully and the campaign was at its crisis.

*   *   *   *

At a conference of the German Naval Commander-in-Chief
with the Fuehrer on August 26, 1942, Admiral Raeder stated:

Evidently the Ally convoy did not sail. We can thus assume that
our submarines and aircraft, which totally destroyed the last convoy, have forced the enemy to give up this route temporarily, or
even fundamentally to change his whole system of supply lines.
Supplies to northern ports of Russia remain decisive for the whole
conduct of the war waged by the Anglo-Saxons. They must preserve Russia's strength in order to keep German forces occupied.
The enemy will most probably continue to ship supplies to northern Russia, and the Naval Staff must therefore maintain submarines
along the same routes. The greater part of the Fleet will also be
stationed in northern Norway. The reason for this, besides making
attacks on convoys possible, is the constant threat of an enemy

invasion. Only by keeping the Fleet in Norwegian waters can we hope to meet this danger successfully. Besides, it is especially important, in view of the whole Axis strategy, that the German "Fleet in being" tie down the British Home Fleet, especially after the heavy Anglo-American losses in the Mediterranean and the Pacific. The Japanese are likewise aware of the importance of this measure. In addition, the danger of enemy mines in home waters has constantly increased, so that the naval forces should be shifted only for repairs and training purposes.

* * * * *

It was not until September that another convoy set off for North Russia. By now the scheme of defence had been revised, and the convoy was accompanied by a close escort of sixteen destroyers, as well as the first of the new escort carriers, the *Avenger,* with twelve fighter aircraft. As before, strong support was provided by the Fleet. This time however the German surface ships made no attempt to intervene, but left the task of attack to the aircraft and U-boats. The result was a particularly fierce battle in the air, in which twenty-four enemy aircraft were destroyed out of about a hundred which came in to the attack. Ten merchant ships were lost in these actions and two more by U-boats, but twenty-seven ships successfully fought their way through.

* * * * *

Not only did almost the whole burden of these convoys fall upon us, but, as the table on page 274 shows, we provided from our strained resources by far the greater number of aircraft and more tanks for Russia, both in 1941 and in 1942. The figures are a conclusive answer to those who suggest that our efforts to help Russia in her struggle were lukewarm. We gave our heart's blood resolutely to our valiant, suffering Ally.

* * * * *

The year 1942 was not to close without its flash of triumph upon the thankless task the Royal Navy had discharged, and we must trench upon the future. After the passage of P.Q.18

SUPPLIES TO NORTH RUSSIA, 1941–1942

Arrivals at Russian Ports

(*Figures are approximate only*)

1941	Ships		Cargoes				
	British Controlled	U.S. Controlled	Vehicles (Number)	Tanks (Number)	Aircraft (Number)	Ammunition & Misc. Stores (Tons)	Oil and Petroleum (Tons)
British supplies	} 34	14{	867	446	676	75,512	Nil
American supplies			1,506	35	29	11,460	24,900
Totals	34	14	2,373	481	705	86,972	24,900
1942							
British supplies	} 68	103{	3,029	1,347	1,312	190,263	Nil
American supplies			18,998	1,448	648	337,429	44,583
Totals	68	103	22,027	2,795	1,960	527,692	44,583
	TOTAL ARRIVALS						
Total arrivals 1941–42	102	117	24,400	3,276	2,665	614,664	69,483
	LOST AT SEA						
Totals for 1941–42	22	42[4]	8,422	1,226	656	232,483	7,373

in September, 1942, convoys to North Russia were again suspended. Later, major operations in North Africa were to claim the whole strength of our naval forces in home waters. But supplies accumulated for delivery to Russia, and the means of protecting future convoys were closely studied. It was not until late in December that the next convoy set out on its hazardous voyage. It sailed in two parts, each escorted by six

4 Some of these losses occurred in the North Atlantic.

or seven destroyers, and covered by the Home Fleet. The first group arrived safely. The second had a more eventful passage. On the morning of December 31 Captain R. Sherbrooke in the destroyer *Onslow,* commanding the escort, was about a hundred and fifty miles northeast of the North Cape when he sighted three enemy destroyers. He immediately turned to engage them. As the action began the German heavy cruiser *Hipper* appeared upon the scene. The British destroyers held off this powerful ship for nearly an hour. The gun-flashes of the action drew to the scene Admiral Burnett with two British cruisers *Sheffield* and *Jamaica* from twenty-five miles away. This force, racing southward, ran into the German pocket-battleship *Lützow,* which, after a short engagement, disappeared to the westward in the twilight. The German admiral, thinking that the British cruisers were the vanguard of a battle squadron, retired hastily. During this brief engagement the *Sheffield* sank a German destroyer at close range. A running fight followed. The two German heavy ships and their six escorting destroyers struck at the convoy which Sherbrooke guarded. But this stroke failed.

The convoy arrived safely in Russian waters with the loss of one destroyer and no more than slight damage to one merchant ship. Captain Sherbrooke, who had been severely wounded in the early stages but continued to fight his ship and personally to direct operations, despite the loss of an eye, was awarded the Victoria Cross for his leadership.

Within the German High Command the repercussions of this affair were far-reaching. Owing to delays in the transmission of signals the High Command first learnt of the episode from an English news broadcast. Hitler was enraged. While waiting impatiently for the outcome of the fight his anger was fostered by Goering, who complained bitterly of wasting squadrons of the German Air Force on guarding the capital ships of the Navy, which he suggested should be scrapped. Admiral Raeder was ordered to report immediately. On January 6 a naval conference was held. Hitler launched a tirade upon the past record of the German Navy. "It should not be considered a degradation if the Fuehrer decides to scrap the larger ships. This would be true only if he were removing a fighting unit which had retained its full usefulness. A parallel to this in the Army would be the removal of all cavalry divisions." Raeder was ordered to report in writing why he objected to putting the capital ships out of commission. When Hitler received this memorandum he treated it with derision, and ordered Doenitz, the designated successor to Raeder, to make a plan to meet his demands. A bitter conflict between Goering and Raeder raged round Hitler over the future of the German Navy compared with that of the Luftwaffe. But Raeder stuck grimly to the defence of the service which he had commanded since 1928. Time and again he had demanded the formation of a separate Fleet Air Arm, and had been opposed successfully by Goering's insistence that the Air Force could accomplish more at sea than the Navy. Goering won, and on January 30 Raeder resigned. He was replaced by Doenitz, the ambitious Admiral of the U-boats. All effective new construction was henceforth to be monopolised by them.

Thus this brilliant action fought by the Royal Navy to protect an allied convoy to Russia at the end of the year led directly to a major crisis in the enemy's naval policy, and ended the dream of another German High Seas Fleet.

16

The Offensive in the Aether

The Bruneval Raid, February 27, 1942 — Invaluable Prizes — A Missing Detail — "Lichtenstein" — A Fine Exploit — Doubts About the Accuracy of Our Bombing — Devices to Guide the Bombers — "Gee" — "Oboe" — H₂S — Plans for a New Bomber Offensive on Germany — Slow Progress in the Production of H₂S — Effects of the Device on the Anti-U-Boat Campaign — The A.S.V. Equipment — A Position-Finding Service Shared with the Enemy — Reactions at Hitler's Headquarters to Our New Bombing Offensive — Combating the German Night-Fighter Attack — The Kammhuber Line — The Device Called "Window" — Our Hesitation in Using it — Its Remarkable Success.

DURING THE WINTER of 1941 our Intelligence suspected that the Germans were using a new radar apparatus for giving the direction and range of our planes to their anti-aircraft guns. This apparatus was believed to look like a large bowl-shaped electric heater. Our secret agents, our listening apparatus, and air photographs soon found out that a chain of stations stretched along the northern coast of Europe, and that one of them, probably containing the new equipment, was established on Cap d'Antifer, not far from Havre. On December 3, 1941, a squadron leader of the Photographic Reconnaissance Unit happened to visit our Intelligence Centre and learnt of our suspicions. On his own initiative he flew over next day and spotted it. On December 5 he made another sortie and took a brilliant and successful photograph. Our scientists found that it was exactly what they expected. Although it was at the top of a four-hundred-foot cliff, a shelving beach nearby provided a possible landing-place, and a Commando raid was planned accordingly.

On the night of February 27, 1942, a Commando raid on Bruneval captured vital portions of a key piece of equipment in the German radar defences and gathered information which greatly helped our air offensive. In the snow and darkness a detachment of paratroops dropped at midnight behind the German station on the cliff summit and held the defenders at bay. With them went a carefully briefed party of sappers and an R.A.F. radio mechanic, with instructions to remove as much of the equipment as they could, sketch and photograph the rest, and if possible capture one of the German operators. In all this they succeeded, although a hitch in the time-table cut down their working period from half an hour to barely ten minutes. Most of the equipment was found, dismantled under fire, and carried to the beach. Here the Navy was waiting and took the party off.

*   *   *   *   *

Supplemented by a rapidly increasing network of agents who were specially briefed in radar intelligence, and by friendly neutrals who brought back information from the occupied countries, our knowledge of the German defences grew all through 1942. In speaking of "agents" and "friendly neutrals" it would be fair to single out the Belgians for special mention. In 1942 they provided about eighty per cent of all "agent" information on this subject, including a vital map, stolen from the German Officer Commanding searchlight and radar equipment for the more northerly of the two sectors of the German night-fighter line in Belgium. It was this map, in conjunction with other information, which enabled our experts to unravel the system of the German air defence. By the end of the year we knew not only how the hostile system worked, but how to cope with it.

One detail however was still missing, and not to be discovered for many months. Towards the end of the year Professor Linde-

mann, now Lord Cherwell, told me that the Germans had
fitted their night fighters with a new kind of radar set. Little
was known about it except that it was called "Lichtenstein"
and was designed for hunting our bombers. It was imperative
to find out more about it before the start of our air offensive.
On the night of December 2, 1942, an aircraft of 192 Squadron
was presented as a decoy. It was attacked many times by an
enemy night fighter radiating the Lichtenstein transmissions.
Nearly all the crew were hit. The special operator listening to
the radiations was severely wounded in the head, but continued
to observe with accuracy. The wireless operator, though badly
injured, was parachuted out of the aircraft over Ramsgate, and
survived with the precious observations. The rest of the crew
flew the plane out to sea and alighted on the water because the
machine was too badly damaged to land on an airfield. They
were rescued by a boat from Deal. The gap in our knowledge
of the German night defences was closed.

*   *   *   *   *

Late in 1940 Professor Lindemann had begun to raise doubts
in my mind about the accuracy of our bombing, and in 1941
I authorised his Statistical Department to make an investigation at Bomber Headquarters. The results confirmed our fears.
We learnt that although Bomber Command believed they
had found the target, two-thirds of the crews actually failed to
strike within five miles of it. The air photographs showed how
little damage was being done. It also appeared that the crews
knew this, and were discouraged by the poor results of so much
hazard. Unless we could improve on this there did not seem
much use in continuing night bombing. On September 3,
1941, I had minuted:

Prime Minister to Chief of Air Staff

This is a very serious paper [by Lord Cherwell, on the results of
our bombing raids on Germany in June and July], and seems to
require your most urgent attention. I await your proposals for
action.

Several methods had been proposed to guide bombers to
their targets by radio aids, but until we recognised how inaccurate our bombing was, there seemed no reason to embark
on such complications. Now attention was focused on them.
We had developed a device called "Gee," by which radio pulses
were sent out simultaneously from three stations far apart in
England. By exact timing of their arrival at an aircraft it
could fix its position within a mile. This was an improvement,
and we began to use it on a large scale about ten days after
the Bruneval raid. With its aid we struck at most of the Ruhr,
but it could not reach deep enough into Germany. Lübeck and
Rostock were also bombed at this time, but not by "Gee."
Another device on similar lines called "Oboe" was much more
accurate. But since it involved flying for a considerable time
in a straight line the bombers were exposed to great dangers
from A.A. fire. And, as with "Gee," the radio waves for which
it was designed were too short to curve round the earth's surface; hence it could only be used up to distances at which the
aircraft was above the horizon — say 200 miles at 25,000 feet.
This limited seriously the regions we could attack. Something
better was needed.

Since 1941, when the idea had been shown to be feasible,
Lindemann had argued that a radar set mounted in the aircraft
itself could throw onto a screen in the cockpit a map of the
ground over which it flew. If the bomber navigated with the
aid of "Gee" or other methods to within say fifty miles of the
target, it could then switch on this apparatus and drop its
bombs through cloud or haze without possibility of jamming
or interference. Distance would not matter, as the plane would
carry its radar eye with it wherever it went and the eye could
see in the dark.

This device, which afterwards became well known by the
code-name H_2S, encountered many obstacles, and I was for
some time warned that it could not be achieved. But, as the
following minutes show, I persisted in pressing the theme, and
eventually it worked well. Special ultra-short waves were used.
The shorter the wave the clearer the picture became on the

aircraft's screen. The transmitting machine for these micro-waves, as they were called, was entirely a British invention, and it revolutionised the radio war both on land and at sea. It was not until it fell into German hands that they were able to copy it. But all this lay in the future. In this critical period there was little to go on except scientific theories. The first step was to make a working model. If that functioned, then we still had to produce it in numbers, fit it into our planes, and teach the crews how to use it. If too much time were spent on experiment, manufacture would be delayed, and so would accuracy of bombing.

*   *   *   *   *

Prime Minister to Secretary of State for Air   14 Apr. 42

We are placing great hopes on our bomber offensive against Germany next winter, and we must spare no pains to justify the large proportion of the national effort devoted to it. The Air Ministry's responsibility is to make sure that the maximum weight of the best type of bombs is dropped on the German cities by the aircraft placed at their disposal. Unless we can ensure that most of our bombs really do some damage it will be difficult to justify the pre-eminence we are according to this form of attack. The following seem to be needful for success: (i) To make sure that crews are practised in the use of blind bombing apparatus, which should be installed by this autumn in most of our night bombers. (ii) To discover any difficulties which navigators may find in the use of sextants for astro-navigation, overcome them, and make sure they employ this method to get them within twelve to fifteen miles of the target, after which the blind bombing equipment comes into play. (iii) To make certain that the large number of bombers we expect to get will not be immobilised by bad weather. This will entail preparing adequate runways, homing devices, and possibly fog-clearing gear on the aerodromes, and de-icing and blind-landing equipment, etc., on the planes. (iv) To insist that a sufficient supply of incendiary and high-charge-weight-ratio bombs is available, even if this implies relaxing the penetration specifications. I raised this matter last July, and was assured there would be no shortage, but I gather that the 1000-lb. and 500-lb. bombs which form the bulk of our loads are still of the old inefficient type.

We must expect that the enemy will improve his defences, both ground and air. Various counter-measures are, I understand, in sight, which we are quite properly holding up for the time being. No doubt you will see that everything is concerted so that we can install and use each of them immediately it is deemed desirable.

Three weeks later I held a meeting and authorised an emergency programme.

Prime Minister to Secretary of State for Air   6 May 42

I am glad to learn that the numerous matters raised in my minute of April 14 are in hand.

I hope that a really large order for H_2S has been placed, and that nothing will be allowed to stand in the way of getting this apparatus punctually. If it fulfils expectations it should make a big difference in the coming winter.

Your statement that the Ministry of Aircraft Production cannot supply medium capacity bombs in quantity before the end of this year is most surprising. Last July I wrote to you on this subject, and you replied that they had been promised at an early date. Now it seems that they are still awaiting hammer tests, etc. Surely it would be better to drop plenty of high explosive in any thin-walled container than waste so large a proportion of our bombing effort.

Although all the essential matters are being dealt with, there are so many facets of the task which have to be completed at the proper time that it might be a good thing to appoint some one man to be responsible for taking the necessary action by the proper dates and rendering a monthly report. I have heard Sir Robert Renwick mentioned as a man of drive and business experience who has already rendered valuable service in connection with "Gee." Perhaps you might think he is a good man for this purpose. It would be most unfortunate if we found later on that the bombing programme was held up because one or other of the items was lagging behind.

The manufacturers had some misgivings, but on June 7 I was able to write:

Prime Minister to Secretary of State for Air   7 June 42

I have learnt with pleasure that the preliminary trials of H_2S

have been extremely satisfactory. But I am deeply disturbed at
the very slow rate of progress promised for its production. Three
sets in August and twelve in November is not even beginning to
touch the problem. We must insist on getting, at any rate, a sufficient number to light up the target by the autumn, even if we
cannot get them into all the bombers, and nothing should be allowed to stand in the way of this.

I propose to hold a meeting to discuss this next week and to see
what can be done. The relatively disappointing results of our
second big raid make it doubly urgent.

I am glad you have arranged with the Minister of Aircraft Production for Sir Robert Renwick to make a personal effort to accelerate production of the needed radio equipment. But I hope you
will not let him disperse his efforts on too many bits of apparatus.
The main thing is to hit the target, and this we can do with H_2S.
All the other items are of course useful, but nothing like so urgent.

It is most necessary that training, aerodromes, runways, and
bombs should all be synchronised, and it was for this reason that
I suggested it might be well to put Sir Robert Renwick in charge
of the whole thing. The difficulty of co-ordinating all these matters is obvious, but the urgent need is clear. If you do not wish Sir
Robert Renwick to undertake it, I trust you will appoint some
other individual to be responsible for ensuring that everything
marches in step, so that we are not faced at the end by some missing item. I do not think it is sufficient to leave this matter to the
ordinary processes of departmental organisation.

As to the bombs, you told me in your minute of July 19, 1941,
that a production order had been placed for 500-lb. special bombs,
and that you were proceeding with the design of a larger one. It
has been stated at several meetings that you entirely agreed that
they were superior to the General Purpose bomb, and I am disappointed that such a large proportion of our efvrt should still be
applied to carrying bombs with only half the blasting power they
might have.

* * * * *

So vital was it to our bomber effort that the Secretary of
State for Air took over the matter himself.

Prime Minister to Secretary of State for Air   15 June 42

It is very good of you to undertake this work yourself. Will you please however keep in touch with Lord Cherwell, so that he can keep you apprised of my point of view?

I hope to have an H₂S meeting on Wednesday at 11 A.M.

Early in 1943 the equipment was ready for operations. It was issued to the pathfinder group which, copying the German example of Kampf Gruppe 100, we had formed some months earlier. Success was immediate. Nor did its usefulness stop at bombing on land. For some time our aircraft had carried airborne radar for detecting surface vessels at sea. This was called A.S.V. But in the autumn of 1942 the Germans had begun to fit their U-boats with special receivers for detecting the signals which it sent out. They were thus enabled to dive in time to avoid attack. As a result Coastal Command successes in sinking U-boats declined and our losses in merchant shipping increased. H₂S was adapted for use in the A.S.V. rôle with striking advantage. In 1943 it made a definite contribution to the final defeat of the U-boats. But until it could be got ready I had to ask President Roosevelt for help, which was granted in full measure.

Former Naval Person to President Roosevelt   20 Nov. 42

One of the most potent weapons for hunting the U-boat and protecting our convoys is the long-range aircraft fitted with A.S.V. equipment.

2. The German U-boats have recently been fitted with a device enabling them to listen to our 1½-metre A.S.V. equipment, and thus dive to safety before our aircraft can appear on the scene. As a result our day patrols in the Bay have become largely ineffective in bad weather, and our night patrols, with searchlight aircraft, have been rendered almost entirely useless. Sightings of U-boats have accordingly declined very sharply from 120 in September to 57 in October. No improvement can be expected until aircraft fitted with a type of A.S.V. to which they cannot at present listen, called "centimetre A.S.V.," become available.

3. One of the main objects of patrolling the Bay is to attack U-boats in transit to and from the American Atlantic seaboard. This region is doubly urgent now that so many American convoys pass in the vicinity.

4. We can deal with the inner zone of the Bay of Biscay by modifying and diverting to our Wellingtons a form of centimetre A.S.V. which has been developed as a target-location device for our heavy bombers.

5. A more difficult situation arises in the outer zone of the Bay, where aircraft of longer range fitted with centimetre A.S.V. are essential.

6. The very heavy sinkings in mid-Atlantic have forced us to convert our own Liberators for work in this area. This leaves us with no aircraft with adequate range for the outer zone of the Bay, unless we make a further diversion from a small force of long-range bombers responsible for the air offensive against Germany. Even if this diversion were made, a considerable time would necessarily elapse before the essential equipment could be modified and installed.

7. I am most reluctant to reduce the weight of bombs we are able to drop on Germany, as I believe it is of great importance that this offensive should be maintained and developed to the utmost of our ability throughout the winter months.   I would therefore ask you, Mr. President, to consider the immediate allocation of some thirty Liberators with centimetre A.S.V. equipment from the supplies which I understand are now available in the United States. These aircraft would be put to work immediately in an area where they would make a direct contribution to the American war effort.

*   *   *   *   *

Submarine detection was not our only problem in this area. The Germans had established two long-range beam stations for enabling their aircraft and U-boats to navigate far out in the Bay and the western approaches. One of these was near Brest, and the other in Northwest Spain. Our Ambassador at Madrid came to hear about the Spanish station, but instead of trying to get the Spaniards to close it down, which would have involved us in endless legal and diplomatic controversy, we were advised by Dr. R. V. Jones [1] to use it ourselves. By taking photographs of the equipment we were able to learn

1 This is the Dr. Jones mentioned in Voiume II, page 384.

how it worked, and henceforward our aircraft and fighting ships were supplied with a first-class position-finding service which they shared happily with the enemy. Coastal Command were in fact able to use it to a greater extent than the Germans themselves, and it was so efficient that we built several similar beacons for service in Australia and the Pacific.

*   *   *   *   *

To anticipate the story, our air offensive in 1943 started well, and the accuracy of the "Oboe" attacks worried the Germans considerably. The news that we were hitting individual factories on cloudy nights in the Ruhr reached Hitler at his head-quarters in Russia. He immediately sent for Goering and General Martini, Director-General of Signals of the Luftwaffe. After haranguing them, he stated that it was a scandal that the British could achieve this feat and that the Germans could not. Martini replied that the Germans were not only able to do it, but had done it in the Blitz with the "X" and "Y" beam systems. The Fuehrer said he would not be convinced by words, and demanded a demonstration. At the cost of considerable effort this was arranged. In the meantime Bomber Command, guided by "Oboe," had wrought great damage in the Ruhr.

*   *   *   *   *

But we still had to deal with the enemy night fighters, which accounted for about three-quarters of our bomber losses. Each German fighter was confined to a narrow area of the sky and was controlled by a separate ground station. These ground stations had originally formed a line across Europe, called the Kammhuber Line, after the name of the German general who built it. As we attempted to pierce or outflank it, so the enemy extended and deepened it. Nearly 750 of these stations spread across Europe ivy fashion from Berlin westward to Ostend, northward to the Skagerrak, and southward to Marseilles. We found all but six of them, but there were too many to destroy by bombing. If they were permitted to stay in operation our bombers would have to drive their way through many hundred miles of night-fighter "boxes" stretching from the North Sea to the target. Although the losses in each "box" would rarely be high, they would rarely be nothing; and in time they might cripple our bomber offensive. A cheap and wholesale method of jamming the entire system was urgently needed.

As early as 1937 Professor Lindemann had prompted me to make a very simple suggestion to the Air Defence Research Committee. This was to scatter from the air packets of tin-foil strips or other conducting material cut to a special length so as to simulate a bomber on the enemy's radar screens. If a cloud of these were dropped by our aircraft the enemy fighters would not be able to tell which were our bombers and which were our tin-foil strips. This was later called "Window." The experts were doubtful, and the idea had not been tested till four years later, when, early in 1942, at Lindemann's instigation, highly secret trials were held. These were conducted by Dr. Jackson, one of our leading spectroscopists, who had joined the Air Force early in the war, and had distinguished himself as a night-fighter pilot. The tests were successful, and thereafter "Window" was rapidly developed. At first sight it seemed that these decoys would have to be as large as aircraft in order to give as good an echo. But if they were cut to the exact length to respond to the enemy radar this was unnecessary and they gave a very much stronger echo for their size than an untuned mass of metal like an aeroplane.

An easy and clever way of making such "tuned dipoles," as they are known technically, was worked out in 1942, after a certain amount of stimulation from above. It was found that strips of paper with one side metallised, such as is often used to wrap up chocolate, were quite sufficient, if cut to the right length, to reflect radio waves strongly. Bundles of strips of this sort, weighing only a few pounds, thrown out of an aeroplane would flutter down in clouds several yards across and give radar echoes almost exactly like those produced by ordinary bombers. It was hoped that we might be able to confuse the German radar if a good many bombers strewed clouds of such paper strips about the sky, which would give spurious radio echoes and make it difficult to distinguish the echo of the real aircraft. As they would only be blown along by the wind, the echo from the aircraft moving at hundreds of miles an hour could in principle be disentangled from the others. But this would be very difficult to do in the few minutes available, and we reckoned that it would hamper, if not prevent, accurate gun-laying by the anti-aircraft batteries, and make it very difficult for the radar operators in charge of the German ground control to guide the defending fighters to the attacking bombers. Our bombers came to hear of it, and wanted to use it at once to save their machines. But the snag was obvious. The device was so simple and so effective that the enemy might copy it and use it against us. If he started to bomb us again as he had done in 1940, our own fighters would be equally baffled and our own defence system equally frustrated. Fighter Command accordingly wanted the secret kept at any rate till we had found an antidote. Tense controversy ensued.

On June 22, 1943, I convened a Staff Conference of the heads of Bomber and Fighter Command to decide upon the use of "Window" in bombing operations. We guessed that the Germans must have thought of the device, but even if they adopted it the decline of their bomber force and the mounting strength of our air attack on Germany would give us the balance of advantage. Our experts were convinced that its large-scale introduction would reduce our bomber casualties by more than a third. We therefore decided at this meeting that "Window" could be used as soon as there was no chance that its imitation by the Germans could affect adversely our operations in Sicily. Highest priority was therefore given to the development, production, and installation of counter-measures in this country.

This work was actively pursued and pressed forward, a leading part being played by Dr. Jackson. The first trial of "Window" was made in a raid on Hamburg on July 24, 1943. Its effects surpassed expectations. Heated controversies, which we intercepted, between the German ground control operators and the pilots in their fighter planes showed the confusion which arose. For some months our bomber losses dropped to nearly half. And up to the end of the war, although the German fighter planes increased fourfold, our bomber losses never reached the same level that had been suffered before "Window" was used. The advantage gained by its introduction was maintained by a series of other new radio counter-measures and tactics.

There was, and still is, some argument as to whether we should have started using "Window" earlier. So many factors have to be considered that it is difficult to give a sharp-cut answer. Nobody could be certain how strong the German bomber force was in the summer of 1943, and it would have been very discouraging for our people if bombing attacks had begun again and our defences had proved less effective than three years earlier. On the whole it may be claimed that we released it about the right time. We learnt after the war that a similar proposal had been made by a German technician. Goering was quick to realise its danger to the defence. All papers relating to it were at once impounded, and the strictest orders issued that it should never be mentioned. Before we started using it they refrained for exactly the same reasons that had made us hesitate for so long. The Germans used it ultimately during the winter and spring of 1943–44, but by then their bombing effort was dying and they pinned their faith to rockets and pilotless weapons.

All this will be recorded in due course. We have already trespassed seriously upon chronology.

17

Malta and the Desert

*Another Four Months' Pause Proposed by General Auchinleck —
He Declines My Invitation to Come Home — Our Grave Differ-
ences with the Commander-in-Chief — Sir Stafford Cripps, on His
Indian Mission, Confers at Cairo — Agreeable but Futile Dis-
cussion — Interrelation Between Malta and the Desert — Malta's
Plight Desperate — Hitler Agrees to Take a Hand — Our Efforts
to Run Convoys — Admiral Vian's Spirited Attempt in March
— Climax of the German Air Attack on the Island — President
Roosevelt Lends Me the "Wasp" Carrier — Malta Gains the Air
Battle — The June Convoy from East and West — Only Two
Ships Out of Seventeen Reach Harbour — German-Italian Con-
ferences — Mussolini Decides on the Assault of the Island —
General Dobbie's Cry for Help — The "Wasp" Stings Again
— General Dobbie's Health Breaks Down — Lord Gort to Suc-
ceed Him — Rommel Plans His Offensive — General Auchin-
leck Seeks Further Delay — We Send Him Definite Orders to
Attack in June — He Obeys — My Telegram to Him of May
20 — His Reply — My Personal Military Views — A Strategic
Principle.*

DURING FEBRUARY it became apparent to us that General
Auchinleck proposed to make another four months' pause
in order to mount a second set-piece battle with Rommel.
Neither the Chiefs of Staff nor I and my colleagues were convinced that another of these costly interludes was necessary.
We were all sure it was lamentable that British and Imperial
armies, already numbering over six hundred and thirty thou-

sand men on ration strength, with reinforcements constantly arriving, should stand idle for so long a period at enormous expense while the Russians were fighting desperately and valiantly along their whole vast front. Moreover, it seemed to us that Rommel's strength might well grow quicker than our own. These considerations were fortified by the German renewal of their air attack on Malta and the consequent breakdown of our means of obstructing German and Italian convoys to Tripoli. Finally, Malta itself was threatened with starvation unless a steady monthly flow of supplies could be maintained. The supreme struggle for the life of Malta now began, and grew in intensity during the whole spring and summer.

General Auchinleck however was not convinced. This chapter will show the increasing pressure we put upon him, culminating in positive and formal orders to attack the enemy and fight a main battle rather than see Malta fall. The Commander-in-Chief complied with these orders and made preparations for a general offensive in the June period of the dark moon, during which we planned to run a vital convoy into the island fortress. His delay had however lost him the initiative, and it was Rommel who struck the blow.

Prime Minister to General Auchinleck   26 Feb. 42

I have not troubled you much in these difficult days, but I must now ask what are your intentions. According to our figures you have substantial superiority in the air, in armour, and in other forces over the enemy. There seems to be danger that he may gain reinforcements as fast as or even faster than you. The supply of Malta is causing us increased anxiety, and anyone can see the magnitude of our disasters in the Far East.

Pray let me hear from you. All good wishes.

General Auchinleck had meanwhile in a paper of fifteen hundred words marshalled his reasons for not being hurried and for making sure on this occasion of victory in his own time.

On February 27 he reported that he held a strong defensive position in the area Gazala-Tobruk-Bir Hacheim, and that enemy attack on it should be repulsed with loss. The real value of this position was that it provided security for Tobruk and therefore formed an admirable base for future offensive action, and his intention was to hold it firmly. He weighed up his own resources and their probable rate of expansion, comparing them with the estimated enemy capabilities, and stated that he thoroughly understood the critical nature of the Malta maintenance situation and the need for recovering landing-grounds in Cyrenaica farther forward than those he already held. Nevertheless he thought it clear that he would not have reasonable numerical superiority before June 1, and that to launch a major offensive before then would be to risk defeat in detail and possibly endanger the safety of Egypt.

He concluded:

To sum up, my intentions for Western Front are:

To continue to build up the armoured striking force in Eighth Army forward area as rapidly as possible.

2. Meanwhile to make the Gazala-Tobruk and Sollum-Maddalena positions as strong as possible and push the railway forward towards El Adem.

3. To build up in the forward area reserves of supplies for the renewal of the offensive.

4. To seize the first chance of staging a limited offensive to regain landing-grounds in area Derna-Mechili, provided this can be done without prejudicing chances of launching major offensive to recapture Cyrenaica or safety of the Tobruk area.

This document engaged the earnest attention of our Chiefs of Staff, and we were agreed that, boiled down, it expressed a standstill till June, or even July, without regard to the fate of Malta or any other consideration in the world — and there were many. After the whole matter had been thrashed out and we found ourselves all together I sent the following telegram:

Prime Minister to General Auchinleck   8 Mar. 42

The situation disclosed by your appreciation is very serious and not likely to be adjusted by correspondence. I should be glad therefore if you would come home for consultation at your earliest convenience, bringing with you any officers you may require, especially an authority on the state of the tanks and their servicing.

Auchinleck declined this invitation on the ground of the need for his presence in Cairo. It seemed to me that he conceived himself stronger in resisting from his own headquarters the requests which he knew would be made to him.

We returned to the sharp point.

Prime Minister to General Auchinleck   15 Mar. 42

Your appreciation of February 27 continues to cause deepest anxiety here, both to the Chiefs of Staff and Defence Committee. I therefore regret extremely your inability to come home for consultation. The delay you have in mind will endanger safety of Malta. Moreover, there is no certainty that the enemy cannot reinforce faster than you, so that after all your waiting you will find yourself in relatively the same or even a worse position. Your losses have been far less than the enemy's, who nevertheless keeps fighting. For instance, the 7th Armoured Division was withdrawn to the Delta to rest although its losses were far less than those of the 15th and 21st German Armoured Divisions, who came back at you with so much vigour. A very heavy German counter-stroke upon the Russians must be expected soon, and it will be thought intolerable that the 635,000 men (exclusive of Malta) on your ration strength should remain unengaged, preparing for another set-piece battle in July.

2. A limited offensive to Derna, of which you hold out some prospect, would have the advantage at any rate of coming to grips with the enemy and forcing him to consume lives, munitions, tanks, and aircraft. In that case, if he beat your armour you would have to retire to your defensive zone. But if you beat his armour no one here understands why you should not press your advantage and go farther. . . .

4. I have done everything in my power to give you continuous support at heavy cost to the whole war. It would give me the greatest pain to feel that mutual understanding had ceased. In order to avoid this, I have asked Sir Stafford Cripps to stop for a day in Cairo about [the] 19th or 20th on his way to India, and put before you the views of the War Cabinet. He will be joined

by General Nye, who is proceeding separately, and is fully possessed
of the Chiefs of Staff's opinion. It is impossible for C.I.G.S. to
leave the centre at this moment.

Prime Minister to General Auchinleck   16 Mar. 42

I ought to have added the following to my message of March 15.
If, as the result of all discussions, it is decided that you must stand
on the defensive until July, it will be necessary at once to consider
the movement of at least fifteen air squadrons from Libya to sustain the Russian left wing in the Caucasus.

At this time Sir Stafford Cripps was passing through Cairo
on his Indian Mission. He had been of course in full agreement
with the line we were taking at home. I therefore hoped that
he might by his personal force bring about a solution on the
spot. However, when he got to Cairo he only touched upon
the surface of things. His mind was no doubt full of the Indian
problem, about which he had high hopes and strong views.

Sir Stafford Cripps to Prime Minister   21 Mar. 42

I am very satisfied with the atmosphere at Cairo after our talks.
Last night I had long and most friendly talk with Auchinleck,
Nye, Tedder, Cunningham's deputy, and Monckton, at which I
went through my telegram to you in detail. They were all most
helpful and co-operative. When I first arrived I felt a rather prickly
atmosphere, which was also apparent on Nye's arrival. That has
now completely disappeared, and everyone, including Nye, was
most happy when we left early this morning. I do not think there
will be any need for you to trouble to come out, and I think you
would find [the] journey long and difficult. I hope ᵧou will get
all additional detail you want from Nye before he returns home.
I have no doubts as to Auchinleck's offensive [spirit], but I think
his Scottish caution and desire not to mislead by optimism cause
him to overstress in statement the difficulties and uncertainties of
[the] situation. I am convinced of his determination to face these,
and am sure that it will help him very much if he can now be
made to feel that all misunderstandings are at an end and there
is no more questioning of his desire to take [the] offensive. If you
accept [the] situation as detailed in my long telegram, as I much

hope you will, it would, I am sure, help if you could send Auchinleck a short, friendly telegram expressing your satisfaction that he
will have all possible help from you to hit the target at the appointed time.

I was very ill-content with all this, and the long telegram
of technical detail which accompanied it. Cripps had gone on
to India, so I telegraphed to General Nye, who had left home
in a robust mood.

Prime Minister to General Nye, Cairo   22 Mar. 42

I have heard from the Lord Privy Seal. I do not wonder everything was so pleasant, considering you seem to have accepted
everything they said, and all *we* have got to accept is the probable
loss of Malta and the Army standing idle, while the Russians are
resisting the German counter-stroke desperately, and while the
enemy is reinforcing himself in Libya faster than we are.

2. Do not hasten your return, but go into the questions of tank
serviceability, armament, and the use of man-power in the Middle
East searchingly.

3. Also let me have precise answers to your twenty questions by
cable in good time before you leave, so that we can comment on
them here.

4. Finally, try to form an opinion about possibility of enemy
offensive, either from the west or across the sea from Greece, the
latter (*a*) by air or (*b*) by ships. This of course would alter the
picture altogether.

*   *   *   *   *

The interrelation between Malta and the Desert operations
was never so plain as in 1942, and the heroic defence of the
island in that year formed the keystone of the prolonged
struggle for the maintenance of our position in Egypt and the
Middle East. In the bitter land fighting in the Western Desert
the outcome of each phase was measured by a hand's-breadth,
and frequently depended on the rate at which supplies could
reach the combatants by sea. For ourselves this meant the two
or three months' voyage round the Cape, subject to all the
perils of the U-boats, and the employment of enormous quanti-

ties of high-class shipping. For the enemy there was only the two or three days' passage across the Mediterranean from Italy, involving the use of a moderate number of smaller ships. But athwart the route to Tripoli lay the island fortress of Malta. We have seen in an earlier volume how the island had been converted into a veritable hornets' nest, and how in the last days of 1941 the Germans had been compelled to make a supreme, and partially successful, effort to curb its action.

In 1942 the air attack on Malta mounted formidably and the plight of the island became desperate. In January, while Rommel's counter-offensive prospered, Kesselring struck chiefly at the Malta airfields. Under German pressure, the Italian Navy used battleships to support their Tripoli convoys. The Mediterranean Fleet, stricken as has been described, could offer only a limited challenge to these movements. Our submarines and air forces from Malta continued however to take their toll.

In February Admiral Raeder, whose repute at that time stood high, sought to convince Hitler of the importance of decisive victory in the Mediterranean. On February 13, the day after the successful passage up the Channel by the German battle-cruisers, he had found the Fuehrer in a receptive mood, and his representations had at last met with some success. The intervention of the Germans in North Africa and the Mediterranean, which had begun as a purely defensive measure to save their weak ally from defeat, was now viewed in a new light as an aggressive means of destroying British power in the Middle East. Raeder dwelt on events in Asia and the irruption of Japanese power into the Indian Ocean. In the course of his statement he said, "Suez and Basra are the western pillars of the British position in the East. Should these positions collapse under the weight of concerted Axis pressure the consequences for the British Empire would be disastrous. . . ." Hitler was impressed, and, having hitherto paid little attention to the unfruitful task of helping the Italians, he now consented to press forward his vast plan for the conquest of the whole of the Middle East. Admiral Raeder insisted that Malta was the key, and urged the immediate preparation of transports for its storm.

The favourable situation in the Mediterranean, so pronounced at the present time, will probably never occur again. All reports confirm that the enemy is making tremendous efforts to pour all available reinforcements into Egypt. . . . It is therefore imperative to take Malta as soon as possible and to launch an offensive against the Suez Canal not later than 1942.

As a weaker alternative he suggested:

If Axis troops do *not* occupy Malta, it is imperative that the German Air Force continue its attacks on the island to the same extent as heretofore. Such attacks alone will prevent the enemy from rebuilding Malta's offensive and defensive capacity.

Hitler and his military advisers did not relish the plan of seaborne assault. The Fuehrer had only recently given orders for the final cancellation of the long-term plans for the invasion of England, which had dragged on since 1940. The slaughter of his cherished airborne troops in Crete a year before was a deterrent factor. It was however agreed at this time that Malta should be captured and that German forces should participate. Hitler had reservations, and continued to hope that the attacks of the Luftwaffe would bring about capitulation, or at least paralyse the defence and its activities. We tried to run supplies through to Malta from the east. Four ships were successful in January, but the February convoy of three ships met disaster by air attack. In March the cruiser *Naiad*, wearing Admiral Vian's flag, was sunk by a U-boat. By May the island would be in danger of famine.

The Admiralty were ready to face all risks to carry in supplies. On March 20 four merchant ships left Alexandria, with a strong escort supported by four light cruisers. Admiral Vian, now in the *Cleopatra*, again commanded. By the morning of the 22d the air attacks had started and heavy Italian warships were approaching. Presently the *Euryalus* sighted four ships to the northward, and the British admiral at once turned to attack, while the convoy headed away to the southwest under cover of smoke. The enemy cruisers retired, but only to return two hours later, supported by the battleship *Littorio* and what appeared to be two more cruisers. For the next two hours the British ships, Vian's squadron, fought a bold and successful action at these fantastic odds to protect the convoy, which meanwhile was under heavy attack from German bombers. Thanks to the effective smoke cover and the fierce defence by the close escort and the merchant ships themselves, not a ship was damaged. In the evening the enemy turned away. Four light cruisers with eleven destroyers, in stormy weather, had held at bay one of the most powerful battleships afloat, supported by two heavy cruisers, one light cruiser, and ten destroyers. Although the *Cleopatra* and three destroyers had been hit, all remained in vigorous action to the end.

I telegraphed:

Prime Minister to Commander-in-Chief Mediterranean   25 Mar. 42

I shall be glad if you will convey to Admiral Vian and all who sailed with him the admiration which I feel at this resolute and brilliant action. . . . That one of the most powerful modern battleships afloat, attended by two heavy cruisers and one light cruiser and a flotilla, should have been routed and put to flight with severe torpedo and gunfire injuries in broad daylight by the fire of British light cruisers and destroyers constitutes a naval episode of the highest distinction and entitles all ranks and ratings concerned, and above all their Commander, to the compliments of the British nation.

The convoy had to make for Malta by itself. Admiral Vian could not refuel there, and so could protect it no farther. Little of its precious cargoes reached the defenders of Malta. The heavy air attacks were renewed as the ships approached the island. The *Clan Campbell* and then the *Breconshire* were sunk when there were only eight miles to go. The two remaining ships reached harbour only to be sunk there while being unloaded. Of 26,000 tons of supplies carried in the four ships only about 5000 were landed. Malta got no more for another three months.

This decided us not to send any more convoys until we could reinforce the island with fighter aircraft. During March the *Eagle* had flown in thirty-four, but this was not nearly enough. Admiral Vian's action had convinced the Germans that the Italian Navy did not mean to fight and that they must rely on their own resources. From the beginning of April Kesselring's air attacks on Malta did very great damage to the dockyard and the ships in the harbour. Naval vessels could no longer use the island as a base, and before the end of the month all that could move were withdrawn.

The Royal Air Force stayed to fight for its life and for that of all the island. In those critical weeks we often had only a handful of serviceable fighters. Our men were pressed to the limit of endurance to prevent their own annihilation and to keep up the constant flow of aircraft that used Malta as a staging base to Egypt. While the air crews fought and the ground crews toiled to service and refuel for the next engagement, the soldiers repaired the stricken airfields. Malta won through only by the narrowest margin, and at home we were very anxious.

* * * * *

I now appealed to President Roosevelt, who clearly saw that the island was the key to all our hopes in the Mediterranean.

Former Naval Person to President Roosevelt 1 Apr. 42

Air attack on Malta is very heavy. There are now in Sicily about four hundred German and two hundred Italian fighters and bombers. Malta can now muster only twenty or thirty serviceable fighters. We keep feeding Malta with Spitfires in packets of sixteen loosed from *Eagle* carrier from about six hundred miles west of Malta.

This has worked a good many times quite well, but *Eagle* is now laid up for a month by defects in her steering gear. There are no Spitfires in Egypt. *Argus* is too small and too slow, and moreover she has to provide the fighter cover for the carrier launching the Spitfires and for the escorting force. We would use *Victorious,* but unfortunately her lifts are too small for Spitfires. Therefore there will be a whole month without any Spitfire reinforcements.

2. It seems likely, from extraordinary enemy concentration on Malta, that they hope to exterminate our air defence in time to reinforce either Libya or their Russian offensive. This would mean that Malta would be at the best powerless to interfere with reinforcements of armour to Rommel, and our chances of resuming offensive against him at an early date ruined.

3. Would you be willing to allow your carrier *Wasp* to do one of these trips provided details are satisfactorily agreed between the Naval Staffs? With her broad lifts, capacity, and length, we estimate that *Wasp* could take fifty or more Spitfires. Unless it were necessary for her to fuel, *Wasp* could proceed through the Straits at night without calling at Gibraltar until on the return journey, as the Spitfires would be embarked in the Clyde.

4. Thus, instead of not being able to give Malta any further Spitfires during April, a powerful Spitfire force could be flown into Malta at a stroke and give us a chance of inflicting a very severe and possibly decisive check on [the] enemy. Operation might take place during third week of April.

The response was generous.

President Roosevelt to Prime Minister   3 Apr. 42

Your proposal does not mention availability of *Furious,* which is scheduled to leave United States April 3 for the Clyde via Bermuda, and whose plans show elevators large enough for Spitfires.

Admiral King will advise Admiral Pound through Ghormley that *Wasp* is at [your] disposal as you request if our estimate as to *Furious* should be incorrect.

The *Wasp* was sent. But Malta had to live as well as fight.

Prime Minister to General Ismay, for C.O.S. Committee   3 Apr. 42

This serious report [from Governor of Malta] should be considered with a view to action. It seems odd that the small-arms ammunition position should be unsatisfactory, having regard to the fact that there has been no rifle or machine-gun fighting.

Are we to understand from paragraph 1 (*c*) that they are entirely meatless? or have they cattle they can kill, and if so how many?

What are the plans for the April convoy?

2. We certainly have not got "large quantities of transport air-craft," but what can be done with additional large submarines or fast ships of the "A" type? What a pity we did not get hold of the *Surcouf* and keep her on this job! How much can a submarine carry? What about sending in vitamins and other concentrates?

Prime Minister to First Sea Lord   12 Apr. 42

Can you give me details of the method of supplying Malta by submarine? I understand that removal of certain batteries greatly increases the carrying capacity of the submarine, and I would like to inform the United States authorities of these details for use in supplying Corregidor.

*   *   *   *   *

During April and May one hundred and twenty-six aircraft were safely delivered to the Malta garrison from the *Wasp* and *Eagle,* with salutary effect. The bombing attacks, which had reached their peak in April, now began to slacken, largely as a result of great air battles on May 9 and 10, when sixty Spit-fires which had just arrived went into action with destructive effect. Daylight raiding was brought to an abrupt end. In June the stage was at last set for another large-scale attempt to relieve the island, and this time it was intended to pass convoys through from the east and west simultaneously. Six ships entered the Mediterranean from the west on the night of June 11, escorted by the A.A. cruiser *Cairo* and nine destroyers. In support was Admiral Curteis with the battleship *Malaya,* the carriers *Eagle* and *Argus,* two cruisers, and eight destroyers. Off Sardinia on the 14th the heavy air attacks began, one merchant ship being sunk and the cruiser *Liverpool* damaged and put out of action. That evening the heavy covering forces withdrew as the convoy approached the Narrows, but next morning when south of Pantelleria an attack developed by two Italian cruisers, supported by destroyers and numerous aircraft. The British ships were outranged, and in the ensuing action the destroyer *Bedouin* was sunk and another heavily damaged before the enemy were driven off, not without loss. Repeated air attacks continued throughout the day, and three more merchant ships were lost. The two surviving ships of the battered convoy reached Malta that night.

The eastern convoy of eleven ships was even less fortunate. Admiral Vian, who again commanded, now had at his disposal much more powerful covering forces of cruisers and destroyers than when he had driven off the enemy in March, but he lacked the support of any battleship or aircraft-carrier, and it was to be expected that the main strength of the Italian Fleet would be deployed against him. After sailing on the 11th the convoy met heavy and continuous air attack on the 14th, when south of Crete. That evening Vian learned that the enemy fleet, including two *Littorio* class battleships, had left Taranto, presumably to intercept him. It was hoped that the British submarines and the land-based air attacks from Cyrenaica and Malta would cripple the enemy during his approach. One Italian cruiser was hit, and later sunk. But this was not enough. The enemy held on to the southeastward, and our interception by an overwhelming force on the morning of the 15th seemed inevitable. The convoy and its escort had to return to Egypt, having lost the cruiser *Hermione* by U-boat, as well as three destroyers and two merchant ships by air attack. The Royal Air Force losses were also considerable. On the Italian side one heavy cruiser was sunk and a battleship damaged, but the approach to Malta from the eastward remained sealed, and no convoy again attempted this passage until November.

Thus, in spite of our greatest efforts, only two supply ships out of seventeen got through, and the crisis in the island continued.

* * * * *

German records show how tense was the interplay in enemy minds between Malta and the Desert operations. As long as Malta could strike with air-power and flotillas upon the enemy's communications these were greatly hampered. The reduction of Malta to impotence, or better still its capture, was the main objective, and for this purpose an ever-growing German air force was gathered on the Sicilian airfields. On the

other hand, when Rommel was active he required the aid of all
the air that could be maintained in Tripoli. But then if the
attack on Malta were lightened, the fortress rapidly recovered
its striking power, and by extreme exertions began at once to
take a heavy toll of the convoys. There was no lasting solution
for the enemy short of the conquest of Malta. Rommel
clamoured for petrol and reinforcements, but above all for
petrol. During March and April all the heat was turned on
Malta, and remorseless air attacks by day and night wore the
island down and pressed it to the last gasp.

Early in April Field-Marshal von Kesselring, having visited
the African front, met Mussolini and General Cavallero.
Kesselring held that the air attack on Malta had put the island
out of action as a naval base for some time to come and had
severely reduced its air menace. He reported that Rommel was
planning to attack in June with the object of destroying the
British forces and capturing Tobruk. This could be achieved
with the additional replenishments which would be able to
reach him while Malta was virtually crippled.

Mussolini decided that all preparations for the capture of
Malta should be hastened. He asked for German help, and
proposed the assault for the end of May. The operation was
called "Hercules," and figures prominently in all the later
April telegrams. Cavallero offered the Italian Parachute Division of two regiments, a battalion of engineers, and five batteries. Hitler gave orders that Germans should co-operate with
two parachute battalions, an engineer battalion, transport aircraft for a lift of one battalion, and, by the German Navy, an
unspecified number of barges.

When Sir Stafford Cripps was on his way back from India
I again felt it right to let him know, on his way through Cairo,
how grievous and urgent was the need for Auchinleck to act,
and how little content we were with the results of the discussions on his outward journey.

Prime Minister to Lord Privy Seal, Cairo   14 Apr. 42
I hope you will not let it be thought that we here are not deeply

concerned with the prolonged inaction of the Libya Army. It seems to me quite possible that Rommel will grow stronger at a greater rate than our people. Now that one submarine flotilla has to go from the Mediterranean to the Indian Ocean and the air attack on Malta makes it impossible to station bombers there, the route from Italy to Tripoli will not be much obstructed. Besides this, the Middle East air will be increasingly drawn upon for the Indian emergency. There is no use pressing a general beyond his better judgment, but I should like you to know that my opinion and that of the Staffs here is unaltered.

*   *   *   *   *

We were all indebted to Mr. Curtin for allowing his division to remain for the Desert battle.

Prime Minister to Mr. Curtin, Australia   15 Apr. 42

I am very much obliged to you for your decision to allow the Australian 9th Division to remain in Middle East for the present. It is fully understood, and was certainly my wish, that United States forces should go to Australia unconditionally, and you have always been, and will be, perfectly free to decide the movement of all your troops.

*   *   *   *   *

Malta cried aloud for help. The strain was at many points more than could be borne. General Dobbie was distressed. In March he had said that his situation was critical, and on April 20 he reported: "It has now gone beyond that point, and it is obvious that the very worst may happen if we cannot replenish our vital needs, especially flour and ammunition, and that very soon. . . . It is a question of survival." A few days later he added that bread consumption was being cut by a quarter and would now last only until mid-June.

I was prepared to run serious naval risks to save Malta, and the Admiralty were in full accord. We prepared, and kept the option in hand, to send Admiral Somerville with all his carriers and the *Warspite* through the Canal into the Mediterranean, and to carry a convoy through to Malta, hoping to bring about a general engagement with the Italian Fleet on the way. I asked President Roosevelt to allow the *Wasp* to do a second trip with Spitfires. "Without this aid I fear Malta will be pounded to bits. Meanwhile its defence is wearing out the enemy's Air Force and effectively aiding Russia." The President responded as I hoped. "I am pleased to say," he replied on April 25, "that *Wasp* is to be made available for the second trip with Spitfires for Malta."

Prime Minister to Chief of Air Staff   25 Apr. 42

Now that the President has agreed about *Wasp,* let me know the programme for feeding Malta with Spitfires, week by week, during the next eight weeks.

Former Naval Person to President Roosevelt   29 Apr. 42

Most grateful for your telegram about Madagascar, for which all goes forward. Also for allowing *Wasp* to have another good sting. . . .

It may be well here to complete the story of the *Wasp.* On May 9 she successfully delivered another all-important flight of Spitfires to struggling Malta. I made her a signal, "Who said a wasp couldn't sting twice?" The *Wasp* thanked me for my "gracious" message. Alas, poor *Wasp!* She left the dangerous Mediterranean for the Pacific, and on September 15 was sunk by Japanese torpedoes. Happily her gallant crew were saved. They had been a link in our chain of causation.

*   *   *   *   *

Disturbing news in April arrived about General Dobbie. Up to this moment he had been magnificent, and from all parts of the Empire eyes were turned on him — a Cromwellian figure at the key point. But the long strain had worn him down. I received this news with very deep regret, and I did not at first accept what I was told. However, a successor had to be chosen. I felt that in Lord Gort, the Governor of Gibraltar, would be found a warrior of the truest mettle. Mr. Casey was flying out via Gibraltar to take up his appointment as Minister of State, and I entrusted him with full explanations to Gort.

Mr. Churchill to Viscount Gort   25 Apr. 42

I avail myself of the Minister of State's journey through Gibraltar and Malta to send you these few lines. It may be that — as he will explain to you — a change will be required at a most critical juncture in the command of Malta. If this should be so, we all feel you are the man of all others to render this vitally important service. You may be sure that I shall do everything in my power to carry a heavy convoy of supplies into Malta in the latter part of June, and that meanwhile the supply of Spitfires from the west will be continual.

I am delighted with all the reports we get of the splendid way in which you have organised Gibraltar and maintained the high morale of its garrison. Should you be required for this further service you will be equipped with ample powers, and will carry with you the full confidence of His Majesty's Government and of your sincere friend.

*   *   *   *   *

Meanwhile Rommel was planning his offensive. About its timing he said, "The Panzer Army is to attack as soon as possible after the capture of Malta. If the operations against Malta should extend beyond June 1 it may be necessary for the Army to attack without waiting for the capture of the island." His plan of April 30 reckoned to destroy the British forces in the field by the evening of the second day, after which Tobruk was to be captured by a surprise attack. This however depended on his getting the reinforcements and the supplies of oil, munitions, vehicles, and food which he had specified. He also asked what extra help he could expect in the air and at sea, and hoped that Italian heavy naval forces and assault boats would "hold down the British Fleet based on Alexandria."

Cavallero visited Africa on May 6 to discuss the forthcoming attack. He considered — and so did we in London — that the capture of Tobruk was an essential condition for further Axis advance. If Tobruk were not taken, the Gazala line, or even west of it, was his limit. All must be completed by June 20, as some of the air forces to be used in Cyrenaica would have to withdraw thereafter "for operations elsewhere." Owing to Benghazi having reached a capacity of two thousand tons a day, Rommel's requirements could be met, but there was no hope of more transport from either German or Italian sources.

* * * * *

Rommel's intentions may be contrasted with General Auchinleck's, who presently sent a telegram in which he offered to stand on the defensive in the Desert and send considerable reinforcements to India. This was entirely contrary to our ideas. I replied:

Prime Minister to General Auchinleck   5 May 42

. . . While we are grateful to you for your offer to denude the Middle East further for the sake of the Indian danger, we feel that the greatest help you could give to the whole war at this juncture would be [to] engage and defeat the enemy on your western front. All our directions upon this subject remain unaltered in their purpose and validity, and we trust you will find it possible to give full effect to them about the date which you mentioned to the Lord Privy Seal.

Soon there arrived another telegram from General Auchinleck seeking further to postpone the engagement of his army. I referred this to all my colleagues, military and political.

Prime Minister to General Auchinleck   8 May 42

The Chiefs of Staff, the Defence Committee, and the War Cabinet have all earnestly considered your telegram in relation to the whole war situation, having particular regard to Malta, the loss of which would be a disaster of first magnitude to the British Empire, and probably fatal in the long run to the defence of the Nile Valley.

2. We are agreed that in spite of the risks you mention you would be right to attack the enemy and fight a major battle, if possible during May, and the sooner the better. We are prepared to take full responsibility for these general directions, leaving you the necessary latitude for their execution. In this you will no doubt

have regard to the fact that the enemy may himself be planning
to attack you early in June.

As the result of these hard discussions it was decided to send
General Auchinleck definite orders which he must obey or be
relieved. This was a most unusual procedure on our part
towards a high military commander.

Prime Minister to General Auchinleck   10 May 42

The Chiefs of Staff, the Defence Committee, and the War Cabinet have again considered the whole position. We are determined
that Malta shall not be allowed to fall without a battle being
fought by your whole army for its retention. The starving out of
this fortress would involve the surrender of over 30,000 men, Army
and Air Force, together with several hundred guns. Its possession
would give the enemy a clear and sure bridge to Africa, with all
the consequences flowing from that. Its loss would sever the air
route upon which both you and India must depend for a substantial part of your aircraft reinforcements. Besides this, it would
compromise any offensive against Italy, and future plans such as
"Acrobat" and "Gymnast." Compared with the certainty of these
disasters, we consider the risks you have set out to the safety of
Egypt are definitely less, and we accept them.

2. We therefore reiterate the views we have expressed, with this
qualification—that the very latest date for engaging the enemy
which we could approve is one which provides a distraction in
time to help the passage of the June dark-period convoy.

There was a considerable pause, during which we did not
know whether he would accept or resign.

Prime Minister to General Auchinleck   17 May 42

It is necessary for me to have some account of your general intentions in the light of our recent telegrams.

At length his answer came.

General Auchinleck to Prime Minister   19 May 42

My intention is to carry out the instructions of your message of
May 10.

2. I am assuming that [your telegram] is not meant to imply that all that is required is an operation solely to provide a distraction to help the Malta convoy, but that the primary object of an offensive in Libya is still to be the destruction of the enemy forces and the occupation of Cyrenaica as a step toward the eventual expulsion of the enemy from Libya. If I am wrong in this assumption, then I should be so informed at once, as plans for a major offensive differ entirely from those designed merely to produce a distraction. I am proceeding as if my assumption is right.

3. Assuming that a major offensive is to be carried out but that its inception must be so timed as to provide distraction to help the Malta convoy, the actual moment of the launching of the offensive will be governed by three considerations — first, the sailing date of the convoy; second, enemy action between now and then; third, the relative air strength of the enemy and ourselves. All these are under close and continuous examination here.

4. There are strong signs that the enemy intends to attack us in the immediate future. If he does attack, our future action must be governed by the results of the battle and cannot be forecast now.

5. Assuming that the enemy does not attack us first, it is my intention that General Ritchie shall launch his offensive in Libya on the date which will best fit in with the object of providing the maximum distraction for the Malta convoy, and at the same time ensure the fullest degree of readiness in the forces carrying out the offensive. These considerations are mutually conflicting, as you will realise, and entail a certain degree of compromise which it will be my responsibility in consultation with the other Commanders-in-Chief to determine. The importance of avoiding an abortive attack has already been fully set out [by us] and does not need further explanation from me. . . .

I replied at once:

Prime Minister to General Auchinleck   20 May 42

Your interpretation of the instructions contained in mine of May 10 is absolutely correct. We feel that the time has come for a trial of strength in Cyrenaica, and that the survival of Malta is involved. . . .

Of course we realise that success cannot be guaranteed. There are no safe battles. But whether this one arises from an enemy

attack and your forestalling or manoeuvring counter-stroke, or
whether it has to be undertaken by you on its own, we have full
confidence in you and your glorious army, and whatever happens
we will sustain you by every means in our power.

I should personally feel even greater confidence if you took
direct command yourself, as in fact you had to do at Sidi Rezegh.
On this however I do not press you in any way.

Ought not the New Zealand Division to be nearer the battle-
front? If you want any help in dealing with the New Zealand
Government pray recur to me.

These last two suggestions were not accepted by General
Auchinleck. He gave his reasons. We shall see how the General
was forced by events to take both these steps. But, alas, too
late!

General Auchinleck to Prime Minister   22 May 42

I am now absolutely clear as to my task, and I will do my utmost
to accomplish it to your satisfaction.

Am most grateful for your most generous expression of confidence in the army I command and in myself and for the assurance
of your support, the measure of which has been proved to us so
often and so amply in the past.

Much as I would like to take command personally in Libya, I
feel it would not be the right course to pursue. I have considered
the possibility most carefully, and have concluded that it would be
most difficult for me to keep a right sense of proportion if I became immersed in tactical problems in Libya. I feel that a situation may arise almost at any time when I shall have to decide
whether I can continue to reinforce and sustain the Eighth Army
without serious hindrance, or whether I must hold back and
consider the building up of our northern front, which I am now
weakening in order to give General Ritchie all the help possible.
On balance I think my place is here, but you can rely on me, I
hope, to adapt myself to the situation and to take hold if need
arises. I am in very close touch with General Ritchie and he is
fully in my mind. I hope all will be well.

I have considered fully the desirability of bringing the New
Zealand Division out of Syria into Egypt. Apart from the political
aspect, which I am sure you could settle as you so kindly offer to

do, there are other considerations. I am loth to denude Syria of troops just now, partly because of the uneasy political situation in the country itself and partly because of the possible effect on the Turks, of whose attitude I am not too sure. . . . I am already bringing 10th Indian Division, a well-trained formation, from Iraq to reinforce Eighth Army should need arise, and have meanwhile sent up a brigade of 4th Indian Division as an interim reinforcement. With these reinforcements the Eighth Army will almost reach saturation point so far as power to provide the Army with food and water is concerned. . . .

Once more I thank you for your most sustaining message. There will be hard fighting, as there was before. I have great confidence in our troops and in our dispositions. I have a firm hope of victory, and pray that it may lead to greater things.

* * * * *

About this time also I drafted a message to the General which expressed my own military convictions. On reflection I did not send it, as I did not wish to trespass too much on his own domain.

The following is quite unofficial and private:

It certainly looks as if the enemy will himself attack you soon. I do not fully share your view that this would give Eighth Army its best chance. Although many famous victories have been won by the repulse of an assailant followed by a counter-stroke, I cannot help thinking at this time of Napoleon's preconceived rupturing counter-stroke at Austerlitz. We have often been inclined to think that Germans are particularly vexed when some well-thought-out plan on which they are working is upset by the unexpected. This would seem to apply all the more in these days when the unimpeded initiative is of special value to armoured forces. In short, the picture of two separate battle plans, theirs and ours, clashing upon each other makes a powerful appeal to the mind. We may be given good opportunities for timing a blow upon the enemy at his most vulnerable moment.

2. Pray excuse these rudimentary thoughts upon an approaching episode which you have been studying so long. Your affairs are so much in my mind that I could not resist.

* * * * *

I have often tried to set down the strategic truths I have comprehended in the form of simple anecdotes, and they rank this way in my mind. One of them is the celebrated tale of the man who gave the powder to the bear. He mixed the powder with the greatest care, making sure that not only the ingredients but the proportions were absolutely correct. He rolled it up in a large paper spill, and was about to blow it down the bear's throat. *But the bear blew first.*

If I venture to set this down at this moment in my story it is because I am emboldened by the words of Socrates: "The genius of Tragedy and Comedy are essentially the same, and they should be written by the same authors."

18

"Second Front Now!"

April 1942

President Roosevelt's Majestic Plan — Arrival of Mr. Hopkins and General Marshall in London — "Operations in Western Europe" — Our Chiefs of Staff Consider the Proposal — My Telegram to the President of April 12 — Conference of the Defence Committee, April 14 — General Marshall's Statement — I Stress Dangers in the Indian Ocean — Mr. Hopkins Sustains General Marshall — The Favourable Reception of the Plan — "Round-up" and "Bolero" — My Report to President Roosevelt of April 17 — His Gratification — My Personal Views — Our Imperial Duty to Defend India — My Accord with a Supreme Cross-Channel Attack in 1943 — General Marshall's Project of a Partial Attempt in 1942: "Sledgehammer" — Other Alternatives: French Northwest Africa or Northern Norway — A Summing Up.

MEANWHILE President Roosevelt was also exercised about Russia, and with his Staff was developing plans for taking the weight off her.

President Roosevelt to Former Naval Person   2 Apr. 42

As I have completed survey of the immediate and long-range problems of the military situations facing the United Nations, I have come to certain conclusions which are so vital that I want you to know the whole picture, and to ask your approval. The whole of it is so dependent on complete co-operation by the United Kingdom and United States that Harry and Marshall will leave for London in a few days to present first of all to you the salient points. It is a plan which I hope Russia will greet with enthusiasm, and, on word from you when you have seen Harry and Marshall, I propose to ask Stalin to send two special representatives to see me at once. I think it will work out in full accord with trend of public opinion here and in Britain. And, finally, I would like to be able to label it the plan of the United Nations.

I soon received the following letter from the President:

The White House, Washington,
3 Apr., 11 P.M.

Dear Winston,

What Harry and Geo. Marshall will tell you all about has my heart and *mind* in it. Your people and mine demand the establishment of a front to draw off pressure on the Russians, and these peoples are wise enough to see that the Russians are today killing more Germans and destroying more equipment than you and I put together. Even if full success is not attained, the *big* objective will be.

Go to it! Syria and Egypt will be made more secure, even if the Germans find out about our plans.

Best of luck. Make Harry go to bed early, and let him obey Dr. Fulton, U.S.N., whom I am sending with him as super-nurse with full authority.

As ever,
F. D. R.

On April 8 Hopkins and General Marshall arrived in London. They brought with them a comprehensive memorandum prepared by the United States Joint Staff and approved by the President.

OPERATIONS IN WESTERN EUROPE

April, 1942

Western Europe is favoured as the theatre in which to stage the first major offensive by the United States and Great Britain. Only there could their combined land and air resources be fully developed and the maximum support given to Russia.

The decision to launch this offensive must be made *at once,* because of the immense preparations necessary in many directions. Until it can be launched the enemy in the West must be pinned down and kept in uncertainty by ruses and raids; which latter would also gain useful information and provide valuable training.

The combined invasion forces should consist of forty-eight divisions (including nine armoured), of which the British share is eighteen divisions (including three armoured). The supporting air forces required amount to 5800 combat aircraft, 2550 of them British.

Speed is the essence of the problem. The principal limiting factors are shortages of landing-craft for the assault and of shipping to transport the necessary forces from America to the United Kingdom. Without affecting essential commitments in other theatres, these forces can be brought over by April 1, 1943, but only if sixty per cent of the lift is carried by non-U.S. ships. If the movement is dependent only on U.S. shipping, the date of the assault must be postponed to the late summer of 1943.

About seven thousand landing-craft will be needed, and current construction programmes must be greatly accelerated to achieve this figure. Concurrently, preparatory work to receive and operate the large U.S. land and air contingents must be speeded up.

The assault should take place on selected beaches between Havre and Boulogne, and be carried out by a first wave of at least six divisions, supplemented by airborne troops. It would have to be nourished at the rate of at least one hundred thousand men a week. As soon as the beachheads are secure armoured forces would move rapidly to seize the line of the Oise-St. Quentin. Thereafter the next objective would be Antwerp.

Since invasion on this scale cannot be mounted before April 1, 1943, at earliest, a plan must be prepared, and kept up to date, for immediate action by such forces as may be available from time to time. This may have to be put into effect as an emergency measure either (a) to take advantage of a sudden German disintegration, or (b) "as a sacrifice" to avert an imminent collapse of Russian resistance. In any such event local air superiority is essential. On the other hand, during the autumn of 1942 probably not more than five divisions could be dispatched and maintained. In this period the chief burden would fall on the U.K. For example, on September 15 the U.S. could find two and a half divisions of the five needed, but only seven hundred combat aircraft; so that the contribution required from the U.K. might amount to five thousand aircraft.

*　　*　　*　　*　　*

Hopkins, much exhausted by his journey, fell ill for two or three days, but Marshall started talks with our Chiefs of Staff at once. It was not possible to arrange the formal conference with the Defence Committee till Tuesday the 14th. Meanwhile I talked the whole position over with the Chiefs of Staff as well as with my colleagues. We were all relieved by the evident strong American intention to intervene in Europe, and to give the main priority to the defeat of Hitler. This had always been the foundation of our strategic thought. On the other hand, neither we nor our professional advisers could devise any practical plan for crossing the Channel with a large Anglo-American army and landing in France before the late summer of 1943. This, as is recorded in the paper I had written on my voyage to Washington in December, 1941, and given to the President, had always been my aim and time-table. There was also before us the new American idea of a preliminary emergency landing on a much smaller but still substantial scale in the autumn of 1942. We were most willing to study this, and also any other plan of diversion, for the sake of Russia and also for the general waging of the war.

Having meditated upon President Roosevelt's memorandum and the views of the Chiefs of Staff, I sent the following message to the President:

Former Naval Person to President Roosevelt   12 Apr. 42

I have read with earnest attention your masterly document about the future of the war and the great operations proposed. I am in entire agreement in principle with all you propose, and so are the Chiefs of Staff. We must of course meet day-to-day emergencies in the East and Far East while preparing for the main stroke. All the details are being rapidly examined, and preparations where action is clear have already begun. The whole matter will be discussed on evening of Tuesday, the 14th, by the Defence Committee, to which Harry and Marshall are coming, and I have no doubt that I shall be able to send you our complete agreement.

I may say that I thought the proposals made for an interim operation in certain contingencies this year met the difficulties and uncertainties in an absolutely sound manner. If, as our experts

believe, we can carry this whole plan through successfully, it will
be one of the grand events in all the history of war.

On the night of the 14th the Defence Committee met our
American friends at 10 Downing Street. This discussion
seemed so important that I asked General Ismay beforehand
to make personally the record which follows.

I opened the Conference by saying that the Committee had met
to consider the momentous proposal which Mr. Hopkins and
General Marshall had brought over, and which had now been
fully discussed and examined by the Staffs. I had no hesitation in cordially accepting the plan. The conception underlying it
accorded with the classic principles of war — namely, concentration
against the main enemy. One broad reservation must however be
made — it was essential to carry on the defence of India and the
Middle East. We could not possibly face the loss of an army of
600,000 men and the whole man-power of India. Furthermore,
Australia and the island bases connecting that country with the
United States must not be allowed to fall. This meant that we
could not entirely lay aside everything in furtherance of the main
object proposed by General Marshall.

GENERAL MARSHALL said that all were in complete agreement as
to what should be done in 1943 and upon developing the strongest
air offensive against Germany. . . . The availability of troops presented no problem. The main difficulties would be found in providing the requisite tonnage, the landing-craft, the aircraft, and
the naval escorts.

There were two points of doubt which had arisen in his discussions with the British Chiefs of Staff. The first was whether
sufficient material would be available from the United States for
the support of the Middle East and India; the second was on the
practicability of making a landing on the Continent, other than a
large-scale raid, in 1942. We might be compelled to do this, and
we must in any case prepare for it. He thought that the difficulties
should not be insoluble, as we should have a great measure of air
control. The size of our joint air programmes showed that this
would be so, particularly as the German campaign against Russia
would absorb great resources and thus reduce the hazards of our
operations. Thus it would be the Germans who would have a taste

of fighting without air support. There had not been much time
before he left the United States to study the problem of operations
in 1942, and, on the data available, he had concluded that they
could not be undertaken before September. If they had to be done
before then the United States contribution would be modest; but
whatever was available in the way of American forces over here at
the time could be used to the full. The President had particularly
emphasised that he wished his armed forces to share to the greatest
extent possible in whatever might be undertaken.

SIR ALAN BROOKE said that the Chiefs of Staff were in entire
agreement with him on the project for 1943. Operations on the
Continent in 1942 were governed by the measure of success achieved
by the Germans in their campaign against Russia. We had felt that
matters would come to a head before September.

The Chiefs of Staff entirely agreed that Germany was the main
enemy. At the same time it was essential to hold the Japanese and
to ensure that there should be no junction between them and the
Germans. If the Japanese obtained control of the Indian Ocean not
only would the Middle East be gravely threatened, but we should
lose the oil supplies from the Persian Gulf. The results of this
would be that Germany would get all the oil she required, the
southern route to Russia would be cut, Turkey would be isolated
and defenceless, the Germans would obtain ready access to the
Black Sea, and Germany and Japan would be able to interchange
the goods of which they stood so much in need.

I then added that we were unable for the next two or three
months to cope unaided with the naval strength which the Japanese
could develop in the Indian Ocean. At the moment we had no sure
knowledge of the United States' naval intentions and movements
in the Pacific. . . . The first essential in that area was to get
superiority over the Japanese in seaborne aircraft. We ourselves
would very shortly have three aircraft-carriers in the Indian Ocean,
and these might be joined in due course by the *Furious*.

MR. HOPKINS said that if public opinion in America had its way
the weight of American effort would be directed against Japan.
Nevertheless, after anxious discussion the President and the American military leaders had decided that it would be right to direct
the force of American arms against Germany. It should not be
thought however that there was any misunderstanding in the minds
of the American Government as to the position in the Middle East

and on the other great fronts, such as Russia, Australia, and the Pacific. The American decision had been governed by two main considerations. First, the United States wished to fight not only on the sea, but on land and in the air. Secondly, they wished to fight in the most useful place, and in the place where they could attain superiority, and they were desirous above all of joining in an enterprise with the British. If such an enterprise were to be launched this year the United States wished to make the greatest contribution that was possible, whenever it might take place. When they had suggested September as the earliest date for moving they had been largely influenced by the fear of promoting an enterprise in which they could not play an adequate part.

He had sensed public opinion both in America and in the United Kingdom, and had found it disturbed as to what the United States Navy was doing. There should be no doubt on this point. The Navy would join with the British to the full in bringing the enemy to action. They were only anxious that they should fight in favourable circumstances.

With regard to the Australian and other theatres, the United States would certainly discharge their obligations, but their whole heart would be fully engaged in the great plan now proposed. The American nation was eager to join in the fight alongside the British.

Sir Charles Portal [Chief of the Air Staff] said that it was necessary to bear in mind the difference between air operations across the Channel and the landing of an Expeditionary Force. The former could be continued or stopped at will. In the latter case however we could not take as much or as little as we liked. We should have to maintain the air effort for as long as the troops remained on the Continent. If therefore we launched an Expeditionary Force we must be sure that the air resources were sufficient to enable operations to be carried through to the end.

In conclusion, I said that, although it remained to work out the details of the plan [for the cross-Channel invasion of 1943], there was complete unanimity on the framework. The two nations would march ahead together in a noble brotherhood of arms. I would prepare a message to the President, conveying to him the conclusions which had been reached, and also put forward to him a request for the vital requirements of the Indian Ocean, without which the whole plan would be fatally compromised. Full preparations could now start, and we could go ahead with the utmost resolution. It would gradually become known that the English-speaking peoples were resolved on a great campaign for the liberation of Europe, and it was for consideration whether a public announcement to this effect should in due course be made.

*   *   *   *   *

The plan itself was now named, though not by me, "Roundup." On this basis all went to work in the utmost good faith and goodwill. I reported to the President:

Former Naval Person to President Roosevelt   17 Apr. 42

Your envoys will take back with them a full note of our memorable meeting last Tuesday and a detailed commentary on your proposals by our Chiefs of Staff. I think however that you would wish to have at once a short account of the conclusions which were reached.

2. We whole-heartedly agree with your conception of concentration against the main enemy, and we cordially accept your plan, with one broad qualification. As you will see from my telegram of April 15, it is essential that we should prevent a junction of the Japanese and the Germans. Consequently, a proportion of our combined resources must for the moment be set aside to halt the Japanese advance. This point was fully discussed at the meeting, and Marshall felt confident that we could together provide what was necessary for the Indian Ocean and other theatres, and yet go right ahead with your main project.

3. The campaign of 1943 is straightforward, and we are starting joint plans and preparations at once. We may however feel compelled to act this year. Your plan visualised this, but put mid-September as the earliest date. Things may easily come to a head before then. Marshall explained that you had been reluctant to press for an enterprise that was fraught with such grave risks and dire consequences until you could make a substantial air contribution; but he left us in no doubt that, if it were found necessary to act earlier, you, Mr. President, would earnestly wish to throw in every available scrap of human and material resources. We are proceeding with plans and preparations on that basis. Broadly speaking, our agreed programme is a crescendo of activity on the Continent, starting with an ever-increasing air offensive both by

night and day and more frequent and large-scale raids, in which United States troops will take part.

4. I agree with the suggestion in your telegram of April 2 that you should ask Stalin to send two special representatives to see you at once about your plans. It will in any case be impossible to conceal the vast preparations that will be necessary, but with the whole coast of Europe, from the North Cape to Bayonne, open to us we should contrive to deceive the enemy as to the weight, the timing, the method, and the direction of our attacks. It is indeed for consideration whether it would not be right to make a public announcement that our two nations are resolved to march forward into Europe together in a noble brotherhood of arms on a great crusade for the liberation of the tormented peoples. I will cable you further on this last point.

The President replied:

President Roosevelt to Former Naval Person   22 Apr. 42

I am delighted with the agreement which was reached between you and your military advisers and Marshall and Hopkins. They have reported to me on the unanimity of opinion relative to the proposal which they carried with them, and I appreciate ever so much your personal message confirming this.

I believe that this move will be very disheartening to Hitler, and may well be the wedge by which his downfall will be accomplished. I am very heartened at the prospect, and you can be sure that our Army will approach the matter with great enthusiasm and vigour.

I would like to think over a bit the question of a public announcement. I will let you know my feeling about this soon.

I believe that any junction between Japanese and Germans is going to take a great deal of doing, but realise that the remote prospect of this is something that must be watched.

In the meantime, as you will have seen in the press, we have had a good crack at Japan by air, and I am hoping that we can make it very difficult for them to keep too many of their big ships in the Indian Ocean. I will have a talk with Pound [who was going to Washington] about this in a day or two.

I have a cordial message from Stalin telling me that he is sending Molotov and a general to visit me. I am suggesting that they come here first before going to England. Will you let me know if you have any other view about this. I am quite pleased about the Stalin message.

While our mutual difficulties are many, I am frank to say that I feel better about the war than at any time in the past two years.

I want to thank you for your cordial reception of Marshall and Hopkins.

*   *   *   *   *

Let me now set out my own view, which was persistent, of what had so far been decided and of what I thought should be done.

In planning the gigantic enterprise of 1943 it was not possible for us to lay aside all other duties. Our first Imperial obligation was to defend India from the Japanese invasion, by which it seemed it was already menaced. Moreover, this task bore a decisive relation to the whole war. To leave four hundred millions of His Majesty's Indian subjects, to whom we were bound in honour, to be ravaged and overrun, as China had been, by the Japanese would have been a deed of shame. But also to allow the Germans and Japanese to join hands in India or the Middle East involved a measureless disaster to the Allied cause. It ranked in my mind almost as the equal of the retirement of Soviet Russia behind the Urals, or even of their making a separate peace with Germany. At this date I did not deem either of these contingencies likely. I had faith in the power of the Russian armies and nation fighting in defence of their native soil. Our Indian Empire however, with all its glories, might fall an easy prey. I had to place this point of view before the American envoys. Without active British aid, India might be conquered in a few months. Hitler's subjugation of Soviet Russia would be a much longer, and to him more costly, task. Before it was accomplished the Anglo-American command of the air would have been established beyond challenge. Even if all else failed this would be finally decisive.

I was in complete accord with what Hopkins called "a frontal assault upon the enemy in northern France in 1943." But what was to be done in the interval? The main armies could not simply be preparing all that time. Here there was a wide diversity of opinion. General Marshall had advanced the proposal that we should attempt to seize Brest or Cherbourg, preferably the latter, or even both, during the early autumn of 1942. The operation would have to be almost entirely British. The Navy, the air, two-thirds of the troops, and such landing-craft as were available must be provided by us. Only two or three American divisions could be found. These, it must be remembered, were very newly raised. It takes at least two years and a very strong professional cadre to form first-class troops. The enterprise was therefore one on which British Staff opinion would naturally prevail. Clearly there must be an intensive technical study of the problem.

Nevertheless I by no means rejected the idea at the outset; but there were other alternatives which lay in my mind. The first was the descent on French Northwest Africa (Morocco, Algeria, and Tunis), which for the present was known as "Gymnast," and which ultimately emerged in the great operation "Torch." I had a second alternative plan for which I always hankered and which I thought could be undertaken as well as the invasion of French North Africa. This was "Jupiter" — namely, the liberation of northern Norway. Here was direct aid to Russia. Here was the only method of direct combined military action with Russian troops, ships, and air. Here was the means, by securing the northern tip of Europe, of opening the broadest flood of supplies to Russia. Here was an enterprise which, as it had to be fought in Arctic regions, involved neither large numbers of men nor heavy expenditure of supplies and munitions. The Germans had got these vital strategic points by the North Cape very cheaply. They might also be regained at a small cost compared with the scale which the war had now attained. My own choice was for "Torch," and if I could have had my full way I should have tried "Jupiter" also in 1942.

The attempt to form a bridgehead at Cherbourg seemed to me more difficult, less attractive, less immediately helpful or ultimately fruitful. It would be better to lay our right claw on French North Africa, tear with our left at the North Cape, and wait a year without risking our teeth upon the German fortified front across the Channel.

Those were my views then, and I have never repented of them. I was however very ready to give "Sledgehammer," as the Cherbourg assault was called, a fair run with other suggestions before the planning committees. I was almost certain the more it was looked at the less it would be liked. If it had been in my power to give orders I would have settled upon "Torch" and "Jupiter," properly synchronised for the autumn, and would have let "Sledgehammer" leak out as a feint through rumour and ostentatious preparation. But I had to work by influence and diplomacy in order to secure agreed and harmonious action with our cherished Ally, without whose aid nothing but ruin faced the world. I did not therefore open any of these alternatives at our meeting on the 14th.

On the supreme issue we welcomed with relief and joy the decisive proposal of the United States to carry out a mass invasion of Germany as soon as possible, using England as the springboard. We might so easily, as will be seen, have been confronted with American plans to assign the major priority to helping China and crushing Japan. But from the very start of our alliance after Pearl Harbour, President Roosevelt and General Marshall, rising superior to powerful tides of public opinion, saw in Hitler the prime and major foe. Personally I longed to see British and American armies shoulder to shoulder in Europe. But I had little doubt myself that study of details — landing-craft and all that — and also reflection on the main strategy of the war, would rule out "Sledgehammer." In the upshot no military authority — Army, Navy, or Air — on either side of the Atlantic was found capable of preparing such a plan, or — so far as I was informed — ready to take the responsibility for executing it. United wishes and good will cannot overcome brute facts.

To sum up: I pursued always the theme set forth in my memorandum given to the President in December, 1941, namely, (1) that British and American liberating armies should land in Europe in 1943. And how could they land in full strength otherwise than from Southern England? Nothing must be done which would prevent this and anything that would promote it. (2) In the meantime, with the Russians fighting on a gigantic scale from hour to hour against the main striking force of the German Army, we could not stand idle. We must engage the enemy. This resolve also lay at the root of the President's thought. What then should be done in the year or fifteen months that must elapse before a heavy cross-Channel thrust could be made? Evidently the occupation of French North Africa was in itself possible and sound, and fitted into the general strategic scheme.

I hoped that this could be combined with a descent upon Norway, and I still believe both might have been simultaneously possible. But in these tense discussions of unmeasurable things it is a great danger to lose simplicity and singleness of purpose. Though I hoped for both "Torch" and "Jupiter," I never had any intention of letting "Jupiter" queer the pitch of "Torch." The difficulties of focusing and combining in one vehement thrust all the efforts of two mighty countries were such that no ambiguity could be allowed to darken counsel. (3) The only way therefore to fill the gap, before large masses of British and United States troops could be brought in contact with the Germans in Europe in 1943, was by the forcible Anglo-American occupation of French Northwest Africa in conjunction with the British advance westward across the desert towards Tripoli and Tunis.

Eventually, when all other plans and arguments had worn themselves out and perished by the way, this became the united decision of the Western Allies.

19

The Molotov Visit

WHEN MR. EDEN had visited Moscow in December, 1941, he had been confronted by specific demands from the Russian Government for the recognition of the Soviet frontiers in the West as they stood at that time. The Russians were particularly anxious to secure within the frame of any general treaty of alliance an explicit recognition of their occupation of the Baltic States and of their new frontier with Finland.

Mr. Eden had refused to make any commitments on this subject, stressing, among other things, the pledge we had given to
the United States Government not to enter into any secret
agreement for territorial revision during the course of the war.

At the end of this conference it was agreed that Mr. Eden
should convey the Soviet demands both to the British Cabinet
and to the United States, and that they should be considered in
the future negotiations for a formal Anglo-Soviet treaty. The
United States Government were fully informed of what had
passed. Their attitude to the Russian proposals was sharp and
negative. In the American view any acceptance of such requests
would be a direct violation of the principles of the Atlantic
Charter.

When I was at Washington on the morrow of the American
entry into the war, and Mr. Eden had reported the wishes of
the Soviet Government to absorb the Baltic States, I had reacted
unfavourably, as the telegrams already printed show. But
now, three months later, under the pressure of events, I did
not feel that this moral position could be physically maintained.
In a deadly struggle it is not right to assume more burdens than
those who are fighting for a great cause can bear. My opinions
about the Baltic States were, and are, unaltered, but I felt that
I could not carry them farther forward at this time.

Former Naval Person to President Roosevelt   7 Mar. 42

If Winant is with you now, he will no doubt explain the Foreign
Office view about Russia. The increasing gravity of the war has
led me to feel that the principles of the Atlantic Charter ought
not to be construed so as to deny Russia the frontiers she occupied
when Germany attacked her. This was the basis on which Russia
acceded to the Charter, and I expect that a severe process of
liquidating hostile elements in the Baltic States, etc., was employed
by the Russians when they took these regions at the beginning
of the war. I hope therefore that you will be able to give us a
free hand to sign the treaty which Stalin desires as soon as possible.
Everything portends an immense renewal of the German invasion
of Russia in the spring, and there is very little we can do to help
the only country that is heavily engaged with the German armies.

The President and the State Department however held to their position, and as will be seen we eventually arrived at a better conclusion.

*   *   *   *   *

A more cordial period now intervened in Anglo-Russian relations.

Prime Minister to Premier Stalin   9 Mar. 42

I have sent a message to President Roosevelt urging him to approve our signing the agreement with you about the frontiers of Russia at the end of the war.

2. I have given express directions that the supplies promised by us shall not in any way be interrupted or delayed.

3. Now that the season is improving we are resuming heavy air offensive both by day and night upon Germany. We are continuing to study other measures for taking some of the weight off you.

4. The continued progress of the Russian armies and the known

terrible losses of the enemy are naturally our sources of greatest encouragement in this trying period.

Premier Stalin to Prime Minister   15 Mar. 42

I am very grateful to you for your message handed in at Kuibyshev on March 12.

I express to you the appreciation of the Soviet Government for your communication regarding measures you have taken to ensure supplies to U.S.S.R. and to intensify air attacks on Germany.

I express the firm conviction that the combined actions of our troops, in spite of incidental reverses, will in the end defeat the forces of our mutual enemy, and that the year 1942 will be decisive in the turn of events at the battle-front against Hitlerism.

As regards the first point of your letter, dealing with frontiers of U.S.S.R., I think that it will still be necessary to exchange views regarding the text of a respective suitable agreement, in the event of its being accepted for the signature of both parties.

*   *   *   *   *

In the general desire to find ways of helping the Soviet armies in the forthcoming German offensive, and the fear that gas, probably mustard gas, would be used upon them, I procured the consent of the Cabinet to our making a public declaration that if gas were used by the Germans against the Russians we would retaliate by gas attacks on Germany.

Prime Minister to Premier Stalin   20 Mar. 42

Many thanks for your reply of the 15th to my latest telegram. Beaverbrook is off to Washington, where he will help smooth out the treaty question with the President in accordance with the communications which have passed between us and between our Governments.

2. Ambassador Maisky lunched with me last week, and mentioned some evidences that the Germans may use gas upon you in their attempted spring offensive. After consulting my colleagues and the Chiefs of Staff, I wish to assure you that His Majesty's Government will treat any use of this weapon of poison gas against Russia exactly as if it was directed against ourselves. I have been building up an immense store of gas bombs for discharge from

aircraft, and we shall not hesitate to use these over all suitable objectives in Western Germany from the moment that your armies and people are assaulted in this way.

3. It is a question to be considered whether at the right time we should not give a public warning that such is our resolve, as the warning might deter the Germans from adding this new horror to the many they have loosed upon the world. Please let me know what you think about this, and whether the evidence of German preparations warrants the warning.

4. There is no immediate hurry, and before I take a step which may draw upon our cities this new form of attack I must of course have ample time to bring all our anti-gas precautions to extreme readiness.

5. I trust you will give our new Ambassador the opportunity of presenting this message himself, and the advantage of personal discussion with you. He comes, as you know, almost direct from close personal contact with General Chiang Kai-shek, which he has maintained during the last four years. He enjoyed, I believe, the General's high regard and confidence; I hope and believe that he will equally gain yours. He is a personal friend of mine of many years' standing.

Premier Stalin to Prime Minister   30 Mar. 42

I thank you for the message recently transmitted to me by Sir A. Clark Kerr. I have had a long talk with Sir A. Clark Kerr, and I am convinced that our joint work will proceed in an atmosphere of perfect mutual confidence.

2. I wish to express to you the Soviet Government's gratitude for the assurance that the British Government will look upon any use by the Germans of poison gas against the U.S.S.R. in the same light as if this weapon had been used against Great Britain, [and] that the British Air Force will immediately use against suitable objectives in Germany the large stocks of gas bombs held in England.

* * * * *

The President was also at this time in pleasant relations with the Soviets, and we have seen in the last chapter his reference to a visit by Molotov to Washington. He would have preferred the envoy to come first to the United States, but Stalin planned otherwise.

Premier Stalin to Prime Minister 23 Apr. 42

Recently the Soviet Government received from Mr. Eden the drafts of two agreements between the U.S.S.R. and Great Britain which differed in some material respects from the text of agreements which were under discussion while Mr. Eden was in Moscow. In view of the fact that these drafts reveal fresh divergences of opinion which it would be difficult to solve by correspondence, the Soviet Government have decided, despite all the obstacles, to send Mr. Molotov to London, in order, by means of personal discussion, to dispose of all the matters which stand in the way of the signing of the agreements. This is all the more necessary because the question of opening a second front in Europe (which was raised in the last message addressed to me by the President of the United States, in which he invited Mr. Molotov to go to Washington to discuss this matter) calls for a preliminary exchange of views between representatives of our two Governments.

Accept my greetings and my wishes for success in your fight against the enemies of Great Britain.

Former Naval Person to President Roosevelt 24 Apr. 42

With regard to what you say in your telegram about Molotov's journeyings, I have had a message from Stalin saying he is sending M. here to discuss certain divergences in the draft texts of our agreement, which he wants settled as soon as possible. He may even be already on his way. You will understand that I cannot now suggest to him a change in the order of his visits. If and when therefore Molotov bears down upon us, I propose to agree to a discussion of our drafts, and would hope to clear main difficulties out of the way. But I will suggest to him that he should then go on to Washington and see you before anything is finally signed.

Prime Minister to Premier Stalin 24 Apr. 42

I am very grateful to you for your message of April 23, and we shall of course welcome M. Molotov, with whom I am confident we shall be able to do much useful work. I am very glad that you feel able to allow this visit, which I am sure will be most valuable.

* * * * *

Molotov did not arrive until May 20, and formal discussions began the following morning. On that day and at the two following meetings the Russians maintained their original position, and even brought up specifically the question of agreeing to the Russian occupation of Eastern Poland. This was rejected as incompatible with the Anglo-Polish Agreement of August, 1939. Molotov also put forward a case for the recognition in a secret agreement of Russia's claims on Rumania. This also was contrary to our understanding with the United States. The conversations at the Foreign Office, which Mr. Eden conducted, though most friendly, therefore moved towards a deadlock.

Apart from the question of the treaty, Molotov had come to London to learn our views upon the opening of a second front. On the morning of May 22 therefore, I had a formal conversation with him.

Molotov began by saying that he had been charged by the Soviet Government to come to London to discuss the question of the establishment of a second front. This was no new problem. It had first been raised nearly ten months ago, and now, more recently, the impetus had come from President Roosevelt, who had suggested to M. Stalin that he (M. Molotov) should go to the United States to discuss this question. Though the initiative for the present inquiry had come from the United States, the Soviet Government had thought it right that he should proceed to the United States via London, since it was upon Great Britain that the main task of organising the second front would initially fall. The coming weeks and months on the Russian front were fraught with serious consequence to the Soviet Union and their Allies. The material aid rendered by Great Britain and the United States was highly prized and appreciated by the Soviet Government. Nevertheless the most urgent issues were involved in the establishment of a second front.

The object of his visit was to learn how the British Government viewed the prospects of drawing off in 1942 at least forty German divisions from the U.S.S.R., where it seemed that at the present time the balance of advantage in armed strength lay with the Germans.

In reply I gave Molotov the essence of our combined thought upon future operations on the Continent. In all previous wars

control of the sea had given the Power possessing it the great advantage of being able to land at will on the enemy's coast, since it
was impossible for the enemy to be prepared at every point to meet
seaborne invasion. The advent of air-power had altered the whole
situation. For example, in France and the Low Countries the
enemy could move his Air Force in a few hours to threatened points
anywhere along the coast; and bitter experience had shown that
landing in the teeth of enemy air opposition was not a sound
military proposition. The inescapable consequence was that large
portions of the Continental coastline were denied to us as places
for disembarkation. We were forced therefore to study our chances
at those parts of the coast where our superior fighter force would
give us control in the air. Our choice was, in fact, narrowed down
to the Pas de Calais, the Cherbourg tip, and part of the Brest
area. The problem of landing a force this year in one or more
of these areas was being studied, and preparations were being
made. Our plans were being based on the assumption that the
landing of successive waves of assault troops would bring about air
battles which, if continued over a week or ten days, would lead
to the virtual destruction of the enemy's air-power on the Continent. Once this was achieved and the air opposition removed,
landings at other points on the coast could be effected under cover
of our superior sea-power. The crucial point in making our plans
and preparations was the availability of the special landing-craft
required for effecting the initial landing on the very heavily defended enemy coastline. Unfortunately, our resources in this
special type of craft were for the time being strictly limited. I
said that as far back as last August, at the Atlantic meeting, I
had impressed upon President Roosevelt the urgent need for the
United States to build as large a number of tank-landing and other
assault craft as possible. Later, in January of this year, the President had agreed that the United States should make an even
larger effort to construct these craft. We, for our part, for more
than a year had been turning out as large a number of assault craft
as our need for constructing ships for the Navy and mercantile
marine, which had suffered grievous losses, permitted.

Two points should however be borne in mind. First, with the
best will and endeavour, it was unlikely that any move we could
make in 1942, even if it were successful, would draw off large
numbers of enemy land forces from the Eastern Front. In the air

however the position was different; in the various theatres of war we were already containing about one-half of the fighter and one-third of the German bomber strength. If our plan for forcing air battles over the Continent proved successful, the Germans might be faced with the choice either of seeing the whole of their fighter air force in the West destroyed in action or of making withdrawals from their air strength in the East.

The second point related to M. Molotov's proposition that our aim should be to draw off (including those now in the West) not less than forty German divisions from Russia. It should be noted that at the present time we had confronting us in Libya eleven Axis divisions, of which three were German, the equivalent of eight German divisions in Norway, and twenty-five German divisions in France and the Low Countries. These totalled forty-four divisions.

But we were not satisfied with that, and if any further effort could be made or plan devised, provided it was sound and sensible, for drawing the weight off Russia this year, we should not hesitate to put it into effect. Clearly, it would not further either the Russian cause or that of the Allies as a whole if, for the sake of action at any price, we embarked on some operation which ended in disaster and gave the enemy an opportunity for glorification at our discomfiture.

MOLOTOV said that he had no doubt that Great Britain genuinely wished for the success of the Soviet Army against the Germans this summer. What, in the view of the British Government, were the prospects of Soviet success? Whatever their views might be, he would be glad to have a frank expression of opinion — good or bad.

I said that, without detailed knowledge of the resources and reserves on both sides, it was difficult to form a firm judgment on this question. Last year the military experts, including those of Germany, had thought that the Soviet Army might be borne down and overcome. They had proved quite wrong. In the event the Soviet forces had defeated Hitler and nearly brought his Army to disaster. Consequently Russia's Allies felt great confidence in the strength and ability of the Soviet Army. The Intelligence available to the British Government did not indicate the massing of vast German forces at any particular point on the Eastern Front. Moreover, the full-scale offensive heralded for May now seemed unlikely to take place before June. In any event, it did not seem that Hitler's attack this year could be as strong or so menacing as that of 1941.

MOLOTOV then asked what, if the Soviet Army failed to hold out during 1942, would be the position and the attitude of the British Government.

I said that if the Soviet military power was seriously reduced by the German onslaught, Hitler would in all probability move as many troops and air forces as possible back to the West, with the object of invading Great Britain. He might also strike down through Baku to the Caucasus and Persia. This latter thrust would expose us to the gravest dangers, and we should by no means feel satisfied that we had sufficient forces to ward it off. Therefore our fortunes were bound up with the resistance of the Soviet Army. Nevertheless, if, contrary to expectation, they were defeated, and the worst came to the worst, we should fight on, and, with the help of the United States, hope to build up overwhelming air superiority, which in the course of the next eighteen months or two years would enable us to put down a devastating weight of air attack on the German cities and industries. We should moreover maintain the blockade and make landings on the Continent against an increasingly enfeebled opposition. Ultimately the power of Great Britain and the United States would prevail. It should not be overlooked that after the fall of France Great Britain had stood alone for a whole year with but a handful of ill-equipped troops between her and Hitler's victorious and numerous divisions. But what a tragedy for mankind would be this prolongation of the war, and how earnest was the hope for Russian victory, and how ardent the desire that we should take our share in conquering the evil foe!

At the end of our talk I asked M. Molotov to bear in mind the difficulty of oversea invasions. After France fell out of the war we in Great Britain were almost naked — a few ill-equipped divisions, less than a hundred tanks and less than two hundred field guns. And yet Hitler had not attempted an invasion, by reason of the fact that he could not get command of the air. The same sort of difficulties confronted us at the present time.

*   *   *   *   *

On May 23 Mr. Eden proposed to substitute for a territorial agreement a general and public Treaty of Alliance for twenty

years, omitting all reference to frontiers. By that evening the
Russians showed signs of giving way. They were impressed by
the solidarity of view of the British and American Governments
with which they had been confronted. The following morning
Molotov requested permission from Stalin to negotiate on the
basis of Mr. Eden's draft. Minor modifications were suggested
from Moscow, mainly stressing the long-term character of the
proposed alliance. The treaty, without any territorial provisions, was signed on May 26. This was a great relief to me,
and a far better solution than I had dared to hope. Eden
showed much skill in the timing of his new suggestion.

With this grave issue settled, Molotov left for Washington to
begin general military talks with the President and his advisers
on the question of opening a second front. It had been agreed
that, having heard the American view, he should return to
London for final discussions upon this matter before going
back to Moscow.

*   *   *   *   *

Our Russian guests had expressed the wish to be lodged in
the country outside London during their stay, and I therefore
placed Chequers at their disposal. I remained meanwhile at the
Storey's Gate Annexe. However, I went down for two nights to
Chequers. Here I had the advantage of having long private
talks with Molotov and Ambassador Maisky, who was the best
of interpreters, translating quickly and easily, and possessing a
wide knowledge of affairs. With the aid of good maps, I tried
to explain what we were doing, and the limitations and peculiar characteristics in the war capacity of an island Power.
I also went at length into the technique of amphibious operations, and described the perils and difficulties of maintaining
our life-line across the Atlantic in the face of U-boat attack.
I think Molotov was impressed with all this, and realised that
our problem was utterly different from that of a vast land
Power. At any rate, we got closer together than at any other
time.

The inveterate suspicion with which the Russians regarded foreigners was shown by some remarkable incidents during Molotov's stay at Chequers. On arrival they had asked at once for keys to all the bedrooms. These were provided with some difficulty and thereafter our guests always kept their doors locked. When the staff at Chequers succeeded in getting in to make the beds they were disturbed to find pistols under the pillows. The three chief members of the mission were attended not only by their own police officers, but by two women who looked after their clothes and tidied their rooms. When the Soviet envoys were absent in London these women kept constant guard over their masters' rooms, only coming down one at a time for their meals. We may claim, however, that presently they thawed a little and even chatted in broken French and signs with the household staff.

Extraordinary precautions were taken for Molotov's personal safety. His room had been thoroughly searched by his police officers, every cupboard and piece of furniture and the walls and floors being meticulously examined by practised eyes. The bed was the object of particular attention; the mattresses were all prodded in case of infernal machines, and the sheets and blankets were rearranged by the Russians so as to leave an opening in the middle of the bed out of which the occupant could spring at a moment's notice, instead of being tucked in. At night a revolver was laid out beside his dressing gown and his dispatch case. It is always right, especially in time of war, to take precautions against danger, but every effort should be made to measure its reality. The simplest test is to ask oneself whether the other side have any interest in killing the person concerned. For myself, when I visited Moscow I put complete trust in Russian hospitality.

* * * * *

Prime Minister to Premier Stalin   23 May 42

We have greatly enjoyed receiving M. Molotov in London, and have had fruitful conversations with him on both military and

political affairs. We have given him a full and true account of
our plans and resources. As regards the treaty, he will explain to
you the difficulties, which are mainly that we cannot go back on
our previous undertakings to Poland, and have to take account of
our own and American opinion.

I am sure that it would be of the greatest value to the common
cause if M. Molotov could come back this way from America. We
can then continue our discussions, which I hope will lead to the
development of close military co-operation between our three countries. Moreover, I shall then be able to give him the latest developments in our own military plans.

Stalin assented at once.

J. V. Stalin to Mr. Churchill   24 May 42

Vyacheslav Molotov as well as I feel that it might be advisable
for him on the return journey from the U.S.A. to stop in London
to complete the negotiations with the representatives of the British
Government on the questions in which our countries are interested.

Prime Minister to Premier Stalin   27 May 42

We are most grateful to you for meeting our difficulties in the
treaty as you have done. I am sure the reward in the United States
will be solid, and our three great Powers will now be able to
march together united through whatever has to come. It has been
a great pleasure to meet M. Molotov, and we have done a great
beating down of barriers between our two countries. I am very
glad he is coming back this way, for there will be more good work
to be done.

2. So far all has been well with the convoy, but it is now at its
most dangerous stage. Many thanks for the measures you are
taking to help it in.

3. Now that we have bound ourselves to be Allies and friends
for twenty years, I take occasion to send to you my sincere good
wishes and to assure you of the confidence which I feel that victory
will be ours.

*   *   *   *   *

I duly reported to the President.

Former Naval Person to President Roosevelt   27 May 42

We have done very good work this and last week with Molotov, and, as Winant will no doubt have informed you, we have completely transformed the treaty proposals. They are now, in my judgment, free from the objections we both entertained, and are entirely compatible with our Atlantic Charter. The treaty was signed yesterday afternoon, with great cordiality on both sides. Molotov is a statesman, and has a freedom of action very different from what you and I saw with Litvinov. I am very sure you will be able to reach good understandings with him. Please let me know your impressions.

So far all has gone well with the northern convoy, but the dangers on the next two days must necessarily be serious.

Mountbatten and Lyttelton will come together to the United States, but the former's visit must be short on account of our common work with which he is charged.

I am fully aware of your preoccupations in the Pacific at the present time, and if you considered it necessary to withdraw the [battleship] *Washington* at once we should quite understand. It is however most important to complete our concentration in the Indian Ocean of *Warspite, Valiant, Nelson,* and *Rodney* by the middle of July. This can be done if we can retain *Washington* until *King George V* finishes refitting at the end of June. . . .

7. The introduction of convoys between Key West and Hampton Roads has evidently had the good effects we all expected, but the Caribbean and Gulf of Mexico are still very sore spots. Admirals King and Pound have been in communication about this, and I hope it may be found possible, even by running risks elsewhere, to provide sufficient escort craft to deal with these areas.

8. I must express my gratitude for your allocation of seventy tankers to build up United Kingdom stocks of oil. Without this help our stocks would have fallen to a dangerous level by the end of the year. This action is the more generous considering recent heavy American tanker losses and the sacrifices involved in releasing so many ships.

*   *   *   *   *

Meanwhile the Soviet envoy was in the air on his return journey.

President Roosevelt to Former Naval Person   27 May 42

The visitor is expected tonight, but will not discuss "Bolero" until Thursday. A short summary of what you and he said to each other about "Bolero" is desired quickly. It would aid me to know.

By "Bolero" the President meant "Sledgehammer," in 1942. This was fully comprehended by us.

Former Naval Person to President Roosevelt   28 May 42

I send in my immediately following report of our formal conversation, which covers "Bolero," "Sledgehammer," and "Super Round-up." [1]

Additional private conversation improved the atmosphere, but did not alter substance. We made great progress in intimacy and good will.

2. We are working hard with your officers, and all preparations are proceeding ceaselessly on the largest scale. Dickie [Mountbatten] will explain to you the difficulties of 1942 when he arrives. I have also told the Staffs to study a landing in the north of Norway, the occupation of which seems necessary to ensure the flow of our supplies next year to Russia. I have told Molotov we would have something ready for him about this to discuss on his return here. We did not go deeply into it in any way. Personally I set great importance upon it if a good plan can be made.

3. So far our northern convoy is fighting its way through, having lost five ships, sunk or turned back, out of thirty-five. Tomorrow we ought to be getting under the Russian air umbrella, if any has been provided. Otherwise, two more days of this.

4. Auchinleck's news tonight indicates that the battle in Libya has begun. This may be the biggest encounter we have ever fought. . . .

5. We must never let "Gymnast" [landing in French North Africa] pass from our minds. All other preparations would help, if need be, towards that.

*   *   *   *   *

[1] See pages 320 ff.

Stalin was almost purring.

Premier Stalin to Prime Minister 28 May 42

I thank you very much for friendly feelings and good wishes expressed by you in connection with the signature of our new treaty. I am sure this treaty will be of the greatest importance for the future strengthening of friendly relations between the Soviet Union and Great Britain, as well as between our countries and the United States of America, and will secure the close collaboration of our countries after the victorious end of the war. I hope also that your meeting with Molotov on his way back from the United States will present the opportunity to bring to an end that part of the work which was left uncompleted.

With regard to the measures concerning protection of convoys, you may rest assured that in this respect everything possible on our side will be done now and in the future.

Please accept my most sincere good wishes, as well as my fullest confidence in our complete joint victory.

* * * * *

When Molotov returned to London after his American visit he was naturally full of the plans for creating a second front by a cross-Channel operation in 1942. We ourselves were still actively studying this in conjunction with the American Staff, and nothing but difficulties had as yet emerged. There could be no harm in a public statement, which might make the Germans apprehensive and consequently hold as many of their troops in the West as possible. We therefore agreed with Molotov to the issue of a communiqué, which was published on June 11, containing the following sentence: "In the course of the conversations full understanding was reached with regard to the urgent task of creating a second front in Europe in 1942."

I felt it above all important that in this effort to mislead the enemy we should not mislead our Ally. At the time of drafting the communiqué, therefore, I handed Molotov personally in the Cabinet Room and in the presence of some of my colleagues an *aide-mémoire* which made it clear that while we were trying our best to make plans we were not committed to action and that we could give no promise. When subsequent reproaches were made by the Soviet Government, and when Stalin himself raised the point personally with me, we always produced the *aide-mémoire* and pointed to the words *"we can therefore give no promise."*

AIDE-MÉMOIRE

We are making preparations for a landing on the Continent in August or September, 1942. As already explained, the main limiting factor to the size of the landing-force is the availability of special landing-craft. Clearly however it would not further either the Russian cause or that of the Allies as a whole if, for the sake of action at any price, we embarked on some operation which ended in disaster and gave the enemy an opportunity for glorification at our discomfiture. It is impossible to say in advance whether the situation will be such as to make this operation feasible when the time comes. *We can therefore give no promise in the matter,* but provided that it appears sound and sensible we shall not hesitate to put our plans into effect.

Molotov sailed off into the air on his somewhat dangerous homeward flight, apparently well satisfied with the results of his mission. Certainly an atmosphere of friendliness had been created between us. He had been deeply interested in his visit to Washington. There was the Twenty Years Anglo-Russian Treaty, upon which high hopes were at that time set by all.

*   *   *   *   *

During these conversations the Eastern Front had flared into activity. Throughout the early months of the year the Russians had, by unrelenting pressure, forced the enemy line back at many points. The Germans, unprepared for the rigours of winter campaigning, suffered great privations and heavy losses.

When spring came Hitler issued a directive, dated April 5, with this preamble:

The winter campaign in Russia is nearing its close. The out-

standing bravery and the self-sacrificing effort of our troops on the
Eastern Front have achieved a great defensive success. The enemy
suffered very severe losses in men and material. In an attempt to
take advantage of what seemed to be initial successes, Russia
during the course of the winter also expended the bulk of her
reserves intended for future operations.

As soon as weather and terrain conditions are favourable the
superior German command and German forces must take the
initiative once again to force the enemy to do our bidding.

The objective is to wipe out the entire defence potential remaining to the Soviets and to cut them off as far as possible from their
most important sources of supply.

To give effect to this, he continued —

It is intended to hold the central part of the front, in the North
to bring about the fall of Leningrad . . . and on the southern wing
of the Army front to force a break-through into the Caucasus. . . .
To begin with all available forces are to be combined for the
main operations in the southern sector, the objective being to
destroy the enemy before the Don in order to gain the oil region
of the Caucasian area and to cross the Caucasus mountains. . . .
We must try to reach Stalingrad, or at least to subject this city to
bombardment of our heavy weapons to such an extent that it is
eliminated as an armament and traffic centre in the future.

As a preliminary to these main operations Sevastopol was
to be captured by Manstein's Eleventh Army and the Russians
ejected from the Crimea.

The Southern Army Group, under Field-Marshal von Bock,
was given very large forces for its task. There were a hundred
divisions, grouped into five armies, of which nearly sixty divisions were German, including eight armoured divisions; the
rest were Rumanian, Italian, or Hungarian. Of a total of
2750 German aircraft on the Eastern Front 1500 were detailed
to support the southern operations.

It was probably intended to open this great campaign at the
end of May, but the Russians struck first. On May 12 Timo-
shenko launched a heavy attack on and south of Kharkov,
making a deep bulge in the German line. But his southern

flank was vulnerable, and a series of German attacks forced him to give up all the ground he had gained. This "spoiling" attack, though it cost the Russians heavy casualties, probably caused a month's delay in plans; if so, the time gained proved invaluable later.

While this battle was still in progress the German Eleventh Army opened its assault on Sevastopol. The great fortress fell after a month of siege and hard fighting.

20

Strategic Natural Selection

"Sledgehammer" Falls of Its Own Weakness — Question of a Tip-and-Run Raid: "Imperator" — I Oppose This Project — My Alternative, "Jupiter" — Memoranda of May 1 and of June 13 — Hostile Air Defence Not Necessarily Decisive — Further Arguments for the Norway Plan — My Thoughts on a Cross-Channel Invasion in 1943 — My Memorandum of June 15 on Operation "Round-Up" — Conception of Scale and Spirit Required — The French North Africa Plan Survives for 1942.

DURING THE WEEKS which followed Molotov's departure, professional opinion marched forward. I gave all my thought to the problem of "Sledgehammer," and called for constant reports. Its difficulties soon became obvious. The storm of Cherbourg by a sea-landed army in the face of German opposition, probably in superior numbers and with strong fortifications, was a hazardous operation. If it succeeded, the Allies would be penned up in Cherbourg and the tip of the Cotentin peninsula, and would have to maintain themselves in this confined bomb and shell trap for nearly a year under ceaseless bombardment and assault. They could be supplied only by the port of Cherbourg, which would have to be defended all the winter and spring against potentially continuous and occasionally overwhelming air attack. The drain which such a task would impose must be a first charge upon all our resources of shipping and air-power. It would bleed all other operations. If we succeeded we should have to debouch in the summer from the narrow waist of the Cotentin peninsula, after storming a succession of German fortified lines defended by whatever troops the Germans might care to bring. Even so there was only one railroad along which our army could advance, and this would certainly have been destroyed. Moreover, it was not apparent how this unpromising enterprise would help Russia. The Germans had left twenty-five mobile divisions in France. We could not have more than nine ready by August for "Sledgehammer," and of these, seven must be British. There would therefore be no need for the recall of German divisions from the Russian front.

As these facts and many more presented themselves in an ugly way to the military staffs, a certain lack of conviction and ardour manifested itself, not only among the British but among our American comrades. I did not have to argue against "Sledgehammer" myself. It fell of its own weakness.

*   *   *   *   *

An alternative scheme for a tip-and-run raid on a large scale was therefore put forward. This was called "Imperator." To this I addressed myself.

Prime Minister to General Ismay, for C.O.S. Committee   8 June 42

The plan "Imperator," which I have seen only in outline, proposes to land on the Continent a division and armoured units to raid as effectively as possible during two or three days, and then to re-embark as much as possible of the remnants of the force. This is to be our response to a *cri de coeur* from Russia in the event of things going very wrong there. Certainly it would not help Russia if we launched such an enterprise, no doubt with world publicity, and came out a few days later with heavy losses. We should have thrown away valuable lives and material, and made ourselves and our capacity for making war ridiculous throughout the world. The Russians would not be grateful for this worsening of the general position. The French patriots who would rise in our aid and their families would be subjected to pitiless Hun revenge, and this would spread far and wide as a warning against similar imprudences in case of larger-scale operations. Many of those who are now egging us on would be the first to point all this out. It would be cited as another example of sentimental politics dominating the calm determination and common sense of professional advisers.

2. In order to achieve this result we have to do the two most difficult operations of war: first, landing from the sea on a small front against a highly prepared enemy, and, second, evacuating by sea two or three days later the residue of the force landed. It may be mentioned that this force would certainly encounter, near the place proposed, superior German armour and good German troops, by whom it would be accompanied on its inland excursion. When we see in Libya that it is only evenly, if evenly, that we fight with German armour, we must regard the stay on shore of the landed force as very hazardous and costly. The arrangements for bringing off the wounded would alone open up a vista of Q problems, unless they are to be left where they fall virtually unattended.

3. However, all this is to be regarded as "bait" to draw the German fighters into combat with British air fighter superiority. The idea is presumably that the German fighter Air Force will feel bound to face extermination rather than let British armoured units go as far as Lille or Amiens. Would they be wise to make this sacrifice? Surely, having regard to the great superiority which they possess in armour and ground troops compared with the force proposed, the farther they let them get into France and the more closely and deeply they let them become involved, the better. They could therefore afford to use their Air Force with great restraint, avoiding action, and thus frustrating what they will divine was our main purpose.

4. Of course, if this were one of a dozen simultaneous operations of a similar kind very different arguments would hold. Such large establishments might be built up and disturbances caused in France as to confront the enemy with a major danger and cause him to use his whole air-power, or even to bring back squadrons from the East. But a single foray of this kind would not have that effect on the mind of the German General Headquarters, and even if it did, as we are only staying a few days there would be no time for any movements to take place. In fact, the result on the fourth day, when our remnants returned to Britain à la Dunkirk, would be that everyone, friend and foe, would dilate on the difficulties of landing on a hostile shore. A whole set of inhibitions would grow up on our side prejudicial to effective action in 1943.

5. I would ask the Chiefs of Staff to consider the following two principles: (a) No substantial landing in France unless we are going to stay; and (b) No substantial landing in France unless the Germans are demoralised by another failure against Russia. It follows from the above that we should not delay or impede the preparations for "Sledgehammer" for the sake of "Imperator"; secondly, that we should not attempt "Sledgehammer" unless the Germans are demoralised by ill-success against Russia; and, thirdly, that we should recognise that, if Russia is in dire straits, it would not help her for us to come a nasty cropper on our own.

6. It would seem wise that all preparations should go forward for "Sledgehammer" on the largest scale possible at the dates mentioned, but that the launching of "Sledgehammer" should be dependent not on a Russian failure, but on a Russian success and consequent proved German demoralisation in the West.

We heard no more of "Imperator" after this.

* * * * *

I now turned back to my constructive plan.

OPERATION "JUPITER"

Prime Minister to General Ismay, for C.O.S. Committee   1 May 42

This must be considered as an alternative to a medium "Sledgehammer" this year.

2. High strategic and political importance must be attached thereto. It may be all that we have to offer to the Russians. In studying it the Planners need not burden themselves with such questions as (a) would not the Russians prefer to use the shipping for more munitions? or (b) would they not prefer us to do "Sledgehammer"? Let us look at it on its merits.

3. About seventy German bombers and a hundred fighters established in the north of Norway in only two airfields, protected by about ten or twelve thousand effective fighting men, are denying us all entry into Norway and taking a heavy toll of our convoys. If we could gain possession of these airfields and establish an equal force there not only would the northern sea route to Russia be kept open, but we should have set up a second front on a small scale from which it would be most difficult to eject us. If the

going was good we could advance gradually southward, unrolling the Nazi map of Europe from the top. All that has to be done is to oust the enemy from the airfields and destroy their garrisons.

4. Surprise can easily be obtained, because the enemy could never tell till the last moment whether it was an ordinary convoy at sea or an expedition.

5. It must be assumed that the Russians will support this movement, though they certainly will not do so until they know that any form of "Sledgehammer" is off. The effects on Sweden and on Finland may also be important.

6. It is essential to plan this operation so as not to put an undue strain upon the Fleet or upon our anti-U-boat vessels. For this purpose the expedition must be entirely self-contained. The troops must be based on the ships which carry them there, they will draw their supplies from them, and in the winter the great bulk of them will live in these ships. We must expect that the enemy will probably destroy the hutments he has erected. After the Navy has convoyed and landed the expedition, the German U-boats will come out to cut its communications. But if the expedition carries three or four months' supplies with it, the U-boats will get tired of waiting and a refresher convoy may have a safe passage. We shall know whether they are there or not.

7. The first step is to establish in Murmansk six squadrons of fighters and two or three squadrons of bombers. This will only be renewing on a larger scale the help we have already given at this end of the northern flank of the Russian line, and the enemy would not necessarily attach significance to it.

8. The second step is the landing of a storm party equal to a division in the Petsamo area. This is a fierce and hazardous operation, but small beer compared with what we are talking about in "Sledgehammer." Simultaneously with the above, the airfield at the head of Parsangerfiord must also be mastered by the equivalent of a brigade group.

9. The British aircraft from Murmansk would then establish themselves on the airfields, and the question to be decided is how they could be expelled therefrom. We should no doubt arrange heavy Russian pressure in the north of Finland, and our operation would be associated with this.

10. There would have to be two waves: first, the fighting expedition; the second, a week later, the supplies. Thereafter the

expedition would fend for itself for at least three months. How would the coming of winter affect our position? Would it make it easier for the enemy to attack us, or harder? This should be patiently thought out. During the winter the new snow tanks should be brought to the scene. Whether we should go south to attack Tromso need not be decided except in harmony with the main war situation.

For six weeks I fought hard for this Northern plan.

Prime Minister to General Ismay, for C.O.S. Committee 13 June 42

The following note on "Jupiter" should be read by the Planning Committee in conjunction with my previous paper on the subject. The Planners should set themselves to making a positive plan and overcoming the many difficulties, and not concern themselves with judging whether the operation is desirable or not, which must be decided by higher authority.

It is possible Russian troops might be used to come in behind a British high-class landing force.

I must have a preliminary report by next Tuesday.

I then wrote my final note upon this scheme, to which after all that has happened I am still faithful.

"JUPITER"

There are two important differences between "Imperator" and "Jupiter." First, in "Jupiter" we can certainly bring superior forces to bear at the point of attack and in the whole region invaded; secondly, if successful, we get a permanent footing on the Continent of constant value to the passage of our convoys and capable of almost indefinite exploitation southward. In fact, we could begin to roll the map of Hitler's Europe down from the top. Once we have established ourselves with growing air-power in the two main airfields, we can attack by parachute and other means under air cover the airfields to the southward and make ourselves masters of this northern region, so that with the spring of 1943 other landings could be made, Tromso and Narvik taken, then Bodo and Mo, by combinations of seaborne landings under shore-based air. No great mass of the enemy could be brought to bear upon them, except by inordinate efforts over bad communications.

The population would rise to aid us as we advanced, and only as we advanced. All this would be a convenient prelude and accompaniment to "Round-up." The distraction caused to the enemy's movements would far exceed the employment of our own resources. The reactions upon Sweden and Finland might be highly beneficial. Here is the best way of acting in the autumn of this year as an alternative to "Sledgehammer," if we judge that the Germans in France are not by then sufficiently demoralised for us to take the plunge.

2. It has come to be accepted by us as an axiom that it is impossible to land anywhere against opposition, including air opposition, however limited, without superior air strength. This is a hard saying, which limits all use of sea-power to the very small portions of the French coast which are under home-based fighter protection, and consequently to those points on the enemy's coasts where his best troops are concentrated and in the highest state of readiness. Without in any way disputing the desirability of having superior air-power and fighter cover, it may be questioned whether it is indispensable if the objective is of sufficient value and there is no other way. The lessons of the Norwegian campaign in the spring of 1940 must not be overstressed. We had practically no anti-aircraft artillery, and we exposed many scores of vessels for a month to the enemy's air attack without any compensating air defence. There were scarcely a dozen anti-aircraft guns available to us on shore. We landed over 20,000 men at Namsos and Andalsnes and brought them off again without undue loss, and the reason we came off was as much the military strength of the enemy as his air-power. It is not intended to press this argument too far, but there is no doubt that even merchant ships which have very powerful Oerlikon and other flak defence can, for a while and for an adequate need, carry out an operation without total destruction. The last Russian convoy was attacked continuously for four or five days with a loss of twenty per cent. It is a question whether it is better to land without fighter cover at a point where the enemy are very weak in armour and troops, or with fighter cover at a point where the enemy are very strong in armour and ground troops. It is a question of emphasis and proportion.

3. Lately Middle East Command gave us detailed calculations of the number of sorties likely to be expected [in their theatre]. The estimate may be right or wrong, but it is anyhow the way to

look at these problems. They must be faced in detail instead of our bowing to a general taboo. Let us take September or October and examine the number of sorties possible by the German Air Force at Murmansk and Petsamo against an expedition of, say, forty ships with escort which was approaching the coast. The armada would probably be sighted at dawn of D minus one, and would have to make the final approach during the dark hours of that day, assaulting before dawn of Day zero. The protection of the armada during the daylight advance would be by four or five auxiliary aircraft-carriers, and every ship would have six or seven Oerlikons or other flak on their decks. The protection at the moment of landing and of the ships when anchored or beached would be by six or seven beach defence ships with their trained floating flak. These would also take part in the protection during the approach. Similarly, the flak of the transports would be used in their own defence on arrival. With all this it seems unlikely that more than one-fifth or one-sixth of the transports and covering craft would be sunk. A military attack is not ruled out simply because a fifth of the soldiers may be shot on the way, provided the others get there and do the job.

4. Naturally, during the approach British and/or Russian forces from Murmansk would heavily attack any enemy airfields within range, and this should further minimise the losses of the armada.

5. The business of landing and assaulting and of capturing the airfields and other key points is a matter for Combined Operations, and need not be touched upon here.

6. It is intended at the moment that the transports carrying the troops should also carry a large part of their stores, and should also serve as the habitations and bases of the troops, in so far as these cannot be found ashore. It is essential that the expedition should be self-contained for three months, so that the Navy is liberated from all need of convoys. Let me have calculations as to the strength of the forces required, say, twenty-five thousand men of high quality; of the number of ships required to carry them; of the most convenient size of the said ships; and of the quantity of stores which they would have to carry for the three months' reserves. Also, whether it would be better to send them all together in one armada, or wait till the first lot have made a landing and then send a second wave.

7. As soon as the airfields are in our hands our fighter aircraft

from Murmansk must occupy them. This may have to begin even before our own flak is in position. We have to fight our way into the air as well as on to the shore. But special arrangements to bring portable flak to the airfields at the earliest moment would be necessary. Three batteries of mobile or portable Bofors would be needed for each airfield, and these should be in position in the first two days. The heavier flak should come in as soon as possible. As we should only have two airfields to work from at the beginning, it is essential that these should bristle with guns.

8. As soon as the airfields are established with flak and fighter protection, the heavy bombers would be flown from Scotland, and would operate from these airfields against the enemy airfields to the south.

* * * * *

I now tried to conceive a plan for the main invasion of France from England and America in the summer of 1943. This had always been my aim since the United States came into the war. I had outlined it in my third paper to the President on December 18, 1941. I was especially anxious that the gigantic scale of the operation should be understood from the outset and plans made accordingly. I threw myself into the mental proposition with such strength as I had. I wanted to give a picture of the size and character of the enterprise, and of the spirit in which alone it could be undertaken. Whatever may be thought about the detail, it struck the note of supreme effort.

Prime Minister to General Ismay   15 June 42

The attached should be considered by the Chiefs of Staff, and I should like to have their thoughts upon it as soon as possible. It may also be shown to the Planning Committee.

2. The preparations for "Sledgehammer" and "Round-up" should be separated from Commander-in-Chief Home Forces. He has enough to do in other directions. Pray show me how this can be achieved.

OPERATION "ROUND-UP"

For such an operation the qualities of magnitude, simultaneity, and violence are required. The enemy cannot be ready everywhere.

At least six heavy disembarkations must be attempted in the first wave. The enemy should be further mystified by at least half a dozen feints, which, if luck favours them, may be exploited. The limited and numerically inferior air force of the enemy will thus be dispersed or fully occupied. While intense fighting is in progress at one or two points, a virtual walk-over may be obtained at others.

2. The second wave nourishes the landings effected, and presses where the going is good. The fluidity of attack from the sea enables wide options to be exercised in the second wave.

3. It is hoped that "Jupiter" will be already in progress. Landings or feints should be planned in Denmark, in Holland, in Belgium, at the Pas de Calais, where the major air battle will be fought, on the Cotentin peninsula, at Brest, at St. Nazaire, at the mouth of the Gironde.

4. The first objective is to get ashore in large numbers. At least ten armoured brigades should go in the first wave. These brigades must accept very high risks in their task of pressing on deeply inland, rousing the populations, deranging the enemy's communications, and spreading the fighting over the widest possible areas.

5. Behind the confusion and disorder which these incursions will create, the second wave will be launched. This should aim at making definite concentrations of armour and motorised troops at strategic points carefully selected. If four or five of these desirable points have been chosen beforehand concentrations at perhaps three of them might be achieved, relations between them established, and the plan of battle could then take shape.

6. If forces are used on the above scale the enemy should be so disturbed as to require at least a week to organise other than local counter-strokes. During that week a superior fighter air force must be installed upon captured airfields, and the command of the air, hitherto fought for over the Pas de Calais, must become general. The R.A.F. must study, as an essential element for its success, the rapid occupation and exploitation of the captured airfields. In the first instance these can only be used as refuelling grounds, as the supreme object is to get into the air at the earliest moment. Altogether abnormal wastage must be expected in this first phase. The landing and installation of the flak at the utmost speed is a matter of high consequence, each airfield being a study of its own.

7. While these operations are taking place in the interior of the

country assaulted, the seizure of at least four important ports must be accomplished. For this purpose at least ten brigades of infantry, partly pedal-cyclists, but all specially trained in house-to-house fighting, must be used. Here again the cost in men and material must be rated very high.

8. To ensure success the whole of the above operations, simultaneous or successive, should be accomplished within a week of zero, by which time not less than four hundred thousand men should be ashore and busy.

9. The moment any port is gained and open the third wave of attack should start. This will be carried from our Western ports in large ships. It should comprise not less than three hundred thousand infantry, with their own artillery, plus part of that belonging to the earlier-landed formations. The first and second waves are essentially assaulting forces, and it is not till the third wave that the formations should be handled in terms of divisions and corps. If by zero 14 seven hundred thousand men are ashore, if air supremacy has been gained, if the enemy is in considerable confusion, and if we hold at least four workable ports, we shall have got our claws well into the job.

10. The phase of sudden violence, irrespective of losses, being over, the further course of the campaign may follow the normal and conventional lines of organisation and supply. It then becomes a matter of reinforcement and concerted movement. Fronts will have developed, and orderly progress will be possible. Unless we are prepared to commit the immense forces comprised in the first three waves to a hostile shore with the certainty that many of our attacks will miscarry, and that if we fail the whole stake will be lost, we ought not to attempt such an extraordinary operation of war under modern conditions.

11. The object of the above notes is to give an idea of the scale and spirit in which alone they can be undertaken with good prospects of success.

*   *   *   *   *

The ceaseless Staff discussions continued during the summer. "Sledgehammer" was knocked out by general assent. "Imperator" never reappeared. On the other hand, I did not receive much positive support for "Jupiter." We were all agreed upon the major cross-Channel invasion in 1943. The question arose irresistibly, what to do in the interval? It was impossible for the United States and Britain to stand idle all that time without fighting, except in the Desert. The President was determined that Americans should fight Germans on the largest possible scale *during* 1942. Where then could this be achieved? Where else but in French North Africa, upon which the President had always smiled? Out of many plans the fittest might survive.

I was content to wait for the answer.

21

Rommel Attacks

Our Defensive Position — Mines and "Boxes" — The German Attack Begins, May 26 — Auchinleck's Communiqué — Our Thousand-Bomber Raid on Cologne, May 30 — Fierce Fighting in the Bridgehead and at Bir Hacheim — Our Mobile Strategic Reserve — My Telegram to Auchinleck of June 9 — Auchinleck's Estimate of Casualties — A Disquieting Feature — The Tank Battle between El Adem and "Knightsbridge," June 12 and 13 — The Minister of State's Telegram of June 14 — Auchinleck and Ritchie: An Unsatisfactory Compromise — Tobruk in Peril — The War Cabinet Telegram of June 15 — Auchinleck's Reply, June 16 — Importance of the Fortress — I Resolve Not to Cancel My Visit to Washington.

A LTHOUGH GENERAL AUCHINLECK had not felt himself strong enough to seize the initiative, he awaited with some confidence the enemy's attack. General Ritchie, commanding the Eighth Army, had under his chief's supervision prepared an elaborate defensive position stretching from Gazala, held by the South African Division on the sea, to Bir Hacheim, forty-five miles due south in the Desert, held by the 1st Free French Brigade Group under General Koenig. The system of defence adopted to hold the front was a series of fortified points called "boxes," held in strength by brigades or larger forces, the whole being covered by an immense spread of minefields. Behind this our armour and the XXXth Corps were held in reserve.[1]

[1] Diagram 1, "Enemy Plan for May 27–28" (page 358), shows the first enemy thrust and the position of our own troops.

357

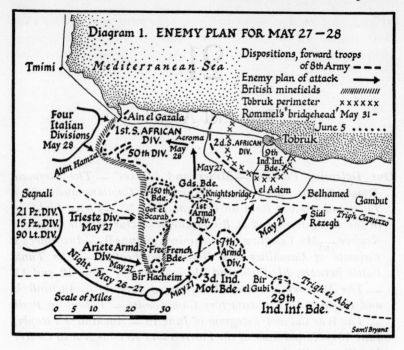

Diagram 1. ENEMY PLAN FOR MAY 27—28

Dispositions, forward troops of 8th Army - - -
Enemy plan of attack →
British minefields ////////////
Tobruk perimeter ×××××
Rommel's "bridgehead" May 31– June 5 ......

Tmimi · — Mediterranean Sea

Four Italian Divisions May 28 — Ain el Gazala
1st. S. AFRICAN DIV. — Acroma
50 th DIV. May 28
2d. S. AFRICAN DIV. — Tobruk
Alem Hamza
May 27
9th Ind. Inf. Bde.

Segnali
21 Pz. DIV.
15 Pz. DIV.
90 Lt. DIV.

150 th Bde.
Gds. Bde.
Knightsbridge
el Adem
Belhamed
Gambut

Trieste Div. May 27
Got el Scarab
1st Armd. Div.
Sidi Rezegh
Trigh Capuzzo

Ariete Armd. Div. — Free French Bde.
May 27
Bir Hacheim
7th. Armd. Div.
May 27

Night May 26–27
May 27
3d. Ind. Mot. Bde.
Bir el Gubi
29th Ind. Inf. Bde.
Trigh el Abd

Scale of Miles
0   5   10   20   30

Sam'l Bryant

All the Desert battles, except Alamein, began by swift, wide
turning movements of armour on the Desert Flank. Rommel
started by moonlight on the night of May 26–27, and swept
forward round Bir Hacheim with all his armour, intending to
engage and destroy the British armour and seize the El Adem-
Sidi Rezegh position by nightfall on the 28th, thus taking the
long-prepared British position in rear. He overran an Indian
motorised brigade, and broke forward at first with great speed.
He was stubbornly resisted by the British armour and all the
formations which had been posted to counter the kind of stroke
he had launched. After several days of hard and bitter fighting
he found that he could make no more headway, and was much
hampered by having to bring all his supplies, and the ammunition for unceasing battle, by a wide détour round Bir Hacheim.
He therefore sought a shorter line of communication, and his
engineers cleared two short-cuts back through the British minefields. These passages, which were continually broadened, lay

on each side of the "box" held with devoted tenacity by the 150th Brigade of the 50th Division. By the 31st he was able to withdraw his mass of armoured and transport vehicles into these two gaps. He formed a so-called "bridgehead" towards us, enclosing behind it the fortified "box" of the 150th Brigade. This enclave, or "cauldron" as it was not unsuitably named, became the main target of our Air Force.

Rommel's original audacious scheme had certainly failed; but once he had retreated into our minefields these became an effective part of his defence. Here he regrouped, and crouched for a further spring.

The opening phase of this severe and disastrous battle is well described in General Auchinleck's communiqué of June 1, which I read almost verbatim to the House of Commons the next day.

General Auchinleck and Air Marshal Tedder to Prime Minister
1 June 42

On evening May 26 General Rommel launched the German Afrika Corps to the attack. He was at pains to explain in an order of the day issued to all Italian and German troops under his command that in the course of great operations they were to carry through a decisive attack against our forces in Libya, and that for this purpose he had made ready and equipped a force superior in numbers with perfected armament and a powerful air force to give it support. In conclusion he hailed His Majesty the King of Italy and Emperor of Ethiopia, the Duce of the Roman Empire, and the Fuehrer of Great Germany. We had foreseen this attack and were ready for it. From captured documents it is clear that Rommel's object was to defeat our armoured forces and capture Tobruk.

The attacks against the northern front of our main positions south of Gazala on the 27th achieved little or nothing. An attempt to break through our defences along the coast road by the Gazala inlet was easily stopped. Throughout May 28, 29, and 30 there was very heavy and continuous fighting between our armoured divisions and brigades and the German Afrika Corps, backed up by the Italian Mobile Corps. The battle swayed backward and forward over a wide area from Acroma in the north to Bir Hacheim forty miles to the south, and from El Adem to our minefields thirty miles to the westward. The enemy, finding himself running short of supplies and water, had to make gaps in our minefields, one along the general line of the Trigh Capuzzo and another ten miles to the south. . . . It is still difficult to give a firm estimate of the number of vehicles and tanks knocked out or disabled by these attacks, but there has been ample confirmation that the effect was very great. Meantime each night our night bombers were attacking enemy forward aerodromes and his communications.

On May 31 the enemy had succeeded in withdrawing many of his tanks and much transport into one or other of these gaps, which he then proceeded to protect from attack from the east by bringing anti-tank guns, with which he is well equipped, into position. A large number of his tanks and many transport vehicles however remained on the wrong side of this barrier, and these are still being ceaselessly harried and destroyed by our troops, vigorously aided by the bombers and fighters of our Air Force.

The country to the east of Bir Hacheim is being mopped up by our troops, which have destroyed many tanks and vehicles in this area and captured two large workshops. Fierce fighting is still proceeding, and the battle is by no means over. Further heavy fighting is to be expected, but whatever may be the result there is no shadow of doubt that Rommel's plans for his initial offensive have gone completely awry and that this failure has cost him dear in men and material. The skill, determination, and pertinacity shown by General Ritchie and his Corps Commanders, Lieutenant-Generals Norrie and Gott, throughout this difficult and strenuous week of hard and continuous fighting have been of the highest order.

I contented myself with the following comment: "From all the above it is clear that we have every reason to be satisfied and more than satisfied with the course that the battle has so far taken, and that we should watch the further development with earnest attention."

I then spoke of the mammoth air raid upon Cologne on the night of May 30–31, when no fewer than 1130 British-manned aircraft crossed the sea. I also reported that "last night 1036 machines of the Royal Air Force again visited the Continent.

Nearly all of these operated on the Essen region. From this second large-scale air raid thirty-five of our bombers are missing. These two great night bombing raids mark the introduction of a new phase in the British air offensive against Germany, which will increase markedly in scale when we are joined, as we soon shall be, by the Air Force of the United States."

While I was content with the way the battle had opened, I was anxious about Malta.

Prime Minister to General Auchinleck and Air Marshal Tedder
2 June 42

There is no need for me to stress the vital importance of the safe arrival of our convoys at Malta, and I am sure you will both take all steps to enable the air escorts, and particularly the Beaufighters, to be operated from landing-grounds as far west as possible. I hope that you have prepared a plan for bringing Martuba into use as an advance refuelling base immediately it is in our possession, including arrangements for guards, A.A. protection, and possibly the transport by air of aviation petrol, oil, and ammunition for operations by our fighters. Even two refuellings might make a decisive difference. Other points will no doubt occur to you both. Let me know as soon as possible that all arrangements are complete.

* * * * *

We now know that Rommel had hoped to seize Tobruk on the second day of his attack, and that General Auchinleck was correct in his belief that Rommel's initial plan had to that extent miscarried. In order to renew his strength for a further effort it was essential for Rommel to hold and develop the bridgehead through our minefield. So long as Bir Hacheim, strongly defended by the 1st Free French Brigade against constant land and air attack, held firm, it was only here that he could be sure of passing his supplies.

During the first week of June the battle was therefore focused on these two points, Bir Hacheim and the bridgehead. Within the latter was the stubborn 150th Brigade. Rommel was

in dire need of supplies and water. If the whole battle were not
to be lost, he must eliminate the brigade so that his convoys
might pass. It was set upon, and destroyed on June 1. This is
Rommel's account in his own words:

Yard by yard the German-Italian units fought their way forward
against the toughest British resistance imaginable. The British
defence was conducted with considerable skill. As usual the British
fought to the last round of ammunition.[2]

For us, all now turned on breaking into the bridgehead, as,
despite the heavy air attacks on his line of communications, it
was only a question of time before the enemy would be sufficiently recovered to burst forth from it again. Days slipped by
in considering alternative plans, and it was not till June 4 that
the effort was made. It was a costly failure, in which an Indian
infantry brigade and four regiments of field artillery were overwhelmed through lack of support and mismanagement. General Auchinleck has rightly called this "the turning-point of the
whole battle." We missed our chance, and Rommel regained
the initiative, punching Ritchie's army when and where he
willed.

Soon the enemy armour sallied from the bridgehead and
renewed its attacks. The Free French were evacuated from Bir
Hacheim after a very fine defence. This was a very heavy blow,
and the next phase of the battle began, in far worse circumstances than the first; nor could the whole-hearted efforts of the
Royal Air Force prevent the collapse that followed.

*   *   *   *   *

The process of having a strategical reserve with sea mobility
at our service was one to which, as has been seen, I was greatly
attached. In the summer of 1941 I had persuaded President
Roosevelt, although the United States were not at war, to lend
us American transports to carry two divisions round the Cape.
These had enabled us to reinforce India when the Japanese

2 *Rommel*, by Desmond Young, page 267.

came into the war. On March 4, 1942, I had again asked the
President for American shipping to carry a second two additional divisions round the Cape in this critical period, while
keeping their destination open.[3] This considerable force was
now at sea and gave us highly convenient options. It seemed
clear that they should go to Egypt to sustain the Desert campaign. Of course, if the Russian front broke in the Caspian-
Caucasus area, and even greater emergencies fell upon us, or if
India or Australia were actually invaded by Japan — which, to
say the least, was most improbable — there was still a month
in hand for a second choice.

I hastened to tell General Auchinleck the good news.

Prime Minister to General Auchinleck   9 June 42

I have been continually thinking about your great battle and
how we can best sustain your army, so that it may be fought out
to a victorious end. Here is some good news.

The 8th Armoured Division is now at the Cape, and the 44th
Division is nearing Freetown. We have deliberately kept an option
on the ultimate destination of these divisions until we could see our
way more clearly. Some time ago I promised the Australian Government that if Australia were seriously invaded we would immediately divert both these divisions to their assistance. Australia up to
date has not been seriously invaded, and in view of the naval losses
which the Japanese have sustained in the battles of the Coral Sea
and off Midway Island we regard a serious invasion in the near
future as extremely improbable. We were also prepared, though we
have never promised Wavell, to send both these divisions to India
if it looked as though the Japanese had an invasion of India in
mind. This also seems extremely improbable at the moment, and
India has already got the 2d, 5th, and 70th British Divisions.

We have therefore decided that the 8th Armoured Division and
the 44th Division should be sent to you unless Australia is threatened with serious invasion within the next few days. You may therefore make your plans for the battle on the assumption that the 8th
Armoured Division will reach Suez at the end of June and the
44th Division by mid-July.

3 See Chapter 11, "The Shipping Stranglehold."

Thereafter, depending on the general situation then prevailing, you should be prepared to send to India one of your Indian divisions and the 252d Indian Armoured Brigade. Pray let us have your proposals so that we may tell General Wavell.

A detailed account of the exact state of the 8th Armoured Division and of the technical preparedness of its tanks, together with the exact loading on the various ships and their dates of arrival, is being sent you separately. You can thus make the best possible plans for disembarking, organising, and bringing it into action in the most effective manner with the least delay. We feel that with this rapidly approaching reserve behind you you will be able to act with greater freedom in using your existing resources. All good wishes.

General Auchinleck to Prime Minister   10 June 42

I feel greatly encouraged by your good wishes. I hope to be able to show you some returns from all the hard and bitter fighting which has taken place during the last two weeks. It is most welcome to know that we may get the 44th and 8th Armoured Divisions in this theatre, and I am at once proceeding with plans to make the best use of them, although I appreciate that this decision may be changed. The 8th Armoured Divisional Commander is now in Cairo.

I note that later I may be ordered to send to India an Indian infantry division and an Indian armoured brigade. It is known to you that I have nothing like enough troops either to face a German attack through Anatolia or to defend Persia, and I must plan to meet these threats, although I realise that they may never materialise. I appreciate that the threat to India may materialise quicker and be of a more serious nature than a threat to my north and northeastern fronts, and that, since the largest strategical issues will be at stake, you alone are in a position to allot troops to meet these eventualities. I only mention commitments in Syria, Iraq, and Persia in order to remind you that unless we are substantially reinforced before the Germans have penetrated too deeply, the chances of a successful defence in these theatres with our present resources are slim.

As you say, the knowledge that these two fresh and powerful divisions are coming will considerably increase my freedom of action with the troops I have at present. You probably know that already, in order to strengthen the Eighth Army, I have moved considerable forces from Iraq to Libya.

We are all most grateful to you.

*   *   *   *   *

On the 10th General Auchinleck sent us an estimate of the casualties on both sides up to June 7. "It has been and still is most difficult to get details of army losses in personnel and equipment while the battle still rages. Our own losses are estimated very approximately at 10,000, of whom some 8000 may be prisoners, but the casualties of the 5th Indian Division are not yet accurately known." He had no figures of the enemy killed and wounded, but he thought they must be "probably equal to, and possibly greater than ours." We had taken 4000 prisoners, of whom 1660 were German. The enemy had lost 400 tanks, of which 211 were "guaranteed certain." Our losses, including tanks which might still be recovered, were 350, leaving our total armoured strength fit for action on June 9, at 254 cruiser and 67 Infantry tanks. We had destroyed 120 enemy guns, and lost ourselves 10 medium and 140 field guns, 42 six-pounders, and 153 two-pounders.

Our aircraft losses from all causes amounted to 176 machines, and 70 pilots killed or missing or wounded. The estimate of enemy air losses was 165 machines destroyed or damaged, of which three-quarters were German.

In the meantime, the 3d Indian Motor Brigade Group (alas, already overrun), the 10th Indian Division, one armoured brigade group, and several other formations had reinforced the Eighth Army, and the 5th Indian Infantry Brigade Group was being got ready. Altogether 25,000 men, 78 field guns, 220 anti-tank guns, and 353 tanks had reached the Army since the battle began.[4]

The figures of tanks, guns, and aircraft were satisfactory and also precise. I was naturally struck by the statement, "Our own losses in personnel are estimated very approximately at ten

---

[4] These figures include the 3d Indian Motor Brigade Group, which was present at the beginning of the battle.

thousand, of whom some eight thousand may be prisoners, but casualties of the 5th Indian Division not yet accurately known." This extraordinary disproportion between killed and wounded on the one hand and prisoners on the other revealed that something must have happened of an unpleasant character. It showed also that the Cairo Headquarters were in important respects unable to measure the event. I did not dwell on this in my reply.

Prime Minister to General Auchinleck   11 June 42

Many thanks for your facts and figures. They seem to me quite good. Although of course one hopes for success by manoeuvre or counter-stroke, nevertheless we have no reason to fear a prolonged *bataille d'usure*. This must wear down Rommel worse than Ritchie because of our superior communications. More especially is this true in view of what is coming towards you as fast as ships can steam. Recovery work is most encouraging and reflects credit on all concerned. Please give my compliments to Ritchie and tell him how much his dogged and resolute fighting is admired by the vast audience which follows every move from day to day.

General Auchinleck replied:

General Auchinleck to Prime Minister   11 June 42

Thank you very much for your most encouraging and understanding telegram of June 11.

Our losses have been heavy, and I am afraid in one engagement avoidably so, but, as you say, our resources are greater than his and his situation is not enviable.

I have passed your message to General Ritchie, who will, I know, be deeply gratified by it.

*   *   *   *   *

With replenished forces and a new freedom of movement granted him by the capture of Bir Hacheim, Rommel now broke out of the "cauldron" with his armour to attack us from the south. Our flank had been turned, and at the extreme northern end of the line the 1st South African and the remaining brigades of the 50th Division, still holding their original positions, were in danger of being cut off.[5]

[5] See Diagram 2, "The Battle for Tobruk."

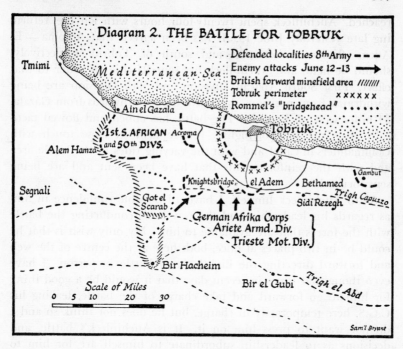

Diagram 2. THE BATTLE FOR TOBRUK

Defended localities 8th Army — — —
Enemy attacks June 12-13 ——→
British forward minefield area /////////
Tobruk perimeter ×××××
Rommel's "bridgehead" ••••••

Throughout June 12 and 13 a fierce battle was fought for possession of the ridges that lie between El Adem and "Knightsbridge." This was the culmination of the tank battle; at its close the enemy were masters of the field, and our own armour gravely reduced. "Knightsbridge," the focus of communications in that neighbourhood, had to be evacuated, after a stubborn defence by the Guards Brigade, supported by the 2d Regiment of Royal Horse Artillery. Only by immediate withdrawal were the 1st South African and 50th Divisions saved from destruction; they accomplished it successfully, thanks in no small degree to the protection given overhead by the Royal Air Force.

By the 14th it became clear that the battle had taken a heavy adverse turn. Mr. Casey, the Minister of State, sent me a telegram which emphasised the Service messages.

Minister of State to Prime Minister   14 June 42

You know the serious stage that the Western Desert battle has

reached. Auchinleck spent twenty-four hours with Ritchie, returning late yesterday June 13. It has been agreed that Acroma — El
Adem (sixteen miles west and south of Tobruk respectively)
should be held, and Auchinleck has sent Ritchie an order to that
effect. First South African Division and 50th Division are being
withdrawn from positions they have held southwards from Gazala,
34 miles west of Tobruk. The battle has ebbed and flowed tactically over the last fortnight. I have kept in close touch with
Commanders-in-Chief and with the varying tides in the battle area
and with the reinforcements that have been sent and are being
sent forward.

As to Auchinleck himself, I have all possible confidence in him
as regards his leadership and the way he is conducting the battle
with the forces that are available to him. My only wish is that he
could be in two places at once, both here at the centre of the web
and forward directing the Eighth Army battle in person. I have
even thought at times in recent days that it would be a good thing
for him to go forward and take charge of the battle, leaving his
C.G.S. here temporarily in charge, but he does not think so and I
do not want to press him on it. It is Auchinleck's battle, and
decisions as to leadership subordinate to himself are for him to
make.

In short, the situation today is anxious, but the enemy is and
will continue to be fought hard and relentlessly. The Royal Air
Force under Tedder are doing well, and I believe it is right to say
that we have air superiority in the battle area. The outcome of
the two convoys to Malta rests on today and tomorrow. The
Western Desert battle will undoubtedly help the westbound convoy
from the air point of view. The greater danger that the westbound
convoy will be exposed to tomorrow will be from surface vessels
of the Italian fleet. Tedder is at Alexandria for these two critical
days, for the westbound convoy with Harwood. Harwood, by the
way, has started very well here and shows common sense and
judgment.

Mr. Casey's remark about the advantages of Auchinleck's
taking personal command of the Desert battle confirmed my
own feelings which I had expressed to the General a month
before. The Commander-in-Chief of the Middle East was embarrassed and hampered by his too extensive responsibilities.

He thought of the battle, on which all in his work depended, only as a part of his task. There was always the danger from the north, to which he felt it his duty to attach an importance to which we at home in a better position to judge no longer subscribed.

The arrangement which he had made was a compromise. He left the fighting of the decisive battle to General Ritchie, who had so recently ceased to be his Deputy Chief of Staff. At the same time he kept this officer under strict supervision, sending him continuous instructions. It was only after the disaster had occurred that he was induced, largely by the urgings of the Minister of State, to do what he should have done from the beginning and take over the direct command of the battle himself. It is to this that I ascribe his personal failure, some of the blame for which undoubtedly falls on me and my colleagues for the unduly wide responsibilities assigned a year before to the Middle East Command. Still, we had done our best to free him from these undue burdens by precise, up-to-date, and superseding advice, which he rejected. Personally I believe that if he had taken command from the outset and, as was fully in his power, left a deputy in Cairo to keep an eye on the north and discharge the mass of varied business belonging to the rest of the immense theatre over which he presided, he might well have won the battle, and certainly when late in the day he took command he saved what was left of it.

The reader will presently see how these impressions bit so deeply into me that in my directive to General Alexander of August 10 I made his main duty clear beyond a doubt. One lives and learns.

I now telegraphed to Auchinleck:

Prime Minister to General Auchinleck   14 June 42

Your decision to fight it out to the end is most cordially endorsed. We shall sustain you whatever the result. Retreat would be fatal. This is a business not only of armour but of will-power. God bless you all.

*   *   *   *   *

Immediately Tobruk glared upon us, and as in the previous year, we had no doubt that it should be held at all costs. Now also, after a month's needless delay, General Auchinleck ordered up the New Zealand Division from Syria, but not in time for it to take part in the battle for Tobruk.

Prime Minister to General Auchinleck   14 June 42

To what position does Ritchie want to withdraw the Gazala troops? Presume there is no question in any case of giving up Tobruk. As long as Tobruk is held no serious enemy advance into Egypt is possible. We went through all this in April, 1941. Do not understand what you mean by withdrawing to "old frontier."

2. Am very glad you are bringing New Zealand Division into the Western Desert. Let me know dates when it can be deployed and where.

3. C.I.G.S. agrees with all this. Please keep us informed.

General Auchinleck to Prime Minister   15 June 42

Have ordered General Ritchie to deny to the enemy general line Acroma-El Adem-El Gubi. This does not mean that this can or should be held as a continuous fortified line, but that the enemy is not to be allowed to establish himself east of it. The two divisions from Gazala position will be available to help in this. Although I do not intend that Eighth Army should be besieged in Tobruk, I have no intention whatever of giving up Tobruk. My orders to General Ritchie are: (*a*) to deny general line Acroma-El Adem-El Gubi to the enemy; (*b*) not to allow his forces to be invested in Tobruk; (*c*) to attack and harass the enemy whenever occasion offers.

Meanwhile I propose to build up strong as possible reserve in Sollum-Maddalena area with object of launching counter-offensive soon as possible.

2. New Zealand Division, already moving, should be fully concentrated in about ten or twelve days, but leading elements will naturally be available earlier if required.

We were not satisfied with the orders to General Ritchie, which did not positively require him to defend Tobruk. To make sure I sent the following telegram:

Prime Minister to General Auchinleck   15 June 42

We are glad to have your assurance that you have no intention
of giving up Tobruk. War Cabinet interpret your telegram to
mean that, if the need arises, General Ritchie would leave as many
troops in Tobruk as are necessary to hold the place for certain.

The reply left no doubt.

General Auchinleck to Prime Minister   16 June 42

War Cabinet interpretation is correct. General Ritchie is putting
into Tobruk what he considers an adequate force to hold it even
should it become temporarily isolated by enemy. Basis of garrison
is four brigade groups, with adequate stocks of ammunition, food,
fuel, and water. Basis of immediate future action by Eighth Army
is to hold El Adem fortified area as pivot of manoeuvre and to
use all available mobile forces to prevent enemy establishing
himself east of El Adem or Tobruk. Very definite orders to this
effect have been issued to General Ritchie, and I trust he will be
able to give effect to them.

Position is quite different to last year, as we and not enemy
now hold fortified positions on frontier, and can operate fighter
aircraft over Tobruk even if use of Gambut landing-ground should
be temporarily denied to us. It seems to me that to invest Tobruk
and to mask our forces in the frontier positions the enemy would
need more troops than our information shows him to have. This
being so, we should be able to prevent the area between the
frontier and Tobruk passing under enemy control.

I have discussed matter with Minister of State and other Commanders-in-Chief, who agree with the policy proposed.

Prime Minister to General Auchinleck   16 June 42

The news of your success in regrouping the Eighth Army on the
new front in close contact with your reinforcements was particularly
welcome, and the Cabinet was glad to know that you intended to
hold Tobruk at all costs.

Of course we cannot judge battle tactics from here at the present
time, but it would certainly seem that it would be advantageous if
the whole of our forces were engaged together at one time and if
you could recover the initiative. It may be that this opportunity
will arise with the new situation, especially if the enemy is given

no breathing-space, as he is evidently himself hard-pressed. Because armoured warfare allows a design to be unfolded step by step it seems to favour the offensive, whereas the defensive, which was so powerful in the last war, has to yield itself continually to the plans of the attacker. We all send you our good wishes.

* * * * *

On this we rested with confidence based upon the experience of the previous year. Moreover, our position, as General Auchinleck had pointed out, appeared on paper much better than in 1941. We had an army deployed on a fortified front, in close proximity to Tobruk, with the newly constructed direct broad-gauge railway sustaining it. We were no longer formed to a flank with our communications largely dependent on the sea, but according to the orthodox principles of war, running back at right-angles from the centre of our front to our main base. In these circumstances, though grieved by what had happened, I still felt from a survey of all the forces on both sides, and of Rommel's immense difficulties of supply, that all would still be well.

We did not however know the conditions prevailing in Tobruk. Considering that Auchinleck's plan had been to await an attack, and all the months that had passed, it was inconceivable that the already well-proved fortifications of Tobruk should not have been maintained in the highest efficiency, and indeed strengthened. For the defensive battle upon which he had resolved, the fortress and sally-port of Tobruk was an invaluable factor.

Finally, the word "temporarily," as applied to the defence of Tobruk, had a significance which was not appreciated in London. Our intention, which we thought the Commander-in-Chief fully shared, was that Tobruk should once again be held as an isolated fortress if the main battle went against us, and that the Eighth Army should fall back along its main line of communication to the Mersa Matruh position. This would have left Rommel with Tobruk still on his flank, having to be invested or masked, while his own communications were ever lengthening and ever more strained. With the New Zealand

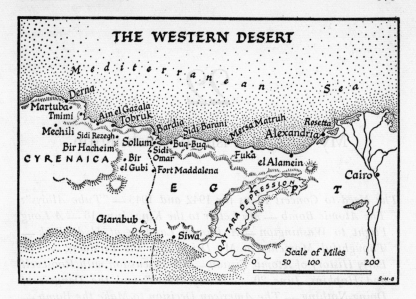

THE WESTERN DESERT

Division now not far away, and with the powerful reinforcements approaching by the sea, I did not myself feel that the continuance of hard fighting in the greatest possible strength on both sides would be to our detriment in the long run. I did not therefore cancel the plans I had made for a second visit to Washington, where business of the highest importance to the general strategy of the war had to be transacted. In this I was supported by my colleagues.

22

My Second Visit to Washington

THE MAIN OBJECT of my journey was to reach a final decision
on the operations for 1942–43. The American authorities
in general, and Mr. Stimson and General Marshall in particular, were anxious that some plan should be decided upon at
once which would enable the United States to engage the
Germans in force on land and in the air in 1942. Failing this,
there was the danger that the American Chiefs of Staff would
seriously consider a radical revision of the strategy of "Germany
first." Another matter lay heavy on my mind. It was the
question of "Tube Alloys," which was our code-word for what

afterward became the atomic bomb. Our research and experiments had now reached a point where definite agreements must be made with the United States, and it was felt this could only be achieved by personal discussions between the President and me. The fact that the War Cabinet decided that I should leave the country and London, with the C.I.G.S. and General Ismay, at the height of the Desert battle, measures the importance which we attached to a settlement of the grave strategic issues which were upon us.

On account of the urgency and crisis of our affairs in these very difficult days, I decided to go by air rather than by sea. This meant that we should be barely twenty-four hours cut off from the full stream of information. Efficient arrangements were made for the immediate transmission of messages from Egypt and for the rapid passage and decoding of all reports, and no harmful delays in taking decisions were expected or in fact occurred.

It is not customary for a Prime Minister to advise the Sovereign officially upon his successor unless he is asked to do so. As it was wartime I sent the King, in response to a request he had made to me in conversation at our last weekly interview, the following letter:

> 10 Downing Street, Whitehall
> June 16, 1942

Sir,

In case of my death on this journey I am about to undertake, I avail myself of Your Majesty's gracious permission to advise that you should entrust the formation of a new government to Mr. Anthony Eden, the Secretary of State for Foreign Affairs, who is in my mind the outstanding Minister in the largest political party in the House of Commons and in the National Government over which I have the honour to preside, and who I am sure will be found capable of conducting Your Majesty's affairs with the resolution, experience, and capacity which these grievous times require.

I have the honour to remain

> Your Majesty's faithful and devoted servant and subject
> WINSTON S. CHURCHILL

Although I now knew the risks we had run on our return voyage flight from Bermuda in January, my confidence in the chief pilot, Kelly Rogers, and his Boeing flying-boat was such that I asked specially that he should take charge. My party was completed by Brigadier Stewart, the Director of Plans at the War Office (who was later killed when flying back from the Casablanca Conference), Sir Charles Wilson, Mr. Martin, and Commander Thompson. We left Stranraer on the night of June 17, shortly before midnight. The weather was perfect and the moon full. I sat for two hours or more in the co-pilot's seat admiring the shining sea, revolving my problems, and thinking of the anxious battle. I slept soundly in the "bridal suite" until in broad daylight we reached Gander. Here we could have refuelled, but this was not thought necessary, and after making our salutes to the airfield we pursued our voyage. As we were travelling with the sun the day seemed very long. We had two luncheons with a six-hour interval, and contemplated a late dinner after arrival.

For the last two hours we flew over the land, and it was about seven o'clock by American time when we approached Washington. As we gradually descended towards the Potomac River I noticed that the top of the Washington Monument, which is over five hundred and fifty feet high, was about our level, and I impressed upon Captain Kelly Rogers that it would be peculiarly unfortunate if we brought our story to an end by hitting this of all other objects in the world. He assured me that he would take special care to miss it. Thus we landed safely and smoothly on the Potomac after a journey of twenty-seven flying hours. Lord Halifax, General Marshall, and several high officers of the United States welcomed us. I repaired to the British Embassy for dinner. It was too late for me to fly on to Hyde Park that night. We read all the latest telegrams — there was nothing important — and dined agreeably in the open air. The British Embassy, standing on the high ground, is one of the coolest places in Washington, and compares very favourably in this respect with the White House.

Early the next morning, the 19th, I flew to Hyde Park. The

President was on the local airfield, and saw us make the roughest bump landing I have experienced. He welcomed me with greatest cordiality, and, driving the car himself, took me to the majestic bluffs over the Hudson River on which Hyde Park, his family home, stands. The President drove me all over the estate, showing me its splendid views. In this drive I had some thoughtful moments. Mr. Roosevelt's infirmity prevented him from using his feet on the brake, clutch, or accelerator. An ingenious arrangement enabled him to do everything with his arms, which were amazingly strong and muscular. He invited me to feel his biceps, saying that a famous prize-fighter had envied them. This was reassuring; but I confess that when on several occasions the car poised and backed on the grass verges of the precipices over the Hudson I hoped the mechanical devices and brakes would show no defects. All the time we talked business, and though I was careful not to take his attention off the driving we made more progress than we might have done in formal conference.

The President was very glad to hear I had brought the C.I.G.S. with me. His field of interest was always brightened by recollections of his youth. It had happened that the President's father had entertained at Hyde Park the father of General Brooke. Mr. Roosevelt therefore expressed keen interest to meet the son, who had reached such a high position. When they met two days later he received him with the utmost cordiality, and General Brooke's personality and charm created an almost immediate intimacy which greatly helped the course of business.

* * * * *

I told Harry Hopkins about the different points on which I wanted decisions, and he talked them over with President Roosevelt, so that the ground was prepared and the President's mind armed upon each subject. Of these, "Tube Alloys" was one of the most complex, and, as it proved, overwhelmingly the most important.

I can best describe the position at this time by quoting

from a statement that I issued on August 6, 1945, after Hiroshima had with one stroke been made a ruin:

By the year 1939 it had become widely recognised among scientists of many nations that the release of energy by atomic fission was a possibility. The problems which remained to be solved before this possibility could be turned into practical achievement were however manifold and immense, and few scientists would at that time have ventured to predict that an atomic bomb could be ready for use by 1945. Nevertheless, the potentialities of the project were so great that His Majesty's Government thought it right that research should be carried on in spite of the many competing claims on our scientific man-power. At this stage the research was carried out mainly in our universities, principally Oxford, Cambridge, London (Imperial College), Liverpool, and Birmingham. At the time of the formation of the Coalition Government responsibility for co-ordinating the work and pressing it forward lay with the Ministry of Aircraft Production, advised by a committee of leading scientists presided over by Sir George Thomson.

At the same time, under the general arrangements then in force for the pooling of scientific information, there was a full interchange of ideas between the scientists carrying out this work in the United Kingdom and those in the United States.

Such progress was made that by the summer of 1941 Sir George Thomson's committee was able to report that in their view there was a reasonable chance that an atomic bomb could be produced before the end of the war. At the end of August, 1941, Lord Cherwell, whose duty it was to keep me informed on all these and other technical developments, reported the substantial progress which was being made. The general responsibility for the scientific research carried on under the various technical committees lay with the then Lord President of the Council, Sir John Anderson. In these circumstances (having in mind also the effect of ordinary high explosive of which we had recently had enough), I referred the matter on August 30, 1941, to the Chiefs of Staff Committee in the following minute:

General Ismay, for C.O.S. Committee

Although personally I am quite content with the existing

explosives, I feel we must not stand in the path of improvement, and I therefore think that action should be taken in the sense proposed by Lord Cherwell, and that the Cabinet Minister responsible should be Sir John Anderson.

I shall be glad to know what the Chiefs of Staff Committee think.

The Chiefs of Staff had recommended immediate action, with the maximum priority. We therefore set up within the Department of Scientific and Industrial Research a special division to direct the work, and Imperial Chemical Industries, Limited, agreed to release Mr. W. A. Akers to take charge of this directorate, which we called, for purposes of secrecy, the "Directorate of Tube Alloys." After Sir John Anderson had ceased to be Lord President and became Chancellor of the Exchequer, I asked him to continue to supervise this work, for which he has special qualifications. To advise him there was set up under his chairmanship a Consultative Council.

On October 11, 1941, President Roosevelt sent me a letter suggesting that our efforts might be jointly conducted. Accordingly all British and American efforts were joined, and a number of British scientists concerned proceeded to the United States. By the summer of 1942 this expanded programme of research had confirmed with surer and broader foundations the promising forecasts which had been made a year earlier, and the time had come when a decision must be made whether or not to proceed with the construction of large-scale production plants.

* * * * *

We had reached this point when I joined the President at Hyde Park. I had my papers with me, but the discussion was postponed till the next day, the 20th, as the President needed more information from Washington. Our talks took place after luncheon, in a tiny little room which juts out on the ground floor. The room was dark and shaded from the sun. Mr. Roosevelt was ensconced at a desk almost as big as the apartment. Harry sat or stood in the background. My two American friends did not seem to mind the intense heat.

I told the President in general terms of the great progress we had made, and that our scientists were now definitely convinced that results might be reached before the end of the present war. He said his people were getting along too, but no one could tell whether anything practical would emerge till a full-scale experiment had been made. We both felt painfully the dangers of doing nothing. We knew what efforts the Germans were making to procure supplies of "heavy water" — a sinister term, eerie, unnatural, which began to creep into our secret papers. What if the enemy should get an atomic bomb before we did! However sceptical one might feel about the assertions of scientists, much disputed among themselves and expressed in jargon incomprehensible to laymen, we could not run the mortal risk of being outstripped in this awful sphere.

I strongly urged that we should at once pool all our information, work together on equal terms, and share the results, if any, equally between us. The question then arose as to where the research plant was to be set up. We were already aware of the enormous expense that must be incurred, with all the consequent grave diversion of resources and brain-power from other forms of war effort. Considering that Great Britain was under close bombing attack and constant enemy air reconnaissance, it seemed impossible to erect in the Island the vast and conspicuous factories that were needed. We conceived ourselves at least as far advanced as our Ally, and there was of course the alternative of Canada, who had a vital contribution herself to make through the supplies of uranium she had actively gathered. It was a hard decision to spend several hundred million pounds sterling, not so much of money as of competing forms of precious war energy, upon a project the success of which no scientist on either side of the Atlantic could guarantee. Nevertheless, if the Americans had not been willing to undertake the venture we should certainly have gone forward on our own power in Canada, or, if the Canadian Government demurred, in some other part of the Empire. I was however very glad when the President said he thought the United States would have to do it. We therefore took this decision jointly, and settled a basis of agreement. I shall continue the story in a later volume. But meanwhile I have no doubt that it was the progress that we had made in Britain and the confidence of our scientists in ultimate success, imparted to the President, that led him to his grave and fateful decision.

* * * * *

On this same day I gave President Roosevelt the following note on the immediate strategic decision before us.

Secret 20 June 42

The continued heavy sinkings at sea constitute our greatest and most immediate danger. What further measures can be taken now to reduce sinkings other than those in actual operations, which must be faced? When will the convoy system start in the Caribbean and Gulf of Mexico? Is there needless traffic which could be reduced? Should we build more escort vessels at the expense of merchant tonnage, and if so to what extent?

2. We are bound to persevere in the preparation for "Bolero," if possible in 1942, but certainly in 1943. The whole of this business is now going on. Arrangements are being made for a landing of six or eight divisions on the coast of Northern France early in September. However, the British Government do not favour an operation that was certain to lead to disaster, for this would not help the Russians whatever their plight, would compromise and expose to Nazi vengeance the French population involved, and would gravely delay the main operation in 1943. We hold strongly to the view that there should be no substantial landing in France this year unless we are going to stay.

3. No responsible British military authority has so far been able to make a plan for September, 1942, which had any chance of success unless the Germans become utterly demoralised, of which there is no likelihood. Have the American Staffs a plan? At what points would they strike? What landing-craft and shipping are available? Who is the officer prepared to command the enterprise? What British forces and assistance are required? If a plan can be found which offers a reasonable prospect of success, His Majesty's Government will cordially welcome it, and will share to the full with

their American comrades the risks and sacrifices. This remains our settled and agreed policy.

4. But in case no plan can be made in which any responsible authority has good confidence, and consequently no engagement on a substantial scale in France is possible in September, 1942, what else are we going to do? Can we afford to stand idle in the Atlantic theatre during the whole of 1942? Ought we not to be preparing within the general structure of "Bolero" some other operation by which we may gain positions of advantage, and also directly or indirectly to take some of the weight off Russia? It is in this setting and on this background that the French Northwest Africa operation should be studied.

* * * * *

Late on the night of the 20th the Presidential train bore us back to Washington, which we reached about eight o'clock the next morning. We were heavily escorted to the White House, and I was again accorded the very large air-conditioned room, in which I dwelt in comfort at about thirty degrees below the temperature of most of the rest of the building. I glanced at the newspapers, read telegrams for an hour, had my breakfast, looked up Harry across the passage, and then went to see the President in his study. General Ismay came with me. Presently a telegram was put into the President's hands. He passed it to me without a word. It said, "Tobruk has surrendered, with twenty-five thousand men taken prisoners." This was so surprising that I could not believe it. I therefore asked Ismay to inquire of London by telephone. In a few minutes he brought the following message, which had just arrived from Admiral Harwood [1] at Alexandria:

Tobruk has fallen, and situation deteriorated so much that there is a possibility of heavy air attack on Alexandria in near future, and in view of approaching full moon period I am sending all Eastern Fleet units south of Canal to await events. I hope to get H.M.S. *Queen Elizabeth* out of dock towards end of this week.[2]

[1] Admiral Harwood had succeeded Admiral Cunningham in the Mediteranean Command on May 31.

[2] Admiral Harwood made this decision because Alexandria could now be attacked by dive-bombers with fighter-cover.

This was one of the heaviest blows I can recall during the war. Not only were its military effects grievous, but it had affected the reputation of the British armies. At Singapore 85,000 men had surrendered to inferior numbers of Japanese. Now in Tobruk a garrison of 25,000 (actually 33,000) seasoned soldiers had laid down their arms to perhaps one-half of their number. If this was typical of the morale of the Desert Army, no measure could be put upon the disasters which impended in Northeast Africa. I did not attempt to hide from the President the shock I had received. It was a bitter moment. Defeat is one thing; disgrace is another. Nothing could exceed the sympathy and chivalry of my two friends. There were no reproaches; not an unkind word was spoken. "What can we do to help?" said Roosevelt. I replied at once, "Give us as many Sherman tanks as you can spare, and ship them to the Middle East as quickly as possible." The President sent for General Marshall, who arrived in a few minutes, and told him of my request. Marshall replied, "Mr. President, the Shermans are only just coming into production. The first few hundred have been issued to our own armoured divisions, who have hitherto had to be content with obsolete equipment. It is a terrible thing to take the weapons out of a soldier's hands. Nevertheless, if the British need is so great they must have them; and we could let them have a hundred 105-mm. self-propelled guns in addition."

To complete the story it must be stated that the Americans were better than their word. Three hundred Sherman tanks, with engines not yet installed, and a hundred self-propelled guns were put into six of their fastest ships and sent off to the Suez Canal. The ship containing the engines for all the tanks was sunk by a submarine off Bermuda. Without a single word from us the President and Marshall put a further supply of engines into another fast ship and dispatched it to overtake the convoy. "A friend in need is a friend indeed."

* * * * *

Shortly afterward, General Brooke and Harry Hopkins joined us for a conference about future strategy. General Ismay has preserved a note of the military conclusions.

Plans and preparations for the "Bolero" operation in 1943, on as large a scale as possible, are to be pushed forward with all speed and energy. It is however essential that the United States and Great Britain should be prepared to act offensively in 1942.

2. Operations in France or the Low Countries in 1942 would, if successful, yield greater political and strategic gains than operations in any other theatre. Plans and preparations for the operations in this theatre are to be pressed forward with all possible speed, energy, and ingenuity. The most resolute efforts must be made to overcome the obvious dangers and difficulties of the enterprise. If a sound and sensible plan can be contrived we should not hesitate to give effect to it. If, on the other hand, detailed examination shows that, despite all efforts, success is improbable, we must be ready with an alternative.

3. The possibilities of French North Africa (Operation "Gymnast") will be explored carefully and conscientiously, and plans will be completed in all details as soon as possible. Forces to be employed in "Gymnast" would in the main be found from "Bolero" units which have not yet left the United States. The possibility of operations in Norway and the Iberian peninsula in the autumn and winter of 1942 will also be carefully considered by the Combined Chiefs of Staff.

4. Planning of "Bolero" will continue to be centred in London. Planning for "Gymnast" will be centred in Washington.

*   *   *   *   *

On June 21, when we were alone together after lunch, Harry said to me, "There are a couple of American officers the President would like you to meet, as they are very highly thought of in the Army, by Marshall, and by him." At five o'clock therefore Major-Generals Eisenhower and Clark were brought to my air-cooled room. I was immediately impressed by these remarkable but hitherto unknown men. They had both come from the President, whom they had just seen for the first time. We talked almost entirely about the major cross-Channel invasion in 1943, "Round-up" as it was then called, on which their thoughts had evidently been concentrated. We had a most agreeable discussion, lasting for over an hour. In order to convince them of my personal interest in the project I gave them a copy of the paper [3] I had written for the Chiefs of Staff on

3 Chapter 20, pages 353–355.

June 15, two days before I started, in which I had set forth my first thoughts of the method and scale of such an operation. At any rate, they seemed much pleased with the spirit of the document. At that time I thought of the spring or summer of 1943 as the date for the attempt. I felt sure that these officers were intended to play a great part in it, and that was the reason why they had been sent to make my acquaintance. Thus began a friendship which across all the ups and downs of war I have preserved with deep satisfaction to this day.

A month later, in England, General Eisenhower, evidently anxious to prove my zeal, asked me if I would send a copy of my paper to General Marshall which I did.

*   *   *   *   *

In the evening, at 9.30, we had another conference in the President's room, at which the three American Chiefs of Staff were present. There were some discussions about the naval position and the alarming U-boat sinkings off the east coast of America. I strongly urged Admiral King to extend the convoy system to the Caribbean and Gulf of Mexico at once. He was in full agreement, but thought it better to wait until he had adequate escort vessels available.

At 11.30 P.M. I had yet another talk with the President, with Marshall, King, Arnold, Dill, Brooke, and Ismay present. The discussion centred around the deterioration of the situation in the Middle East, and the possibility of sending large numbers of American troops, starting with the 2d Armoured Division, which had been specially trained in desert warfare, to that theatre as soon as possible. It was agreed that the possibility should be carefully studied with particular reference to the shipping position, and that in the meanwhile I should, with the full approval of the President, inform General Auchinleck that he might expect a reinforcement of a highly trained American armoured division, equipped with Sherman or Lee tanks, during August.

*   *   *   *   *

Meanwhile the surrender of Tobruk reverberated round the

world. On the 22d Hopkins and I were at lunch with the President in his room. Presently Mr. Elmer Davis, the head of the Office of War Information, arrived with a bunch of New York newspapers, showing flaring headlines about "ANGER IN ENGLAND," "TOBRUK FALL MAY BRING CHANGE OF GOVERNMENT." "CHURCHILL TO BE CENSURED," etc. I had been invited by General Marshall to visit one of the American army camps in South Carolina. We were to start by train with him and Mr. Stimson on the night of June 23. Mr. Davis asked me seriously whether, in view of the political situation at home, I thought it wise to carry out the programme, which of course had been elaborately arranged. Might it not be misinterpreted if I were inspecting troops in America when matters of such vital consequence were taking place both in Africa and London? I replied that I would certainly carry out the inspections as planned, and that I doubted whether I should be able to provoke twenty members into the lobby against the Government on an issue of confidence. This was in fact about the number which the malcontents eventually obtained.

Accordingly I started by train next night for South Carolina, and arrived at Fort Jackson the next morning. The train drew up, not at a station, but in the open plain. It was a very hot day, and we got out of the train straight onto the parade ground, which recalled the plains of India in the hot weather. We went first to an awning and saw the American armour and infantry march past. Next we watched the parachute exercises. They were impressive and convincing. I had never seen a thousand men leap into the air at once. I was given a "walkie-talkie" to carry. This was the first time I had ever handled such a convenience. In the afternoon we saw the mass-produced American divisions doing field exercises with live ammunition. At the end I said to Ismay (to whom I am indebted for this account), "What do you think of it?" He replied, "To put these troops against continental troops would be murder." Whereupon I said, "You're wrong. They are wonderful material and will learn very quickly." To my American hosts however I consistently pressed my view that it takes two years or more to make a soldier. Certainly two years later the troops we saw in Carolina bore themselves like veterans.

I must here record what I said after the war, in 1946, when as a private person I was received by the assembled Chiefs of the three American Services in the Pentagon Building, Washington.

I greatly admired the manner in which the American Army was formed. I think it was a prodigy of organisation, of improvisation. There have been many occasions when a powerful State has wished to raise great armies, and with money and time and discipline and loyalty that can be accomplished. Nevertheless the rate at which the small American Army of only a few hundred thousand men, not long before the war, created the mighty force of millions of soldiers is a wonder in military history.

I was here two or three years ago, and visited with General Marshall an Army Corps being trained in South Carolina, and we saw there the spectacle of what you may call the mass production of divisions. In great and rapid rotation they were formed, and moved on to further stages of their perfection. I saw the creation of this mighty force — this mighty army, victorious in every theatre against the enemy in so short a time and from such a very small parent stock. This is an achievement which the soldiers of every other country will always study with admiration and with envy.

But that is not the whole story, nor even the greatest part of the story. To create great armies is one thing; to lead them and to handle them is another. It remains to me a mystery as yet unexplained how the very small staffs which the United States kept during the years of peace were able not only to build up the armies and air force units, but also to find the leaders and vast staffs capable of handling enormous masses and of moving them faster and farther than masses have ever been moved in war before.

*   *   *   *   *

We flew back to Washington on the afternoon of the 24th, where I received various reports.

And later:

General Auchinleck to Prime Minister   24 June 42

I deeply regret that you should have received this severe blow at so critical a time as a result of the heavy defeat suffered by the

forces under my command. I fear that the position is now much
what it was a year ago when I took over command, except that the
enemy now has Tobruk, which may be of considerable advantage
to him, not only from the supply point of view, but because he has
no need to detach troops to contain it. . . .

After explaining his dispositions he said:

We are deeply grateful to you and to the President of the
United States for the generous measure of help which you propose to give us, and for the speed with which you are arranging to
send it. The 2d United States Armoured Division will indeed be a
welcome reinforcement, as will the Grant and Lee tanks diverted
from India. Your assurance that the Indian infantry division and
the Indian armoured brigade need not now be sent back to India
will greatly ease my difficulties in regard to the internal security
problem in Iraq and Persia, especially in the oilfield areas. Air
Marshal Tedder informs me that the diversion of aircraft to this
theatre will strengthen our hands immensely.

I thank you personally and most sincerely for all your help and
support during the past year, and deeply regret the failures and setbacks of the past month, for which I accept the fullest responsibility.

Before I left Washington I assured Auchinleck of my entire
confidence.

Prime Minister to General Auchinleck   25 June 42

I told you that President Roosevelt proposed to send you the 2d
United States Armoured Division, and that it would leave for Suez
about July 5. We find that the shipping of this division within the
next month presents very grave difficulties.

General Marshall has therefore put forward a proposal which
C.I.G.S. considers even more attractive from your point of view,
since you will be getting a generous hamper of the most modern
equipment, and your reinforcements from England are not affected.
We have therefore accepted following proposal:

The Americans will send three hundred Sherman (M.4) tanks
and one hundred self-propelling 105-mm.-gun howitzers to the
Middle East as an urgent move. These equipments will sail for Suez
about July 10 in two sea trains taken from the Havana sugar traffic,
doing fifteen and thirteen knots respectively, and their passage will

be expedited by every possible means. A small number of American key personnel will accompany the tanks and guns. . . .

Do not have the slightest anxiety about course of affairs at home. Whatever views I may have about how the battle was fought or whether it should have been fought a good deal earlier, you have my entire confidence, and I share your responsibilities to the full. . . .

Please tell Harwood that I am rather worried about reports of undue despondency and alarm in Alexandria and of the Navy hastening to evacuate to the Red Sea. Although various precautionary moves may be taken and *Queen Elizabeth* should be got out at earliest, I trust a firm, confident attitude will be maintained. The President's information from Rome is that Rommel expects to be delayed three or four weeks before he can mount a heavy attack on the Mersa Matruh position. I should think the delay might well be greater.

I hope the crisis will lead to all uniformed personnel in the Delta and all available loyal man-power being raised to the highest fighting condition. You have over seven hundred thousand men on your ration strength in the Middle East. Every fit male should be made to fight and die for victory. There is no reason why units defending the Mersa Matruh position should not be reinforced by several thousands of officers and administrative personnel ordered to swell the battalions or working parties. You are in the same kind of situation as we should be if England were invaded, and the same intense, drastic spirit should reign.

* * * * *

On the 25th I met the representatives of our Dominions and India, and attended a meeting of the Pacific War Council. That evening I set out for Baltimore, where my flying-boat lay. The President bade me farewell at the White House with all his grace and courtesy, and Harry Hopkins and Averell Harriman came to see me off. The narrow, closed-in gangway which led to the water was heavily guarded by armed American police. There seemed to be an air of excitement, and the officers looked serious. Before we took off I was told that one of the plain-clothes men on duty had been caught fingering a pistol and heard muttering that he would "do me in," with some other expressions of an unappreciative character. He had been pounced upon and arrested. Afterwards he turned out to be a lunatic. Crackpates are a special danger to public men, as they do not have to worry about the "getaway."

We came down at Botwood the next morning in order to refuel, and took off again after a meal of fresh lobsters. Thereafter I ate at stomach-time — i.e., with the usual interval between meals — and slept whenever possible. I sat in the co-pilot's seat as, after flying over Northern Ireland, we approached the Clyde at dawn, and landed safely. My train was waiting, with Peck, one of my personal secretaries, and a mass of boxes, and four or five days' newspapers. In an hour we were off to the South. It appeared that we had lost a by-election by a sweeping turn-over at Maldon. This was one of the by-products of Tobruk.

This seemed to me to be a bad time. I went to bed, browsed about in the files for a while, and then slept for four or five hours till we reached London. What a blessing is the gift of sleep! The War Cabinet were on the platform to greet me on arrival, and I was soon at work in the Cabinet Room.

23

The Vote of Censure

The Strength of the National Government — A Long Succession of Military Misfortunes and Defeats — A Convenient Motion of Censure, June 25 — Offers to Withdraw It Declined — Sir Stafford Cripps' Report — The First Day, July 1 — An Able Speech by Sir John Wardlaw Milne — His Ill-Conceived Digression — Sir Roger Keyes as Seconder — A Contradictory Line — Lord Winterton's Attack — A Specimen of Free Criticism — Mr. Hore-Belisha Speaks — I Wind Up the Debate — Unbridled Freedom of Parliamentary Discussion — Our Sudden Disasters — The Surprising Fall of Tobruk — Distorted Accounts in the United States of British Opinion — Tank Shortcomings and Pre-War Causes — Auchinleck and Ritchie — I Demand a Division — The Prime Minister Must Have Power in War — Only Twenty-Five Hostile Votes — My American Friends' Delight — An Historical Coincidence.

THE CHATTER AND CRITICISMS of the press, where the sharpest pens were busy and many shrill voices raised, found its counterpart in the activities of a few score of Members in the House of Commons, and a fairly glum attitude on the part of our immense majority. A party government might well have been overturned at this juncture, if not by a vote, by the kind of intensity of opinion which led Mr. Chamberlain to relinquish power in May, 1940. But the National Coalition Government, fortified by its reconstruction of February, was massive and overwhelming in its strength and unity. All its principal Ministers stood together around me, with never a thought that

391

was not loyal and robust. I seemed to have maintained the
confidence of all those who watched with full knowledge the
unfolding story and shared the responsibilities. No one
faltered. There was not a whisper of intrigue. We were a
strong, unbreakable circle, and capable of withstanding any
external political attack and of persevering in the common
cause through every disappointment.

We had had a long succession of misfortunes and defeats —
Malaya, Singapore, Burma; Auchinleck's lost battle in the
Desert; Tobruk, unexplained, and, it seemed, inexplicable; the
rapid retreat of the Desert army and the loss of all our conquests
in Libya and Cyrenaica; four hundred miles of retrogression
towards the Egyptian frontier; over fifty thousand of our men
casualties or prisoners. We had lost vast masses of artillery,
ammunition, vehicles, and stores of all kinds. We were back
again at Mersa Matruh, at the old positions of two years before,
but this time with Rommel and his Germans triumphant,
pressing forward in our captured lorries fed with our oil supplies, in many cases firing our own ammunition. Only a few
more marches, one more success, and Mussolini and Rommel
would enter Cairo, or its ruins, together. All hung in the
balance, and after the surprising reverses we had sustained, and
in face of the unknown factors at work, who would predict how
the scales would turn?

The Parliamentary situation required prompt definition. It
seemed however rather difficult to demand another Vote of
Confidence from the House so soon after that which had preceded the collapse at Singapore. It was therefore very convenient when the discontented Members decided among themselves to place a Vote of Censure on the Order Paper.

*   *   *   *   *

On June 25 a motion was placed upon the paper in the
following terms:

That this House, while paying tribute to the heroism and endurance of the Armed Forces of the Crown in circumstances of

exceptional difficulty, has no confidence in the central direction
of the war.

It stood in the name of Sir John Wardlaw-Milne, an influential
member of the Conservative Party. He was chairman of the
powerful all-party Finance Committee, whose reports of cases
of administrative waste and inefficiency I had always studied
with close attention. The Committee had a great deal of information at their disposal and many contacts with the outer
circle of our war machine. When it was also announced that
the motion would be seconded by Admiral of the Fleet Sir
Roger Keyes, and supported by the former Secretary of State
for War, Mr. Hore-Belisha, it was at once evident that a serious
challenge had been made. Indeed, in some newspapers and in
the lobbies the talk ran of an approaching political crisis which
would be decisive.

I said at once that we would give full opportunity for public
debate, and fixed July 1 for the occasion. There was one announcement I felt it necessary to make.

Prime Minister to General Auchinleck   29 June 42
     When I speak in the Vote of Censure debate on Thursday, about
4 P.M., I deem it necessary to announce that you have taken the
command in supersession of Ritchie as from June 25.

The battle crisis in Egypt grew steadily worse, and it was
widely believed that Cairo and Alexandria would soon fall to
Rommel's flaming sword. Mussolini indeed made preparations
to fly to Rommel's headquarters with the idea of taking part
in the triumphal entry to one or both of these cities. It seemed
that we should reach a climax on the Parliamentary and Desert
fronts at the same moment. When it was realised by our critics
that they would be faced by our united National Government,
some of their ardour evaporated, and the mover of the motion
offered to withdraw it if the critical situation in Egypt rendered public discussion untimely. We had however no intention of letting them escape so easily. Considering that for
nearly three weeks the whole world, friend or foe, had been

watching with anxiety the mounting political and military tension, it was impossible not to bring matters to a head.

Mr. Churchill to Sir John Wardlaw-Milne   30 June 42

I brought your letter of June 30 before the War Cabinet this morning, and they desired me to inform you that in view of the challenge to the competence and authority of the Government, which has now for some days been spread throughout the world, it is imperative that the matter should go forward to an immediate issue, and for this all arrangements have been made.

Before the debate opened, Commander King-Hall rose to ask Sir John Wardlaw-Milne to defer moving his motion until the conclusion of the battle then raging in Libya. Sir John replied that if the Government had desired postponement on the ground of national interest he would have immediately acquiesced, but no such suggestion had come from the Government. I then made this statement:

I have carefully considered this matter, and I have had at no time any doubt but that if an appeal were made on the grounds of the urgency and seriousness of the situation the debate would be postponed. But, after all, this Vote of Censure has been on the Order Paper for some time, and it has been flashed all over the world. When I was in the United States I can testify to the lively excitement which was created by its appearance, and although we in this country may have our own knowledge of the stability of our institutions and of the strength of the Government of the day, yet that is by no means the opinion which is shared or felt in other countries. Now that this has gone so far, and this matter has been for more than a week the subject of comment in every part of the world, it would be, in my opinion, even more injurious to delay a decision than to go forward with this issue.

*   *   *   *   *

As I reserved myself for the end of the debate I had the advantage of considering a report from Sir Stafford Cripps upon what he considered were the substantial points of criticism to be met.

Sir Stafford Cripps to Prime Minister   2 July 42 [1]

There is no doubt that there is a very grave disturbance of opinion both in the House of Commons and in the country. But it is also clear that the Vote of Censure does not in any way represent the general reaction of the country to the news. At the same time the very significant result of the Maldon by-election, in which the Government candidate only polled 6226 votes out of a total of nearly 20,000, was undoubtedly largely due to results in Libya, and shows the profound disquiet and lack of confidence of the electors. I do not think that the feeling is in any sense a personal one against the Prime Minister, but a general feeling of dissatisfaction that something is wrong and should be put right without delay. As far as I can gather, the critical feeling is concentrated upon six main points, which are the following:

(1) *Overoptimistic News Reports from Cairo.* It is true that these reports are in no sense official, but they must necessarily be influenced by the information given to the press by the military authorities, and their general tenor has been such as to lead the correspondents to give a picture which has been much too optimistic, and there has been no countervailing official communiqués to damp down this optimism. The impression created is that the military authorities did not appreciate the seriousness of the situation and that the military intelligence is not accurate and has tended to mislead our commanders in the field. The general line of this reporting has undoubtedly done much to emphasise the shock of the loss of Tobruk and the retreat to Mersa Matruh.

(2) *Generalship.* There is a very general view that with better generalship Rommel could have been defeated, especially at the critical moment when, according to General Auchinleck, he had been forced to exhaustion. The view taken is that there has been a lack of leadership, and that the whole campaign has been conceived too much on the basis of a defensive action without the necessary vigour in counter-stroke at the critical moment.

This line of criticism has led to doubts as to whether either the Commander-in-Chief or the Army Commander has a real appreciation of the tactics and strategy of modern mechanised warfare, and as to whether it is not necessary to have a complete change in the Command, putting in the place of those now there men more experienced in and with more aptitude for mechanical warfare.

[1] This paper was available to me when I began my work on July 2.

(3) *Supreme Command.* The criticisms under head (2) above
are reflected in wider doubts as to whether the supreme military
command is similarly out of date and unable to appreciate the correct method of fighting Rommel and his forces. Coupled with this
is the feeling that the co-operation between the air and land forces
was not as effective as it might have been, and that there is still a
lack of common effort and planning at the top.

(4) *Weapons.* Perhaps the strongest line of criticism is that after
nearly three years of war we still find ourselves inferior in vital
weapons such as tanks and anti-tank guns, and that this inferiority
has been largely responsible for the débâcle.

(5) *Research and Invention.* There is a considerable feeling that
although we have in this country very skilled research workers,
scientists, and inventors we have somehow or other failed to make
good use of their abilities in the race for efficient equipment, and
that there is room for some improvement in the method of organisation in order to get the full benefit from this important branch
of war effort.

(6) *Air Force.* People fail to understand how it can be said,
as was stated by General Auchinleck, that we had maintained
moral superiority in the air while at the same time we were unable
to stop the advance. This leads to doubts as to the availability of
the correct aerial weapons, and has raised again the whole question of dive-bombers and other questions as to types of aircraft.
There is in this sphere an uneasiness that the outlook is too rigid
as regards types, and that this rigidity is preventing us, even with
air superiority, from being as effective in fighting from the air as
the enemy.

The question as to the stopping of reinforcements reaching the
enemy in Libya is also raised in the form of whether we might not
have made a greater use of long-range aircraft in view of our naval
weakness in the Mediterranean.

The above, I think, summarises the main points of disquietude
in the minds of the more seriously thinking part of the population.

*   *   *   *   *

The debate was opened by Sir John Wardlaw-Milne in an
able speech in which he posed the main issue. This motion was
"not an attack upon officers in the field. It is a definite attack
upon the central direction here in London, and I hope to show

that the causes of our failure lie here far more than in Libya or elsewhere. The first vital mistake that we made in the war was to combine the offices of Prime Minister and Minister of Defence." He dilated upon the "enormous duties" cast upon the holder of the two offices. "We must have a strong, full-time leader as the Chief of the Chiefs of Staff Committee. I want a strong and independent man appointing his generals and his admirals and so on. I want a strong man in charge of all three branches of the Armed Forces of the Crown . . . strong enough to demand all the weapons which are necessary for victory . . . to see that his generals and admirals and air-marshals are allowed to do their work in their own way and are not interfered with unduly from above. Above all, I want a man who, if he does not get what he wants, will immediately resign. . . . We have suffered both from the want of the closest examination by the Prime Minister of what is going on here at home, and also by the want of that direction which we should get from the Minister of Defence, or other officer, whatever his title might be, in charge of the Armed Forces. . . . It is surely clear to any civilian that the series of disasters of the past few months, and indeed of the past two years, is due to fundamental defects in the central administration of the war."

All this was making its point, but Sir John then made a digression. "It would be a very desirable move — if His Majesty the King and His Royal Highness would agree — if His Royal Highness the Duke of Gloucester were to be appointed Commander-in-Chief of the British Army — without of course, administrative duties." This proved injurious to his case, as it was deemed a proposal to involve the Royal Family in grievous controversial responsibilities. Also the combination of a Supreme War Commander with almost unlimited powers and his association with a Royal Duke seemed to have some flavour of dictatorship about it. From this moment the long and detailed indictment seemed to lose some of its pith. Sir John concluded, "The House should make it plain that we require one man to give his whole time to the winning of the war, in complete charge of all the armed forces of the Crown, and when we have got him let the House strengthen him to carry out the task with power and independence."

The motion was seconded by Sir Roger Keyes. The Admiral, who had been pained by his removal from the position of Director of Combined Operations, and still more by the fact that I had not always been able to take his advice while he was there, was hampered in his attack by his long personal friendship with me. He concentrated his criticism mainly upon my expert advisers — meaning of course the Chiefs of Staff. "It is hard that three times in the Prime Minister's career he should have been thwarted — in Gallipoli, in Norway, and in the Mediterranean — in carrying out strategical strokes which might have altered the whole course of two wars, each time because his constitutional naval adviser declined to share the responsibility with him if it entailed any risk." The inconsistency between this argument and that of the mover did not pass unnoticed. One of the members of the Independent Labour Party, Mr. Stephen, interrupted to point out that the mover had proposed "a Vote of Censure on the ground that the Prime Minister has interfered unduly in the direction of the war; whereas the seconder seems to be seconding because the Prime Minister has not sufficiently interfered in the direction of the war." This point was apparent to the House.

"We look to the Prime Minister," said Admiral Keyes, "to put his house in order, and to rally the country once again for its immense task." Here another Socialist made a pertinent intervention. "The motion is directed against the central direction of the war. If the motion is carried the Prime Minister has to go; but the honourable and gallant Member is appealing to us to keep the Prime Minister there." "It would be," said Sir Roger, "a deplorable disaster if the Prime Minister had to go." Thus the debate was ruptured from its start.

Nevertheless, as it continued the critics increasingly took the lead. The new Minister of Production, Captain Oliver Lyttelton, who dealt with the complaints made against our equipment, had a stormy passage in the full, detailed account which he gave of this aspect. Strong Conservative support was given to the Government from their back benches, Mr. Boothby in particular making a powerful and helpful speech. Lord Winterton, the father of the House, revived the force of the attack, and concentrated it upon me.

Who is the Minister of the Government who practically controlled the Narvik operation? It is the present Prime Minister, who was then First Lord of the Admiralty. . . . No one dares put the blame, where it should be put constitutionally, on the Prime Minister. . . . If whenever we have disasters we get the same answer, that whatever happens you must not blame the Prime Minister, we are getting very close to the intellectual and moral position of the German people — "The Fuehrer is always right." . . . During the thirty-seven years in which I have been in this House I have never seen such attempts to absolve a Prime Minister from Ministerial responsibility as are going on at present. . . . We never had anything in the last war comparable with this series of disasters. Now, see what this Government gets off with — because "the Fuehrer is always right." We all agree that the Prime Minister was the Captain-General of our courage and constancy in 1940. But a lot has happened since 1940. If this series of disasters goes on, the Right Honourable Gentleman, by one of the greatest acts of self-abnegation which any man could carry out, should go to his colleagues — and there is more than one suitable man for Prime Minister on the Treasury Bench now — and suggest that one of them should form a Government, and that the Right Honourable Gentleman himself would take office under him. He might do so, perhaps, as Foreign Secretary, because his management of our relations with Russia and with the United States has been perfect.

It was not possible for me to listen to more than half the speeches of the animated debate, which lasted till nearly three in the morning. I had of course to be shaping my rejoinder for the next day; but my thoughts were centred on the battle which seemed to hang in the balance in Egypt.

*   *   *   *   *

The debate, which had talked itself out in the small hours of its first day, was resumed with renewed vigour on July 2.

Certainly there was no denial of free speech or lack of it. One
Member even went so far as to say:

We have in this country five or six generals, members of other
nations, Czechs, Poles, and French, all of them trained in the use
of these German weapons and this German technique. I know it is
hurtful to our pride, but would it not be possible to put some of
those men temporarily in charge in the field, until we can produce
trained men of our own? Is there anything wrong in sending out
these men, of equal rank with General Ritchie? Why should we
not put them in the field in charge of our troops? They know
how to fight this war; our people do not, and I say that it is far
better to win battles and save British soldiers' lives under the leadership of other members of the United Nations than to lose them
under our own inefficient officers. The Prime Minister must realise
that in this country there is a taunt on everyone's lips that if Rommel had been in the British Army he would still have been a
sergeant.[2] Is that not so? It is a taunt right through the Army.
There is a man in the British Army — and this shows how we are
using our trained men — who flung 150,000 men across the Ebro
in Spain, Michael Dunbar. He is at present a sergeant in an
armoured brigade in this country. He was Chief of Staff in Spain;
he won the battle of the Ebro, and he is a sergeant in the British
Army. The fact of the matter is that the British Army is ridden
by class prejudice. You have got to change it, and you will have
to change it. If the House of Commons has not the guts to make
the Government change it, events will. Although the House may
not take any notice of me today, you will be doing it next week.
Remember my words next Monday and Tuesday. It is events
which are criticising the Government. All that we are doing is
giving them a voice, inadequately perhaps, but we are trying to do
it.

The main case against the Government was summed up by
Mr. Hore-Belisha, the former Secretary of State for War. He
concluded, "We may lose Egypt or we may not lose Egypt — I
pray God we may not — but when the Prime Minister, who
said that we would hold Singapore, that we would hold Crete,

2 This of course showed complete ignorance of Rommel's long and distinguished
professional career in both wars.

that we had smashed the German army in Libya . . . when I read that he had said that we are going to hold Egypt, my anxieties became greater. . . . How can one place reliance in judgments that have so repeatedly turned out to be misguided? That is what the House of Commons has to decide. Think what is at stake. In a hundred days we lost our Empire in the Far East. What will happen in the next hundred days? Let every Member vote according to his conscience."

I followed this powerful speech in winding up the debate. The House was crammed. Naturally I made every point which occurred to me.

This long debate has now reached its final stage. What a remarkable example it has been of the unbridled freedom of our Parliamentary institutions in time of war! Everything that could be thought of or raked up has been used to weaken confidence in the Government, has been used to prove that Ministers are incompetent and to weaken their confidence in themselves, to make the Army distrust the backing it is getting from the civil power, to make the workmen lose confidence in the weapons they are striving so hard to make, to represent the Government as a set of nonentities over whom the Prime Minister towers, and then to undermine him in his own heart, and, if possible, before the eyes of the nation. All this poured out by cable and radio to all parts of the world, to the distress of all our friends and to the delight of all our foes! I am in favour of this freedom, which no other country would use, or dare to use, in times of mortal peril such as those through which we are passing. But the story must not end there, and I make now my appeal to the House of Commons to make sure that it does not end there.

The military misfortunes of the last fortnight in Cyrenaica and Egypt have completely transformed the situation, not only in that theatre, but throughout the Mediterranean. We have lost upwards of fifty thousand men, by far the larger proportion of whom are prisoners, a great mass of material, and, in spite of carefully organised demolitions, large quantities of stores have fallen into the enemy's hands. Rommel has advanced nearly four hundred miles through the desert, and is now approaching the fertile Delta of the Nile. The evil effects of these events, in Turkey, in Spain, in

France, and in French North Africa, cannot yet be measured. We are at this moment in the presence of a recession of our hopes and prospects in the Middle East and in the Mediterranean unequalled since the fall of France. If there are any would-be profiteers of disaster who feel able to paint the picture in darker colours they are certainly at liberty to do so.

A painful feature of this melancholy scene was its suddenness. The fall of Tobruk, with its garrison of about 25,000 men, in a single day, was utterly unexpected. Not only was it unexpected by the House and the public at large, but by the War Cabinet, by the Chiefs of the Staff, and by the General Staff of the Army. It was also unexpected by General Auchinleck and the High Command in the Middle East. On the night before its capture we received a telegram from General Auchinleck that he had allotted what he believed to be an adequate garrison, that the defences were in good order, and that ninety days' supplies were available for the troops. It was hoped that we could hold the very strong frontier positions which had been built up by the Germans and improved by ourselves, from Sollum to Halfaya Pass, from Capuzzo to Fort Maddalena. From this position our newly built railroad ran backward at right angles, and we were no longer formed to a flank — as the expression goes — with our backs to the sea, as we had been in the earlier stages of the new Libyan battle. General Auchinleck expected to maintain these positions until the powerful reinforcements which were approaching, and have in part arrived, enabled him to make a much stronger bid to seize the initiative for a counter-offensive. . . .

When on the morning of Sunday, the 21st, I went into the President's room, I was greatly shocked to be confronted with a report that Tobruk had fallen. I found the news difficult to believe, but a few minutes later my own telegram, forwarded from London, arrived. I hope the House will realise what a bitter pang this was to me. What made it worse was being on an important mission in the country of one of our great Allies. Some people assume too readily that, because a Government keeps cool and has steady nerves under reverses, its members do not feel the public misfortunes as keenly as do independent critics. On the contrary, I doubt whether anyone feels greater sorrow or pain than those who are responsible for the general conduct of our affairs. It was an aggravation in the days that followed to read distorted accounts of the feeling in Britain and in the House of Commons. The House can have no idea how its proceedings are represented across the ocean. Questions are asked [here], comments are made by individual members or by independents who represent no organised grouping of political power, which are cabled verbatim, and often quite honestly taken to be the opinion of the House of Commons. Lobby gossip, echoes from the smoking-room, and talk in Fleet Street are worked up into serious articles seeming to represent that the whole basis of British political life is shaken, or is tottering. A flood of expectation and speculation is let loose. Thus I read streamer headlines like this: "Commons Demand Churchill Return to Face Accusers," or "Churchill Returns to Supreme Political Crisis." Such an atmosphere is naturally injurious to a British representative engaged in negotiating great matters of State upon which the larger issues of the war depend. That these rumours coming from home did not prejudice the work I had to do was due solely to the fact that our American friends are not fair-weather friends. They never expected that this war would be short or easy, or that its course would not be chequered by lamentable misfortunes. On the contrary, I will admit that I believe in this particular case the bonds of comradeship between all the men at the top were actually strengthened.

All the same, I must say I do not think any public man charged with a high mission from this country ever seemed to be barracked from his homeland in his absence — unintentionally, I can well believe — to the extent that befell me while on this visit to the United States; and only my unshakable confidence in the ties which bind me to the mass of the British people upheld me through those days of trial. I naturally explained to my hosts that those who were voluble in Parliament in no way represented the House of Commons, just as the small handful of correspondents who make it their business to pour out damaging tales about our affairs to the United States, and I must add to Australia, in no way represent the honourable profession of journalism. I also explained that all this would be put to the proof when I returned, by the House of Commons as a whole expressing a responsible, measured, and deliberate opinion. And that is what I am going to ask it to do today.

Mr. Hore-Belisha had dwelt upon the failures of the British

tanks and the inferiority of our equipment in armour. He was not in a very strong position to do this on account of the pre-war record of the War Office. I was able to turn the tables upon him.

The idea of the tank was a British conception. The use of armoured forces as they are now being used was largely French, as General de Gaulle's book shows. It was left to the Germans to convert those ideas to their own use. For three or four years before the war they were busily at work with their usual thoroughness upon the design and manufacture of tanks, and also upon the study and practice of armoured warfare. One would have thought that even if the Secretary of State for War of those days could not get the money for large-scale manufacture he would at any rate have had full-size working models made and tested out exhaustively, and the factories chosen and the jigs and gauges supplied, so that he could go into mass production of tanks and anti-tank weapons when the war began.

When what I may call the Belisha period ended we were left with some 250 armoured vehicles, very few of which carried even a two-pounder gun. Most of these were captured or destroyed in France. . . .

I willingly accept, indeed I am bound to accept, what the noble Lord [Earl Winterton] has called the "constitutional responsibility" for everything that has happened, and I consider that I discharged that responsibility by not interfering with the technical handling of armies in contact with the enemy. But before the battle began I urged General Auchinleck to take the command himself, because I was sure nothing was going to happen in the vast area of the Middle East in the next month or two comparable in importance to the fighting of this battle in the Western Desert, and I thought he was the man to handle the business. He gave me various good reasons for not doing so, and General Ritchie fought the battle. As I told the House on Tuesday, General Auchinleck on June 25 superseded General Ritchie and assumed command himself. We at once approved his decision, but I must frankly confess that the matter was not one on which we could form any final judgment, so far as the superseded officer is concerned. I cannot pretend to form a judgment upon what has happened in this battle. I like commanders on land and sea and in the air to feel that between them and all forms of public criticism the Government stands like a strong bulkhead. They ought to have a fair chance, and more than one chance. Men may make mistakes and learn from their mistakes. Men may have bad luck, and their luck may change. But anyhow you will not get generals to run risks unless they feel they have behind them a strong government. They will not run risks unless they feel that they need not look over their shoulders or worry about what is happening at home, unless they feel they can concentrate their gaze upon the enemy. And you will not, I may add, get a government to run risks unless they feel that they have got behind them a loyal, solid majority. Look at the things we are being asked to do now, and imagine the kind of attack which would be made on us if we tried to do them and failed. In wartime if you desire service you must give loyalty. . . .

I wish to speak a few words "of great truth and respect" — as they say in the diplomatic documents — and I hope I may be granted the fullest liberty of debate. This Parliament has a peculiar responsibility. It presided over the beginning of the evils which have come on the world. I owe much to the House, and it is my hope that it may see the end of them in triumph. This it can do only if, in the long period which may yet have to be travelled, the House affords a solid foundation to the responsible Executive Government, placed in power by its own choice. The House must be a steady stabilising factor in the State, and not an instrument by which the disaffected sections of the press can attempt to promote one crisis after another. If democracy and Parliamentary institutions are to triumph in this war it is absolutely necessary that Governments resting upon them shall be able to act and dare, that the servants of the Crown shall not be harassed by nagging and snarling, that enemy propaganda shall not be fed needlessly out of our own hands, and our reputation disparaged and undermined throughout the world. On the contrary, the will of the whole House should be made manifest upon important occasions. It is important that not only those who speak, but those who watch and listen and judge, should also count as a factor in world affairs. After all, we are still fighting for our lives, and for causes dearer than life itself. We have no right to assume that victory is certain; it will be certain only if we do not fail in our duty. Sober and constructive criticism, or criticism in Secret Session, has its high virtue; but the duty of the House of Commons is to sustain the Government or to change the Government. If it cannot change it it should sustain it. There is no working middle course in wartime. Much harm was done abroad by the two days' debate in May. Only the hostile speeches are reported abroad, and much play is made with them by our enemy.

A division, or the opportunity for a division, should always follow a debate on the war, and I trust therefore that the opinion of the overwhelming majority of the House will be made plain not only in the division, but also in the days which follow, and that the weaker brethren, if I may so call them, will not be allowed to usurp and almost monopolise the privileges and proud authority of the House of Commons. The majority of the House must do their duty. All I ask is a decision one way or another.

There is an agitation in the press, which has found its echo in a number of hostile speeches, to deprive me of the function which I exercise in the general conduct and supervision of the war. I do not propose to argue this today at any length, because it was much discussed in a recent debate. Under the present arrangement the three Chiefs of Staff, sitting almost continuously together, carry on the war from day to day, assisted not only by the machinery of the great departments which serve them, but by the Combined General Staff, in making their decisions effective through the Navy, Army, and Air Forces over which they exercise direct operational control. I supervise their activities, whether as Prime Minister or Minister of Defence. I work myself under the supervision and control of the War Cabinet, to whom all important matters are referred, and whom I have to carry with me in all major decisions. Nearly all my work has been done in writing, and a complete record exists of all the directions I have given, the inquiries I have made, and the telegrams I have drafted. I shall be perfectly content to be judged by them.

I ask no favours either for myself or for His Majesty's Government. I undertook the office of Prime Minister and Minister of Defence, after defending my predecessor to the best of my ability, in times when the life of the Empire hung upon a thread. I am your servant, and you have the right to dismiss me when you please. What you have no right to do is to ask me to bear responsibilities without the power of effective action, to bear the responsibilities of Prime Minister but "clamped on each side by strong men," as the honourable Member said. If today, or at any future time, the

House were to exercise its undoubted right, I could walk out with a good conscience and the feeling that I have done my duty according to such light as has been granted to me. There is only one thing I would ask of you in that event. It would be to give my successor the modest powers which would have been denied to me.

But there is a larger issue than the personal issue. The mover of this Vote of Censure has proposed that I should be stripped of my responsibilities for Defence in order that some military figure or some other unnamed personage should assume the general conduct of the war, that he should have complete control of the Armed Forces of the Crown, that he should be the Chief of the Chiefs of Staff, that he should nominate or dismiss the generals or the admirals, that he should always be ready to resign — that is to say, to match himself against his political colleagues, if colleagues they could be considered — if he did not get all he wanted, that he should have under him a Royal Duke as Commander-in-Chief of the Army, and finally, I presume, though this was not mentioned, that this unnamed personage should find an appendage in the Prime Minister to make the necessary explanations, excuses, and apologies to Parliament when things go wrong, as they often do and often will. That is at any rate a policy. It is a system very different from the Parliamentary system under which we live. It might easily amount to or be converted into a dictatorship. I wish to make it perfectly clear that as far as I am concerned I shall take no part in such a system.

Sir John J. Wardlaw-Milne here interjected: "I hope my Right Honourable Friend has not forgotten the original sentence, which was 'subject to the War Cabinet'?"

I continued:

"Subject to the War Cabinet," against which this all-powerful potentate is not to hesitate to resign on every occasion if he cannot get his way. It is a plan, but it is not a plan in which I should personally be interested to take part, and I do not think that it is one which would recommend itself to this House.

The setting down of this Vote of Censure by Members of all parties is a considerable event. Do not, I beg of you, let the House underrate the gravity of what has been done. It has been trumpeted all round the world to our disparagement, and when every nation, friend and foe, is waiting to see what is the true resolve and conviction of the House of Commons, it must go forward to the end. All over the world, throughout the United States, as I can testify, in Russia, far away in China, and throughout every subjugated country, all our friends are waiting to know whether there is a strong, solid Government in Britain and whether its national leadership is to be challenged or not. Every vote counts. If those who have assailed us are reduced to contemptible proportions and their Vote of Censure on the National Government is converted to a vote of censure upon its authors, make no mistake, a cheer will go up from every friend of Britain and every faithful servant of our cause, and the knell of disappointment will ring in the ears of the tyrants we are striving to overthrow.

The House divided, and Sir John Wardlaw-Milne's motion of "No Confidence" was defeated by 475 votes to 25.

My American friends awaited the issue with real anxiety. They were delighted by the result. I woke to receive their congratulations.

President Roosevelt to the Prime Minister   2 July 42
  Good for you.

Harry Hopkins to Prime Minister   2 July 42
  Action of Commons today delighted me. These have been some of the bad days. No doubt there will be others. They who run for cover with every reverse, the timid and faint of heart, will have no part in winning the war. Your strength, tenacity, and everlasting courage will see Britain through, and the President, you know, does not quit. I know you are of good heart, for your military defeats and ours and our certain victories to come will be shared together. More power to you.

I replied:

Prime Minister to Mr. Harry Hopkins   3 July 42
  Thank you so much, my friend. I knew you and the President would be glad of this domestic victory. I hope one day I shall have something more solid to report.

*   *   *   *   *

A curious historical point had been made in the debate by Mr. Walter Elliot when he recalled Macaulay's account of Mr. Pitt's administration. "Pitt was at the head of a nation engaged in a life-and-death struggle. . . . But the fact is that after eight years of war, after a vast expenditure of life and . . . wealth, the English Army under Pitt was the laughing-stock of all Europe. They could not boast of a single brilliant exploit. It had never shown itself on the Continent but to be beaten, chased, forced to re-embark." However, Macaulay proceeded to record that Pitt was always sustained by the House of Commons. "Thus through a long and calamitous period every disaster that happened without the walls of Parliament was regularly followed by triumph within them. At length he had no longer an opposition to encounter, and in the eventful year 1799 the largest majority that could be mustered to vote against the Government was twenty-five." "It is odd," said Mr. Elliot, "how history is in some ways repeated." He could not know before the division how true this was. I too was astonished that the figure of twenty-five was almost exactly the one I had named to the President and Harry Hopkins when I was with them at the White House on the day of the Tobruk news.

END OF BOOK ONE

★

Book Two

Africa redeemed

1

The Eighth Army at Bay

*Auchinleck and the Defence of Tobruk — Telegrams in the Crisis
— General Klopper's Task — Rommel Attacks — A Desperate
Situation — Confusion and Surrender — Complete Change of
Enemy Plans — Malta No Longer Their Objective — Retreat of
the Eighth Army — Views of the Middle East Defence Com-
mittee, June 21 — My Telegram to General Auchinleck of June
22 — Rommel's Pursuit — Auchinleck Assumes Command —
Superb Behaviour of the New Zealand Division — Devoted Aid of
the Air Force — Preparations for Resistance in the Delta —
Auchinleck's Stubborn Stand — General Smuts and the Tobruk
Surrender — My Letter of July 11 to Mr. Fraser and Mr. Curtin
— Rommel at a Standstill — The Eighth Army Weathers the
Storm.*

GENERAL AUCHINLECK had issued instructions in February
that whereas Tobruk was essential as a supply base for
offensive operations, yet if we were forced to withdraw "it is
not my intention to continue to hold it once the enemy is in a
position to invest it effectively. Should this appear inevitable,
the place will be evacuated and the maximum amount of
destruction carried out in it." In consequence of these orders,
the defences had not been maintained in good shape. Many
mines had been lifted for use elsewhere, gaps had been driven
through the wire for the passage of vehicles, and the sand had
silted up much of the anti-tank ditch so that in places it was
hardly an obstacle. Only on the western and southwestern faces
of the perimeter were the defences strong; elsewhere, and

especially to the east, they were in bad condition. At the same time masses of supplies, ammunition, and petrol were accumulated in the place.

General Ritchie proposed to make use of the Tobruk western defences by incorporating them as part of a general defensive line running southeastward to El Adem, supported by a mobile force farther south to prevent encirclement. He reported to Auchinleck that this arrangement might involve the investment of Tobruk by the enemy, if only for a short time. If this was not acceptable there was no option but to withdraw the entire garrison. Auchinleck would not at first countenance the plan. He telegraphed to Ritchie on June 14: "Tobruk must be held and the enemy not allowed to invest it. This means that the Eighth Army must hold the line Acroma-El Adem and southward"; and later: "The defences of Tobruk and other strong places will be used as pivots of manoeuvre, but on no account will any part of the Eighth Army be allowed to be surrounded in Tobruk and invested there."

At home we had no inkling that the evacuation of Tobruk had ever entered into the plans or thoughts of the Commanders. It was certainly the Cabinet view that if the Eighth Army were beaten back, Tobruk should remain, as in the previous year, a thorn in the enemy's side. In order to confirm that this view was shared by Auchinleck, I had, as set forth in an earlier chapter, telegraphed to him on June 14 before I left for Washington: "Presume there is no question in any case of giving up Tobruk."

Auchinleck had replied next day that he did not intend that the Eighth Army should be besieged in Tobruk but had no intention whatever of giving up Tobruk. His orders to General Ritchie were not to allow his forces to be invested in Tobruk. As this seemed to us equivocal, we put the point precisely. "War Cabinet interpret your telegram to mean that if the need arises General Ritchie would have as many troops as are necessary to hold the place for certain."

To this on June 16 Auchinleck had replied:

War Cabinet interpretation is correct. General Ritchie is putting what he considers an adequate force to hold it, even should it become temporarily isolated.

At the same time he sent the following to General Ritchie. "Although I have made it clear to you that Tobruk must not be invested, I realise that its garrison may be isolated for short periods until our counter-offensive can be launched."

Had I seen this order, I should not have been content with it.

*   *   *   *   *

General Klopper, commanding the 2d South African Division, was placed in charge of the fortress. Supplies and ammunition for the garrison were sufficient for ninety days, and General Klopper was confident that Tobruk could play its part in the plan, which included the retention by the Eighth Army of the strong points of El Adem and Belhamed outside the perimeter. The garrison included four infantry brigades (fourteen battalions), a tank brigade and sixty-one Infantry tanks, five regiments of field and medium artillery, and about seventy anti-tank guns.[1] In addition there were about ten thousand men in administrative and transport units centred round the port and its base installations. In all, a total of about thirty-five thousand men were within the perimeter, a force about equal to that which had held Tobruk when it was first besieged a year before. The dispositions for the defence are shown in the map on page 416.

*   *   *   *   *

After a lull of only two days, on June 16 Rommel renewed his offensive. In a series of rapid blows he took El Adem, Belhamed, and Acroma. On June 17 he defeated our 4th

---

[1] Tobruk Order of Battle: *H.Q. 2d South African Division.*
4th and 6th South African Infantry Brigades.
Two composite South African battalions from 1st South African Division.
7th South African Reconnaissance battalion (armoured cars).
11th Indian Infantry Brigade.
201st Guards Brigade.
32d Army Tank Brigade (4th and 7th Battalions).
2d and 3d South African Field Artillery Regiments.
25th Field Artillery Regiment.
67th and 68th Medium Artillery Regiments.

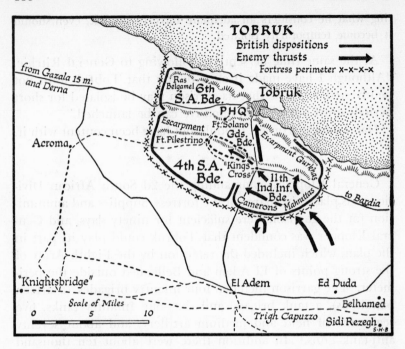

TOBRUK
British dispositions ——
Enemy thrusts ➔
Fortress perimeter x-x-x-x

from Gazala 15 m.
and Derna

Ras
Belgamel **6th
S.A.Bde.**   Tobruk

PHQ
Escarpment Ft.Solano
Ft.Pilestrino   Gds.
Bde.

Acroma.

**4th S.A.
Bde.**   "Kings
Cross"   **11th
Ind.Inf.
Bde.**
Camerons Mahrattas   to Bardia

"Knightsbridge"   El Adem   Ed Duda

Scale of Miles   Belhamed
0   5   10   Trigh Capuzzo
Sidi Rezegh

Armoured Brigade at Sidi Rezegh, reducing them to a
strength of only twenty tanks. By the 19th, Tobruk was isolated
and surrounded, and until tank replenishments came to hand
there was no effective armoured force to support or relieve the
garrison from outside. At 6 A.M. on June 20 the enemy opened
a heavy bombardment with guns and dive-bombers on the
southeastern part of the Tobruk perimeter, held by the 11th
Indian Infantry Brigade. Half an hour later the attack was
launched, led by the 21st Panzer Division, supported by the
15th Panzer Division, together with the Italian armoured division and a motorised infantry division. With our own armour
outside Tobruk temporarily disposed of, Rommel could afford
to put his full weight into this single blow. It fell mainly on
a battalion of the Indian Brigade, in a sector where the defences
were at their weakest. They were soon deeply penetrated. No
fighter protection could be given to our troops as our Air Force
was withdrawn to distant landing-grounds.

General Klopper ordered a counter-attack by his tanks and part of the Coldstream Guards. This effort, hastily organised and delivered piecemeal, failed. All remaining British tanks were thrown into the cauldron southeast of the road junction called "King's Cross," where the remnants of the Indians were fighting it out. But it was of no avail. By noon only a handful of our tanks survived and our supporting batteries were overrun. Enemy tanks swung west and north, but the main body drove straight for "King's Cross." At 2 P.M. Rommel himself was there. He ordered one group directly on to Tobruk. It suffered heavily from artillery fire, but reached the Solaro ridge at 3.30 P.M., and by 6 P.M. was on the outskirts of Tobruk. Another group was sent due west from "King's Cross," along the ridge towards Pilastrino, where they met the Guards Brigade hastily forming front to meet attack from this unexpected direction.

All that afternoon and evening the Guards Brigade, strongly supported by our artillery, fought a stern battle, and suffered heavy losses. Some ground was lost and the brigade head-quarters was captured, but at nightfall the enemy had been brought to a halt. The situation was parlous. The western and southern sides of the perimeter were intact and the Gurkhas on the extreme left were holding out, but the enemy were in possession of a great part of the Tobruk fortress. All our reserve troops were pinned down. Demolition was ordered of the closely threatened base installations. In Tobruk itself the reserve of transport, necessary if the remnants of the garrison were to be evacuated, was immobilised and soon to be destroyed.

* * * * *

At 8 P.M. on June 20 General Klopper reported to Eighth Army Headquarters: "My H.Q. surrounded. Infantry on per-imeter still fighting hard. Am holding out, but I do not know how long." He asked for instruction, and was told: "Come out tomorrow night preferably, if not tonight." He called his senior officers to conference and asked their views. Some said that effec-tive resistance was no longer possible. With the main supplies in enemy hands, ammunition was running short; to continue fighting meant heavy casualties to no purpose. Let all who could break out. But others were for fighting on. The transport, without which escape was not possible, had been captured. There was hope that a relieving column might come from the south. Let what remained be concentrated in the southwest corner of the perimeter and fight on till relieved. At 2 A.M. the moon set and a breakout through the minefields, even if hitherto practicable, became impossible. General Klopper held a radio telephone conversation with General Ritchie and told him that the situation was a "shambles." If resistance were continued terrible casualties would result; he was "doing the worst." General Ritchie instructed him: "Every day and hour of resistance materially assists our cause. I cannot tell the tactical situation, and must therefore leave you to act on your own judgment regarding capitulation.... The whole of the Eighth Army has watched with admiration your gallant fight."

At dawn on the 21st General Klopper sent out a parlementaire with an offer to capitulate, and at 7.45 A.M. German officers came to his headquarters and accepted his surrender. His orders were received by many of his troops, some of whom had hardly been engaged, with incredulity and dismay. To some of his commanding officers he had to issue personal instructions, for they would accept them from no other source. According to German records 33,000 of our men were taken prisoners. Despite General Klopper's orders many attempts were made by small parties to escape, but without transport nearly all failed. Only one considerable group was successful. Defiant and undaunted, 199 officers and men of the Coldstream Guards and 188 South Africans, having collected some lorries, set out together, and, breaking through the perimeter, made a wide sweep that brought them at nightfall to the Egyptian frontier seventy miles away.

The hopes of the garrison of help from a relieving force had been vain. The 7th Armoured Division was re-form-

ing in the desert to the south, and on the 20th received orders
to dispatch a force in aid. But Rommel was too quick for them.
Before it had even started all was over.

*   *   *   *   *

The Germans captured vast quantities of stores. Here is the
account of Rommel's Chief of Staff:

The booty was gigantic. It consisted of supplies for 30,000 men
for three months and more than 10,000 cubic metres of petrol.
*Without this booty adequate rations and clothing for the armoured
divisions would not have been possible in the coming months.*
Stores arriving by sea had only on one occasion — in April, 1942 —
been enough to supply the army for one whole month.[2]

The news of the capture of Tobruk without the need of a
long siege revolutionised the Axis plans. Hitherto it had been
intended that after Tobruk was taken Rommel should stand
on the Egyptian frontier and that the next major effort should
be the capture of Malta by airborne and seaborne forces. As
late as June 21 Mussolini reiterated these orders. The day after
Tobruk fell Rommel reported that he proposed to destroy the
small British forces left on the frontier, and thus open the way
to Egypt. The condition and morale of his forces, the large
captures of munitions and supplies, and the weakness of the
British position prompted pursuit "into the heart of Egypt."
He requested approval. A letter also arrived from Hitler pressing Rommel's proposals upon Mussolini.

Destiny has offered us a chance which will never occur twice in
the same theatre of war. . . . The Eighth Army has been practically
destroyed. In Tobruk the port installations are almost intact. You
now possess, Duce, an auxiliary base whose significance is all the
greater because the English themselves have built from there a railway leading almost into Egypt. If, at this moment, the remains of
this British Army are not pursued to the last breath of each man,
the same thing will happen as when the British were deprived of
success when they nearly reached Tripoli and suddenly stopped in
order to send forces to Greece. . . .

2 *Heer in Fesseln,* by Westphal, page 180.

The God of Battles visits warriors only once. He who does not
grasp her at such a moment never reaches her again. . . .[3]

The Duce needed no persuasion. Elated at the prospect of
conquering Egypt, he postponed the assault on Malta till the
beginning of September, and Rommel — now a Field-Marshal,
rather to Italian surprise — was authorised to occupy the relatively narrow passage between Alamein and the Qattara
Depression as the starting-point for future operations whose
final objective was the Suez Canal. Kesselring held a different
view. Believing that the Axis position in the Desert would never
be secure until Malta was captured, he was alarmed at the
change of plan. He pointed out to Rommel the dangers of this
"foolhardy enterprise."

*   *   *   *   *

Hitler himself had not been confident of success against
Malta, as he mistrusted the ability of the Italian troops who
would have formed the major part of the expedition. The
attack might well have failed. Nevertheless, it now seems
certain that the shattering and grievous loss of Tobruk spared
the island from the supreme trial. This is a consolation of
which no good soldier, whether involved or not, should avail
himself. The burden falls upon the High Command rather
than on General Klopper, and still less upon his troops.

General Ritchie proved himself both a competent Staff
Officer and later a resolute Corps Commander. Nevertheless
it was a bad arrangement by which he left his desk as General
Auchinleck's deputy Chief of Staff to become the commander
of the Eighth Army. The rôles are different and should be
divorced. The personal association of Auchinleck and Ritchie
did not give Ritchie a chance of those independent conceptions
on which the command of violent events depends. The lack of
clear thought and the ill-defined responsibility between General Auchinleck and his staff officer, General Ritchie, had led
to a mishandling of the forces, which in its character and con-

[3] Quoted in *Comando Supremo,* by Cavallero, page 277.

THUNDERBIRD LANES
York & Fitzwatertown Roads
Willow Grove, PA 19090

PITNEY BOWES

U.S. POSTAGE $00.23⁰ P635714776
NOV 28 2005
19090
19288 MAILED FROM ZIP CODE

Saul Hansell
588 Glenluros Ave.
Wyndmoor, PA 19038

C033

THANK YOU
FOR VISITING
OUR CENTER

ONE FREE GAME

Compliments of

THUNDERBIRD LANES

York & Fitzwatertown Roads

Willow Grove, PA 19090

215/659-1715

www.PHILLYBOWL.com

One Coupon per Person per Day   Expires_____

sequences constitutes an unfortunate page in British military history. It was not possible to judge the event at the time. The Tobruk commanders were prisoners of war. But now that the salient facts are known the truth should not be obscured.

* * * * *

What remained of the Eighth Army was now drawn back behind the frontier. In a telegram of June 21 the Middle East Defence Committee at Cairo described as the alternative courses open to them:

First, to fight the enemy on the frontier defences. Without adequate armoured forces this entails risking the loss of all our infantry holding the frontier position. Second course, to delay the enemy on the frontier with forces which are kept fully mobile, while withdrawing main body of Eighth Army to the Matruh defences. This, coupled with delaying action by our air forces, gives us the best chance of gaining time in which to reorganize and build up a striking force for an offensive. . . . We have decided on the second course.

I did not welcome this decision, and telegraphed from Washington as follows:

Prime Minister to General Auchinleck   22 June 42

The Chief of the Imperial General Staff Dill and I earnestly hope stern resistance will be made on the Sollum frontier line. Stresses which enemy has undergone are doubtless severe. Very important reinforcements are on their way. A week gained may be decisive. We do not know exact dates of the deployment of the New Zealand Division, but had expected it would be by the end of the month. 8th Armoured and 44th are approaching and near. We agree with General Smuts that you may draw freely upon Ninth and Tenth Armies as the danger from north is more remote. Thus you can effect drastic roulement with the three divisions now east of the Canal.

2. I was naturally disconcerted by your news, which may well put us back to where we were eighteen months ago and leave all the work of that period to be done over again. However, I do not feel that the defence of the Delta cannot be effectively maintained,

and I hope no one will be unduly impressed by the spectacular blows which the enemy has struck at us. I am sure that with your perseverance and resolution and continued readiness to run risks the situation can be restored, especially in view of the large rein-forcements approaching.

3. Here in Washington the President is deeply moved by what has occurred, and he and other high United States authorities show themselves disposed to lend the utmost help. They authorise me to inform you that the 2d United States Armoured Division, specially trained in desert warfare in California, will leave for Suez about July 5, and should be with you in August. You need not send the Indian Division and 288th Indian Armoured Brigade back to India as proposed. Measures are also being taken in addi-tion to those described in the Chief of Staff's telegram, to divert India-bound aircraft to the Libyan theatre. . . .

4. The main thing now is for you to inspire all your forces with an intense will to resist and strive and not to accept the freak decisions produced by Rommel's handful of heavy armour. Make sure that all your man-power plays a full part in these critical days. His Majesty's Government is quite ready to share your responsi-bilities in making the most active and daring defence.

However, Auchinleck adhered to his opinion.

*   *   *   *   *

Rommel swiftly organised his pursuit, and on June 24 crossed the frontier to Egypt, opposed only by our light mobile columns, and the stubborn and magnificent fighter squadrons of the Royal Air Force, who really covered the retreat of the Eighth Army to Mersa Matruh. Their position here was not strong. About the town itself there was an organised defensive system, but south of it were only some lines of unconnected minefields inadequately guarded. As in the case of the rejected frontier position, the Matruh line, if it were to be successfully held, needed a powerful armoured force to guard its southern flank. The 7th Armoured Division, though now rebuilt to nearly a hundred tanks, was not yet capable of such a task.

General Auchinleck himself came forward to Matruh on June 25 and decided to take over direct operational command

of the Army from General Ritchie. He should have done this
when I asked him to in May.

Prime Minister to General Auchinleck   28 June 42

I am very glad you have taken command. Do not vex yourself
with anything except the battle. Fight it out wherever it flows.
Nothing matters but destroying the enemy's armed and armoured
force. A strong stream of reinforcements is approaching. We are
sure you are going to win in the end.

General Auchinleck quickly concluded that it was not
possible to make a final stand at Matruh. Arrangements were
already in hand for the preparation and occupation of the
Alamein position, a hundred and twenty miles farther back. To
halt the enemy, if only for a time, the following dispositions
were made: The Xth Corps, with the 10th Indian and
50th British Infantry Divisions, held the Matruh defences.
Farther south, under command of the XIIIth Corps, were the

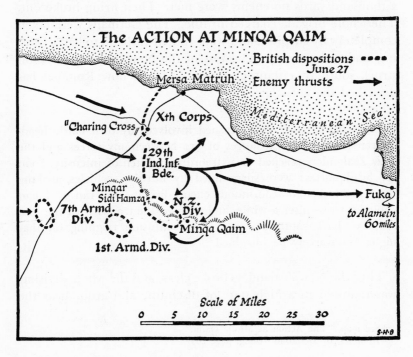

29th Indian Infantry Brigade, covering a six-mile gap in the minefields, and the New Zealand Division. The 1st Armoured Division and the 7th Armoured Division guarded the desert flank.[4]

The New Zealand Division, which had arrived at Matruh from Syria on June 21, was at length moved on the 26th into action on the ridge about Minqa Qaim. That evening the enemy broke through the front of the 29th Indian Infantry Brigade, where the minefield was incomplete. The next morning they streamed through the gap, and then, passing behind the New Zealanders, encircled and attacked them from three sides. Desperate fighting continued all day, and at the end it seemed that the division was doomed. General Freyberg had been severely wounded. But he had a worthy successor. Brigadier Inglis was determined to break out. Shortly after midnight the 4th New Zealand Brigade moved due east across country with all its battalions deployed and bayonets fixed. For a thousand yards no enemy were met. Then firing broke out. The whole brigade charged in line. The Germans were taken completely by surprise, and were routed in hand-to-hand fighting under the moon. The rest of the New Zealand Division struck south by circuitous routes. This is how Rommel has described the episode:

The wild flare-up which ensued involved my own battle headquarters. . . . The exchanges of fire between my forces and the New Zealanders reached an extraordinary pitch of intensity. Soon my headquarters were surrounded by burning vehicles, making them the target for continuous enemy fire at close range. I had enough of this after a while, and ordered the troops with the staff to move back southeastwards. The confusion reigning on that night can scarcely be imagined.[5]

Thus the New Zealanders broke clear, and the whole division was reunited in a high state of discipline and ardor near the

---

4 See map, "The Action at Minqa Qaim."
5 *Rommel,* by Desmond Young, page 269.

Alamein position, eighty miles away. So little were they disorganised that they were used forthwith to stiffen the defences
at Alamein.

Prime Minister to General Freyberg   4 July 42

Deeply moved to hear of your new wound and new glory. Trust
that your injury is not serious and that you will soon be back commanding your splendid division. All good wishes to you and to
them.

* * * * *

The two divisions of the Xth Corps around Matruh were
also brought back to safety, though with difficulty. On June 27
they had struck southward at the enemy break-through, without bringing it to a halt. The enemy pressed on and threatened
the coastal road. The Corps was ordered to retire eastward.
They fought their way down the road until blocked by an
enemy force. Then they struck south across the desert to Alamein.
The XXXth Corps had been withdrawn earlier to Alamein.
When joined there by the Xth and XIIIth Corps the whole
army, on June 30, was ranged on or behind the new position.
The troops were amazed rather than depressed.

* * * * *

Casey had been active and helpful in this convulsion.
I requested him to grip the situation at the rear and in the
Cairo stewpot.

Prime Minister to Minister of State   30 June 42

I wished to let you know how much I appreciate the part you
have played not only in the main situation, but also in the change
of command, which I have long desired and advocated. While
Auchinleck fights at the front you should insist upon the mobilisa-
tion for battle of all the rearward services. Everybody in uniform
must fight exactly like they would if Kent or Sussex were invaded.
Tank hunting-parties with sticky bombs and bombards, defence
to the death of every fortified area or strong building, making
every post a winning-post and every ditch a last ditch. This is the

spirit you have got to inculcate. No general evacuation, no playing for safety. Egypt must be held at all costs.

I was also aware that the Army would never have escaped in good order without the devoted aid of the Air Force, who fought from the advanced airfields till these were actually overrun. Now they could work from well-established bases in Egypt against the advancing enemy.

Prime Minister to Air Chief Marshal Tedder   4 July 42

Here at home we are all watching with enthusiasm the brilliant, supreme exertions of the Royal Air Force in the battle now proceeding in Egypt. From every quarter the reports come in of the effect of the vital part which your officers and men are playing in this Homeric struggle for the Nile Valley. The days of the Battle of Britain are being repeated far from home. We are sure you will be to your glorious army the friend that endureth to the end.

*   *   *   *   *

The Alamein position runs from the railway station of that name to the impassable Qattara Depression, thirty-five miles to

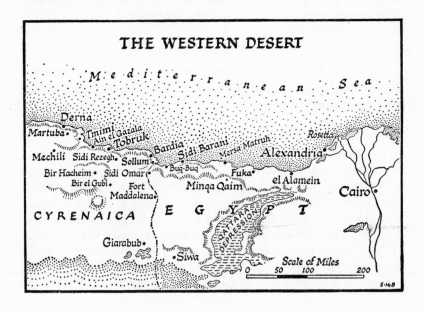

the southward.[6] This was a long line for the forces available to hold. Much work had been done, but except for semi-permanent fortifications around Alamein itself the line consisted chiefly of disconnected works. The flanks however were secure and the Eighth Army had been strongly reinforced. The New Zealand Division was in perfect order after the fine action it had fought. The 9th Australian Division was also soon to arrive and win high distinction. With the advantage of short communications, and with Alexandria only forty miles away, the reorganisation of the Eighth Army did not take long. Auchinleck, once in direct command, seemed a different man from the thoughtful strategist with one eye on the decisive battle and the other on the vague and remote dangers in Syria and Persia. He sought at once to regain the tactical initiative. As early as July 2 he made the first of a series of counter-attacks which continued until the middle of the month. These challenged Rommel's precarious ascendancy. I sent my encouragement, on the morrow of the Vote of Censure debate, which had been an accompaniment to the cannonade.

Prime Minister to General Auchinleck   4 July 42

I cannot help liking very much the way things seem to be going. If fortune turns I am sure you will press your advantage, as you say, "relentlessly."

*   *   *   *   *

The surrender of the South African Division under a South African commander at Tobruk had been a dire stroke to General Smuts in the political as well as the military sphere.

Prime Minister to General Smuts   4 July 42

I have been so much harried by the weaker brethren in the House of Commons since my return from America last week that this is the first chance I have had of telling you how deeply I grieve for the cruel losses you have sustained in your gallant South African divisions, and how I admire the indomitable manner in which you have inspired South Africa to face this heavy blow.

6 See map on page 426.

2. We have been through so much together and are so often
in harmony of thought that I do not need to say much now about
the lamentable events of the last three weeks. I am still hopeful
that all can be retrieved. President Roosevelt gave me three hundred of their latest Sherman tanks, which are far superior to the
Grants, and a hundred 105-mm. self-propelled gun howitzers as
anti-tank weapons. These should reach Egypt by the beginning of
September. The President is also sending Liberators up to about
one hundred, which should arrive during July. Two heavy Halifax bombing squadrons from England will be in action during
the next ten days. Another sixty American fighters are being
rushed across the Atlantic via Takoradi. All this is additional to
our regular reinforcement of the air. As you probably know, the
8th Armoured Division, with 350 tanks, mostly Valentines, is landing now. The 44th British Infantry Division should land July 23,
and the 51st a month later. Whether these forces will be able to
play their part depends upon the battle now proceeding at Alamein.

General Smuts was imperturbable. His mind moved majes-
tically amid the vagaries of Fortune. No one better than he
knew how to

> . . . meet with Triumph and Disaster,
> And treat those two impostors just the same.

General Smuts to Prime Minister   7 July 42

What with your most heartening message and news from Middle
East foreshadowing that tide is turning at El Alamein, yesterday
was one of my happiest recent days. I do believe Rommel has over-
stretched himself, and if Auchinleck remains in personal charge
not only will Tobruk be avenged, but our counter-stroke may carry
us right on to Tripoli and save both Egypt and Malta. The reinforcements you foreshadow will go far to assist in achieving this
great object, and I hope it will not again be necessary to deflect
them to some other theatre. Not only would Egypt be secured, but
a base thus established for the coming offensive against the weakest
Axis partner may have other important results. I believe possible
German attempt to reach Iraq oil through Syria may also thus be
thwarted. I am thus for fullest exploitation of victory which I
believe is in sight owing to Rommel's overreaching audacity.

Auchinleck may meet with serious difficulties. His transport has
suffered seriously in long retreat, and enemy will try to destroy pipe-
line and railways to delay his advance, while enemy reinforcements may be expected. Our air superiority and relentless bombing of enemy ports and communications will however have their
effect.

As America is now our great strategic reserve for the final blows,
much of your time will have to be devoted to wisely guiding Washington in its war effort and not letting vital war direction slip out
of our hands. I think your service in this respect can now be at
least as great as your Empire war service. Your contacts with
Roosevelt are now a most valuable war asset, and I hope your
weaker brethren with their purely domestic outlook will be made
to realise this.

* * * * *

Prime Minister to Mr. Fraser and Mr. Curtin [7]   11 July 42

The division which you consented to leave in the Middle East
is doing splendid work in the Western Desert, and has already
brought fresh fame to New Zealand's arms at this vital keypoint
of the war.

... The unforeseeable tide of disaster which drove us from Gazala
to Alamein with the loss of Tobruk and fifty thousand men has now
for the time being been stemmed. General Auchinleck has received
strong reinforcements, raising his army to a hundred thousand
men, with another twenty thousand well forward in the Delta
behind them. He is thus about double Rommel in men. He has a
fair equality in artillery, but is still somewhat weaker in armour.
This imposes prudence upon him for two reasons. First, a retirement is much worse for him than for Rommel, who has nothing
but deserts behind him, and, secondly, far more strength is coming
to General Auchinleck than to the enemy.

It was very fortunate that four months ago I obtained from
President Roosevelt the shipping to carry an additional forty
thousand men to the East without deciding on their destination till
they rounded the Cape. Without these, the reinforcements now
proved so needful by the hazards of war could not have been at
hand.

[7] *To Mr. Curtin only*: "I am very glad that the 9th Australian Division is
now in action in the Western Desert, and am very thankful to you for making
it available for this vital key point of the war."

When in Washington I obtained from the President three hundred of the latest and finest tanks [Shermans] in the American Army. They were taken from the very hands of the American troops, who eagerly awaited them, and were sent by special convoy direct to Suez. With them went one hundred 105-mm. self-propelled guns, which definitely outmatch the 88-mm., the whole being accompanied by a large number of American key-men. These should arrive early September. Apart from the 8th Armoured Division, and in addition to the two armoured and one Army tank brigades now in action forward, we have in the Delta the personnel of four armoured brigades awaiting re-equipment. About half of these men are desert-trained in tanks. We should therefore be able to bring into action incomparably the most powerful and best-trained armoured division yet seen in the Middle East or indeed anywhere. But I hope the issue will be decided in our favour earlier. This is especially desirable because of dangers that may, though I do not say they will, develop on the northern approaches to Egypt.

Scarcely less important are the air reinforcements given me by the President on the morrow of Tobruk. As you know, we have not been hitherto able, for technical as well as military reasons, to provide heavy bomber squadrons for the Middle East, though they have often asked for them. But now the President has assigned to the defence of Egypt the group of 20 Liberators which was on its way to India, after bombing Rumanian oilfields, ten other Liberators which had already reached India, and a group of 35 Liberators from the United States. These with our own Liberators make up about 85 of these heavy bombers, which should all be available this month. At the same time our two Halifax squadrons will come into action, making up to 127 heavy bombers in all. It is this force I rely upon to beat up the ports of Tobruk and Benghazi, hampering Rommel's reinforcements, besides of course playing the part of a battle-fleet in preventing a seaborne invasion of Egypt. We have great enterprises in preparation for the revictualling of Malta, but as these deal with future operations you will not, I am sure, wish me to mention details.

Besides this, every preparation has been made to defend the Delta should the battles in the Desert go against us. Here we have very large numbers of men, all of whom have been ordered to take part in the defence of Egypt exactly as if it were England that was invaded. The cultivation and irrigation of the Delta make it literally the worst ground in the world for armoured vehicles, and armour as a factor would lose a great deal of its predominance. All ideas of evacuation have been repressed, the intention being to fight for every yard of ground to the end. As I have said however I do not think this situation will arise.

The House of Commons has proved a rock in these difficult days, as it did in the struggle against Napoleon, and I have also been greatly encouraged by the good will of your Government and people. I never felt more sure that complete ultimate victory will be ours. But the struggle will be long and we must not relax for an instant.

*   *   *   *   *

Rommel's communications were indeed strained to the utmost limit and his troops exhausted. Only a dozen German tanks were still fit for action, and the superiority of the British Air Force, especially in fighters, was again becoming dominant. Rommel reported on July 4 that he was suspending his attacks and going over to the defensive for a while in order to regroup and replenish his forces. He was still confident however of taking Egypt, and his opinion was shared by Mussolini and by Hitler. The Fuehrer indeed, without reference either to the Italians or to his own naval command, postponed the attack on Malta until the conquest of Egypt was complete.

Auchinleck's counter-attacks pressed Rommel very hard for the first fortnight of July. He then took up the challenge, and from July 15 to July 20 renewed his attempts to break the British line. On the 21st he had to report that he was checked: "The crisis still exists." On the 26th he was contemplating withdrawal to the frontier. He complained that he had received little in the way of replenishments; he was short of men, tanks, and artillery; the British Air Force was extremely active. And so the battle swayed back and forth until the end of the month, by which time both sides had fought themselves to a standstill. The Eighth Army under Auchinleck had weathered the storm, and in its stubborn stand had taken several thousand prisoners. Egypt was still safe.

2

Decision for "Torch"

Need to Reach Strategic Decisions with the United States — My Minute to C.O.S. Committee of July 5 — Telegram to President Roosevelt, July 8 — Choice of Commanders — We Suggest General Marshall for the Cross-Channel Task — Clarification of Code-Words — I Ask General McNaughton, Canadian Army, to Study "Jupiter" — President Roosevelt's Reply about Code-Names — The Pith of My Thought, July 14 — Tensions at Washington — The President's Decision to Send His Principal Advisers to Confer with Us — Dill's Full Account of the Washington Scene — The Delegation Arrives — The President's Massive Document of July 16 — "Franklin D. Roosevelt, Commander-in-Chief" — Chiefs of Staff's Meeting at Chequers, July 16 — My Notes for the Conference of July 20 — My Minute to the Chiefs of Staff, July 23 — "Gymnast" Rechristened "Torch" [1] — I Rejoice at the Decisions — The President's Satisfaction — Telegrams from Dill of July 30 — My Suggestions to the President about Commands — I Start on a Journey.

D URING THIS MONTH of July, when I was politically at my weakest and without a gleam of military success, I had to procure from the United States the decision which, for good or ill, dominated the next two years of the war. This was the aban-

---

[1] The following shortly explain the code-names occurring in this chapter:

ACROBAT: The advance into Tripolitania.

BOLERO: Preparations for the main invasion of France, afterwards the foundation of "Overlord."

GYMNAST: The landing in Northwest Africa, later called "Torch."

JUPITER: Operations in Northern Norway.

ROUND-UP: The invasion of German-dominated Europe, afterwards called "Overlord."

SLEDGEHAMMER: The attack on Brest or Cherbourg in 1942.

donment of all plans for crossing the Channel in 1942 and the occupation of French North Africa in the autumn or winter by a large Anglo-American expedition. I had made a careful study of the President's mind and its reactions for some time past, and I was sure that he was powerfully attracted by the North African plan. This had always been my aim, as was set forth in my papers of December, 1941. Everyone in our British circle was by now convinced that a Channel crossing in 1942 would fail, and no military man on either side of the ocean was prepared to recommend such a plan or to take responsibility for it. There was by now general agreement on the British side that no major cross-Channel operation could take place before 1943, but that all preparation for mounting it in the greatest strength should continue with the utmost zeal.

On June 11 the War Cabinet had agreed that preparations for "Sledgehammer," the attack on Brest and Cherbourg, should be vigorously pressed forward, "on the understanding that the operation would not be launched except in conditions which held out a good prospect of success." The position was studied again by the Chiefs of Staff at the beginning of the following month. On July 2 they drafted a memorandum commenting on the earlier discussions in the War Cabinet. They stated that "at the War Cabinet on June 11 the Prime Minister laid down, and the War Cabinet generally approved, that operations in 1942 should be governed by the following two principles: (1) no substantial landing in France in 1942 unless we are going to stay, and (2) no substantial landing in France unless the Germans are demoralised by failure against Russia. It seems to us that the above conditions are unlikely to be fulfilled, and that therefore the chances of launching Operation 'Sledgehammer' this year are remote."

It was therefore necessary to simplify our policy. The moment had come to bury "Sledgehammer," which had been dead for some time. With the general agreement of all my colleagues and the Chiefs of Staff I stated the case with whatever force I could command and in the plainest terms in an important telegram to the President.

Former Naval Person to President Roosevelt   8 July 42

No responsible British general, admiral, or air marshal is prepared to recommend "Sledgehammer" as a practicable operation in 1942. The Chiefs of Staff have reported, "The conditions which would make 'Sledgehammer' a sound, sensible enterprise are very unlikely to occur." They are now sending their paper to your Chiefs of Staff.

2. The taking up of the shipping is being proceeded with by us for camouflage purposes, though it involves a loss in British imports of perhaps 250,000 tons. But far more serious is the fact that, according to Mountbatten, if we interrupt the training of the troops we should, apart from the loss of landing-craft, etc., delay "Round-up" or 1943 "Bolero" for at least two or three months, even if the enterprise were unsuccessful and the troops had to be withdrawn after a short stay.

3. In the event of a lodgment being effected and maintained it would have to be nourished, and the bomber effort on Germany would have to be greatly curtailed. All our energies would be involved in defending the bridgehead. The possibility of mounting a large-scale operation in 1943 would be marred, if not ruined. All our resources would be absorbed piecemeal on the very narrow front which alone is open. It may therefore be said that premature action in 1942, while probably ending in disaster, would decisively injure the prospect of well-organised large-scale action in 1943.

4. I am sure myself that French North Africa ["Gymnast"] is by far the best chance for effecting relief to the Russian front in 1942. This has all along been in harmony with your ideas. In fact, it is your commanding idea. Here is the true second front of 1942. I have consulted Cabinet and Defence Committee, and we all agree. Here is the safest and most fruitful stroke that can be delivered this autumn.

5. We of course can aid in every way, by transfer of either American or British landing-forces from the United Kingdom to "Gymnast," and with landing-craft, shipping, etc. You can, if you choose, put the punch in partly from here and the rest direct across the Atlantic.

6. It must be clearly understood that we cannot count upon an invitation or a guarantee from Vichy. But any resistance would not be comparable to that which would be offered by the German

Army in the Pas de Calais. Indeed, it might be only token resistance. The stronger you are, the less resistance there would be and the more to overcome it. This is a political more than a military issue. It seems to me that we ought not to throw away the sole great strategic stroke open to us in the Western theatre during this cardinal year.

7. Besides the above we are studying very hard the possibility of an operation in northern Norway, or, if this should prove impracticable, elsewhere in Norway. The difficulties are great owing to the danger of shore-based aircraft attack upon our ships. We are having frightful difficulties about the Russian convoys. All the more is it necessary to try to clear the way and maintain the contact with Russia.

*   *   *   *   *

All this involved the choosing of commanders, and I sent two further messages to the President.

Former Naval Person to President Roosevelt   8 July 42

We have been deeply considering the question of command of maximum "Bolero" [the main crossing of the English Channel]. It would be agreeable to us if General Marshall would undertake this supreme task in 1943. We shall sustain him to the last inch.

2. The War Cabinet authorise me to convey the above to you.

8 July 42

I hope, Mr. President, you will make sure that the appointment of a United States commander over "Bolero," 1943, does not prejudice operations of immediate consequence, such as "Gymnast."

Another thing was to clear up the nomenclature. Under the ever-changing pressure of events the labels describing the many and various plans had become sadly confused or obsolete. The mere process of re-writing the labels was salutary and helpful.

Former Naval Person to President Roosevelt   6 July 42

Our code-words need clarification. By "Bolero" we British mean the vast arrangements necessary both in 1942 and 1943 for the operation against the Continent. The Joint Anglo-American Staffs Committees are all working on this basis. They are not operational,

but purely administrative. What you in conversation have called
"One-third Bolero" we have hitherto been calling "Sledgehammer."
The name "Round-up" has been given to the 1943 operation. I
do not much like this name, as it might be thought overconfident
or overgloomy, but it has come into considerable use. Please let
me know whether you have any wishes about this. The "Gymnast"
you and I have in view is, I think, the variant called by your Staffs
"Semi-Gymnast." I also use the word "Jupiter" to describe an
operation in the Far North.

*   *   *   *   *

I still hoped for "Jupiter." Little or no progress had been
made with its detailed planning. I thought that this operation
would give a glorious opportunity to the Canadian Army,
which had now for two years been eating its heart out in
Britain, awaiting the invader. I therefore had a long talk on
this subject in the garden at Chequers with General McNaughton, of whom I had a high opinion, and whose influence with
the Canadian Government was powerful. I explained the
whole position to him in all its bearings, and asked him
whether he would conduct a personal inquiry into the scheme
and make a plan, for which all aid would be given him by our
technical departments. He agreed to do this, and promised to
do his best.

Prime Minister to C.I.G.S. and C.O.S. Committee   8 July 42
General McNaughton should be entrusted with the preliminary
study and planning of "Jupiter," being given all the necessary
assistance by the Chiefs of Staff organisation. Climate proclaims
that the Canadian Army should undertake this task, if it is thought
feasible. The decision whether or not to adopt the plan will be
reserved.

I did not hear from the General for a long time.

*   *   *   *   *

President Roosevelt replied about the labels in a manner
which showed how clearly and deeply he comprehended the
issues involved. He made three proposals:

That the term "Bolero" be used to designate the preparation for and movement of United States forces into the European theatre, preparations for their reception therein, and the production, assembly, transport, reception, and storage of equipment and supplies necessary for support of the United States forces in operation against the European continent.

2. That the term "Sledgehammer" be used to designate an offensive operation of the British and American troops against the European continent in 1942, to be carried out in case of German internal collapse, or imminent Russian military collapse which necessitates an emergency attack in order to divert German forces from the Russian front.

3. That the term "Round-up," or any other name which you may desire, be used to designate an offensive operation against German-dominated Europe, to be carried out by combined American and British forces in 1943 or later.

I therefore minuted to the Chiefs of Staff:

Prime Minister to Brigadier Hollis   15 July 42

I fear that to change the name "Round-up" would make the Americans think there was some change of purpose. Therefore we must stick to this boastful, ill-chosen name, and hope it does not bring us bad luck.

I think we had better not alter the President's wording. We are not now dealing with policy, but only with nomenclature.

Draft accordingly and promulgate after obtaining American agreement.

*   *   *   *   *

On the eve of grave decisions I sent to the President the pith of my thought.

Former Naval Person to President Roosevelt   14 July 42

I am most anxious for you to know where I stand myself at the present time. I have found no one who regards "Sledgehammer" as possible. I should like to see you do "Gymnast" as soon as possible, and that we in concert with the Russians should try for "Jupiter." Meanwhile all preparations for "Round-up" in 1943

should proceed at full blast, thus holding the maximum enemy
forces opposite England. All this seems to me as clear as noonday.

* * * * *

But before the final decision for action could be obtained
there was a pause. Strong tensions grew in the supreme
American war direction. General Marshall was divided from
Admiral King as between Europe and the Pacific. Neither was
inclined to the North African venture. In this deadlock the
President's liking for North Africa grew steadily stronger.
Field-Marshal Dill's qualities had won him the confidence of
all the rival schools of thought, and his tact preserved their good
will. My correspondence with him throws an intimate light on
the processes at work.

Prime Minister to Field-Marshal Dill (Washington)   12 July 42

I have had the full text of the Staff paper sent to you by air.
You should draw particular attention to Mountbatten's Note
showing the mortal injury that would be done to "Round-up"
by "Sledgehammer." Apart altogether from this, no one is able
to solve the problems of "Sledgehammer" itself.

2. "Gymnast" affords the sole means by which United States
forces can strike at Hitler in 1942. If "Gymnast" were successful
our resulting threat to Italy would draw important German air
forces off Russia. "Gymnast" does not interrupt the vast preparation and training for "Round-up" now proceeding on this side. It
only means that six United States divisions will be withdrawn
intact from "Round-up." These might surely be replaced by new
U.S. divisions, which would be ready before the transportation
schedule is accomplished.

3. However, if the President decides against "Gymnast" the
matter is settled. It can only be done by troops under the American flag. The opportunity will have been definitely rejected. Both
countries will remain motionless in 1942, and all will be concentrated on "Round-up" in 1943.

4. There could be no excuse in these circumstances for the
switch of United States effort [to the Pacific], and I cannot think
that such an attitude would be adopted.

It was felt by all who met at the White House to decide these issues that a visit to England offered the only hope of reaching accord. I learned that the President proposed to send his most trusted friends and officers over to see us.

Field-Marshal Dill to Prime Minister 15 July 42

Marshall leaves for England with Harry Hopkins and King tomorrow evening.

Broadly, objection to "Gymnast" are: (*a*) It would necessitate drawing naval forces from Pacific, particularly carriers, which are urgently required for operations U.S. have in hand there, and of which you are aware. (*b*) It would necessitate new line of sea communications, which they would have difficulty in maintaining together with other commitments. (*c*) To strike only at Casablanca, where landings are difficult and facilities for maintenance poor, would withdraw nothing from Russian front, and to strike inside Mediterranean, at, say, Algiers, and even Bizerta, would be too hazardous, particularly in view of ease with which Axis could cut communication through Straits of Gibraltar. (*d*) "Gymnast" would build up into such a large commitment as to destroy any possibility of "Round-up" in 1943.

Vague plans for action in Pacific have been put to [the] President. . . .

All these activities would use up shipping at present earmarked for "Bolero," and would reduce the U.S. air forces sent to Britain by some two-thirds. . . . It is quite clear that Pacific ventures can give no immediate relief to Russia, and will be slow to obtain anything decisive against Japan.

There is no doubt that Marshall is true to his first love, but he is convinced that there has been no real drive behind the European project. Meetings are held, discussions take place, and time slips by. Germany will never again be so occupied in the East as she is today, and if we do not take advantage of her present preoccupation we shall find ourselves faced with a Germany so strong in the West that no invasion of the Continent will be possible. We can then go on pummelling each other by air, but the possibility of a decision will have gone. Marshall feels, I believe, that if a great businessman were faced with pulling off this *coup* or going bankrupt he would strain every nerve to pull off the *coup,* and would probably succeed.

King's war is against the Japanese.

I have a feeling (based on nothing more than the American thought that the Pacific could be a substitute for "Bolero" and the strong American desire to build up an army of seven millions) that there are highly placed Americans who do not believe that anything better than a stalemate with Germany is possible.

May I suggest with all respect that you must convince your visitors that you are determined to beat the Germans, that you will strike them on the continent of Europe at the earliest possible moment even on a limited scale, and that anything which detracts from this main effort will receive no support from you at all? Marshall believes that your first love is "Gymnast," just as his is "Bolero," and that with the smallest provocation you always revert to your old love. Unless you can convince him of your unswerving devotion to "Bolero" everything points to a complete reversal of our present agreed strategy and the withdrawal of America to a war of her own in the Pacific, leaving us with limited American assistance to make out as best we can against Germany.

*   *   *   *   *

President Roosevelt was conscious of the strength of the arguments against "Sledgehammer." If he placed it in the forefront of his communications to us, it was to convince General Marshall that it should have every chance. But if no one would touch it, what then? There was the wave of American Staff opinion which argued, "If nothing can be done this year in Europe let us concentrate on Japan, and thus bring the United States Army and Navy thought together and unite General Marshall with Admiral King." July 15, when the Vote of Censure was being debated in the House of Commons, when Auchinleck's battle for the defence of Cairo hung in the balance, was also "a very tense day in the White House." We are told, "The United States Chiefs of Staff were in a 'fish or cut bait' mood," and that the President said this would amount to "taking up your dishes." The meaning of these homely expressions was of course "If Britain won't or can't do 'Sledgehammer' in 1942, let us leave the European theatre and concentrate on Japan." This, said the President, in effect amounted to abandoning the European side of the war. There is no evidence that either General Marshall or Admiral King harboured such ideas. But there was a strong surge of feeling in the powerful second rank of the American Staff. The President withstood and brushed aside this fatal trend of thought.

His second conviction was that the United States Army must fight against the Germans in 1942. Where then could this be but in French North Africa? "This was," says Mr. Stimson, "his secret war baby." The movement of the force of the argument and of the President's mind to this conclusion was remorseless. The purpose of my visit to Washington three weeks earlier had been to obtain this decision. The fall of Tobruk, the political clamour at home, and the undoubted loss of prestige which our country, and I as its representative, suffered from this disaster had rendered it impossible for me to obtain satisfaction. But the grim questions had to be answered none the less. I was certain that the clarity and unity of our views would earn their reward.

* * * * *

Our American visitors landed at Prestwick on Saturday, July 18, and travelled by train to London. Here they went into immediate conference with the American Service Chiefs now established in the capital, Eisenhower, Clark, Stark, and Spaatz. The debate on "Sledgehammer" was renewed. Opinion among the American leaders was still strongly in favour of pressing on exclusively with this operation. Only the President himself seemed to have been impressed by my arguments. He had drafted for the delegation the most massive and masterly document on war policy that I ever saw from his hand.

MEMORANDUM FOR HON. HARRY L. HOPKINS,
GENERAL MARSHALL, AND ADMIRAL KING

Subject: Instructions for London Conference, July 1942   16 July 42

You will proceed immediately to London as my personal representatives for the purpose of consultation with appropriate British authorities on the conduct of the war.

2. The military and naval strategic changes have been so great since Mr. Churchill's visit to Washington that it became necessary

to reach immediate agreement on joint operational plans between the British and ourselves along two lines:

(a) Definite plans for the balance of 1942.

(b) Tentative plans for the year 1943, which of course will be subject to change in the light of occurrences in 1942, but which should be initiated at this time in all cases involving preparation in 1942 for operations in 1943.

3. (a) The common aim of the United Nations must be the defeat of the Axis Powers. There cannot be compromise on this point.

(b) We should concentrate our efforts and avoid dispersion.

(c) Absolute co-ordinated use of British and American forces is essential.

(d) All available U.S. and British forces should be brought into action as quickly as they can be profitably used.

(e) It is of the highest importance that U.S. ground troops be brought into action against the enemy in 1942.

4. British and American material promises to Russia must be carried out in good faith. If the Persian route of delivery is used, preference must be given to combat material. This aid must continue as long as delivery is possible, and Russia must be encouraged to continue resistance. Only complete collapse, which seems unthinkable, should alter this determination on our part.

5. In regard to 1942, you will carefully investigate the possibility of executing "Sledgehammer." Such an operation would definitely sustain Russia this year. "Sledgehammer" is of such grave importance that every reason calls for accomplishment of it. You should strongly urge immediate all-out preparations for it, that it be pushed with utmost vigour, and that it be executed whether or not Russian collapse becomes imminent. In the event Russian collapse becomes probable, "Sledgehammer" becomes not merely advisable but imperative. The principal objective of "Sledgehammer" is the positive diversion of German air forces from the Russian front.

6. Only if you are completely convinced that "Sledgehammer" is impossible of execution with reasonable chance of serving its intended purpose inform me.

7. If "Sledgehammer" is finally and definitely out of the picture I want you to consider the world situation as it exists at that time, and determine upon another place for U.S. troops to fight in 1942.

It is my present view of the world picture that:

(a) If Russia contains a large German force against her, "Round-up" becomes possible in 1943, and plans for "Round-up" should be immediately considered and preparations made for it.

(b) If Russia collapses and German air and ground forces are released, "Round-up" may be impossible of fulfilment in 1943.

8. The Middle East should be held as strongly as possible whether Russia collapses or not. I want you to take into consideration the effect of losing the Middle East. Such loss means in series:

(1) Loss of Egypt and the Suez Canal.

(2) Loss of Syria.

(3) Loss of Mosul oil wells.

(4) Loss of the Persian Gulf through attack from the north and west, together with access to all Persian Gulf oil.

(5) Joining hands between Germany and Japan and the probable loss of the Indian Ocean.

(6) The very important probability of German occupation of Tunis, Algiers, Morocco, Dakar, and the cutting of the ferry route through Freetown and Liberia.

(7) Serious danger to all shipping in the South Atlantic and serious danger to Brazil and the whole of the east coast of South America. I include in the above possibilities the use by the Germans of Spain, Portugal, and their territories.

(8) You will determine the best methods of holding the Middle East. These methods include definitely either or both of the following:

(a) Sending aid and ground forces to the Persian Gulf, to Syria, and to Egypt.

(b) A new operation in Morocco and Algeria intended to drive in against the back door of Rommel's armies. The attitude of French Colonial troops is still in doubt.

9. I am opposed to an American all-out effort in the Pacific against Japan with the view to her defeat as quickly as possible. It is of the utmost importance that we appreciate that defeat of Japan does not defeat Germany and that American concentration against Japan this year or in 1943 increases the chance of complete German domination of Europe and Africa. On the other hand, it is obvious that defeat of Germany or the holding of Germany in 1942 or in 1943 means probable eventual defeat of Germany in the European and African theatre and in the Near East.

Defeat of Germany means the defeat of Japan, probably without firing a shot or losing a life.

10. Please remember three cardinal principles — speed of decision on plans, unity of plans, attack combined with defence but not defence alone. This affects the immediate objective of U.S. ground forces fighting against Germans in 1942.

11. I hope for total agreement within one week of your arrival.

FRANKLIN D. ROOSEVELT
Commander-in-Chief

That same evening I held a meeting of the Chiefs of Staff Committee at Chequers. The essential part of the minutes reads as follows:

The discussion showed that there was complete agreement between the Prime Minister on the one hand and the Chiefs of Staff on the other.

In respect of action in 1942, the only feasible proposition appeared to be "Gymnast." It would be much to our advantage to get a footing in North Africa cheaply in the same way as the Germans got Norway cheaply by getting there first.

"Gymnast" would in effect be the right wing of our "second front." An American occupation of Casablanca and district would not be sufficient. The operations would have to extend to Algiers, Oran, and possibly farther east. If the Americans could not supply the forces for all of these, we might undertake the more easterly operations with British troops accompanied by small American contingents. It was probable that the United States would be unable to supply all the naval forces necessary for "Gymnast" in addition to those necessary for their "Bolero" convoys. In that event we should have to help them out.

I was naturally aware that the American war leaders, now gathered in London, still had to be convinced that our view was the only practicable one. Hopkins came to Chequers over the week-end, and we went over informally the divergence between us.

On Monday morning, July 20, the first meeting with the American delegates was held in the Cabinet room.

My summary of the attitude of the British Government is on record.

PRIME MINISTER'S NOTES FOR MEETING ON JULY 20, 1942

I do not desire to discuss this morning the merits of the various grave major proposals which are before us, but rather to survey the general scene and suggest the most convenient method and sequence of our conferences. We must reach decisions, and though these affect the whole future of the war there is no reason why the process should be protracted.

The first question is "Sledgehammer." Should we do it or not? But here also arises immediately the question, in what form? Our visitors may be thinking of one thing, while we have been working mainly at another. If we have been unable to devise a satisfactory plan ourselves, we will give the most earnest, sympathetic attention to any American plan. It is most important that no one should come to these discussions with a closed mind, either for or against any particular project. It is of course necessary to consider not only whether a thing can be done, but whether on balance it would be a profitable use of our resources at the present time.

We must consider the effect of doing or not doing "Sledgehammer" on the future of "Round-up," for which all the "Bolero" preparations are proceeding. We are ardently in favour of "Round-up." But here again, what is "Round-up"? Is it necessarily confined to an attack upon the western seaboard of France? Is the idea of a second front necessarily confined within those limits? Might it not be extended even more widely, and with advantage? We have been inclined to think that "Sledgehammer" might delay or even preclude "Round-up." On the other hand, it may be contended that the fortunes of "Round-up" do not depend to any large extent on what we do, but on what happens in Russia.

We have hitherto discussed "Sledgehammer" on the basis that Russia is either triumphant or crushed. It is more probable that an intermediate situation will confront us. The Russian battle may long hang in the balance; or, again, the result may be indeterminate, and the Russian front will be maintained, though somewhat farther to the east.

If "Sledgehammer" is excluded what are we to do pending "Round-up"? Or, if it is held that the exclusion of "Sledgehammer" destroys "Round-up," what are we to do anyway?

Here I will come to the second chapter, the operation "Gymnast." This should certainly be examined in all its various forms and from every angle. The Germans will probably not wait indefinitely before occupying the "Gymnast" area and drawing Spain and Portugal into their system. Even though not strong enough to invade Britain with Russia still on their hands, they might easily find enough for that. We have to face the prospect of a German occupation of the North African and West African coasts. How serious would be the disadvantages of this?

The case for or against "Gymnast" is powerfully affected by the course of the battle now raging in Egypt. Should General Auchinleck win, his advance westward may be very rapid. "Acrobat" might then again come into view, with possibilities of action against Sicily and Italy, and also of regaining the air control of the Southern Mediterranean, with all the saving of shipping that would result therefrom.

A wide gap now exists in our defences. The Levant-Caspian front is almost bare. If General Auchinleck wins the Battle of Egypt we could no doubt build up a force of perhaps eight divisions, which, with the four Polish divisions when trained, would play a strong part in delaying a German southward advance. But if General Auchinleck cannot drive the enemy to a safe distance away from Egypt, or if, having driven them, he pursues them into "Acrobat," then the only shield for the vital region south of the Caspian is the Russian southern armies. We cannot yet say how they will fare. It is far too early to assume that they will break. Even at the worst they should retire in force through the Caucasus and hold the mountain range through the winter and retain, possibly with our air assistance, the naval command of the Caspian Sea. These are great bulwarks. At present they are our only bulwarks. . . .

There was also a brief discussion on "Anakim" (operations in Burma) and on what steps we could take to help in the Pacific theatre.

*   *   *   *   *

The next meeting was held on the afternoon of July 22. General Marshall opened the discussion by saying that he and his colleagues had reached a deadlock in their talks with the British Chiefs of Staff, and therefore that they would have to report to the President for instructions.

I replied that I fully shared the ardent desire of the President and his Service advisers "to engage the enemy in the greatest possible strength at the earliest possible moment," but that I felt sure that, with the limited forces at our disposal, we should not be justified in attempting "Sledgehammer" in 1942. I pointed to the number of ugly possibilities looming in front of us. There might, for example, be a collapse in Russia, or the Germans might move into the Caucasus, or they might beat General Auchinleck and occupy the Nile Delta and the Suez Canal, or again they might establish themselves in North Africa and West Africa and thereby put an almost prohibitive strain on our shipping. Nevertheless, disagreement between Great Britain and America would have far greater consequences than all the above possibilities. It was therefore agreed that the American Chiefs of Staff should report to the President that the British were not prepared to go ahead with "Sledgehammer" and ask for instructions.

President Roosevelt replied at once that he was not surprised at the disappointing outcome of the London talks. He agreed that it was no use continuing to press for "Sledgehammer" in the face of British opposition, and instructed his delegation to reach a decision with us on some operation which would involve American land forces being brought into action against the enemy in 1942.

Thus "Sledgehammer" fell by the wayside and "Gymnast" came into its own. Marshall and King, though naturally disappointed, bowed to the decision of their Commander-in-Chief, and the greatest goodwill between us all again prevailed.

I now hastened to rechristen my favourite. "Gymnast," "Super-Gymnast," and "Semi-Gymnast" vanished from our code-words. On July 24 in an instruction from me to the Chiefs of Staff "Torch" became the new and master term. On July 25 the President cabled to Hopkins that plans for landings in North Africa to take place "not later than October 30" should go ahead at once. That evening our friends set off on their journey back to Washington.

*   *   *   *   *

All was therefore agreed and settled in accordance with my long-conceived ideas and those of my colleagues, military and political. This was a great joy to me, especially as it came in what seemed to be the darkest hour. At every point except one the plans I cherished were adopted. "Jupiter" alone (the Norway enterprise) I could not carry, although its merits were not disputed. I did not give this plan up yet, but in the end I failed to establish it. For months past I had sought "No 'Sledgehammer,' " but instead the North African invasion *and* "Jupiter." "Jupiter" fell by the way.

But I had enough to be thankful for.

*   *   *   *   *

Former Naval Person to President Roosevelt   27 July 42

I was sure you would be as pleased as I am, indeed as we all are here, at the results of this strenuous week. Besides reaching complete agreement on action, relations of cordial intimacy and comradeship have been cemented between our high officers. I doubt if success would have been achieved without Harry's invaluable aid.

2. We must establish a second front this year and attack at the earliest moment. As I see it this second front consists of a main body holding the enemy pinned opposite "Sledgehammer" and a wide flanking movement called "Torch" (hitherto called "Gymnast"). Now that everything is decided we can, as you say, go full steam ahead. All depends on secrecy and speed and on having a regular schedule of political and military action. Every hour counts, and I agree with you that October 30 is the latest date which should be accepted.

3. Secrecy can only be maintained by deception. For this purpose I am running "Jupiter," and we must also work up "Sledgehammer" with the utmost vigour. These will cover all movements in the United Kingdom. When your troops start for "Torch" everyone except the secret circles should believe that they are going to Suez or Basra, thus explaining tropical kit. The Canadian Army here

will be fitted for Arctic service. Thus we shall be able to keep the enemy in doubt till the last moment.

4. Meanwhile I hope "Bolero" processes will continue at full blast, subject only to any necessary impingement upon them made by "Torch," which impingement eventuates only in a certain delay. Thus we shall be able to strike left-handed, right-handed, or both-handed.

The President was as pleased as I was to find such complete agreement between all the experts upon what we had both long cherished.

President Roosevelt to Prime Minister   28 July 42

The Three Musketeers arrived safely this afternoon, and the wedding is still scheduled. I am of course very happy in the result, and especially in the successful meeting of minds. I cannot help feeling that the past week represented a turning-point in the whole war and that now we are on our way shoulder to shoulder. I agree with you that secrecy and speed are vital, and I hope the October date can be advanced. I will talk with Marshall in regard to scale of supplies and equipment in terms of tonnage and in terms of the United Kingdom importations of food and raw materials. Also I will do my best to get the air squadrons on the Russian southern flank. I fully agree that this should be done.

The commanders had now to be settled.

Field-Marshal Dill to Prime Minister   30 July 42

I would urge that you should at once clear question of command with the President. I feel myself that Marshall is the man for the job, and I believe he would accept. Equally clearly he cannot be spared from here at present, but Eisenhower could well act with his authority. President has not yet approached Marshall on this question. This may be due to President's fear of losing him, but Eisenhower deputy idea may be welcome.

If this were agreed, then Eisenhower would be able to collect his Combined Staff and really function. In doing this it would be wise if Eisenhower were to delegate the planning and preparations for "Sledgehammer" to someone else, obviously a Britisher, so that Eisenhower with his own staff could be free, apart from a general supervision of "Sledgehammer," to concentrate entirely on "Torch." Surely "Torch" is what matters now above all else, and "Torch" requires much detailed planning, and the allotment of forces and tasks and training and what not. It will require furious work from now till its launching, and the sooner it can be launched, clearly the better.

May I express my admiration for the way in which you have steered these difficult negotiations to so successful a conclusion? I hope to be in London early next week, when I would like, if I may, to come and see you.

About the commanders I telegraphed to the President.

Former Naval Person to President Roosevelt   31 July 42

I should be grateful for a decision about the command of "Bolero," "Sledgehammer," "Round-up," and "Torch." [This meant the "Bolero," "Sledgehammer," and "Round-up" group and "Torch."] It would be agreeable to us if General Marshall were designated for the Supreme Command of "Round-up," and that in the meanwhile General Eisenhower should act as his deputy here. We would appoint General Alexander as Task Force Commander in the first instance, to work with and under General Eisenhower. Both these men would work at "Torch," and General Eisenhower would also for the time being supervise the "Bolero"-"Sledgehammer" business. He will thus be able to draw for "Torch" the necessary forces with the least injury to "Bolero" and "Round-up." As soon as "Torch" has taken shape he would command it, with Alexander and an American commander as Task Force Commanders of the two forces starting from United Kingdom and United States. When this party starts out to do the job we should be glad if you would nominate either General Marshall or another [as] *locum tenens* to carry forward the work of "Bolero," "Sledgehammer," and "Round-up." We will supply him also with a deputy.

2. It seems important to act quickly, as committees are too numerous and too slow. If you prefer other arrangements pray let me know your wishes.

Field-Marshal Dill to Prime Minister   1 Aug. 42

President has gone [to] Hyde Park for short rest, but before going he issued orders for full steam ahead "Torch" at earliest possible moment. He has asked Combined Chiefs of Staff to tell him on August 4 earliest date when landing could take place. Risk of whittling to Pacific may still exist, but President entirely sound on this point.

2. In the American mind, "Round-up" in 1943 is excluded by acceptance of "Torch." We need not argue about that. A one-track mind on "Torch" is what we want at present, and I conclude you would accept Marshall for this command if President so desired, and not stipulate that he should be reserved for "Round-up," in spite of what you say in your telegram to President of July 31.

3. May what you are at have the success which courage and imagination deserve.

This message reached me at midnight on the Lyneham Airfield, where I was about to set forth upon a journey of which the next chapter will offer both explanation and account.

3

My Journey to Cairo

Changes in Command

Decision that I Should Visit Cairo and Moscow — Stalin's Invitation — Journey in the "Commando" — Dawn Above the Nile — I Visit the Alamein Positions with General Auchinleck, August 5 — My Meeting with General Gott — At the Air Force Headquarters — Telegrams to the Cabinet of August 5 and 6 — Proposed Changes in Command and Organisation — Further Explanations to the Cabinet, August 7 — General Gott Killed in Action — An Acute Moment in the War Cabinet — General Montgomery Appointed to Command the Eighth Army — Changes in Eisenhower's British Commanders for "Torch" — My Day with the Yeomanry Division, August 8 — My Letter to General Auchinleck, August 8 — A Note in Colonel Jacob's Dairy — Arrival of General Alexander, August 9 — General Auchinleck Declines the Command of the Iraq-Persia Theatre — My Directive to General Alexander and his Eventual Reply.

T HE DOUBTS I HAD about the High Command in the Middle East were fed continually by the reports which I received from many quarters. It became urgently necessary for me to go there and settle the decisive questions on the spot. It was at first accepted that this journey would be by Gibraltar and Takoradi and thence across Central Africa to Cairo, involving five or even six days' flying. As this would carry me through tropical and malarious regions, a whole series of protective injections was prescribed. Some of these would take ten days to give their immunity, and involved considerable discomfort and even inactivity meanwhile. Several members of the War

Cabinet also took a very close and friendly interest in my health and became an opposing factor to be reasoned with.

However, at this juncture there arrived in England a young American pilot, Captain Vanderkloot, who had just flown from the United States in the aeroplane "Commando," a Liberator plane from which the bomb-racks had been removed and some sort of passenger accommodation substituted. This machine was certainly capable of flying along the route prescribed with good margins in hand at all stages. Portal, the Chief of the Air Staff, saw this pilot and cross-examined him about "Commando." Vanderkloot, who had already flown a million miles, asked why it was necessary to fly all round by Takoradi, Kano, Fort Lamy, El Obeid, etc. He said he could make one bound from Gibraltar to Cairo, flying from Gibraltar eastward in the afternoon, turning sharply south across Spanish or Vichy territory as dusk fell, and then proceeding eastward till he struck the Nile about Assiout, when a turn to the northward would bring us in another hour or so to the Cairo landing-ground northwest of the Pyramids. This altered the whole picture. I could be in Cairo in two days without any trouble about Central African bugs and the inoculations against them. Portal was convinced.

We were all anxious about the reaction of the Soviet Government to the unpleasant though inevitable news that there would be no crossing of the Channel in 1942. It happened that on the night of July 28 I had the honour of entertaining the King to dinner with the War Cabinet in the propped-up garden-room at Number 10, which we used for dining. I obtained His Majesty's approval privately, and, immediately he had gone, brought the Ministers, who were in a good frame of mind, into the Cabinet Room and clinched matters. It was settled that I should go to Cairo in any case, and should propose to Stalin that I should go on to see him. I therefore telegraphed to him as follows:

Prime Minister to Premier Stalin   30 July 42

We are making preliminary arrangements for another effort

to run a large convoy through to Archangel in the first week of
September.

2. I am willing, if you invite me, to come myself to meet you in
Astrakhan, the Caucasus, or similar convenient meeting-place. We
could then survey the war together and take decisions hand-in-
hand. I could then tell you plans we have made with President
Roosevelt for offensive action in 1942. I would bring the Chief of
the Imperial General Staff with me.

3. I am starting for Cairo forthwith. I have serious business
there, as you may imagine. From there I will, if you desire it, fix a
convenient date for our meeting, which might, so far as I am concerned, be between August 10 and 13, all being well.

4. The War Cabinet have endorsed my proposals.

Premier Stalin to Premier Churchill   31 July 42

On behalf of the Soviet Government I invite you to the U.S.S.R.
to meet the members of the Government. I should be very grateful
if you could come to the U.S.S.R. to consider jointly the urgent
questions of war against Hitler, as the menace from these quarters
to Great Britain, the United States of America, and the U.S.S.R.
has now reached a special degree of intensity.

I think the most suitable meeting-place would be Moscow, as
neither I nor the members of the Government and the leading men
of the General Staff could leave the capital at the moment of such
an intense struggle against the Germans.

The presence of the Chief of the Imperial General Staff would
be extremely desirable.

The date of the meeting please fix yourself in accordance with
the time necessary for completion of your business at Cairo. You
may be sure beforehand that any date would suit me.

Let me express my gratitude for your consent to send the next
convoy with war materials for the U.S.S.R. at the beginning of
September. In spite of the extreme difficulty of diverting aircraft
from the battle-front we will take all possible measures to increase
the aerial protection of the convoy.

Prime Minister to Premier Stalin   1 Aug. 42

I will certainly come to Moscow to meet you, and will fix the
date from Cairo.

*   *   *   *   *

Meanwhile the battle on the Alamein position centring on the Ruweisat Ridge continued, and seemed to hang in the balance, although in fact by this time the energy of Rommel's thrust required replenishment and our defence was more than holding its own. Plans were now made for me to fly to Cairo and I cabled to General Auchinleck accordingly:

Prime Minister to General Auchinleck   31 July 42

I hope to arrive in Cairo on Monday, August 3. The C.I.G.S. should arrive by a different route on the same day. I have asked Field-Marshal Smuts and General Wavell to try to come there during the same week. Let nothing take your eye off the ball.

General Brooke, the Chief of the Imperial General Staff was already at Gibraltar flying to Cairo via Malta. I cabled to him as follows:

Prime Minister to General Brooke   1 Aug. 42

How necessary it is for us to get to the Middle East at once is shown by the following extract from Auchinleck's telegram received yesterday:

"An exhaustive conference on tactical situation held yesterday with Corps Commanders. Owing to lack of resources and enemy's effective consolidation of his positions we reluctantly concluded that in present circumstances it is not feasible to renew our efforts to break enemy front or turn his southern flank. It is unlikely that an opportunity will arise for resumption of offensive operations before mid-September. This depends on enemy's ability to build up his tank force. Temporarily therefore our policy will be defensive, including thorough preparations and consolidations in whole defensive area. In the meantime we shall seize at once any opportunity of taking the offensive suddenly and surprising the enemy. . . . "

It had been arranged that Sir Alexander Cadogan should come with me to represent the Foreign Office. We started after midnight on Sunday, August 2, from Lyneham in the bomber "Commando." This was a very different kind of travel from the comforts of the Boeing flying-boats. The bomber was at this time unheated, and razor-edged draughts cut in through many chinks. There were no beds, but two shelves in the after cabin enabled me and Sir Charles Wilson, my doctor, to lie down. There were plenty of blankets for all. We flew low over the South of England in order to be recognised by our batteries, who had been warned, but who were also under Alert conditions. As we got out to sea I left the cockpit and retired to rest, fortified by a good sleeping cachet.

We reached Gibraltar uneventfully on the morning of August 3, spent the day looking round the fortress, and started at 6 P.M. for Cairo, a hop of two thousand miles or more, as the détours necessary to avoid the hostile aircraft around the Desert battle were considerable. Vanderkloot, in order to have more petrol in hand, did not continue down the Mediterranean till darkness fell, but flew straight across the Spanish zone and the Vichy quasi-hostile territory. Therefore, as we had an armed escort till nightfall of four Beaufighters, we in fact openly violated the neutrality of both these regions. No one molested us in the air, and we did not come within cannon-shot of any important town. All the same I was glad when darkness cast her shroud over the harsh landscape and we could retire to such sleeping accommodation as "Commando" could offer. It would have been very tiresome to make a forced landing on neutral territory, and even descent in the desert, though preferable, would have raised problems of its own. However, all "Commando's" four engines purred happily, and I slept sound as we sailed through the starlit night.

It was my practice on these journeys to sit in the co-pilot's seat before sunrise, and when I reached it on this morning of August 4, there in the pale, glimmering dawn the endless winding silver ribbon of the Nile stretched joyously before us. Often had I seen the day break on the Nile. In war and peace I had traversed by land or water, almost its whole length, except the "Dongola Loop," from Lake Victoria to the sea. Never had the glint of daylight on its waters been so welcome to me.

Now for a short spell I became "the man on the spot." Instead of sitting at home waiting for the news from the front I could send it myself. This was exhilarating.

*   *   *   *   *

The following issues had to be settled in Cairo. Had General
Auchinleck or his staff lost the confidence of the Desert Army?
If so, should he be relieved, and who could succeed him? In
dealing with a commander of the highest character and quality,
of proved ability and resolution, such decisions are painful. In
order to fortify my own judgment I had urged General Smuts
to come from South Africa to the scene, and he was already at
the Embassy when I arrived. We spent the morning together
and I told him all our troubles and the choices that were open.
In the afternoon I had a long talk with Auchinleck, who explained the military position very clearly. The next morning
at his request I saw General Corbett, of whom the Commander-
in-Chief had a very high opinion. He told me that Auchinleck
was anxious to lay down the command of the Eighth Army at
the earliest moment and return to his wider sphere in Cairo.
He then surprised me by saying, "I am to succeed him in command of the Army. In fact I have been living with my kit
packed for the last week." This arrangement had certainly not
been considered by us. After luncheon General Wavell arrived
from India, and at six o'clock I held a meeting about the
Middle East, attended by all the authorities — Smuts, Casey,
the C.I.G.S., Wavell, Auchinleck, Admiral Harwood, and
Tedder for the Air. We did a lot of business with a very great
measure of agreement. But all the time my mind kept turning
to the prime question of the command.

It is not possible to deal with changes of this character without reviewing the alternatives. In this part of the problem the
Chief of the Imperial General Staff, whose duty it was to ap-
praise the quality of our generals, was my adviser.* Alexander
and Montgomery had both fought with him in the battle which
enabled us to get back to Dunkirk in May, 1940. We both
greatly admired Alexander's magnificent conduct in the hopeless campaign to which he had been committed in Burma.
Montgomery's reputation stood high. If it were decided to
relieve Auchinleck we had no doubt that Alexander must be
ordered to carry the load in the Middle East. But the feelings
of the Eighth Army must not be overlooked. Might it not be

* See footnote on page 471.

taken as a reproach upon them and all their commanders of every grade if two men were sent from England to supersede all those who had fought in the desert? Here General Gott seemed in every way to meet the need. The troops were devoted to him and he had not earned the title "Strafer" by nothing. But then there was the view which Brooke reported to me, that he was very tired and needed a rest. It was at this moment too early to make decisions. I had travelled all this way to have the chance of seeing and hearing what was possible in the short time which might be claimed and spared.

* * * * *

The hospitality of Sir Miles Lampson was princely. I slept in his air-cooled bedroom and worked in his air-cooled study. It was intensely hot, and those were the only two rooms in the house where the temperature was comfortable. In these otherwise agreeable surroundings we dwelt for more than a week, sensing the atmosphere, hearing opinions, and visiting the front or the large camps to the east of Cairo in the Kassassin area, where our powerful reinforcements were now steadily arriving.

On August 5 I visited the Alamein positions. I drove with General Auchinleck in his car to the extreme right flank of the line west of El Ruweisat, which was held by the Australian 9th Division. Thence we proceeded along the front to his headquarters behind the Ruweisat Ridge, where we were given breakfast in a wire-netted cube, full of flies and important military personages. I had asked for various officers to be brought, but above all General "Strafer" Gott. It was said that he was worn down with his hard service. This was what I wanted to find out. Having made the acquaintance of the various Corps and Divisional Commanders who were present, I therefore asked that General Gott should drive with me to the airfield, which was my next stop. Objection was raised by one of Auchinleck's staff officers that this would take him an hour out of his way; but I insisted he should come with me. And here was my first and last meeting with Gott. As we rumbled and jolted over the rough tracks I looked into his clear blue eyes and questioned him about himself. Was he tired, and had he any views to give? Gott said that no doubt he was tired, and that he would like nothing better than three months' leave in England, which he had not seen for several years, but he declared himself quite capable of further immediate efforts and of taking any responsibilities confided to him. We parted at the airfield at two o'clock on this afternoon of August 5. By the same hour two days later he had been killed by the enemy in almost the very air spaces through which I now flew.

At the airfield I was handed over to Air Vice Marshal Coningham, who, under Tedder, commanded all the air-power which had worked with the Army, and without whose activity the immense retreat of five hundred miles could never have been accomplished without even greater disasters than we had suffered. We flew in a quarter of an hour to his headquarters, where luncheon was provided, and where all the leading air officers, from Group Captains upwards, were gathered. I was conscious of an air of nervousness in my hosts from the moment of my arrival. The food had all been ordered from Shepheard's Hotel. A special car was bringing down the dainties of Cairo. But it had gone astray. Frantic efforts were being made to find it. At last it arrived.

This turned out to be a gay occasion in the midst of care — a real oasis in a very large desert. It was not difficult to perceive how critical the Air was of the Army, and how both Air and Army were astonished at the reverse which had befallen our superior forces. In the evening I flew back to Cairo and sent the following:

Prime Minister to Deputy Prime Minister 5 Aug. 42

Just returned from a long but invigorating day with Eighth Army, visiting Alamein and Ruweisat and seeing South African and Australian troops, interviewing Generals Morshead, Ramsden, and Gott, spending morning with Auchinleck and afternoon with Tedder, Coningham, and the Royal Air Force. Troops were very cheerful, and all seem confident and proud of themselves, but bewildered at having been baulked of victory on repeated occasions.

I propose to visit all the formations, both forward and rear, while pondering on the recommendations I shall have to make to the Cabinet.

2. I am discussing the whole situation with Smuts, who is a fount of wisdom. Wherever the fault may lie for the serious situation which exists, it is certainly not with the troops, and only to a minor extent with their equipment.

3. I am purposely keeping my future movements vague. I am very glad the House was contented with the statement. This change and open air are doing me a great deal of good.

All the next day, the 6th, I spent with Brooke and Smuts, and in drafting the necessary telegrams to the Cabinet. The questions that had now to be settled not only affected the high personalities, but also the entire structure of command in this vast theatre. I had always felt that the name "Middle East" for Egypt, the Levant, Syria, and Turkey was ill-chosen. This was the Near East. Persia and Iraq were the Middle East; India, Burma, and Malaya the East; and China and Japan the Far East. But, far more important than changing names, I felt it necessary to divide the existing Middle East Command, which was far too diverse and expansive. Now was the time to effect this change in organisation.

Prime Minister to Deputy Prime Minister   6 Aug. 42, 8.15 P.M.

As a result of such inquiry as I have made here, and after prolonged consultations with Field-Marshal Smuts and C.I.G.S. and Minister of State, I have come to the conclusion that a drastic and immediate change is needed in the High Command.

2. I therefore propose that the Middle East Command shall be reorganised into two separate Commands, namely: (*a*) "Near East Command," comprising Egypt, Palestine, and Syria, with its centre in Cairo, and (*b*) "Middle East Command," comprising Persia and Iraq, with its centre in Basra or Baghdad.

The Eighth and Ninth Armies fall within the first and the Tenth Army in the second of these Commands.

3. General Auchinleck to be offered the post of C.-in-C. the new Middle East Command. The title remains the same, but its scope is reduced. It may however become more important later.

It also preserves General Auchinleck's association with India. It must be remembered that General Wavell's appointment as C.-in-C. India was for the duration of the war, and that the India Office have always desired that Auchinleck should return there if possible. I know of nothing that should prevent the eventual realisation of this plan, though of course no promise can be made in respect of events which are unforeseeable.

4. General Alexander to be Commander-in-Chief the Near East.

5. General Montgomery to succeed Alexander in "Torch." I regret the need of moving Alexander from "Torch," but Montgomery is in every way qualified to succeed [him in that].

6. General Gott to command the Eighth Army under Alexander.

7. General Corbett to be relieved as C.G.S. Near East.

8. General Ramsden to be relieved as G.O.C. XXXth Corps.

9. General Dorman Smith to be relieved as Deputy C.G.S.

10. It will be necessary to find two Corps Commanders for the Eighth Army in the place of Gott and Ramsden. We have ideas for both these posts, but it would be better for the C.I.G.S. to discuss these and a number of junior changes which require to be made with Gott and Alexander when the last-named arrives. . . .

12. The above constitute the major simultaneous changes which the gravity and urgency of the situation here require. I shall be grateful to my War Cabinet colleagues if they will approve them. Smuts and C.I.G.S. wish me to say they are in full agreement that amid many difficulties, and alternatives, this is the right course to pursue. The Minister of State is also in full agreement. I have no doubt the changes will impart a new and vigorous impulse to the Army and restore confidence in the Command, which I regret does not exist at the present time. Here I must emphasise the need of a new start and vehement action to animate the whole of this vast but baffled and somewhat unhinged organisation. The War Cabinet will not fail to realise that a victory over Rommel in August or September may have a decisive effect upon the attitude of the French in North Africa when "Torch" begins.

13. I hope I may receive Cabinet approval at the earliest possible moment, and that Alexander will start forthwith. It is necessary that he should reach here before I and the C.I.G.S. start for Russia. This I hope to do Sunday or Monday. The changes should become effective from Monday, and public announcements must follow at

the earliest moment, compatible with the interests of the fighting front. Meanwhile the utmost secrecy must be observed.

The War Cabinet accepted my view about drastic and immediate changes in the High Command. They warmly approved the selection of General Alexander and said that he would leave England at once. They did not however like the idea of reorganising the Middle East Command into two separate Commands. It seemed to them that the reasons which led to the setting up of the Unified Command were now stronger than they had been when the decision to do so was taken in December, 1941. They agreed that Montgomery should take Alexander's place in "Torch" and had summoned him to London at once. Finally they were content to leave it to me to settle the other appointments.

The next morning I sent the following further explanation of my proposals:

Prime Minister to Deputy Prime Minister   6/7 Aug. 42

Our proposal to divide the Command is made entirely on merits. I doubt if the disasters would have occurred in the Western Desert if General Auchinleck had not been distracted by the divergent considerations of a too widely extended front. . . . He would have taken direct command of the battle which began at the end of May but for reluctance to become "immersed in tactical problems in Libya." This phrase in itself reveals the false proportion engendered by extraneous responsibilities. It is in fact "the tactical problems of Libya" which dominate our immediate affairs.

2. The two Commands are separated by desert areas of three or four hundred miles, and the only lateral communications between them are by the railway through Turkey, which we cannot use for the passage of troops, by motor tracks across the desert, and by sea voyage round Arabia taking nearly fourteen days. Both Commands have entirely different bases of supply. . . . We are all convinced that the arrangement now proposed is sound on geographical, strategic, and administrative grounds. . . . Only the need of making an abrupt and decisive change in the command against Rommel and giving the Army the sense of a new start has induced me to propose the redistribution of Commands. I should be most reluctant

to embarrass Alexander with remote cares at a moment when all our fortunes turn upon the speedy and decisive defeat of Rommel.

I earnestly hope that my colleagues will find themselves able on further consideration of this most difficult problem to authorise me to proceed as I propose. In all this I have the complete agreement of Smuts and C.I.G.S. A decision has now become most urgent, since Alexander has already started and Auchinleck has of course no inkling of what is in prospect. I must apprise him to-morrow.

I am most grateful for the agreement of the Cabinet to the other parts of my plan, grave though they may be.

The War Cabinet replied that my telegram had not entirely removed their misgivings, but that as I was on the spot with Smuts and C.I.G.S., who both agreed with the proposal, they were prepared to authorise the action proposed. They strongly represented however that the continuance of the title of Commander-in-Chief, Middle East, if General Auchinleck were appointed to command in Persia and Iraq, would lead to confusion and misrepresentation. I saw this was right and accepted their advice.

* * * * *

I spent all August 7 visiting the 51st Scottish Division who had just landed. As I went up the stairs after dinner at the Embassy I met Colonel Jacob. "This is bad about Gott," he said. "What has happened?" "He was shot down this afternoon flying into Cairo." I certainly felt grief and impoverishment at the loss of this splendid soldier, to whom I had resolved to confide the most direct fighting task in the impending battle. All my plans were dislocated. The removal of Auchinleck from the Supreme Command was to have been balanced by the appointment to the Eighth Army of Gott, with all his Desert experience and prestige, and the whole covered by Alexander's assumption of the Middle East. What was to happen now?

Prime Minister to Deputy Prime Minister   7 Aug. 42

Deeply regret Gott has just been shot down in the air and killed.

There could be no doubt who his successor should be.

Prime Minister to Deputy Prime Minister

C.I.G.S. decisively recommends Montgomery for Eighth Army. Smuts and I feel this post must be filled at once. Pray send him by special plane at earliest moment. Advise me when he will arrive.

It appeared that the War Cabinet had already assembled at 11.15 P.M. on August 7 to deal with my telegrams of that day, which had just been decoded. Discussion was still proceeding upon them when a secretary came in with my new messages, stating that Gott was dead, and secondly asking that General Montgomery should be sent out at once. I have been told this was an acute moment for our friends in Downing Street. However, as I have several times observed, they had been through much and took it doggedly. They sat till nearly dawn, agreed in all essentials to what I had proposed, and gave the necessary orders about Montgomery.

*   *   *   *   *

When sending my message to the Cabinet telling them of Gott's death I had asked that General Eisenhower should not be told that we had proposed to give him Montgomery in place of Alexander. But this was too late: he had been told already. The further change of plan involved a consequent dislocation of a vexatious kind in the preparation of "Torch." Alexander had been chosen to command the British First Army in that great enterprise. He had already started to work with General Eisenhower. They were getting on splendidly together, as they always did. Now Alexander had been taken from him for the Middle East. Ismay was sent to convey the news and my apologies to Eisenhower for this break in continuity and disturbance of contacts which the hard necessity of war compelled. Ismay dilated upon Montgomery's brilliant qualities as a commander in the field. Montgomery arrived at Eisenhower's headquarters almost immediately, and all the civilities of a meeting of this kind between the commanders of armies of different nations woven into a single enterprise had been discharged. The very next morning,

the 8th, Eisenhower had to be informed that Montgomery must
fly that day to Cairo to command the Eighth Army. This task
also fell to Ismay. Eisenhower was a broad-minded man, practical, serviceable, dealing with events as they came, in cool selflessness. He naturally however felt disconcerted by the two
changes in two days in this vital post in the vast operation confided to him. He was now to welcome a third British Commander. Can we wonder that he asked Ismay, "Are the British
really taking 'Torch' seriously?" Nevertheless the death of Gott
was a war fact which a good soldier understood. General
Anderson was appointed to fill the vacancy, and Montgomery
started for the airfield with Ismay, who thus had an hour or
more to give him the background of these sudden changes.

A story — alas, not authenticated — has been told of this conversation. Montgomery spoke of the trials and hazards of a
soldier's career. He gave his whole life to his profession, and
lived long years of study and self-restraint. Presently fortune
smiled, there came a gleam of success, he gained advancement,
opportunity presented itself, he had a great command. He won
a victory, he became world-famous, his name was on every lip.
Then the luck changed. At one stroke all his life's work
flashed away, perhaps through no fault of his own, and he was
flung into the endless catalogue of military failures. "But,"
expostulated Ismay, "you ought not to take it so badly as all
that. A very fine army is gathering in the Middle East. It may
well be that you are not going to disaster." "What!" cried
Montgomery, sitting up in the car. "What do you mean? I was
talking about Rommel!"

* * * * *

I spent the 8th with the Yeomanry Division. These fine
troops, hitherto wasted and never yet effectively engaged with
the enemy, were camped along the Kassassin road. For two
years they had served in the Middle East, mainly in Palestine,
and I had not been able to have them equipped and worked up
to the high quality of which they were capable. At last they
had reached the back of the front and were to go into action.

Now, at this moment in their career, it had been necessary to take all their tanks from them in order to feed and rearm the fighting line. This was a staggering blow for these eager men. It was my task to go from brigade to brigade and explain to all the officers gathered together, two or three hundred at a time, why they must suffer this mutilation after all their zeal and toil. But I had good news as well. The three hundred Shermans were already approaching through the Red Sea, and in a fortnight the division would begin to be armed with the most powerful armoured vehicles current at that time. I told them the story of my morning with the President and General Marshall on the morrow of Tobruk; how these Shermans had been longed and thirsted for by the 1st United States Armoured Division, and how they had been taken from them almost as soon as they had been issued in order to give us a chance — or perhaps I said the certainty — of saving Alexandria, Cairo, and Egypt from conquest. They had the Shermans. They would become the leading armoured unit in the world. I think they were consoled by this.

I clattered back on the long road to Cairo, and reached the city before 5 P.M.

* * * * *

I now had to inform General Auchinleck that he was to be relieved of his command, and, having learned from the past that that kind of unpleasant thing is better done by writing than orally, I sent Colonel Jacob by air to his headquarters with the following letter:

CAIRO
August 8, 1942

Dear General Auchinleck,

On June 23 you raised in your telegram to the C.I.G.S. the question of your being relieved in this Command, and you mentioned the name of General Alexander as a possible successor. At that time of crisis for the Army His Majesty's Government did not wish to avail themselves of your high-minded offer. At the same time you had taken over the effective command of the battle, as I had long desired and had suggested to you in my telegram of May 20. You stemmed the adverse tide, and at the present time the front is stabilised.

2. The War Cabinet have now decided, for the reasons which you yourself had used, that the moment has come for a change. It is proposed to detach Iraq and Persia from the present Middle Eastern theatre. Alexander will be appointed to command the Middle East, Montgomery to command the Eighth Army, and I offer you the command of Iraq and Persia, including the Tenth Army, with headquarters at Basra or Baghdad. It is true that this sphere is today smaller than the Middle East, but it may in a few months become the scene of decisive operations, and reinforcements for the Tenth Army are already on the way. In this theatre, of which you have special experience, you will preserve your associations with India. I hope therefore that you will comply with my wish and directions with the same disinterested public spirit that you have shown on all occasions. Alexander will arrive almost immediately, and I hope that early next week, subject of course to the movements of the enemy, it may be possible to effect the transfer of responsibility on the Western battle-front with the utmost smoothness and efficiency.

3. I shall be very glad to see you at any convenient time if you should so desire.

Believe me
Yours sincerely
WINSTON S. CHURCHILL

PS. Colonel Jacob, who bears this letter, is also charged by me to express my sympathy in the sudden loss of General Gott.

I kept the President fully informed.

Former Naval Person to President Roosevelt   8 Aug. 42

You will no doubt have seen the cables sent by the British Chiefs of Staff, London, to the combined Chiefs of Staff, Washington, about accelerating the date of "Torch." I am sure that nothing is more vital than this, and that superhuman efforts should be made. Every day counts. I have already telegraphed to London welcoming the appointment of General Eisenhower as Allied Commander-in-Chief for "Torch," and the British Chiefs are co-operating with him to the full. . . .

I have been busy here with a reorganisation of the High Command which was necessary. I am detaching Iraq and Persia from the Middle East Command and transferring General Auchinleck there. Alexander will succeed him as Commander-in-Chief, Middle East. General Gott, who was to have been appointed to command Eighth Army under Alexander, was killed yesterday. I propose to appoint General Montgomery in his place. This will promote the utmost concentration upon the battle. A victory here might have a decisive effect upon the attitude of the French towards "Torch."

*   *   *   *   *

In the evening Jacob returned. Auchinleck had received this stroke with soldierly dignity. He was unwilling to accept the new command, and would come to see me the next day.

Jacob's diary records:

The Prime Minister was asleep. He awoke at six o'clock, and I had to recount to him as best I could what had passed between me and General Auchinleck. C.I.G.S. joined us . . . . The Prime Minister's mind is entirely fixed on the defeat of Rommel, and on getting General Alexander into complete charge of the operations in the Western Desert. He does not understand how a man can remain in Cairo while great events are occurring in the Desert and leave the conduct of them to someone else. He strode up and down declaiming on this point, and he means to have his way. "Rommel, Rommel, Rommel, Rommel!" he cried. "What else matters but beating him?"

On the morning of August 9 General Alexander arrived, and breakfasted with the C.I.G.S. and me.

General Auchinleck reached Cairo just after midday, and we had an hour's conversation, which was at once bleak and impeccable.

I telegraphed accordingly.

Prime Minister to General Ismay   10 Aug. 42

. . . General Auchinleck is disinclined to accept the command of the Iraq-Persia theatre. . . . As however I am convinced that he is the best man for the job, I have given him a few days more to consider the matter further. I shall not press him unduly, but I am anxious that he should not take his decision while under the immediate effects of the blow, which he has accepted with dignity, but naturally not without distress.

Appropriate military authorities are studying the problem connected with the proposed institution of a separate command for Iraq and Persia and the administrative changes consequent thereupon. I should be glad if at the same time the Chiefs of Staff would also propose the best methods for giving effect to the policy. General Smuts has returned to South Africa, but C.I.G.S. and General Alexander share my conviction that this separation is desirable at the present time. . . .

I wrote further to General Auchinleck the same day:

On my return journey I propose to hold a conference at Baghdad on the 14th or 15th in order to discuss, *inter alia,* the machinery of an independent command for Iraq and Persia. . . .

By then I should like to know whether you feel able to undertake the very difficult and serious task which I proposed to you. If, as I trust will be the case, you feel wholeheartedly that you can take your station in the line I hope you will meet me in Baghdad, providing of course that the transference of command has been effected here.

General Alexander came to see me that evening, and final arrangements for the changes in command were drafted. I reported the details to London:

Prime Minister to General Ismay, for those concerned   10 Aug. 42

You should announce at once that General Gott has been killed in action.

2. On the 8th I informed General Auchinleck by letter of the decision which had been reached, and yesterday, 9th, he visited me here. The transfer of responsibility will be effected in three days from the 9th unless General Alexander asks for a few more days, which is unlikely. Alexander will inform you when the transfer is complete, and thereupon you should make an announcement in the following form:

(*a*) General Alexander has assumed command of His Majesty's forces in the Middle East, in succession to General Auchinleck.

Most Secret

**BRITISH EMBASSY,
CAIRO.**

Direction to General Alexander
Commander in Chief in the Middle East

1. Yr prime & main duty will be to take
or destroy at the earliest opportunity the German-
Italian Army commanded by Field Marshal
Rommel together with all its supplies &
establishments in Egypt & Libya.

2. You will discharge or cause to be discharged
such other duties as pertain to Yr Command
without prejudice to the task described in
paragraph 1, wh. must be considered paramount
in His Majesty's interests.

W.C.
10. Aug. 42

[signature]
10.8.42

(*b*) General Montgomery has been appointed to command the Eighth Army, in succession to General Ritchie.

(*c*) General McCreery has been appointed Chief of Staff to General Alexander.

(*d*) General Lumsden, who has recovered from his wound, has been appointed to the command of the XXXth Corps, vice General Gott, killed in action.

3. While strict secrecy must be observed till General Alexander's report that he has taken over is received, it would seem desirable that the Minister of Information should explain to the newspaper proprietors and/or editors in confidence beforehand what is intended, and impress upon them the importance of giving the Army of the Western Desert the utmost stimulus from these drastic changes in the High Command. Similar action will be taken here by the Minister of State.

7. I have given General Alexander the following directive, which is most agreeable to him, and in which C.I.G.S. concurs:

> "Your prime and main duty will be to take or destroy at the earliest opportunity the German-Italian Army commanded by Field-Marshal Rommel, together with all its supplies and establishments in Egypt and Libya.
>
> "2. You will discharge or cause to be discharged such other duties as pertain to your Command, without prejudice to the task described in paragraph 1, which must be considered paramount in His Majesty's interests."

It may no doubt be possible in a later phase of the war to alter the emphasis of this directive, but I am sure that simplicity of task and singleness of aim are imperative now.[2]

Alexander's reply sent six months later will be recorded in due course.

2 See page 457.

I first offered the Middle East Command to General Brooke. He would of course have greatly liked this high operational appointment, and I knew that no man would fill it better. He thought it over, and had a long talk the next morning with General Smuts. Finally he replied that he had been C.I.G.S. for only eight months, he believed he had my full confidence, and the Staff machine was working very smoothly. Another change at this moment might cause a temporary dislocation at this critical time. It may well be also that out of motives of delicacy he did not wish to be responsible for advising General Auchinleck's supersession and then taking the post himself. His reputation stood too high for such imputations; but I had now to look elsewhere.

4

Moscow

The First Meeting

*My Journey to Moscow — Mr. Harriman Comes with Me — Over
the Mountains to Teheran — The Shah's Summer Palace —
Conference about the Trans-Persian Railway — Teheran to
Moscow — The Caspian and the Volga — Arrival in Moscow —
State Villa Number Seven — Meeting with Stalin in the Kremlin
— A Bleak Opening — "No Second Front in 1942" — Hard
Words — A Dark Background Created — I Unfold the "Torch"
Plan — I Draw My Crocodile — Stalin's Masterly Comprehen-
sion — "May God Prosper this Undertaking" — The End of a
Long Day.*

URING MY STAY in Cairo preparations had gone forward
for the journey to Moscow.

On August 4 I had telegraphed to Stalin:

Prime Minister to Premier Stalin   4 Aug. 42

We plan to leave here one day, arriving Moscow the next with
intermediate stop at Teheran.

Details will have to be arranged in part by our R.A.F.
authorities in Teheran in consultation with yours. I hope you
may instruct latter to give the benefit of their assistance in every
way.

I cannot yet give any indication regarding dates beyond what
I have already suggested to you.

I was also anxious that the Americans should play a close
part in the coming talks.

Former Naval Person to President Roosevelt 5 Aug. 42

I should greatly like to have your aid and countenance in my talks with Joe. Would you be able to let Averell come with me? I feel that things would be easier if we all seemed to be together. I have a somewhat raw job. Kindly duplicate your reply to London. Am keeping my immediate movements vague.

President Roosevelt to Former Naval Person (Cairo) 5 Aug. 42

I am asking Harriman to leave at earliest possible moment for Moscow. I think your idea is sound, and I am telling Stalin Harriman will be at his and your disposal to help in any way.

Harriman joined me in Cairo in time to come with us.

* * * * *

Late on the night of August 10, after a dinner of notables at the genial Cairo Embassy, we started for Moscow. My party, which filled three planes, now included the C.I.G.S., General Wavell, who spoke Russian, Air Marshal Tedder, and Sir Alexander Cadogan. Averell Harriman and I travelled together. By dawn we were approaching the mountains of Kurdistan. The weather was good and Vanderkloot in high spirits. As we drew near to these serrated uplands I asked him at what height he intended to fly them. He said nine thousand feet would do. However, looking at the map I found several peaks of eleven and twelve thousand feet, and there seemed one big one of eighteen or twenty thousand, though that was farther off. So long as you are not suddenly encompassed by clouds, you can wind your way through mountains with safety. Still, I asked for twelve thousand feet, and we began sucking our oxygen tubes. As we descended about 8.30 A.M. on the Teheran airfield and were already close to the ground I noticed the altimeter registered four thousand five hundred feet, and ignorantly remarked, "You had better get that adjusted before we take off again." But Vanderkloot said, "The Teheran airfield is over four thousand feet above sea-level."

Sir Reader Bullard, His Majesty's Minister in Teheran, met

me on arrival. He was a tough Briton, with long experience of Persia and no illusions.

We were too late to leap the northern range of the Elburz Mountains before dark, and I found myself graciously bidden to lunch with the Shah in a palace with a lovely swimming-pool amid great trees on an abrupt spur of the mountains. The mighty peak I had noticed in the morning gleamed brilliant pink and orange. In the afternoon, in the garden of the British Legation, there was a long conference with Averell Harriman and various high British and American railway authorities, and it was decided that the United States should take over the whole Trans-Persian railway from the Gulf to the Caspian. This railway, newly completed by a British firm, was a remarkable engineering achievement. There were 390 major bridges on its track through the mountain gorges. Harriman said the President was willing to undertake the entire responsibility for working it to full capacity, and could provide locomotives, rolling-stock, and skilled men in military units to an extent impossible for us. I therefore agreed to this transfer, subject to stipulations about priority for our essential military requirements. On account of the heat and noise of Teheran, where every Persian seems to have a motorcar and blows his horn continually, I slept amid tall trees at the summer residence of the British Legation about a thousand feet above the city.

At 6.30 next morning, Wednesday, August 12, we started, gaining height as we flew through the great valley which led to Tabriz, and then turned northward to Enzeli, on the Caspian. We passed this second range of mountains at about eleven thousand feet, avoiding both clouds and peaks. Two Russian officers were now in the plane, and the Soviet Government assumed responsibility for our course and safe arrival. The snow-clad giant gleamed to the eastward. I noticed that we were flying alone, and a wireless message explained that our second plane, with the C.I.G.S., Wavell, Cadogan, and others, had had to turn back over Teheran because of engine trouble. In two hours the waters of the Caspian Sea shone ahead.

Beneath was Enzeli. I had never seen the Caspian, but I remembered how a quarter of a century before I had, as Secretary of State for War, inherited a fleet upon it which for nearly a year ruled its pale, placid waters. We now came down to a height where oxygen was no longer needed. On the western shore, which we could dimly see, lay Baku and its oilfields. The German armies were now so near the Caspian that our course was set for Kuibyshev, keeping well away from Stalingrad and the battle area. This took us near the delta of the Volga. As far as the eye could reach, spread vast expanses of Russia, brown and flat and with hardly a sign of human habitation. Here and there sharp rectilineal patches of ploughed land revealed an occasional State farm. For a long way the mighty Volga gleamed in curves and stretches as it flowed between its wide, dark margins of marsh. Sometimes a road, straight as a ruler, ran from one wide horizon to the other. After an hour or so of this I clambered back along the bomb bay to the cabin and slept.

I pondered on my mission to this sullen, sinister Bolshevik State I had once tried so hard to strangle at its birth, and which, until Hitler appeared, I had regarded as the mortal foe of civilised freedom. What was it my duty to say to them now? General Wavell, who had literary inclinations, summed it all up in a poem. There were several verses, and the last line of each was, "No Second Front in nineteen forty-two." It was like carrying a large lump of ice to the North Pole. Still, I was sure it was my duty to tell them the facts personally and have it all out face to face with Stalin, rather than trust to telegrams and intermediaries. At least it showed that one cared for their fortunes and understood what their struggle meant to the general war. We had always hated their wicked régime, and, till the German flail beat upon them, they would have watched us being swept out of existence with indifference and gleefully divided with Hitler our Empire in the East.

The weather being clear, the wind favourable, and my need to get to Moscow urgent, it was arranged to cut the corner of

Kuibyshev and go on straight to the capital. I fear a splendid
banquet and welcome in true Russian hospitality was thus left
on one side. At about five o'clock the spires and domes of
Moscow came in sight. We circled around the city by carefully
prescribed courses along which all the batteries had been
warned, and landed on this airfield which I was to revisit
during the struggle.

Here was Molotov at the head of a concourse of Russian
generals and the entire Diplomatic Corps, with the very large
outfit of photographers and reporters customary on these
occasions. A strong guard of honour faultless in attire and
military punctilio was inspected, and marched past after the
band had played the national anthems of the three Great
Powers whose unity spelt Hitler's doom. I was taken to the
microphone and made a short speech. Averell Harriman spoke
on behalf of the United States. He was to stay at the American
Embassy. M. Molotov drove me in his car to my appointed
residence, eight miles out of Moscow, "State Villa No. 7."
While going through the streets of Moscow, which seemed
very empty, I lowered the window for a little more air, and
to my surprise felt that the glass was over two inches thick.
This surpassed all records in my experience. "The Minister
says it is 'more prudent,' " said Interpreter Pavlov. In a little
more than half an hour we reached the villa.

*   *   *   *   *

Everything was prepared with totalitarian lavishness. There
was placed at my disposal, as aide-de-camp, an enormous,
splendid-looking officer (I believe of a princely family under
the Czarist régime), who also acted as our host and was a model
of courtesy and attention. A number of veteran servants in
white jackets and beaming smiles waited on every wish or
movement of the guests. A long table in the dining-room and
various sideboards were laden with every delicacy and stimulant
that supreme power can command. I was conducted through a
spacious reception room to a bedroom and bathroom of almost
equal size. Blazing, almost dazzling, electric lights displayed

the spotless cleanliness. The hot and cold water gushed. I longed for a hot bath after the length and the heat of the journey. All was instantly prepared. I noticed that the basins were not fed by separate hot and cold water taps and that they had no plugs. Hot and cold turned on at once through a single spout, mingled to exactly the temperature one desired. Moreover, one did not wash one's hands in the basins, but under the flowing current of the taps. In a modest way I have adopted this system at home. If there is no scarcity of water it is far the best.

After all necessary immersions and ablutions we were regaled in the dining-room with every form of choice food and liquor, including of course caviare and vodka, but with many other dishes and wines from France and Germany, far beyond our mood or consuming powers. Besides, we had but little time before starting for Moscow. I had told Molotov that I should be ready to see Stalin that night, and he proposed seven o'clock.

I reached the Kremlin, and met for the first time the great Revolutionary Chief and profound Russian statesman and warrior with whom for the next three years I was to be in intimate, rigorous, but always exciting, and at times even genial, association. Our Conference lasted nearly four hours. As our second airplane had not arrived with Brooke, Wavell, and Cadogan, there were present only Stalin, Molotov, Voroshilov, myself, Harriman, and our Ambassador, with interpreters. I have based this account upon the record which we kept, subject to my own memory, and to the telegrams I sent home at the time.

The first two hours were bleak and sombre. I began at once with the question of the Second Front, saying that I wished to speak frankly and would like to invite complete frankness from Stalin. I would not have come to Moscow unless he had felt sure that he would be able to discuss realities. When M. Molotov had come to London I had told him that we were trying to make plans for a diversion in France. I had also made it clear to M. Molotov that I could make no promises about 1942, and had given M. Molotov a memorandum to this

effect. Since then an exhaustive Anglo-American examination
of the problem had been carried out. The British and American Governments did not feel themselves able to undertake a
major operation in September, which was the latest month in
which the weather was to be counted upon. But, as M. Stalin
knew, they were preparing for a very great operation in 1943. For
this purpose a million American troops were now scheduled to
reach the United Kingdom at their point of assembly in the
spring of 1943, making an expeditionary force of twenty-seven
divisions, to which the British Government were prepared to
add twenty-one divisions. Nearly half of this force would be
armoured. So far only two and a half American divisions had
reached the United Kingdom, but the big transportation would
take place in October, November, and December.

I told Stalin that I was well aware that this plan offered no
help to Russia in 1942, but thought it possible that when the
1943 plan was ready it might well be that the Germans would
have a stronger army in the West than they now had. At this
point Stalin's face crumpled up into a frown, but he did not
interrupt. I then said I had good reasons against an attack on
the French coast in 1942. We had only enough landing-craft
for an assault landing on a fortified coast — enough to throw
ashore six divisions and maintain them. If it were successful,
more divisions might be sent, but the limiting factor was
landing-craft, which were now being built in very large numbers in the United Kingdom, and especially in the United
States. For one division which could be carried this year it
would be possible next year to carry eight or ten times as many.

Stalin, who had begun to look very glum, seemed unconvinced
by my argument, and asked if it was impossible to attack any
part of the French coast. I showed him a map which indicated
the difficulties of making an air umbrella anywhere except
actually across the Straits. He did not seem to understand, and
asked some questions about the range of fighter planes. Could
they not, for instance, come and go all the time? I explained
that they could indeed come and go, but at this range they
would have no time to fight, and I added that an air umbrella

to be of any use had to be kept open. He then said that there
was not a single German division in France of any value, a
statement which I contested. There were in France twenty-five
German divisions, nine of which were of the first line. He
shook his head. I said that I had brought the Chief of the
Imperial General Staff and General Sir Archibald Wavell with
me in order that such points might be examined in detail with
the Russian General Staff. There was a point beyond which
statesmen could not carry discussions of this kind.

Stalin, whose glumness had by now much increased, said that,
as he understood it, we were unable to create a second front
with any large force and unwilling even to land six divisions. I
said that this was so. We could land six divisions, but the
landing of them would be more harmful than helpful, for it
would greatly injure the big operation planned for next year.
War was war but not folly, and it would be folly to invite a
disaster which would help nobody. I said I feared the news I
brought was not good news. If by throwing in 150,000 to
200,000 men we could render him aid by drawing away from
the Russian front appreciable German forces, we would not
shrink from this course on the grounds of loss. But if it drew
no men away and spoiled the prospects for 1943 it would be a
great error.

Stalin, who had become restless, said that his view about war
was different. A man who was not prepared to take risks could
not win a war. Why were we so afraid of the Germans? He
could not understand. His experience showed that troops must
be blooded in battle. If you did not blood your troops you had
no idea what their value was. I inquired whether he had ever
asked himself why Hitler did not come to England in 1940,
when he was at the height of his power and we had only 20,000
trained troops, 200 guns, and 50 tanks. He did not come. The
fact was that Hitler was afraid of the operation. It is not so
easy to cross the Channel. Stalin replied that this was no
analogy. The landing of Hitler in England would have been
resisted by the people, whereas in the case of a British landing
in France the people would be on the side of the British. I

pointed out that it was all the more important therefore not to expose the people of France, by a withdrawal, to the vengeance of Hitler and to waste them when they would be needed in the big operation in 1943.

There was an oppressive silence. Stalin, at length said that if we could not make a landing in France this year he was not entitled to demand it or to insist upon it, but he was bound to say that he did not agree with my arguments.

*   *   *   *   *

I then unfolded a map of Southern Europe, the Mediterranean, and North Africa. What was "A Second Front"? Was it only a landing on a fortified coast opposite England? Or could it take the form of some other great enterprise which might be useful to the common cause? I thought it better to bring him southward by steps. If, for instance, we could hold the enemy in the Pas de Calais by our concentration in Britain, and at the same time attack elsewhere — for instance, in the Loire, the Gironde, or alternatively the Scheldt — this was full of promise. There indeed was a general picture of next year's big operation. Stalin feared that it was not practicable. I said that it would indeed be difficult to land a million men, but that we should have to persevere and try.

We then passed on to the bombing of Germany, which gave general satisfaction. M. Stalin emphasised the importance of striking at the morale of the German population. He said he attached the greatest importance to bombing, and that he knew our raids were having a tremendous effect in Germany.

After this interlude which relieved the tension, Stalin observed that from our long talk, it seemed that all we were going to do was no "Sledgehammer," no "Round-up," and pay our way by bombing Germany. I decided to get the worst over first and to create a suitable background for the project I had come to unfold. I did not therefore try at once to relieve the gloom. Indeed I asked specially that there should be the plainest speaking between friends and comrades in peril. However, courtesy and dignity prevailed.

*   *   *   *   *

The moment had now come to bring "Torch" into action. I said that I wanted to revert to the question of a second front in 1942, which was what I had come for. I did not think France was the only place for such an operation. There were other places, and we and the Americans had decided upon another plan, which I was authorised by the American President to impart to Stalin secretly. I would now proceed to do so. I emphasised the vital need of secrecy. At this Stalin sat up and grinned and said that he hoped that nothing about it would appear in the British press.

I then explained precisely Operation "Torch."

As I told the whole story Stalin became intensely interested. His first question was what would happen in Spain and Vichy France. A little later on he remarked that the operation was militarily right, but he had political doubts about the effect on France. He asked particularly about the timing, and I said not later than October 30, but the President and all of us were trying to pull it forward to October 7. This seemed a great relief to the three Russians.

I then described the military advantages of freeing the Mediterranean, whence still another front could be opened. In September we must win in Egypt, and in October in North Africa, all the time holding the enemy in Northern France. If we could end the year in possession of North Africa we could threaten the belly of Hitler's Europe, and this operation should be considered in conjunction with the 1943 operation. That was what we and the Americans had decided to do.

To illustrate my point I had meanwhile drawn a picture of a crocodile, and explained to Stalin with the help of this picture how it was our intention to attack the soft belly of the crocodile as we attacked his hard snout. And Stalin, whose interest was now at high pitch, said: "May God prosper this undertaking."

I emphasised that we wanted to take the strain off the Russians. If we attempted that in Northern France we should meet with a rebuff. If we tried in North Africa we had a good chance of victory, and then we could help in Europe. If we

could gain North Africa Hitler would have to bring his Air
Force back, or otherwise we would destroy his allies, even, for
instance, Italy, and make a landing. The operation would have
an important influence on Turkey and on the whole of
Southern Europe, and all I was afraid of was that we might be
forestalled. If North Africa were won this year we could make
a deadly attack upon Hitler next year. This marked the turning-point in our conversation.

Stalin then began to present various political difficulties.
Would not an Anglo-American seizure of "Torch" regions be
misunderstood in France? What were we doing about de
Gaulle? I said that at this stage we did not wish him to intervene in the operation. The [Vichy] French were likely to fire
on de Gaullists but unlikely to fire on Americans. Harriman
backed this very strongly by referring to reports, on which the
President relied, by American agents all over "Torch" territories and also to Admiral Leahy's opinion.

*   *   *   *   *

At this point Stalin seemed suddenly to grasp the strategic
advantages of "Torch." He recounted four main reasons for it.

First, it would hit Rommel in the back;

Second, it would overawe Spain;

Third, it would produce fighting between Germans and
Frenchmen in France; and,

Fourth, it would expose Italy to the whole brunt of the war.

I was deeply impressed with this remarkable statement. It
showed the Russian Dictator's swift and complete mastery of
a problem hitherto novel to him. Very few people alive could
have comprehended in so few minutes the reasons which we
had all so busily been wrestling with for months. He saw it all
in a flash.

I mentioned a fifth reason, namely, the shortening of the sea
route through the Mediterranean. Stalin was concerned to
know whether we were able to pass through the Straits of
Gibraltar. I said, it would be all right. I also told him about
the changes of command in Egypt, and of our determination

to fight a decisive battle there in late August or September. Finally, it was clear that they all liked "Torch," though Molotov asked whether it could not be in September.

I then added: "France is down and we want to cheer her up." France had understood Madagascar and Syria. The arrival of the Americans would send the French nation over to our side. It would intimidate Franco. The Germans might well say at once to the French, "Give us your fleet and Toulon." This would stir anew the antagonisms between Vichy and Hitler.

I then opened the prospect of our placing an Anglo-American Air Force on the southern flank of the Russian armies in order to defend the Caspian and the Caucasian mountains and generally to fight in this theatre. I did not however go into details, as of course we had to win our battle in Egypt first, and I had not the President's plans for the American contribution. If Stalin liked the idea we would set to work in detail upon it. He replied that they would be most grateful for this aid, but that the details of location, etc., would require study. I was very keen on this project, because it would bring about more hard fighting between the Anglo-American air-power and the Germans, all of which aided the gaining of mastery in the air under more fertile conditions than looking for trouble over the Pas de Calais.

We then gathered round a large globe, and I explained to Stalin the immense advantages of clearing the enemy out of the Mediterranean. I told Stalin I should be available should he wish to see me again. He replied that the Russian custom was that the visitor should state his wishes and that he was ready to receive me at any time. He now knew the worst and yet we parted in an atmosphere of good will.

The meeting had now lasted nearly four hours. It took half an hour or more to reach State Villa No. 7. Tired as I was, I dictated my telegram to the War Cabinet and President Roosevelt after midnight, and then, with the feeling that at least the ice was broken and a human contact established, I slept soundly and long.

5

MOSCOW

A RELATIONSHIP ESTABLISHED

A Talk with Molotov — Amenities of the State Villa — Second Meeting with Stalin in the Kremlin — His Complaints about Supplies — He Demands Higher Sacrifices from the Allies — My Rejoinder — Painful Passages — The Problem of the Caucasus — Stalin's Aide-Mémoire — My Reply of August 14 — Banquet at the Kremlin, August 14 — A Friendly Interlude — We Stir Old Quarrels — "The Past Belongs to God" — Abortive Meeting of the Military Staffs — General Brooke's Misgivings about the Caucasus — I Go to Say Good-bye to Stalin, August 15 — His Confidence about the Caucasus — He Invites Me to an Improvised Dinner — Molotov Joins Us — Six Hours of Talk — Stalin on the Collective Farm Policy — The Joint Anglo-Soviet Communiqué — Arrival at Teheran — My Report to the War Cabinet and to President Roosevelt — A Sense of Encouragement.

LATE THE NEXT MORNING I awoke in my luxurious quarters. It was Thursday, August 13 — to me always "Blenheim Day." I had arranged to visit Molotov in the Kremlin at noon in order to explain to him more clearly and fully the character of the various operations we had in mind. I pointed out how injurious to the common cause it would be if owing to recriminations about dropping "Sledgehammer" we were forced to argue publicly against such enterprises. I also explained in more detail the political setting of "Torch." He listened affably, but contributed nothing. I proposed to him that I should see Stalin at 10 that night, and later in the day got word that eleven o'clock would be more convenient, and that, as the subjects to be dealt with would be the same as those of the night before, would I wish to bring Harriman? I said "Yes," and also Cadogan, Brooke, Wavell, and Tedder, who had meanwhile arrived safely from Teheran in a Russian plane. They might have had a very dangerous fire in their Liberator.

Before leaving this urbane, rigid diplomatist's room I turned to him and said, "Stalin will make a great mistake to treat us roughly when we have come so far." For the first time Molotov unbent. "Stalin," he said, "is a very wise man. You may be sure that, however he argues, he understands all. I will tell him what you say."

* * * * *

I returned in time for luncheon to State Villa Number Seven. Out of doors the weather was beautiful. It was just like what we love most in England — when we get it. I thought we would explore the domain. State Villa Number Seven was a fine, large, brand-new country house standing in its own extensive lawns and gardens in a fir wood of about twenty acres. There were agreeable walks, and it was pleasant in the beautiful August weather to lie on the grass or pine-needles. There were several fountains, and a large glass tank filled with many kinds of goldfish, which were all so tame that they would eat out of your hand. I made a point of feeding them every day. Around the whole was a stockade, perhaps fifteen feet high, guarded on both sides by police and soldiers in considerable numbers. About a hundred yards from the house was an air-raid shelter. At the first opportunity we were conducted over it. It was of the latest and most luxurious type. Lifts at either end took you down eighty or ninety feet into the ground. Here were eight or ten large rooms inside a concrete box of massive thickness. The rooms were divided from each other by heavy sliding doors. The lights were brilliant. The furniture was stylish "Utility," sumptuous and brightly coloured. I was more attracted by the goldfish.

* * * * *

We all repaired to the Kremlin at 11 P.M., and were received only by Stalin and Molotov, with their interpreter. Then began a most unpleasant discussion. Stalin handed me a document. When it was translated I said I would answer it in writing, and that he must understand we had made up our minds upon the course to be pursued and that reproaches were vain. Thereafter we argued for about two hours, during which he said a great many disagreeable things, especially about our being too much afraid of fighting the Germans, and if we tried it like the Russians we should find it not so bad; that we had broken our promise about "Sledgehammer"; that we had failed in delivering the supplies promised to Russia and only sent remnants after we had taken all we needed for ourselves. Apparently these complaints were addressed as much to the United States as to Britain.

I repulsed all his contentions squarely, but without taunts of any kind. I suppose he is not used to being contradicted repeatedly, but he did not become at all angry, or even animated. He reiterated his view that it should be possible for the British and Americans to land six or eight divisions on the Cherbourg peninsula, since they had domination of the air. He felt that if the British Army had been fighting the Germans as much as the Russian Army it would not be so frightened of them. The Russians, and indeed the R.A.F., had shown that it was possible to beat the Germans. The British infantry could do the same provided they acted at the same time as the Russians.

I interposed that I pardoned the remarks which Stalin had made on account of the bravery of the Russian Army. The proposal for a landing in Cherbourg overlooked the existence of the Channel. Finally Stalin said we could carry it no further. He must accept our decision. He then abruptly invited us to dinner at eight o'clock the next night.

Accepting the invitation, I said I would leave by plane at dawn the following morning — i.e., 15th. Joe seemed somewhat concerned at this, and asked could I not stay longer. I said certainly, if there was any good to be done, and that I would wait one more day anyhow. I then exclaimed there was no ring of comradeship in his attitude. I had travelled far to establish good working relations. We had done our utmost to help Russia, and would continue to do so. We had been left entirely alone for a year against Germany and Italy. Now that the three great nations were allied, victory was certain, provided we did not fall apart, and so forth. I was somewhat animated in this passage, and before it could be translated he made the remark that he liked the tone of my utterance. Thereafter the talk began in a somewhat less tense atmosphere.

He plunged into a long discussion of two Russian trench mortars firing rockets, which he declared were devastating in their effects, and which he offered to demonstrate to our experts if they could wait. He said he would let us have all information about them, but should there not be something in return? Should there not be an agreement to exchange information about inventions? I said that we would give them everything without any bargaining, except only those devices which, if carried in aeroplanes over the enemy lines and shot down, would make our bombing of Germany more difficult. He accepted this. He also agreed that his military authorities should meet our generals, and this was arranged for three o'clock in the afternoon. I said they would require at least four hours to go fully into the various technical questions involved in "Sledgehammer," "Round-up," and "Torch." He observed at one moment that "Torch" was "militarily correct," but that the political side required more delicacy — i.e., more careful handling. From time to time he returned to "Sledgehammer," grumbling about it. When he said our promise had not been kept I replied, "I repudiate that statement. Every promise has been kept," and I pointed to the *aide-mémoire* I gave Molotov. He made a sort of apology, saying that he was expressing his sincere and honest opinions, that there was no mistrust between us, but only a difference of view.

Finally I asked about the Caucasus. Was he going to defend the mountain chain, and with how many divisions? At this he sent for a relief model, and, with apparent frankness and evi-

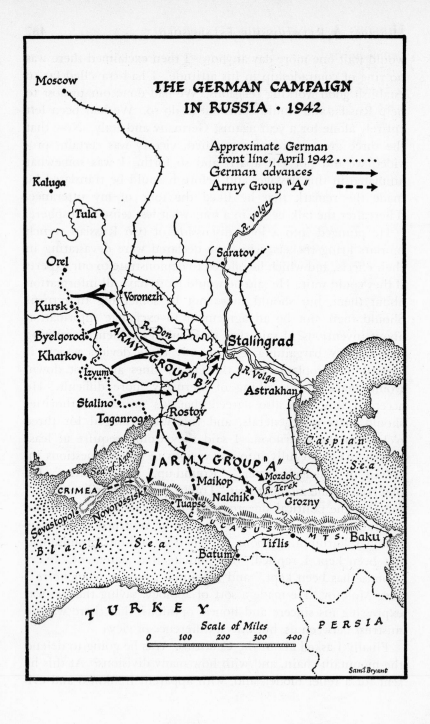

THE GERMAN CAMPAIGN
IN RUSSIA · 1942

Approximate German
front line, April 1942 · · · · · · ·
German advances
Army Group "A"

Moscow

Kaluga

Tula

Orel

Kursk

Byelgorod

Kharkov

Izyum

Stalino

Taganrog

Voronezh

R. Don

ARMY GROUP "B"

Rostov

Saratov

R. Volga

Stalingrad

R. Volga

Astrakhan

ARMY GROUP "A"

Sea of Azov

CRIMEA

Sevastopol

Novorossisk

Tuapse

Maikop

Nalchik

CAUCASUS

Mozdok

R. Terek

Grozny

Caspian
Sea

Black   Sea

Batum

Tiflis

MTS. Baku

TURKEY

PERSIA

Scale of Miles
0   100   200   300   400

Sam'l Bryant

dent knowledge, explained the strength of this barrier, for which he said twenty-five divisions were available. He pointed to the various passes and said they would be defended. I asked were they fortified, and he said, "Yes, certainly." The Russian front line, which the enemy had not yet reached, was north of the main range. He said they would have to hold out for two months, when the snow would make the mountains impassable. He declared himself quite confident of their ability to do this, and also recounted in detail the strength of the Black Sea Fleet, which was gathered at Batum.

All this part of the talk was easier, but when Harriman asked about the plans for bringing American aircraft across Siberia, to which the Russians had only recently consented after long American pressing, he replied, curtly, "Wars are not won with plans." Harriman backed me up throughout, and we neither of us yielded an inch nor spoke a bitter word.

Stalin made his salute and held out his hand to me on leaving, and I took it.

*   *   *   *   *

I reported to the War Cabinet on August 14:

We asked ourselves what was the explanation of this performance and transformation from the good ground we had reached the night before. I think the most probable is that his Council of Commissars did not take the news I brought as well as he did. They may have more power than we suppose, and less knowledge. Perhaps he was putting himself on the record for future purposes and for their benefit, and also letting off steam for his own. Cadogan says a similar hardening up followed the opening of the Eden interview at Christmas, and Harriman says that this technique was also used at the beginning of the Beaverbrook mission.

It is my considered opinion that in his heart, so far as he has one, Stalin knows we are right, and that six divisions on "Sledgehammer" would do him no good this year. Moreover, I am certain that his surefooted and quick military judgment makes him a strong supporter of "Torch." I think it not impossible that he will make amends. In that hope I persevere. Anyhow, I am sure it was better to have it out this way than any other. There was never at any time the slightest suggestion of their not fighting on, and I think myself that Stalin has good confidence that he will win.

When I thanked Stalin for the forty Boston aircraft he made a half-disdainful gesture, saying, "They are American planes. When I give you Russian planes then you may thank me." By this he did not mean to disparage the American planes, but said that he counted on his own strength.

I make great allowances for the stresses through which they are passing. Finally, I think they want full publicity for the visit.

*   *   *   *   *

The following was the *aide-mémoire* which Stalin had handed me:

13 Aug. 42

As the result of an exchange of views in Moscow which took place on August 12 of this year, I ascertained that the Prime Minister of Great Britain, Mr. Churchill, considered the organisation of a second front in Europe in 1942 to be impossible. As is well known, the organisation of a second front in Europe in 1942 was pre-decided during the sojourn of Molotov in London, and it found expression in the agreed Anglo-Soviet communiqué published on June 12 last. It is also known that the organisation of a second front in Europe has as its object the withdrawal of German forces from the Eastern Front to the West and the creation in the West of a serious base of resistance to the German-Fascist forces, and the affording of relief by this means to the situation of the Soviet forces on the Soviet-German front in 1942. It is easy to grasp that the refusal of the Government of Great Britain to create a second front in 1942 in Europe inflicts a mortal blow to the whole of Soviet public opinion, which calculates on the creation of a second front, and that it complicates the situation of the Red Army at the front and prejudices the plan of the Soviet command. I am not referring to the fact that the difficulties arising for the Red Army as a result of the refusal to create a second front in 1942 will un-doubtedly be detrimental to the military situation of England and all the remaining Allies. It appears to me *and my colleagues* [1] that the most favourable conditions exist in 1942 for the creation of a second front in Europe, inasmuch as almost all the forces of the

[1] My italics — Author.

German Army, and the best forces to boot, have been withdrawn to the Eastern Front, leaving in Europe an inconsiderable amount of forces, and these of inferior quality. It is unknown whether the year of 1943 will offer conditions for the creation of a second front as favourable as 1942.

We are of opinion therefore that it is particularly in 1942 that the creation of a second front in Europe is possible and should be effective. I was however unfortunately unsuccessful in convincing Mr. Prime Minister of Great Britain thereof, while Mr. Harriman, the representative of the President of the United States, fully supported Mr. Prime Minister in the negotiations held in Moscow.

The next morning, August 14, having rested well, I prepared, with the aid of the C.I.G.S. and Cadogan, the following reply, which seemed to me suitable and conclusive:

The best second front in 1942 and the only large-scale operation possible from the Atlantic is "Torch." If this can be effected in October it will give more aid to Russia than any other plan. It also prepares the way for 1943, and has the four advantages mentioned by Premier Stalin in the conversation of August 12. The British and United States Governments have made up their minds about this, and all preparations are proceeding with the utmost speed.

2. Compared with "Torch," the attack with six or eight Anglo-American divisions on the Cherbourg peninsula and the Channel Islands would be a hazardous and futile operation. The Germans have enough troops in the West to block us in this narrow peninsula with fortified lines, and would concentrate all their air forces in the West upon us. In the opinion of all the British naval, military, and air authorities, the operation could only end in disaster. Even if the lodgment were made it would not bring a single division back from Russia. It would also be far more a running sore for us than for the enemy, and would use up wastefully and wantonly the key men and the landing-craft required for real action in 1943. This is our settled view. The C.I.G.S. will go into details with the Russian commanders to any extent that may be desired.

3. No promise has been broken by Great Britain or the United States. I point to paragraph 5 of my *aide-mémoire* given to Mr.

Molotov on June 10, 1942, which distinctly says, "We can there-fore give no promise." This *aide-mémoire* followed upon lengthy conversations, in which the very small chance of such a plan being adopted was made abundantly clear. Several of these conversations are on record.

4. However, all the talk about an Anglo-American invasion of France this year has misled the enemy, and has held large air forces and considerable military forces on the French Channel coast. It would be injurious to all common interests, especially Russian interests, if any public controversy arose in which it would be necessary for the British Government to unfold to the nation the crushing arguments which they conceive themselves to possess against "Sledgehammer." Widespread discouragement would be caused to the Russian armies, who have been buoyed up on this subject, and the enemy would be free to withdraw further forces from the West. The wisest course is to use "Sledgehammer" as a blind for "Torch," and proclaim "Torch" when it begins as the second front. This is what we ourselves mean to do.

5. We cannot admit that the conversations with M. Molotov about the second front, safeguarded as they were by reservations both oral and written, formed any ground for altering the strategic plans of the Russian High Command.

6. We reaffirm our resolve to aid our Russian Allies by every practicable means.

*   *   *   *   *

That evening we attended the official dinner at the Kremlin, where about forty people, including several of the military commanders, members of Politburo, and other high officials were present. Stalin and Molotov did the honours in cordial fashion. These dinners were lengthy, and from the beginning many toasts were proposed and responded to in very short speeches. Silly tales have been told of how these Soviet dinners became drinking-bouts. There is no truth whatever in this. The Marshal and his colleagues invariably drank their toasts from tiny glasses, taking only a sip on each occasion. I had been well brought up.

During the dinner Stalin talked to me in lively fashion through the interpreter Pavlov. "Some years ago." he said, "we had a visit from Mr. George Bernard Shaw and Lady Astor." Lady Astor suggested that Mr. Lloyd George should be invited to visit Moscow, to which Stalin had replied, "Why should we ask him? He was the head of the intervention." On this Lady Astor said, "That is not true. It was Churchill who misled him." "Anyhow," said Stalin, "Lloyd George was head of the Government and belonged to the Left. He was responsible, and we like a downright enemy better than a pretending friend." "Well, Churchill is finished finally," said Lady Astor. "I am not so sure," Stalin had answered. "If a great crisis comes, the English people might turn to the old war-horse." At this point I interrupted, saying, "There is much in what she said. I was very active in the intervention, and I do not wish you to think otherwise." He smiled amicably, so I said, "Have you forgiven me?" "Premier Stalin, he say," said Interpreter Pavlov, "all that is in the past, and the past belongs to God."

* * * * *

In the course of one of my later talks with Stalin I said, "Lord Beaverbrook has told me that when he was on his mission to Moscow in October, 1941, you asked him, 'What did Churchill mean by saying in Parliament that he had given me warnings of the impending German attack?' I was of course," said I, "referring to the telegram I sent you in April '41," and I produced the telegram which Sir Stafford Cripps had tardily delivered. When it was read and translated to him Stalin shrugged his shoulders. "I remember it. I did not need any warnings. I knew war would come, but I thought I might gain another six months or so." In the common cause I refrained from asking what would have happened to us all if we had gone down for ever while he was giving Hitler so much valuable material, time, and aid.

* * * * *

As soon as I could I gave a more formal account of the banquet to Mr. Attlee and the President.

Former Naval Person to Deputy Prime Minister and
President Roosevelt   17 Aug. 42

The dinner passed off in a very friendly atmosphere and the
usual Russian ceremonies. Wavell made an excellent speech in
Russian. I proposed Stalin's health, and Alexander Cadogan proposed death and damnation to the Nazis. Though I sat on
Stalin's right I got no opportunity of talking about serious things.
Stalin and I were photographed together, also with Harriman.
Stalin made quite a long speech proposing the "Intelligence Service," in the course of which he made a curious reference to the
Dardanelles in 1915, saying that the British had won and the Germans and Turks were already retreating, but we did not know
because the intelligence was faulty. This picture, though inaccurate, was evidently meant to be complimentary to me.

2. I left about 1.30 A.M., as I was afraid we should be drawn into
a lengthy film and was fatigued. When I said good-bye to Stalin
he said that any differences that existed were only of method. I
said we would try to remove even those differences by deeds. After
a cordial handshake I then took my departure, and got some way
down the crowded room, but he hurried after me and accompanied
me an immense distance through corridors and staircases to the
front door, where we again shook hands.

3. Perhaps in my account to you of the Thursday night meeting
I took too gloomy a view. I feel I must make full allowance for
the really grievous disappointment which they feel here that we
can do nothing more to help them in their immense struggle. In
the upshot they have swallowed this bitter pill. Everything for us
now turns on hastening "Torch" and defeating Rommel.

*   *   *   *   *

It had been agreed between Stalin and me that there should
also be meetings between the high military authorities on
both sides. Two conferences were held on August 15.

I reported the results to Mr. Attlee and President Roosevelt
as follows:

At a conference in Moscow on Saturday [August 15], Voroshilov
and Shaposhnikov [2] met Brooke, Wavell, and Tedder, who offered
detailed reasons about no "Sledgehammer." No impression was made,

---

[2] The Russian Chief of Staff.

as the Russians, though entirely good-humoured, were acting under strict instructions. They did not even attempt to argue the matter in serious detail. After some time C.I.G.S. asked for details about the Caucasus position, to which Voroshilov replied he had no authority to speak on this point, but would ask for it. Accordingly, in the afternoon a second meeting was held, at which the Russians repeated what Stalin had said to us, to the effect that twenty-five divisions would be assigned to the defence of the Caucasus mountain line and the passages at either end, and that they believed they could hold both Batum and Baku and the Caucasus range until the winter snows greatly improved their position. However, C.I.G.S. is by no means reassured. For instance, Voroshilov stated that all the passes were fortified, but when C.I.G.S. had flown at 150 feet all up the west bank of the Caspian he only saw the northern line of defence being begun with anti-tank obstacles, pill-boxes, etc. In my private conversation with Stalin he revealed to me other solid reasons for his confidence, including a counter-offensive on a great scale, but as he asked me to keep this specially secret I will not refer to it further here. My own feeling is that it is an even chance they will hold, but C.I.G.S. will not go so far as this.

* * * * *

I had been offended by many things which had been said at our conferences. I made every allowance for the strain under which the Soviet leaders lay, with their vast front flaming and bleeding along nearly two thousand miles, and the Germans but fifty miles from Moscow and advancing towards the Caspian Sea. The technical military discussions had not gone well. Our generals had asked all sorts of questions to which their Soviet colleagues were not authorised to give answers. The only Soviet demand was for "A Second Front *now*." In the end Brooke was rather blunt, and the military conference came to a somewhat abrupt conclusion.

We were to start at dawn on the 16th. On the evening before, I went at seven o'clock to say good-bye to Stalin. We had a useful and important talk. I asked particularly whether he would be able to hold the Caucasus mountain passes, and also prevent the Germans reaching the Caspian, taking the oilfields

round Baku, with all that meant, and then driving southward
through Turkey or Persia. He spread out the map, and then
said with quiet confidence, "We shall stop them. They will
not cross the mountains." He added, "There are rumours that
the Turks will attack us in Turkestan. If they do I shall be
able to deal with them as well." I said there was no danger of
this. The Turks meant to keep out, and would certainly not
quarrel with England.

Our hour's conversation drew to its close, and I got up to
say good-bye. Stalin seemed suddenly embarrassed, and said
in a more cordial tone than he had yet used with me, "You
are leaving at daybreak. Why should we not go to my house
and have some drinks?" I said that I was in principle always
in favour of such a policy. So he led the way through many
passages and rooms till we came out into a still roadway within
the Kremlin, and in a couple of hundred yards gained the
apartment where he lived. He showed me his own rooms,
which were of moderate size, simple, dignified, and four in
number — a dining-room, working-room, bedroom, and a large
bathroom. Presently there appeared, first a very aged housekeeper and later a handsome red-haired girl, who kissed her
father dutifully. He looked at me with a twinkle in his eye,
as if, so I thought, to convey, "You see, even we Bolsheviks have
family life." Stalin's daughter started laying the table, and in
a short time the housekeeper appeared with a few dishes. Meanwhile Stalin had been uncorking various bottles, which began
to make an imposing array. Then he said, "Why should we not
have Molotov? He is worrying about the communiqué. We
could settle it here. There is one thing about Molotov — he
can drink." I then realised that there was to be a dinner. I
had planned to dine at State Villa No. 7, where General Anders,
the Polish commander, was awaiting me, but I told my new
and excellent interpreter, Major Birse, to telephone that I
should not be back till after midnight. Presently Molotov
arrived. We sat down, and, with the two interpreters, were
five in number. Major Birse had lived twenty years in Moscow,
and got on very well with the Marshal, with whom he for some

time kept up a running conversation, in which I could not share.

We actually sat at this table from 8.30 till 2.30 the next morning, which, with my previous interview, made a total of more than seven hours. The dinner was evidently improvised on the spur of the moment, but gradually more and more food arrived. We pecked and picked, as seemed to be the Russian fashion, at a long succession of choice dishes, and sipped a variety of excellent wines. Molotov assumed his most affable manner, and Stalin, to make things go, chaffed him unmercifully.

Presently we talked about the convoys to Russia. This led him to make a rough and rude remark about the almost total destruction of the Arctic convoy in June. I have recounted this incident in its place. I did not know so much about it then as I do now.

"Mr. Stalin asks," said Pavlov, with some hesitation, "has the British Navy no sense of glory?" I answered, "You must take it from me that what was done was right. I really do know a lot about the Navy and sea war." "Meaning," said Stalin, "that I know nothing." "Russia is a land animal," I said; "the British are sea animals." He fell silent and recovered his good-humour. I turned the talk on to Molotov. "Was the Marshal aware that his Foreign Secretary on his recent visit to Washington had said he was determined to pay a visit to New York entirely by himself, and that the delay in his return was not due to any defect in the aeroplane, but because he was off on his own?"

Although almost anything can be said in fun at a Russian dinner, Molotov looked rather serious at this. But Stalin's face lit with merriment as he said:

"It was not to New York he went. He went to Chicago, where the other gangsters live."

Relations having thus been entirely restored, the talk ran on. I opened the question of a British landing in Norway with Russian support, and explained how, if we could take the North Cape in the winter and destroy the Germans there,

the path of the convoys would henceforth be open. This idea
was always, as has been seen, one of my favourite plans. Stalin
seemed much attracted by it, and, after talking of ways and
means, we agreed we must do it if possible.

* * * * *

It was now past midnight, and Cadogan had not appeared
with the draft of the communiqué.

"Tell me," I asked, "have the stresses of this war been as
bad to you personally as carrying through the policy of the
Collective Farms?"

This subject immediately aroused the Marshal.

"Oh, no," he said, "the Collective Farm policy was a terrible
struggle."

"I thought you would have found it bad," said I, "because
you were not dealing with a few score thousands of aristocrats
or big landowners, but with millions of small men."

"Ten millions," he said, holding up his hands. "It was
fearful. Four years it lasted. It was absolutely necessary for
Russia, if we were to avoid periodic famines, to plough the land
with tractors. We must mechanise our agriculture. When we
gave tractors to the peasants they were all spoiled in a few
months. Only Collective Farms with workshops could handle
tractors. We took the greatest trouble to explain it to the
peasants. It was no use arguing with them. After you have said
all you can to a peasant he says he must go home and consult
his wife, and he must consult his herder." This last was a new
expression to me in this connection.

"After he has talked it over with them he always answers
that he does not want the Collective Farm and he would rather
do without the tractors."

"These were what you call Kulaks?"

"Yes," he said, but he did not repeat the word. After a pause,
"It was all very bad and difficult — but necessary."

"What happened?" I asked.

"Oh, well," he said, "many of them agreed to come in with
us. Some of them were given land of their own to cultivate in

the province of Tomsk or the province of Irkutsk or farther north, but the great bulk were very unpopular and were wiped out by their labourers."

There was a considerable pause. Then, "Not only have we vastly increased the food supply, but we have improved the quality of the grain beyond all measure. All kinds of grain used to be grown. Now no one is allowed to sow any but the standard Soviet grain from one end of our country to the other. If they do they are severely dealt with. This means another large increase in the food supply."

I record as they come back to me these memories, and the strong impression I sustained at the moment of millions of men and women being blotted out or displaced for ever. A generation would no doubt come to whom their miseries were unknown, but it would be sure of having more to eat and bless Stalin's name. I did not repeat Burke's dictum, "If I cannot have reform without injustice, I will not have reform." With the World War going on all round us it seemed vain to moralise aloud.

About 1 A.M. Cadogan arrived with the draft, and we set to work to put it into final form. A considerable sucking-pig was brought to the table. Hitherto Stalin had only tasted the dishes, but now it was half-past one in the morning and around his usual dinner hour. He invited Cadogan to join him in the conflict, and when my friend excused himself, our host fell upon the victim single-handed. After this had been achieved he went abruptly into the next room to receive the reports from all sectors of the front, which were delivered to him from 2 A.M. onwards. It was about twenty minutes before he returned, and by that time we had the communiqué agreed. Finally, at 2.30 A.M. I said I must go. I had half an hour to drive to the villa, and as long to drive back to the airport. I had a splitting headache, which for me was very unusual. I still had General Anders to see. I begged Molotov not to come and see me off at dawn, for he was clearly tired out. He looked at me reproachfully as if to say, "Do you really think I would fail to be there?"

The following was the published text of the communiqué.

Prime Minister of Great Britain, Mr. Winston Churchill, with the President of the Council of the People's Commissars of U.S.S.R., J. V. Stalin.

Negotiations have taken place in Moscow between President of the Council of the People's Commissars of U.S.S.R., J. V. Stalin, and Prime Minister of Great Britain, Mr. Winston Churchill, in which Mr. Harriman, representing the President of the United States of America, participated. There took part in the discussions the People's Commissar for Foreign Affairs, V. M. Molotov, Marshal K. E. Voroshilov, from the Soviet side; the British Ambassador, Sir A. Clark Kerr, C.I.G.S. Sir A. Brooke, and other responsible representatives of the British armed forces, and the Permanent Under-Secretary of State for Foreign Affairs, Sir A. Cadogan, from the British side.

A number of decisions were reached covering the field of the war against Hitlerite Germany and her associates in Europe. This just war of liberation both Governments are determined to carry on with all their power and energy until the complete destruction of Hitlerism and any similar tyranny has been achieved. The discussions, which were carried on in an atmosphere of cordiality and complete sincerity, provided an opportunity of reaffirming the existence of the close friendships and understanding between the Soviet Union, Great Britain, and the United States of America, in entire accordance with the Allied relationships existing between them.

*   *   *   *   *

We took off at 5.30 A.M. I was very glad to sleep in the plane, and I remember nothing of the landscape or journey till we reached the foot of the Caspian and began to climb over the Elburz Mountains. At Teheran I did not go to the Legation, but to the cool, quiet glades of the summer residence, high above the city. Here a great press of telegrams awaited me. I had planned a conference for the next day at Baghdad with most of our high authorities in Persia and Iraq, but I did not feel I could face the heat of Baghdad in the August noonday, and it was quite easy to change the venue to Cairo. I dined with the Legation party that night in the agreeable woodland, and was content to forget all cares till morning.

From Teheran I sent a message to Stalin:

Prime Minister to Premier Stalin   16 Aug. 42

On arriving at Teheran after a swift and smooth flight I take occasion to thank you for your comradeship and hospitality. I am very glad I came to Moscow: firstly, because it was my duty to tell the tale; and, secondly, because I feel sure our contacts will play a helpful part in furthering our cause. Give my regards to Molotov.

I also reported as usual to the War Cabinet and President Roosevelt.

16 Aug. 42

I went to wind up with M. Stalin at 7 P.M. yesterday, and we had an agreeable conversation, in the course of which he gave me a full account of the Russian position, which seemed very encouraging. He certainly speaks with great confidence of being able to hold out until the winter. At 8.30 P.M., when I got up to leave, he asked when was the next time he was going to see me. I said that I was leaving at dawn. He then said, "Why do not you come over to my apartment in the Kremlin and have some drinks?" I went, and stayed to dinner, to which M. Molotov was also summoned. M. Stalin introduced me to his daughter, a nice girl, who kissed him shyly, but was not allowed to dine. The dinner and the communiqué lasted till 3 this morning. I had a very good interpreter and was able to talk much more easily. The greatest good will prevailed, and for the first time we got on to easy and friendly terms. I feel that I have established a personal relationship which will be helpful. We talked a great deal about "Jupiter," which he thinks essential in November or December. Without it I really do not see how we are going to be able to get through the supplies which will be needed to keep this tremendous fighting army equipped. The Trans-Persian route is only working at half what we hoped. What he requires most of all are lorries. He would rather have lorries than tanks, of which he is making two thousand a month. Also he wants aluminium.

"On the whole," I ended, "I am definitely encouraged by my
visit to Moscow. I am sure that the disappointing news I
brought could not have been imparted except by me personally
without leading to really serious drifting apart. It was my duty
to go. Now they know the worst, and having made their protest
are entirely friendly; this in spite of the fact that this is their
most anxious and agonising time. Moreover, M. Stalin is entirely convinced of the great advantages of 'Torch,' and I do
trust that it is being driven forward with superhuman energy
on both sides of the ocean."

6

Return to Cairo

ON MY RETURN to Cairo I received congratulations from the King.

His Majesty the King to Prime Minister   17 Aug. 42

I am delighted that your talks with Stalin ended on such a friendly note. As a bearer of unwelcome news your task was a very disagreeable one, but I congratulate you heartily on the skill with which you accomplished it. The personal relationship which you have established with Stalin should be valuable in the days to come; and your long journey has, I am sure, been well worth while.

I hope that you are not too tired, and that you will be able to take things more easily now.

My best wishes for a safe and comfortable journey home when your business is completed.

I replied on the following day:

Prime Minister to the King   18 Aug. 42

Mr. Churchill, with his humble duty to Your Majesty, has been much encouraged by Your Majesty's most gracious message.

2. Mr. Churchill hopes to deal with a number of important and urgent problems here during the present week. He is in the best of health and not at all tired. Your Majesty is always so kind, and these fresh marks of your confidence are most agreeable.

I also heard from General Smuts.

General Smuts to Prime Minister   19 Aug. 42

I have read your Moscow messages with deepest interest, and congratulate you on a really great achievement. Your handling of a critical psychological situation was masterly, and final effect on my mind is that you have achieved even more than you appear to realise and have firmly and finally bound Russia to us for this war at least. The quarrelsome interlude was evidently a clumsy attempt by Stalin to save appearances for himself while really accepting "Torch" as a better plan than "Sledgehammer." Your introduction of air assistance for Caucasus was a shrewd point, and well worth pursuing with Roosevelt. I must say after reading your account of talks I feel much happier about Russia than I had felt before. There appears now to be a good prospect of Hitler having to spend another winter in Russian mud, while we clear [the] Mediterranean basin and establish a firm base for second front next year. For the moment all depends on Alexander's success, and [on] "Torch" being undertaken as soon as possible consistent with firm prospect of success. We dare not fail with this venture, on which so much depends for our victory.

After your recent Herculean labours I implore you to relax.
You cannot continue at the present pace. Please follow Charles
Wilson's advice, as you expect [the] nation to follow yours.

*   *   *   *   *

During my visit to Moscow several affairs of high importance
in which I was deeply interested had reached their climax.
The disappointments of the June convoys to Malta showed that
only large-scale and speedy relief could save the fortress. The
suspension of the North Russian convoys after the disaster in
July enabled the Admiralty to draw heavily upon the Home
Fleet. Admiral Syfret in the *Nelson,* with the *Rodney,* three
large carriers, seven cruisers, and thirty-two destroyers, entered
the Mediterranean on August 9 for Operation "Pedestal." The
Furious was added to fly aircraft into Malta. The enemy had
meanwhile strengthened his air forces in Sardinia and Sicily.

On August 11 Admiral Syfret's fleet, escorting fourteen fast
merchant ships loaded with supplies, was off Algiers. The
carrier *Eagle* was sunk by a U-boat, but the *Furious* successfully
flew off her Spitfires to Malta. The next day the expected air
attacks began. One merchant ship and a destroyer were sunk,
and the carrier *Indomitable* damaged. Thirty-nine enemy aircraft and an Italian U-boat were destroyed. On approaching
the Narrows that evening Admiral Syfret with the battleships
withdrew according to plan, leaving Rear-Admiral Burrough to
continue with the convoy. The night that followed brought a
crescendo of attacks by U-boats and E-boats, and by morning
seven merchant ships had been lost, as well as the cruisers
Manchester and *Cairo.* Two other cruisers and three of the
merchant ships, including the American tanker *Ohio,* whose
cargo was vital, were damaged.

Undaunted, the survivors held on for Malta. Daylight on
the 13th brought a renewal of the air attacks. The *Ohio* was
hit again and stopped, as well as another merchant ship. By
now the remnants of the convoy were within supporting distance of the Malta defences, and that evening three ships, the
Port Chalmers, Melbourne Star, and *Rochester Castle,* at last

entered the Grand Harbour. Valiant efforts were now made to
bring in the three cripples still afloat. The *Brisbane Star*
arrived successfully the next day, and on the 15th the *Ohio,*
in tow and growing ever more unmanageable under ceaseless
air attack, was at last brought triumphantly into port. Thus in
the end five gallant merchant ships out of fourteen got through
with their precious cargoes. The loss of three hundred and
fifty officers and men and of so many of the finest ships in the
Merchant Navy and in the escorting fleet of the Royal Navy was
grievous. The reward justified the price exacted. Revictualled
and replenished with ammunition and vital stores, the strength
of Malta revived. British submarines returned to the island,
and, with the striking forces of the Royal Air Force, regained
their dominating position in the Central Mediterranean.

It should have been within the enemy's power, as it was
clearly his interest, to destroy this convoy utterly. Two Italian
cruiser squadrons sailed to intercept it on the morning of the
13th south of Pantelleria, when it was already heavily damaged
and dispersed. They needed strong air support to enable them
to operate so close to Malta, and here the effects of Admiral
Vian's earlier action in March against the Italian Fleet bore
fruit. Unwilling again to co-operate with the Italian Navy,
the German air forces insisted on attacking alone. A heated
controversy arose at headquarters, and a German admiral
records that an appeal was made to Mussolini, on whose intervention the cruisers were withdrawn before they got to the
Sicilian Narrows. Two of them were torpedoed by British submarines while returning to harbour. The German continues:
"A more useless waste of fighting power cannot be imagined.
The British operation, in spite of all the losses, was not a defeat,
but a strategical failure of the first order by the Axis, the repercussions of which will one day be felt."

On August 17 I telegraphed:

Prime Minister to First Lord and First Sea Lord　　　　17 Aug. 42

Please convey my compliments to Admirals Syfret, Burrough,
and Lyster and all officers and men engaged in the magnificent

crash through of supplies to Malta, which cannot fail to have an important influence on the immediate future of the war in the Mediterranean.

2. Papers here report thirteen enemy aircraft shot down, but this was only by the Malta force, and I have seen no mention of the thirty-nine additional shot down by the carriers, which puts a very different complexion on the air fighting.

The safe arrival of the convoy enabled me to invite Lord Gort to Cairo. I greatly desired to hear all about Malta from him. Gort and his aide-de-camp, Lord Munster (who was a Minister when the war began, but insisted on going to the front), arrived safely. They were both very thin and looked rather haggard. The General and his staff had made a point of sharing rigorously the starvation rations of the garrison and civil population. They were cautiously renourished at the Embassy. We had long talks, and when we parted I had the Malta picture clearly in my mind.

*   *   *   *   *

During my absence from London a crisis had arisen in India. The Congress Party committed themselves to an aggressive policy taking the form of sabotage of railways and of fomenting riots and disorder. Mob violence became rampant over large tracts of the countryside. This threatened to jeopardise the whole war effort of India in face of the Japanese invasion menace. The Viceroy's Council, upon which there was only one Englishman, proposed unanimously to arrest and intern Gandhi, Nehru, and the principal members of the Congress Party. The War Cabinet, advised by their Committee on India, immediately endorsed this drastic policy. When the news of the arrests was published, Generalissimo Chiang Kai-shek, at that time regarded in the United States as the supreme champion of Asiatic freedom, sent voluminous protests to the President, which he forwarded to me. I resented this Chinese intervention. "The Government of India," I wrote to the President, "have no doubt of their ability to maintain order and carry on government with efficiency and secure India's maximum contribution to the war, whatever the Indian Congress may say or do, provided of course that their authority is not undermined." The President responded helpfully.

President Roosevelt to Former Naval Person (*Cairo*)   9 Aug. 42

In view of the message you have sent me, I have replied to Chiang Kai-shek that it does not seem to me to be wise or expedient for the time being to consider taking any of the steps which he suggested in his message to me. I have emphasised the fact that we would of course not wish to pursue any course which would undermine the authority of the Indian Government at this critical time. I have, however, told him that I would be glad to have him keep in close touch with me with regard to this and any other questions which affect the vital interests of the United Nations because of my belief that it is wiser to have him feel that his suggestions sent to me receive friendly consideration. I fear that if I did not do so he would be more inclined to take action on his own initiative, which I know you will agree might be very dangerous at this moment. I have, therefore, left the door open for him to make any further suggestions which he may have in mind later on, and should he think the need therefor exists.

To the Viceroy I sent the strongest assurances of support, to which he replied:

Viceroy of India to Prime Minister   20 Aug. 42

I am much encouraged by your kind message. We are confronted by an awkward situation and I am by no means confident that we have yet seen the worst. But I have good hope we may clear up position before either Jap or German is well placed to put direct pressure upon us.

The fact that a number of crises break out at the same time does not necessarily add to the difficulty of coping with them. One set of adverse circumstances may counter-balance and even cancel out another. American opinion remained quiescent in view of the struggle with Japan. The measures proposed by the Viceroy and confirmed by the War Cabinet were soon effective. They proved the superficial character of the Congress Party's influence upon the masses of the Indian peoples, among

whom there was deep fear of being invaded by Japan and who
looked to the King-Emperor to protect them. During the whole
of this direct trial of strength with the Congress leaders, many
thousands of fresh volunteers came forward to join the India
Army. What was at one time feared to become the most serious
rebellion in India since the Sepoy Mutiny of 1857, fizzled out
in a few months with hardly any loss of life.

*   *   *   *   *

On the 17th I received news of the attack on Dieppe, plans
for which had been started in April after the brilliant and
audacious raid on St. Nazaire. On May 13, the outline plan
(Operation "Rutter") was approved by the Chiefs of Staff
Committee as a basis for detailed planning by the Force Commanders. Above ten thousand men were to be employed by
the three Services. This was of course the most considerable
enterprise of its kind which we had attempted against the
Occupied French coastline. From available intelligence it appeared Dieppe was held by German low-category troops amounting to one battalion with supporting units making no more
than fourteen hundred men in all. The assault was originally
fixed for July 4 and the troops embarked at ports in the Isle of
Wight. The weather was unfavourable and the date was postponed till July 8. Four German aircraft made an attack upon
the shipping which had been concentrated. The weather continued bad and the troops disembarked. It was now decided to
cancel the operation altogether. General Montgomery who, as
Commander-in-Chief, Southeastern Command, had hitherto
supervised the plans, was strongly of opinion that it should not
be remounted, as the troops concerned had all been briefed
and were now dispersed ashore.

However, I thought it most important that a large-scale
operation should take place this summer, and military opinion
seemed unanimous that until an operation on that scale was
undertaken, no responsible general would take the responsibility of planning for the main invasion.

In discussion with Admiral Mountbatten it became clear

that time did not permit a new large-scale operation to be
mounted during the summer, but that Dieppe could be remounted (the new code-name was "Jubilee") within a month,
provided extraordinary steps were taken to ensure secrecy.

For this reason no records were kept but, after the Canadian
authorities and the Chiefs of Staff had given their approval, I
personally went through the plans with the C.I.G.S., Admiral
Mountbatten, and the Naval Force Commander, Captain
J. Hughes-Hallett. It was clear that no substantial change between "Jubilee" and "Rutter" was suggested, beyond substituting Commandos to silence the Flank Coastal Batteries in
place of airborne troops. This was now possible as two more
infantry landing-ships had become available to carry the Commandos, and the chances of weather conditions causing "Jubilee" once more to be abandoned were considerably reduced by
omitting the airborne drop. In spite of an accidental encounter
between the landing-craft carrying one of the Commandos and
a German coastal convoy, one of the batteries was completely
destroyed and the other prevented from seriously interfering
with the operation; so that this change in no way affected the
outcome of the operation.

Our post-war examination of their records shows that the
Germans did not receive, through leakages of information, any
special warning of our intention to attack. However, their
general estimate of the threat to the Dieppe sector led
to an intensification of defence measures along the whole
front. Special precautions were ordered for periods like
that between August 10 and August 19, when moon and
tide were favourable for landings. The division responsible for the defence of Dieppe sector had been reinforced
during July and August and was at full strength and on
routine alert at the moment of the raid. The Canadian Army
in Britain had long been eager and impatient for action, and
the main part of the landing force was provided by them. The
story is vividly told by the official historian of the Canadian
Army [1] and in other official publications and need not be repeated here. Although the utmost gallantry and devotion were

---

[1] *The Canadian Army (1939–1945)*, by Colonel C. P. Stacey.

shown by all the troops and by the British Commandos and by the landing-craft and their escorts, and many splendid deeds were done, the results were disappointing and our casualties were very heavy. In the Canadian 2nd Division eighteen per cent of the five thousand men embarked lost their lives and nearly two thousand of them were taken prisoner.

*   *   *   *   *

Looking back, the casualties of this memorable action may seem out of proportion to the results. It would be wrong to judge the episode solely by such a standard. Dieppe occupies a place of its own in the story of the war, and the grim casualty figures must not class it as a failure. It was a costly but not unfruitful reconnaissance-in-force. Tactically it was a mine of experience. It shed revealing light on many shortcomings in our outlook. It taught us to build in good time various new types of craft and appliances for later use. We learnt again the value of powerful support by heavy naval guns in an opposed landing and our bombardment technique, both marine and aerial, was thereafter improved. Above all it was shown that individual skill and gallantry without thorough organisation and combined training would not prevail, and that team work was the secret of success. This could only be provided by trained and organised amphibious formations. All these lessons were taken to heart.

Strategically the raid served to make the Germans more conscious of danger along the whole coast of Occupied France. This helped to hold troops and resources in the West, which did something to take the weight off Russia. Honour to the brave who fell. Their sacrifice was not in vain.

*   *   *   *   *

While in Cairo I pressed the question of giving strong air support to the Soviet southern flank.

Prime Minister (Cairo) to Deputy Prime Minister,
Foreign Secretary, General Ismay, and C.A.S.   19 Aug. 42

I agree that there is no possibility of influencing the situation in the next sixty days. I also agree that nothing can be moved before the decision here, which will certainly be reached in forty days, and may come much sooner.

2. Matter must be viewed as long-term policy; namely, to place on the southern flank of the Russian armies a substantial British and, later on, American Air Force, (a) in order to strengthen the Russian air-power generally; (b) in order to form the advance shield of all our interests in Persia and Abadan; (c) for moral effect of comradeship with the Russians, which will be out of all proportion to the forces employed. We must have the means to do them a friendly act, especially in view of the difficulties of P.Q. convoys after September; and (d) because this is no dispersion of forces, but a greater concentration on the supreme Air Force target, namely, wearing down the German Air Force by daily fighting contact. We can fight them at more advantage in the ordinary conditions of the battle-front than by looking for trouble over the Channel. It pays us to lose machine for machine.

3. I have committed H.M.G. to this policy in my talks with Stalin, and I must ask the Cabinet for support. See also, when it reaches you, the account of the military conversations in Moscow, and also my correspondence with President Roosevelt on the matter, to which he attaches great importance.

4. C.A.S. should prepare a draft project for a movement of the kind outlined by Air Chief Marshal Tedder, which can be first sent to the President by me with a covering telegram. If his reply is satisfactory I will then make a firm offer to Stalin, which might not be operative till November, but which would enable immediate work to be started on surveying and preparing the landing-grounds and would give us access to the Russian sphere in Persia and the Caucasus. If things go well we will advance with the Russians' southern wing; if ill, we shall anyhow have to put forces of this order in North Persia. I wish to telegraph to the President before I leave here. Final decision can be taken at home when we hear what he says.

5. Everybody always finds it convenient to ease themselves at the expense of Russia, but grave issues depend upon preserving a good relationship with this tremendous army, now under dire distress. It will take a lot to convince me that action within the limits mentioned by Tedder will interfere with "Torch."

*   *   *   *   *

I was also able to complete the important business about transferring the Persian railway to American management which we had discussed at Teheran.

Prime Minister to Deputy Prime Minister, General Ismay, and others concerned   21 Aug. 42

As a result of conferences which we held in Teheran and Cairo with Mr. Harriman and his American railway experts we are all agreed that I should accept the President's offer to take over the working of the Trans-Persian railway and the port of Khorramshahr. We cannot run it unless they provide sixty per cent of the total personnel required. Their offer is to take it over as a task, becoming our servants so far as all movement is concerned, but managing everything on American lines, with American personnel, military and civil. Transference would be gradual and spread over a good many months. When completed it will release about two thousand British railway personnel, who will be urgently required on other parts of our military railway system. You will see my telegram to the President as it passes through.

Former Naval Person to President Roosevelt   22 Aug. 42

I have delayed my reply until I could study the Trans-Persian situation on the spot. This I have now done, both at Teheran and here, and have conferred with Averell, General Maxwell, General Spalding, and their railway experts. The traffic on the Trans-Persian railway is expected to reach three thousand tons a day for all purposes by the end of the year. We are all convinced that it ought to be raised to six thousand tons. Only in this way can we ensure an expanding flow of supplies to Russia while building up the military forces which we must move into northern Persia to meet a possible German advance.

2. To reach the higher figure it will be necessary to increase largely the railway personnel and to provide additional quantities of rolling-stock and technical equipment. Furthermore, the target will only be attained in reasonable time if enthusiasm and energy are devoted to the task and a high priority accorded to its requirements.

3. I therefore welcome and accept your most helpful proposal contained in your telegram, that the railway should be taken over, developed, and operated by the United States Army. With the railway should be included the ports of Khorramshahr and Bandar-

shahpur. Your people would thus undertake the great task of
opening up the Persian corridor, which will carry primarily your
supplies to Russia. All our people here agree on the benefits which
would follow your approval of this suggestion. We should be
unable to find the resources without your help, and our burden in
the Middle East would be eased by the release for use elsewhere
of the British units now operating the railway. The railway and
ports would be managed entirely by your people, though the allocation of traffic would have to be retained in the hands of the British
military authorities, for whom the railway is an essential channel of
communication for operational purposes. I see no obstacle in this
to harmonious working. . . .

*   *   *   *   *

The Australian cruiser *Canberra* had been sunk on the night
of August 9 by the Japanese near Guadalcanal, in the Solomons.

Prime Minister to First Lord and First Sea Lord   23 Aug. 42

Australia has lost her eight-inch cruiser, *Canberra*. It might
have lasting effect on Australian sentiment if we gave freely
and outright to Royal Australian Navy one of our similar ships.
Please give your most sympathetic consideration to the project
and be ready to tell me about it when I return. Meanwhile I am
not mentioning it to anyone.

This suggestion was adopted and the cruiser *Shropshire* was
presented to the Australian Government.

*   *   *   *   *

On August 19 I paid another visit to the Desert Front. I
drove with Alexander in his car out from Cairo past the
Pyramids, about a hundred and thirty miles through the desert
to the sea at Abusir. I was cheered by all he told me. As the
shadows lengthened we reached Montgomery's headquarters at
Burg-el-Arab. Here the afterwards famous caravan was drawn
up amid the sand dunes by the sparkling waves. The General
gave me his own wagon, divided between office and bedroom.
After our long drive we all had a delicious bathe. "All the
armies are bathing now at this hour all along the coast," said
Montgomery as we stood in our towels. He waved his arm to

the westward. Three hundred yards away, about a thousand of our men were disporting themselves on the beach. Although I knew the answer, I asked, "Why do the War Office go to the expense of sending out white bathing drawers for the troops? Surely this economy should be made." They were in fact tanned and burnt to the darkest brown everywhere except where they wore their short pants.

How fashions change! When I marched to Omdurman forty-four years before, the theory was that the African sun must at all costs be kept away from the skin. The rules were strict. Special spine-pads were buttoned on to the back of all our khaki coats. It was a military offence to appear without a pith helmet. We were advised to wear thick underclothing, following Arab custom enjoined by a thousand years of experience. Yet now, halfway through the twentieth century, many of the white soldiers went about their daily toil hatless and naked except for the equal of a loincloth. Apparently it did them no harm. Though the process of changing from white to bronze took several weeks and gradual application, sunstroke and heat-stroke were rare. I wonder how the doctors explain all this.

After we had dressed for dinner — my zip hardly takes a minute to put on — we gathered in Montgomery's map wagon, and he explained in detail his plans for the offensive battle.[1] He must however have six weeks to get the Eighth Army into order. He would reform the divisions as integral tactical units. We must wait till the new divisions had taken their place at the front and until the Sherman tanks were broken in. Then there would be three Army Corps, each under an experienced officer, whom he and Alexander knew well. Above all, the artillery would be used as had never been possible before in the Desert. He spoke of the end of September. I was disappointed at the date, but even this was dependent upon Rommel. Our information showed that a blow from him was imminent. I was myself already fully informed, and was well content that he should try a wide turning movement round our Desert Flank

[1] He gave us a masterly exposition of the situation, showing that in a few days he had firmly gripped the whole problem. He accurately predicted Rommel's next attack, and explained his plans to meet it. All of which proved true and sound. He then described his plans for taking the offensive himself.

in order to reach Cairo, and that a manoeuvre battle should be fought on his communications.

At this time I thought much of Napoleon's defeat in 1814. He too was poised to strike at the communications, but the allies marched straight on into an almost open Paris. I thought it of the highest importance that Cairo should be defended by every able-bodied man in uniform not required for the Eighth Army. Thus alone would the field army have full manoeuvring freedom and be able to take risks in letting its flank be turned before striking. It was with great pleasure that I found we were all in agreement. Although I was always impatient for offensive action on our part at the earliest moment, I welcomed the prospect of Rommel breaking his teeth upon us before our main attack was launched. But should we have time to organise the defence of Cairo? Many signs pointed to the audacious commander who faced us only a dozen miles away striking his supreme blow before the end of August. Any day indeed, my friends said, he might make his bid for continued mastery. A fortnight or three weeks' delay would be all to our good.

*   *   *   *   *

On August 20 we sallied forth early to see the prospective battlefield and the gallant troops who were to hold it. I was taken to the key point southeast of the Ruweisat Ridge. Here, amid the hard, rolling curves and creases of the desert, lay the mass of our armour, camouflaged, concealed, and dispersed, yet tactically concentrated. Here I met the young Brigadier Roberts, who commanded the whole of our armoured force in this vital position. All our best tanks were under him. He certainly had a great part to play should Rommel come. Montgomery explained to me the disposition of our artillery of all natures. Every crevice of the desert was packed with camouflaged concealed batteries. Three or four hundred guns would fire at the German armour before we hurled in our own.

Although of course no gathering of troops could be allowed under the enemy's continuous air reconnaissance, I saw a great

many soldiers that day, who greeted me with grins and cheers.
I inspected my own regiment, the 4th Hussars, or as many of
them as they dared to bring together — perhaps fifty or sixty —
near the field cemetery, in which a number of their comrades
had been newly buried. All this was moving, but with it all
there grew a sense of the reviving ardour of the Army. Everybody said what a change there was since Montgomery had taken
command. I could feel the truth of this with joy and comfort.

* * * * *

We were to lunch with Bernard Freyberg. My mind went
back to a similar visit I had paid him in Flanders, at his battle-
post in the valley of the Scarpe, a quarter of a century before,
when he already commanded a brigade. Then he had blithely
offered to take me for a walk along his outposts. But knowing
him and knowing the line as I did, I declined. Now it was the
other way round. I certainly hoped to see at least a forward
observation post of these splendid New Zealanders, who were
in contact about five miles away. Alexander's attitude showed
he would not forbid but rather accompany the excursion. But
Bernard Freyberg flatly refused to take the responsibility, and
this was not a matter about which orders are usually given,
even by the highest authority.

Instead we went into his sweltering mess tent, and were
offered a luncheon far more magnificent than the one I had
eaten on the Scarpe. This was an August noonday in the
Desert. The set-piece of the meal was a scalding broth of
tinned New Zealand oysters, to which I could do no more
than was civil. Presently Montgomery, who had left us some
time before, drove up. Freyberg went out to salute him, and
told him his place had been kept and that he was expected to
luncheon. But "Monty," as he was already called, had, it appeared, made it a rule not to accept hospitality from any of
his subordinate commanders. So he sat outside in his car eating
an austere sandwich and drinking his lemonade with all for-
malities. Napoleon also might have stood aloof in the interests
of discipline. *Dur aux grands* was one of his maxims. But he

would certainly have had an excellent roast chicken, served him from his own *fourgon*. Marlborough would have entered and quaffed the good wine with his officers — Cromwell, I think, too. The technique varies, and the results seem to have been good in all these cases.

We spent all the afternoon among the Army, and it was past seven when we got back to the caravan and the pleasant waves of its beach. I was so uplifted by all I had seen that I was not at all tired and sat up late talking. Before Montgomery went to bed at ten o'clock, in accordance with his routine, he asked me to write something in his personal diary. I did so now and on several other occasions during the long war. Here is what I wrote this time:

"May the anniversary of Blenheim which marks the opening of the new Command, bring to the Commander-in-Chief of the Eighth Army and his troops the fame and fortune they will surely deserve."

* * * * *

I sent the following report home:

Prime Minister to Deputy Prime Minister, for War Cabinet General Ismay, and others concerned   21 Aug. 42

Have just spent two days in the Western Desert visiting H.Q. Eighth Army. Brooke, Alexander, Montgomery, and I went round together, seeing 44th Division, 7th Armoured Division, and 22nd Armoured Brigade, and representatives of the New Zealand Division. I saw a great number of men and all the principal commanders in the XIIIth Corps area, also again Air Marshal Coningham, who shares headquarters with General Montgomery.

2. I am sure we were heading for disaster under the former régime. The Army was reduced to bits and pieces and oppressed by a sense of bafflement and uncertainty. Apparently it was intended in face of heavy attack to retire eastward to the Delta. Many were looking over their shoulders to make sure of their seat in the lorry, and no plain plan of battle or dominating will power had reached the units.

3. So serious did this appear that General Montgomery insisted

Note: August 13 Gen. Montgomery assumed command of the Desert Army. (Feb. 4. 1943)

May the anniversary of Blenheim which marks the opening of the new command bring to the Commander in Chief of the Eighth Army & his troops the fame & fortune they will surely deserve.

Aug. 20. 1942 Winston S. Churchill.

on taking command of the Eighth Army as soon as he had visited
the front, and by Alexander's decision the whole command in the
Middle East was transferred on the 13th.

4. Since then, from what I could see myself of the troops and
hear from their commanders, a complete change of atmosphere
has taken place. Alexander ordered Montgomery to prepare to
take the offensive and meanwhile to hold all positions, and Montgomery issued an invigorating directive to his commanders, of which
I will circulate the text on my return. The highest alacrity and
actively prevail. Positions are everywhere being strengthened, and
extended forces are being sorted out and regrouped in solid units.
The 44th and the 10th Armoured Divisions have already arrived
in the forward zone. The roads are busy with the forward movement of troops, tanks, and guns. General Horrocks commands the
XIIIth Corps. Ramsden will remain with the XXXth Corps. General Lumsden is forming the Xth Corps for a mass of manoeuvre
for the offensive battle towards the end of September. For this
a bold and comprehensive plan has been made.

5. However, it seems probable that Rommel will attack during
the moon period before the end of August. He has lost valuable
shipments, on which he counted, and underrates our strength, but
we must not underrate his. We must expect a very wide turning
movement by perhaps twenty thousand Germans and fifteen thousand Italians, comprising formations of two Panzer and four or five
Axis motorised divisions. The ensuing battle will be hard and
critical, but I have the greatest confidence in Alexander and Montgomery, and I feel sure the Army will fight at its best. If Rommel
does not attack in August he will be attacked himself at greater
relative disadvantage in September. This would fit in well with
"Torch."

6. For an August battle we should have at the front about 700
tanks, with 100 replacements, about 700 serviceable aircraft, 500
field guns, nearly 400 six-pounder and 440 two-pounder anti-tank
guns, but as we have only 24 medium guns, we are definitely weaker
in medium artillery. As parachute descents must be expected on a
large scale and Rommel will no doubt bid high for victory, the
Army will be extended to the full.

7. To give the fullest manoeuvring power to the Eighth Army
in the event of its being attacked next week, a strong line of defence
is being developed along the Delta from Alexandria to Cairo.

The 51st [Highland] Division is taking station there. I shall visit
it tomorrow. I drew General Alexander's attention to the inunda-
tion plans which we made two years ago, and action has been taken
at various points.

8. To sum up, while I and others would prefer the September
to the August battle, because of our growing strength I am
satisfied that we have lively, confident, resolute men in command,
working together as an admirable team under leaders of the highest
military quality. Everything has been done and is being done that
is possible, and it is now my duty to return home, as I have no part
to play in the battle, which must be left to those in whom we
place our trust. I have still a good deal of business to settle. As
you will see from other telegrams, Gort is here and Platt arrives
tomorrow. C.I.G.S. and I plan to start Sunday night by a route
which you will learn in a separate telegram. I hope to be available
for my weekly luncheon with the King on Tuesday if that should
be His Majesty's wish.

9. My general impression of "Jubilee" [Dieppe] is that the results
fully justified the heavy cost. The large-scale air battle alone justified the raid.

10. I thank you all most warmly for the support you have given
me while engaged in these anxious and none too pleasant tasks.

*   *   *   *   *

On August 22 I visited the Tura caves near Cairo where vital
repair work was being done. Out of these caves the stones of
the Pyramids had been cut some time before. They came in
very handy now. The reader will have seen my perpetual complaints of the bad servicing and slowness of repairs of our aircraft and tanks. Everything looked very smart and efficient on
the spot, and an immense amount of work was being done day
and night by masses of skilled men. But I had my tables of facts
and figures and remained dissatisfied. The scale was far too
small. The original fault lay with the Pharaohs for not having
built more and larger Pyramids. Other responsibilities were
more difficult to assign. We spent the rest of the day flying
from one airfield to another, inspecting the installations and
addressing the ground staffs. At one point two or three thousand airmen were assembled. I also visited, brigade by brigade,

the Highland Division just landed. It was late when we got
back to the Embassy.

*   *   *   *   *

During these last days of my visit all my thought rested upon
the impending battle. At any moment Rommel might attack
with a devastating surge of armour. He could come in by the
Pyramids with hardly a check except a single canal till he
reached the Nile, which flowed serenely by at the bottom of the
Residency lawn. Lady Lampson's baby son smiled from his
pram amid the palm trees. I looked out across the river at
the flat expanses beyond. All was calm and peaceful, but I
suggested to the mother that it was very hot and sultry in
Cairo and could not be good for children. "Why not send the
baby away to be braced by the cool breezes of the Lebanon?"
But she did not take my advice, and none can say she did not
judge the military situation rightly.

In the fullest accord with General Alexander and the
C.I.G.S., I set on foot a series of extreme measures for the defence of Cairo and the water-lines running northward to the
sea. Rifle-pits and machine-gun posts were constructed, bridges
mined and their approaches wired, and inundations loosed
over the whole wide front. All the office population of Cairo,
numbering thousands of staff officers and uniformed clerks,
were armed with rifles and ordered to take their stations, if
need be, along the fortified water-line. The 51st Highland
Division was not yet regarded as "desert-worthy," but these
magnificent troops were now ordered to man the new Nile
front. The position was one of great strength because of the
comparatively few causeways which cross the canalised, flooded
or floodable area of the Delta. It seemed quite practicable to
arrest an armoured rush along the causeways. The defence of
Cairo would normally have belonged to the British general
who commanded the Egyptian Army, all of whose forces were
also arrayed. I thought it better however to place the responsibility, should an emergency occur, upon General Maitland-
Wilson — "Jumbo" — who had been appointed to the Persia-

Iraq Command, but whose headquarters during these critical weeks were forming in Cairo. To him I issued a directive to inform himself fully of the whole defence plan, and to take responsibility from the moment when General Alexander told him that Cairo was in danger.

I had now to go home on the eve of battle and return to far wider but by no means less decisive affairs. I had already obtained the Cabinet's approval to the directive to be given to General Alexander. He was the supreme authority with whom I now dealt in the Middle East. Montgomery and the Eighth Army were under him. So also, if it became necessary, was Maitland-Wilson and the defence of Cairo. "Alex," as I had long called him, had already moved himself and his personal headquarters into the Desert by the Pyramids. Cool, gay, comprehending all, he inspired quiet, deep confidence in every quarter.

* * * * *

We sailed off from the Desert airfield at 7 P.M. on August 23, and I slept the sleep of the just till long after daylight. When I clambered along the bomb bay to the cockpit of the "Commando" we were already approaching Gibraltar. I must say it looked very dangerous. All was swathed in morning mist. One could not see a hundred yards ahead, and we were not flying more than thirty feet above the sea. I asked Vanderkloot if it was all right, and said I hoped he would not hit the Rock of Gibraltar. His answers were not particularly reassuring, but he felt sufficiently sure of his course not to go up high and stand out to sea, which personally I should have been glad to see him do. We held on for another four or five minutes. Then suddenly we flew into clear air, and up towered the great precipice of Gibraltar, gleaming on the isthmus and strip of neutral ground which joins it to Spain and the mountain called the Queen of Spain's Chair. After three or four hours' flying in mist, Vanderkloot had been exact. We passed the grim rock-face a few hundred yards away without having to alter our course, and made a perfect landing. I still think it would have been better to go aloft and circle round for an hour or two. We had the petrol and were not pressed for time. But it was a fine performance.

We spent the morning with the Governor, and flew home in the afternoon, taking a wide sweep across the Bay of Biscay when darkness fell.

7

The Final Shaping of "Torch"

General Eisenhower to Command — Agreement with President Roosevelt — Agreeable Contacts with the United States Generals — Need for a Simple Directive — A Bombshell from Washington — American Apprehension of Going Inside the Mediterranean — My Telegram to President Roosevelt of August 27 — The President's Reply of August 30 — American Belief that the French Would Not Fire on Their Troops — My Telegram to President Roosevelt of September 1 — The President's Reply of September 3 — My Proposal that Eisenhower Should Fly to Washington to Explain — An Unsent Letter from Me to Harry Hopkins — A Survey of the Deadlock and its Causes — Better News from the President, September 4 — We Agree: Hurrah! — O.K., Full Blast — Planning and Timing — Further Discussion with Generals Eisenhower and Clark — My Fears that Delay Would Destroy Secrecy — My Telegram to the President, September 15 — "An American Enterprise in Which We Are Your Helpmeets" — Date of "Torch" Fixed for November 8 — Rommel's Last Thrust for Cairo — The Combat of Alam Halfa.

WHEN I LEFT LONDON on my missions to Cairo and Moscow the Commander for "Torch" had not been chosen. I had suggested on July 31 that if General Marshall were designated for the Supreme Command of the cross-Channel operation in 1943, General Eisenhower should act as his deputy and forerunner in London, and work at "Torch," which he would himself command with General Alexander as his second. Opinion moved forward on these lines and before

525

I started from Cairo to Moscow President Roosevelt sent me
the two following telegrams:

President Roosevelt to Former Naval Person (Cairo)   6 Aug. 42

The proposals of the British Chiefs of Staff dated August 6 that
General Eisenhower be designated as Commander-in-Chief for the
"Torch" operation is acceptable to me and to the United States
Chiefs of Staff. The formal directive for General Eisenhower's
guidance submitted by the British Chiefs of Staff is being studied,
and will be reported upon shortly.

And on the 8th:

I wholly agree date for "Torch" should be advanced, and I am
asking three weeks' advance over the selected date.

Announcement of Eisenhower command I leave to discretion of
Chiefs of Staff in London and Washington.

*   *   *   *   *

When on August 24 I returned from Cairo to London, much
remained to be decided about the final shaping of our plans
and on the following day Generals Eisenhower and Clark came
to dine with me to discuss the state of the operation.

I was at this time in very close and agreeable contact with
these American officers. From the moment they arrived in June
I had arranged a weekly luncheon at Number 10 on Tuesdays.
These meetings seemed to be a success. I was nearly always
alone with them, and we talked all our affairs over, back and
forth, as if we were all of one country. I set great value on
these personal contacts. Irish stew turned out to be very
popular with my American guests, and especially with General
Eisenhower. My wife was nearly always able to get this. I soon
began to call him "Ike." For Mark Clark and Bedell Smith,
the latter of whom arrived early in September as Chief of Staff
to Eisenhower, I coined the titles "the American Eagle" and
"the American Bulldog." We also had a number of informal conferences in our downstairs dining-room, beginning at about
ten o'clock at night and sometimes running late. Several times

the American generals came for a night or a week-end to Chequers. Nothing but shop was ever talked on any of these occasions.

One of General Eisenhower's aides-de-camp, a friend from civil life, has suggested in his book that all these meetings were a great burden upon the already overworked American officers. If this be true they showed great politeness and address in concealing their feelings. Anyhow, I am sure these close relationships were necessary for the conduct of the war, and I could not have grasped the whole position without them. At one of our meetings on September 28, I certainly rendered a service to Bedell Smith and his chief. It was not very late at night, but I noticed that "the Beetle," as he was also called, looked frightfully tired and ill. I suggested to him to go to bed, but he insisted on remaining. There was a moment when I thought he was going to faint and fall off his chair. I therefore closed the discussion. On the way upstairs I asked Eisenhower to come alone with me into the Cabinet room. I closed the door and said, "If you want Bedell in this battle you should send him to hospital this very night, no matter what he says. Otherwise you will lose him altogether." Eisenhower acted with his customary decision. The next day Bedell Smith was in the hospital. He had to have two blood transfusions in the next two days, and was kept a fortnight from all work and mostly in bed. Thus he was able to play his important part in the design which dominated our minds.

* * * * *

After my talk with the American generals I telegraphed to the President:

Former Naval Person to President Roosevelt　　　　26 Aug. 42

I am concentrating my main thought upon "Torch" from now on, and you may trust me to do my utmost to make your great strategic conception a decisive success. It seems to me from talks I have had with Eisenhower, Clark, and our own people here that the best, and indeed the only, way to put this job through is to fix a date for the party and make everything conform to that, rather than saying it will start when everything is ready. It would be an immense help if you and I were to give Eisenhower a directive something like this:

> You will start "Torch" on October 14, attacking with such troops as are available and at such places as you deem fit.

This will alter the whole character of the preparations. Eisenhower will really have the power he should have as the Allied Commander-in-Chief. Endless objections, misgivings, and well-meant improvements will fall back into their proper places, and action will emerge from what will otherwise be almost unending hummings and hawings. I think Eisenhower would like this, and it would anyhow give him a chance which he has not now got.

2. As I see this operation, it is primarily political in its foundations. The first victory we have to win is to avoid a battle; the second if we cannot avoid it, to win it. In order to give us the best chances of the first victory, we must (a) present the maximum appearance of overwhelming strength at the moment of the first attack, and (b) attack at as many places as possible. This is an absolutely different kind of operation from the Dieppe business or any variants of "Sledgehammer." There we were up against German efficiency and the steel-bound, fortified coasts of France. In "Torch" we have to face at the worst weak, divided opposition and an enormous choice of striking-points at which to land. Risks and difficulties will be doubled by delay and will far outstrip any increase of our forces. Careful planning in every detail, safety first in every calculation, far-seeing provisions for a long-term campaign, to meet every conceivable adverse contingency, however admirable in theory, will ruin the enterprise in fact. Anything later than the date I have mentioned enormously increases the danger of leakage and forestalment.

3. In order to lighten the burden of responsibility on the military commanders, I am of opinion that you and I should lay down the political data and take this risk upon ourselves. In my view, it would be reasonable to assume (a) that Spain will not go to war with Britain and the United States on account of "Torch"; (b) that it will be at least two months before the Germans can force their way through Spain or procure some accommodation from her; (c) that the French resistance in North Africa will be largely token resistance, capable of being overcome by the suddenness and scale

of the attack, and that thereafter the North African French may
actively help us under their own commanders; (*d*) that Vichy will
not declare war on the United States and Great Britain; (*e*) that
Hitler will put extreme pressure on Vichy, but that in October he
will not have the forces available to overrun Unoccupied France
while at the same time we keep him pinned in the Pas de Calais,
etc. All these data may prove erroneous, in which case we shall have
to settle down to hard slogging. For this we have already been
prepared, but a bold, audacious bid for a bloodless victory at the
outset may win a very great prize. Personally, I am prepared to
take any amount of responsibility for running the political risks
and being proved wrong about the political assumptions.

4. It is evident that these assumptions would be greatly helped
by a battle won in the Western Desert. Either Rommel attacks us
by the August moon, or we shall attack him by the end of September. Either way there will be a decision, and I feel very confident
that the decision will be helpful.

5. I have refrained, as you know, from going into any details
here because I feel that a note must be struck now of irrevocable
decision and superhuman energy to execute it.

*   *   *   *   *

But at this moment a bombshell arrived from Washington.
Serious divergences had opened between the British and
American Staffs on the character and scope of our plan to
invade and occupy French North Africa. The United States
Chiefs of Staff disliked very much the idea of committing
themselves to large operations beyond the Straits of Gibraltar.
They seemed to have the feeling that in some sort of way their
armies would be cut off in the inland sea. General Eisenhower,
on the other hand, fully shared the British view that powerful
action inside the Mediterranean, above all including Algeria,
was vital to success. His views, so far as he may have pressed
them, did not seem to influence his military superiors. He was
also hampered in his planning by the insistence of various
American departments concerned that all must be delayed until
their respective consignments of men or store ships had definitely started. In so vast an operation there were bound to be

laggard items, and to wait for the last of these would impose an indefinite delay in fixing zero day.

The American Chiefs of Staff now pressed their view, which I and my advisers resisted.

Former Naval Person to President Roosevelt   27 Aug. 42

We are all profoundly disconcerted by the memorandum sent us by the United States Joint Chiefs of Staff on the 25th instant about "Torch." It seems to me that the whole pith of the operation will be lost if we do not take Algiers as well as Oran on the first day. In Algiers we have the best chance of a friendly reception, and even if we got nothing except Algeria a most important strategic success would have been gained. General Eisenhower, with our cordial support, was in fact planning landings at Philippeville and Bone for Day 3. We cannot of course be sure of getting to Tunis before the Germans, but neither is it certain that the Germans would be well received by the French in Tunis even if Vichy gave them permission.

2. Strongly established in Algeria, with Oran making good the communications, we could fight the Germans for Tunis even if they got there. But not to go east of Oran is making the enemy a present not only of Tunis but of Algiers. An operation limited to Oran and Casablanca would not give the impression of strength and of widespread simultaneous attack on which we rely for the favourable effect on the French in North Africa. We are all convinced that Algiers is the key to the whole operation. General Anderson, to whom this task has been assigned by Eisenhower, is confident of his ability to occupy Algiers. The occupation of Algeria and the movement towards Tunis and Bizerta is an indispensable part of the attack on Italy, which is the best chance of enlisting French co-operation and one of the main objects of our future campaign.

3. We are all agreed about Oran, and of course we should like to see Casablanca occupied as well, but if it came to choosing between Algiers and Casablanca it cannot be doubted that the former is incomparably the more hopeful and fruitful objective. Inside the Mediterranean, landings can be made in October on four days out of five. On the Atlantic shores of Morocco the proportion is exactly reversed, only one day in five being favourable.

4. Nevertheless, if the operations at Oran and Algiers yield good

reactions and results, entry might easily be granted to a force appearing off Casablanca, and a feint would certainly be justified. It is however by far the most difficult point of attack, and the one most remote from the vital objectives in the Mediterranean. Casablanca might easily become an isolated failure and let loose upon us for a small reward all the perils which have anyway to be faced in this great design. So far as Algiers is concerned, all we ask from you is an American contact team to show the [American] flag. We [ourselves] cannot however do Algiers and Oran at the same time. If therefore you wish to do Casablanca on a large scale with all its risks, it is indispensable that United States forces should continue to be directed on Oran as now planned by the Allied Commander-in-Chief.

5. A complete change in the plans such as the memorandum suggests would of course be fatal to the date, and thus possibly to the whole plan. In October Hitler will not have the power to move into Spain or into Unoccupied France. In November and with every week that passes his power to bring pressure upon the Vichy and Madrid Governments increases rapidly.

6. I hope, Mr. President, you will bear in mind the language I have held to Stalin, supported by Harriman with your full approval. If "Torch" collapses or is cut down as is now proposed, I should feel my position painfully affected. For all these reasons I most earnestly beg that the memorandum may be reconsidered, and that the American Allied Commander-in-Chief may be permitted to go forward with the plans he has made, upon which we are all now working night and day. The Staffs are communicating similar views to their American colleagues.

On August 30 I received the President's reply.

President Roosevelt to Former Naval Person　　　　　　30 Aug. 42

I have considered carefully your telegram in reference to the "Torch" operation. It is my earnest desire to start the attack at the earliest possible moment. Time is of the essence, and we are speeding up preparations vigorously.

I feel very strongly that the initial attacks must be made by an exclusively American ground force, supported by your naval, transport, and air units. The operation should be undertaken on the assumption that the French will offer less resistance to us than they will to the British. I would even go so far as to say I am reasonably sure a simultaneous landing by British and Americans would result in full resistance by all French in Africa, whereas an initial American landing without British ground forces offers a real chance that there would be no French resistance, or only a token resistance. I need a week, if possible, after we land to consolidate the poistion for both of us by securing the non-resistance of the French. I sincerely hope I can get this.

Then your force can come in to the eastward. I realise full well that your landing must be made before the enemy can get there. It is our belief that German air and parachute troops cannot get to Algiers or Tunis in any large force for at least two weeks after the initial attack. Meanwhile your troops would be ashore, we hope, without much opposition, and would be moving eastward. As to the place of the landings, it seems to me that we must have a sure and permanent base on the northwest coast of Africa, because a single line of communications through the Straits is far too hazardous in the light of our limited joint resources.

I propose therefore that: (a) American troops land simultaneously near Casablanca and near Oran; (b) that they seek to establish road and rail communication with each other back of the mountains. The distance is little more than three hundred miles. This gives to the enterprise a supply base in Morocco, which is outside the Straits and can be used to reinforce and supply the operations in Algiers and Tunis. The real problem seems to be that there is not enough cover and combat loadings for more than two landings. I realise it would be far better to have three, with you handling the one to the eastward a week after we get it. To this end I think we should re-examine our resources and strip everything to the bone to make the third landing possible. We can give up the Russian convoy temporarily at that time and risk or hold up other merchant shipping.

It is essential of course that all ships now assigned to Eisenhower for his two landings remain intact. Hence the eastward landing must be made on ships not now available to "Torch." I will explore this at our end. Can we not get an answer on this within forty-eight hours or less?

I want to emphasise however that under any circumstances one of our landings must be on the Atlantic.

The directive to the Commander-in-Chief of the operation should prescribe that the attack should be launched at the earliest practicable date. The date should be consistent with the preparation necessary for an operation with a fair chance of success, and accordingly it should be determined by the Commander-in-Chief; but in no event later than October 30. I still would hope for October 14.

* * * * *

As can be seen from this telegram, another series of difficulties arose from the strength of the American view that while United States forces would probably be admitted by the French without fighting, or perhaps even welcomed, any appearance of the British would entail fierce and obstinate resistance. Certain memories of Oran, Dakar, Syria, Madagascar, and our blockade were grave causes of antagonism between Britain and Vichy. The American Ambassador, Admiral Leahy, on the other hand, was intimate and friendly with Pétain. We were always anxious to preserve the American character of the expedition, and I was so anxious for them to agree to it that from the outset I had welcomed President Roosevelt's assuming the leadership. However, when it came to working out the plan it was found necessary that very large numbers of the troops, the bulk of the transportation, at least an equal contribution in the air, and two-thirds of the naval force engaged would have to be British. I did not wholly share the American view that either they were so beloved by Vichy or we so hated as to make the difference between fighting and submission, but I was very willing that provided the necessary forces were set in motion and the operation was not fatally restricted in its scope, we should keep as much in the background as was physically possible. I would even have agreed to such British troops as had to be used in the first assaults wearing American uniform. Nothing mattered but success. But that must not be compromised for lack of the necessary force, or by unsound restrictions on its employment. As all agreement between the Staffs had failed, the issue had to be settled personally between the President and me.

* * * * *

Former Naval Person to President Roosevelt   1 Sept. 42

We have carefully considered your last. The Chiefs of Staff have also talked things over with Eisenhower.

2. We could not contest your wish, if you so desire it, to take upon the United States the whole burden, political and military, of the landings. Like you I assign immense importance to the political aspect. I do not know what information you have of the mood and temper of Vichy and North Africa, but of course if you can get ashore at the necessary points without fighting or only token resistance, that is the best of all. We cannot tell what are the chances of this.

3. I hope however that you have considered the following points:

(*a*) Will not British participation be disclosed by the assembly of British small craft and aircraft at Gibraltar for some time beforehand?

(*b*) Would it not be disclosed at the time of landing whatever flag we wear?

(*c*) Would not initial fighting necessarliy be between French and British aircraft and French batteries and British ships?

(*d*) If the approach and landing take place in the dark, as is indispensable to surprise, how will the Americans be distinguished from British? In the night all cats are grey.

(*e*) What happens if, as I am assured is 4–1 probable, surf prevents disembarkation on Atlantic beaches?

4. Moreover, if, contrary to your hopes, the landings are stubbornly opposed and even held up, we shall not be able to give you the follow-up help for some considerable time, because all our assault vessels would have been used for your troops and our reinforcements would be embarked in vessels which can only enter by captured harbours. Thus, if the political bloodless victory, for which I agree with you there is a good chance, should go amiss, a military disaster of very great consequence will supervene. We could have stormed Dakar in September, 1940, if we had not been cluttered up with preliminary concilatory processes. It is that hard experience that makes our military experts rely so much upon the simplicity of force. Will you have enough American trained and equipped forces to do this all by yourselves, or at any rate to impress the enemy by the appearance of ample strength?

5. This sudden abandonment of the plan on which we have hitherto been working will certainly cause grievous delay. Gen-

eral Eisenhower says that October 30 will be the very earliest date. I myself think that it may well mean the middle of November. Orders were given to suspend loadings yesterday in order that, if necessary, all should be recast. I fear the substitution of November for October will open up a whole new set of dangers far greater than those which must anyhow be faced.

6. Finally, in spite of the difficulties, it seems to us vital that Algiers should be occupied simultaneously with Casablanca and Oran. Here is the most friendly and hopeful spot where political reaction would be most decisive throughout North Africa. To give up Algiers for the sake of the doubtfully practicable landing at Casablanca seems to us a very serious decision. If it led to the Germans forestalling us not only in Tunis but in Algeria, the results on balance would be lamentable throughout the Mediterranean.

7. Mr. President, to sum up, "Torch," like "Gymnast" before it, has always been viewed as primarily a United States enterprise. We have accepted an American command and your leadership, and we will do our utmost to make a success of any plan on which you decide. We must however say quite plainly that we are sure that the best course is to persevere along the general lines so clearly set out in the agreed directive handed to General Eisenhower on August 14. I am sure that if we both strip ourselves to the bone, as you say, we could find sufficient naval cover and combat loadings for simultaneous attempts at Casablanca, Oran, and Algiers.

President Roosevelt to Prime Minister   3 Sept. 42

Your message of September 1 has been received and given careful consideration.

2. Your willingness to co-operate by agreeing that all initial landings will be made by United States ground forces is appreciated. It is true that British participation in the form of naval and air support will be disclosed to the defenders early in the operation. However, I do not believe that this will have quite the same effect that British forces making the first beach landing would have.

3. Bad surf conditions on the Atlantic beaches is a calculated risk. The use of numerous small lightly defended ports may be necessary.

4. It will be necessary to use all available combat loaders in the first assault. The assaulting troops, regardless of whether they are

British or American, must seize a port before follow-up forces can be landed. Regardless of what troops arrive subsequent to the initial landing, the situation will be the same.

5. In view of your urgent desire that Algiers should be occupied simultaneously with Casablanca and Oran we offer the following solution:

(1) Simultaneous landings at Casablanca, Oran, and Algiers, with assault and immediate follow-up troops generally as follows:

(a) Casablanca (United States troops): 34,000 in the assault and 24,000 in the immediate follow-up to land at a port.

(b) Oran (United States troops): 25,000 in the assault and 20,000 in the immediate follow-up to land at a port.

(c) Algiers (United States and British troops): in the beach landing 10,000 United States troops, followed within the hour by British troops, to make the landing secure, the follow-up to be determined by the Commander-in-Chief. This follow-up to land at a port in non-combat-loaded ships.

(2) *Troops*. For the above landings the United States can furnish:

(a) from the United States, Casablanca force, and

(b) from the United Kingdom, the Oran force and 10,000 men for the Algiers force.

As immediate follow-up forces we have one armoured division in the United States and one armoured division in the United Kingdom (both less elements included in the assault echelons), with supporting and service troops, including ground echelons of air units. Later, additional infantry and armoured divisions can be furnished from the United States and the remaining United States troops in the United Kingdom can be made available.

(3) *Shipping*. The following shipping can be made available by the United States to sail from United States ports October 20.

(a) Combat loaders with a lift of 34,000 men.

(b) Transports, other than combat loaders, with a lift of 52,000 men, with sufficient cargo vessels to support this personnel. In addition to this shipping there will be available in the United Kingdom United States transports with personnel lift of 15,000 and nine cargo vessels which have been previously set aside by agreement to transport United States troops from the United Kingdom for this operation. In round numbers, the shipping shown as available in the United States is estimated to be sufficient to move the first, second, and third convoys of the Casablanca force.

(4) *Naval.* The United States cannot provide forces for escort and support in this operation in excess of those now available in the Atlantic, plus all ships which can be expedited in readiness for service as is now being done.

6. The above shows the total ground, naval, and shipping effort which the United States can put into this operation. If the operation is to be executed along the lines indicated, namely, simultaneous landings at Casablanca, Oran, and Algiers, all the remaining requirements must be furnished from British sources. As we see it, this would mean, in general, that it will be necessary for you to furnish:

(a) all shipping (including combat loaders) required for the Oran and Algiers forces, except the United States shipping now in the United Kingdom earmarked for "Torch";

(b) the additional troops required for the Algiers assault and follow-up forces; and

(c) the naval forces required for the entire operation, less the United States naval force indicated above.

7. In order that I may continue with vigorous preparations for the execution of "Torch" at the earliest practicable date, please confirm by cable that the United Kingdom will provide the trooplift, troops, naval forces, and shipping noted herein as necessary.

8. I reiterate the belief expressed in my telegram of August 30 that the Commander-in-Chief should be directed to execute the operation at the earliest practicable date, and that this date should be fixed by him. I am convinced of the absolute necessity for an early decision. I feel that the operation as outlined herein is as far as I can go towards meeting your views, and seems to me to be a practical solution which retains the Algiers operation and is sufficiently strong to be a good risk throughout.

9. Our latest and best information from North Africa is as follows:

An American expedition led in all three phases by American officers will meet little resistance from the French Army in Africa. On the other hand, a British-commanded attack in any phase or with de Gaullist co-operation would meet with determined resistance. . . .

Because of this information I consider it vital that some re-

sponsibility be placed [on] high American for relations with French
military and civil authorities in Africa.

As you and I decided long ago, we were to handle the French
in North Africa, while you were to handle the situation in Spain.

Former Naval Person to President Roosevelt   3 Sept. 42

We have spent the day looking into physical possibilities.
Accepting your general outlines, we think that a working plan
can be made on the basis that the emphasis is shifted somewhat,
namely, reducing Casablanca by ten or twelve thousand (making
up deficiency in the follow-ups). These troops, with their combat-
loaded ships, would give sufficient strength inside, while making
the entire assault American. This evens up the three landings and
gives the essential appearance of strength at all vital points. Without such a transference there is no hope of Algiers, on account of
shortage of combat loaders and landing-craft. We all think this
would be a great blemish to the plan.

2. Tomorrow we suggest that either General Clark or General
Eisenhower should come with Admiral Ramsay, who knows the
whole transportation escort story and the naval aspect from our
end, and Mountbatten on the landing details, which are crucial,
party reaching you Sunday morning. We do not here know what
naval forces you are able to supply. Please let these be imparted
to Admiral Cunningham, to whom, in view of the importance of
the operation, we propose to give the naval command, under the
Allied Commander-in-Chief.

3. Delay due to change already extends three weeks. Free French
have got inkling and are leaky. Every day saved is precious. We
have therefore already ordered work to go forward on these lines,
but of course the decision rests with you.

At this time, when all hung in the balance, I thought it
right to give Harry Hopkins the whole of my thought, and
leave to his discretion how he would press the matter upon
the President.

Prime Minister to Mr. Harry Hopkins   4 Sept. 42

I send you by hand of Dickie Mountbatten this letter, because
I know how wholly your heart is centred in the cause and the
peerless services you have rendered it. You should use your own

discretion about showing it to our great friend, and if you think it would vex him in any way do not do so. I leave it to your judgment, it being entirely an "off the record" document.

I am deeply perturbed by the way "Torch" is being knocked about, and above all at the needless delays, which add so much to our joint troubles. It had been a long and slow business getting rid of "Sledgehammer," but when you left here on July 25, all was set for full steam ahead, and I certainly thought that Marshall had reconciled himself to the President's final decision. We gladly accepted General Eisenhower as the Allied Commander-in-Chief, and he and Clark, these two very fine officers, set to work at once. It was not however until the 14th of August that a definite directive was received from the Combined Staffs in Washington. Upon this all thoughts were concentrated. An amphibious operation like this has to fit together like a jewelled bracelet; for each particular landing-place the right ships must be chosen, and these ships must be loaded in accordance with the needs of the particular work each landing party has to do. This does not affect all the ships, as many can work common service, but quite a proportion have to be fitted to their rôle and to the slope of the beaches and depth of the water off the coasts they are to strike. I do not wish to exaggerate this, because naturally one has to take a chance in a good many things, but the more careful the arrangements the better the results.

2. At any rate, all was going forward, and until a week ago there was no reason why we should not have made the date October 15. Then suddenly out of the blue arrived the shattering memorandum of the United States Chiefs of Staff, which altered the whole character and emphasis of the operation — discarding Algiers, the softest and most paying spot, and throwing all the major weight upon Casablanca and the Atlantic shore, which after prolonged study we think may be quite impossible on account of the surf for a sea landing, and which is certainly four to one against, even in October. It seemed so easy no doubt to say "Abandon Algiers; switch around to Casablanca; find other troops for Oran," but look at the effect this had on all the work which had been done. I have been a witness of the distresses into which your two brilliant officers have been thrown by the delays and by the changes in policy coming from the United States Chiefs of Staff. Indeed, Eisenhower's position has been a very painful one. On the one hand, below him British and American Staff Officers clamouring for decisions on a

whole host of points of detail; on the other, the restriction of the
rigid and at the same time changeable control from across the ocean.
What is the use of putting up an Allied Commander-in-Chief or
Supreme Commander if he cannot have the slightest freedom in
making his plan or deciding how, when, and where to apply his
forces? We are prepared to take his decisions and to obey. Even if
we do not agree we will obey, after having put the facts before you.
We are only out to help him in every way to give effect to the President's great strategic conception. Now the whole matter has to go
back across the Atlantic and completely new schemes are set us.
I do not see how a united command is possible if the Supreme
Commander is not allowed to act.

3. Frankly, I do not understand what is at the back of all this.
I thought there was agreement with Marshall and that King had
been paid off with what he needed for his Pacific war. But now
it seems there is a bad comeback from the professional circles in
the American Army, and I have a deep and growing fear that the
whole of the President's enterprise may be wrecked bit by bit. With
it will fall the brightest hope of the Allies and the only hope this
year. One change of plan after another will produce delays; the
enormous numbers of people in our two countries who will get
wind of what is going on will make it sure that the enemy will be
informed. With every day's delay the Germans have a better chance
of forestalling us. Now the earliest that can be hoped for is the
first week of November, but I should be very much surprised if it
was not the last week. What will have happened by then in other
quarters no one can predict.

4. What particularly puzzles me is that I do not know what are
the reasons which make the United States Staffs so reluctant to go
inside the Mediterranean, and especially to Algiers, and so eager
to concentrate all the weight on Casablanca. Let us take first the
resistance of the French. Generally speaking, I agree with the
President's views and hopes about this. I think there is at least a
fifty-fifty chance that the French will not shed American blood
and have a massacre of American youth on the beaches of North
Africa. The past and still more the future of France would forbid
such an episode. At any rate, I think the risk is not disproportionate, and should be run because the prize is so great. But if this
assumption is correct and the French make no resistance or only
token resistance and thereafter come over to our side, as follows
inevitably from their not resisting, this would apply simultaneously

at Casablanca and Oran, and above all at Algiers, where the atmosphere is most favourable. If then you succeed in getting these ports easily and swiftly, as it must be, on the first day, the world is confronted with a new fact and we need not anticipate any trouble from Spain. There will be a peaceful occupation for liberation purposes of French North Africa, and the next step will be to build up the attack on Sicily and Italy, as well as on Rommel's back at Tripoli.

5. But take the other alternative. Let us assume that there is fighting, that the batteries fire, that the ports are denied, and that French aircraft bombard Gibraltar harbour, as they did when the Dakar show was on. Then indeed the Spaniards may be tempted by the bribes and the threats of the Germans to take a hand in rendering Gibraltar untenable. I think myself they would wait until they were quite sure things had gone wrong before exposing themselves to our vengeance. Our hope in this case is surely to make the landings inside the Mediterranean in as great a force and at as great a speed as possible, and overcome the French resistance, and get on shore and get some ports. This is why we do not understand the Casablanca emphasis, because it will be made at the expense of the landings inside, and if there is resistance inside *a fortiori* there will be resistance on the Atlantic shore, with this difference — that you can overcome the resistance inside and cannot overcome it outside unless the surf is favourable, which is four to one against. In short, the place to determine French action is inside, and if it is determined there in a favourable sense there will be no difficulty in occupying Casablanca by agreement later. On the other hand, what happens if there is a rebuff at Casablanca? What are all the troops to do that cannot land on the beaches through the surf and cannot go up the creeks and small harbours in the big ships by which they have crossed the Atlantic, and will have to face the shore batteries and the machine-gun defences of the harbour if they try a frontal attack on Casablanca port?

This letter was never sent to Hopkins, nor did Mountbatten have to cross the Atlantic. Before I had need to send it I received the following most helpful and hopeful telegram from the President:

President Roosevelt to Former Naval Person　　　　4 Sept. 42

... We are getting very close together. I am willing to reduce the

Casablanca force by the number of combat loaders capable of carrying a force of one regimental combat team. Approximately 5000 men. Since a similar reduction was made in original Oran assault force, this releases a total of British and United States combat loaders for some 10,000 men for use at Algiers. The combat-loaded force of American troops can be used as the nucleus on which to complete that force. I am sure that the additional troops can be found in the United Kingdom.

I do not see advantage of Eisenhower or Clark coming over at this time. I know they have heavy and pressing responsibilities in organising slowly arriving American forces, and I am sure we have a full understanding of their viewpoint. Furthermore, I do want to see Eisenhower later on before final take-off, and two trips appear out of the question. We would be glad to see Ramsay and Mountbatten if you wish to send them, but I do not desire that their visit shall cause any delay. I am directing all preparations to proceed. We should settle this whole thing with finality at once.

I hope to cable you today a list of United States naval craft which can be made available for the operation.

Former Naval Person to President Roosevelt   5 Sept. 42

We agree to the military layout as you propose it. We have plenty of troops highly trained for landing. If convenient, they can wear your uniform. They will be proud to do so. Shipping will be all right.

2. I have just had your telegram,[1] and it is evident that you too have skinned yourselves to the bone. Unless we suffer serious losses in P.Q., we consider that naval forces now jointly to be provided justify us in going full speed ahead with staging the operations.

3. I am sending Admiral Ramsay,[2] with the agreement of General Eisenhower, over at once to furnish Admiral Cunningham with the means of going into naval details with you. It is impera-

---

[1] *President Roosevelt to Former Naval Person*   5 Sept. 42

[Admiral] King reports maximum number of American naval vessels that can be made available for "Torch" operation: one modern battleship, two old battleships, one aircraft-carrier, two small converted aircraft-carriers (tentative planes carried total seventy-eight fighters, thirty dive-bombers), two eight-inch cruisers, three large six-inch cruisers, forty destroyers, six fast mine-sweepers; total, fifty-seven vessels.

[2] Admiral Ramsay, who had commanded at Dover with conspicuous ability since the beginning of the war, had been selected to undertake the naval planning of "Torch."

tive now to drive straight ahead and save every hour. In this way alone shall we realise your strategical design and the only hope of doing anything that really counts this year.

4. We strongly endorse the request which we understand Eisenhower has already made to Marshall that the force you are releasing from Casablanca may be sent over here complete with its regimental combat team.

Kindest regards.

President Roosevelt to Prime Minister   5 Sept. 42
Hurrah!

Former Naval Person to President Roosevelt   6 Sept. 42
O.K., full blast.

*   *   *   *   *

It now remained to press forward the planning and timing of the operation.

Prime Minister to Brigadier Hollis   6 Sept. 42
There is no need for anyone to get excited for fear "Torch" should happen too early. Intense efforts must be made to strike on October 31. To ensure this it would be well to aim at October 29. I propose to telegraph to the President in this sense. Surely if the Americans can be ready at their end we can conform at ours?

We must beware lest we give orders which lead to a general slacking off. If you announce October 31 as the earliest date it will certainly be ten days later.

On September 8 Eisenhower and Clark dined with me. It was our regular Tuesday meeting. I had come back from speaking in the House of Commons upon the results of my recent journey. The main purpose of our talk that evening was to discuss the final date of attack in North Africa. The planners were still aiming at November 4. I asked "Ike" for his view. "November 8 — sixty days from today," was his answer.[3] The new delay was apparently due to the need for equipping the American regimental combat teams. I offered,

[3] *Three Years with Eisenhower*, by Harry C. Butcher (English edition), page 82.

as before, to place our highly trained Commandos in American
uniform in order to avoid further delay. "Ike" however was
anxious to keep to the all-American character of the operation.

On September 15 I telegraphed to the President:

Former Naval Person to President Roosevelt   15 Sept. 42

I entirely agree with your political outlook on "Torch." It
is sound unless we are forestalled. There is no sign that the enemy
is aware, and the mood of France is now at its very best. I count
the days.

In the whole of "Torch," military and political, I consider
myself your lieutenant, asking only to put my viewpoint plainly
before you. We shall have a wireless station of overriding power
available by zero, so that if you dictate your appeals to France and
other propaganda material to gramophone records beforehand,
these can be blared out over everything during the performance.
We British will come in only as and when you judge expedient.
This is an American enterprise, in which we are your helpmeets.

I had however my own anxieties about Spain.

Prime Minister to Secretary of State for Foreign Affairs,
Brigadier Hollis, for C.O.S. Committee   16 Sept. 42

We shall have to watch very carefully Spanish reactions to preparations for "Torch" which will become evident at Gibraltar. I
should like to have a short report on what we shall be putting into
Gibraltar in preparation for "Torch," with time-table. How much
of these preparations would exceed the normal for a big Malta
convoy?

2. The arrival of large numbers of aircraft will be the crux of
the problem, and the use of the neutral ground will be involved.

3. What will happen if, about a fortnight before zero "Torch,"
the Germans put pressure on Spain for an explanation of these
preparations and demand either that the neutral ground is cleared
or that they are allowed to install their own aircraft in the Valencia
airfields? What are the likely Spanish reactions to this pressure,
and what should be our attitude? We might be faced with a show-
down with Franco over this at an awkward moment. I think we
should have our plans prepared.

The final decision was taken on September 22 at a Chiefs of Staff meeting at which I presided and Eisenhower was present. The date of "Torch" was fixed for November 8.

* * * * *

In the midst of all the tense correspondence with the President about our major operation Rommel made his determined, but as it proved, his last thrust towards Cairo. Until this was over my thoughts lay in the Desert and the trial of strength impending there. I had full confidence in our new Commanders and was sure that our numerical superiority in troops, armour and airpower was higher than it had ever been before. But after the unpleasant surprises of the past two years it was difficult to banish anxiety. As I had been so lately over the very ground where the battle was to be fought, and had the picture of the creased and curving rocky desert with its hidden batteries and tanks and our army crouched for a counter-spring so vividly in my mind's eye, the whole scene was fiercely lighted. Another reverse would not only be disastrous in itself but would damage British prestige and influence in the discussions we were having with our American Allies. On the other hand if Rommel were repulsed, growing confidence and the feeling that the tide was about to turn in our favour would help carry all our other affairs to agreement.

* * * * *

General Alexander had promised to send me the word "Zip" (which I took from the clothes I so often wore) when it actually began.

"What do you now think," I asked him on August 28, "of the probabilities of 'Zip' coming this moon? Military intelligence opinion now does not regard it as imminent. All good wishes."

" 'Zip,' now equal money every day," he replied, "from now onwards. Odds against it are increasing till September 2 when it can be considered unlikely." On the 30th I received the monosyllabic signal "Zip" and telegraphed to Roosevelt and

Stalin. "Rommel has begun the attack for which we have been preparing. An important battle may now be fought."

Rommel's plan, correctly deduced by Montgomery, was to pass his armour through the weakly defended mine belt in the southern part of the British front and then swing north to roll up our position from flank and rear. The critical ground for the success of this manoeuvre was the Alam Halfa ridge, and Montgomery's dispositions were made principally to ensure that this did not fall into enemy hands.

During the night of August 30 the two armoured divisions of the German Afrika Corps penetrated the mine belt, and next morning moved to the Ragil Depression. Our 7th Armoured Division withdrawing steadily before them took station on the eastward flank. To the north of the German armour, two Italian armoured divisions, and one motorised, also attempted to cross the minefield. They had little success. It was deeper than they had expected, and they found themselves under severe harassing fire from the enfilading artillery of the New Zealand Division. The German 90th Light Division however successfully penetrated, to form a hinge for the armour's northern swing. At the other end of the line simultaneous holding attacks were made on the 5th Indian and 9th Australian Divisions; these were repulsed after some stiff fighting. From the Ragil Depression the German-Italian armour had the option of striking north against the Alam Halfa ridge, or northeast towards Hammam. Montgomery hoped that they would not take the latter course. He preferred to fight on his chosen battleground, the ridge. A map which showed easy going for tanks in that direction, and bad going farther east, had been planted upon Rommel. General von Thoma, captured two months later, stated that this false information had its intended effect. Certainly the battle now took the precise form that Montgomery desired.

On the evening of the 31st a northward thrust was repulsed and the enemy's armoured mass went into laager for a night, uncomfortably spent under continuous artillery fire and violent air bombardment. Next morning they advanced against

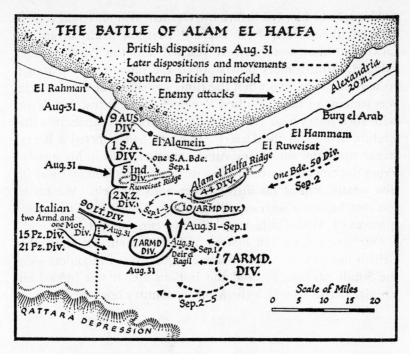

the centre of the British line, where the 10th Armoured Division were now concentrated to meet them. The sand was much heavier than they had been led to believe and the resistance far stronger than they had hoped. The attack, though renewed in the afternoon, failed. Rommel was now deeply committed. The Italians had foundered. He had no hope of reinforcing his forward armour and the heavy going had consumed much of his scanty fuel. He had probably heard also of the sinking of three more tankers in the Mediterranean. So on September 2 his armour took up a defensive posture and awaited attack.

Montgomery did not accept the invitation and Rommel had no alternative but to withdraw. On the 3d the movement began, harassed in flank by the 7th British Armoured Division, which took a heavy toll of unarmoured transport vehicles. That night the British counter-attack began, not on the enemy armour, but on the 90th Light and the Trieste Motorised Divisions. If these could be broken, then the gaps in the minefield might be blocked before the German armour could return through them. The New Zealand Division made strong attacks, but they were fiercely resisted and the Afrika Corps escaped. Montgomery now stopped the pursuit. He planned to seize the initiative when the time was ripe, but not yet. He was content to have repulsed Rommel's final thrust for Egypt with such heavy loss. At relatively little cost to themselves the Eighth Army and the Desert Air Force had inflicted a heavy stroke upon the enemy and caused another crisis in his supply. From documents captured later we know that Rommel was in dire straits, and of his insistent demands for help. We know too that he was a wearied ailing man at the time. The consequences of Alam Halfa were effective two months later.

Our losses were 110 officers and 1640 men. Of these the British lost 984; the Australians 257; the New Zealanders 405; the South Africans 65, and the Indians 39. It was indeed an Empire battle, in which the Mother Country bore the brunt.

8

Suspense and Strain

*A Trying Interlude — An Unbroken Catalogue of Misfortunes —
The Top of the Pass — Unity and Strength of the War Cabinet
— Lord Trenchard Advocates Concentration on the Air — My
Reply of September 4 — Sir Stafford Cripps Criticises Our War
Methods — My Discussion with Him — He Wishes to Resign
from the Government — My Letter to Him of September 22 —
My Colleagues Urge Him to Delay His Resignation — He De-
cides to Remain Till After the Battle — He Becomes Minister
of Aircraft Production — Consequential Changes in the Gov-
ernment — The Four-Power Plan — My Minute to the Foreign
Secretary, October 21 — I Look Forward to the United States
of Europe.*

ALTHOUGH OUR TWO GREAT OPERATIONS at both ends of the
Mediterranean were now settled and all preparations for
them were moving forward, the period of waiting was one of
suppressed but extreme tension. The inner circle who knew
were anxious about what would happen. All those who did
not know were disquieted that nothing was happening.

I had now been twenty-eight months at the head of affairs, during which we had sustained an almost unbroken series of military
defeats. We had survived the collapse of France and the air
attack on Britain. We had not been invaded. We still held
Egypt. We were alive and at bay; but that was all. On the
other hand, what a cataract of disasters had fallen upon us!
The fiasco of Dakar, the loss of all our Desert conquests from
the Italians, the tragedy of Greece, the loss of Crete, the unre-
lieved reverses of the Japanese war, the loss of Hong Kong,

549

the overrunning of the A.B.D.A. Command and all its territories, the catastrophe of Singapore, the Japanese conquest of
Burma, Auchinleck's defeat in the Desert, the surrender of
Tobruk, the failure, as it was judged, at Dieppe — all these
were galling links in a chain of misfortune and frustration to
which no parallel could be found in our history. The fact that
we were no longer alone but instead had the two most mighty
nations in the world in alliance, fighting desperately at our
side, gave indeed assurances of ultimate victory. But this, by
removing the sense of mortal peril, only made criticism more
free. Was it strange that the whole character and system of the
war direction, for which I was responsible, should have been
brought into question and challenge?

It is indeed remarkable that I was not in this bleak lull dismissed from power or confronted with demands for changes in
my methods, which it was known I should never accept. I
should then have vanished from the scene with a load of
calamity on my shoulders, and the harvest, at last to be reaped,
would have been ascribed to my belated disappearance. For indeed the whole aspect of the war was about to be transformed.
Henceforward increasing success, marred hardly by a mishap,
was to be our lot. Although the struggle would be long and
hard, requiring the most strenuous effort from all, we had
reached the top of the pass, and our road to victory was not only
sure and certain, but accompanied by constant cheering events.
I was not denied the right to share in this new phase of the
war, because of the unity and strength of the War Cabinet, the
confidence which I preserved of my political and professional
colleagues, the steadfast loyalty of Parliament, and the persist-
ing good will of the nation. All this shows how much luck
there is in human affairs, and how little we should worry about
anything except doing our best.

A number of eminent people with whom I was in various
degrees of intimacy felt the stress of these two months acutely.
One of the most important and able of the Dominion's High
Commissioners wrote a weighty letter which reached me, and
was also circulated in our select circle. This document began:

"The emotional value of Mr. Churchill is no doubt very great,
but . . . " There followed a long catalogue of my failures and
a wealth of proposals for lightening my burdens by taking
power out of my hands.

*   *   *   *   *

My friend Lord Trenchard, whom I had known and often
worked with over a quarter of a century, wrote a powerful
paper, of which he sent me a copy, advocating a concentration
on bombing *in excelsis*.

29 Aug. 42

We and the Americans are in course of organising huge armies
(maybe as much as six to eight millions for the United States alone).
These armies will need enormous quantities of material and industrial man-power to maintain them; of merchant shipping to
convey that material, and other ships (and aircraft) to protect it
in convoy. It is doubtful if the sources of raw material available
to the Allies will be sufficient to equip these forces and on a scale
which will enable them to *sustain* heavy operations in the face of
setbacks and wastage. . . .

Time is short and we are at a parting of the ways. The risk is
that we shall try to go down two roads and that our air-power will
be inextricably entangled in large schemes and protracted operations of two-dimensional warfare.

For the country to get mixed up this year or next in land warfare on the continent of Europe is to play Germany's game — it is
to revert to 1914–18. It is to bring in against us the one enormously
powerful military asset remaining to the enemy — namely, the
German Army. Our strength and advantage over Germany is in
the air — the British and the American Air Force. . . .

The strategy of warfare today is undergoing a greater change
than that caused by the invention of gunpowder or the coming of
the modern battleship. The power of the air grows every day. It
has progressed enormously since 1939. The bombs and the bomber
today are vastly different from those in use when war broke
out. . . .

Britain and America are growing stronger in the air every day.
There is no realisable limit to the power we can achieve in this arm

if we concentrate our efforts on a policy which realises what we can do — and do quickly. . . .

The policy of victory by land forces entails stupendous drains on material and on man-power. Air, the new dimension, the power in military science, has given the Allied nations the great alternative. If we decide to use it with determination and concentration we can not only save millions of lives, but we can shorten the war by months, perhaps by years. . . .

As the enemy conquered Poland and France by their "tank blitz," so can we smash the German machine by the "bomber blitz." . . .

Finally, the carrying out of this policy requires that there should be one brain responsible for the purely military (in its widest sense) strategical conception of the war in Europe, supported of course by a staff representative of all three Services. It would be essential that this commander should be one who believes in his weapon, the power of the air, and should have had experience of command in this war. There are many such.

*   *   *   *   *

Making all allowances for the shoemaker who said there is nothing like leather, I considered this paper, coming from a high authority like Lord Trenchard, so important that I had it printed and circulated, together with a similar document by Air Marshal Harris, to the War Cabinet and Chiefs of Staff, with the following note:

I do not myself adopt or endorse the views expressed. . . . Nevertheless, as these papers are written with force and vigour I thought they might be of interest to my colleagues. They also serve as a considerable answer to those who attack the usefulness of our bombing policy.

To Lord Trenchard I wrote:

Prime Minister to Viscount Trenchard   4 Sept. 42

Many thanks for your interesting paper. As you may have heard, I am a champion of Bomber Command, and I do my utmost to strengthen it in every way and to prevent it from being wrongfully inroaded upon.

While admitting and admiring the force of your arguments, I think you spoil a good case by overstating it. You certainly push it to lengths where very few people here or in the United States would agree with you. However, as I am most anxious to combat the attacks made upon what is called "the luxury bombing of Germany" and the campaign of disparagement which has been pressed upon bombing from so many quarters, I am circulating your paper to the War Cabinet, as I did a recent document by Air Marshal Harris.

With regard to your last paragraph, it is very difficult to divorce the head of the executive in any country from the chief responsibility for the conduct of the war. In the United States and Russia the head of the executive is also Commander-in-Chief, although neither Mr. Roosevelt nor Premier Stalin has any military experience or training. In this country it would be even more difficult to separate the chief constitutional authority from all control over the war sphere, which is identical with the whole life and fortunes of the nation. To pick an airman, give him plenary powers, and tell him to win the war is certainly a policy, but I wonder whether you have thought it out in all its implications. He would certainly have great difficulty with the other two Services. He would also have difficulty with the Allies, who adopt quite different systems, and particularly with the United States, who hold rigidly to a subordinate Air Force. There might also be trouble with the House of Commons, the Cabinet, and all those sorts of things. Should the right man be found however, many of these difficulties could be overcome by his becoming at the same time Prime Minister. If I were convinced that this solution would bring about a speedy victory I should be very glad to make way for him. Would it be too much to inquire whom you have in mind? You say there are many. I was not aware that our Services were so rich in talent as to have a number of officers who have already commanded in this war who take your view about the air, and who are capable of being the "one brain responsible for the purely military (in its widest sense) strategical conception of the war in Europe."

With good wishes . . .

Trenchard replied on September 8:

. . . My paper was not written for you, as I know too well that you are keen on hitting our chief enemy in Germany. It was written for a certain number of people who I thought might be influenced by the views of a complete outsider like myself. . . .

My last paragraph was not intended in any shape or form to have the meaning you have attached to it. I was not suggesting that the head of the executive should be divorced from the chief responsibility for the war. I have never expressed or held such a view. What I was trying to say was this. In many newspapers and discussions it has been suggested that there should be one Commander-in-Chief appointed for Europe — a man like Marshall or Wavell — and I wanted to combat the idea that it must necessarily be an Army man. If air is the dominant force, the force that can give us victory, why *must* the commander be a military man? Why is our strategy to be based on the "ground" view when we know now that it is the air which decides? . . .

*   *   *   *   *

But the most serious comment on our war methods came from Sir Stafford Cripps, the Lord Privy Seal. As Leader of the House of Commons his position was one of prime importance. On him fell the burden of explaining our successive defeats and disappointments to the House of Commons, and he certainly discharged his task with skill and loyalty. Severance between him and me during this period of oppressive pause would have created a political crisis. I was therefore very gravely concerned to find, on my return from abroad at the end of August, that he had developed serious doubts about the state of the national morale and the effectiveness of our machinery for the central direction of the war. In the mood of public opinion at home he detected a widespread sense of frustration and discontent. Workers, he believed, were suffering a demoralising sense of futility when they heard that the weapons which they had strained every nerve to produce had been found wanting in Libya. Scientists and technicians with ideas for operational devices were receiving no encouragement. Businessmen were exasperated at official delays and indecisions and at the wasteful proliferation of committees. In the Services officers and men were baffled and disturbed by evidence of inadequate military leadership. There was, he thought, an urgent need to infuse a new spirit of vigour and enthusiasm into the nation's war effort. For this purpose he proposed a series of reforms in our machinery of government. With some of these I found myself in full sympathy, and initiated action to give effect to them. But on the main question of the technical direction of the war I was profoundly at variance with the views expressed by the Lord Privy Seal. He did not, it is true, suggest that I should be superseded or displaced from my position; he proposed instead that as Minister of Defence I should have associated with me, as advisers, three persons of the calibre of the Chiefs of Staff who would supervise the Joint Planning Staffs and would be free to devote the whole of their time to military planning in its broadest sense. These three were to form an independent War Planning Directorate, which would keep under review the whole strategy of the war and consider all future operations; and for these purposes they were to supersede the Chiefs of Staff Committee. In each theatre of war there would be a single Commander, with full power over all the naval, land, and air forces. These Commanders, advised by a small joint staff, would be responsible directly to the War Planning Directorate. The conception was, in brief, that the Minister of Defence should turn himself into a Supreme Commander-in-Chief directly commanding all three Services all over the world, so that from the Minister downward there would be an unbroken chain of foresight, planning, and action.

This was, in truth, a planner's dream. The new Directorate, concerned solely with planning and armed with full powers of direction and control, would be free to go its way without distraction by the daily cares which beset the Chiefs of Staff in controlling the forces over which they exercised command. These manifold cares would continue to be left to the Chiefs of Staff and the staffs which served them in their individual and collective capacities, while the Supreme Command elaborated its strategy and plans in splendid isolation. I did not believe that such a dualism could succeed, and I addressed myself with zeal and vigour to the Lord Privy Seal's proposals. I judged them to be misconceived in theory and unworkable in practice. The guiding principle of war direction is, in my opinion, that war plans should be formulated by those who have the power and the responsibility for executing them. Under the system which we had evolved in the hard school of experience the need for inter-Service planning was fully met by the Chiefs of Staff Committee and its subordinate bodies, in which those carrying the responsibility for execution came together to make jointly the plans which they were to carry out. The establishment of a War Planning Directorate divorced from the Service staffs responsible for action would have been vicious in principle, for it would have created two rival bodies, one responsible and one irresponsible, yet both nominally of equal status. It would have confronted Ministers with the constant need to disregard the advice of one or other of these bodies. It would have led at once to immediate and violent friction. Was an Admiral to be appointed to the War Planning Directorate with power to tell the First Lord how to move the Fleet, or an Air Marshal "of equal calibre" to criticise by implication the Chief of the Air Staff? It was easy to see the dangers and antagonisms inherent in such a system. Any clever person can make plans for winning a war if he has no responsibility for carrying them out. Such ingenuity and resource is to be encouraged in the members of Planning Staffs, so long as they are definitely and effectively subordinated in status to the Service chiefs who carry the executive responsibility. I was not however prepared to invite a disembodied Brains Trust to browse about among our secrets and add to the already immense volume of committees and reports. My long experience in these matters had taught me that a Minister of Defence must work with and through responsible advisers — that is to say, war chiefs who can give effect to the decisions taken and are accountable for the results. There had never been a period, in this war or the last, when the relations between the Prime Minister and the three Service chiefs were so good and smooth, or when there was such complete identity of view upon all the measures to be taken. Why then should I withdraw my confidence from those professional advisers whom I considered to be the best that the Services had at this time, in order to bestow it in part at least upon officers who would be not only less responsible but less capable? It was a delusion to suppose that there was a large supply of officers "of equal calibre" to those whom I had chosen to discharge the heavy responsibilities of the Chiefs of Staff.

With these and similar arguments I wrestled with the Lord Privy Seal and strove to win him over to my point of view. This stern discussion occupied the larger part of September. But I did not succeed in convincing him, and on September 21 he intimated to me that he felt it his duty to resign his position in the Government, in which he held so commanding an office. Since his return from India, he said, he no longer felt that I relied upon his help, and found himself increasingly out of touch with my mind on a wide range of subjects on which, as Leader of the House of Commons, he ought to have an intimate knowledge. He was deeply anxious about the war situation, and, in the light of the developments of recent months and the heavy responsibilities weighing upon all members of the War Cabinet, he was anxious to know how I viewed the future. To this I replied:

22 Sept. 42

My dear Cripps,

I am surprised and somewhat pained to receive your letter. I was certainly not aware of any change in our relationship since you first took office seven months ago. I thought we were on the most cordial terms when I set out on my journey at the beginning of August. In the seven weeks that have passed since then I have been away for nearly a month, and you, later, for more than a week. Apart from Cabinets (of which we have had three, aggregating six hours and a half, in the last twenty-four hours) I always do my best to see my principal colleagues. I have always found our conversations agreeable and stimulating. I hope you will not fail to come and see me whenever you wish.

With regard to the further memorandum which you have been good enough to send me on the whole system and method by which, for good or for ill, I endeavour to discharge my task of presiding over the Government and the conduct of the war, no one knows better than you the controversial significance of all that you write. I also have convictions on these matters, which are the result of long experience and heavy responsibility. Another would no doubt do differently.

I do not intend to argue here, as it would be endless, but I am sure you would not underrate the wisdom, knowledge, and precision of mind of the First Sea Lord if you had worked with him as closely as I have under the hard stresses of this war. Indeed, I cannot help saying that I feel you are less than generous to the Admiralty achievement by which we have lived.

You ask me how I view the future. I view it with hope, and, I trust, with undiminished firmness of spirit. Great operations impend which are in full accordance with your own conceptions and on which we are all agreed. We must have the fibre and fortitude to endure the delays and await the outcome. As I myself find waiting more trying than action, I can fully understand the uneasiness you say you feel.

Yours very sincerely
WINSTON S. CHURCHILL

I realised, none the less, that he would not again give me his full confidence and that he could not for long take his full share of responsibility as a colleague in the War Cabinet. It was clear to me that if he resigned from the Government on this account keen political controversy must follow; and, although I was resolved to face this, I hoped that it would not take place while all hung in the balance in Africa. Several of my colleagues in the War Cabinet urged him to consider whether his resignation at this juncture would not be injurious to the public interest, having regard to the great operations which were now drawing ever nearer to their decisive moment. Although it was evident that if we won the impending battles in North Africa my position would be overwhelmingly strengthened and his proportionately reduced, his patriotism ruled his conduct.

3 Oct. 42

My dear Prime Minister,

In accordance with my promise when I saw you yesterday, I am writing to you about my position in the War Cabinet, which we have been discussing during the last few days.

You have not convinced me that the changes which I have suggested in the central direction of the war are unnecessary. I firmly believe that alterations of that nature are essential if we are to make the most of our war potential.

Such a conviction would have led me to ask you to place my resignation in the hands of H.M. the King, were it not for the special circumstances to which you and my other colleagues have drawn my attention.

I fully realise however, as you have impressed upon me, that this precise moment is one of great anxiety for the country and for the Government. In such circumstances it is clear that nothing avoidable should be done during these particularly critical days by the suggestion of disunity or of differences as to the central direction of the war which might disturb the morale of our fighting men or increase our international difficulties.

These temporary considerations seem to me to override even the necessity for the changes that I have suggested, and I have therefore decided that it is my duty, in the interest of the successful prosecution of the coming operations, to delay taking any further action as regards my position in the War Cabinet until the operations are at least well launched.

When the time arrives I will revert to this matter.

It is, I am sure, unnecessary for me to add that in the meantime I shall do my utmost to assist you in every possible way and that I shall give you my utmost energetic support wherever and whenever I can.

P.S. — I have shown this letter to Anthony Eden and Clem Attlee, and have told the other members of the War Cabinet of the general line of my action.

3 Oct. 42

My dear Stafford Cripps,

I am sure that you are right to withhold your resignation until the great operations upon which we have all agreed have been, as you say, at least well launched. The discussions attending your departure from the Government could not fail at the present time to be harmful to the public interest and to the safety of British and American troops. It would be very difficult for me to take

part in them without saying something from which the enemy
might draw conclusions. On the other hand, you are fully entitled
to bring our differences to an issue at a later stage. Meanwhile I
thank you for your assurance that you will give me all possible
help in the interval, and I shall certainly reciprocate your aid and
courtesy to the full.

*   *   *   *   *

In the event, Sir Stafford Cripps did not withdraw entirely
from the Government. Although he was no longer willing to
accept the full responsibilities entailed by membership of the
War Cabinet itself, I was anxious to find some other field of
service within the Government in which his talents and energies could continue to be used. In November, when the battle
in Africa was fairly launched, I prevailed upon him to take
Ministerial charge of the Ministry of Aircraft Production, an
office which he held with increasing skill and effectiveness until
the end of the war. I am glad to be able to acknowledge my
sense of obligation to him for the loyal and efficient service
which he rendered as a Production Minister during those three
difficult years. Elsewhere in this book I have said that an
exalted brooding over the work of others is only too often the
lot of a Minister without departmental duties. For a man of
his keen intellect, as yet untempered by administrative experience, his exalted ideals and his skill in theoretical exposition,
this form of activity held a strong though dangerous appeal.
His great intellectual energy needed to be harnessed to a more
practical task; and the success which he achieved as Minister
of Aircraft Production, no less than the sense of frustration
which he suffered as Lord Privy Seal, only deepens my regret
that he should have declined my original proposal that he
should join the Government in the first instance as Minister
of Supply.

*   *   *   *   *

It will be convenient if at this point, in defiance of chronology, I complete this part of my story by recording the other
Cabinet changes which became necessary at the end of Novem-

ber. I had long felt the need to have a Minister resident in Washington to handle the numerous supply problems which arose with the United States Administration and could best be settled at a Ministerial level. Colonel J. J. Llewellin readily agreed to make way for Sir Stafford Cripps at the Ministry of Aircraft Production and to assume instead this responsible role in Washington. Viscount Cranborne, who had a heavy task as Leader of the House of Lords, accepted the office of Lord Privy Seal and surrendered his departmental duties at the Colonial Office to Colonel Oliver Stanley, who was willing at this time to abandon his military work and to resume Ministerial office. Mr. Anthony Eden agreed to add to his duties as Foreign Secretary the task of leading the House of Commons.

Sir Stafford Cripps' transfer to the Ministry of Aircraft Production left a vacancy in the War Cabinet, which was filled by Mr. Herbert Morrison. As Home Secretary and Minister of Home Security he had used his great administrative ability to advantage in adapting our Civil Defence organisation to meet the varying challenges of 1940 and 1941; now he had rather more time in which to deploy his political agility. My War Cabinet colleagues were glad to have his assistance in their councils.

* * * * *

Amid these internal political stresses I found some relief in examining the proposals which the Foreign Office were elaborating, in consultation with the State Department in Washington, on the future of world government after the war. The Foreign Secretary circulated to the War Cabinet in October an important document on this subject entitled "The Four-Power Plan," under which the supreme direction would have come from a council composed of Great Britain, the United States, Russia, and China. I am glad that I found strength to put my own opinions on record in the following minute.

Prime Minister to Foreign Secretary   21 Oct. 42

In spite of the pressure of events, I will endeavour to write a reply. It sounds very simple to pick out these four Big Powers. We cannot however tell what sort of a Russia and what kind of Russian demands we shall have to face. A little later on it may be possible. As to China, I cannot regard the Chungking Government as representing a great world Power. Certainly there would be a faggot vote on the side of the United States in any attempt to liquidate the British overseas Empire.

2. I must admit that my thoughts rest primarily in Europe — the revival of the glory of Europe, the parent continent of the modern nations and of civilisation. It would be a measureless disaster if Russian barbarism overlaid the culture and independence of the ancient States of Europe. Hard as it is to say now, I trust that the European family may act unitedly as one under a Council of Europe. I look forward to a United States of Europe in which the barriers between the nations will be greatly minimised and unrestricted travel will be possible. I hope to see the economy of Europe studied as a whole. I hope to see a Council consisting of perhaps ten units, including the former Great Powers, with several confederations — Scandinavian, Danubian, Balkan, etc. — which would possess an international police and be charged with keeping Prussia disarmed. Of course we shall have to work with the Americans in many ways, and in the greatest ways, but Europe is our prime care, and we certainly do not wish to be shut up with the Russians and the Chinese when Swedes, Norwegians, Danes, Dutch, Belgians, Frenchmen, Spaniards, Poles, Czechs, and Turks will have their burning questions, their desire for our aid, and their very great power of making their voices heard. It would be easy to dilate upon these themes. Unhappily the war has prior claims on your attention and on mine.

*   *   *   *

Thus we approached the great military climax upon which all was to be staked.

9

Soviet "Thank You"

I RETURNED from Moscow with new resolve to aid Russia to the very limits of our power. It was clear that the coming winter campaign would be the supreme crisis of the struggle in the East, that the Russian southern flank in the Don and Caucasus regions was to be the theatre, and the oilfields of Baku and the domination of the Caspian area the immediate German goal. I had been impressed by Stalin's solid confidence that he would win, and knew from what he had told me at the Kremlin that he planned some tremendous counter-stroke.

There was little enough that we could do to sway this gigantic
conflict. We must send supplies at all costs by every route to
the Russian armies. We must maintain the Arctic convoys and
develop the Trans-Persian railway. The only direct military
help we could give was to place a strong Anglo-American air
force in the Caspian area. Even this must wait for its fulfilment
till victory was gained in the Western Desert. Meanwhile all
preparations for it would go forward, under the name of
Operation "Velvet."

As soon as I got home I presented the project formally to the
President.

Former Naval Person to President Roosevelt   30 Aug. 42

The project of placing on the southern flank of the Russian
armies a British and presently American air force must be viewed
as a long-term policy in our co-operation with Russia and for the
defence of the Persian oilfields. The main reasons appear to be:
(*a*) to strengthen the Russian air-power generally; (*b*) to form
the advance shield of all our interests in Persia and Abadan; (*c*) for
moral effect of comradeship with the Russians, which will be out
of all proportion to the forces employed; and (*d*) because this is
no dispersion of forces, but a greater concentration on the supreme
Allied Air Force target, namely, wearing down the German Air
Force by daily fighting contact.

2. Following on the various references to this subject which occur
in our correspondence, and to the favour with which you have
viewed it in principle, I have committed His Majesty's Government
in my talks with Stalin to the general policy and have stated that
you also took a great interest in the matter. I now submit, Mr. President, a formal draft on which you may feel disposed to give me
your decision:

(i) The proposal is to establish in Trans-Caucasia an Anglo-
American Air Force to assist the Russian land and air forces in
holding the line of the Caucasus Mountains and the Black Sea
coast. The necessary air forces would be withdrawn from Egypt
as soon as the situation in the Western Desert is such that they
can be spared from that front, and could be concentrated in the
Baku-Batum area in about two months from that time.

(ii) This proposal has already been offered in general terms to

Premier Stalin, who accepted it gratefully and indicated that the details of the plan should receive further study. In discussion between the C.I.G.S., Air Marshal Tedder, and Marshal Voroshilov it was agreed that combined planning and preparation should start at once, and the suggestion put that Allied air representatives should go to Moscow for this purpose.

3. Subject to American agreement, the force envisaged would comprise the following units: eight short-range fighter squadrons, one long-range fighter squadron, three light bomber squadrons, two medium bomber squadrons, one United States heavy bombardment group, and possibly, later, one general reconnaissance squadron.

4. Owing to the extreme difficulties which the lack of good ground communications will impose on the maintenance of this force, ample air transport will be essential for its maintenance. One United States transport group of approximately fifty aircraft is considered the minimum necessary for this purpose.

5. Thus, the American contribution suggested is one heavy bombardment group now in Egypt and one transport group, which is not at present available in the Middle East. The former will require an adequate flow of aircraft and trained crews to meet attrition. In addition it is of the utmost importance that every effort should be made to ensure that at least the aircraft and air crews, both first-line and replacements, together with minimum maintenance parties of the United States Pursuit and Medium Bomber groups scheduled for the Middle East, should be operationally fit in Egypt by the dates agreed. Even if Rommel is driven out of Cyrenaica, the air defence of Egypt and our long line of communications in the Western Desert will be a heavy commitment. It is also vitally important that the R.A.F. allocations of American fighters for Egypt be fully and promptly supplied, since we must expect a high rate of attrition in the Caucasus area, not only in air fighting, but on account of the poor communications and lack of adequate repair facilities in that area.

6. The force will have to rely for the protection of its bases and line of communications mainly on the Russian forces, but we should be prepared to send light anti-aircraft units for the defence of aerodromes. We might also have to send some engineer units for work on aerodromes.

7. It is important that the ground echelon of the force should

be kept as small as possible consistent with the effective operation of the aircraft, since it can only be concentrated and maintained at the expense of Russian supplies through the Persian Gulf route. The interference with these supplies should not be serious. The concentration of the force will involve a movement on the rail and sea communications between Iraq and the Caucasus of the order of 12,000 personnel, 2000 vehicles, and 4000 tons of stores. Its subsequent maintenance, on the assumption that petrol and lubricants can be supplied by the Russians, should not exceed 200 tons a day, of which a substantial proportion should be lifted by air.

8. The force will operate under the strategic control of the Russian High Command, but will remain a homogeneous Allied force under a British air officer, with the right of appeal to his own Government.

9. The foregoing should constitute the basis of instructions to a mission consisting of British and American Air Force officers, who should be despatched forthwith to Russia to undertake the necessary planning reconnaissance and practical preparations in combination with the Russians. It is urgently important that this be put in hand without delay.

The President, who was at this time engaged in the Congressional elections, replied briefly.

President Roosevelt to Prime Minister   31 Aug. 42

I will let you know by Tuesday in regard to your telegram. I am in full accord with desirability of it, and will make every effort to dovetail it into the other operations.

Also we are working on the Persian railway problem, and I will advise you.

I was most anxious that everything in our power should be done to send convoys to Stalin.

*   *   *   *   *

Prime Minister to First Sea Lord   26 Aug. 42

It is true that no one can tell how far an enterprise like "Torch," once begun, will carry us. Nevertheless we should now make plans to resume the P.Q. convoys late in October or the beginning of November. It may be that losses in "Torch," or great and hopeful developments there, will force or induce us to concentrate all our efforts in the Mediterranean. But the results of battle explain themselves and we have to accept them.

2. Although I indicated in my conversations with Stalin, and it is upon the record, that "Torch" would affect the P.Q.'s, I think it would be a great mistake at this crisis to send him news, which amounts to the fact that he will get nothing more after the September convoy this year. We should therefore get the utmost help we can from the President, and push ahead with plans for the P.Q.s until or unless we have to give them up by main force. I still think means may be found to run them. If not, there will be overwhelming reasons for not doing so.

At the beginning of September a further Arctic convoy sailed. Its adventures have been described in an earlier chapter.[1] I informed Stalin of this movement.

Prime Minister to Premier Stalin   6 Sept. 42

Convoy P.Q.18, with forty ships, has started. As we cannot send our heavy ships within range of enemy shore-based aircraft, we are providing a powerful destroyer striking force, which will be used against the enemy's surface ships should they attack us east of Bear Island. We are also including in the convoy escort, to assist in protecting it against air attack, an auxiliary aircraft-carrier just completed. Further, we are placing a strong line of submarine patrols between the convoy and the German bases. The risk of an attack by German surface ships still however remains serious. This danger can only be effectively warded off by providing, in the Barents Sea, air striking forces of such strength that the Germans will not risk their heavy ships any more than we will risk ours in that area. For reconnaissance we are providing eight Catalina flying-boats and three Photographic Reconnaissance Unit Spitfires to operate from North Russia. To increase the scale of air attack we have sent thirty-two torpedo-carrying aircraft, which have suffered loss on the way, though we hope that at least twenty-four will be available for operation. These, with the nineteen bombers, the ten torpedo-carrying aircraft, the forty-two short-range and forty-three long-range fighters which we understand you are providing, will almost certainly not be enough to act as a final deterrent. What

[1] Book I, Chapter 15.

is needed is more long-range bombers. We quite understand that the immense pressure put upon you on the main line of battle makes it difficult to supply any more Russian Army long-range bombers; but we must stress the great importance of this convoy, in which we are using seventy-seven warships, requiring to take in fifteen thousand tons of fuel during the operation. If you can transfer more long-range bombers to the north temporarily, please do so. It is most needful for our common interests.

2. Rommel's attack in Egypt has been sharply rebuffed, and I have good hopes we may reach a favourable decision there during the present month.

3. The operation "Torch," though set back about three weeks beyond the earliest date I mentioned to you, is on, full blast.

4. I am awaiting the President's answer to definite proposals I have made him for bringing a British-American air contingent into action during the winter on your southern flank. He agrees in principle, and I am expecting to receive his plans in detail. I will then cable you again. Meanwhile I hope that planning with regard to airfields and communications may proceed as was agreed, subject to your approval, by your officers while I was in Moscow. For this purpose we are anxious to send Staff officers from Egypt to Moscow, in the first instance, as soon as you are ready for us to do so.

5. We are watching with lively admiration the continued magnificent resistance of the Russian armies. The German losses are certainly heavy and winter is drawing nearer. I shall give, when I address the House of Commons on Tuesday, an account of my visit to Moscow, of which I retain most pleasing memories, in what I hope you will regard as agreeable terms.

6. Please give my good wishes to Molotov and thank him for his congratulations on my safe return. May God prosper all our undertakings.

Premier Stalin to Premier Churchill   8 Sept. 42

I received your message on September 7. I understand all the importance of safe arrival of convoy P.Q.18 in Soviet Union and necessity of taking measures for its defence. Difficult as it is for us to transfer at the present moment an additional number of long-range bombers for this task, we have decided to do so. Today orders have been given to send additional long-range bombers for the purpose mentioned by you.

I wish you success in the outcome of operations against Rommel in Egypt, and also full success in Operation "Torch."

The heavy losses sufferel by the Arctic convoys, including twelve ships in P.Q.18, the deteriorating position in the Atlantic, and the increased demands upon our shipping for "Torch," forced us to consider whether or not we could keep up these sailings on the northern route to Russia. I had already warned President Roosevelt of this.

President Roosevelt to Former Naval Person 16 Sept. 42

We are prepared to take over the Persian railway and all plans are now being developed. We are examining closely the Anglo-American Air Force in southern Russia, and I hope to have word for you very soon in regard to this. I fully appreciate the importance of Stalin knowing that we mean business. . . . If the decision is against sending further convoys I will of course do everything I can with Stalin.

The urgency of this question of convoys lay behind the increased attention which I now gave to the "Jupiter" project. The reader will remember that I asked General McNaughton, the Canadian Commander-in-Chief in England, to report on this plan. On September 16, I commented upon his paper to the Chiefs of Staff.

Operation "Jupiter" [2]

Prime Minister to General Ismay for C.O.S. Committee 16 Sept. 42

To keep contact with Russia and to keep the Russian armies equipped and in the field by a continued stream of supplies must be considered one of the three or four most important vital objects before us. For this the greatest sacrifices and exertions must be made by the Allies. The total defeat of Russia or the reduction of that country to a minor military factor would let the whole mass of the German armies loose upon us. The President has stated that he regards the maintenance of the P.Q. convoys as an operation of equal magnitude with "Torch," although he is ready to skip one or perhaps two for the sake of "Torch."

2 See Book I, Chapter 20, page 348.

2. The alternative before us is therefore: (a) to go on with the P.Q. convoys (perhaps missing one or two) in addition to "Torch" and all it implies, all through 1943. Indeed, the scale of the convoys must be increased. The Russians have been solemnly promised larger quotas, and they will become more dependent on imported arms as their own territory is reduced by enemy invasion; or (b) to clear the Germans out of the north of Norway by some form of the operation "Jupiter."

When we consider the losses attendant on the sending of these convoys, that they have to take place at least three times in every two months, and the grievous consequences of our announcing, on the other hand, that we can send no more, it may well be that "Jupiter," with all its cost and risk, will be found not only necessary but cheapest in the long run.

3. I have now read the McNaughton report, which certainly does not err on the side of underrating the difficulties before us. Making allowances for this, the McNaughton report can be taken as a basis for further discussions.

4. When the winter comes the Russians must take the offensive against the German lines. Here in the north is as good a place as any, and, having regard to their vital need of Allied munitions, I have no doubt, after my conversations with Premier Stalin, that they not only will resist attacks upon the Murmansk and Archangel railways, but also would be willing to set on foot a heavy offensive towards Petsamo. At any rate, before dogmatising about it we must find out what they would be prepared to do. I am assuming however that they would not only bring enough forces to the north to attack the enemy, as proposed by General McNaughton, but also would if necessary undertake part of the landings themselves.

5. The fitting of Operation "Jupiter" into our war plans can only be considered in relation to "Torch." We cannot yet judge what "Torch" will involve. If the French come over to us the whole of the "Torch" area may be formed up against Germany in a week, or even a night. If this were so, we should have harbours with proper defences, airfields, eight or nine French divisions, a certain amount of air, and perhaps the French fleet in Toulon. In this case the British troops could be railed rapidly through to attack Tripoli from the west. There is no question of the Germans being able in the time mentioned — a fortnight, or even a month —

to mount and launch a heavy attack. They have not got, above all, the air force to spare. We must expect that very heavy operations in Egypt and Libya will have been already in progress. Therefore, I think, if things go well for us on the North African shore, it may be that a large number of assault ships and tank-landing craft will be free to go north for "Jupiter." To these would be added all the additions to our tank-landing force and assault ships, over and above those assigned to "Torch," which were coming into Britain under "Bolero" for the purposes of "Round-up." It is no use saying the Americans have cancelled all this, because we have not yet given them the reasons against such improvident action. I am sure I can claim from the United States for the purposes of "Jupiter" all the craft which were being prepared under "Bolero" for an April "Round-up," or at any rate enough of them. I admit the escorts are the pinch.

6. On the other hand, if the French fight the Americans in "Torch" and ask the Germans to come and help them, and the Germans come, or the Spaniards turn against us and we have to fight neck or nothing in the "Torch" area, naturally in that case "Jupiter" does not have to be argued about.

7. I have no doubt we could have a couple of Arctic-trained American divisions, and with the Canadian Corps and also several Russian divisions, apart from the Russian offensive, we could get together quite enough forces to conquer the "Jupiter" area. But if we don't make preparations, not mere paper plans, now (which, anyhow, may come in for 1943–44), order the equipment, train the troops, etc., we are not even going to have the option.

8. It follows that if "Jupiter" as well as "Torch" should get going there could be no "Round-up" till 1944. This is already the United States view. But "Torch" by itself is no substitute for "Round-up."

I thought it wise to present this plan to Stalin, and proposed sending McNaughton himself to explain it to the Russian High Command. It was also necessary to make clear to Stalin that whereas we were prepared to consider an operation on the lines of "Jupiter," the commitments of "Torch" would inevitably lead to a temporary reduction in the scale of supplies to Russia, and that another convoy on the scale of P.Q.18 was out of the question. On September 22 I telegraphed to the President as follows:

Former Naval Person to President Roosevelt   22 Sept. 42

Following is text of telegram which I wish to send to Stalin:

As I told you in Moscow, we are convinced that the most effective contribution that we and the United States can make in 1942 to the defeat of Germany is to launch "Torch" at the earliest possible date.

2. The date which has now been finally fixed with the President is early in November.

3. The effect of "Torch" must be either (*a*) to oblige the Germans to divert air and land forces to counter our move, or (*b*) to compel them to accept the new position created by the success of "Torch," which would then create a further diversion by the threat of attack against Sicily and the south of Europe.

4. The considerable success of the last convoy operation was achieved only because no less than seventy-seven warships were employed in the operation. Protection on anything like this scale will be impossible until the end of the year, when the naval escorts which must now assemble for "Torch" can again be made available in northern waters.

5. In the meanwhile we are trying to find means of sending you supplies on a reduced scale by the Northern route during the rest of 1942.

6. We intend to resume the full flow of supplies from January 1943.

7. In order to reduce losses of merchant ships by enemy action, and thus make the convoys in 1943 as effective as possible, we are anxious to examine with you the possibility of carrying out Operation "Jupiter" during this winter.

8. I therefore suggest to you that I send to Moscow General McNaughton, Commander-in-Chief of the Canadian Army, arriving in the early days of October, so that he may discuss the matter fully with your Staff. He has already made a preliminary examination of this question.

It was a disagreeable issue to face, and the President had not yet returned to Washington. On September 27 I received the following reply:

President Roosevelt to Prime Minister 27 Sept. 42

I agree with you that the realities of the situation require us to give up P.Q.19. While I think that is a tough blow for the Russians, I nevertheless think that the purposes for which the escorts are to be used both as to time and place make that decision inevitable. P.Q.19 however would not have sailed under any circumstances for another ten days, and I feel very strongly that we should not notify the Russians until that time arrives and we know with finality that the convoy will not go. I can see nothing to be gained by notifying Stalin sooner than is necessary, and indeed much to be lost. Furthermore, I believe that within ten days we could come to a final conclusion about the air force in Trans-Caucasia, regarding which Stalin should be notified at the same time.

For security reasons I think it would be unwise to unload any of the ships at Iceland. While it is true that we are short of shipping, we probably do not need those particular ships for "Torch," and I think we had better make the sacrifice of letting the ships remain idle in Iceland rather than risk giving the enemy the information that we are not running the next convoy. I believe that "Torch" should not be delayed a single day. We are going to put everything in that enterprise, and I have great hopes for it.

I will be back in Washington Thursday, and will cable you then regarding the air force in the Caucasus and other matters. I am having a great trip. The training of our forces is far advanced and their morale excellent. Production is good, but must be better.

Former Naval Person to President 28 Sept. 42

Earliest date P.Q.19 could have sailed is October 2 — i.e., five days from date of your message of September 27. However, if you think well we can keep it, as if it really was sailing, till 7th or even later. Bulk of the ships are in Scottish ports. Agree it is most important to make a firm offer about Caucasus air support.

* * * * *

The situation in the Caucasus still caused anxiety, though I did not believe the Germans would reach Baku. I had a standing bet on this with the C.I.G.S., on which I used to chaff him weekly at Cabinet: "How is our bet going this week?" On the view taken of this depended whether General Wilson's Tenth Army in Persia should move forward.

All turned on timing.

Prime Minister to General Ismay, for C.O.S. Committee 28 Sept. 42

General Wilson's proposals for taking up advanced positions in Persia are sound in principle and seem to be well worked out.

The price to be paid in cutting down Russian supplies is heavy, and the moment when P.Q.19 is cancelled is by no means the best for notifying the Russians. The question is therefore one of timing, and the answer depends upon the view taken of the German advance into the Caucasus. In the six weeks that have passed since the C.I.G.S. and I were in Moscow the Caucasus situation has improved markedly. More than forty of the sixty days for which Premier Stalin told me he would have to hold out have passed. The Russian resistance has been most vigorous. Their artillery still commands the borders of Novorossisk. The intruders over the high passes made no headway. Snow is falling on the Caucasian Mountains. The Grozny oilfield has not yet been taken. The fortifications which the C.I.G.S. saw just beginning on the Caspian shore must now be much further advanced. Personally I have always felt that the Russians would hold the line of the Caucasus Mountains until the spring, and that Baku would not be taken this year. I must admit that this view is temperamental rather than scientific. Nevertheless we must all feel that things have turned out better than many people expected.

2. In the light of the above, it would certainly seem that we could afford to wait for another fortnight before embarking on the forward move of the Tenth Army. By the middle of October it should be possible to see more clearly over the whole scene, and I suggest we wait until then before addressing the Russians and the Americans on the subject of trans-Persian tonnages.

3. President Roosevelt has now promised to give an answer, presumably favourable, about "Velvet" by October 7. A draft time-table should be prepared on the assumption that the answer is favourable. I am not clear whether the twenty squadrons of "Velvet" involve all the aircraft, including the Army components, at the disposal of our Tenth Army. They will certainly be in advance of it and a shield to it, and if things go badly they will fall back on it. It would be convenient to have all the air units set out on a table even before the President's message is received.

4. It is not yet necessary or possible to make up our minds what to do with the Tenth Army if the German attack on Russia in 1942 should present itself as a definite failure. But this question

will assume a greater precision when we see how "Lightfoot" [the Desert offensive] and "Torch" go.

* * * * *

The Russians showed neither appreciation of our efforts nor understanding of our difficulties, and the following minor incident was a gloomy example of the state of our relations.

Prime Minister to M. Molotov 27 Sept. 42

The Foreign Secretary tells me that he has sent you a message about the British Naval Hospital at Vaenga being ordered to close and go home. I should be glad if you would look into the matter personally yourself. Terrible cases of mutilation through frost-bite are now arriving back here, and I have to consider constantly the morale of the merchant seamen, who have hitherto gone so willingly to man the merchant ships to Russia. The British hospital unit was sent simply to help, and implied no reflection on Russian arrangements under the pressure of air bombardment, etc. It is hard on men in hospital not to have nurses who speak their own language. At any rate, I hope you will give me some solid reason which I can give should the matter be raised in Parliament, as it very likely will be.

This was all I got:

M. Molotov to Prime Minister 2 Oct. 42

In my letter to Mr. Eden I asked him to acquaint you, Mr. Prime Minister, with the contents of my reply on the question of the British medical personnel in Archangel and Vaenga (Murmansk). I think that if you glance at the memorandum of the Soviet Foreign Office of August 27 and my letter of September 12 addressed to the British Ambassador you will have the full information on the matter and will be in a position to draw the necessary conclusions as to the real state of affairs, particularly in regard to certain irregularities in the actions of the respective British naval authorities.

This grimace is a good example of how official jargon can be used to destroy any kind of human contact, or even thought itself.

* * * * *

On October 5 I received the President's comments upon my proposed message of September 22 to Stalin.

President Roosevelt to Prime Minister   5 Oct. 42

I have gone over carefully your proposed message to Stalin of September 22.

I feel very strongly that we should make a firm commitment to put an air force in the Caucasus, and that that operation should not be contingent on any other.

The Russian front is today our greatest reliance, and we simply must find a direct manner in which to help them other than our diminishing supplies. We shall on our part undertake to replace in the Middle East all of our own planes which are transferred, and assist you in every way possible with your own air problems in the Middle East.

In so far as P.Q.19 is concerned, I feel most strongly that we should not tell Stalin that the convoy will not sail. After talk with Admiral King I would like to urge that a different technique be employed, in which evasion and dispersion are the guiding factors. Thus let P.Q.19 sail in successive groups, comprising the fastest ships now loaded and loading for Russia. These groups would comprise two or three ships each, supported by two or three escorts, and sail at twenty-four- to forty-eight-hour intervals. They might have to go without the full naval covering support that would protect the convoy from the *Tirpitz* or heavy cruisers, but that must simply be a risk that we have to take. We know that in so far as air attack is concerned the weather would in all probability not be against us every day and that the longer nights will be of help.

I believe we would stand a good chance of getting as high a proportion of the ships through as we did with P.Q.18. Under any circumstances I think it is better that we take this risk than endanger our whole relations with Russia at this time. I know that you and Pound will give this proposal of mine every consideration. I should tell you that our Ambassador, Admiral Standley, has asked to come home to deliver in person a very important message, and I have some fears as to what that message might be.

About "Velvet" the President proposed that I should send the following to Stalin:

You will recall our conversation about putting a British-American air force in the Caucasus. I have examined this matter with the President, and we have determined to move to accomplish this without delay. I will let you know the extent of the air force that we can make available, and our plans for building the force up during succeeding months.

He ended:

Please let me know when you send [your] message to Stalin, and I will immediately send him a similar message, but I am certain both our messages should be so phrased as to leave a good taste in his mouth.

* * * * *

Throughout the following weeks discussions continued between the President and myself upon the possibilities of Operation "Velvet" and ways and means of maintaining the Arctic convoys. On October 5, after nearly a month's silence, I received through M. Maisky the following telegram from Stalin:

5 Oct. 42

I have to inform you that the situation in the Stalingrad area deteriorated since the beginning of September. The Germans were able to concentrate in this area great reserves of aviation, and in this way managed to secure superiority in the air in the ratio of two to one. We have not enough fighters for the protection of our forces from the air. Even the bravest troops are helpless if they lack the air protection. We more particularly require Spitfires and Air-Cobras. I told about all that in great detail to Mr. Wendell Willkie.

2. The ships with arms arrived at Archangel and are being unloaded. This is a great help. In view however of the scarcity of tonnage we would be prepared temporarily to forgo some forms of assistance, and in this way secure the increased number of the fighter aircraft.

3. The information of your intelligence to the effect that Germany manufactures not more than 1300 combat machines a month is not confirmed by our sources. According to our information, the German aircraft works, together with the works in the occupied countries engaged in making of aircraft parts, are producing not less than 2500 combat machines a month.

I passed this to the President, with the following comments:

Former Naval Person to President Roosevelt   7 Oct. 42

There is no possibility of letting P.Q.19 sail in successive groups with reduced escorts as you suggest. Neither can the fact that the convoy is not sailing be concealed from the Russians any longer. Maisky is already aware of the position, though not officially informed, and I expect he has let Stalin know the general prospect. We are preparing ten ships to sail individually during the October dark.[3] They are all British ships, for which the crews will have to volunteer, the dangers being terrible, and their sole hope if sunk far from help being Arctic clothing and such heating arrangements as can be placed in the lifeboats. Absolutely nothing else is possible unless you are able to help by providing some American ships for independent sailing after November 9, should experience have proved that the chances are sufficiently good.

2. I believe that the blunt truth is best with Stalin, but that there has been advantage in the delay of a fortnight in telling him, which you proposed. I feel strongly that he should be told now.

3. With regard to "Velvet," nothing can move before the battle in Egypt. There is the danger that the Germans will pull their Air Force off Russia and turn it on to Egypt. There is also the probability that they will be forced anyway to turn a large proportion on to "Torch."

But, although we cannot be definite about an early date, it seems to me that we could be more definite as to the composition of the force. We have for weeks had the exact composition of the twenty squadrons planned out, subject to your concurrence and help. I should like to state the actual detail of the force and the time required for it to move and come into action.

4. I am puzzled to know what message Admiral Standley is bringing home to you, but I cannot believe it threatens a separate peace. So far the Russian campaign has been very adverse to Hitler, and though they are angry with us both they are by no means in despair.

5. If therefore we offer "Velvet" as now defined, plus increased aircraft deliveries and the individual ships on the P.Q. route, I trust this will be sufficient to bridge the gap before "Torch" opens.

[3] Thirteen merchant ships sailed independently to Russia at this time. Five arrived.

*   *   *   *   *

On October 9 I telegraphed Stalin, outlining the "Velvet" plan.

Prime Minister to Premier Stalin   9 Oct. 42

We shall attack in Egypt towards the end of this month, and "Torch" will begin early in November. The effect of these operations must be either: (*a*) to oblige the Germans to send air and land forces to counter our move; or (*b*) to compel them to accept the new position created by our success, which would then create a diversion by the threat of attack against Sicily and the south of Europe.

2. Our attack in Egypt will be in good force. "Torch" will be a heavy operation, in which, in addition to the United States Navy, 240 British warships and more than half a million men will be engaged. This is all rolling forward irrevocably.

3. The President and I are anxious to put an Anglo-American air force on your southern flank and operate it under the strategic control of the Soviet High Command. Orders have been issued by us to assemble this force and take their station so that they would be available for combat early in the New Year. Most of this force will come from Egypt as soon as they can be disengaged from the battle there, which we believe will be successful on our part.

4. In the letter which M. Maisky delivered to me on October 5 you asked for a great increase in fighter aircraft supplied to Russia by this country and the United States. We will send you as soon as possible, by the Persian Gulf route, one hundred and fifty Spitfires, with the equivalent of fifty more in the form of spares, to be sent as they become available, as a special reinforcement, which we cannot repeat. This special reinforcement is over and above the protocol supplies by the Northern route so far as it can be used. President Roosevelt will cable separately about the United States contribution.

5. I was greatly relieved that so large a proportion of the last convoy reached Archangel safely. This success was achieved only because no less than seventy-seven warships were employed on the operation. Naval protection will be impossible until our impending operations are completed. As the necessary escorts are withdrawn from "Torch" they can again be made available in northern waters.

6. Nevertheless we intend in the meanwhile to do our best to send

you supplies by the Northern route by means of ships sailed independently instead of in escorted convoys. Arrangements have been made to sail ships from Iceland during the moonless period October 28 to November 8. Ten of ours are preparing in addition to what the Americans will do. The ships will sail singly, at about 200-mile intervals, with occasional larger gaps, and rely on evasion and dispersion.

7. We hope to resume the flow of supplies in strongly escorted convoys from January 1943.

8. It would of course greatly help both you and us if the Germans could be denied the use of airfields in northern Norway. If your staffs could make a good plan the President and I would at once examine the possibility of co-operating up to the limit of our ability.

The President took similar steps.

President Roosevelt to Prime Minister   9 Oct. 42

I am sending the following message to Premier Stalin today:

"The Prime Minister has sent me copy of his message to you. We are going to move as rapidly as possible to place an air force under your strategic command in the Caucasus. I am now trying to find additional planes for you immediately, and will advise you soon. I am also trying to arrange to have some of our merchant ships transferred to your flag to increase your flow of materials in the Pacific. I have just ordered an automobile tyre plant to be made available to you. We are sending very substantial reinforcements to the Persian Gulf to increase the flow of supplies over the route, and are confident that this can be done. We are sending a large number of engines and other equipment as well as personnel. I am confident that our contemplated operation will be successful. Everyone in America is thrilled by the gallant defence of Stalingrad, and we are confident that it will succeed. Roosevelt."

On October 13 I received a communication from Stalin. It was neither informative nor helpful.

Premier Stalin to Prime Minister   13 Oct. 42

I received your message of October 9. Thank you.

*   *   *   *   *

The atmosphere was heavily charged with suspicion. The Moscow press made great and belated play with the Hess episode. On October 15 Molotov made a public speech demanding the immediate trial of Hess as a war criminal by an international tribunal. On October 27 a leading Soviet publicist in a lecture denounced "the machinations of Lady Astor and the 'Cliveden Set,' " who were alleged to be working for a separate peace.

None of this stuff affected in any way the views or feelings of the President or myself. We were doing our best. On October 27 I minuted to the Foreign Secretary:

I am sure it would be a great mistake to run after the Russians in their present mood; and still less to run around with them chasing a chimera. By all means let the Lord Privy Seal, Sir Stafford Cripps, focus and refresh in our minds the Hess story. When it is ready the Cabinet can consider whether the facts should be imparted to the Russian Government. I assure you the only thing that will do any good is fighting hard and winning victories. A great deal of fighting is now going on, and more is to come. Should success crown our efforts you will find we shall be in a very different position. Meanwhile I should treat the Russians coolly, not getting excited about the lies they tell, but going steadily on with our task. You must remember the Bolsheviks have undermined so many powerful Governments by lying, machine-made propaganda, and they probably think they make some impression on us by these methods.

2. I am awaiting the President's answer to my query about whether he has heard from Stalin in reply to his and my telegrams. As soon as I hear I will draft a telegram to Stalin myself. It will be quite short, asking if his "Thank you" was in reply to my long telegram, and if so what steps does he propose to take about the twenty squadrons on the southern flank, anything additional about the Spitfires which we are sending, and the ships which are to slip through, one by one, in the dark period. Now that *Tirpitz* has gone south to Trondheim it may be possible after the first part of "Torch" is over to reconsider the convoy question, but the problem will still be escort craft.

At the same time the President sent me the following telegram:

President Roosevelt to Prime Minister   28 Oct. 42

I am not unduly disturbed about our respective responses or lack
of responses from Moscow. I have decided they do not use speech
for the same purposes as we do.

I had not heard of any difficulty at our end about arrangements
for landing-fields on the Russian southern flank, but I shall explore
that from my end at once.

I feel very sure the Russians are going to hold this winter, and
that we should proceed vigorously with our plans both to supply
them and set up an air force to fight with them. I want us to be
able to say to Mr. Stalin that we have carried out our obligations
one hundred per cent.

*   *   *   *   *

The strains and stresses of the winter months were to be
relieved by Alamein and "Torch" and the great Russian victory at Stalingrad. In the Arctic a brilliant operation was,
before the end of the year, to carry a convoy safely through.
In retrospect it seems as if Soviet behaviour was in part due
to the feeling that if they could survive the winter they could
reject any direct military aid from the West, which they
regarded as an infecting contact and as a blow to their
prestige.

I feel we at least deserve credit for our patience in the face
of ceaseless affront from a Government which had been hoping
to work with Hitler, until it was assaulted and almost destroyed
by him.

*   *   *   *   *

This is however the point at which to tell, all too briefly, the
tale of the magnificent struggle and decisive victory of the
Russian Armies.*

The drive of the German Army Group A to reach the
Caucasus had been led by Kleist's First Panzer Army of fifteen
divisions. Once across the Don they made much headway
against little opposition. They reached Maikop on August 9
to find the oilfields thoroughly destroyed. Another column
took Mozdok on August 25 but was held on the river Terek

* See footnote on page 585.

and failed to reach the Grozny oilfields. Those of Baku, the greatest of them all, were still three hundred miles away. On the shore of the Black Sea Novorossisk was taken on September 10 and the Russian Black Sea Fleet, which had sheltered there when Sevastopol fell, sailed to Tuapse where they remained. Hitler's orders to seize the whole of the Black Sea littoral could not be carried out. In the centre the Germans reached the foothills of the Caucasus, but no farther. Russian resistance, reinforced by fresh troops sent down by railway along the western shore of the Caspian, was everywhere firm. Kleist, weakened by diversions for the Stalingrad effort, struggled on till November. He took Nalchik on November 2. Winter conditions then intervened. His bolt was shot.

On the front of the German Army Group B, worse than failure befell. The lure of Stalingrad fascinated Hitler; its very name was a challenge. The city was important as a centre of industry and also a strong-point on the defensive flank protecting his main thrust to the Caucasus. It became a magnet drawing to itself the supreme effort of the German Army and Air Force.

The deflection southward of the Fourth Panzer Army to help Army Group A to cross the Don also had serious consequences. It delayed the drive on Stalingrad, and by the time this Army turned east again, the Russian forces that had withdrawn across the river were reorganising. Resistance grew daily stiffer. It was not till September 15 that after heavy fighting between the Don and the Volga the outskirts of Stalingrad were reached. The battering-ram attacks of the next month made some progress at the cost of terrible slaughter. Nothing could overcome the Russians fighting with passionate devotion amid the ruins of their city.

The German Generals, long uneasy, had good cause for their anxiety. After three months of fighting, the main objectives of the campaign, the Caucasus, Stalingrad, and Leningrad were still in Russian hands. Casualties had been very heavy and replacements insufficient. Hitler, instead of sending fresh contingents forward to replace losses, was forming them into

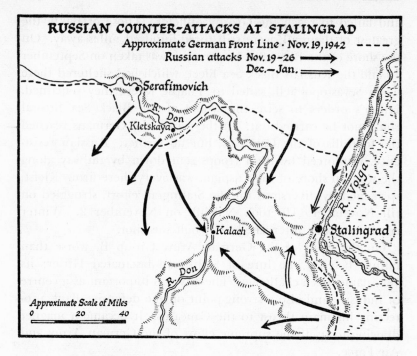

RUSSIAN COUNTER-ATTACKS AT STALINGRAD
Approximate German Front Line · Nov. 19, 1942 - - - -
Russian attacks Nov. 19-26 ⟶
Dec.-Jan. ⟹

new and untrained divisions. In military opinion it was high time to call a halt, but "The Carpet Eater" would not listen. At the end of September Halder, Hitler's Chief of Staff, finally resisted his master and was dismissed. Hitler scourged his armies on.

By the middle of October the German position had markedly worsened. The frontage of Army Group B stretched over seven hundred miles. General Paulus' Sixth Army had expended its efforts at Stalingrad and now lay exhausted with its flanks thinly protected by allies of dubious quality. Winter was near, when the Russians would surely make their counter-stroke. If the Don front could not be held, the safety of the armies on the Caucasus front would be undermined. But Hitler would not countenance any suggestion of withdrawal. On November 19 the Russians delivered their long and valiantly prepared encircling assault, striking both north and south of Stalingrad upon the weakly defended German flanks.

Four days later the Russian pincers met and the Sixth German Army was trapped between the Don and the Volga. Paulus proposed to break out. Hitler ordered him to hold his ground. As the days passed his army was compressed into an ever lessening space. On December 12, in bitter weather, the Germans made a desperate effort to break through the Russian cordon and relieve their besieged Sixth Army. They failed. Thereafter, though Paulus and his army held out for seven more terrible weeks, their doom was certain.[4]

4 See page 582.

In order to free the way for the south-easterly drive to the Caucasus, Rostov had to be taken and the Russians cleared from within the bend of the Lower Don. The first thrusts, on May 28, were from north of Kursk and Byelgorod. By July 7 the former had reached the outskirts of Rostov, but could not capture it. The long defensive flank from Orel to Voronezh was left to be guarded largely by Hungarians, while the German Fourth Panzer Army drove down the western bank of the Don. A later thrust broke through the Russian defences before Izyum and joined the southerly drive. Finally, a third attack from Stalino swept round to reach the Lower Don above Rostov. All this went very much according to plan, though not quite so swiftly as had been hoped. Russian resistance was strong, but the several penetrations of their line by armoured and motorised troops enforced a general withdrawal, much harassed by the enemy, to behind the river Don.

After three weeks the first phase was virtually over and Hitler issued his orders for the next. The Southern Army Group was now divided into Army Group A, commanded by List, and Army Group B, under Bock. Hitler's directive of July 23 gave them their tasks. Army Group A was to capture the entire eastern shore of the Black Sea. After the capture of the Maikop oilfields a mobile force was to take Grozny. "Subsequently the Baku area is to be captured by an advance along the Caspian Sea." Army Group B, having established a defensive flank along the river Don, was to advance on Stalingrad, "smash the enemy forces being assembled there, and occupy the city." Mobile forces were to proceed down the Volga to Astrakhan.

Local operations by the Central Army Group were to take place in order to prevent the Russians withdrawing troops from that front, and in the north Leningrad was to be captured in early September. For this purpose Hitler ordered five divisions of the Eleventh Army, released by the capture of Sebastopol, to join the Northern Army Group, an improvident weakening of his major attack. They arrived in time not to attack, but to defend a German line sagging under Russian assault.

10

The Battle of Alamein

*Preparations for the Desert Offensive — An Unwelcome Delay —
General Alexander's Justification — The Battle Date Draws Near
— "Zip," October 23, 1942 — Montgomery's Dispositions —
Bombardment by a Thousand Guns — General Assault — The
Struggle Ebbs and Flows — Fruitful Thrust by the 9th Australian
Division — Fierce Fighting of October 27 and 28 — Report to
the Dominions Prime Ministers — My Congratulations to the
Commanders — British Casualties — Montgomery's Final Plan:
Operation "Supercharge" — Forward Drive of the Australians
— Rommel's Front Pierced — Our Armour Pursues — Alexan-
der's Telegram of November 4 — Defeat and Destruction of the
Enemy — "Ring Out the Bells!" — Old-Fashioned Tactics —
The Hinge Turns.*

IN THE WEEKS which followed the changes in command,
planning preparations and training went forward ceaselessly
in Cairo and at the front. The Eighth Army was strengthened
to an extent never before possible. The 51st and 44th Divisions
had arrived from home and become "desert-worthy." Our
strength in armour rose to seven brigades of over a thousand
tanks, nearly half of them Grants and Shermans from the
United States; we now had a two-to-one superiority in numbers
and at least a balance of quality. A powerful and highly trained
artillery was for the first time in the Western Desert massed to
support the impending attack.

The Air Force in the Middle East was, in accordance with
the directive of October 7, 1941, subordinated to the military

conceptions and requirements of the Commander-in-Chief. However, under Air Marshal Tedder there was no need for hard-and-fast precedents. The relations between the Air Command and the new generals were in every way agreeable. The Western Desert Air Force, under Air Marshal Coningham, had now attained a fighting strength of 550 aircraft. There were two other groups, in addition to the aircraft based on Malta, numbering 650 planes, whose task it was to harry enemy ports and supply routes across both the Mediterranean and the desert. Together with a hundred United States fighters and medium bombers, our total strength amounted to about 1200 serviceable aircraft.

While all this was going forward it was necessary that I should have the earliest possible information of Alexander's intentions. Accordingly, on September 17:

Prime Minister to General Alexander   17 Sept. 42

I am anxiously awaiting some account of your intentions. My understanding with you was the fourth week in September. Since then you have stated that the recent battle, which greatly weakened the enemy, has caused delay in regrouping, etc. I do not wish to know either your plan or the exact date, but I must know which week it falls in, otherwise I cannot form the necessary judgments affecting the general war.

Alexander told us in various telegrams that about October 24 had been chosen for "Lightfoot," as the operation was to be called. "Since there is no open flank, the battle," he said, "must be so stage-managed that a hole is blown in the enemy's front." Through this the Xth Corps, comprising the main armour, which was to be the spearhead of our attack, would advance in daylight. This corps would not have all its weapons and equipment before October 1. It would then require nearly a month's training for its rôle. "In my view it is essential that the initial break-in attack should be launched in the full moon period. This will be a major operation, which will take some time, and an adequate gap in the enemy's lines must be made if our armoured forces are to have a whole day in which to

make their operation decisive. A full moon is in fact essential
to my whole plan. I have carefully considered the timing in
relation to 'Torch,' and have come to the conclusion that the
best date for us to start would be minus 13 of 'Torch' [then
fixed for November 4]."

Prime Minister to Commander-in-Chief Middle East   23 Sept. 42

We are in your hands, and of course a victorious battle makes
amends for much delay. Whatever happens we shall back you up
and see you through.

There is a point about the fortifications which the enemy will
make in the interval which I should like to put to you. Instead
of a crust through which a way can be cleared in a night, may you
not find twenty-five miles of fortifications, with blasted rock, gun-
pits, and machine-gun posts? The tank was originally invented
to clear a way for the infantry in the teeth of machine-gun fire.
Now it is the infantry who will have to clear a way for the tanks,
and it seems to me their task will be a very hard one now that
fire-power is so greatly increased. No doubt you are thinking about
all this and how so to broaden your front of attack as to make your
superior numbers felt.

*   *   *   *   *

Nearly a month passed, and the battle date drew near.

Prime Minister to General Alexander   20 Oct. 42

Events are moving in our favour both in North Africa and Vichy
France, and "Torch" goes forward steadily and punctually. But
all our hopes are centred upon the battle you and Montgomery
are going to fight. It may well be the key to the future. Give my
warmest regards to Montgomery and also Coningham. Let me
have the word "Zip" when you start.

The Air Force had already begun their battle, attacking
enemy troops, airfields, and communications. Special attention
was paid to their convoys. In September thirty per cent of Axis
shipping supplying North Africa was sunk, largely by air
action. In October the figure rose to forty per cent. The loss
of petrol was sixty-six per cent. In the four autumn months

over 200,000 tons of Axis shipping was destroyed. This was a severe injury to Rommel's army.

At last the word came:

C.-in-C. to Prime Minister and C.I.G.S.   23 Oct. 42
"Zip!"

I duly informed the President.

Former Naval Person to President Roosevelt   23 Oct. 42

The battle in Egypt began to-night at 8 P.M. London time. The whole force of the Army will be engaged. I will keep you informed. A victory there will be most fruitful to our main enterprise. All the Shermans and self-propelled guns which you gave me on that dark Tobruk morning will play their part.

*   *   *   *   *

General Montgomery had at his immediate disposal three armoured and the equivalent of seven infantry divisions. The concentration of so large a force demanded a number of ingenious deceptive measures and precautions. It was especially necessary that enemy aircraft should be prevented from overlooking the preparations. All this was attended by great success and the attack came as a complete surprise.

In the full moon of October 23 nearly a thousand guns opened upon the enemy batteries for twenty minutes, and then turned onto their infantry positions. Under this concentration of fire, deepened by bombing from the air, the XXXth (General Leese) and XIIIth Corps (General Horrocks) advanced. Attacking on a front of four divisions, the whole XXXth Corps sought to cut two corridors through the enemy's fortifications. Behind them the two armoured divisions of the Xth Corps (General Lumsden) followed to exploit success. Strong advances were made under heavy fire, and by dawn deep inroads had been made. The engineers had cleared the mines behind the leading troops. But the minefield system had not been pierced in its depth, and there was no early prospect of our armour breaking through. Farther south the 4th Indian Division launched raids from the Ruweisat Ridge, while

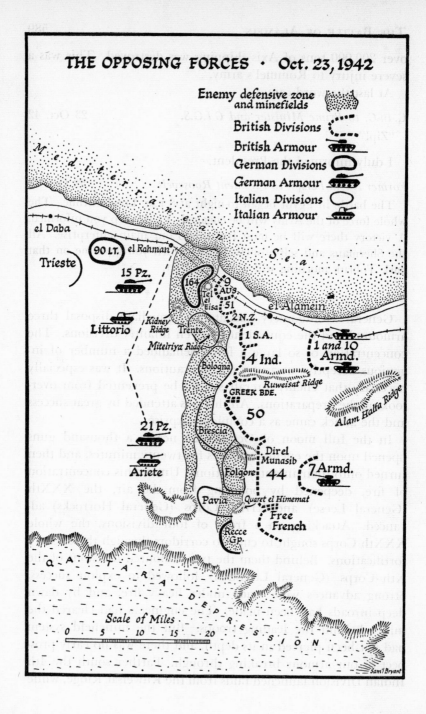

THE OPPOSING FORCES · Oct. 23, 1942

Enemy defensive zone and minefields
British Divisions
British Armour
German Divisions
German Armour
Italian Divisions
Italian Armour

Mediterranean

Sea

el Daba

90 LT. el Rahman

Trieste

15 Pz.

164 9 AUS

Tel el Eisa 51 el Alamein

2 N.Z.

Littorio Kidney Ridge Trente

1 S.A.

Mitelriya Ridge

4 Ind. 1 and 10 Armd.

Bologna

Ruweisat Ridge

GREEK BDE.

21 Pz. Brescia 50

Alam Halfa Ridge

Ariete Dir el Munasib

Folgore 44 7 Armd.

Pavia Quaret el Himemat

Recce Gp. Free French

QATTARA DEPRESSION

Scale of Miles

0   5   10   15   20

Sam'l Bryant

the 7th Armoured and 44th Divisions of the XIIIth Corps broke into the enemy defences opposite to them. This achieved its object of inducing the enemy to retain his two armoured divisions for three days behind this part of the front while the main battle developed in the north.

So far however no hole had been blown in the enemy's deep system of minefields and defences. In the small hours of the 25th Montgomery held a conference of his senior commanders, at which he ordered the armour to press forward again before dawn in accordance with his original instructions. During the day more ground was indeed gained, after hard fighting; but the feature known as Kidney Ridge became the focus of an intense struggle with the enemy's 15th Panzer and Ariete armoured divisions, which made a series of violent counter-attacks. On the front of the XIIIth Corps the attack was pressed no farther, in order to keep the 7th Armoured Division intact for the climax.

There had been serious derangements in the enemy's command. Rommel had gone to hospital in Germany at the end of September, and his place was taken by General Stumme. Within twenty-four hours of the start of the battle Stumme died of a heart attack. Rommel, at Hitler's request, left hospital and resumed his command late on the 25th.

Hard fighting continued on October 26 all along the deep bulge so far forced into the enemy line, and especially again at Kidney Ridge. The enemy Air Force, which had been quiescent on the previous two days, now made its definite challenge to our air superiority. There were many combats, ending mostly in our favour. The efforts of the XIIIth Corps had delayed but could not prevent the movement of the German armour to what they now knew was the decisive sector of their front. This movement however was severely smitten by our Air Force.

At this moment a new and fruitful thrust was made by the 9th Australian Division, under General Morshead. They struck northwards from the bulge towards the sea. Montgomery was prompt to exploit this notable success. He held

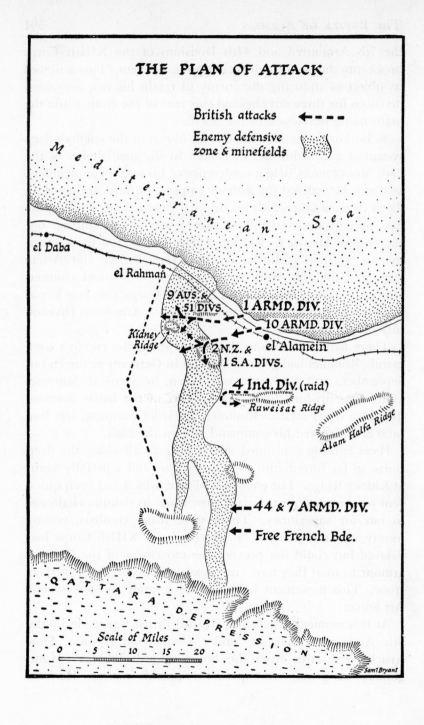

THE PLAN OF ATTACK

British attacks ← – – –

Enemy defensive
zone & minefields

Mediterranean Sea

el Daba

el Rahman

9 AUS. &
51 DIVS

1 ARMD. DIV.

10 ARMD. DIV.

Kidney
Ridge

el Alamein

2 N.Z. &
1 S.A. DIVS.

4 Ind. Div. (raid)

Ruweisat Ridge

Alam Halfa Ridge

44 & 7 ARMD. DIV.

Free French Bde.

QATTARA DEPRESSION

Scale of Miles

0   5   10   15   20

Sam't Bryant

back the New Zealanders from their westward drive and ordered the Australians to continue their advance towards the north. This threatened the retreat of part of the German infantry division on the northern flank. At the same time he now felt that the momentum of his main attack was beginning to falter in the midst of the minefields and strongly posted anti-tank guns. He therefore regathered his forces and reserves for a renewed and revived assault.

All through the 27th and the 28th a fierce conflict raged for Kidney Ridge against the repeated attacks of the 15th and 21st Panzer Divisions, now arrived from the southern sector. General Alexander has described the struggle in these words:[1]

On October 27 came a big armoured counter-attack in the old style. Five times they attacked with all available tanks, both German and Italian, but gained no ground and suffered heavy and, worse still, disproportionate casualties, for our tanks, fighting on the defensive, suffered but lightly. On October 28 [the enemy] came again, [after] prolonged and careful reconnaissance all the morning, to find the weak spots and locate our anti-tank guns, followed by a smashing concentrated attack in the afternoon with the setting sun behind him. The reconnaissance was less successful than in the old days, since both our tanks and anti-tank guns could engage him with longer range. When the enemy attempted to concentrate for the final attack the R.A.F. once more intervened on a devastating scale. In two and a half hours bomber sorties dropped eighty tons of bombs in his concentration area, measuring three miles by two, and the enemy's attack was defeated before he could even complete his forming up. This was the last occasion on which the enemy attempted to take the initiative.

In these days of October 26 and 28 three enemy tankers of vital importance were sunk by air attack, thus rewarding the long series of air operations which were an integral part of the land battle.

*   *   *   *   *

Although the issue still hung in suspense I thought the time had come to report the situation to the Dominions Prime Ministers.

[1] In a telegram dated November 9, sent to me after the battle.

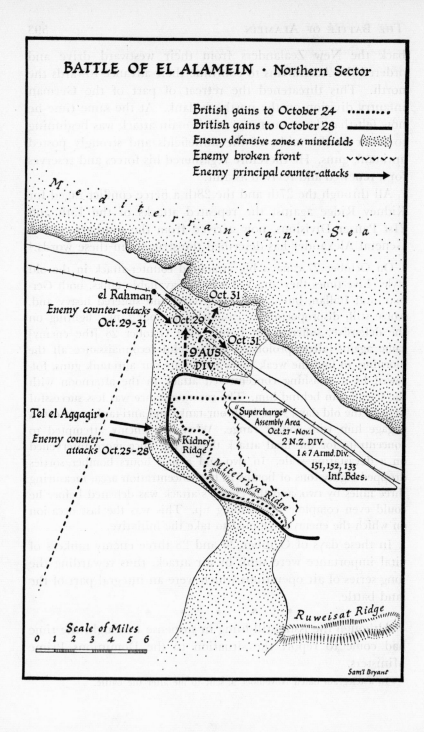

BATTLE OF EL ALAMEIN · Northern Sector

British gains to October 24 ············
British gains to October 28 ▬▬▬▬▬
Enemy defensive zones & minefields ⣿⣿⣿
Enemy broken front ∨∨∨∨∨
Enemy principal counter-attacks ⟶

Mediterranean Sea

el Rahman
Enemy counter-attacks
Oct. 29-31

Oct. 31

Oct. 29

Oct. 31

9 AUS
DIV

Tel el Aggagir

Enemy counter-
attacks Oct. 25-28

Kidney
Ridge

Mitelriya Ridge

"Supercharge"
Assembly Area
Oct. 27 - Nov. 1
2 N.Z. DIV.
1 & 7 Armd. Div.
151, 152, 133
Inf. Bdes.

Ruweisat Ridge

Scale of Miles
0 1 2 3 4 5 6

Sam'l Bryant

Prime Minister to Prime Ministers of Canada, New Zealand,
and Australia   28 Oct. 42

The great battle in Egypt has opened well, although one cannot
yet forecast its result. The enemy are short of ammunition and
fuel, and we have just destroyed a most important tanker on which
they must have been counting. Our forces are substantially superior
in the air, in armour, including best armour, in artillery fire, and
in numbers, and they have far easier lines of communication. Rommel is seriously ill, and has only been brought back as an extreme
measure. In Alexander and Montgomery we have generals determined to fight the battle out to the very end. Should they succeed
it will be very difficult for the enemy army to make a good retreat
on account of his shortage of transport and fuel. It is therefore
much better for us to fight him to a finish on this ground than
farther west.

To Mr. Fraser:

You will have seen with pride and pleasure all that your valiant
New Zealanders are doing and the part they are playing in what
may well be a memorable event.

To Mr. Curtin:

You will have observed with pride and pleasure the distinguished
part which the 9th Australian Division are playing in what may
be an event of first magnitude.

And to General Alexander:

29 Oct. 42

The Defence Committee of the War Cabinet congratulate you
on the resolute and successful manner in which the decisive battle
which is now proceeding has been launched by you and General
Montgomery. The Defence Committee feel that the general situation justifies all the risks and sacrifices involved in the relentless
prosecution of this battle, and we assure you that whatever the
cost you will be supported in all the measures which you take to
shake the life out of Rommel's army and to make this a fight to
the finish.

2. The brilliant success of the Air in sinking the tankers so
vitally needed, the conditions of intense anxiety and strain behind

the enemy's front, provide solid grounds for confidence in your final success. We should be glad to receive any general outline over and above what is contained in the reports which you may care to give of your immediate intentions.

3. In the meantime "Torch" moves forward with complete secrecy and good fortune, so far, and we shall keep the date punctually.

4. *The following for you and Montgomery alone.* Clark has visited "Torch" area and held long conference with friendly French generals. We have reason to believe that not only will little opposition be encountered, but that powerful assistance will be forthcoming. Events may therefore move more quickly, perhaps considerably more quickly, than had been planned. Decisive reactions may well be expected in France; nothing sinister has yet cropped up in Spain. So far as we know the enemy have no idea of what is in store for them, and certainly no idea of its scale or imminence. Every good wish to you and Montgomery. Your battle continuing at full blast will play a memorable part.

General Alexander to Prime Minister and C.I.G.S.   30 Oct. 42

Montgomery and I [are] fully agreed utmost pressure of our offensive must be maintained. Enemy minefields and anti-tank guns have caused a lot of trouble and delay. We are now however about to put in a large-scale attack with infantry and tanks to break a way through for the Xth Corps. If this is successful it will have far-reaching results.

Prime Minister to Air Chief Marshal Tedder   30 Oct. 42

Many congratulations on the magnificent way in which you are cutting into the enemy in the air, on the ground, and on the sea. Pray give my compliments to Coningham, and also to all the officers and men who welcomed me so cordially in the Desert. I was sure then that great days lay ahead. Those days have come, and you are all playing a glorious part in them.

Air Chief Marshal Tedder to Prime Minister   31 Oct. 42

On behalf of all of us I wish to thank you most sincerely for your inspiring mesasge of encouragement. We are all at full throttle and determined to make a job of it.

General Alexander to Prime Minister   31 Oct. 42

Thank you for your encouraging message. Enemy is fighting desperately, but we are hitting him hard and continuously and boring into him without mercy. Have high hopes he will crack soon.

General Alexander to Prime Minister and C.I.G.S.   1 Nov. 42

Best estimate of casualties up to 6 A.M., October 31: killed, wounded, and missing — officers, 695; other ranks, 9,435.

Formations with most casualties are 51st Highland Division and 9th Australian Division, each about 2000. 10th Armoured Division, 1350.

Recovery of wounded tanks is getting on well. During first six days 213 tanks were recovered. Of these only 16 were condemned as unrepairable.

*   *   *   *   *

Montgomery now made his plans and dispositions for the decisive breakthrough (Operation "Supercharge"). He took out of the line the 2d New Zealand and the 1st British Armoured Divisions, the latter being in special need of reorganisation after its notable share in the repulse of the German armour at Kidney Ridge. The British 7th Armoured and 51st Divisions and a brigade of the 44th were brought together and the whole welded into the new reserve. The breakthrough was to be led by the 2d New Zealand Division, the 151st and 152d British Infantry Brigades, and the 9th British Armoured Brigade.

Meanwhile, in Alexander's words,

On the night of October 28 and again on October 30 the Australians attacked northwards towards the coast, succeeding finally in isolating in the pocket thus formed the four [German] battalions remaining there. The enemy appear to have been firmly convinced that we intended to strike up the road and railway, and he reacted to our thrust most vigorously. He moved up his 21st Armoured Division from its position west of our salient, added to it his 90th Light Division, which was guarding the northern flank of the salient, and used both in furious attacks to relieve his encircled troops. Into the position vacated by the 21st Armoured Division he put the Trieste Division, his last uncommitted reserve formation. While he was thus fully extended and was eking out his last remaining fresh formations in an attempt to extricate one regiment, we were able to carry out, undisturbed, the reorganisation of our forces for Operation "Supercharge."

The magnificent forward drive of the Australians, achieved by ceaseless bitter fighting, had swung the whole battle in our favour. At 1 A.M. on November 2 "Supercharge" began. Under a barrage of three hundred guns the British brigades attached to the New Zealand Division broke through the defended zone, and the 9th British Armoured Brigade drove on ahead. They found however that a new line of defence strong in anti-tank weapons was facing them along the Rahman track. In a long engagement the brigade suffered severely, but the corridor behind was held open and the 1st British Armoured Division moved forward through it. Then came the last clash of armour in the battle. All the remaining enemy tanks attacked our salient on each flank, and were repulsed. Here was the final decision; but even next day, the 3d, when our air reports indicated that the enemy's retirement had begun, his covering rearguard on the Rahman track still held the main body of our armour at bay. An order came from Hitler forbidding any retreat, but the issue was no longer in German hands. Only one more hole had to be punched. Very early on November 4, five miles south of Tel el Aggagir, the 5th Indian Brigade launched a quickly mounted attack which was completely successful. The battle was now won, and the way finally cleared for our armour to pursue across the open desert.

General Alexander to Prime Minister   4 Nov. 42

After twelve days of heavy and violent fighting the Eighth Army has inflicted a severe defeat on the German and Italian forces under Rommel's command. The enemy's front has broken, and British armoured formations in strength have passed through and are operating in the enemy's rear areas. Such portions of the enemy's forces as can get away are in full retreat, and are being harassed by

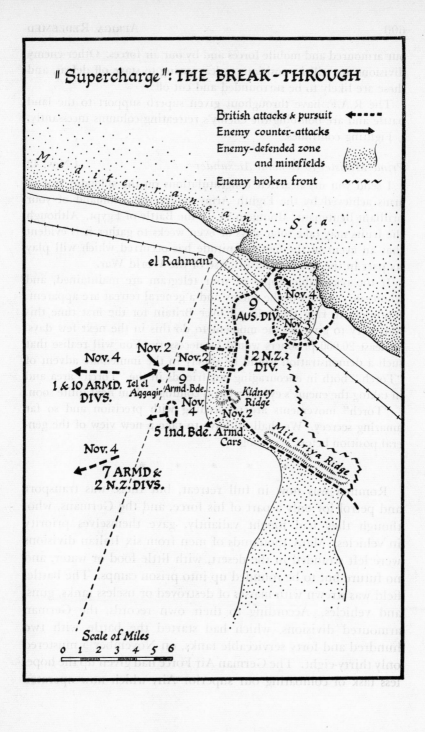

"Supercharge": THE BREAK-THROUGH

British attacks & pursuit
Enemy counter-attacks
Enemy-defended zone
and minefields
Enemy broken front

Mediterranean   Sea

el Rahman

Nov. 4

9
AUS. DIV.

Nov. 3

2 N.Z.
DIV.

Nov. 2

Nov. 2   Nov. 2

Nov. 4

1 & 10 ARMD.
DIVS.

9
Tel el   Armd. Bde.
Aggagir   Nov.
Kidney
Ridge

Nov.
4

Nov. 2

5 Ind. Bde. Armd.
Cars

Mitelriya Ridge

Nov. 4

7 ARMD &
2 N.Z. DIVS.

Scale of Miles

0 1 2 3 4 5 6

our armoured and mobile forces and by our air forces. Other enemy divisions are still in position, endeavouring to stave off defeat, and these are likely to be surrounded and cut off.

The R.A.F. have throughout given superb support to the land battle and are bombing the enemy's retreating columns incessantly.

Fighting continues.

Prime Minister to General Alexander   4 Nov. 42

I send you my heartfelt congratulations on the splendid feat of arms achieved by the Eighth Army under the command of your brilliant lieutenant, Montgomery, in the Battle of Egypt. Although the fruits may take some days or even weeks to gather it is evident that an event of the first magnitude has occurred which will play its part in the whole future course of the World War.

If the reasonable hopes of your telegram are maintained, and wholesale captures of the enemy and a general retreat are apparent, I propose to ring the bells all over Britain for the first time this war. Try to give me the moment to do this in the next few days. At least 20,000 prisoners would be necessary. You will realise that such a demonstration would be timely in the immediate advent of "Torch," both in encouraging our friends in the "Torch" area and in taking the enemy's eye off what is coming to him next quite soon.

"Torch" movements are proceeding with precision and so far amazing secrecy. We shall all have to take a new view of the general position before very long.

*   *   *   *   *

Rommel was now in full retreat, but there was transport and petrol for only a part of his force, and the Germans, who, though they had fought valiantly, gave themselves priority in vehicles. Many thousands of men from six Italian divisions were left stranded in the desert, with little food or water, and no future but to be rounded up into prison camps. The battle-field was strewn with masses of destroyed or useless tanks, guns, and vehicles. According to their own records, the German armoured divisions, which had started the battle with two hundred and forty serviceable tanks, on November 5 mustered only thirty-eight. The German Air Force had given up the hopeless task of combating our superior Air, which now operated almost unhindered, attacking with all its resources the great columns of men and vehicles struggling westward. Rommel has himself paid notable tribute to the great part played by the Royal Air Force.[2] His army had been decisively beaten; his lieutenant, General von Thoma, was in our hands, with nine Italian generals.

There seemed good hopes of turning the enemy's disaster into annihilation. The New Zealand Division was directed on Fuka, but when they reached it on November 5 the enemy had already passed. There was still a chance that they might be cut off at Mersah Matruh, upon which the 1st and 7th British Armoured Divisions had been thrust. By nightfall on the 6th they were nearing their objective, while the enemy were still trying to escape from the closing trap. But then rain came and forward petrol was scarce. Throughout the 7th our pursuit was halted. The twenty-four-hour respite prevented complete encirclement. Nevertheless four German divisions and eight Italian divisions had ceased to exist as fighting formations. Thirty thousand prisoners were taken, with enormous masses of material of all kinds. Rommel has left on record his opinion of the part played by our gunners in his defeat: "The British artillery demonstrated once again its well-known excellence. Especially noteworthy was its great mobility and speed of reaction to the requirements of the assault troops."[3]

The account of this rout may end with an extract from General Alexander's telegram of November 9:

This great battle can be divided into four stages: The grouping and concentration of our forces for battle and deception methods employed, which gained for us surprise, that battle-winning factor. The break-in attack — that great concentration of force of all arms which punched a hole deep into his defences, and by its disruption created artificial flanks which gave us further opportunities for exploitation. The thrust now here, now there, which drew off his forces and made him use up his reserves in stopping holes and in repeated counter-attacks. The final thrust, which disrupted his last

2 *Rommel*, by Desmond Young, page 258.
3 *Ibid.*, page 279.

remaining line of defence and broke a way through — through which poured our armoured and mobile formations.

General Alexander to Prime Minister   6 Nov. 42

Ring out the bells! Prisoners estimated now 20,000, tanks 350, guns 400, M.T. several thousand. Our advanced mobile forces are south of Mersa Matruh. Eighth Army is advancing.

Recalling what happened after Cambrai in 1917, I decided on second thoughts not to ring the bells till after "Torch," now on the verge, had begun successfully. I hoped however to do so within the week, and I so informed General Alexander.

*   *   *   *   *

The Battle of Alamein differed from all previous fighting in the Desert. The front was limited, heavily fortified, and held in strength. There was no flank to turn. A breakthrough must be made by whoever was the stronger and wished to take the offensive. In this way we are led back to the battles of the First World War on the Western Front. We see repeated here in Egypt the same kind of trial of strength as was presented at Cambrai at the end of 1917, and in many of the battles of 1918, namely, short and good communications for the assailants, the use of artillery in its heaviest concentration, the "drum-fire barrage," and the forward inrush of tanks.

In all this General Montgomery and his chief, Alexander, were deeply versed by experience, study, and thought. Montgomery was a great artillerist. He believed, as Bernard Shaw said of Napoleon, that cannons kill men. Always we shall see him trying to bring three or four hundred guns into action under one concerted command, instead of the skirmishing of batteries which was the inevitable accompaniment of swoops of armour in wide desert spaces. Of course everything was on a far smaller scale than in France and Flanders. We lost more than thirteen thousand men at Alamein in twelve days but nearly sixty thousand on the first day of the Somme. On the other hand, the fire-power of the defensive had fearfully increased since the previous war, and in those days it was always considered that a concentration of two or three to one was required, not only in artillery but men, to pierce and break a carefully fortified line. We had nothing like this superiority at Alamein. The enemy's front consisted not only of successive lines of strong-points and machine-gun posts, but of a whole deep area of such a defensive system. And in front of all there lay the tremendous shield of minefields of a quality and density never known before. For these reasons the Battle of Alamein will ever make a glorious page in British military annals.

There is another reason why it will survive. It marked in fact the turning of "the Hinge of Fate." It may almost be said, "Before Alamein we never had a victory. After Alamein we never had a defeat."

11

The Torch Is Lit

General de Gaulle's Position — General Giraud, "King-pin," Arrives at Gibraltar — The Armadas Approach the Scene — President Roosevelt's Message to Pétain and Others — Eisenhower Flies to Gibraltar, November 5 — The Rock in the War — General Giraud's Illusions — Explosion Hour! — A Curious Complication — Admiral Darlan in Algiers — Mr. Murphy and General Juin Appeal to Him — His Hideous Plight — The British and American Landings Begin — The American Attack on Oran, November 8 — French Resistance Ceases at Oran and Algiers — The All-American Landing in Morocco — General Béthouart's Loyalty — Resident-General Noguès Regains Control — He Orders Resistance — The "Western Task Force" Lands — Fierce Action Between the French Ships and the United States Fleet — Noguès Surrenders, November 11 — Generals Giraud and Clark Fly to Algiers — Icy Reception of Giraud by the French Commanders — The Germans Invade Unoccupied France — Darlan Orders a General "Cease Fire" Throughout North Africa — Laval Learns the News — He Dominates Marshal Pétain — And is Summoned to Berchtesgaden — General Clark Finally Rallies Admiral Darlan — General Anderson Assumes Command in Algeria — Rapid Progress Eastward — The Germans Reinforce Tunis by Air — The Fate of the French Fleet in Toulon.

PRESIDENT ROOSEVELT'S PREJUDICES against General de Gaulle, the contacts he possessed through Admiral Leahy with Vichy, and our memories of the leakage about Dakar two years before led to a decision to withhold all information about "Torch" from the Free French. I did not contest these resolves. I was none the less conscious of our British relationships with de Gaulle, and the gravity of the affront which he would have to suffer by being deliberately excluded from all share in the design. I planned to tell him just before the blow fell. As some means of softening this slight to him and his Movement, I arranged to confide the trusteeship of Madagascar to his hands. All the facts before us in the months of preparation and everything we have learnt since justify the view that bringing de Gaulle into the business would have been deeply injurious to French reactions in North Africa.

Former Naval Person to President Roosevelt   5 Nov. 42

It will be necessary for me to explain "Torch" to de Gaulle some time during D minus 1, when it is certain the weather is all right. You will remember that I have exchanged letters with him of a solemn kind in 1940 recognising him as the leader of Free Frenchmen. I am confident his military honour can be trusted.

2. I shall explain to him that the reason I have not mentioned "Torch" to him is that it is a United States enterprise and a United States secret, and that the reason he and his friends are not in on it is not any want of good will on our part toward him and his Movement, but because of the local complications in the "Torch" area and the need to have as little fighting as possible. I am arranging to let him announce General Le Gentilhomme as Governor-General of Madagascar some time Friday. This we have been keeping for his consolation prize. It will be a proof that we do not think of throwing over the Free French. As for his relations with Giraud, I should think myself they will join forces politically, though under what conditions I cannot foresee. I hope you will approve of the course I propose.

President Roosevelt to Prime Minister   5 Nov. 42

I am very apprehensive in regard to the adverse effect that any introduction of de Gaulle into the "Torch" situation would have on our promising efforts to attach a large part of the French African forces to our expedition.

Therefore I consider it inadvisable for you to give de Gaulle any information in regard to "Torch" until subsequent to a successful landing. You would then inform him that the American com-

mander of an American expedition with my approval insisted on
complete secrecy as a necessary safety precaution.

De Gaulle's announcement on Friday of a Governor-General of
Madagascar will not be of any assistance to "Torch," and it should
be sufficient at the present time to maintain his prestige with his
followers.

Admiral Leahy agrees wholly with the thoughts expressed above.

The need to find some oustanding French figure was obvious,
and to British and American eyes none seemed more appropriate than General Giraud, the fighting General of high rank
whose dramatic, audacious escape from his prison in Germany
was a famous tale. I have already described my meeting with
Giraud at Metz in 1937,[1] when I visited the Maginot Line, of
which he commanded the principal sector. He told me about
his adventures in the First World War as an escaped prisoner
behind the German lines. As a fellow escapee this gave us
something in common. Now he had as an Army Commander
repeated his youthful exploits in an even more sensational
fashion. It is curious that I had telegraphed to the President
in April while "Torch," the President's "secret war baby," still
lay in the womb of the future.

29 Apr. 42

I am highly interested in the escape of General Giraud and his
arrival at Vichy. This man might play a decisive part in bringing
about things of which you had hopes. Please tell me anything you
know.

Now after six months all this had become vital. The Americans entered into secret parleys with the General, and plans
were made to bring him from the Riviera to Gibraltar at the
decisive moment. Many hopes were based on "King-pin" as
he was called in our code. On November 3 I had telegraphed
to the President:

"King-pin" has wirelessed us saying that he has decided to come
over at once, and asking for an airplane to fetch him to Gibraltar.

1 See *The Gathering Storm*, Book II, Chapter 5, page 475.

Eisenhower has replied advising that he use the British submarine under a United States captain which is already off the coast.

Not without danger from the sea, Giraud and his two sons were safely transported.

*   *   *   *   *

Meanwhile our great armadas were approaching the scene. We were determined to spare nothing to safeguard their passage. Most of the convoys which sailed from British ports had to cross the Bay of Biscay, traversing all the U-boat routes. Heavy escorts were needed, and we had somehow to conceal not only the concentration of shipping, which from the beginning of October began to crowd the Clyde and other western ports, but also the actual sailing of the convoys. We were completely successful. The Germans were led by their own Intelligence to believe that Dakar was again our aim. By the end of October about forty German and Italian U-boats were stationed to the south and east of the Azores. They were successful in severely mauling a large convoy homeward bound from Sierra Leone, and sank thirteen ships. In the circumstances this could be borne. The first of the "Torch" convoys left the Clyde on October 22. By the 26th all the fast troopships were under way and American forces were sailing for Casablanca direct from the United States. The whole expedition of about six hundred and fifty ships was now launched upon the enterprise. They traversed the Bay of Biscay or the Atlantic unseen by the U-boats or by the Luftwaffe.

All our resources were at full strain. Far to the north our cruisers watched the Denmark Strait and the exits from the North Sea to guard against intervention by enemy surface ships. Others covered the American approach near the Azores, and Anglo-American bombers attacked the U-boat bases along the French Atlantic seaboard. Despite apparent U-boat concentrations towards the Gibraltar Straits, the leading ships began to enter the Mediterranean on the night of November 5th–6th still undetected. It was not until the 7th, when the Algiers convoy was less than twenty-four hours from its destination, that it was sighted, and even then only one ship was attacked.

The time had come to launch the President's manifesto. I was concerned at the first draft he sent me, in which he addressed Marshal Pétain as "My dear old friend" and revived the somewhat outdated glories of Verdun in 1916. I thought this would be the final touch with the de Gaullists.

Former Naval Person to President Roosevelt   3 Nov. 42

Will you allow me to say that your proposed message to Pétain seems to me too kind? His stock must be very low now. He has used his reputation to do our cause injuries no lesser man could have done. I beg you to think of the effect on the de Gaullists, to whom we have serious obligations, and who have now to go through the great trial of being kept outside. I am advised that unfavourable reactions would be produced in various other quarters. Of course it is absolutely right to send him a friendly message, but will you consider toning it down a bit.

President Roosevelt to Prime Minister   4 Nov. 42

I agree that message to Pétain should be toned down, and I have rewritten it so that I am sure it will not offend the friends of France.

The alterations which the President made were satisfactory, and may be studied in the published Hopkins Papers.[2]

* * * * *

On November 5 Eisenhower by a hazardous flight reached Gibraltar. I had placed the fortress within his command as the temporary headquarters of the leader of this first large-scale American and British enterprise.

Gibraltar's climax in the war had now come. Military measures of defence were of course put into effect from September, 1939, to prepare for a possible siege. Facing the Spanish frontier, a strong defensive system was gradually built up, overlooked by the Rock itself, out of which galleries were blasted

2 Hopkins, pages 644–45.

for guns commanding the isthmus. Measures had to be taken
also against attack from the sea and air, as well as by airborne
forces. The vital need was water, and by the middle of 1940
distillation plants were completed in the solid rock affording
ample supplies and storage. This was a prodigious work.

Gibraltar's greatest positive contribution to the war was the
development of its new airfield and the use that was made of it.
Starting from a mere landing-strip on the racecourse, this was
developed from 1942 onwards into a broad runway over a mile
long, its western end built out into Gibraltar Bay with the
rubble from the tunnelling. Here the great concentration of
aircraft for "Torch" was made. The whole isthmus was
crowded with machines, and fourteen squadrons of fighters
were assembled for zero hour. All this activity necessarily took
place in full view of German observers, and we could only
hope they would think it was for the reinforcement of Malta.
We did all we could to make them think so. Apparently they
did.

Well may General Eisenhower write, "Britain's Gibraltar
made possible the invasion of North-West Africa." [3]

General Eisenhower to Prime Minister   7 Nov. 42

Arrived here safely yesterday.

I have hopes of getting "King-pin" to North Africa before [we
land], but the arrangements are dependent upon good weather to
enable him to transfer from submarine to airplane. I will report on
this officially.

I should like once again to express to you personally my grateful
thanks for your constant support and encouragement during the
last few months. We are of good heart, and have every confidence
that good fortune will continue to be ours.

Giraud duly arrived at this rendezvous, and to help make
things go well I sent him the following message:

As a fellow escapee I am delighted that we are at work together.
I remember all our talks at Metz. For thirty-five years I have had
faith in France, and I rejoice that our two nations and the United

[3] Eisenhower, *Crusade in Europe,* page 95.

States are now going to strike the first great blow together for the recovery of Alsace-Lorraine.

General Eisenhower to Prime Minister   8 Nov. 42

"King-pin" was manifestly pleased to receive your message, and has asked me to transmit to you following reply:

"Thank you for your kind telegram. I too remember our frank talks at Metz. Like you, through difficulties and trials, I have never had any doubts of the final victory. I am certain today that, thanks to the efforts of all, Alsace and Lorraine will remain French."

Giraud had come with the idea that he would be appointed Supreme Commander in North Africa, and that the American and British armies, of whose strength he had no prior knowledge, would be placed under his authority. He himself strongly urged a landing in France instead of or in addition to Africa, and for some time seemed to imagine that this picture possessed reality. Argument, protracted over forty-eight hours, proceeded between him and General Eisenhower before this brave Frenchman could be convinced of the proportion of affairs. We had all counted overmuch upon "King-pin," but no one was to be more undeceived than he about the influence he had with the French governors, generals, and indeed the Officer Corps, in North Africa.

The moment of the explosion had at last come. General Eisenhower, in *Crusade in Europe*,[4] has given a vivid account of his anxious experiences during the night of November 7–8, and all through the next few days. He was always very good at bearing stresses of this kind. The immensity of the stake that was being played, the uncertainty of the weather, by which all might be wrecked, the fragmentary news which arrived, the extraordinary complications of the French attitude, the danger from Spain — all, apart from the actual fighting, must have made this a very hard trial to the Commander, whose responsibilities were enormous and direct.

*   *   *   *   *

A curious but in the upshot highly fortunate complication

---

[4] Eisenhower, *Crusade in Europe*, pages 99 ff.

now descended upon us. Admiral Darlan, having completed his tour of inspection in North Africa, returned to France. His son was stricken by infantile paralysis and taken into hospital at Algiers. The news of his dangerous condition led the Admiral to fly back on November 5. He thus happened to be in Algiers on the eve of the Anglo-American descent. This was an odd and formidable coincidence. Mr. Murphy hoped he would depart before the assault struck the shores. But Darlan, absorbed in his son's illness, tarried for a day, staying in the villa of a French official, Admiral Fénard.

Our leading hope in Algiers in recent weeks had been General Juin, the French Military Commander. His relations with Mr. Murphy had been intimate, although the actual date had not been imparted to him. A little after midnight on the 7th Murphy visited Juin to tell him that the hour had struck. A mighty Anglo-American army, sustained by overwhelming naval and air forces, was approaching, and would begin landing in Africa in a few hours. General Juin, although deeply engaged and loyal to the enterprise, was staggered by the news. He had conceived himself to possess full command of the situation in Algiers. But he knew that Darlan's presence completely overrode his authority. At his disposal were a few hundred ardent young Frenchmen. He knew only too well that all control of the military and political government had passed from his hands into those of the Minister-Admiral. Now he would certainly not be obeyed. Why, he asked, had he not been told earlier of zero hour? The reasons were obvious, and the fact would have made no difference to his authority. Darlan was on the spot and Darlan was master of all Vichy-French loyalties. Murphy and Juin decided to ask Darlan by telephone to come to them at once. Before two in the morning Darlan, roused from slumber by the urgent message from General Juin, came. On being told of the imminent stroke he turned purple and said, "I have known for a long time that the British were stupid, but I always believed that the Americans were more intelligent. I begin to believe that you make as many mistakes as they do."

Darlan, whose aversion to Britain was notorious, had for a long time been committed to the Axis. In May, 1941, he had agreed to grant facilities to the Germans both at Dakar and for the passage of supplies to Rommel's armies through Tunisia. At the time this treacherous move had been stopped by General Weygand, who commanded in North Africa, and who succeeded in persuading Pétain to refuse this German demand. Hitler, at that time fully preoccupied with the impending Russian campaign, did not press the matter, despite contrary advice from his naval staff. In November of the same year Weygand, deemed unreliable by the Germans, was relieved of his command. Although nothing more was heard of the Axis plans to use Dakar against us, the Tunisian ports were later opened to Axis shipping, and played a part in feeding Rommel's armies during the summer of 1942. Now circumstances had changed, and with them Darlan's attitude, but whatever thoughts he might have nourished of aiding an Anglo-American occupation of Northwest Africa he was still bound to Pétain in form and in fact. He knew that if he went over to the Allies he would become personally responsible for the inevitable invasion and occupation by Germany of Unoccupied France. The most he could be prevailed upon to do therefore was to ask Pétain by telegram for liberty of action. In the hideous plight in which he had become involved by the remorseless chain of events this was his only course.

Meanwhile the design unfolded. Very soon bands of young anti-Vichy Frenchmen, armed with rifles, surrounded the villa, resolved to make sure how its inmates intended to act. Ingress and exit were barred. Before daybreak fifty *gardes mobiles,* sent as a matter of routine by the police authority, arrived at the villa and dispersed the law-breaking band. They in their turn took charge of the party and placed Juin, Murphy, and his assistant, Mr. Kenneth, the American Vice-Consul at Marrakech, who was with him, under arrest. They looked to Darlan for further instructions. He authorised Mr. Pendar to take his telegram to Pétain to the French naval headquarters in Algiers. The French admiral on duty, after making sure the message

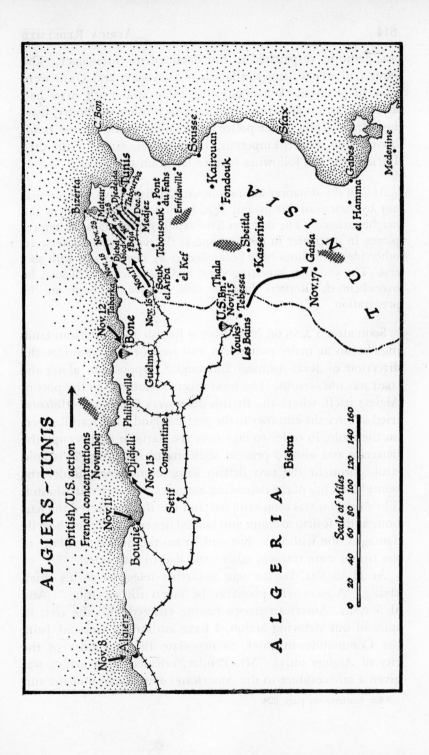

ALGIERS ~ TUNIS

British/U.S. action

French concentrations
November

Scale of Miles
0 20 40 60 80 100 120 140 160

C. Bon

Bizerta
Mateur
Nov. 28
Djedeida
Nov. 18 Tunis
Abiod Nov. 17 Tebourba Dec. 3
Djebel Nov. 17 Beja
Tabarka Medjez
Nov. 12 Souk
Nov. 16 el Arba
Bone

Enfidaville
Pont
du Fahs

Sousse

Sfax

Kairouan
Fondouk

el Kef

U.S. Bn. Thala
Nov. 15
Youks Tebessa
Les Bains

Sbeitla
Kasserine

Gafsa
Nov. 17

el Hamma

Gabes

Medenine

T U N I S I A

Philippeville
Nov. 13

Djidjelli
Nov. 15

Guelma

Constantine

Setif

Bougie
Nov. 11

Algiers
Nov. 8

A L G E R I A

Biskra

was genuine, dispatched it, but detained the messenger. The hour had struck, and the landings at Algiers and Oran were now in progress. When morning came and much news had arrived, Darlan and Juin, watching each other vigilantly, leaving Mr. Murphy under police arrest, went to the Algiers headquarters in Fort l'Empereur, from which, timed 7.40 A.M., Darlan sent the following further telegram to Pétain:

At 7.30 the situation was as follows: Landings have been carried out by American troops and British ships at Algiers and in the neighbourhood. The defences have repulsed the attacks in several places, in particular in the port and at the naval headquarters. In other places landings have been effected by surprise and with success. The situation is getting worse and the defences will soon be overwhelmed. Reports indicate that massive landings are in preparation.

Soon after 1 A.M. on November 8 British and American landings began at many points east and west of Algiers under the direction of Rear-Admiral Burrough.[5] Opposition along the coast was not serious. The most severe action was in the port of Algiers itself, where the British destroyers *Broke* and *Malcolm* tried to force the entrance to the port and land American Rangers on the mole, in order to take over the harbour and occupy the batteries and also to prevent scuttling of shipping. This bold stroke brought the two British ships immediately under the point-blank fire of the defending batteries, and ended in disaster. The *Malcolm* was soon crippled, but the *Broke* entered the harbour at the fourth attempt and landed her troops. Later, heavily damaged, she withdrew, but sank at sea the next day. Many of the troops were trapped ashore and had to surrender.

At 11.30 A.M. Darlan sent a further telegram to his chief, saying, "Algiers will probably be taken this evening." And at 5 P.M., "American troops having entered into the city, in spite of our delaying action, I have authorised General Juin, the Commander-in-Chief, to negotiate the surrender of the city of Algiers only." Mr. Pendar, released from arrest, was given a safe-conduct to the American commander, and the sur-

5 See footnote on page 628.

render of Algiers took effect from 7 P.M. From that moment Admiral Darlan was in American power, and General Juin resumed control of his command under Allied direction.

* * * * *

At Oran the attack was made by the United States "Centre Task Force," which had been trained and had embarked in Britain. The main assault was made in the Bay of Arzeu, to the east of the town, about 1 A.M. on November 8, while two secondary landings took place to the westward. There was stronger French opposition here than at Algiers. Various regular French units who had fought the British in Syria, and those forces under naval command whose memories of the British attack on Mers-el-Kebir in 1940 were bitter, resisted. Because of these earlier events the Americans had expected greater opposition here than anywhere else, but the landings were effected as planned. Meanwhile misfortune befell two subsidiary operations. The first was the audacious airborne descent which had been planned to seize the airfields behind Oran. A battalion of American parachute infantry set out from England on this daring adventure, but the formation became scattered over Spain in stormy weather. The leading elements pressed on, but their navigation was faulty and they landed some miles from their target. Later they joined their comrades, already ashore, and played their part in capturing the airfield at Tafaroui.

The second misfortune attended the gallant attempt by two small British warships to land a party of American troops in Oran harbour. Their object, as at Algiers, was to seize the port installations and so prevent the French from sabotaging them or scuttling shipping. The party therefore included many skilled technicians. The importance of this venture lay in the fact that it was imperative to bring the port of Oran into use as an Allied base at the earliest moment. Led by Captain F. T. Peters, R.N., the *Walney* entered the harbour, followed by the *Hartland,* soon after the main landings had been launched. Both were ex-American coastguard cutters transferred to us under Lend-Lease. They encountered murderous fire at point-blank range, and both ships were destroyed, with most of those on board. Captain Peters miraculously survived, only to meet his death a few days later in an aircraft disaster while returning to England. He was posthumously awarded the Victoria Cross and the American Distinguished Service Cross.

By dawn the French destroyers and submarines were active in Oran Bay, but were met with overwhelming force and either sunk or dispersed. Coastal batteries continued to oppose the landings, but were bombarded and bombed effectively by British naval forces, including the *Rodney*. Fighting continued until the morning of the 10th, when the American forces ashore launched their final attack on the city, and by noon the French capitulated.

Although French resistance had ceased at Oran and Algiers German reactions along the North African coast now rapidly increased, and our vital supply route by sea was soon threatened by a swarm of U-boats. They had some successes, including the sinking of three large liners returning empty from the landing-beaches; but our counter-measures were vigorous, and by the end of November nine U-boats were destroyed in these waters.

* * * * *

For the all-American landing in Morocco there was hope of active local support. General Béthouart, the French Divisional Commander at Casablanca, had fought at Narvik. He was zealous against the Germans. He was in charge of the land defences of the greater part of the Moroccan coast. At a late stage he had been brought into the secret, and was prepared to accept Giraud as Supreme French Commander. He hoped that when the moment came both the Resident-General, Noguès, and Admiral Michelier would rally to the cause. The Allied agents had wished him to take no chances and arrest the Resident-General. This Béthouart was not prepared to do. He did not want to be accused of supplanting his chief. At 11 P.M. on November 7 he assembled at his headquarters those officers whom he had made privy to the design. He told them,

"The Americans are landing tomorrow morning at five o'clock." At midnight the party left Casablanca in three cars, and two hours later took over the headquarters in Rabat, the capital, together with the telephone exchanges of the General Staff and the post office. Unluckily General Noguès' secret line was overlooked, and during the next fateful hours the Resident-General was able to communicate freely with the commanders of the main bases throughout Morocco.

On arrival at Rabat Béthouart sent his aide-de-camp to Noguès with written details of the discussions between Giraud and Murphy and of the imminent Allied landings. On Béthouart's orders Noguès was surrounded in his residence by a company of colonial infantry. He was enraged. He arrested the aide-de-camp, who was his own nephew, and at once rang up Admiral Michelier at the naval base at Casablanca. He was told that there was no evidence of any Allied approach to the coast. This negative news determined Noguès' action. He ordered the "Alert," and told Michelier to supersede Béthouart, now in Rabat. At that moment the American fleet of more than a hundred ships, carrying General Patton's landing-force was in fact but thirty miles away; but no word had yet reached Noguès even about the landings which were already in progress in Algeria. In this tense situation General Béthouart had every reason for anxiety. He alone had direct knowledge of the impending attack, but his *coup* in Rabat with his small band of supporters had merely placed all Morocco in a state of siege behind Noguès.

At 5 A.M. Noguès received from the American Vice-Consul in Rabat a personal letter from President Roosevelt calling on him to aid the Allies. Two hours later, after the landings had begun, he informed Darlan in Algiers that he had rejected this United States ultimatum. Béthouart and his few adherents were surrounded. Noguès himself telephoned threatening to shoot the officers of the colonial regiment involved. All were arrested forthwith. Béthouart was tried by court-martial two days later, and was not finally released till November 17.

*   *   *   *   *

The assault on the exposed Atlantic coast of Morocco had given more anxiety during the planning than those within the Mediterranean. Not only had the whole expedition to be brought direct from American ports to their landing-beaches over the North Atlantic, and in conformity with a fixed time-table, but grave concern was felt lest the weather along the coast should render landing impossible on the selected day, particularly so late in the season. On November 7 the weather forecasts received in Admiral Hewitt's flagship from London and Washington boded no good, and the Admiral had then to decide at once whether to adhere to his original plan or adopt the alternative, which entailed taking his whole force through the Gibraltar Straits and landing General Patton near Nemours on little-known beaches close to the frontier of Spanish Morocco. Apart from other considerations, this plan involved serious and possibly fatal delay. Fortunately his staff confidently predicted a temporary local improvement in the weather, and the Admiral boldly, and as it turned out correctly, backed their judgment. The die was cast, and the fleet dispersed before dark to their several destinations.

The "Western Task Force" reached the Moroccan coast before dawn on November 8. To allow for a longer approach in darkness the time chosen for this assault was three hours later than the landings in Algeria. This had been criticised beforehand by General Patton, as he believed, not without reason, that the broadcast appeal by the President to the French people of North Africa, which was timed for the Algerian landings at 1 A.M., would serve merely to warn the defences in Morocco. In the event the broadcast to Morocco was of no importance, but, as we have seen, the defences had none the less been "Alerted." The operations comprised three landings. In the centre the main attack was made at Fedala, close to Casablanca. Flanking attacks took place at Port Lyautey in the north and at Safi in the south. The weather in the morning was fair but hazy, and the surf on the beaches less severe than had been feared. Later the surf got worse, but by then a firm foothold had been gained in all areas. In some places the

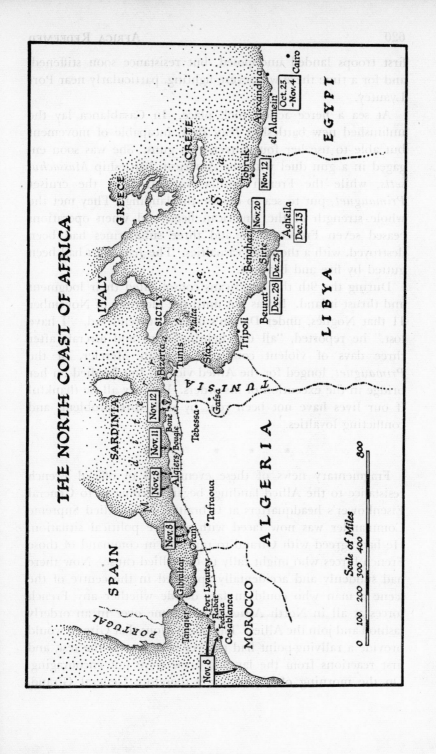

THE NORTH COAST OF AFRICA

first troops landed unopposed, but resistance soon stiffened, and for a time there was severe fighting, particularly near Port Lyautey.

At sea a fierce action took place. In Casablanca lay the unfinished new battleship *Jean Bart,* incapable of movement but able to use her four fifteen-inch guns. She was soon engaged in a gun duel with the American battleship *Massachusetts,* while the French flotilla, supported by the cruiser *Primauguet,* put to sea to oppose the landing. They met the whole strength of the American fleet, and when operations ceased seven French ships and three submarines had been destroyed, with a thousand casualties. The *Jean Bart* had been gutted by fire and beached.

During the 9th the Americans consolidated their lodgment and thrust inland. It was not until the morning of November 11 that Noguès, under Darlan's orders, surrendered. "I have lost," he reported, "all our fighting ships and aircraft after three days of violent combat." Captain Mercier, of the *Primauguet,* longed for the Allied victory, but he died on her bridge in the execution of his orders. We may all be thankful if our lives have not been rent by such dire problems and conflicting loyalties.

*   *   *   *   *

Fragmentary news of these events and of official French resistance to the Allied landings began to come in to General Eisenhower's headquarters at Gibraltar. The Allied Supreme Commander was now faced with a grave political situation. He had agreed with Giraud to put him in command of those French forces who might rally to the Allied cause. Now there had suddenly and accidentally appeared in the centre of the scene a man who could in fact decide whether any French forces at all in North Africa would come over in an orderly fashion and join the Allies. The calculations that Giraud would provide a rallying-point had not yet been put to the test, and first reactions from the landing areas were not encouraging. On the morning of November 9 therefore General Giraud, and a little later General Clark, acting as General Eisenhower's personal deputy, flew to Algiers to arrange with the French authorities the immediate ending of all hostilities.

The reception of Giraud by the leading French commanders was icy. The local Resistance organisation, so long fostered by both American and British agents, had already collapsed. The first conference held by Clark that evening with Darlan produced no agreement. It was obvious that Giraud would not be accepted by any one of importance as Supreme French Commander. On the morning of November 10 General Clark arranged a second meeting with the Admiral. He told Eisenhower by radio that a deal with Darlan was the only solution. There was no time to engage in telegraphic discussions with London and Washington. Giraud was not present at this meeting. Darlan hesitated on the grounds of lack of instructions from Vichy. Clark gave him half an hour in which to make up his mind. The Admiral at length agreed to order a general "cease fire" throughout North Africa. "In the name of the Marshal" he assumed complete authority throughout the French North African territories, and ordered all officials to remain on duty.

Later that day came the important news that the Germans had begun to invade Unoccupied France. This simplified Darlan's position. He could now maintain, and his word would be accepted by local officials and commanders, that Marshal Pétain was no longer a free agent. The German move also struck Darlan's vital nerve. Very soon advanced German elements would be entering the great French naval base at Toulon. As in 1940, the fate of the French Fleet was now again in the balance. The only man whose prestige would be sufficient to get the French battle fleet to sea under these circumstances would be Darlan.

He now acted decisively and telegraphed on the afternoon of November 11 to Metropolitan France that the Toulon fleet was to put to sea if in danger of imminent capture by the Germans. Allied naval and air dispositions were taken to protect the sortie of the French ships in such an event.

*   *   *   *   *

In the event the German High Command did not know where the great Allied convoys steaming towards North Africa were going until almost the last moment. The wide arc of U-boat patrols had been traversed at many points. But once the main armada had passed the Straits of Gibraltar their destination was more definite. Even then the Germans seem to have thought that the Allied expedition might be aiming at Italy or reinforcing Malta. In his diary the chief of the Italian General Staff, Marshal Cavallero, records a telephone conversation overheard between Goering and Kesselring.[6]

Goering: "According to our calculations the convoy will be within the next forty to fifty hours in range of our Air Force, and therefore everything must be held in readiness."

Kesselring: "Herr Reichsmarshal, and supposing a convoy attempts a landing in Africa?"

Goering: "To my mind a landing will be attempted in Corsica, in Sardinia, or at Derna or Tripoli."

Kesselring: "It is more probable at a North African port."

Goering: "Yes, but not in a French one."

Kesselring: "If the convoy has to pass through the Sicily channel I shall have time."

Goering: "If it doesn't aim at Sardinia it will certainly pass through the channel, where the Italians have not mined the waters, and this should be pointed out to them."

Not until midnight on November 7 was there official contact between the German authorities and Vichy. The head of the German Armistice Commission at Wiesbaden then summoned one of the French officers attached to that body and informed him that the objective of the large Allied convoys now in the Mediterranean would probably be Algeria and Tunisia. An offer of German military aid was sent to Vichy.

*   *   *   *   *

During the early hours of November 8 reports began to flow into Vichy of the Allied approach. Laval, sleeping at his house hard by, was rung up by the German political representative at

6 Cavallero, *Commando Supremo*, page 371.

Vichy, who repeated the offer of German support should the
landings develop in force in North Africa. Laval hastened to
the centre of government. At 4 A.M. the American Chargé
d'Affaires, Mr. Pinckney Tuck, arrived at Marshal Pétain's
private office with the letter from the President. Laval took
control. He collected his close supporters and drafted a negative and hostile reply for the Marshal to sign in the morning.
An hour later the Vichy Admiralty informed Darlan in Algiers
of the German offer to give air support against Allied landings.
The reply from Darlan suggested that the German air forces
based on Sicily and Sardinia should attack the Allied transports
at sea.

It was not until 7 A.M. that the Marshal was awakened to
hear the news. He showed little visible emotion or even interest in Laval's draft reply to the American President. He
accepted it without demur, whistling a little hunting-tune to
himself. At nine he received Mr. Pinckney Tuck to hand him
his reply. There are several accounts of the climate of this
meeting. It is said that when Pétain handed the document to
the American he gave him a knowing tap on the shoulder.
The aged Marshal acted throughout these days like a man in
a dream.

But any illusions of Vichy that a double game could still be
played by them between the Allies and the Germans were soon
dispelled. Nazi pressure hardened, and at 11.30 A.M. the Vichy
Cabinet accepted the German offer of air support from Sicily
and Sardinia. This caitiff decision enabled the Germans to
take the quick, decisive action of occupying airfields in Tunisia,
with all its costly consequences upon our campaign.

Later in the day a second Cabinet meeting accepted a formal
rupture of diplomatic relations with the United States.

*   *   *   *   *

That evening Hitler summoned Laval to Berchtesgaden.
Laval set out by car in the morning, but only reached Munich
in thick fog early on the 10th. He was therefore on the road
during the hours when Darlan was negotiating with the Allies

in Algiers, and while the news of these parleys was injecting
a little hope into those few men at Vichy who still wanted the
Marshal to come out on the Allied side. Both Weygand, who
had come to Vichy on purpose to dissuade the Marshal from
giving in, and Admiral Auphan, Minister of Marine, tried
their best. They even got him to agree to a draft telegram to
Darlan approving his move. When Laval at Munich learnt
of these moves, both at Algiers and at Vichy, he was enraged,
and under threat of resignation extorted the Marshal's withdrawal of his telegram to Darlan.

Laval met Hitler late that afternoon. The Fuehrer, with his
theatrical sense of history, treated the Frenchman to a discourse
on past Franco-German relations, going back a long way. He
also confronted him with a joint German-Italian note demanding French consent to Axis landings in Tunisia. Ciano, who
was present, says Laval cut a pitiable figure. This may well be
believed. Early in the morning of November 11 Laval was
woken up by Abetz to be told that the Fuehrer had ordered
the German Army to occupy the free zone of France. The same
day the Italians occupied Nice and Corsica. So much for Vichy.

*   *   *   *   *

The Germans had intercepted Darlan's message to Vichy,
and Laval under their pressure forced Pétain to send a message
to Algiers disowning Darlan's actions. General Clark, when
confronted with Darlan's apparent readiness to withdraw the
orders he had issued, put the Admiral under arrest. The
arrival of a secret message from Pétain however in a special
naval code and the news of further German advances into Unoccupied France restored both the situation and the tempers
of those concerned in Algiers. On the following day, November 11, it was agreed that Darlan should send categorical instructions to the Toulon fleet to put to sea, and further
messages were sent to the French Resident-General in Tunisia,
Admiral Esteva, to join the Allies.

*   *   *   *   *

Admiral Esteva was a faithful servant of Vichy. He followed

the cataract of events with mounting confusion and alarm. As he was closer to the enemy in Sicily and on his eastern frontier, his position was worse than that of either Darlan or Noguès. His high subordinates matched him in equal indecision. Already on November 9 units of the German Air Force occupied the important airfield at El Aouina. On the same day German and Italian troops arrived in Tunisia. Depressed and wavering, Esteva clung to a formal allegiance to Vichy, while the Axis forces in Tripolitania were coming from the east and the Allies hastened from the west. The French General Barré, at first baffled by a problem the like of which, gentle reader, you have not yet been asked to solve, finally moved the bulk of the French garrison westwards and placed himself under the orders of General Giraud. At Bizerta however four destroyers and six submarines surrendered to the Axis.

In Alexandria, where the French naval squadron had been immobilised since 1940, parleys took place without effect. Admiral Godefroy, its commander, persisted in his loyalty to Vichy and refused to recognise the authority of Admiral Darlan. In his view, until the Allies had conquered Tunisia they could not claim that it was in their power to liberate France. Thus his ships continued in idleness until in the fullness of time we conquered Tunis.

At Dakar the Vichy Governor-General Boisson accepted Darlan's order to cease resistance on November 23, but the units of the French Navy there refused to join the Allies. Only after the completion of our conquest of all North Africa did the battleship *Richelieu* and the three cruisers with her rally to our cause.

*   *   *   *   *

As soon as the Algiers landing was well established General Anderson, as previously arranged, took over command from the United States General Ryder. He dispatched his 36th Infantry Brigade by sea to Bougie, which they took unopposed on November 11; one of its battalions reached Djidjelli airfield

next day. Two British parachute companies dropped on Bone
on the 12th, and were supported by Commandos from the sea;
others on Souk-el-Arba airfield on the 16th, whence they advanced to Beja, and farther on met Germans in position. The
36th Brigade, pressing on rapidly by road, crossed into Tunisia,
and at Djebel Abiod on November 17 met German troops.
Meanwhile United States parachutists had dropped at Youks-
les-Bains on the 15th, and reached Gafsa also two days later.

These rapid and unopposed movements had secured the
eastern airfields of Algeria necessary for the support of ground
forces which could no longer be covered from Gibraltar, now
eight hundred miles behind. Great dash and enterprise had
been shown in gaining ground so fast, but now that the enemy
were met the pace must slacken. The Germans had taken
prompt measures. Their first contingents arrived by air on
November 9, and soon two parachute regiments and four
battalions of reinforcements originally destined to reinforce
Rommel sought to bar the way. These were followed by advanced elements of the 10th Panzer Division, two Bersaglieri
battalions, and six battalions of the Italian Superga Infantry
Division. By the end of the month the Axis forces in Tunisia
amounted to fifteen thousand fighting troops, with a hundred
tanks, sixty field guns, and thirty anti-tank guns. Their dive-
bombers, based on the good airfields of Tunisia, were beginning to prove troublesome. But already we had brought a relief
to the Russian armies. During November the Germans withdrew four hundred operational aircraft, mostly long-range
bombers, from the Eastern Front for use in the Mediterranean.
In this latter theatre a quarter of the whole German Air Force
was now deployed, as compared with only a twelfth eighteen
months before.

*   *   *   *   *

The Anglo-American descent in North Africa brought an
immediate sequel in France. Since 1940 the Germans had
drawn up detailed plans for the occupation of the free zone of
France. The code-word was "Attila," and the directive was

issued by Hitler on December 10 of that year. The original purpose was to counteract any move of Weygand in North Africa. Each time that there was a tension in Franco-German relations the question of putting "Attila" into force arose. The main object of such an operation would be the capture intact of the main units of the French Fleet, which lay at Toulon. But both Hitler and Raeder were consistent in working for collaboration with Vichy, wishing to avoid the commitments which would follow the total occupation of Metropolitan France.

The Allied landings in North Africa however revolutionised the position. It may well be that Laval's description to the Germans at Berchtesgaden of Darlan's talks with the Allies at Algiers was decisive. General Eisenhower was as anxious to lay his hands on the French Fleet as were the Germans. The main justification for negotiating with Darlan at all was his authority with the Vichy admirals and officers. The Germans clearly could not afford to take any risks, and while Darlan was sending messages to Vichy and to Toulon urging the French Fleet to put to sea in the direction of Allied controlled ports the Germans were marching rapidly towards the Mediterranean coast.

Admiral Auphan, the Minister of Marine at Vichy, wished to stand by Darlan, but he was powerless in the face of Laval and of the attitude of the French commanders at Toulon. Admiral de Laborde, the Commander of the French Mediterranean Fleet, was fanatically anti-British. On learning the news of the landings he wished to put to sea and attack the Allied convoys. He rejected Darlan's appeals to come over, and when the Germans arrived at the perimeter of the French naval base an agreement was made whereby a free zone round the harbour was to be garrisoned by French troops. Auphan reluctantly endorsed this arrangement, and attempts were made to put the port in a serious state of defence. But on November 18 the Germans demanded the withdrawal of all French troops from the zone, which could only be garrisoned by naval units. The following day Auphan resigned.

The Germans now planned a *coup de main* against the Fleet. The operation took place on November 27. The courage and resource of a few officers, including Laborde, who rallied at last, made possible the wholesale scuttling of the Fleet. One battleship, two battle cruisers, seven cruisers, twenty-nine destroyers and torpedo boats, and sixteen submarines were among the seventy-three ships which sank in the port.

*   *   *   *   *

The assault phase of "Torch" had been a brilliant success, and was in itself a remarkable operation. The fall of Algiers and Casablanca had been obtained cheaply, partly through the intervention of Admiral Darlan. Through the vacillation of the French commanders in Tunisia we were robbed of complete success. In his report on these events Admiral Cunningham said: "It is a matter for lasting regret to me that the bolder conception for the initial assault on Bone was not implemented. The enemy were surprised and off their balance. We failed to give the final push which would have tipped the scales." [7]

---

[7] See page 614.

Most careful preparations had been made for guiding the landing-craft to the chosen beaches. In the west, leading units of the British 11th Brigade were completely successful, but farther east the ships and craft carrying the Americans were driven some miles from their planned positions by an unexpected tidal set and in the darkness there was some confusion and delay. Fortunately we gained surprise and opposition along the coast was nowhere serious. After daylight, with the arrival of reinforcements mastery was soon complete. An aircraft of the Fleet Air Arm observing friendly signals from the ground, landed at Blida airfield and with the co-operation of the local French Commander held it until Allied troops from the beaches arrived in support.

12

The Darlan Episode

The Position of General de Gaulle and the Free French — My Telegram to President Roosevelt of November 11 — His Reply, November 12 — Eisenhower Flies to Algiers — Darlan's Authority Prevails with the French in North and West Africa — Widespread Disquiet in England — I Warn the President, November 17 — His Public Statement — General Smuts' View from the Spot — Passion Mounts in England — "The Darlan Deal" — The Secret Session, December 10 — French Military and Official Mentality — "In the Name of the Marshal" — The House of Commons Convinced — Assassination of Admiral Darlan, December 24 — A Tragic Career.

THE FACTS of the story told in the last chapter show briefly what happened on the spot and in what order. Although these events were political they were as much a part of the battle as the movement of troops or ships. General Clark dealt with Darlan in the only way which would accord with the prime theme of the enterprise, namely, the procuring of the utmost French support and the avoidance of bloodshed between the French and the Allies. He showed daring, sagacity, and power of decision. On Eisenhower fell the responsibility of accepting and sustaining what had been done. The conduct of both these American officers, who only a year before had been Brigadier-Generals, reached a high level of courage and good sense. Nevertheless their action raised issues of a moral and sentimental character of cardinal importance to the peoples of the United States and Great Britain, and reverberated

through the Allied world. Hoping always that I understood
the soul of France, I was at this time anxious about the President's vehement hostility to de Gaulle and his Movement.
After all, this was the core of French resistance and the flame
of French honour.

Former Naval Person to President Roosevelt   11 Nov. 42

It is surely of the highest importance to unify in every possible
way all Frenchmen who regard Germany as the foe. The invasion
of Unoccupied France by Hitler should give the opportunity for
this. You will, I am sure, realise that His Majesty's Government
are under quite definite and solemn obligations to de Gaulle and
his Movement. We must see they have a fair deal. It seems to me
that you and I ought to avoid at all costs the creation of rival
French *émigré* Governments, each favoured by one of us. We
must try to fuse all anti-German French forces together and make
a united Government. This may take some time, and nothing
must prejudice the military operations, but we ought to make it
clear to all parties what we want and what we are going to work for.

Meanwhile it became apparent that a decisive victory had
been gained at Alamein.

President Roosevelt to Prime Minister   12 Nov. 42

I am very happy with the latest news of your splendid campaign
in Egypt, and of the success that has attended our joint landing in
West and North Africa. This brings up the additional steps that
should be taken when and if the south shore of the Mediterranean
is cleared and under our control. It is hoped that you with your
Chiefs of Staff in London and I with the Combined Staff here may
make a survey of the possibilities, including a forward movement
directed against Sardinia, Sicily, Italy, Greece, and other Balkan
areas, and including the possibility of obtaining Turkish support
for an attack through the Black Sea against Germany's flank.

In regard to de Gaulle, I have hitherto enjoyed a quiet satisfaction in leaving him in your hands. Apparently I have now acquired
a similar problem in brother Giraud. I wholly agree that we must
prevent rivalry between the French *émigré* factions, and I have no
objection to a de Gaulle emissary visiting Giraud in Algiers. We
must remember that there is also a cat-fight in progress between

Giraud and Darlan, each claiming full military command of French forces in North and West Africa.

The principal thought to be driven home to all three of these prima donnas is that the situation is today solely in the military field, and that any decision by any one of them, or by all of them, is subject to review and approval by Eisenhower.

Also I think it would be well to find out before de Gaulle's man leaves for Africa just what his instructions are.

*   *   *   *   *

On November 13 General Eisenhower flew from Gibraltar to Algiers to take the responsibility for the bargain which Clark had just made with Darlan and assume direct control. The Allied commanders and officials on the spot were unanimous that Darlan was the only Frenchman who could rally Northwest Africa to the Allies. Giraud, whose power to command French allegiance was already exposed as a myth, had offered to work with Darlan when he heard of the German invasion of Unoccupied France. Darlan's authority was proved by the obedience to his "cease fire" order at Oran, in Morocco, and throughout Algeria. A final and formal agreement was therefore signed between Darlan and Eisenhower on the same day. In London I thought that Eisenhower's action was overwhelmingly justified on military grounds. On November 14 I sent him the following message: "Anything for the battle, but the politics will have to be sorted out later on."

To the President I cabled:

Former Naval Person to President Roosevelt   15 Nov. 42

We cannot say that our doubts or anxieties are removed by what is proposed or that the solution will be permanent or healthy. Nevertheless, in view of the dominating importance of speed and of the fact that the Allied Commander-in-Chief's opinion is so strongly and ably expressed and that it is endorsed by our officers, including Admiral Cunningham, who were with him on the spot, we feel we have no choice but to accept General Eisenhower's arrangements for maintaining local and interim equilibrium and for securing the vital positions in Tunis.

2. We feel sure you will consult us on the long-term steps,

pursuing always the aim of uniting all Frenchmen who will fight
Hitler.

*　　*　　*　　*　　*

As the facts of the Darlan agreement became known they
caused widespread disquiet at home. I was conscious of the
rising tide of opinion around me. I was grieved to find the
success of our immense operation, and the victory of Alamein,
overshadowed in the minds of many of my best friends by
what seemed to them a base and squalid deal with one of our
most bitter enemies. I considered their attitude unreasonable
and not sufficiently considerate of the severities of the struggle
and the lives of the troops. As their criticisms became sharper
I grew resentful, and also somewhat contemptuous of their
sense of proportion; but I understood what was troubling them
and felt it myself. The reaction in the United States was not
so violent as in England, but many were agog. I did not think
that President Roosevelt was sufficiently impressed with the
surge of feeling, and certainly not of British feeling.

Former Naval Person to President Roosevelt   17 Nov. 42

I ought to let you know that very deep currents of feeling are
stirred by the arrangement with Darlan. The more I reflect upon
it the more convinced I become that it can only be a temporary
expedient, justifiable solely by the stress of battle. We must not
overlook the serious political injury which may be done to our
cause, not only in France but throughout Europe, by the feeling
that we are ready to make terms with the local Quislings. Darlan
has an odious record. It is he who has inculcated in the French
Navy its malignant disposition by promoting his creatures to command. It is but yesterday that French sailors were sent to their
death against your line of battle off Casablanca, and now, for the
sake of power and office, Darlan plays the turncoat. A permanent
arrangement with Darlan or the formation of a Darlan Government in French North Africa would not be understood by the great
masses of ordinary people, whose simple loyalties are our strength.

2. My own feeling is that we should get on with the fighting and
let that overtake the parleys, and we are all very glad to hear that
General Eisenhower expects to be able to order the leading elements

of our First Army to attack the Germans in Tunis and Bizerta in the course of the next few days.

The President replied:

President Roosevelt to Prime Minister   18 Nov. 42

I too have encountered the deep currents of feeling about Darlan. I felt I should act fast, so I have just given out a statement at my Press conference which I hope you will like, and I trust it will be accepted at face value.

I was relieved by his public statement,[1] which he had cabled me:

I have accepted General Eisenhower's political arrangements made for the time being in Northern and Western Africa. I thoroughly understand and approve the feeling in the United States and Great Britain and among all the other United Nations that in view of the history of the past two years no permanent arrangement should be made with Admiral Darlan. People in the United Nations likewise would never understand the recognition of a reconstitution of the Vichy Government in France or in any French territory. We are opposed to Frenchmen who support Hitler and the Axis.

No one in our Army has any authority to discuss the future Government of France and the French Empire. The future French Government will be established, not by any individual in Metropolitan France or overseas, but by the French people themselves after they have been set free by the victory of the United Nations. The present arrangement in North and West Africa is only a temporary expedient, justified solely by the stress of battle.

His statement proceeded:

Our first military objective was to save American and British lives on the one hand, and French lives on the other hand. The second was the vital factor of time. . . . Every day of delay in the current operation would have enabled the Germans and Italians to build up a strong resistance, to dig in, and make a huge operation on our part essential before we could win. Here again many more lives will be saved under the present speedy offensive than if we had had to

1 Abridged.

delay it for a month or more. . . . Reports indicate that the French
of North Africa are subordinating all political questions to the
formation of a common front against the common enemy.

This met my view and the public need.

Former Naval Person to President Roosevelt   19 Nov. 42

Your public statement about Darlan has settled the matter in
the best possible way. I am as anxious however as you and Eisenhower that we should profit to the full in the actions which are
impending by French co-operation. Also, I fully recognise that if
Darlan and Company render real services during the operations
these would naturally count in their favour. I feel pretty sure we
are looking at it from exactly the same point of view. Every good
wish.

*   *   *   *   *

General Smuts was with us at home in these days, and it was
a comfort to find how close was our agreement. He now flew
off, after a long talk, to the scene of action on his way back
to South Africa. After a full discussion in Algiers he expressed
himself in the following practical manner:

Field Marshal Smuts to Prime Minister   20 Nov. 42

After arrival this morning I had a long talk with Eisenhower and
Cunningham, which I summarise for your information. As regards
coming operation next Sunday or Monday, it is doubtful whether
Anderson is strong enough to take Bizerta, but Tunis appears more
hopeful. In any case, every effort will be made to press the enemy
into as small an area or bridgehead as possible, so that air and other
attack may finish him later. Farther south attempt will be made to
clean up small pockets of enemy at Sfax and elsewhere, but no large
forces will be employed in the Tripoli direction at present. Sea
losses so far have been made good. Loss of personnel ships have
been compensated by equal number of French ships acquired, and
for every merchant vessel lost a U-boat has been sunk.

As regards Darlan, statements published have had unsettling
effect on local French leaders, and it would be dangerous to go
farther on those lines. Noguès has threatened to resign, and as he
controls the Morocco population the results of such a step might be

far-reaching. From the point of view of securing French co-operation and stabilising the situation nothing could be worse than impression that we were merely using leaders to discard them as soon as they have served our purpose. There can be no doubt that Darlan and his friends have burnt their boats and are doing their best to fight the Axis and consolidate French behind us in this fight. French are co-operating in non-combatant tasks, and even in fighting on small scale, but their fighting value is at present low for want of proper arms. Darlan was not Eisenhower's choice, but that of other French leaders, some of whom were his enemies and our strong supporters, and who all agreed that his leadership in co-operation was essential for our operations. It would be great mistake to create impression that he is to be discarded at early date. Military situation may call for his retention for fairly long period, and meanwhile an impression to contrary should not be publicly created.

I explained to Eisenhower that I do not think there was any intention to repeat or go beyond statements already made, which were only intended to correct impression that political accord with Vichy elements had been come to. Future political arrangements should be left to Governments concerned and agreement of French among themselves. I think it would be wise to pass on to President Roosevelt my strong impression that further anti-Darlan statements might be harmful to our cause, and indeed are not called for. We leave late this afternoon, and I shall signal you again from Cairo. Your company and talks last night were a great honour, and most deeply enjoyed. Thanks very much.

The President kept me in touch with his own mood.

President Roosevelt to Prime Minister　　　　　　　　20 Nov. 42

I told the Press yesterday in confidence an old Orthodox Church proverb used in the Balkans that appears applicable to our present Darlan-de Gaulle problem: "My children, it is permitted you in time of grave danger to walk with the devil until you have crossed the bridge."

In regard to North Africa and possibly additional future areas, I think you and I might give some consideration to the idea of appointing one Britisher and one American to whom would be given authority not to administer civil functions but to hold a veto

power over French civil administrators, and to direct them in rare
instances to follow out certain policies. For example, I sent word
to Eisenhower that all political prisoners in North and West
Africa must be released. If Darlan fails to carry out this directive
Eisenhower must at once exercise his authority as Supreme Commander and take independent action in the matter.

On December 5 General Eisenhower telegraphed to me:

... I assure you again that we are not entering a cabal designed
to place Darlan at the head of anything except the local organisation. Here he is entirely necessary, for he and he alone is the
source of every bit of practical help we have received. If you will
contemplate the situation existing along our lines of communication, which extend five hundred miles from here through mountainous country to Tunisia, you will understand that the local
French could, without fear of detection, so damage us that we
would have to retreat hurriedly back to ports from which we could
supply ourselves by sea. Giraud quickly gave up trying to help us,
and it was only through Darlan's help that we are now fighting the
Boche in Tunisia instead of somewhere in the vicinity of Bone or
even west of that. It appears to us that both Boisson and Darlan
are committed irrevocably to an Allied victory. ...

Darlan had been smitten by the President's reference to a
"temporary expedient," and was beginning to feel his growing
isolation. At this time he wrote to General Clark:

Monsieur le Général,
    Information from various sources tends to substantiate the view
that I am "only a lemon which the Americans will drop after they
have squeezed it dry."
    In the line of conduct which I have adopted out of pure French
patriotic feeling, in spite of the serious disadvantages which it
entails for me, at the moment when it was extremely easy for me to
let events take their course without my intervention, my own personal position does not come into consideration.
    I acted only because the American Government has solemnly
undertaken to restore the integrity of French sovereignty as it
existed in 1939, and because the armistice between the Axis and

France was broken by the total occupation of Metropolitan France, against which the Marshal has solemnly protested.

I did not act through pride, ambition, or calculation, but because the position which I occupied in my country made it my duty to act.

When the integrity of France's sovereignty is an accomplished fact — and I hope it will be in the least possible time — it is my firm intention to return to private life and to end my days, in the course of which I have ardently served my country, in retirement.

* * * * *

The Admiral held on only because he felt that for the moment he was indispensable to the Allied Command in North Africa and held the key of power. On November 22 the so-called Clark-Darlan Agreements were signed, setting up provisional machinery for administering the region. Two days later Governor-General Boisson, under persuasion from Darlan's emissaries, brought over French West Africa, with the great base of Dakar, to the Allies.

But passion ran high in England about the Darlan deal. It affected poignantly some of my friends who had been most affronted by Munich, with whose impulses I had moved at crucial moments before the war. "Is this then what we are fighting for?" they asked. Many of those with whom I was in closest mental and moral harmony were in extreme distress. All these emotions were fanned by the de Gaulle Committee and organisation in our midst. The press gave full expression to this mood. Certainly there was a real and vivid case to be made and to be met. Not only Parliament but the nation found it hard to swallow "De Gaulle banned; Darlan uplifted." At the same time the facts could not be stated nor the arguments deployed in public. While in my mind, rightly or wrongly, I never had the slightest doubt that it was my duty to support General Eisenhower and to save the lives of the soldiers committed to the enterprise, I was acutely sensitive to the opposite argument, and understood, if only to override, the discarded alternative conviction.

* * * * *

On December 9 I voiced my disquiet to the President:

Former Naval Person to President Roosevelt　　　　　9 Dec. 42

I have been disturbed by reports received during the last few days from North Africa about conditions in French Morocco and Algeria. These reports, which come from independent and reliable sources, all paint the same picture of the results which follow from our inability in existing circumstances to exercise a proper control over the local French authorities in internal administrative matters. You are, I am sure, fully aware of this state of affairs, but I think it my duty to let you know the position as it appears in the light of our own reports.

2. These reports show that the S.O.L. [Service d'Ordre Légionnaire, a Vichy organisation of ex-servicemen] and kindred Fascist organisations continue their activities and victimise our former French sympathisers, some of whom have not yet been released from prison. The first reaction of these organisations to the Allied landing was, rightly, one of fear, but it seems that they have now taken courage to regroup themselves and continue their activities. Well-known German sympathisers who had been ousted have been reinstated. Not only have our enemies been thus encouraged, but our friends have been correspondingly confused and cast down. There have been cases of French soldiers being punished for desertion because they tried to support the Allied forces during their landing. . . .

The next day, December 10, a month after the landing, the mounting pressures in the circles of which I was conscious led me to seek refuge in Secret Session of the House of Commons. The speech which I then made was conceived with the sole purpose of changing the prevailing opinion, and I chose with the greatest care the points to make. I began with some severe understatements.

The question which we must ask ourselves is not whether we like or do not like what is going on, but what are we going to do about it. In war it is not always possible to have everything go exactly as one likes. In working with allies it sometimes happens that they develop opinions of their own. Since 1776 we have not been in the position of being able to decide the policy of the United States.

This is an American expedition in which they will ultimately have perhaps two or three times as large ground forces as we have, and three times the air force.

This was true at the time, but, as we shall see, was soon to be contradicted by events.

On sea the proportion is overwhelmingly in our favour, and we have of course given a vast amount of organisation and assistance in every way. Nevertheless the United States regards this as an American expedition under the ultimate command of the President of the United States, and they regard Northwest Africa as a war sphere which is in their keeping, just as we regard the Eastern Mediterranean as a theatre for which we are responsible. We have accepted this position from the outset and are serving under their command. That does not mean we have not got a great power of representation, and I am of course in the closest touch with the President. It does mean however that neither militarily nor politically are we directly controlling the course of events. It is because it would be highly detrimental to have a debate upon American policy or Anglo-American relations in public that His Majesty's Government have invited the House to come into Secret Session. In Secret Session alone can the matter be discussed without the risk of giving offence to our great Ally, and also of complicating the relationships of Frenchmen, who, whatever their past, are now firing upon the Germans.

I hold no brief for Admiral Darlan. Like myself, he is the object of the animosities of Herr Hitler and of Monsieur Laval. Otherwise I have nothing in common with him. But it is necessary for the House to realise that the Government and to a large extent the people of the United States do not feel the same way about Darlan as we do. He has not betrayed them. He has not broken any treaty with them. He has not vilified them. He has not maltreated any of their citizens. They do not think much of him, but they do not hate him and despise him as we do over here. Many of them think more of the lives of their own soldiers than they do about the past records of French political figures. Moreover, the Americans have cultivated up to the last moment relations with Vichy which were of a fairly intimate character and which in my opinion have conduced to our general advantage. At any rate, the position of the

Americans at Vichy gave us a window on that courtyard which otherwise would not have existed. . . .

Admiral Leahy has been Ambassador to Vichy until quite recently. He lived on terms of close intimacy with Marshal Pétain. He has at all times used his influence to prevent Vichy France becoming the ally of Germany or declaring war upon us when we have had to fire on Vichy troops at Oran or Dakar, in Syria or in Madagascar. On all these occasions I have believed, and have recorded my opinion beforehand, that France would not declare war; but a factor in forming that opinion was the immense American influence upon all Frenchmen, which influence of course increased enormously after the United States entered the war. Admiral Leahy is a close friend of President Roosevelt and was recently appointed his personal Chief of the Staff. The attitude of the United States Executive and State Department towards Vichy and all its works must be viewed against this background.

*   *   *   *   *

I now turn to examine a peculiar form of French mentality, or rather of the mentality of a large proportion of Frenchmen in the terrible defeat and ruin which has overtaken their country. I am not at all defending, still less eulogising, this French mentality. But it would be very foolish not to try to understand what is passing in other people's minds, and what are the secret springs of action to which they respond. The Almighty in His infinite wisdom did not see fit to create Frenchmen in the image of Englishmen. In a State like France, which has experienced so many convulsions — Monarchy, Convention, Directory, Consulate, Empire, Monarchy, Empire, and finally Republic — there has grown up a principle founded on the *droit administratif* which undoubtedly governs the action of many French officers and officials in times of revolution and change. It is a highly legalistic habit of mind, and it arises from a subconscious sense of national self-preservation against the dangers of sheer anarchy. For instance, any officer who obeys the command of his lawful superior or of one whom he believes to be his lawful superior is absolutely immune from subsequent punishment. Much therefore turns in the minds of French officers upon whether there is a direct, unbroken chain of lawful command, and this is held by many Frenchmen to be more important than moral, national, or international considerations. From this point of view many Frenchmen who admire General de Gaulle and envy him in his rôle nevertheless regard him as a man who has rebelled against the authority of the French State, which in their prostration they conceive to be vested in the person of the antique defeatist who to them is the illustrious and venerable Marshal Pétain, the hero of Verdun and the sole hope of France.

Now all this may seem very absurd to our minds. But there is one point about it which is important to us. It is in accordance with orders and authority transmitted or declared to be transmitted by Marshal Pétain that the French troops in Northwest Africa have pointed and fired their rifles against the Germans and Italians instead of continuing to point and fire their rifles against the British and Americans. I am sorry to have to mention a point like that, but it makes a lot of difference to a soldier whether a man fires his gun at him or at his enemy; and even the soldier's wife or father might have a feeling about it too. . . .

All this is done in the sacred name of the Marshal, and when the Marshal bleats over the telephone orders to the contrary and deprives Darlan of his nationality the Admiral rests comfortably upon the fact or fiction — it does not much matter which — that the Marshal is acting under the duress of the invading Hun, and that he, Darlan, is still carrying out his true wishes. In fact, if Admiral Darlan had to shoot Marshal Pétain he would no doubt do it in Marshal Pétain's name. . . .

I must however say that personally I consider that in the circumstances prevailing, General Eisenhower was right; and even if he was not quite right I should have been very reluctant to hamper or impede his action when so many lives and such vitally important issues hung in the balance. I do not want to shelter myself in any way behind the Americans or anyone else.

I ended with some bitterness, the outcome of the stresses which I felt.

I must say I think he is a poor creature with a jaundiced outlook and disorganised loyalties who in all this tremendous African episode, West and East alike, can find no point to excite his interest except the arrangements made between General Eisenhower and Admiral Darlan. The struggle for the Tunisian tip is now rising to its climax and the main battle impends. Another trial of strength

is very near on the frontiers of Cyrenaica. Both these battles will
be fought almost entirely by soldiers from this Island. The First
and Eighth British Armies will be engaged to the full. I cannot
take my thoughts away from them and their fortunes, and I expect
that will be the feeling of the House of Commons. . . .

I ask them to treat with proper reprobation that small, busy, and
venomous band who harbour and endeavour to propagate unworthy and unfounded suspicions, and so to come forward unitedly
with us in all the difficulties through which we are steadfastly and
successfully making our way.

I do not remember any speech out of hundreds which I made
where I felt opinion change so palpably and decisively. This
was no case for applause, but only for results. The Commons
were convinced, and the fact that all further Parliamentary
opposition stopped after the Secret Session quenched the hostile
press and reassured the country. There was also the growing
exhilaration of victory after so many hard months of disappointment or defeat.

General Eisenhower in his post-war book [2] contributes from
his own angle a practical and soldierly confirmation:

It is possible to understand why de Gaulle was disliked within
the ranks of the French Army. At the time of France's surrender
in 1940 the officers who remained in the Army had accepted the
position and orders of their Government and had given up the
fight. From their viewpoint, if the course chosen by de Gaulle was
correct, then every French officer who obeyed the orders of his
Government was a poltroon. If de Gaulle was a loyal Frenchman
they had to regard themselves as cowards. Naturally the officers
did not choose to think of themselves in this light; rather they
considered themselves as loyal Frenchmen carrying out the orders
of constituted civilian authority, and it followed that they officially
and personally regarded de Gaulle as a deserter.

*   *   *   *   *

Political affairs in North Africa deteriorated rapidly during
the last days of 1942. Not only was there a desperate struggle

[2] Eisenhower, *Crusade in Europe*, page 84.

against Giraud for power and recognition among the recent adherents to the Allied cause, Darlan, Noguès, Boisson, and others, but also active discontent among those men who had helped the Allied landings on November 8, and among the small but active group which was ardent for de Gaulle. In addition there was growing support for a movement to place the Comte de Paris, at this time living quietly near Tangier, at the head of a provisional wartime administration in North Africa in opposition to Vichy. The patchwork arrangement whereby Darlan was at the head of civil affairs and Giraud was in command of the French armed forces in North Africa came under increasing strain.

On December 19 the first emissary of de Gaulle, General François d'Astier de la Vigerie, arrived unofficially in Algiers to explore the ground on behalf of his leader. He was the brother of Henri, who had played a leading part in the rising in the town of Algiers on November 8, and who was now implicated in the Royalist conspiracy which aimed at bringing the Comte de Paris to power. The Gaullist visit was exploratory. The military co-operation of the Free French forces was formally offered both to Giraud and Eisenhower in discussions on December 20, but no decisions were taken. The practical result of General d'Astier de la Vigerie's visit was to stimulate the Gaullist opposition to Darlan. Simultaneously with these talks the Monarchist elements in Algiers decided to press Darlan to abdicate and hand over to an all-party administration. It is not even now clear how much support they had.

On the afternoon of December 24 Darlan drove down from his villa to his offices in the Palais d'Eté. At the door of his bureau he was shot down by a young man of twenty named Bonnier de la Chapelle. The Admiral died within the hour on the operating table of a near-by hospital. The youthful assassin had, according to some stories, been connected with Henri d'Astier, and under much persuasion had worked himself into an exalted state of mind as the saviour of France from wicked leadership. Apart from a small circle of personal friends

grouped round d'Astier, there was no open support in Algiers
for his act. He was tried by court-martial under Giraud's
orders, and, much to his surprise, was executed by a firing
squad shortly after dawn on December 26.

On receiving the news of Darlan's assassination General
Eisenhower hurried back from the Tunisian front. In the circumstances the only thing to do was to nominate Giraud to fill
the vacant place. We could not run the risk of civil disorder
behind the front, and indirect though decisive pressure was
exerted by the American authorities to achieve the appointment of Giraud to supreme though transitory political power
in North Africa.

Darlan's murder, however criminal, relieved the Allies of
their embarrassment at working with him, and at the same
time left them with all the advantages he had been able to
bestow during the vital hours of the Allied landings. His authority had passed smoothly to the organisation created in
agreement with the American authorities during the months of
November and December. Giraud filled the gap. The path
was cleared for the French forces now rallied in North and
Northwest Africa to unite with the Free French Movement
round de Gaulle, and comprising all Frenchmen throughout
the world outside German control. On learning of Darlan's
fate de Gaulle made the first approach. He was about to leave
for Washington for a long-delayed first meeting with the
President when the news reached London. He at once drafted
and dispatched through Allied channels a message to Giraud.
It seemed to me wise to put off the Washington visit in the
hope of uniting French Resistance. I explained the position
in a telegram to the President, and sent him a copy of de
Gaulle's message to Giraud.

Former Naval Person to President Roosevelt   27 Dec. 42

As I told Harry, I had already asked United States Headquarters,
London, to delay for forty-eight hours the plane which was to carry
de Gaulle, to see how the "Torch" situation develops. It seems
to me that we ought to try above anything to bring them all to-

gether and have some French nucleus, solid and united, to work with. I am seeing de Gaulle today, and will cable you further.

2. I am sure that North African settlement cannot be held up for "Symbol" [our conference at Casablanca]. We have received news that "King-pin" has been unanimously elected High Commissioner and Commander-in-Chief by the French group of notabilities. I have already informed Eisenhower that so far as we are concerned we entirely agree with this solution.

3. The War Cabinet attach much importance to Macmillan's appointment and arrival [at Algiers]. We feel quite unrepresented there, yet our fortunes are deeply involved, and we are trying to make a solid contribution to your enterprise. Murphy's appointment has already been announced, and I hope you will agree to my publishing Macmillan's. He will be, I am sure, a help. He is animated by the friendliest feelings towards the United States, and his mother hails from Kentucky.

Here followed de Gaulle's message to Giraud, sent through the American Embassy in London:

27 Dec. 42

The assassination at Algiers is an indication and warning: an indication of the exasperation into which the tragedy of France has thrown the mind and soul of Frenchmen; a warning of the consequences of every kind which necessarily result from the absence of a national authority in the midst of the greatest national crisis of our history. It is more than ever necessary that this national authority should be established. I propose, my General, that you should meet me as soon as possible on French soil, either in Algeria or in Chad, in order to study the means of grouping under a provisional central authority all French forces inside and outside the country and all the French territories which are in a position to struggle for the liberation and the salvation of France.

*   *   *   *   *

Few men have paid more heavily for errors of judgment and failure of character than Admiral Darlan. He was a professional figure, and a strong personality. His life's work had been to recreate the French Navy, and he had raised it to a position it had never held since the days of the French kings.

He commanded the allegiance not only of the Naval Officer
Corps, but of the whole Naval Service. In accordance with
his repeated promises, he ought in 1940 to have ordered the
fleets to Britain, to the United States, the African ports, anywhere out of German power. He was under no treaty or
obligation to do so except assurances which he had voluntarily
given. But this was his resolve until on that deadly June 20,
1940, he accepted from Marshal Pétain's hands the office of
Minister of Marine. Then, perhaps influenced by motives of a
departmental character, he gave his allegiance to Marshal
Pétain's Government. Ceasing to be a sailor and becoming a
politician, he exchanged a sphere in which he had profound
knowledge for one where his chief guide was his anti-British
prejudices, dating, as I have mentioned, from the Battle of
Trafalgar, where his great-grandfather had fallen.

In this new situation he showed himself a man of force and
decision who did not wholly comprehend the moral significance
of much that he did. Ambition stimulated his errors. His
vision as an Admiral had not gone beyond his Navy, nor as a
Minister beyond immediate local or personal advantages. For
a year and a half he had been a great power in shattered France.
At the time when we descended upon North Africa he was the
undoubted heir of the aged Marshal. Now suddenly a cataract
of amazing events fell upon him. By a strange chance the illness of his son had drawn him to Algiers, where he fell into
Anglo-American power.

We have recounted the stresses which he underwent. All
French North and West Africa looked to him. The invasion
of Vichy France by Hitler gave him the power, and it may be
the right, to make a new decision. He brought to the Anglo-
American Allies exactly what they needed, namely, a French
voice which all French officers and officials in this vast theatre,
now plunged in the war, would obey. He struck his final blow
for us, and it is not for those who benefited enormously from
his accession to our side to revile his memory. A stern, impartial judge may say that he should have refused all parley
with the Allies he had injured, and defied them to do their

worst with him. We may all be glad he took the opposite
course. It cost him his life, but there was not much left in life
for him. It seemed obvious at the time that he was wrong in
not sailing the French Fleet to Allied or neutral ports in June
1940; but he was right in this second fearful decision. Probably his sharpest pang was his failure to bring over the Toulon
fleet. Always he had declared it should never fall into German
hands. In this undertaking before history he did not fail. Let
him rest in peace, and let us all be thankful we have never had
to face the trials under which he broke.

13

Problems of Victory

AMERICAN MILITARY OPINION, not only in the highest circles, was convinced that the decision for "Torch" ruled out all prospect of a major crossing of the Channel into Occupied France in 1943. I had not yet brought myself to accept this view. I still hoped that French Northwest Africa, including the Tunisian tip, might fall into our hands after a few months' fighting. In this case the main invasion of Occupied France from England would still be possible in July or August, 1943. I was therefore most anxious that the strongest build-up of American power in Britain which our shipping would allow should proceed at the same time as "Torch." This idea of being able to use our left as well as our right hand, and the fact that the enemy must prepare himself against blows from either, seemed wholly in accordance with the highest economy of war. Events would decide whether we should thrust across the Channel or follow our luck in the Mediterranean, or do both. It seemed imperative, in the interests of the war as a whole and especially of aiding Russia, that the Anglo-American armies should enter Europe either from the west or from the east in the coming year.

There was however a danger that we might do neither. Even if our campaign in Algeria and Tunisia prospered swiftly, we should content ourselves with capturing Sardinia or Sicily or both, and put off crossing the Channel till 1944. This would mean a wasted year for the Western Allies, with results which might be fatal, not indeed to our survival, but to a decisive victory. We could not go on losing five or six hundred thousand tons of shipping a month indefinitely. A stalemate was Germany's last hope.

Before we knew what was going to happen at Alamein or to "Torch," and while the terrific struggle in the Caucasus seemed undecided, the British Chiefs of Staff were weighing all these issues. The Planners under them were also busy. Their reports were in my opinion unduly negative, and I commented on them to the Chiefs of Staff on November 9, while the landings in Africa were still proceeding:

It would be most regrettable to make no more use of the success of "Torch" and Alamein in 1943 than the occupation of Sicily and Sardinia. We have already committed ourselves with the Americans to "Round-up" in 1943, an operation on the greatest scale. The interposition of "Torch" is no excuse for lying down during 1943, content with descents on Sicily and Sardinia and a few more operations like Dieppe (which can hardly be taken as a pattern).

The effort for the campaign of 1943 should clearly be a strong pinning down of the enemy in Northern France and the Low Countries by continuous preparations to invade, and a decisive attack on Italy, or, better still, Southern France, together with operations not involving serious shipping expense, and other forms of pressure to bring in Turkey and operate overland with the Russians into the Balkans. If French North Africa is going to be made an excuse for locking up great forces on the defensive and calling it a "commitment," it would be better not to have gone there at all. Is it really to be supposed that the Russians will be content with our lying down like this during the whole of 1943, while Hitler has a third crack at them? However alarming the prospect may seem, we must make an attempt to get on to the mainland of Europe and fight in the line against the enemy in 1943.

And further on the 18th:

. . . Under the agreements made about "Round-up" and "Bolero" with General Marshall we were to have by April 1, 1943, twenty-seven American and twenty-one British divisions ready for the Continent, together with all the necessary landing-craft, etc. This task was solemnly undertaken and an immense amount of work has been done. . . . We then went off to "Torch," which is now in progress. But "Torch" is only thirteen divisions, whereas we had been prepared to move forty-eight divisions against the enemy in 1943. We have therefore reduced our striking intent against the enemy by thirty-five divisions. Allowance should no doubt be made for the larger distances from here to "Torch" compared with those across the Channel. But we have given Stalin to understand that the great attack on the Continent will come in 1943, and we are now working on a basis of thirty-five divisions short of what was purposed in the period April-July, or, in other words, little more than a quarter.

It is no use blinking at this or imagining that the discrepancy will not be perceived. I have no doubt myself that we and General Marshall overestimated our capacity as measured by shipping, and also by the rate at which United States forces as well as special landing-craft, etc., could be ready. But there is a frightful gap between what the Chiefs of Staff contemplated as reasonable in the summer of 1942 for the campaign of 1943 and what they now say we can do in that campaign. I am not making criticisms, because I am in this myself to the full. But I feel we have got to get much closer to grips with this whole business. I fear I shall have to go to the United States in the near future. No doubt we were planning too much for 1943 in the summer, but we are certainly planning too little now. I must repeat that "Torch" is no substitute for "Round-up." It must also be remembered that we had proposed to continue the campaign in the Middle East while "Round-up" was going forward, and now we have an easement there through the virtual destruction of Rommel. We have, in fact, pulled in our horns to an almost extraordinary extent, and I cannot imagine what the

Russians will say or do when they realise it. My own position is that I am still aiming at a "Round-up" retarded till August. I cannot give this up without a massive presentation of facts and figures which prove physical impossibility. These figures will however if they prove the case stultify our ambitions and judgment of this summer, and that of the Americans. . . . I never meant the Anglo-American Army to be stuck in North Africa. It is a springboard and not a sofa. . . .

It may be that we should close down the Mediterranean activities by the end of June with a view to "Round-up" in August. The issues will have to be settled on the highest levels after we have reached agreement among ourselves.

We were thus reaching from both sides of the Atlantic a sort of combined deadlock. The British Staffs favoured the Mediterranean and an attack upon Sardinia and Sicily, with Italy as the goal. The United States experts had given up all hopes of crossing the Channel in 1943, but were most anxious not to be entangled in the Mediterranean in such a way as to prevent their great design in 1944. "It would seem," as I wrote, "that the sum of all American fears is to be multiplied by the sum of all British fears, faithfully contributed by each Service."

* * * * *

The American staffs, swayed by that undue liking for logical, clear-cut decisions, however desirable they may be, which I have ventured to note in earlier chapters, had in fact slowed down with a sweeping gesture the build-up of "Bolero" in Great Britain after the "Torch" decision had been taken. Late in November a written notification reached us from the administrative side of the United States machine which caused general astonishment. The following message which I sent to the President should incidentally, but I trust finally, dispose of the many American legends that I was inveterately hostile to the plan of a large-scale Channel crossing in 1943, and, still more, of the post-war Soviet assertions that I used the operation "Torch" with the deliberate intention of preventing "a Second Front in 1943."

Former Naval Person to President Roosevelt   24 Nov. 42

We have had a letter from General Hartle stating that under
directive from the United States War Department "any construction in excess of the requirements for a force of 427,000 must be
accomplished entirely by your own labour and with your own
materials," and that "Lend-Lease materials cannot be furnished in
these instances." This has caused us very great concern, not so
much from the standpoint of Lend-Lease, but on ground of grand
strategy. We have been preparing under "Bolero" for 1,100,000
men, and this is the first intimation we have had that this target is
to be abandoned. We had no knowledge that you had decided to
abandon for ever "Round-up," and all our preparations were proceeding on a broad front under "Bolero."

2. It seems to me that it would be a most grievous decision to
abandon "Round-up." "Torch" is no substitute for "Round-up,"
and only engages thirteen divisions as against the forty-eight contemplated for "Round-up." All my talks with Stalin, in Averell's
presence, were on the basis of a postponed "Round-up," but never
was it suggested that we should attempt no second front in Europe
in 1943, or even 1944.

3. Surely, Mr. President, this matter requires most profound
consideration. I was deeply impressed with all General Marshall's
arguments that only by "Round-up" could the main forces be
thrown into France and the Low Countries, and only in this area
could the main strength of the British Metropolitan and United
States Overseas Air Forces be brought into action. One of the
arguments we used against "Sledgehammer" was that it would eat
up in 1942 the seed-corn needed for the much larger "Round-up"
in 1943. No doubt we have all been sanguine of our shipping resources, but that is a matter which time can correct. Only by the
building up of a "Round-up" force here as rapidly and regularly
as other urgent demands on shipping allow can we have the means
of coming to grips with the main strength of the enemy and
liberating the European nations. It may well be that, try as we will,
our strength will not reach the necessary levels in 1943. But if so
it becomes all the more important to make sure we do not miss
1944.

4. Even in 1943 a chance may come. Should Stalin's offensive
reach Rostov-on-the-Don, which is his aim, a first-class disaster may
overtake the German southern armies. Our Mediterranean opera-

tions following on "Torch" may drive Italy out of the war. Widespread demoralisation may set in among the Germans, and we must be ready to profit by any opportunity which offers.

5. I do beg of you, Mr. President, to let me know what has happened. At present we are completely puzzled by this information and the manner in which it has reached us. It seems to me absolutely necessary either that General Marshall and Admiral King with Harry should come over here or that I should come with my people to you.

The President lost no time in correcting this misunderstanding which had arisen at a lower level.

President to Prime Minister   26 Nov. 42

We of course have no intention of abandoning "Round-up." No one can possibly know now whether or not we may have the opportunity to strike across the Channel in 1943, and if the opportunity comes we must obviously grasp it. However, the determination as to the size of the force which we should have in "Bolero" in 1943 is a matter which should require our joint strategic consideration. It is my present thought that we should build up as rapidly as present active operations permit a growing striking force in the United Kingdom to be used quickly in the event of a German collapse, or a very large force later if Germany remains intact and assumes a defensive position.

The conclusions of the Combined Chiefs of Staff at the meeting last summer in London indicated that the mounting of "Torch" necessarily postponed the assembling of the required forces in the United Kingdom. In view of our requirements for the initiation and maintenance of "Torch" our studies indicated that we could not send forces and material to the United Kingdom at this time in excess of that stated by General Hartle. Until we have provided adequately against the possible reactions from Spanish Morocco and are clear as to the situation in Tunisia, North Africa must naturally take precedence. We are far more heavily engaged in the Southwest Pacific than I anticipated a few months ago. Nevertheless we shall continue with "Bolero" as rapidly as our shipping and other resources permit.

*   *   *   *   *

I now tried to survey the Mediterranean scene.

NOTE BY THE MINISTER OF DEFENCE
November 25, 1942

In settling what to do in a vast war situation like this it may sometimes be found better to take a particular major operation to which one is committed and follow that through vigorously to the end, making other things subordinate to it, rather than to assemble all the data from the whole world scene in a baffling array. After the needs of the major operation have been satisfied so far as possible, other aspects of the war will fall into their proper places. Moreover, it is by the continued stressing of the major operation that our will may be imposed upon the enemy and the initiative regained.

2. The paramount task before us is, first, to conquer the African shores of the Mediterranan and set up there the naval and air installations which are necessary to open an effective passage through it for military traffic; and, secondly, using the bases on the African shore to strike at the under-belly of the Axis in effective strength and in the shortest time.

3. There are therefore two phases — consolidation and exploitation. Dealing with consolidation first, we may hope that General Alexander will become master of the whole of Cyrenaica during the present month, and that he will be pressing the enemy in the Agheila position or even at Sirte. We may also assume that in the same period or not long after the American and British forces will become masters of the whole of French North Africa, including Tunis, provided they press forward with their present energy and violence.

4. It will be necessary to set up air stations at suitable intervals along all the African shore in our power, but particularly and urgently in the Tunisian tip. The largest installations for American bombers ought to be set up here so that long-range bombers sent by the United States to North Africa, together with American bombers already based on the Middle East, can operate against Italian targets. The United States form of daylight attack would have its best chance in the better weather of the Mediterranean.

5. The bombing weight of the British night attack should be brought to bear on Italy whenever the weather is more favourable than for bombing Germany.

6. It will no doubt be necessary also to act against the Catania and Cagliari airfields so as to keep down the attack on Tunis in the period of consolidation.

7. As soon as we are sure of ourselves, and consolidated, in French North Africa, including especially Tunis, two successive operations present themselves. The first is the advance to Tripoli. It is possible that General Alexander may be able to take this important prize from the east, and I have asked him how he feels about it, and how long he thinks he would require; but we must also be prepared for a rapid advance from the west. Would General Anderson's two British divisions be sufficient, assuming that Tunis itself can be held by American and French Allied troops? I should like the best possible estimate of the time that this will take.

8. The second immediate objective is obviously either Sardinia or Sicily. The possession of one of these islands and of the airfields in the South would create an air triangle, in which we should fight for and secure air mastery. Moreover, from either of them continuous intensified short-range attacks on Naples, Rome, and the Italian fleet bases would raise the war against Italy to an intense degree. Let an immediate report be prepared in order that a decision can be taken. Whichever it may be, the fight for air control in the Central Mediterranean should be undertaken as a great air battle with extreme priority, the fullest advantage being taken of the Axis shortage of aircraft. . . . Note that the preparations to attack Sardinia may take as long as those to attack Sicily, and that Sicily is by far the greater prize.

The rest of this paper dealt with the need for drawing Turkey into the war. These arguments will find their own place later in the story.

* * * * *

I now turn back to the supreme project of crossing the Channel in 1943.

NOTE BY THE MINISTER OF DEFENCE

December 3, 1942

In April last General Marshall unfolded to us the plan subsequently called "Round-up," of which "Bolero" is the administrative counterpart. A massive argument was that "Round-up" is the only way in which large American and British forces can be brought into direct contact with the enemy, and the British Metropolitan and United States Overseas Air Forces exercise their maximum power. American military opinion was solidly ranged behind this enterprise, and since then preparations under "Bolero" have gone forward steadily, subject only to "Torch." As an addition to "Round-up," "Sledgehammer" was proposed in July. It was agreed by the combined Staffs that "Torch" should be executed instead of "Sledgehammer." Meanwhile "Bolero" was to continue with preparations for a retarded or opportunist "Round-up."

2. However, the opinion was held by the American Staffs that the abandonment of "Sledgehammer" and the adoption of "Torch" in fact rendered "Round-up" impossible in 1943, even though retarded. One reason for this was the probability of Russia being so seriously weakened that Hitler could bring back very large armies from the East, thus making the forces available for "Round-up" in 1943 altogether insufficient. They also founded their opinion on the fact that the assembly of forces for "Round-up" would be so delayed by the diversion of shipping to "Torch" that we should not be strong enough during the 1943 season to effect an entry into the Continent, even against comparatively weak forces. The American military staff thus foresaw their troops being held idle in the United Kingdom, a situation which the President and General Marshall were anxious to avoid.

3. Besides the above, the shipping stringency has become pronounced. The progress of constructing landing-craft and training-crews has been slowed down, if not largely arrested. "Torch" is in full progress, with its serious demands on shipping, and we have in prospect the variants of "Brimstone" (Sardinia), which, though secondary, are substantial operations.

4. On the other hand, the Russians have been led to believe that we were going to open a second front in 1943. "Round-up" was explained to them by me in the presence of the United States representative, Mr. Harriman. These conversations at Moscow were duly reported to the President. I feel that Premier Stalin would have grave reasons to complain if our land offensive against Germany and Italy in 1943 were reduced to the scale of about thirteen divisions instead of nearly fifty, which have been mentioned to him. Moreover, apart from any Russian obligations, I feel that

our offensive war plans for 1943 are on altogether too small a scale compared with the resources and power of Britain and the United States.

5. Recent most important events have altered, and are altering, the data on which thought on both sides of the Atlantic has hitherto proceeded. The Russians have not been defeated or weakened in the campaign of 1942. On the contrary, it is Hitler who has been defeated and the German Army which has been very grievously reduced. General von Thoma [1] was heard to say that the one hundred eighty German divisions on the Russian front are in many cases little more than brigades. The demoralisation among the Hungarian, Rumanian, and Italian troops on the Eastern Front is marked. The Finns are no longer fighting, except for a few mountain troops.

6. The great battles now in progress at Stalingrad and in the central sector of the Russian front have not yet been decided. It may well be that the Russian offensives will produce far-reaching effects upon the German power. If the Sixth German Army, which is now encircled before Stalingrad, is destroyed the Russian southern offensive may reach its objective at Rostov-on-the-Don. In this case the position of the three remaining German armies in the Northern Caucasus, already closely engaged by the Russians, may be seriously and perhaps even mortally compromised, again with measureless results. The Russian offensive in the central sector and the counter-attacks they are making at many points along the front may lead to a withdrawal of the German line to winter positions. The winter will impose formidable privations and ordeals upon the weakened German armies, in spite of the better railway system they now have. Before the end of 1942 it may be possible for us to draw with certainty at least the conclusion *that no important transfers of German troops can be made in 1943 from the Eastern to the Western theatre*. This would be a new fact of the first magnitude. . . .

9. The events which have taken place in France have compelled the Germans, in order to defend the southern coasts of France, to withdraw eleven divisions from the forty which stood opposite Britain in France and the Low Countries. Their task of maintaining internal security in France has been rendered more onerous. They will probably be compelled to find another four or even six

[1] Taken prisoner at Alamein.

divisions to protect and hold down Italy against the menace of
"Torch," "Brimstone," etc., and to garrison Sicily and perhaps
Sardinia. The Yugoslav resistance continues, and no relief can be
expected by the Axis in any part of the Balkan peninsula. On
the contrary, they have the need to reinforce Greece, Rumania, and
Bulgaria, on account of the general situation, as well as of the
possible entry of Turkey against them, for which we are to work.
None of these facts were present when "Round-up" and "Sledgehammer" were considered at the London conferences of July.

10. I am therefore of opinion that the whole position must be
completely re-surveyed, with the object of finding means for engaging United States and British armies directly upon the Continent. For this purpose the assumptions set forth in the preceding
paragraphs should be accepted as data. Besides these, it should be
assumed that the North African shore is adequately equipped with
air forces, and that the Mediterranean is open for military traffic
by the end of March, thus securing a substantial relief in shipping;
that any Sardinian operations are concluded by the beginning of
June; that all landing-craft, etc., needed for "Round-up" should
be back in Great Britain by the end of June; that July should be
devoted to preparation and rehearsal; and that August, or, if the
weather is adverse, September, should be taken as the striking
target.

I was very glad to find my argument was welcomed by
General Marshall, whom I had kept fully informed through
Dill.

Field-Marshal Dill to Prime Minister   14 Dec. 42

I have had a private talk with Marshall. He is very encouraged
to know that your thoughts and his are running on the same lines,
but he has made it clear to me that until he sees the full development of operations in North Africa and has the views of Eisenhower
his opinions as to our future strategy cannot be firm.

2. He is however getting more and more convinced that we
should be in a position to undertake a modified "Round-up" before
the summer [of 1943] if, as soon as North Africa is cleared of Axis
forces, we start pouring American forces into England instead of
sending them to Africa for the exploitation of "Torch." Such an
operation would, he feels, be much more effective than either

"Brimstone" or "Husky," less costly in shipping, more satisfying to the Russians, engage many more German air forces, and be the most effective answer to any German attack through Spain.

3. Marshall would of course have liked to discuss these questions with you and the Chiefs of Staff, but as American and British ideas now appear to be so close there is, he considers, less need for such personal discussions.

*   *   *   *   *

I have thus laid before the reader the position as I saw it at the close of 1942. It will no doubt be said that the course of events proved that I took too sanguine a view about the prospects in Northwest Africa, and the United States Staffs were right in believing that the decision for "Torch" which we had taken in July closed the possibility of "Round-up" in 1943. Certainly that was what happened. No one could foresee at this time that Hitler would make his immense effort to reinforce the Tunisian tip by sending thither by air and sea, in spite of heavy losses, nearly a hundred thousand of his best troops. This was on his part a grave strategic error. It certainly delayed for several months our victory in Africa. If he had held the forces which were captured or destroyed there in May he might either have reinforced his retreating front against Russia, or have gathered the strength in Normandy which would have deterred us, even if we were so resolved, from trying "Round-up" in 1943. Hardly anyone now disputes the wisdom of the decision to wait until 1944. My conscience is clear that I did not deceive or mislead Stalin. I tried my best. On the other hand, provided we invaded the mainland of Europe from the Mediterranean in the coming campaign and that the Anglo-American armies were in full contact with the enemy, I was not ill-content with the decision which Fate and facts were to impose.

14

Our Need to Meet

THERE NOW CAME a definite check and setback in North
Africa. Although we had the initiative and the advantage
of surprise, our build-up was inevitably slow. Shipping imposed its harsh limits. Unloading was hampered by air attacks
on Algiers and Bone. Road transport was lacking. The single-
line coastal railway, five hundred miles long, was in poor condition, with hundreds of bridges and culverts, any one of which
might be sabotaged. With the arrival of German troops in
large numbers by air in Tunis a high-class, stubborn, and
violent resistance began. The French forces who had now
joined our cause were over a hundred thousand strong. The
majority were native troops of good quality, but as yet ill-
equipped and unorganised. General Eisenhower thrust forward to Anderson's command every American unit on which

he could lay his hands. We put in all we could. A British infantry brigade, with part of the United States 1st Armoured Division, attacked and captured Medjez, and on November 28 nearly reached Djedeida, only twelve miles from Tunis. This was the climax of the winter fighting.

Now came the rainy season. It poured. Our improvised airfields became quagmires. The German Air Force, though not yet strong in numbers, worked from good all-weather airfields. On December 1 they counter-attacked, frustrating the advance we had planned, and in a few days the British brigade was forced back to Medjez. Supplies could only reach the forward troops by sea on a small scale. Indeed, it was barely possible to nourish them, far less to make any accumulations. It was not till the night of December 22 that a renewed attack could be launched. This met with some initial success, but at dawn began three days of torrential rain. Our airfields became useless and vehicles could only move along the indifferent roads.

At a conference on Christmas Eve General Eisenhower decided to give up the plan for the immediate capture of Tunis and, until campaigning could begin again, to guard his forward airfields on the general line already gained. Although the Germans suffered important losses at sea, their strength in Tunisia continually grew. By the end of December their numbers approached fifty thousand.

* * * * *

While these operations were in progress the Eighth Army had covered immense distances. Rommel succeeded in withdrawing his shattered forces from Alamein to Agheila. His rearguards were heavily pressed, but an attempt to head him off south of Benghazi failed. He paused at Agheila, while Montgomery, after his long advance, contended with the same difficulties of transport and supply on which his predecessors had foundered. On December 13 Rommel was dislodged and nearly cut off by a wide turning movement of the 2d New Zealand Division. He suffered severely, and the Desert Air Force took heavy toll of his transport on the coast road. Mont-

gomery could follow at first only with light forces. The Eighth
Army had advanced twelve hundred miles since Alamein.
After occupying Sirte and its landing-grounds on Christmas
Day our troops closed with Rommel's next main position near
Buerat at the end of the year.

*   *   *   *   *

President Roosevelt's telegram to me of November 26, partly
quoted in the preceding chapter, had also contained his proposal for a triple conference between representatives of the
three staffs.

President Roosevelt to Former Naval Person   26 Nov. 42

I believe that as soon as we have knocked the Germans out of
Tunisia we should proceed with a military strategical conference
between Great Britain, Russia, and the United States. I am hoping
that our military position in Africa will be such that a conference
might be held in a month or six weeks. Our own Combined Chiefs
of Staff will, I believe, have a recommendation for us within a few
days as to what the next steps should be, but I feel very strongly
that we have got to sit down at the table with the Russians. My
notion would be a conference in Cairo or Moscow: that each of us
would be represented by a small group, meeting very secretly. The
conclusions of the conference would of course be approved by the
three of us. I would probably send Marshall to head up our group,
but I presume that all services should be represented. I think it
would be wise to keep the numbers down to three from each of us.

Will you let me know as soon as you can what you think of my
proposal.

I replied the same day, saying that I did not believe a conference of experts would meet our need.

Former Naval Person to President Roosevelt   26 Nov. 42

I entirely agree in principle that there should be a conference
with the Russians, but I doubt very much whether a conference on
general war policy, apart from some special point, between officers
would be of much value. Certainly if a Russian delegation went
to Cairo, which I deem unlikely, they would be so tied up that
they would have to refer every point of substance back to Stalin at

Moscow. If the conference were held in Moscow there would be less delay, but I trust that before British and United States Missions went to Moscow they would have a joint and agreed view, to serve at least as a basis for discussion. I hope also that if General Marshall were sent by you he would not bypass this country.

I think I can tell you in advance what the Soviet view will be. They will say to us both, "How many German divisions will you be engaging in the summer of 1943? How many have you engaged in 1942?" They will certainly demand a strong second front in 1943 by the heavy invasion of the Continent either from the west or from the south or from both. This sort of argument, of which I had plenty in Moscow, requires to be met either by principals or by naval and shipping authorities, who would certainly have to be present. It would be very difficult to spare all our chiefs for so long at this time.

Stalin talked to me in Moscow in the sense of being willing to come to meet you and me somewhere this winter, and he mentioned Iceland. I pointed out that England was no farther and more convenient. He neither accepted nor rejected the idea. At the same time, apart from the climate, there is a lot to be said for a new triple Atlantic Conference in Iceland. Our ships might lie together in Halfjord, and we would place a suitable ship at Stalin's disposal wearing the Soviet flag *pro tem*. He talked with some zest of his desire to fly and of his confidence in the Russian machines. Only at a meeting between principals will real results be achieved. What about proposing it for January? By that time Africa should be cleared and the great battle in South Russia decided.

I may add that if ever I can persuade you to come to Iceland I shall never be satisfied unless you look in on this small place before returning.

* * * * *

On December 3 the President cabled me again.

President Roosevelt to Former Naval Person   3 Dec. 42

I have been giving a good deal of thought to our proposed joint conference with the Russians, and I agree with you that the only satisfactory way of coming to the vital strategic conclusions the military situation requires is for you and me to meet personally with Stalin. My thought would be that each of us could be accompanied by a very small staff made up of our top Army, Air, and

Naval Chiefs of Staff. I should bring Harry and Averell, but no
State Department representative, although I believe we should
arrive at tentative procedures to be adopted in event of a German
collapse. I should like to see the conference held about January 15,
or soon thereafter. Tunis and Bizerta should have been cleared up
and Rommel's army liquidated before the conference. As to the
place, Iceland or Alaska are impossible for me at this time of year,
and I believe equally so for Stalin. I should prefer a secure place
south of Algiers or in or near Khartoum. I don't like mosquitoes.
I think the conference should be very secret and that the Press
should be excluded. I would question the advisability of Marshall
and the others going to England prior to the conference, because
I do not want to give Stalin the impression that we are settling
everything between ourselves before we meet him.

I think that you and I understand each other so well that prior
conferences between us are unnecessary and when the time comes
we can work things out from day to day. Our military people will
also be in close co-operation at all times from now on.

I think that this conference may well result in knocking out Germany sooner than we anticipated. As you know, Stalin has already
agreed to a purely military conference to be held in Moscow, and
I have to-day sent him a message urging him to meet you and me.
I believe he will accept.

I prefer a comfortable oasis to the raft at Tilsit.

I replied at once:

Former Naval Person to President Roosevelt   3 Dec. 42

I am delighted at your proposal, which is the only way of making
a good plan for 1943. At present we have no plan for 1943 which
is on the scale or up to the level of events. It is grand of you to
come, and I will meet you anywhere. I am telegraphing Stalin to
reinforce your invitation.

2. Meanwhile I deprecate sending our military representatives
to Moscow. It will only lead to a deadlock and queer the pitch.
We still think that Marshall, King, and Arnold should come here
in advance so that at least we have some definite plans as a basis
for discussion when we all meet in January "somewhere in Africa."
Otherwise Stalin will greet us with the question, "Have you then
no plan for the second front in Europe you promised me for 1943?"

3. Khartoum is at your disposal, and would be most satisfactory

as regards weather, security, and communications. I will report on accommodation to-morrow. We should be honoured to be the hosts. I am not informed, though quite ready to learn, about the oases south of Algiers. Marrakech I can personally vouch for as regards accommodation, climate, and, barring any extraordinary lapse, weather.

4. A supreme war conference, as this would be, ought to have the necessary staffs. For ourselves, I should like to bring Eden from the War Cabinet with me and three Chiefs or Vice-Chiefs of the Staff, supported by a powerful secretariat, cipher staff, map room, etc. — say about twenty-five.

5. As to timing, the sooner the better. Every day counts. We may reasonably expect that Tunis will be settled by the end of December and Tripolitania by the end of January. We ought not to be dependent on the actual working out of these operations. All prospect of attack in Europe in 1943 depends on early decision.

6. However, everything hangs on whether "Barkis is willin'."

* * * * *

He proved unwilling, as the following interchange of telegrams shows.

Prime Minister to Premier Stalin 3 Dec. 42

The President tells me he has proposed a meeting for us three in January somewhere in North Africa. This is far better than the Iceland project we talked over in Moscow. You could get to any point desired in three days, I in two, and the President in about the same time as you. I earnestly hope you will agree. We must decide at the earliest moment the best way of attacking Germany in Europe with all possible force in 1943. This can only be settled between the heads of Governments and States with their high expert authorities at their side. It is only by such a meeting that the full burden of the war can be shared according to capacity and opportunity.

Premier Stalin to Premier Churchill 6 Dec. 42

I welcome the idea of a meeting between the heads of the Governments of the three countries being arranged in order to fix a common line of military strategy.

To my great regret however I will not be in a position to leave

the Soviet Union. Time presses us, and it would be impossible
for me to be absent even for a day, as it is just now that important
military operations of our winter campaign are developing. These
operations will not be relaxed in January, probably to the contrary.

I am waiting your reply to the paragraph of my preceding letter
dealing with the establishment of the second front in Western
Europe in the spring of 1943.

The operations in the Stalingrad area as well as on the central
front are developing. In the Stalingrad area we are keeping a
large group of the German troops surrounded, and we hope to
annihilate them completely.

The President in reply to our identical message expressed
his deep disappointment to Stalin. To me he said:

I think it would be a mistake for our Staff people to discuss in
Moscow any major moves planned for this coming summer. From
the practical point of view they could not bind your Government
or mine, nor could final plans be approved by you or me without
careful study with our Staffs at home.

What would you think therefore of suggesting that Staff conversations between military officials from U.K., Russia, and America
take place in Africa, either in Algiers, Khartoum, or some other
suitable place? The results and recommendations of such a meeting
would of course have to be taken up in all three capitals before
final approval.

My opinion was unchanged. I was glad that the President
saw the disadvantages of an expert conference at Moscow, but
I did not like one at Khartoum or Algiers much better. I was
sure that for the military representatives to meet at some distant place alone and without any prior agreement on our joint
affairs between us and the Americans would only waste time
and might well result, after many long telegrams had been sent
in cypher, in a deadlock on the spot, and even higher up. Only
the heads of States or Governments face to face could settle
the fearful questions that were open. Why should the refusal
of Stalin to be present at a Three-Power Conference preclude
an early Anglo-American meeting? The President however
seemed determined to have a Triple Military meeting, and

this I thought it necessary to agree to in principle. On the larger issue he forwarded to me on December 17 his latest news from Stalin.

I too must express my deep regret that it is impossible for me to leave the Soviet Union either in the near future or even at the beginning of March. Front business absolutely prevents it demanding my constant presence near our troops.

So far I do not know what exactly are the problems which you, Mr. President, and Mr. Churchill intend to discuss at our joint conference. I wonder whether it would not be possible to discuss these problems by way of correspondence between us as long as there is no chance of arranging our meeting? I admit that there will be no disagreement between us.

Allow me also to express my confidence that the time is not being lost, and that the promises about the opening of a second front in Europe given by you, Mr. President, and by Mr. Churchill in regard to 1942, and in any case in regard to the spring of 1943, will be fulfilled, and that a second front in Europe will be actually opened by the joint forces of Great Britain and the United States of America in the spring of the next year.

In view of all sorts of rumours about the attitude of the Union of Soviet Socialist Republics towards the use made of Darlan or other men like him, it may not be unnecessary for me to tell you that, in my opinion, as well as in that of my colleagues, Eisenhower's policy with regard to Darlan, Boisson, Giraud, and others is perfectly correct. I think it a great achievement that you succeeded in bringing Darlan and others into the waterway [? mainstream] of the Allies fighting Hitler. Some time ago I made this known also to Mr. Churchill.

* * * * *

The President now sent me a very genial letter, by courier asking for an answer yes or no.

> The White House
> Washington
>
> December 14, 1942

Dear Winston,

I have not had an answer to my second invitation to our Uncle Joe, but, on the assumption that he will again decline, I think that in spite of it you and I should get together, as there are things which can be definitely determined only by you and me in conference with our Staff people. I am sure that both of us want to avoid the delays which attended the determination on "Torch" last July.

1. On the grounds of vile climate and icing on the wings, Iceland must be definitely out for both of us.

2. England must be out for me for political reasons.

3. There will be a commotion in this country if it is discovered that I have flown across any old seas. Therefore Bermuda would be just as much out for me as Africa. However on condition that I can get away in absolute secrecy and have my trip kept secret until I get back, I have just about made up my mind to go along with the African idea — on the theory that public opinion here will gasp, but be satisfied when they hear about it after it is over.

4. One mitigating circumstance would be the knowledge that I had seen our military leaders in North and West Africa, and that is why I think it would be best if we could meet somewhere in that neighbourhood instead of Khartoum. Incidentally, I could actually see some of our troops.

5. Incidentally also, it would do me personally an enormous amount of good to get out of the political atmosphere of Washington for a couple of weeks.

6. My thought is, therefore, that if the time suits your plans we could meet back of Algiers or back of Casablanca about January 15. That would mean that I would leave about January 11, and pray for good weather. My route would be either from here to Trinidad and thence to Dakar and thence north, or from here to Natal (Brazil), and across to Liberia or Freetown, and north from there.

7. In view of Stalin's absence, I think you and I need no foreign affairs people with us, for our work will be essentially military. Perhaps your three top men and my three top men could meet at the same place four or five days in advance of our arrival and have plans in fairly good tentative shape by the time we get there. I asked General (Bedell) Smith, who left here four or five days ago, to check up confidentially on some possible tourist oasis as far from any city or large population as possible. One of the dictionaries says "an oasis is never wholly dry." Good old dictionary!

8. Here is an alternative plan in case Uncle Joe says he will meet us about March 1st:

I would suggest that your Staff people and mine should meet with the Russian Staff people somewhere in Africa, or even as far as Baghdad, and come to certain recommendations which would at least get the preliminaries of new moves started. The three of us could, when we meet, close up the loose ends, and also take up some of the post-war matters.

With my warmest regards
As ever yours
FRANKLIN D. ROOSEVELT

To save time Mr. Roosevelt also cabled the substance of his letter.

In spite of Stalin's inability to meet with us I think we should plan a meeting at once with our respective military staffs. I should like to meet in Africa about January 15. There is, I believe, a satisfactory and safe place just north of Casablanca. It might be wise for some of our military men to precede us by a few days to clear the ground. I should think if we could have four or five days together we could clear up all of our business. Will you let me know what you think of this?

I was naturally pleased with this solution and was sure it would replace the purely technical meeting of experts which would only have ended in a deadlock. I hastened to reply:

Former Naval Person to President Roosevelt   21 Dec. 42

Yes, certainly. The sooner the better. I am greatly relieved. It is the only thing to do. All arrangements here will be made on basis that it is a staff meeting only. Suggested code-name "Symbol."

*   *   *   *   *

The following weeks were spent in drafting Staff appreciations for the forthcoming meeting. There were not only issues of military strategy to be worked out, but also the consideration of the grave political issues arising in North Africa as the result of "Torch" and the assassination of Darlan. I had obtained the President's agreement to the appointment of Mr. Harold Macmillan to assist the American political representative in

North Africa, Mr. Robert Murphy, and he went out to study the position on the spot.

Meanwhile the arrangements for "Symbol" went smoothly ahead.

Former Naval Person to President Roosevelt　　　30 Dec. 42

I sent Brigadier Jacob to North Africa on Christmas Day to consult with Generals Eisenhower and Bedell Smith about arrangements for "Symbol." Jacob has now telegraphed that they have found admirable accommodation, and that General Bedell Smith, who is in full agreement, is telegraphing the results of their reconnaissance to you.

2. I do not think we can do better than accept these proposals, and as time is short I am going ahead on the assumption that you approve.

3. My intention is that H.M.S. *Bulolo,* which is a specially fitted headquarters ship, should leave the United Kingdom on about January 4 with the more junior staff officers of my delegation, cypher staff, clerical staff, etc. *Bulolo* will be berthed in the harbour and serve as signal ship.

4. You suggested that some of our military men should precede us by a few days to clear the ground. I entirely agree, and will arrange for British Chiefs of Staff to arrive by air at rendezvous on whatever day it may be possible for American Chiefs of Staff to reach there. Can you give me a date?

5. It would also be helpful if you could let me know as soon as possible your own programme, and I will make my own arrangements.

6. Many thanks about Macmillan's appointment. I agree to what you say about Eisenhower's final authority.

The President and I now had a number of agreeable interchanges on questions of security. He proposed to call himself "Admiral Q."

Former Naval Person to President Roosevelt　　　3 Jan. 43

However did you think of such an impenetrable disguise? In order to make it even harder for the enemy and to discourage irreverent guesswork, propose Admiral Q and Mr. **P.**

N.B. — We must mind our P's and Q's.

De Gaulle. I think it far better his visit should be postponed till "Torch" affairs are "Symbolised."

* * * * *

The Chiefs of Staff Committee produced two papers for the War Cabinet summarising their considered views upon future strategy. In reaching their conclusions they emphasised a serious divergence of view between themselves and their American colleagues. It was one of emphasis rather than principle. It would in fact be the purpose of the coming conference to arrive at a common agreement. The British Chiefs of Staff took the view that the best policy to adopt would be to follow up "Torch" vigorously, accompanied by as large a "Bolero" preparation for "Round-up" as possible, while the American Chiefs of Staff favoured putting our main European effort into "Round-up" and standing fast in North Africa. In their first paper the British Chiefs of Staff, commenting on the American proposals, set forth their points as follows.

We consider that our policy should be:

1. To exploit "Torch" as vigorously as possible with a view to (a) Knocking Italy out of the war; (b) Bringing Turkey into the war; and (c) Giving the Axis no respite for recuperation.

2. Increased bombing of Germany.

3. Maintenance of supplies to Russia.

4. The build-up of "Bolero" on the greatest scale that the above operations admit, in order that we may be ready to re-enter the Continent with about twenty-one divisions in August or September, 1943, if the conditions are such that there is a good prospect of success.

We believe that this policy will afford earlier and greater relief, both direct and indirect, to Russia than if we were to concentrate on "Bolero" to the exclusion of all other operations, observing that at the best we could not put a force of more than twenty-five divisions on to the Continent in late summer of 1943.

I informed Stalin of our plans to meet. He replied:

Premier Stalin to Premier Churchill   5 Jan. 43

Many thanks for your communication concerning the impending

conversations between you and the President. I will be very grateful for information on the results of these conversations.

The final arrangements were now made. We did not go empty-handed to the Conference on which so much depended. Alexander's and Montgomery's plans for advance on Tripoli were now complete.

General Alexander to Prime Minister   5 Jan. 43

Administrative situation of Eighth Army makes it impossible for its main body to move forward before night January 14–15. Montgomery intends however to move forward in strength on this date. Operations will continue intensively until Tripoli is reached.

2. On January 4 heavy gale caused extensive damage to ships and unloading facilities in Benghazi. This may cause a few days' postponement of forward move or restrict size of force. Am asking him whether his intentions altered.

General Alexander to Prime Minister   6 Jan. 43

Further to my last. No change in Montgomery's date.

General Alexander to Prime Minister and C.I.G.S.   9 Jan. 43

The plan for operations is as follows:

The advance will start night January 14–15 with XXXth Corps. The 7th Armoured Division and 2d New Zealand Division will advance to Sedada. There will probably be opposition from the Gheddahia area. After this has been dealt with, direction of advance will be Beni Ulid-Tarhuna, 7th Armoured Division leading; 51st Division will follow the line of the main coastal road; 22d Armoured Brigade is with Army Command; Xth Corps is not being brought up. Heavy bombing of Tripoli and bottlenecks on coastal road start January 8.

XXXth Corps will have approximately five hundred miles of petrol and ten days rations and water for the whole force. Ammunition echelons will be full and generally the administration situation is reasonably good for a period of ten days. Xth Corps will help by carrying supplies from Tobruk to Benghazi. When we get to Tripoli, until the port is opened we shall be on very short commons. The supplies which can be brought to XXXth Corps by road are about eight hundred tons a day, which should be sufficient provided we do not have to fight a battle after we have captured Tripoli until the port is opened.

The capture of the port of Tripoli would be a most welcome prize. It would carry the Eighth Army two hundred miles nearer to Tunisia, and thus bring a new favourable factor of decisive importance into the North African scene.

15

The Casablanca Conference

Flight to Casablanca — The Anfa Suburb — President Roosevelt Arrives — Generals Eisenhower and Alexander Join Us — Hopes of Taking Tripoli — My First Report to the War Cabinet, January 18 — Differences between the Chiefs of Staff and the Joint Planners — My Talks with General Eaker about the Flying Fortresses — He Converts Me to Their Support — Invitation to General de Gaulle — He Arrives — Stiff Conversations — A Tribute to General de Gaulle — Further Reports to the War Cabinet of January 20 — "Unconditional Surrender" — The Full Story — "Verify Your Quotations" — The Final Report on the Conference by the Combined Chiefs of Staff — "Conduct of the War in 1943" — The Press Conference of January 24 — The President and I Motor to Marrakech — The Villa Taylor — The President Departs at Dawn on the 25th.

O~N JANUARY~ 12 I left for North Africa. My journey by air was a little anxious. In order to heat the "Commando" they had established a petrol engine inside which generated fumes and raised various heating-points to very high temperatures. I was woken up at two in the morning, when we were over the Atlantic five hundred miles from anywhere, by one of these heating-points burning my toes, and it looked to me as if it might soon get red-hot and light the blankets. I therefore climbed out of my bunk, and woke up Peter Portal, who was sitting in the well beneath, asleep in his chair, and drew his attention to this very hot point. We looked around the cabin and found two others, which seemed equally on the verge of becoming red-hot. We then went down into the bomb alley (it was a converted bomber), and found two men industriously keeping alive this petrol heater. From every point of view I thought this was most dangerous. The hot points might start a conflagration, and the atmosphere of petrol would make an explosion imminent. Portal took the same view. I decided that it was better to freeze than to burn, and I ordered all heating to be turned off, and we went back to rest shivering in the ice-cold winter air about eight thousand feet up, at which we had to fly to be above the clouds. I am bound to say this struck me as rather an unpleasant moment.

When we got to Casablanca we found beautiful arrangements made. There was a large hotel in the suburb of Anfa, with ample accommodation for all the British and American Staffs, and big conference rooms. Around this hotel were dotted a number of extremely comfortable villas which were reserved for President Roosevelt, for me, for General Giraud, and also for General de Gaulle, should he come. The whole enclave was wired in and closely guarded by American troops. I and the Staff were there two days before the President arrived. I had some nice walks with Pound and the other Chiefs of Staff on the rocks and the beach. Wonderful waves rolling in, enormous clouds of foam, made one marvel that anybody could have got ashore at the landing. There was not one calm day. Waves fifteen feet high were roaring up terrible rocks. No wonder so many landing-craft and ships' boats were turned over with all their men.

My son, Randolph, had come across from the Tunisian front. There was plenty to think about, and the two days passed swiftly by. Meanwhile the Staffs consulted together for long hours every day.

*   *   *   *   *

The President arrived in the afternoon of the 14th. We had a most warm and friendly meeting, and it gave me intense pleasure to see my great colleague here on conquered or liberated territory which he and I had secured in spite of the

advice given him by all his military experts. The next day
General Eisenhower arrived, after a very hazardous flight. He
was most anxious to know what lines the Combined Chiefs of
Staff would take, and to keep in touch with them. Their plane
of command was altogether above his. A day or two later
Alexander came in, and reported to me and the President
about the progress of the Eighth Army. He made a most
favourable impression upon the President, who was greatly
attracted by him and also by his news, which was that the
Eighth Army would take Tripoli in the near future. He explained how Montgomery, who had two strong Army Corps,
had dismounted one and taken all the vehicles to bring the
other on alone, and that this would be strong enough to drive
Rommel right back through Tripoli to the Mareth frontier
line, which was a very serious obstacle. Everyone was much
cheered by this news, and the easy smiling grace of Alexander
won all hearts. His unspoken confidence was contagious.

I reported home as follows:

Prime Minister to Deputy Prime Minister and War Cabinet
18 Jan. 43

The Chiefs of Staff have been in session two or three times each
day either alone or with their American colleagues. The whole
field of the war is being surveyed theatre by theatre. Admiral King
of course considers the Pacific should be a first charge on all resources, and both American Army and Navy authorities are very
keen on more vigorous action in Burma to help China, culminating
in a large-scale "Anakim" [Burma] later in the year. General Marshall is also keen on this, but otherwise his emphasis seemed to
lie towards building up "Round-up" [or] "Sledgehammer" at the
expense of the Mediterranean.

On the other hand, I am satisfied the President is strongly in
favour of the Mediterranean being given prime place. He also
seems increasingly inclined to Operation "Husky" [Sicily] which he
suggested to me last night should be called "Belly," and I advised
"Bellona." Although nothing definite has been settled between us
pending results of the Staff conversations, I feel sure that we are
in solid agreement on the essentials.

Meanwhile, at the Combined Staff meetings it has become

apparent that the Americans are increasingly turning towards Sicily instead of Sardinia. This is what I should like. Admiral King even went so far as to say that if it was decided to do Sicily he would find the necessary escorts.

The Mediterranean situation is being decisively changed by the victorious advance of the Desert Army. Alexander, who is here, made a great impression on all present at the President's conference on the 15th by his clear, precise, confident accounts of his progress and intentions. He hoped to have Tripoli by the 26th, and to deploy as much as six divisions against the Mareth position by the middle of March. A smaller number of divisions could be deployed at an earlier date. Thus with Anderson's four divisions we may expect ten British divisions in the First and Eighth Armies to be available for the final battle for the Tunisian tip.

As the U.S. will not have more than two divisions in Tunisia by then and the French are so underequipped, we shall have an overwhelming British preponderance in this theatre. In these circumstances, should all go well in the battle now in progress for Tripoli and should the clearance of Tripoli harbour not be too difficult, the arrival of the Desert Army in the highest fettle in the Tunisian theatre should be decisive. So great a reinforcement of British numbers would evidently justify increased representation for us in the high command. The President received very well last night a suggestion which I made in agreement with C.I.G.S. that at the right time Alexander should fill the vacancy of Deputy C.-in-C. to Eisenhower which has been created by the appointment of Clark to the Fifth U.S. Army. This avoids difficulties with the French which might follow the appointment of a British officer to the command of all forces in Tunisia.

It was fortunate indeed that we all met here and that I brought General Alexander to the scene. General Eisenhower was about to begin an operation most daring and spirited but also most hazardous against Sfax, which he intended to try to hold, supplying himself partly from Malta. This operation ought evidently to be concerted with Alexander's advance, for otherwise the Americans might find themselves heavily attacked in Sfax just at the very period when the Desert Army would be motionless in Tripoli, regathering petrol and supplies and dependent upon the conditions of the port.

I therefore brought Alexander and Eisenhower, who get on

extremely well, together both alone and also with C.I.G.S. and Marshall. The result has been a perfect understanding between them and arrangements for visits when necessary. Eisenhower is greatly relieved to realise how soon and with what great forces Alexander can arrive, and instead of an isolated operation to keep things going he is now in a position to make a really good combination. The feeling of all four generally was that we have very good prospects in Tunisia provided we do not make a mistake. Personally I am very well satisfied with the way this has gone.

*   *   *   *   *

Neither I nor the President attended the Staff conferences, but we were informed of the whole position and consulted with our own officers every day. The differences did not run along national lines, but were principally between the Chiefs of Staff and Joint Planners. I was myself sure that Sicily should be the next step, and the Combined Chiefs of Staff took the same view. The Joint Planners, on the other hand, together with Lord Mountbatten, felt that we should attack Sardinia rather than Sicily, because they thought it could be done three months earlier; and Mountbatten pressed this view on Hopkins and others. I remained obdurate, and, with the Combined Chiefs of Staff solid behind me, insisted on Sicily. The Joint Planners, respectful but persistent, then said that this could not be done until August 30. At this stage I personally went through all the figures with them, and thereafter the President and I gave orders that D-Day was to be during the favourable July moon period (or, if possible, the favourable June moon period). In the event, the airborne troops went in on the night of July 9, and the landings started on the morning of July 10.

*   *   *   *   *

In these January days I received a request from General Eaker, the Commander of the American Air Forces in England, to see me. I asked him to luncheon alone. We discussed the question of the American scheme of the daylight bombing of Germany by the armoured Flying Fortresses. I was personally sceptical of this method. I had regretted that so much

effort had been put into the daylight bombing, and still thought
that a concentration upon night bombing by the Americans
would have resulted in a far larger delivery of bombs on Germany, and we should have gradually worked up complete accuracy by scientific methods, as we did later. I put these points to
Eaker, who knew my view and was much troubled by it. He
stated the case for the daylight Fortress bomber with powerful
earnestness, and pointed out what immense preparations had
already been made in England — the transfer of many squadrons from America, the piling up of men, materials, spare parts,
and so forth, and also the preparation of airfields now at length
ready.

I pointed out in reply that here we were at the beginning
of 1943. The Americans had been in the war for more than
a year. They had all the time been building up their air-power
in England, but so far they had never thrown a single bomb
on Germany by their daylight methods, except perhaps on one
occasion when a very short raid was protected by British
fighters. We had been led to believe at Washington the year
before that in four or five months very heavy deliveries of
bombs would be taking place by American aircraft, but nothing had happened, though an immense expenditure of resources had been made. Eaker however pleaded his cause with
skill and tenacity. He said it was quite true that they had not
yet struck their blow — give them a month or two more and
they would come into action on an ever-increasing scale.

Considering how much had been staked on this venture by
the United States and all they felt about it, I decided to back
Eaker and his theme, and I turned round completely and withdrew all my opposition to the daylight bombing by the Fortresses. He was much pleased with this, because he had feared
that his own Government had already lost a good deal of faith
in the daylight bombing method. It was certainly a terrible
thing that in the whole of the last six months of 1942 nothing
had come of this immense deployment and effort, absolutely
nothing, not a single bomb had been dropped on Germany.
There must have been twenty thousand men and five hundred

machines all laid out in East Anglia — and nothing so far, as it seemed, to show for it at all. However, when I turned round and pressed no longer the formidable point I was having developed, there was a great easement, and the American plans were no longer subject to British criticism. They went ahead and soon began to pay dividends. All the same, I still think that if at the beginning they had put their money on night bombing we should have reached our climax much sooner. General Eaker afterwards said on several occasions that I saved the Fortress bombers from abandonment by the United States at the moment when they were about to come into their own. If this is true I saved them by leaving off opposing them.

*   *   *   *   *

The question was then raised about de Gaulle. I was now most anxious for him to come, and the President agreed generally with this view. I asked the President also to telegraph inviting him. The General was very haughty and refused several times. I then got Eden to put the utmost pressure upon him, even to the point of saying that if he would not come we should insist on his being replaced by someone else at the head of the French Liberation Committee in London. It is very odd to see the account which the President's son, Elliott Roosevelt, gives of this in the book which he hastened to write about the confidential talks he heard at the meals to which he was brought by his father. He seems to suggest that the President suspected me of trying to stop de Gaulle coming, and objecting to his being brought there, whereas I was putting the utmost pressure possible to get him to come. This rubbish has had a wide and long currency. The telegrams dismiss it for ever.

Prime Minister to Foreign Secretary   18 Jan. 43

If you think well you should give the following message to de Gaulle from me:

"I am authorised to say that the invitation to you to come here was from the President of the United States of America as well as from me.

"I have not yet told General Giraud, who came attended only by two Staff officers, and is waiting here, of your refusal. The consequences of it, if persisted in, will in my opinion be unfavourable for you and your movement. First, we are about to make arrangements for North Africa, on which we should have been glad to consult you, but which must otherwise be made in your absence. The arrangements when concluded will have the support of Great Britain and the United States.

"The fact that you have refused to come to the meeting proposed will in my opinion be almost universally censured by public opinion and serve as a complete answer to any complaints. There can of course be no question of your being invited to visit the United States in the near future if you reject the President's invitation now. My attempt to bridge the difficulties which have existed between your movement and the United States will have definitely failed. I should certainly not be able to renew my exertions in this direction while you remain the leader of the above movement.

"The position of His Majesty's Government towards your movement while you remain at its head will also require to be reviewed. If with your eyes open you reject this unique opportunity we shall endeavour to get on as well as we can without you. The door is still open."

I leave you latitude to make any alteration in the message which you may think desirable so long as its seriousness is not impaired. The difficulty is that on account of secrecy we cannot appeal over his head to the French National Committee. Here I have been all these days fighting de Gaulle's battle and making every arrangement for a good reconciliation between the different sections of Frenchmen. If he rejects the chance now offered I shall feel that his removal from the headship of the Free French Movement is essential to the further support of this movement by H.M.G. I hope you will put as much of this as you think fit to him. For his own sake, you ought to knock him about pretty hard.

*   *   *   *   *

At last, on January 22, de Gaulle arrived. He was taken to his villa, which was next to Giraud's. He would not call upon Giraud, and it was some hours before he could be prevailed upon to meet him. I had a very stony interview with de Gaulle, making it clear that if he continued to be an obstacle we would not hesitate to break with him finally. He was very formal, and stalked out of the villa and down the little garden with his head high in the air. Eventually he was prevailed upon to have a talk with Giraud, which lasted for two or three hours and must have been extremely pleasant to both of them. In the afternoon he went to see the President, and to my relief they got on unexpectedly well. The President was attracted by "the spiritual look in his eyes"; but very little could be done to bring them into accord.

*   *   *   *   *

In these pages various severe statements, based on events of the moment, are set down about General de Gaulle, and certainly I had continuous difficulties and many sharp antagonisms with him. There was however a dominant element in our relationship. I could not regard him as representing captive and prostrate France, nor indeed the France that had a right to decide freely the future for herself. I knew he was no friend of England. But I always recognised in him the spirit and conception which, across the pages of history, the word "France" would ever proclaim. I understood and admired, while I resented, his arrogant demeanour. Here he was — a refugee, an exile from his country under sentence of death, in a position entirely dependent upon the good will of the British Government, and also now of the United States. The Germans had conquered his country. He had no real foothold anywhere. Never mind; he defied all. Always, even when he was behaving worst, he seemed to express the personality of France — a great nation, with all its pride, authority, and ambition. It was said in mockery that he thought himself the living representative of Joan of Arc, with whom it is said one of his ancestors served as a faithful adherent. This did not seem to me as absurd as it looked. Clemenceau, with whom it was said he also compared himself, was a far wiser and more experienced statesman. But they both gave the same impression of being unconquerable Frenchmen.

*   *   *   *   *

I made a further report to the War Cabinet.

Prime Minister to Deputy Prime Minister and War Cabinet
20 Jan. 43

Admiral "Q" [the President] and I called a plenary conference this afternoon, at which the Combined Chiefs of Staff reported progress. It was a most satisfactory meeting. After five days' discussions and a good deal of apparent disagreement the Combined Chiefs of Staff are now, I think, unanimous in essentials about the conduct of the war in 1943. Their final report is not yet ready, but the following is the gist of the statement which C.I.G.S. made on their behalf. The security of sea communications was agreed to be the first charge upon our combined resources, and the principle reaffirmed that we must concentrate first on the defeat of Germany. Full preparations for taking Sicily are to go ahead at once with a view to carrying out the operations at the earliest possible moment. In addition we hope to mount the Burma plan towards the end of this year. The Americans have undertaken to supply the lion's share [for the latter] of the assault shipping and landing-craft, which will be American-manned, and also to help us out with naval covering forces. At home "Bolero" is to go ahead as fast as our commitments allow, with a view to a "Sledgehammer" of some sort this year or a return to the Continent with all available forces if Germany shows definite signs of collapse. In the Pacific, operations for the capture of Rabaul and the clearing of New Guinea are to continue in order to retain the initiative and hold Japan. Whether this offensive should subsequently be carried forward to Truk will be a matter for decision later in the year.

Admiral "Q" and I were in complete agreement with the above outline.

2. Having learned that in the course of the discussions of the Combined Chiefs of Staff the fear had been expressed by the American representatives that we might pull out once Germany was defeated, I thought it right to say in categorical terms that our interest and our honour were alike engaged and that the determination of British Parliament and people to devote their whole resources to the defeat of Japan after Germany had been brought to her knees was not in doubt. I added that I was sure that the War Cabinet would be fully prepared to enter into a formal

treaty or pact with the United States on this point. Admiral "Q"
brushed aside the idea, saying he was confident that the United
States and the British Empire were entirely of one mind in this
matter. He added however that it would be very desirable, if it
were at all possible, to get a definite engagement — secret if necessary — from Russia that they would join in the struggle against
Japan once Germany was out of the war.

3. Having reached agreement on broad principles, the Chiefs of
Staff will have to spend the next ten days examining ways and
means. There is a good deal of detailed work to be done, and I
do not think they ought to separate for several days. It will in any
event be necessary to have another conference of this kind within
the next six months. The necessity for this was particularly stressed
by General Marshall.

4. I thought it a good opportunity to broach in plenary session
the question that at the right time Alexander should become
Deputy Commander-in-Chief to Eisenhower. It was warmly welcomed by Marshall and King. The difficult question of air command is under active consideration, and will, I am assured, be
settled satisfactorily.

5. The War Cabinet should know that General Marshall asked
to place on formal record his admiration of the profound contribution which had been rendered to the Allied cause in North
Africa by Admiral Cunningham. His naval leadership and skill
had been outstanding, and his wisdom and counsel had been of the
greatest help to General Eisenhower. Admiral "Q" also paid a
warm tribute to Field-Marshal Sir John Dill. He had come to be
regarded by the Americans as an indispensable link between the
United States and British Chiefs of Staff on military policy.

6. We propose to draw up a statement of the work of the conference for communication to the press at the proper time. I
should be glad to know what the War Cabinet would think of our
including in this statement a declaration of the firm intention of
the United States and the British Empire to continue the war relentlessly until we have brought about the "unconditional surrender" of Germany and Japan. The omission of Italy would be to
encourage a break-up there. The President liked this idea, and it
would stimulate our friends in every country.

7. It will also be necessary on the conclusion of the conference
to draw up a statement for communication to Premier Stalin. Our

idea is that this statement should set out our combined intentions, but should contain no promises.

8. While the above, which has been drawn up under my direction by General Ismay, represents the present position of our discussions and is, as my colleagues know, in the closest harmony with ideas we have shared, it must be admitted that all our military operations taken together are on a very small scale compared with the mighty resources of Britain and the United States, and still more with the gigantic effort of Russia. I am inclined to think that the President shares this view, as Hopkins spoke to me on the subject yesterday, saying in effect, "It is all right, but it is not enough." Making all allowances for our tremendous efforts on the sea and in the air, I still feel this most strongly, and during the remaining days of our conference we must bend ourselves to the task of weighting our blows more heavily.

* * * * *

The reader should note paragraph 6 of the above message, as the use by the President at the meeting with the press of the words "unconditional surrender" raised issues which will recur in this story and certainly be long debated. There is a school of thought, both in England and America, which argues that the phrase prolonged the war and played into the dictators' hands by driving their peoples and armies to desperation. I do not myself agree with this, for reasons which the course of this narrative will show. Nevertheless, as my own memory has proved defective on some points it will be well to state the facts as my records reveal them. Elliott Roosevelt asserts in his book that the words were used by the President at one of our dinners. I am reported by him to have thought, frowned, thought, finally grinned, and at length announced Perfect, and also that the nightcap toast proposed by me that evening was "Unconditional Surrender." I have no recollection of these private and informal interchanges where conversation was free and unguarded. The matter must certainly however have cropped up in my official talks with the President. Hence paragraph 6.

The records of the War Cabinet show that this was brought

before them at their afternoon meeting on January 20. The
discussion seems to have turned, not upon the principle of
"unconditional surrender," but on making an exception in
favour of Italy. Accordingly on January 21 the following
message was sent, which of course I soon received.

Deputy Prime Minister and Foreign Secretary to Prime Minister

The Cabinet was unanimously of opinion that balance of advantage lay against excluding Italy, because of misgivings which would
inevitably be caused in Turkey, in the Balkans, and elsewhere.
Nor are we convinced that effect on Italians would be good.
Knowledge of all rough stuff coming to them is surely more likely
to have desired effect on Italian morale.

There can therefore be no doubt that the phrase "unconditional surrender" in the proposed joint statement that was
being drafted was mentioned by me to the War Cabinet, and
not disapproved in any way by them. On the contrary, their
only wish was that Italy should not be omitted from its scope.
I do not remember, nor have I any record, of anything that
passed between the President and me on the subject after I
received the Cabinet message, and it is quite possible that in
the pressure of business, especially the discussions about the
relations of Giraud and de Gaulle and interviews with them,
the matter was not further referred to between us. Meanwhile
the official joint statement was being prepared by our advisers
and by the Chiefs of Staff. This was a careful and formally
worded document, which both the President and I considered
and approved. It seems probable that as I did not like applying
unconditional surrender to Italy I did not raise the point again
with the President, and we had certainly both agreed to the
communiqué we had settled with our advisers. There is no
mention in it of "unconditional surrender." It was submitted
to the War Cabinet, who approved it in this form.

It was with some feeling of surprise that I heard the President say at the Press Conference on January 24 that we would
enforce "unconditional surrender" upon all our enemies. It
was natural to suppose that the agreed communiqué had super-

seded anything said in conversation. General Ismay, who knew exactly how my mind was working from day to day, and was also present at all the discussions of the Chiefs of Staff when the communiqué was prepared, was also surprised. In my speech which followed the President's I of course supported him and concurred in what he had said. Any divergence between us, even by omission, would on such an occasion and at such a time have been damaging or even dangerous to our war effort. I certainly take my share of the responsibility, together with the British War Cabinet.

The President's account to Hopkins seems however conclusive.

We had so much trouble getting those two French generals together that I thought to myself that this was as difficult as arranging the meeting of Grant and Lee — and then suddenly the Press Conference was on, and Winston and I had had no time to prepare for it, and the thought popped into my mind that they had called Grant "Old Unconditional Surrender," and the next thing I knew I had said it.[1]

I do not feel that this frank statement is in any way weakened by the fact that the phrase occurs in the notes from which he spoke.

* * * * *

Memories of the war may be vivid and true, but should never be trusted without verification, especially where the sequence of events is concerned. I certainly made several erroneous statements about the "unconditional surrender" incident, because I said what I thought and believed at the moment without looking up the records. Mine was not the only memory at fault, for Mr. Bevin in the House of Commons on July 21, 1949, gave a lurid account of the difficulties he had had to encounter in rebuilding Germany after the war through the policy of "unconditional surrender," on which he said neither he nor the War Cabinet had ever been consulted at the time. I replied on the spur of the moment, with equal

[1] *Roosevelt and Hopkins*, by Robert E. Sherwood, page 696.

inaccuracy and good faith, that the first time I heard the words was from the lips of the President at the Casablanca press conference. It was only when I got home and searched my archives that I found the facts as they have been set out here. I am reminded of the professor who, in his declining hours, was asked by his devoted pupils for his final counsel. He replied, "Verify your quotations."

*   *   *   *   *

The use of the expression "unconditional surrender," although widely hailed at the time, has since been described by various authorities as one of the great mistakes of Anglo-American war policy. It requires to be dealt with at this point. It is said that it prolonged the struggle and made recovery afterwards more difficult. I do not believe that this is true. I took occasion at the Guildhall on June 30, 1943, to say:

We, the United Nations, demand from the Nazi, Fascist, and Japanese tyrannies unconditional surrender. By this we mean that their will power to resist must be completely broken, and that they must yield themselves absolutely to our justice and mercy. It also means that we must take all those far-sighted measures which are necessary to prevent the world from being again convulsed, wrecked, and blackened by their calculated plots and ferocious aggressions. It does not mean, and it never can mean, that we are to stain our victorious arms by inhumanity or by mere lust of vengeance, or that we do not plan a world in which all branches of the human family may look forward to what the American Declaration of Independence finely calls "life, liberty, and the pursuit of happiness."

President Roosevelt also said on December 24, 1943:

The United Nations have no intention to enslave the German people. We wish them to have a normal chance to develop in peace, as useful and respectable members of the European family. But we most certainly emphasise the word "respectable," for we intend to rid them once and for all of Nazism and Prussian militarism and the fantastic and disastrous notion that they constitute the "Master Race."

My principal reason for opposing, as I always did, an alternative statement on peace terms, which was so often urged, was that a statement of the actual conditions on which the three great Allies would have insisted and would have been forced by public opinion to insist, would have been far more repulsive to any German peace movement than the general expression "unconditional surrender." I remember several attempts being made to draft peace conditions which would satisfy the wrath of the conquerors against Germany. They looked so terrible when set forth on paper, and so far exceeded what was in fact done, that their publication would only have stimulated German resistance. They had in fact only to be written out to be withdrawn.

On this point I submitted a note to my colleagues dated January 14, 1944, just after the Russians had made clear to us their attitude at Teheran.

By "unconditional surrender" I mean that the Germans have no *rights* to any particular form of treatment. For instance, the Atlantic Charter would not apply to them as *a matter of right*. On the other hand, the victorious nations owe it to themselves to observe the obligations of humanity and civilisation.

The question is, whether we should go further at the present time. It is perhaps well to look at what is actually going to happen to Germany before deciding whether more precise statements would induce them to surrender.

First, they are to be completely disarmed and deprived of all power to rearm.

Second, they are to be prohibited from all use of aviation, whether civil or military, and from practising the art of flying.

Third, large numbers of persons alleged to be guilty of atrocities are to be handed over for judgment to the countries where their crimes were committed. Premier Stalin mentioned at Teheran that he would certainly require at least four million Germans to work for many years in building up the ruin they had caused in Russia. I have no doubt the Russians will insist upon the handing over to them of vast quantities of German machinery to make up in a generous fashion for what has been destroyed. It may well be that similar claims will be made by others of the victorious Powers. In view of the great severity practised upon immense numbers of French, Italian, and Russian prisoners-of-war and internees, such retribution would not appear to be devoid of justice.

Fourth, the British, United States, and Russian Governments are I understand agreed that Germany is to be decisively broken up into a number of separate States. East Prussia and Germany east of the river Oder are to be alienated for ever and the population shifted. Prussia itself is to be divided and curtailed. The Ruhr and other great centres of coal and steel must be put outside the power of Prussia.

Fifth, the entire core of the German Army comprised in its General Staff must be entirely broken up, and it may be that the Russians will claim that very large numbers of the General Staff of the German Army shall be either put to death or interned for many years. I have myself wished to publish a list of some fifty to one hundred outlaws of first notoriety with a view to dissociating the mass of the people from those who will suffer capital punishment at the hands of the Allies and of avoiding anything in the nature of mass executions. This would tend to reassure the ordinary people. But these proposals were scouted at Teheran as being far too lenient, though I am not sure how far Marshal Stalin was serious in this part of the conversation.

Enough at any rate is set down above to show that a frank statement of what is going to happen to Germany would not necessarily have a reassuring effect upon the German people and that they might prefer the vaguer terrors of "unconditional surrender," mitigated as they are by such statements as the President has made.

Finally I said in the House of Commons on February 22, 1944:

The term "unconditional surrender" does not mean that the German people will be enslaved or destroyed. It means however that the Allies will not be bound to them at the moment of surrender by any pact or obligation. There will be, for instance, no question of the Atlantic Charter applying to Germany as a matter of right and barring territorial transferences or adjustments in enemy countries. No such arguments will be admitted by us as were used by Germany after the last war, saying that they surrendered in consequence of President Wilson's "Fourteen Points." Unconditional surrender means that the victors have a free hand.

It does not mean that they are entitled to behave in a barbarous manner, nor that they wish to blot out Germany from among the nations of Europe. If we are bound, we are bound by our own consciences to civilisation. We are not to be bound to the Germans as the result of a bargain struck. That is the meaning of "unconditional surrender."

It cannot be contended that in the closing years of the war there was any misconception in Germany.

*   *   *   *   *

At length, after ten days' work on the main issues, the Combined Chiefs of Staff reached agreement. Both the President and I kept in daily touch with their work and agreed between ourselves about it. It was settled that we should concentrate all upon taking Tunis, both with the Desert Army and with all forces that could be found by the British, and from Eisenhower's Army, and that Alexander should be Eisenhower's deputy and virtually in charge of all the operations. In addition we had the executive command of the Navy and Air Force under Admiral Cunningham and Air Marshal Tedder. It was evident that should the Eighth Army succeed in arriving on the scene with its six or seven divisions, these, added to the four or five under General Anderson in the First British Army, would give the British about twelve divisions compared with the Americans' three and possibly four, which was all that they could spare for the Tunis climax after garrisoning Morocco and Algeria. Two years later General Marshall told me at Malta how astonished he was that we British had not suggested any transfer of the command from Eisenhower to a British commander, although we had such an enormous superiority of divisions engaged in the fighting for Tunis. This idea never crossed my mind. It was contrary to the whole basis on which the President and I had worked. The relations between Eisenhower and Alexander will be referred to later. Both were selfless men and played the game with each other. Eisenhower confided the entire conduct of the battle to Alexander.

*   *   *   *   *

We were now to wind up our affairs. Our last formal and
plenary meeting with the Chiefs of Staff took place on January
23, when they presented to us their final report on "The
Conduct of the War in 1943." It may be epitomised as follows:

The defeat of the U-boat must remain a first charge on the resources of the United Nations. The Soviet forces must be sustained
by the greatest volume of supplies that can be transported to Russia.

Operations in the European theatre will be conducted with the
object of defeating Germany in 1943 with the maximum forces that
can be brought to bear upon her by the United Nations.

The main lines of offensive action will be:

In the Mediterranean
    (a) The occupation of Sicily with the object of:
        (i) Making the Mediterranean line of communications
more secure.
        (ii) Diverting German pressure from the Russian front.
        (iii) Intensifying the pressure on Italy.
    (b) To create a situation in which Turkey can be enlisted as
an active ally.

In the United Kingdom
    (c) The heaviest possible air offensive against German war
effort.
    (d) Such limited offensive operations as may be practicable
with the amphibious forces available.
    (e) The assembly of the strongest possible force in constant
readiness to re-enter the continent as soon as German resistance is
weakened to the required extent.

Operations in the Pacific and Far East shall continue with the
object of maintaining pressure on Japan, and for the full scale
offensive against Japan as soon as Germany is defeated. These
operations must be kept within such limits as will not, in the
opinion of the Joint Chiefs of Staff, jeopardise the capacity of the
United Nations to take advantage of any favourable opportunity
for the decisive defeat of Germany in 1943. Subject to this, plans
and preparations shall be made for the recapture of Burma
("Anakim") beginning in 1943, and for operations against the
Marshalls and Carolines, if time and resources allow, without prejudice to Anakim.

In giving our approval to this policy which we had shaped at each stage with our expert advisers, the President and I added a letter to the respective Chiefs of Staff:

In cordially approving the report of the combined Chiefs of Staff drawn up after thorough examination of problems, the President and Prime Minister wish to emphasise the following points, which should be steadily pressed in all preparations:

(i) The desirability of finding means of running the W.J.[2] Russian convoys even through the "Husky" period.

(ii) The urgency of sending air reinforcements to General Chenault's forces in China and of finding personnel to make them fully operative.

(iii) The importance of achieving the favourable June moon for Sicily and the grave detriment to our interest which will be incurred by an apparent suspension of activities during summer months.

(iv) The need to build up more quickly the U.S. striking force in U.K., so as to be able to profit by favourable August weather for some form of "Sledgehammer." For this purpose not only the allowances of initial equipment and monthly maintenance should be searchingly re-examined, but the priorities of material and manpower shipment from U.S. to Great Britain should be adjusted to the tactical situation likely to be presented at the target date.

* * * * *

Finally on the morning of the 24th we came to the Press Conference where de Gaulle and Giraud were made to sit in a row of chairs alternating with the President and me, and we forced them to shake hands in public before all the reporters and photographers. They did so, and the pictures of this event cannot be viewed even in the setting of these tragic times without a laugh. The fact that the President and I were at Casablanca had been a well-kept secret. When the press reporters saw us both they could scarcely believe their eyes, and, when they were told we had been there for nearly a fortnight, their ears.

2 "Winston-Joe."

After the compulsory, or "shotgun" marriage (as it is called in the United States) of the bride and bridegroom, about whom such pains had been taken, the President made his speech to the reporters and I supported him.

*   *   *   *   *

The President prepared to depart. But I said to him, "You cannot go all this way to North Africa without seeing Marrakech. Let us spend two days there. I must be with you when you see the sunset on the snows of the Atlas Mountains." I worked on Harry Hopkins also in this sense. It happened there was a most delightful villa, of which I knew nothing, at Marrakech which the American Vice-Consul, Mr. Kenneth Pendar, had been lent by an American lady, Mrs. Taylor. This villa would accommodate the President and me, and there was plenty of outside room for our entourages. So it was decided that we should all go to Marrakech. Roosevelt and I drove together the one hundred and fifty miles across the desert — already it seemed to me to be beginning to get greener — and reached the famous oasis. My description of Marrakech was "the Paris of the Sahara," where all the caravans had come from Central Africa for centuries to be heavily taxed *en route* by the tribes in the mountains and afterwards swindled in the Marrakech markets, receiving the return, which they greatly valued, of the gay life of the city, including fortune-tellers, snake-charmers, masses of food and drink, and on the whole the largest and most elaborately organised brothels in the African continent. All these institutions were of long and ancient repute.

It was agreed between us that I should provide the luncheon, and Tommy was accordingly charged with the task. The President and I drove together all the way, five hours, and talked a great deal of shop, but also touched on lighter matters. Many thousand American troops were posted along the road to protect us from any danger, and aeroplanes circled ceaselessly overhead. In the evening we arrived at the villa, where we were very hospitably and suitably entertained by Mr.

Pendar. I took the President up the tower of the villa. He was carried in a chair, and sat enjoying a wonderful sunset on the snows of the Atlas. We had a very jolly dinner, about fifteen or sixteen, and we all sang songs. I sang, and the President joined in the choruses, and at one moment was about to try a solo. However, someone interrupted and I never heard this.

My illustrious colleague was to depart just after dawn on the 25th for his long flight by Lagos and Dakar and so across to Brazil and then up to Washington. We had parted the night before, but he came round in the morning on the way to the aeroplane to say another good-bye. I was in bed, but would not hear of letting him go to the airfield alone, so I jumped up and put on my zip, and nothing else except slippers, and in this informal garb I drove with him to the airfield, and went on the plane and saw him comfortably settled down, greatly admiring his courage under all his physical disabilities and feeling very anxious about the hazards he had to undertake. These aeroplane journeys had to be taken as a matter of course during the war. None the less I always regarded them as dangerous excursions. However all was well. I then returned to the Villa Taylor, where I spent another two days in correspondence with the War Cabinet about my future movements, and painting from the tower the only picture I ever attempted during the war.

16

Adana and Tripoli

*Need to Bring Turkey into the War — My Note to the Chiefs of
Staff of November 18 — My Telegram to Stalin of November 24
— I Wish to Meet the Turkish President — Objections by the
Cabinet — President Roosevelt's Agreement with My Plan — I
Repeat My Request to My Colleagues — They at Length Ac-
quiesce — Off Over the Atlas Mountains — The Turkish Gov-
ernment Welcome the Conference — We Fly to Adana — My
Memorandum to the Turks — A Wooing Letter — Full Account
to Them of Our Position — Our Discussions in President
Inönü's Train — "Morning Thoughts" — My Report to the War
Cabinet of January 31 — Turkish Suspicions of Russia — Russian Triumph at Stalingrad — My Telegram to Stalin of February 2 — His Reply, February 6 — Lost Opportunities.*

THE STRATEGIC SCENE in the Mediterranean had been transformed by the Allied occupation of Northwest Africa,
and with the acquisition of a solid base on its southern shores
a forward movement against the enemy became possible. President Roosevelt and I had long sought to open a new route to
Russia and to strike at Germany's southern flank. Turkey was
the key to all such plans. To bring Turkey into the war on
our side had for many months been our aim. It now acquired
new hope and urgency.

As soon as the results of Alamein and "Torch" were manifest, I had sent, on November 18, a note to the British Chiefs
of Staff on this sphere. We had considerable forces already

stationed in Egypt and the Middle East which must in any case remain in that theatre, but which in the improved situation should be made to play an active part. The following is the substance of my note:

A supreme and prolonged effort must be made to bring Turkey into the war in the spring. We must expect that our naval forces and shipping, landing-craft, etc., will be fully engaged in the Central Mediterranean, and that only minor amphibious facilities will be available in the Levant. Access can however be had to Turkey by the railways through Syria, as well as by coastal shipping, and by a gradual build-up of air protection, not only Adalia but the Dardanelles itself might become open to supplies for Turkey. Troops can move by rail and road from Syria.

I wish to record my opinion that Turkey may be won if the proper measures are taken. Turkey is an ally. She will wish to have a seat among the victors at the Peace Conference. She has a great desire to be well armed. Her army is in good order except for the specialised modern weapons in which the Bulgarians have been given so great an advantage by the Germans. The Turkish Army has been mobilised for nearly three years, and is warlike. Hitherto Turkey has been restrained by fear from fulfilling her obligations, and we have taken an indulgent view of her policy on account of our own inability to help. The situation has now changed. By the destruction of Rommel's army large forces may presently become available in Egypt and Cyrenaica. By a strengthened Russian resistance and a possible counter-stroke in the Caucasus, which we should urge upon the Russians with all emphasis, great easement will be secured in Persia, and our Tenth Army may be drawn upon. There is also the Ninth Army in Syria. From all these sources it should be possible, on the assumption of the Russians maintaining themselves in the Caucasus north of the mountain line and holding the Caspian, to build up a powerful British land and air force to assist the Turks. A target date for the concentration should be April or May. Let me have proposals.

The following is the order of procedure, political and military:

(a) Turkey should be offered a Russian-American-British guarantee of territorial integrity and *status quo*. The Russians have already agreed with us upon this. The addition of the United States would probably be a decisive reassurance. This should be

followed by the despatch to Turkey of a strong Anglo-American
Military Mission.

(*b*) All through the winter from now on Turkey must be
equipped from Egypt and from the United States with tanks,
A.T. and A.A. guns, and active construction of airfields must be
undertaken. We have been working upon airfield construction in
Turkey for two years. What progress has been made so far? Now
that Rommel has been beaten there is evidently a surplus of
material in Egypt. We had over 2500 tanks at the disposal of the
Middle East Army. Much enemy material has been captured, both
German and Italian. This is also true of anti-tank and A.A. guns.
Experts must be provided to assist the Turks in learning to use
and maintain this material. A ceaseless flow of weapons and equipment must go into Turkey. We have already promised a consignment, but the moment Turkey agrees secretly with the plan above
far greater quantities must be sent. What is the capacity of the
railways from Syria to the Bosphorus and the Dardanelles? It
would seem a great mistake to attack Rhodes and other islands
in enemy hands in the Eastern Mediterranean until we have got
Turkey on our side. Any attacks can then be supported by heavy
shore-based air-power. We have to creep round this coast by land
and sea, building up our air as we go.

(*c*) In conjunction with the above, we should urge the Russians
to develop their strength on their southern flank, to try to clear
the Caucasus, to regain Novorossisk, and above all to resume at
the earliest date their intention, explained to me by Premier Stalin,
of striking southwest from the region north of Stalingrad towards
Rostov-on-the-Don. An ultimate result of these operations, if successful, would be the opening of the Dardanelles, under heavy air
protection, to the passage of supplies to Russian Black Sea ports,
and to any naval assistance the Russians might require in the Black
Sea. . . .

This document of mine represented the preliminary stage.
On November 24 I informed Stalin of the train of my thought.

I have communicated to President Roosevelt some preliminary
ideas about Turkey, and have found that he independently had
formed very similar views. It seems to me that we ought all of us
to make a new effort to have Turkey enter the war on our side.
For this purpose I should like the United States to join in an

Anglo-Soviet Guarantee of the territorial integrity and status of Turkey. Secondly, we are already sending Turkey a considerable consignment of munitions, including two hundred tanks, from the Middle East. . . . Thirdly, I hope by the early spring to assemble a considerable army in Syria . . . so as to go to the help of Turkey, either if she were threatened or were willing to join us. It is evident that your operations in the Caucasus or north of it may also exercise a great influence. If Turkey were to join us we could not only proceed with operations designed to open the shipping route to your left flank on the Black Sea, but we could also bomb heavily, from Turkish bases, the Rumanian oilfields, which are of such vital importance to the Axis, in view of your successful defence of the main oil supplies of the Caucasus.

On November 28 Stalin replied that he was in full agreement with the President and myself on the question of Turkey. "It would be desirable to do everything possible to have Turkey enter the war on our side in the spring. This would be of great importance in order to accelerate the defeat of Hitler and his accomplices."

* * * * *

There the subject rested until the Casablanca Conference. It had been one of the main points in our discussions. Our general agreement on the need to bring Turkey into the war was set forth in the combined report and covering letter. I now wished to clinch the matter by a personal meeting with President Inönü on Turkish soil. There was also much business to be done in Cairo, and I hoped on the way home to visit the Eighth Army in Tripoli, if it were taken, and also to call at Algiers. There were many things I could settle on the spot, and more which I needed to see with my own eyes. On January 20 therefore I telegraphed from Casablanca to the Deputy Prime Minister and the Foreign Secretary as follows:

I raised the Turkish question, having explored the ground beforehand, with President Roosevelt. It was agreed that we play the hand in Turkey, whether in munitions or diplomacy, the Americans taking the lead in China, and of course in French North

Africa. You will be pleased at this. . . . As soon as the President has gone I shall, if the weather is good, fly from Marrakech to Cairo, where I propose to stay for two or three days and settle several important matters. . . . Is this not the opportunity and the moment for me to get into direct touch with the Turks? . . . If you both think well of this the Foreign Secretary should make the proposal to the Turks without delay.

On the following day I received a reply to this telegram stating that Mr. Attlee and Mr. Eden had consulted the War Cabinet, and that as a result they urged my return direct to London to give an account to Parliament of my meeting with the President. My colleagues were opposed to my going to Cairo, on the grounds of extending my risks unnecessarily. Even more strongly did they resist the Turkish proposal. They were convinced that the moment was not ripe for an approach, and that if I persisted I should court either "a rebuff or a failure."

I was by no means content with these arguments.

Prime Minister to Foreign Secretary   21 Jan. 43

I am very sorry about Turkey. I think a golden opportunity may be lost. It had not been my intention to extort any pledge, but only to explain to them the ways in which we can now help them to place their country in a position of security. They are three: (1) by the guarantees; (2) by substantial munitions aid; (3) by sending them reinforcements in the event of attack — the necessary specialist flak units, tanks, and aircraft. anti-tank weapons, radar, and so on. If the Turks were afraid to come in I should not feel at all rebuffed.

Mr. Eden sent me a personal message saying that he felt that the arguments put forward by the War Cabinet were sound, and that the result which I thought important could be achieved by other means. I discussed the question with the President in the light of these messages from London. On January 24, therefore, I telegraphed again as follows:

Prime Minister to Deputy Prime Minister and   24 Jan. 43
Foreign Secretary

I must ask seriously that this matter be reviewed by Cabinet and that I may know as soon as possible their decision. I now wish and ask that the following telegram should be sent, either from me to President Inönü or to the Turkish Prime Minister, as may be thought best.

"I shall shortly be visiting Cairo after my conference in North Africa with President of the United States. I have been charged with the duty of speaking for both Great Britain and the U.S. on the equipment of the Turkish Army with the latest weapons, which are now at last coming forward in large numbers, and also of touching generally upon the matters affecting general defensive security of Turkey. I should be willing therefore to come to a most secret rendezvous with the Turkish Prime Minister, and I could also arrange, if desired, for C.I.G.S. to meet Marshal Chakmak or other high Turkish military authorities. Cyprus would afford a completely sure and secret meeting-place for a friendly talk about general situation, and I should be quite willing to come there if this were agreeable to you."

President Roosevelt attaches much importance to action on these lines, and in the event of my colleagues being willing to send the above message he will himself telegraph to President Inönü as follows:

"President Inönü: The Prime Minister, who has been conferring with me, is going shortly to Cairo. He will in all probability wish to confer with you or with your Prime Minister at some convenient secret place. In case Prime Minister Churchill does seek a conference I earnestly hope you or your Prime Minister will find it possible to meet him. Roosevelt."

Even if the Turks should say "No" it will do no harm. I have no false pride in these matters. The capture of Tripoli, the increasing Russian victories, and the fact that I speak for the two great Allies creates a most favourable occasion. Do not, I beg you, lightly dismiss it.

The flight from Marrakech to Cairo has been very carefully reconnoitred and considered, and is not thought to present any difficulties. It does not go over any enemy territory nor near any fighting fronts. The C.A.S. and the pilot think it a perfectly good and simple flight. The Chief of the Imperial General Staff and I need to go there in any case in order to discuss the whole question with Wilson of his new command and the dispositions of the Tenth Army, on which we are now about to draw heavily for Sicily.

I trust that you and my colleagues will give me such latitude in my personal movements as I deem necessary to the public interest.

The War Cabinet reiterated their arguments against my proposed meeting with the Turkish leaders. They were in favour of the Staff talks continuing, and thought that an approach to Turkey on the highest level, without previous preparation, particularly in regard to shipping and communications in the event of supplies being sent as a result of an agreement, would be premature. I got quite upset by the obstruction of the Cabinet as I lay in my luxurious bed in the Taylor Villa looking at the Atlas Mountains, over which I longed to leap in the "Commando" airplane which awaited me so patient and contented on the airfield.

I was moreover convinced of the rightness of my view, and the President was entirely at one with me on this. I therefore replied again on January 25.

Prime Minister to Deputy Prime Minister and   25 Jan. 43
War Cabinet

Neither the President nor I are at all convinced by arguments put forward. There never was any idea of persuading Turkey to come into war without regard to circumstances and conditions. These have to be created and prepared beforehand. In the first place, Turkey has to be well kitted up. In the second, the situation developing against Italy and induced by the Russian advances must first of all produce its solid results upon safety of Turkey. However, it seems to me a subject of surprise, if right conditions were created, that any one should have doubt about the advantages of Turkey entering the war on our side. No one would propose to urge the Turks to step outside their bounds, but mere occupation by us and use of Turkish aerodromes would give us the power to paralyse Ploesti oilfields, with consequences judged by Chiefs of Staff to be of far-reaching importance. Besides this, there could surely be no doubt that the arrival of Turkey on the Allied side in four or five months' time, when the great operations on which we are resolved will be afoot, would be an invaluable makeweight to our war effort against our enemies. I have not the slightest doubt that Combined Chiefs of Staff would take this view, but they are unhappily now dispersed. I can only say that C.I.G.S. takes the same view as the President and his advisers.

2. I asked most earnestly that telegram in question should be sent. I am sure, and President agreed with me, that what you call the "rebuff," if received, which is questionable, would not have any noticeable consequences. If, on the other hand, the Turks accept, it would surely not be in their interest to let this important contact with the winning side lapse into a failure. As to their pressing inordinate demands for munitions upon the President and me, I should naturally report these to you before agreeing to them.

3. Therefore I wish to request you should send my telegram. The President, who departs in a few hours (Monday morning), has left me authority to release his as soon as your decision has been made.

This of course brought matters to a head. The same afternoon I received an answer from the War Cabinet acquiescing in my plan, and I telegraphed to London in a more easy mood:

Prime Minister to Deputy Prime Minister and   25 Jan. 43
Foreign Secretary

I am most grateful to you for allowing me to try my plan. We may only get a snub, in which case it will be my fault, but I do not think it will do for me to wait for the Turkish answer. I think there is a shade of odds in favour of their coming. If they come, I think I can get things pushed on a bit. How difficult everything becomes once one cannot talk together!

2. Apart from Turkey, there are tremendous possibilities open in Southern Tunisia. I shall try to make sure that these are exploited to the full. The arrival of the glorious Desert armies, whom I last saw in such despondency and disarray, at this stage in their 1500-mile march is the greatest factor alive on the North African shore. It is rather odd to think that this morning up to noon I had the option of either answering my questions tomorrow in the House of Commons or of meeting General Wilson in Cairo (D.V.).

I could not resist sending this:

Prime Minister to Deputy Prime Minister and   26 Jan. 43
Foreign Secretary

We are just off over the Atlas Mountains, which are gleaming

with their sunlit snows. You can imagine how much I wish I were
going to be with you tomorrow on the Bench, but duty calls.

*   *   *   *   *

Accordingly on the afternoon of the 26th we sailed off in
the "Commando" and after having an extremely good dinner,
provided by Mr. Pendar at the Taylor Villa, I slept soundly
till once again, after an eight months' interval, I went to the
co-pilot's seat and sat by Captain Vanderkloot, my young
American pilot, and we saw together for the second time dawn
gleam upon the waters of the Nile. This time we had not to
go so far to the south, because the victory of Alamein had
swept our foes fifteen hundred miles farther to the west. We
arrived at the airfield, ten miles from the Pyramids, and were
welcomed by the Ambassador, Lord Killearn, and received by
the Cairo Command. We then repaired to the Embassy. Here
I was joined by Sir Alexander Cadogan, Permanent Under-
Secretary of State at the Foreign Office, sent from England by
the Cabinet at my desire. We were all able to contrast the
situation with what it had been in August, 1942, with feelings
of relief and satisfaction.

Messages now reached me to say that the Turkish President,
Ismet Inönü, was delighted at the idea of the proposed meeting. Several suggestions were made as to time and place. One
plan was that I should go myself to Angora. This was strongly
opposed by the Foreign Office, particularly in view of the lack
of security, as had been shown by the recent attempt to murder
the German Ambassador, von Papen, by a bomb. Another
suggestion, made by the Turkish President, was that I should
meet his Prime Minister, Mr. Saracoglu, in Cyprus on January
31, whither he would travel after dining at the German Embassy. A much more convenient proposal, made from the
Turkish side, was that the President and his staff should meet
me in his special train in secrecy anywhere agreeable to me on
Turkish territory. Arrangements were therefore made for a
meeting to take place at Adana, on the coast near the Turkish-
Syrian border, on January 30. I hastened to inform both the
President and Stalin of this decision.

Prime Minister to President Roosevelt   27 Jan. 43

The Turk is delighted, as you will see from his message to you. I am now in Cairo, and shall start in a day or two for a secret rendezvous in Turkey, name of which I will telegraph later. I will keep you fully informed. Hope all is well with you and that you are not at all fatigued. We seem to have got a good world press.

And:

Prime Minister to Premier Stalin   27 Jan. 43

It was agreed between President Roosevelt and me that I should propose to the Turkish President a meeting between him and me in order to arrange for the better and more speedy equipment of the Turkish Army with a view to future eventualities. The Turkish President has replied cordially welcoming this plan for increasing "the lateral defensive strength" of Turkey, and he is willing, if I wish, that our meeting should become public in due course after it has taken place. You know my views already in this matter from the telegrams exchanged between us, and you may be sure I shall keep you promptly and fully informed.

Pray accept my renewed expression of admiration at the continued marvellous feats of the Soviet armies.

*   *   *   *   *

I went in the "Commando" to meet the Turks. It is only a four-hour flight across the Mediterranean, most of it in sight of Palestine and Syria, and we landed at Adana. I had with me in another plane Cadogan, Generals Brooke, Alexander, Wilson, and their officers. We landed not without some difficulty on the small Turkish airfield, and we had hardly completed the salutations and ceremonial before a very long enamelled caterpillar began to crawl out of the mountain defiles, containing the President, the entire Turkish Government, and Marshal Chakmak. They received us with the utmost cordiality and enthusiasm. Several saloon carriages had been put on the train for our accommodation, there being none other in the neighbourhood. We spent two nights in this train, having long daily discussions with the Turks and very agreeable talks at meals with President Inönü. I had meanwhile on the journey prepared a statement addressed to the Turks and written for their consumption. It was meant to be a wooing letter containing an offer of platonic marriage both from me and the President.

The danger to Turkey on her northern flank has been removed for the time being by the shattering victories of the Russians over the Germans, and on her southern flank by the fact that Generals Alexander and Montgomery have chased Rommel 1600 miles away from Cairo, with the destruction of three-quarters of his army and nine-tenths of his equipment. There remains however the Germans' need of oil and of the *Drang nach Osten,* and they may in the summer try to force their way through the centre. Turkey must be in the best possible condition to resist any such act of aggression by force of arms. We have come here to find out how we can best help our Ally at this serious but at the same time hopeful juncture. To this end we are prepared to speed up and increase the supply of the modern munitions which the Turkish Army unhappily lacks. The President of the United States has asked me to handle this matter for him as well as for my own country. This of course does not mean that I can draw a blank cheque on the United States, and I shall have to refer back on particular points. However, the President was most anxious this meeting should take place, as he is desirous that Turkey should be safe and strong, and that she should be closely associated with the two great Western democracies not only during the concluding stages of the war, but in the general work of world rehabilitation which will follow. I think therefore we may expect most sympathetic consideration for anything we recommend.

2. In what directions can we increase the flow and speed up the efficient use of the weapons we supply? What is the present state of the communications, and what measures should be taken to reduce any congestion on them? What measure should be taken to make sure that the equipment is properly handled by our Ally? We [British] have ourselves no false pride on these points and think only of getting stronger and better equipped. For instance, the Americans have sent out teachers to train us in the use of their various tanks and weapons they have supplied to us in the Middle East. They even sent out a large number of skilled engineers in plain clothes before they came into the war in order to teach us how to keep the machines in running order and how to

make repairs. Another instance is the railway through Persia. We thought we were running it very well, but the Americans made a number of criticisms and offered to take it over with larger strength and help us to run it better. They are now taking it over from us section by section. I say this to show that we are not making any derogatory suggestion in asking that a considerable number of experts and technicians in plain clothes should come in to assist in the working up of the material so that it can get into the hands of the troops and be kept in good condition. Also, we are very ready to send officers with the latest experience in tank warfare and other branches of technical warfare and to give all possible information that could be desired.

I have been particularly distressed at the spectacle of the Turkish Army, which has the finest infantry and a good field artillery, but has not been able to get during the whole three and a half years of this war the modern equipment which is decisive on the battle-field, and which the Germans, from their looted stores, have been able to give, for instance, to the Bulgarians. This has made me fully comprehend the attitude of Turkey at every stage we have so far travelled. The time has come when these disparities can and must be removed with the greatest speed.

. . . . .

The British and Americans will certainly send together, immediately on Turkey being drawn into the war, at least twenty-five Air squadrons. A number of airfields have already been prepared and a good deal of material is already on the sites. However, there is a second series of airfields, the preparation of which was discontinued about a year ago, the construction of which should be actively proceeded with. Materials, spare parts, and field workshops must all be put in place. The nests must be made so that the birds can fly there at once. Unless the nests are ready birds cannot live and cannot strike. The work, which is really vital to the defence of Turkey, should be pushed forward with frantic energy, and British and American engineers and Air Force officers volunteer their services to any extent that may be needed. The moment the Staff arrangements have been made not a day should be lost. . . .

5. It is not possible for the Turkish Army fully to equip itself with all the technical weapons should the emergency arise in the early summer of this year. The British could make available cer-

tain special units which are already fully trained, which do not involve the movement of great masses of men across the communications, but which are essential to the holding of the airfields and also the repulse of tank attacks. To this end we will hold ready at convenient places, with such American assistance as we may need and can obtain, as many regiments of anti-tank artillery as can be conveniently received, including some of our very latest 17-pounders, which have never yet been in action. We will also have ready a number of regiments of anti-aircraft artillery to reinforce the forces which will already have been moved into position. We will also prepare to move two battle-experienced armoured divisions in at the earliest moment. In addition to this, there will be the Ninth and Tenth Armies. We are drawing somewhat upon the Tenth Army for future operations in the Central Mediterranean, but the Polish Corps, which is three-quarters equipped and is of very high-class personnel, would be available unless the Russian Caucasian front should break and the Germans be found advancing towards Persia. This is not at all likely. Besides this, the Ninth Army in Syria is being built up to perhaps five divisions. It is felt however that the movement of these masses might congest the communications and that it is far better in the first instance to push the specialised units through with the maximum celerity....

6. I will now tell you about the Casablanca Conference and the great concentration of forces we have decided to make in the Central Mediterranean. Naturally, we cannot give details about the exact plans and dates, but our intention is to destroy Italy; shatter her entirely; beat her out of the war, both by terrific bombing from Tunis and from Great Britain and by heavy attacks over the sea, for which great preparations are required and are being made. The breaking down of Italy would lead to contact with the Western Balkans and with the highly hopeful resistance maintained both by General Michailovitch in Serbia and the Partisans in Croatia and Slovenia. According to our expectations and reasonable hopes, we shall drive the enemy from the coasts of Africa into the sea before the summer, and perhaps much earlier. In that event the summer months will see in the Mediterranean the largest operations it is in the power of Great Britain and United States to conduct. These operations, and above all the Italian attitude, will cause the very greatest agitation throughout the Balkans. The further advance of the Russian armies cannot be excluded. Operations across the Black Sea must be considered a

possibility, with their superior fleet. It is therefore in the summer that we must consider the crisis temperature will rise very high and the need for Turkey to be secure will be paramount.

7. I know that Premier Stalin is most anxious to see Turkey well armed and ready to defend herself against aggression. I know it is President Roosevelt's wish, as it is certainly that of His Majesty's Government, that Turkey should be a full partner in the Peace Conference, where all questions of changes in the existing *status quo* will have to be settled. It is not possible to say when this world war will end. We British and Americans are quite sure that we shall win. That is why the President has called the Casablanca Conference the "Unconditional Surrender Conference." It must be remembered that we were peaceful nations who had made very little preparation for the war. But we are now becoming warlike nations with far greater resources of men and munitions than the Germans, Japanese, and Italians can produce. We are absolutely resolved to go on to the end and make a good job of it this time. You probably know as well as we, and perhaps even better, what is the interior state of Germany. We are not counting on an early or sudden collapse, but of course no one can be sure that it will not come suddenly, as it did last time. We must be ready, both for the worst and for the best.

8. I have not been in Turkey since 1909, when I met many of the brave men who laid the foundations of the modern Turkey. There is a long story of the friendly relations between Great Britain and Turkey. Across it is a terrible slash of the last war, when German intrigues and British and Turkish mistakes led to our being on opposite sides. We fought as brave and honourable opponents. But those days are done, and we and our American Allies are prepared to make vigorous exertions in order that we shall all be together and continue together to move forward into a world arrangement in which peaceful peoples will have a right to be let alone and in which all peoples will have a chance to help one another.

This document I handed to the Turkish President at the first meeting in his train on the late afternoon of our arrival.

* * * * *

The general discussion which followed turned largely on to two questions, the structure of the post-war world and the arrangements for an international organisation, and the future relations of Turkey and Russia. I give only a few examples of the remarks which, according to the record, I made to the Turkish leaders. I said that I had seen Molotov and Stalin, and my impression was that both desired a peaceful and friendly association with the United Kingdom and the United States. In the economic sphere both Western Powers had much to give to Russia, and they could help in the reparation of Russia's losses. I could not see twenty years ahead, but we had nevertheless made a treaty for twenty years. I thought Russia would concentrate on reconstruction for the next ten years. There would probably be changes: Communism had already been modified. I thought we should live in good relations with Russia, and if Great Britain and the United States acted together and maintained a strong air force they should be able to ensure a period of stability. Russia might even gain by this. She possessed vast undeveloped areas, for instance, in Siberia.

The Turkish Prime Minister observed that I had expressed the view that Russia might become imperialistic. This made it necessary for Turkey to be very prudent. I replied that there would be an international organisation to secure peace and security, which would be stronger than the League of Nations. I added that I was not afraid of Communism. Mr. Saracoglu remarked that he was looking for something more real. All Europe was full of Slavs and Communists. All the defeated countries would become Bolshevik and Slav if Germany was beaten. I replied that things did not always turn out as bad as was expected; but if they did so it was better that Turkey should be strong and closely associated with the United Kingdom and the United States. If Russia, without any cause, were to attack Turkey the whole international organisation of which I had spoken would be applied on behalf of Turkey, and the guarantees after the present war would be much more severe, not only where Turkey was concerned, but in the case of all Europe. I would not be a friend of Russia if she imitated Germany. If she did so we should arrange the best possible combination against her, and I would not hesitate to say so to Stalin. Molotov had asked for a treaty by which the Baltic States would be regarded as Russian provinces. We had refused to agree to this, (a) because territorial rearrangements were to be postponed for settlement after the war, and (b) because we felt it necessary to make a reservation for free determination for individuals.

* * * * *

Early the following morning I lay in bed in my saloon on the train composing, in the light of the general discussion which had taken place, a note on my views on post-war security. I called this paper "Morning Thoughts." One paragraph is possibly worthy of preservation in the light of subseqent events:

It is the intention of the Chiefs of the United Nations to create a world organisation for the preservation of peace, based upon conceptions of freedom and justice and the revival of prosperity. As a part of this organisation an instrument of European government will be established which will embody the spirit but not be subject to the weaknesses of the former League of Nations. The units forming this body will not only be the great nations of Europe and Asia Minor as long established, but a number of Confederations formed among the smaller States, among which a Scandinavian Bloc, a Danubian Bloc, and a Balkan Bloc appear to be obvious. A similar instrument will be formed in the Far East, with different membership, and the whole will be held together by the fact that the victorious Powers intend to continue fully armed, especially in the air, while imposing complete disarmament upon the guilty. No one can predict with certainty that the victors will never quarrel among themselves, or that the United States may not once again retire from Europe, but after the experiences which all have gone through, and their sufferings, and the certainty that a third struggle will destroy all that is left of the culture, wealth, and civilisation of mankind and reduce us to the level almost of wild beasts, the most intense effort will be made by the leading Powers to prolong their honourable association, and by sacrifice and self-restraint win for themselves a glorious name in human annals.

Great Britain will certainly do her utmost to organise a coalition resistance to any act of aggression committed by any Power, and it is believed that the United States will co-operate with her, and even possibly take the lead of the world, on account of her numbers and strength, in the good work of preventing such tendencies to aggression before they break into open war.

*   *   *   *   *

During these general political discussions military conversations were conducted by the C.I.G.S. and our other high commanders. The two main points to be considered were the provision of equipment for the Turkish forces, prior and subsequent to any political move by Turkey, and the preparation of plans for the reinforcement of the Turkish forces by British units in the event of their coming into the war. The results of these talks were embodied in a military agreement.

*   *   *   *   *

We must now revert to the tremendous drama unfolding around Stalingrad. As has been described, Paulus' Sixth German Army had been caught by the Russian pincers and encircled as the result of the November conflict. Manstein's supreme effort from the southwest in December to break through the Russian cordon and relieve the beleaguered garrison had failed. He pierced the Russian line to a depth of forty miles but there he was stopped, still fifty miles from Stalingrad. A new Russian offensive from the north threatened his flank and forced him into a retreat which spread to all the German southern front, including the Caucasus, and ended only when it was back behind Rostov-on-the-Don.

There was now no hope of further succour for Paulus. Great efforts were made to supply him from the air but little got through, and at the expense of heavy losses in aircraft. The cold was intense; food and ammunition were scarce and an outbreak of typhus added to the miseries of his men. On January 8 he rejected an ultimatum to surrender and next day the last phase began with violent Russian attacks from the west. The Germans fought strongly, so that only five miles were

gained in as many days. But at last they began to crack and by
January 17 the Russians were within ten miles of Stalingrad
itself. Paulus threw into the fight every man who could bear
arms, but it was no use. On January 22 the Russians surged
forward again until the Germans were thrown back on the outskirts of the city they had tried in vain to take. Here the remains of a once-great army were pinned in an oblong only
four miles deep by eight long. Under intense artillery fire and
air bombardment, the survivors defended themselves in violent
street fighting, but their plight was hopeless, and as the
Russians pressed forward, exhausted units began to surrender
wholesale. Paulus and his staff were captured on January 31
and on February 2 Marshal Voronov reported that all resistance
had ceased and that ninety thousand prisoners had been taken.
These were the survivors of twenty-one German and one
Rumanian divisions. This crushing disaster to the Germans
ended Hitler's prodigious effort to conquer Russia by force of
arms, and destroy Communism by an equally odious form of
totalitarian tyranny.

*   *   *   *   *

Prime Minister to Premier Stalin   2 Feb. 43

Thank you for your telegram about Turkey. I met all the chief
Turks at Adana on the 30th, and had long and most friendly
talks. There is no doubt they have come a long way towards us
both, and also that their news from Germany convinces them of a
bad condition there. The first thing is to equip them with modern
weapons, of which we have so far been able to spare only a few.
I have arranged to press forward everything they can take over the
Taurus railway, which is the only road, and also to lend them some
ships to carry more supplies from Egypt. I am also giving them some
German material which we have captured in the Desert. We are
setting up at Angora a Joint Anglo-Turkish Military Commission to
improve communications for the transit of munitions. We are
making joint plans to aid them if they are attacked by Germany or
Bulgaria.

2. I have not asked for any precise political engagement or
promise about entering the war on our side, but it is my opinion that

they will do so before the year is out, and that possibly earlier,
by a strained interpretation of neutrality similar to that of the
United States before she came in, they may allow us to use their
airfields for refuelling for British and American bombing attacks
on the Ploesti oil-wells, which are of vital importance to Germany,
especially now that your armies have recovered Maikop. I repeat,
I have not asked for or received a definite political engagement, and
have told them they are free to say so. Nevertheless, their meeting
me, their whole attitude, and the joint communiqué, which I am
telegraphing you, ranged them more plainly than before in the
anti-Hitler system, and will be so taken all over the world.

3. They are of course apprehensive of their position after the
war in view of the great strength of the Soviet Republic. I told
them that in my experience the U.S.S.R. had never broken an
engagement or treaty; that the time for them to make a good arrangement was now, and that the safest place for Turkey was to
have a seat with the victors, as a belligerent, at the peace table.
All this I said in our common interest in accordance with our
alliance, and I hope you will approve. They would, I am sure,
be very responsive to any gesture of friendship on the part of the
U.S.S.R. I should be very glad to have your candid opinion on
all this. I have established very close personal relations with
them, particularly with President Inönü.

4. In your recent telegram which you sent to President Roosevelt you asked about the slowing down of the Allied operations in
North Africa. So far as the British Eighth Army is concerned, we
have since then taken Tripoli, and hope shortly to enter Tunisia
in force and drive the enemy from the Mareth and Gabes positions.
The clearing and restoring of the harbour at Tripoli is proceeding
with all speed, but at present our line of communications runs to
Benghazi, and part even to Cairo, 1500 miles away. Our First
Army, reinforced by strong American forces, is bringing its supplies forward, and will attack in conjunction with the Eighth Army
as soon as possible. The wet weather is a serious factor, as are also
the communications, which, both by road and rail, are slender and
500 miles long. However, it is my hope that the enemy will be
completely destroyed or driven from the African shore by the end
of April, and perhaps earlier. My own estimate, which is based on
good information, is that the Fifth Panzer Army in Tunisia has a
ration strength of 80,000 Germans, and with them 25,000 to 30,000

Italians. Rommel has 150,000 Germans and Italians on his ration strength, of which perhaps 40,000 only are fighting troops and weak in weapons. The destruction of these forces is our immediate aim.

5. I will reply later to your most proper inquiries of me and the President about the concrete operations settled at Casablanca.

6. Pray accept my congratulations on the surrender of Field-Marshal Paulus and the end of the German Sixth Army. This is indeed, a wonderful achievement.

Victory did not make the Soviet more genial. On February 6 I received a somewhat cool reply.

Premier Stalin to Premier Churchill 6 Feb. 43

Many thanks for information on your talks with the leading Turkish personalities in Adana.

2. In connection with your suggestion that the Turks would reciprocate any friendly gesture from the Soviet Union, I would like to mention that we have already made a number of statements, the friendly character of which is well known to the British Government, some months before the Soviet-German war, as well as after its beginning. However, the Turks did not react to our steps. Apparently they were afraid to incur the wrath of the Germans. I am afraid that a similar reception will be accorded to the gesture suggested by you.

3. The international position of Turkey remains very delicate. On the one hand Turkey has the treaty of neutrality and friendship with the U.S.S.R. and the treaty of mutual assistance against aggression with Great Britain; on the other hand she has the treaty of friendship with Germany, signed three days before the German attack against the U.S.S.R. It is not clear to me how in the present circumstances Turkey thinks to combine her obligation *vis-à-vis* the U.S.S.R. and Great Britain with her obligations *vis-à-vis* Germany. Still, if Turkey wishes to make her relations with the U.S.S.R. more friendly and intimate let her say so. In this case the Soviet Union would be willing to meet Turkey halfway.

4. Of course I have no objection against your making a statement that I was kept informed on the Anglo-Turkish meeting, although I cannot say that the information was very full.

5. I wish the First and the Eighth British Armies, as well as the American troops in North Africa, every success in the coming offen-

sive, and a speedy expulsion of the German-Italian forces from African soil.

6. Let me thank you for your friendly congratulations on the surrender of Field-Marshal Paulus and on the successful annihilation of the encircled enemy troops near Stalingrad.

It was not till March 2 that I received another message from Stalin on Soviet-Turkish relations. Some progress had been made.

. . . On my part I would like to convey to you that on February 13 the Turkish Foreign Minister told the Soviet Ambassador at Angora that the Turkish Government would wish to start negotiations with the Soviet Government for the improvement of the Soviet-Turkish relations. The Soviet Government replied through their Ambassador at Angora that it welcomes this desire of the Turkish Government, and expressed willingness to commence such negotiations. We expect at present the return of the Turkish Ambassador from Angora. It is contemplated to open negotiations thereafter.

*   *   *   *   *

My parleys with Turkey were intended to prepare the way for her entry into the war in the autumn of 1943. That this did not take place after the collapse of Italy and with the further Russian advances against Germany north of the Black Sea, was due to unfortunate events in the Aegean later in the year which will be described in some detail later on.

Of course, when you win everything looks all right, but at this time many long and terrible struggles lay ahead, and I am sure that had I been allowed to carry out my theme, the plain purpose of which was clearly set forth, I could have had Turkey in the war on our side before the end of 1943, without damage to our main plans, and with all kinds of advantages to the Allies, and especially for Turkey. Now in these years after the war when we see the United States sustaining Turkey with her whole power all has been put right, except that we did not have the considerable advantages of Turkish aid and all that this implied in the Balkan situation in the early months of 1944.

17

Home to Trouble

Course of the North African Campaign — Advance of the Eighth Army — Tripoli Captured January 23 — I Fly to Tripoli via Cyprus and Cairo — Triumphal Entry of the Eighth Army — General Alexander's Reply to My Directive of August 10 — Business at Algiers — Safely Home — My Statement to the House of Commons on February 11 — Mr. Eden's Visit to the United States — I get Pneumonia — I am Presented with a Lion — General Sylvester Churchill — Letter from the King — My Reply, February 22 — President Roosevelt is Laid Up — Mr. Gandhi on Hunger Strike — The Stalingrad and "Desert Victory" Films — The President's Letter of March 17.

AFTER THE FAILURE to conquer Tunis in December the force of our initial blow in Northwest Africa was spent, and the German High Command was able temporarily to restore stability in Tunisia. Refusing to recognise that he could not safeguard by sea or air even on the short passage between Sicily and Tunis, Hitler ordered the creation of a new army in Tunisia to meet the impending Allied attacks from both east and west. Rommel's battered Afrika Corps was left to continue its retreat under the hard pressure of the Eighth Army.

In the Central Mediterranean, Malta had been revictualled and rearmed and had again sprung into full activity. From our new bases in Algeria and Cyrenaica our naval and air forces ranged widely, protecting Allied shipping and taking heavy toll of enemy supplies and reinforcements. Besides blockading

Tunis, where German air forces were still strong, we reached out to the ports on the Italian mainland. Palermo, Naples, and Spezia all felt the lash as our strength mounted, and R.A.F. bombers from home took over the attack on Northern Italy. The Italian Fleet made no attempt to interfere. Apart from the presence of the British Fleet the lack of oil was serious. There were days when there was not one ton of fuel in all Sicily for the vessels escorting supplies to Tunis.

On land General Eisenhower had seen that his forces in Northwest Africa must be given a pause in which to reorganise and build their strength. In the north the ground won by the British 78th and 6th Armoured Divisions had to be consolidated. Farther south the long tenuous front, held lightly by the French XIXth Corps in the centre and part of the U.S. IId Corps on the right, offered the enemy a tempting chance to break through and turn the whole Allied line. Allied units were much intermingled, and the problem was complicated by General Giraud's refusal to allow French troops to be placed under British command. A sharp attack on the French XIXth Corps in mid-January led to the detachment of yet more British and American units to support them, and it became necessary for Eisenhower to issue an order, accepted by Giraud, putting the whole front under the orders of General Anderson, Commander of the British First Army.

*   *   *   *   *

During January the Eighth Army made good progress in its advance. At the beginning of the month it was halted in front of the enemy position at Buerat. General Montgomery felt it necessary to delay his attack until he was reasonably assured that he could exploit it rapidly. The Army was supplied from Benghazi, Tobruk, and at the earliest moment from Tripoli. On January 15 Montgomery attacked with the 51st Division along the coastal road, and the 22d Armoured Brigade in the centre, while the 7th Armoured and 2d New Zealand Divisions turned the Desert flank. Tripoli was taken punctually on January 23. The port was found severely damaged. The entrance had been completely blocked by sunken ships, and the approaches lavishly sown with mines. This had been foreseen, and the first supply ship entered the harbour on February 2. A week later two thousand tons a day were being handled. Although the Eighth Army had still great distances to travel, its maintenance during the fifteen-hundred-mile advance from Alamein, crowned by the rapid opening up of Tripoli, was an administrative feat for which credit lay with General Lindsell in Cairo, and General Robertson with the Eighth Army. At the end of the month the Eighth Army was joined by General Leclerc, who had led a mixed force of Free French about twenty-five hundred strong, fifteen hundred miles across the desert from French Equatorial Africa. Leclerc placed himself unreservedly under Montgomery's orders. He and his troops were to play a valuable part in the rest of the Tunisian campaign.

The Eighth Army crossed the frontier into Tunisia on February 4, thus completing the conquest of the Italian Empire by Great Britain. In accordance with the decisions taken at the Casablanca Conference, this army now came under General Eisenhower, with General Alexander as his deputy in executive command of land operations.

* * * * *

I flew back from Adana to Cyprus, where I spent two nights, and inspected for the second time in the war the 4th Hussars, of whom I am Colonel. The last occasion had been a month before Alamein. Everything in Cyprus seemed blooming, and the people as friendly and enthusiastic as I have seen them anywhere. They were all feeling much safer than they had been in 1941, and both the Turkish and Greek elements in the island were very thankful that the Allies were winning and not at all inclined to object to British rule. I made some agreeable contacts with the population, and addressed all the notables in the garden of the Governor's palace. This was my third visit to the island — the first in 1907, as Under-Secretary for the Colonies in Campbell-Bannerman's Government, the second on a cruise in Walter Moyne's yacht in 1936, and now this third visit in 1943. All the time I had followed attentively their affairs, and I am glad to have played a part in abolishing the tribute which Treasury rigour had imposed on the island so wrongfully.

We had another two nights at Cairo, and then flew to Tripoli, where Montgomery, a victor at the end of his historic march, awaited me at the airfield. The enemy had been pushed forty or fifty miles west of the city. I spent two days in Tripoli, and witnessed the magnificent entry of the Eighth Army through its stately streets. At their head were the pipers of the 51st Highland Division. Spick and span they looked after all their marching and fighting. In the afternoon I inspected massed parades of two divisions. I stayed in Montgomery's caravan, which I had not slept in since our meeting before Alamein. I addressed about two thousand officers and men of his head-quarters. I spoke to them about

> Yet nightly pitch our moving tent
> A day's march nearer home.

But they were still a long way from home; nor was the route to be direct.

I had planned to fly to Malta, and in consequence of the directions I had given at Cairo all had been set in readiness by Montgomery. As the flight was considered dangerous, on account of the presence of the enemy, I was to go in a small two-seater plane with an escort of half a dozen Spitfires. However, when I expressed my pleasure and surprise at these excellent arrangements having been made by Montgomery he realised that he had taken what was only my wish as an order. He then began to make objections about the danger of the flight, and finally I deferred to his advice. I am sorry for this, as I should have liked to have a memory of Malta while it was still in its struggle.

The reader may remember that on leaving Cairo six months earlier I had given General Alexander the following directive:

Prime Minister to General Alexander,   10 Aug. 42
Commander-in-Chief in the Middle East

Your prime and main duty will be to take or destroy at the

earliest opportunity the German-Italian army commanded by Field-Marshal Rommel, together with all its supplies and establishments in Egypt and Libya.

2. You will discharge or cause to be discharged such other duties as pertain to your command, without prejudice to the task described in paragraph 1, which must be considered paramount in His Majesty's interests.

He sent me the following reply:

General Alexander to Prime Minister
Sir:

The orders you gave me on August [10], 1942, have been fulfilled. His Majesty's enemies, together with their impedimenta, have been completely eliminated from Egypt, Cyrenaica, Libya, and Tripolitania. I now await your further instructions.[1]

*   *   *   *   *

After these two long and vivid days I set off with my party from Tripoli to visit Eisenhower and all the others at Algiers.

Prime Minister to General Eisenhower (Africa)   3 Feb. 43

According to my present plans, I should arrive on the 5th. I hope that it will be agreeable to you if I lunch with you in a small circle. I hope to see Giraud and Murphy, and of course Macmillan. I do not wish General Anderson to be brought back from the front unless you consider it absolutely convenient and desirable. I plan to leave for Gibraltar after early luncheon. I am looking forward very much to seeing you. Please tell only Admiral Cunningham.

At Algiers the tension was acute. The murder of Darlan still imposed many precautions on all prominent figures. The Cabinet still continued to show concern about my safety, and evidently wanted me home as soon as possible. This at least was complimentary. On the other hand I soon saw that I should have to stay longer in Algiers.

Prime Minister to Deputy Prime Minister   5 Feb. 43

We are here in the Admiral's villa, which is next door to General Eisenhower's. Both are surrounded by barbed wire and heavily

1 See facsimile on page 722.

TO Prime Minister.

FROM Gen. Alexander

Originator's Number	Date
	Aug 15d

Sir, the orders you gave me on Aug 15d
1942 have been fulfilled. His majesty's
enemies together with their impedimenta
have been completely eliminated from EGYPT
CYRENAICA, LIBYA and TRIPOLITANIA ①
I now await your further instructions

1915 MT/g

guarded and patrolled. We came here by circuitous route in bullet-proof car. I do not propose leaving precincts. No one considers in these circumstances there is any danger, provided precautions are taken.

I am planning flying direct from here to England as soon as thoroughly satisfactory weather conditions are established. I should be glad of a day's rest, however, after a very strenuous week. Yesterday I reviewed over forty thousand of our troops in Tripoli. The Italians were second to none in their enthusiasm.

Please do not worry about my personal safety, as I take the utmost care of myself and am very quick to see where danger lies. I hope to take my questions in the House on Tuesday. I must ask a few days' grace on my return before making a statement, which I expect to do on Thursday.

The day was a full one. I had long talks with Eisenhower, and learned from him and from the Admiral much that could not have been put in telegrams. The villas were but a hundred yards apart. At luncheon both de Gaulle and Giraud were present. There was so much to settle that I could not leave till late on Saturday. Eisenhower and I dined together at the Admiral's villa in a small, pleasant circle. On February 6, I met Noguès and Peyrouton. Both these Frenchmen were in positions of authority and of extreme difficulty. In spite of his actions at the American landing Noguès was still Governor-General of Morocco. Peyrouton had just arrived on American invitation from the Argentine, where he had been the Vichy Ambassador, to take up the Governor-Generalship of Algeria. I told them that if they marched with us we would not concern ourselves with past differences. They were dignified, but anxious.

Before midnight I left for the airfield. We all took our places in the plane and waited for it to start; but it would not start. One of my assistant secretaries was of very small stature, and I could not help remarking, "Your light weight is a great advantage in flying, but if we come down in the desert you will not keep us going very long." At last I got impatient and decided to drive back to the Admiral's comfortable villa. My physician, Sir Charles Wilson, had already gone to sleep. He did not hear us leave, and was locked up for the night in the plane. He was only liberated at daybreak. It was necessary to spend another day at Algiers. There was no lack of business. To the Foreign Secretary I cabled:

We were delayed in starting last night for two and a half hours by a magneto failure, and as this would have meant the approach to England in broad daylight, probably without escort, we all thought it better to wait another twenty-four hours. It was obliging of the magneto to cut out before we started rather than later on.

At last, on Sunday night, the 7th, we took off and this time flew directly and safely home. This was my last flight in "Commando," which later perished with all hands, though with a different pilot and crew.

*   *   *   *   *

My first task on getting home was to make a full statement to the House of Commons on the Casablanca Conference, my tour of the Mediterranean, and on the general position. As I wished to announce on this occasion the important military appointments which had been agreed between us, I cabled to President Roosevelt as follows:

Former Naval Person to President Roosevelt   8 Feb. 43

I propose to give the House of Commons some account of our joint affairs on Thursday, 11th, at noon.

I have received from General Alexander a message saying that the directive I gave him on August 15 has been fully accomplished, as the enemy have been driven out of Egypt, Cyrenaica, and Tripolitania. Moreover, the advance forces of the Desert Army are already advancing into Tunisia. This therefore is the moment when the Eighth Army should come under the command of General Eisenhower. I propose to announce this, as it should certainly come from this end. I therefore propose to you that Alexander's and Tedder's appointments should be released to synchronise with my statement in Parliament. I hope that no advance information about the Eighth Army will get out before I tell Parliament.

I have just returned from Algiers, where I had very satisfactory talks with Eisenhower, Smith, Giraud, Murphy, and others. I have been travelling almost continuously since I saw you last, and will send you a further report in a few days. Every good wish to you, Harry, and all friends.

The President replied at once.

President Roosevelt to Prime Minister 9 Feb. 43

I agree to your announcing on February 11 the placing of your Eighth Army under the command of General Eisenhower and the appointment of Alexander as Deputy under Eisenhower, and also the appointment of Tedder. It is my opinion that co-operation by French forces will be best if the American Supreme Command in North Africa is stressed, and I consider it inadvisable to release and thereby make available to the enemy any information whatever as to the details of the duties of Alexander or Tedder. I am so glad you are safely back. You have accomplished marvels.

I thought it well that the President should take the rough with the smooth about British public opinion.

Former Naval Person to President Roosevelt 10 Feb. 43

I will act in the way you wish, but I cannot guarantee that there will be no criticism. I have received the attached note from Brendan Bracken [Minister of Information], who is in close touch with the British and American press here:

"I am having quite a lot of trouble in persuading some of the newspapers not to criticise the American handling of the North African campaign. If General Eisenhower's appointment as Supreme Commander is stressed and General Alexander's and Air Chief Marshal Tedder's respective functions are left vaguely undefined, I think we must expect a spate of criticism from the British press. In this respect I have no doubt that the press would be reflecting the general feeling in the country, and there would be far too many people who would honestly feel that British commanders and troops had been unfairly ignored for the sake of some move in international politics.

"The British Government is accustomed to criticism and is not likely to be unduly ruffled. But the Americans will very much resent the almost inevitably resulting criticism of General Eisenhower's appointment or any comparison between his military qualifications and those possessed by General Alexander. I think it is

important therefore that the public should be told that General
Eisenhower is Generalissimo, that Alexander is commanding the
forces of the United Nations fighting in Tunis, and that Tedder
is commanding the Air Forces."

I shall utter the most solemn warning against controversy in
these matters and every effort will be made by Bracken behind
the scenes. Please do the like on your side to help your faithful
partner. The Russian successes seem to me to be opening altogether a new situation. My hearty congratulations on Guadalcanal.[2]

*   *   *   *   *

It took me more than two hours on February 11 to make my
speech. I thought I had a good tale to tell. The high spot was
of course my directive to General Alexander of August, 1942,
and the reply which had reached me at Montgomery's headquarters in Tripoli on February 2, 1943. I proceeded to outline the general situation in French Northwest Africa and made
the announcements I had settled with the President about
commands, and the appointment of General Eisenhower as
Supreme Commander.

There were so many complicated questions open that I
thought it would be well for the Foreign Secretary to visit
Washington for the first time during the war and establish
intimate personal relations with the President, and also get
into close touch with Mr. Hull and the State Department. The
President welcomed the idea, and I prepared myself to take
over the Foreign Office in Mr. Eden's absence.

President Roosevelt to Prime Minister   12 Feb. 43

That is an excellent thought about Anthony Eden. Delighted
to have him. The sooner the better. Your speech was grand and
will do lots of good everywhere.

*   *   *   *

I was more tired by my journeying than I had realised at
the time, and I must have caught a chill. A few days later a
cold and sore throat obliged me to lie up. In the evening of
the 16th, when I was alone with Mrs. Churchill, my tempera-

2 The conquest of Guadalcanal was completed on February 9. Events there
will be described in the next volume.

ture suddenly rose, and Lord Moran, who had been watching me, took a decided view and told me that I had inflammation of the base of a lung. His diagnosis led him to prescribe a drug called M and B. The next day elaborate photographs were taken and confirmed the diagnosis, and Dr. Geoffrey Marshall of Guy's Hospital was called in consultation. All my work had come to me hour by hour at the Annexe, and I had maintained my usual output though feeling far from well. But now I became aware of a marked reduction in the number of papers which reached me. When I protested, the doctors, supported by my wife, argued that I ought to quit my work entirely. I would not agree to this. What should I have done all day? They then said I had pneumonia, to which I replied, "Well, surely you can deal with that. Don't you believe in your new drug?" Doctor Marshall said he called pneumonia "the old man's friend." "Why?" I asked. "Because it takes them off so quietly." I made a suitable reply, but we reached an agreement on the following lines. I was only to have the most important and interesting papers sent me, and read a novel. I chose *Moll Flanders,* about which I had heard excellent accounts, but had not found time to test them. On this basis I passed the next week in fever and discomfort, and I sometimes felt very ill. There is a blank in my flow of minutes from the 19th to the 25th.

The Speaker, Captain Fitzroy, had been taken ill on almost the same days as I. He too developed pneumonia, and at first we interchanged inquiries. I was not reassured by the replies I got. The Speaker was five years older than I, and his case was serious.

*   *   *   *   *

For me the days passed very slowly, but not without some enlivening diversions. A gentleman, Mr. Thomson, kindly presented me with a lion, who sent me a beautiful photograph of himself, with good wishes for my recovery. "Rota" was the lion's name, and I had to invoke the aid of the Duke of Devonshire, who had been Mr. Thomson's intermediary, to provide him with a home. He was a male lion of fine quality, and in eight years became the father of many children. The assistant secretary, who had been with me in the airplane, came with some papers. He was a charming man, highly competent, but physically on the small side. Indulging in chaff, I now showed him a magnificent photograph of Rota with his mouth open, saying, "If there are any shortcomings in your work I shall send you to him. Meat is very short now." He took a serious view of this remark. He reported to the office that I was in a delirium.

To the Duke I wrote:

I shall have much pleasure in becoming the possessor of the lion, on condition that I do not have to feed it or take care of it, and that the Zoo makes sure that it does not get loose.

You are quite right in your assumption that I do not want the lion at the moment either at Downing Street or at Chequers, owing to the Ministerial calm which prevails there. But the Zoo is not far away, and situations may arise in which I shall have great need of it.

I hope to come to see the lion some time when the weather is better, also my black swans.

I consider you personally bound to receive the lion at Chatsworth should all else fail.

*   *   *   *   *

Soon President Roosevelt, General Smuts, and other friends who had heard about my illness sent repeated telegrams urging me to obey the doctor's orders, and I kept faithfully to my agreement. When I finished *Moll Flanders* I gave it to Doctor Marshall to cheer him up. The treatment was successful.

About this time also there arrived from the President a portrait of an American general named Sylvester Churchill, who had died in 1862 and was undoubtedly a direct descendant of the Dorsetshire Churchills. His pedigree was attached to the photograph. The President thought we looked very much alike.

THE WHITE HOUSE
WASHINGTON
March 2, 1943

Dear Winston,

When you and the family have a spare minute give this a glance. It needs no reply. I do think, however, that Mrs. Harrison is right in regard to a certain resemblance. She is the wife of our Minister to Switzerland.

As ever yours

FRANKLIN D. ROOSEVELT

[*Enclosure*]

27 Feb. 43

Dear Mr. President,

I am sending you a photograph of a portrait which I have of our great-great-grandfather, General Sylvester Churchill.[3]

[3] GENERAL SYLVESTER CHURCHILL

Born Woodstock, Vermont, 1783.
Died Washington, D.C., 1862.

General Churchill was a Captain of Infantry in the War of 1812, a Colonel in the Mexican War in 1846, and was credited with having won the Battle of Buena Vista, in which, assuming command, he "saved the whole army from disaster and won the victory." For this he was promoted to Brigadier-General by brevet. Until 1856 he was Inspector-General of the Army, and travelled over 10,000 miles a year inspecting frontier posts. He was retired in 1856, and died in Washington in 1862.

CHURCHILLS of
Dorsetshire
|
JOHN CHURCHILL,
London.
(Merchant,
supplying
Geo. Endicott of
the Mass. Bay
Colony.)
|

JOHN CHURCHILL
Born England. Emigrated to
Plymouth, Mass., in 1642. Died 1662.
|
JOSEPH CHURCHILL
Born Plymonth, Mass., 1647.
|
BARNABAS CHURCHILL
Born Plymouth, Mass., 1686.
|
JOSEPH CHURCHILL
Born Plymouth, Mass., 1721.
|
JOSEPH CHURCHILL
Born Plymouth, Mass., 1748.
|
SYLVESTER CHURCHILL
Born Woodstock, Vermont, 1783.
Died Washingtor., D.C., 1862.

So many people who see it in my house, without knowing his
name, exclaim, "Why, there is Winston Churchill!" and I reply,
"He was a Churchill, an *American one!*" They are very interested.
Thinking you might be so too, Mr. President, I had the portrait
photographed, and here it is.

I replied:

Former Naval Person to President Roosevelt   19 Mar. 43

Thank you so much for your letter of March 2. I have shown
the photograph and Mrs. Harrison's letter to Mrs. Churchill, and
we are both much interested in them. Would you please thank
Mrs. Harrison so much for letting us see the photograph?

Several good judges think there is a singular resemblance.

*   *   *   *   *

Although the speed of the advance from the east had surpassed expectations, the Allied situation in mid-February was
anxious. The severe losses inflicted by sea and air had not
prevented the enemy from building up a force of fourteen
divisions, including those of Rommel's army. Most of the Germans came in by air. Four divisions, three German and one
Italian, were armoured. The Allies had only nine divisions
available for operation, of which two of the French XIXth Corps
were ill-equipped. The U.S. IId Corps was still incomplete; of
its four divisions only the 1st Infantry and 1st Armoured Division were on the front. The northern sector from the sea to
Bou Arada,[4] was held by the British Vth Corps, of three divisions. On their right was the French XIXth Corps, composed
of one French division, the 1st U.S. Infantry Division, and two
British brigades. This corps held the passes of the mountainous
ridge overlooking the coastal plain. Farther south the line was
continued by the U.S. IId Corps, comprising the U.S. 1st
Armoured Division and a French division, with another U.S.
infantry division assembling. These also were spread to hold
the passes on their front, with the important exception of the
Faid Pass, which the Germans had captured on January 30.

[4] See Map, "Setback in the Desert, 1942," page 32.

Rommel, promoted to command all the Axis troops in Tunisia, concentrated a striking force of two German armoured divisions east of Faid in order to throw back the U.S. IId Corps and prevent them from coming down on his flank and rear while he was engaged against the Eighth Army. The attack began on February 14. It had been mistakenly expected that the main blow would come through Fondouk and not Faid. Consequently the 1st U.S. Armoured Division, under General Anderson's orders, was much dispersed; only half of it was south of Fondouk to take the shock. It was overborne and there was much confusion. On the 17th Kasserine, Feriana, and Sbeitla were in German hands.

Rommel now had a choice: he could advance through the Kasserine Pass on Tebessa, a main centre of communications, with the important airfield of Youks-les-Bains behind it, or strike northward. He struck northward and was met and held by the 1st Guards Brigade and a detachment of the U.S. 9th Division, which Anderson had hastened there. On the Thala road the 21st Panzer Division, which led the attack, encountered our 26th Armoured Brigade and two British battalions, together with American infantry and artillery. A fierce fight ensued, but by noon on the 22d Rommel began a general withdrawal. It was carried out in good order. Kasserine and Feriana were reoccupied by our forces on February 27 and Sbeitla on the 28th. Later our original line was re-established. But Rommel had not yet finished his aggressive attempts to retain at least a foothold in Tunisia. On February 26 he began a series of strong attacks on the front of the British Vth Corps. South of Medjez the enemy were repulsed without significant gains; to the north they won several miles, leaving the town itself in an awkward salient. Near the coast our troops were forced back twenty miles to Djebel Abiod, but at this point they held firm.

* * * * *

I now received a letter from the King, who followed the course of the war with the closest attention, and was not without anxiety on some aspects of it.

My dear Winston,

I am very sorry to hear that you are ill, and I hope that you will
soon be well again. But do please take this opportunity for a rest,
and I trust you will not forget that you have earned one after your
last tour, and you must get back your strength for the strenuous
coming months. I missed being able to have a talk to you last
Tuesday, and I understand we may not meet next Tuesday either,
so I am writing to you instead.

I do not feel at all happy about the present political situation
in North Africa. I know we had to leave the political side of
"Torch" to the Americans, while we were able to keep Spain and
Portugal friendly during the time the operation was going on.
I know we had to tread warily at the start, but is there nothing we
can do now to strengthen Macmillan's and Alexander's hands in
both the political and military sphere, to make the two French
sides come together?

Now I hear that from the American point of view the date of
"Husky" will have to be postponed to the later one, whereas we
can plan for the earlier one, which will be an aggravation of our
difficulties in preparing the operation.

This fact will throw out all our careful calculations for convoys
and escorts, and will upset our import programme again. I should
not think of bothering you with these questions at this moment,
but I do feel worried about them, and I would like an assurance
from you that they are being carefully watched.

I cannot discuss these vital matters with anyone but yourself.

> Believe me,
> Yours very sincerely,
> GEORGE R.I.

I replied forthwith, and once I began dictating it seemed
easy to cover the ground.

February 22, 1943

Sir,

It is very good of Your Majesty to write with your own hand
to me.

I do not feel seriously disturbed by the course of events in North
Africa, either political or even military, although naturally there
is much about both aspects which I would rather have different.

I have been reading all the key telegrams with attention up till two days ago, when I must admit I have fallen a little behind. I am sure that Murphy's aim is to uphold Giraud and to procure a quiet, tranquil Government for the sixteen million people living in French North Africa. In this way alone would he gain any credit. It is quite true that we have for this purpose and to safeguard our vital communications to work with a mass of French officials who were appointed by Vichy; but without them I really do not know how the country could be governed. Even in Syria we have done this to some extent. I do not myself see any danger of these officials changing their sides or obstructing our operation. Their own bread and butter depends upon their good behaviour, and possibly their lives as well.

The irruption of de Gaulle or his agents into this field, especially if forcibly introduced by us, would cause nothing but trouble. It is entirely his fault that a good arrangement was not made between the two French factions. The roughness with which he refused the President's invitation (and mine) to come and make a friendly settlement at Casablanca put him and his French National Committee practically out of court with the Americans.

As I told Your Majesty the last time we met, I tried all I could to bring the operation "Husky" forward to June. In this I was splendidly seconded by the Chiefs of Staff and all concerned. General Eisenhower however expressed a decided opinion that a June operation would be "unlikely to succeed," and was for July at the earliest. Our Chiefs of Staff therefore sent their paper to the Combined Chiefs of Staff in Washington, and I also telegraphed to Hopkins asking him to put this through, with the result that, according to my latest information, the Combined Chiefs of Staff — who are the supreme and official body through which command is exercised — have ordered General Eisenhower to prepare for the June operation with the utmost zeal, and to report to them by April 10 what progress has been made. Thus you see the American Chiefs of Staff took the same view as ours did, and, if I may say so, as I did. That is how the matter stands now.

As to the battle, I suspend judgment till we hear from Alexander. The IId American Army Corps sustained a heavy defeat, and apparently was deprived of about half its important weapons without inflicting any serious loss upon the enemy. However, we have about six of our finest infantry brigade groups and the 6th Armoured Division as well as a brigade of heavy Churchill tanks there. More are on the way. The supplies have come in better. Already the 1st Guards Brigade have come into action at Sbeitla, and have made the enemy feel that they have come up against bone.

In order to make this new offensive, not foreseen in their original plan, the enemy have stripped the Mareth Line pretty thin. Montgomery, who has the whole picture before him, and who has been receiving splendid daily deliveries in Tripoli harbour as well as from Benghazi, sometimes reaching a total of six thousand tons from the two ports together, will soon be able to bring the Xth Corps up, whose transport he has had to use to maintain himself so far and to build up reserves. I look forward to both the Xth and XXXth Corps being in action in Tunisia by the middle of March, or it may be earlier. Nevertheless, matters may not wait so long, because if Montgomery feels the enemy is wilting on his front he will certainly use his strength against them.

I suppose Your Majesty realises that these two corps of the Eighth Army, comprising together about 160,000 men, are perhaps the best troops in the world. Therefore I look confidently forward to their entry into action. Moreover, we have General Alexander under Eisenhower to concert and combine the entire movements. It may well be that the enemy is wasting strength on a false assumption and will give Montgomery an earlier chance.

I need scarcely say that no word of mine is intended in disparagement of the Americans. They are brave but not seasoned troops, who will not hesitate to learn from defeat, and who will improve themselves by suffering until all their strongest martial qualities have come to the front. What a providential thing it was that I perpetually pressed for General Eisenhower to take the command, as the defeat of the American corps, if it had been under a British general, would have given our enemies in the United States a good chance to blaspheme.

Generally I feel we may await with reasonable confidence the development of the situation in North Africa, and I look forward to an improvement before long.

Although I have been hampered by fever from reading all the telegrams, I think I have the picture truly in my mind, and I wish indeed that I could have given this account to Your Majesty verbally at luncheon. I send this instead.

                                        With my humble duty
                                        WINSTON S. CHURCHILL

                        *   *   *   *   *

The Tripoli tonnage rate mounted magnificently. I tele-

graphed to the Port Commandant on the 24th: "Tell them
from me they are unloading history."

From what I read in the boxes, which kept a steady, though
diminished flow, I formed an unfavourable picture of the manner in which the British First Army had been handled in the
severe battle which had developed in Tunisia.

Prime Minister to General Alexander   24 Feb. 43

About Christmas time all ideas of offensive were given up in the
First Army, and for the last two months every effort has been made
to push supplies forward and bring up reinforcements. It is quite
true the French falling out of the line was a complication, but the
Americans came in in large force. However, these same Americans
came under Anderson's command, and were spread about by him
or someone over a large, loosely held line in bits and pieces as you
yourself describe. There was no proper spirit or knowledge of what
was going on in the First Army. They were very much in the
condition of the Eighth Army when you and Monty took over.
It might have been wise to withdraw the line in the south to the
hills, but neither a vigorous front was made nor a prudent withdrawal. Before the attack took place our Intelligence gave ample
warning. Even then a withdrawal would have been very sensible.
Nobody cared about these places, whose names they had never
heard of till they were lost. A kind of false-front manoeuvre might
have been very clever, but there was none of this, with the result
that the American IId Army Corps was left to be mauled, and took
it very badly under the attack of the 150 enemy tanks set against
them.

2. The situation has now been restored, but the past must be
searchingly reviewed. I am relying upon you and your judgment,
feeling sure that you will not shield incompetence or inadequacy.

3. I am so glad to read that the much-abused Churchills acquitted themselves well. Of course my main idea in them was
armour, and I believe they can take a lot of punishment. Any
information you can send or have sent by one of your officers would
interest me.

4. I have been free of the fever for a few hours today, and I
hope this is the beginning of recovery from a very disagreeable
experience. Every good wish to you. I am sure you have in
your hands now all the threads necessary to bring about a very

fine event before the middle of April. How glad I am you are there! The unloadings at Tripoli are splendid. Please keep me informed.

To Mr. Harry Hopkins   24 Feb. 43

Have had a bad time, and might easily have been worse. Am feeling definitely better now. I think the Tunis battle is good, and going to be better; and our men, British and American, are fighting like brothers, mingled together and side by side. A reward lies ahead of them all. Tripoli unloaded 6300 tons yesterday. Montgomery is sharpening his claws.

Thank you so much for helping to get the target date [for Sicily] settled for June. None of this recent fighting should affect it, though some will try to say so.

My warmest regards to the President.

To General Eisenhower (Algiers)   25 Feb. 43

Thank you so much for your kind message. I was sure the Kasserine battle would turn out all right in the end.

It was now the President's turn to be laid up.

Former Naval Person to President Roosevelt   27 Feb. 43

I do hope you are all right and that the fever will soon go. I have got rid of mine, which was heavy and long, I hope for good. Every good wish.

*   *   *   *   *

While I was myself hard-pressed I had to think deeply about the health of another invalid whose bulletins filled the papers. Several hundred Indian Congress members had been arrested and interned by the Viceroy, with the full authority of the War Cabinet, given during my absence in Cairo. Early in February Mr. Gandhi announced he would fast for three weeks. He was in detention under the most favourable conditions in a small palace at Poona, watched with ceaseless vigilance both by British and his own Indian doctors. He continued obdurately to fast, and most active world-wide propaganda was set on foot that his death was approaching. It was certain however at an early stage that he was being fed with glucose whenever he drank water, and this, as well as his intense vitality and lifelong austerity, enabled this frail being to maintain his prolonged abstention from any visible form of food. Nearly all the Indian members of the Viceroy's Executive Council demanded his release, and resigned in protest at our refusal. In the end, being quite convinced of our obduracy, he abandoned his fast, and his health, though he was very weak, was not seriously affected.

I kept the President fully informed throughout, and no pressure was put upon us from the United States. The incident was one which at the time caused me much anxiety, because Mr. Gandhi's death could have produced a profound impression throughout India, where his saintly qualities commanded intense admiration. We however had judged the situation rightly.

* * * * *

Stalin at this time sent me a film of the Stalingrad victory with all its desperate fighting wonderfully portrayed, and with the final surrender of Field-Marshal Paulus and his appearance before the Soviet court-martial. The Russian Government treated this important German war chief with the greatest consideration, and he has been in their service ever since. A less agreeable fate awaited the endless lines of German prisoners, whom the film shows marching wearily forward over the limitless wastes of snow.

I had a cinema installed near my bedroom, and was able to go from my bed to see it about February 24. It was a production of the highest merit, and well commemorates this glorious episode in the struggle on the Eastern Front. I was able in return to send to Stalin, to the President, and to the Dominions Governments our own film, just completed, of the Battle of Alamein, called *Desert Victory*. These photographs, like the Russian, were all taken by the operators under heavy fire and at some loss of life. The sacrifice was not made in vain, for the fruits of their work excited the greatest admiration and enthusiasm throughout the Allied world and brought us all closer together in our common task.

To the President, who was still ailing, I wrote:

Former Naval Person to President Roosevelt

I hope you will accept the accompanying copy of the new film *Desert Victory,* which I saw last night and thought very good. It gives a vivid and realistic picture of the battles, and I know that you will be interested in the photographs of the Sherman tanks in action. I am having the film sent to you by air so that you may see it as soon as possible.

I was so sorry to see that you have been ill, and I hope that you have fully recovered. I am feeling very much better, and hope soon to return to full work.

With kindest regards, and all best wishes to Mrs. Roosevelt, Harry, and yourself . . .

The President replied:

17 Mai. 43

Dear Winston,

That new film *Desert Victory* is about the best thing that has been done about the war on either side. Everyone here is enthusiastic. I gave a special showing for the White House staff, and to-night the Interior Department employees are having a special showing, because everybody in town is talking about it; and I understand that within ten days it will be in the picture houses. Great good will be done.

I think I picked up sleeping sickness or Gambia fever or some kindred bug in that hell-hole of yours called Bathurst. It laid me low — four days in bed — then a lot of sulphathiazole, which cured the fever and left me feeling like a wet rag. I was no good after 2 P.M., and after standing it for a week or so I went to Hyde Park for five days; got full of health in glorious zero weather — came back here last week, and have been feeling like a fighting cock ever since.

Anthony has spent three evenings with me. He is a grand fellow, and we are talking everything, from Ruthenia to the production of peanuts!

It is an interesting fact that we seem to agree on about ninety-five per cent of all the subjects — not a bad average.

He seems to think that you will manage rather well with the Leadership in the House of Commons — but both of us are concerned over what you will do with the Foreign Office! We fear that he will not recognise it when he gets back.

Please, please, for the sake of the world, don't overdo these days. You must remember that it takes about a month of occasional let-ups to get back your full strength.

Harry is in grand form and all goes well here.

Tell Mrs. Churchill that when I was laid up I was a thoroughly model patient, and that I hope you will live down the reputation in our press of having been the "world's worst patient."

God bless you.

18

Russia and the Western Allies

THE SPRING of 1943 marked the turning-point of the war on the Eastern Front. Even before the German Army at Stalingrad had been overwhelmed the mounting Russian tide had swept the enemy back all along the line. The German army of the Caucasus was skilfully withdrawn, half of it to Rostov; the rest formed strong bridgeheads at Novorossisk and in the Kuban peninsula. The Russians pressed the enemy from the Don and back beyond the Donetz River, the starting line of Hitler's offensive of the previous summer. Farther north again the Germans lost ground until they were more than two hundred and fifty miles from Moscow. The investment of Leningrad was broken. The Germans and their satellites suffered immense losses in men and material. The ground

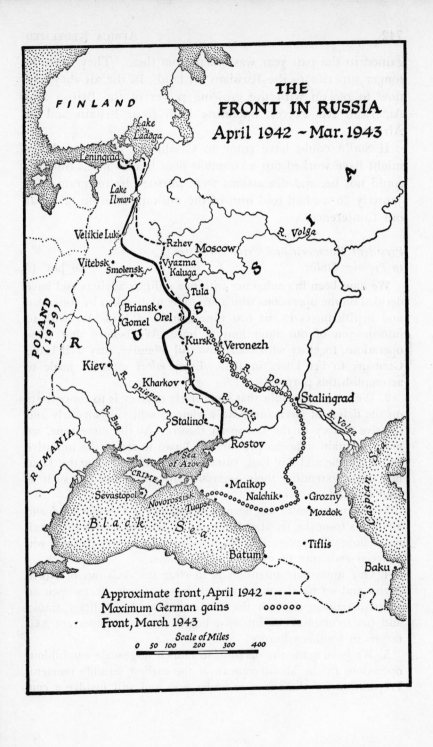

THE
FRONT IN RUSSIA
April 1942 ~ Mar. 1943

FINLAND

Lake Ladoga

Leningrad

Lake Ilman

R. Volga

Velikie Luki

Rzhev Moscow

Vitebsk Smolensk Vyazma
Kaluga

POLAND (1939)

Briansk Tula

Gomel Orel

Kursk Veronezh

Kiev

R. Dnieper Kharkov R. Don

R. Bug R. Donetz Stalingrad

Stalino R. Volga

RUMANIA Rostov

Sea of Azov

CRIMEA Maikop
Nalchik Grozny

Sevastopol Novorossisk Mozdok
Tuapse

Black Sea Tiflis

Batum Caspian Sea

Baku

Approximate front, April 1942 - - - -
Maximum German gains ooooooo
Front, March 1943 ▬▬▬▬

Scale of Miles
0 50 100 200 300 400

gained in the past year was taken from them. They were no longer superior to the Russians on land. In the air they had now to reckon with the growing power of the British and American Air Forces, operating both from Britain and in Africa.

If Stalin could have come to Casablanca the three Allies might have worked out a common plan face to face. But this could not be, and discussions were pursued by telegram. On January 26 we had told him of the military decision taken at our Conference.

President Roosevelt and Prime Minister
to Premier Stalin   26 Jan. 43

We have been in conference with our military advisers and have decided on the operations which are to be undertaken by American and British forces in the first nine months of 1943. We wish to inform you of our intentions at once. We believe that these operations, together with your powerful offensive, may well bring Germany to her knees in 1943. Every effort must be made to accomplish this purpose.

2. We are in no doubt that our correct strategy is to concentrate on the defeat of Germany, with a view to achieving an early and decisive victory in the European theatre. At the same time, we must maintain sufficient pressure on Japan to retain the initiative in the Pacific and Far East, sustain China, and prevent the Japanese from extending their aggression to other theatres, such as your maritime provinces.

3. Our main desire has been to divert strong German land and air forces from the Russian front and to send to Russia the maximum flow of supplies. We shall spare no exertion to send you material assistance by every available route.

4. Our immediate intention is to clear the Axis out of North Africa and set up the naval and air installations: (i) to open an effective passage through the Mediterranean for military traffic; and (ii) to maintain an intensive bombardment of important Axis targets in Southern Europe.

5. We have made the decision to launch large-scale amphibious operations in the Mediterranean at the earliest possible moment. Preparation for these is now under way and will involve a con-

siderable concentration of forces, including landing-craft and shipping in Egyptian and North African ports.

In addition, we shall concentrate in the United Kingdom a strong American land and air force. These, combined with the British forces in the United Kingdom, will prepare themselves to re-enter the continent of Europe as soon as practicable. All this will certainly be known to our enemies, but they will not know where or when, or on what scale, we propose striking. They will therefore be compelled to divert both land and air forces to all the shores of France, the Low Countries, Corsica, Sardinia, Sicily, the heel of Italy, Yugoslavia, Greece, Crete, and the Dodecanese.

6. In Europe we shall increase the Allied bomber offensive from the United Kingdom against Germany at a rapid rate and by mid-summer it should be more than double its present strength. Our experiences to date have shown that the day bombing attacks result in destruction and damage to large numbers of German fighter aircraft. We believe an increased tempo and weight of daylight and night attacks will lead to greatly increased material and morale damage in Germany and rapidly deplete German fighter strength. As you are aware, we are already containing more than half the German air force in Western Europe and the Mediterranean. We have no doubt our intensified and diversified bombing offensive, together with the other operations which we are undertaking, will compel further withdrawals of German air and other forces from the Russian front.

7. In the Pacific it is our intention to eject the Japanese from Rabaul within the next few months and thereafter to exploit the success in the general direction of Japan. We also intend to increase the scale of our operations in Burma in order to reopen our channel of supply to China. We intend to increase our air force in China at once. We shall not, however, allow our offensives against Japan to jeopardise our capacity to take advantage of every opportunity that may present itself for the decisive defeat of Germany in 1943.

8. Our ruling purpose is to bring to bear upon Germany and Italy the maximum forces by land, sea, and air which can be physically applied.

And further, on my return home, with the President's authority, I sent the following additional explanation:

(*a*) There are a quarter of a million Germans and Italians in Eastern Tunisia. We hope to destroy or expel these during April, if not earlier.

(*b*) When this is accomplished we intend in July, or earlier if possible, to seize Sicily, with the object of clearing the Mediterranean, promoting an Italian collapse, with the consequent effect on Greece and Yugoslavia, and wearing down the German Air Force. This is to be closely followed by an operation in the Eastern Mediterranean, probably against the Dodecanese.

(*c*) This operation will involve all the shipping and landing-craft we can get together in the Mediterranean, and all the troops we can have trained in assault-landing, and will be of the order of 300,000 or 400,000 men. We shall press any advantage to the utmost once ports of entry and landing bases have been established.

(*d*) We are also pushing preparations to the limit of our resources for a cross-Channel operation in August, in which both British and United States units would participate. Here again shipping and assault landing-craft will be limiting factors. If the operation is delayed by weather or other reasons it will be prepared with stronger forces for September. The timing of this attack must of course be dependent upon the condition of German defensive possibilities across the Channel at that time.

(*e*) Both the operations will be supported by very large United States and British air forces, and that across the Channel by the whole Metropolitan Air Force of Great Britain. Together these operations will strain to the very utmost the shipping resources of Great Britain and the United States.

(*f*) The President and I have enjoined upon our Combined Chiefs of Staff the need for the utmost speed and for reinforcing the attacks to the extreme limit that is humanly and physically possible.

And a few days later.

Prime Minister to Premier Stalin   14 Feb. 43
The series of prodigious victories which tonight brings us the news of the liberation of Rostov-on-the-Don leaves me without power to express to you the admiration and gratitude which we feel to the Russian arms. My most earnest wish is to do more to aid you.

He replied promptly:

Premier Stalin to Premier Churchill   16 Feb. 43

I received your message concerning the contemplated Anglo-American military operations on February 12. Many thanks for your additional information on the Casablanca decisions. I cannot refrain however from making certain observations on your message, which, as you state, represents also the view-point of the President.

2. It is evident from your message that, contrary to your previous calculations, the end of operations in Tunis is expected in April instead of February. I hardly need to tell you how disappointing is such a delay. Strong activity of the Anglo-American troops in North Africa is more than ever necessary at this moment, when the Soviet armies are still in a position to maintain their powerful general offensive. With simultaneous pressure on Hitler from our front and from your side we could achieve great results. Such a situation would create serious difficulties for Hitler and Mussolini. In this way the intended operations in Sicily and the Eastern Mediterranean could be expedited.

3. It is evident from your message also that the establishment of the second front, in particular in France, is envisaged only in August-September. It seems to me that the present situation demands the greatest possible speeding up of the action contemplated — i.e., of the opening of the second front in the West at a considerably earlier date than indicated. In order not to give enemy any respite it is extremely important to deliver the blow from the West in the spring or in the early summer and not to postpone it until the second half of the year.

4. We have reliable information to the effect that since the end of December, when the Anglo-American operations in Tunis for some reason were slowed down, the Germans transferred twenty-seven divisions, including five Panzer divisions, from France, Belgium, Holland, and Germany herself to the Soviet-German front. Thus, instead of helping the Soviet Union by diversion of the German forces from the Soviet-German front, the position of Hitler was alleviated. It is just because the military operations in Tunis slackened that Hitler was able to throw in some additional troops against the Russians.

5. All this brings us to the conclusion that the sooner we jointly

take advantage of Hitler's difficulties at the front the more reasons
we shall have to expect his early defeat. Unless we take all this
into consideration, unless we use the present moment to our common interest, it may happen that the Germans, after having a
respite, which will enable them to remuster their forces, may once
more recover their strength. It is clear to every one of us how
undesirable it would be to allow this to occur.

I deemed it necessary to send this reply also to Mr. Roosevelt.

Many thanks for your very warm congratulations on the liberation of Rostov. Our troops today captured Kharkov.

This message reached me during my illness.

Prime Minister to Premier Stalin   24 Feb. 43

I much regret I have not been able to answer your last telegram
to me. I had the answer all in draft, but my fever got so high that
I thought it better to leave it for a while. In a few days I hope to
send you more information on the whole scene. Meanwhile what
you are doing is simply indescribable. The battle in Tunisia is
all right. The enemy have shot their bolt and will now be brought
into the grip of the vice. Every good wish.

The President sent me on March 5 a copy of his own reply
to Stalin:

I have received your message of February 16, in which you present certain considerations that you have communicated to Mr.
Chuchill in reply to his message to you of February 12.

I regret equally with you that the Allied effort in North Africa
did not proceed in accordance with the schedule, which was interrupted by unexpected heavy rains that made the roads extremely
difficult for both troops and supplies *en route* from our landing
ports to the front lines, and made the fields and mountains impassable.

I realise fully the adverse effect of this delay on the common
Allied effort, and I am taking every possible step to begin at the
earliest possible moment successful aggressive action against the
Axis forces in Africa with the purpose of accomplishing their
destruction.

You are fully informed in regard to the wide dispersion of American transportation facilities at the present time, and I can assure

you that we are making a maximum effort to increase the output of ships to improve our transportation.

I understand the importance of a military effort on the continent of Europe at the earliest practicable date in order to reduce Axis resistance to your heroic army, and you may be sure that the American war effort will be projected on to the continent of Europe at as early a date, subsequent to success in North Africa, as transportation facilities can be provided by our maximum effort.

We hope that the success of your heroic army, which is an inspiration to all of us, will continue.

* * * *

I thought it right to present our whole case in my own words.

Prime Minister to Premier Stalin   11 Mar. 43

Mr. Roosevelt has sent me a copy of his reply to your full message of February 16. I am now well enough to reply myself.

2. Our first task is to clear the Axis out of North Africa by an operation the code-name of which is "Vulcan." We hope this will be accomplished towards the end of April, by which time about a million Axis troops will be engaged by us. . . .

5. The Anglo-American attempt to get Tunis and Bizerta at a run was abandoned in December because of the strength of the enemy, the impending rainy season, the already sodden character of the ground, and the fact that the communications stretched 500 miles from Algiers and 160 miles from Bone through bad roads and a week of travelling over single-track French railways. It was only possible to get supplies up to the Army by sea on a small scale owing to the strength of the enemy air and submarine attack. Thus it was not possible to accumulate the petrol or other supplies in the forward areas. Indeed, it was only just possible to nourish the troops already there. The same was true of the air, and improvised airfields became quagmires. When we stopped attacking there were about 40,000 Germans in Tunisia, apart from Italians and from Rommel, who was still in Tripoli. The German force in North Tunisia is now more than double that figure, and they are rushing over every man they can in transport aircraft and destroyers. Some sharp local reverses were suffered towards the end of last month, but the position has now been restored. We hope that the delays

caused by this setback will be repaired by the earlier advance of Montgomery's army, which should have six divisions (say 200,000 men) operating from Tripoli with sufficient supplies against the Mareth position before the end of March. Already on March 6 Montgomery's army repulsed Rommel's forestalling attack with heavy losses. The British and American army in the northern sector of Tunisia will act in combination with Montgomery's battle.

6. I thought that you would like to know these details of the story, although it is on a small scale compared with the tremendous operations over which you are presiding.

7. The British Staffs estimate that about half the number of divisions which were sent to the Soviet-German front from France and the Low Countries since last November have already been replaced mainly by divisions from Russia and Germany and partly by new divisions formed in France. They estimate that at the present time there are thirty German divisions in France and the Low Countries.

8. I am anxious that you should know, for your own most secret information, exactly what our military resources are for an attack upon Europe across the Mediterranean or the Channel. By far the larger part of the British Army is in North Africa, in the Middle East, and in India, and there is no physical possibility of moving it back by sea to the British Islands. By the end of April we shall have about 200,000 men, in Northern Tunisia, in addition to General Montgomery's army of some six divisions, and we are bringing two specially trained British divisions from Persia and sending one from this country to reinforce them for Sicily, a total of fourteen. We have four mobile British divisions, the two Polish divisions, one Free French division, and one Greek division in the Middle East. There is the equivalent of four static divisions in Gibraltar, Malta, and Cyprus. Apart from garrison and frontier troops, there are ten or twelve divisions formed and forming in India for reconquering Burma after the monsoon and reopening contact with China (Operation "Anakim"). Thus we have under the British command, spread across a distance of some 6300 miles from Gibraltar to Calcutta, thirty-eight divisions, including strong armour and powerful proportionate air forces. For all these forces active and definite tasks are assigned for 1943.

9. The gross strength of a British division, including corps, army, and line of communication troops, may be estimated at about

40,000 men. There remain in the United Kingdom about nineteen formed divisions, four Home Defence divisions, and four drafting divisions, of which sixteen are being prepared for a cross-Channel operation in August. You must remember that our total population is forty-six millions, and that the first charge upon it is the Royal Navy and Mercantile Marine, without which we could not live. Thereafter come our very large Air Force, about twelve hundred thousand strong, and the needs of munitions, agriculture, and air-raid defence. Thus the entire manhood and womanhood of the country is and has been for some time fully absorbed.

10. The United States had the idea in July last to send twenty-seven divisions, of a gross strength each of between forty and fifty thousand men, to the United Kingdom for the invasion of France. Since then they have sent seven divisions to the Operation "Torch," and three more are to go. In this country there is now only one, in addition to a strong air force. This is no disparagement of the American effort. The reason why these performances have fallen so far short of the expectations of last year is not that the troops do not exist, but that the shipping at our disposal and the means of escorting it do not exist. There is in fact no prospect whatever of bringing anything more than I have mentioned into the United Kingdom in the period concerned. . . .

After a paragraph describing the bombing offensive against Germany I ended:

12. With regard to the attack across the Channel, it is the earnest wish of the President and myself that our troops should be in the general battle in Europe which you are fighting with such astounding prowess. But in order to sustain the operations in North Africa, the Pacific, and India, and to carry supplies to Russia, the import programme into the United Kingdom has been cut to the bone and we have eaten, and are eating, into reserves. However, in case the enemy should weaken sufficiently we are preparing to strike earlier than August, and plans are kept alive from week to week. If he does not weaken, a premature attack with inferior and insufficient forces would merely lead to a bloody repulse, Nazi vengeance on the local population if they rose, and a great triumph for the enemy. The Channel situation can only be judged nearer the time, and in making this declaration of our intentions there for your

own personal information I must not be understood to limit our freedom of decision.

* * * * *

It was clear that the most effective aid which we could offer the Russians was the speedy clearing of the Axis forces from North Africa and the stepping up of the air war against Germany. Stalin of course repeated his demands for a second front.

Premier Stalin to Premier Churchill   15 Mar. 43

It is evident that the Anglo-American operations in North Africa have not only not been expedited, but on the contrary they have been postponed till the end of April. Even this date is not quite definite. Thus at the height of our fighting against the Hitler forces — i.e., in February-March — the weight of the Anglo-American offensive in North Africa has not only not increased, but there has been no development of the offensive at all, and the limit for the operations set by yourself was extended. Meanwhile Germany succeeded in transferring thirty-six divisions (including six armoured divisions) from the West against the Soviet troops. It is easy to see what difficulties this created for the Soviet armies and how the position of the Germans on the Soviet-German front was alleviated.

Fully realising the importance of Sicily, I must however point out that it cannot replace the second front in France. Still I welcome by all means the contemplated acceleration of this operation.

Now as before I see the main task in hastening of the second front in France. As you remember, you admitted the possibility of such a front already in 1942, and in any case not later than the spring of 1943. There were serious reasons for such an admission. Naturally enough I underlined in my previous message the necessity of the blow from the West not later than the spring or the early summer of this year.

The Soviet troops spent the whole winter in the tense fighting which continues even now. Hitler is carrying out important measures with a view to replenish and increase his army for the spring and summer operations against the U.S.S.R. In these circumstances it is for us extremely important that the blow from the West should not be put off, that it should be struck in the spring or in the early summer.

I studied your observations, contained in the paragraphs 8, 9, and 10, on the difficulties of the Anglo-American operations in Europe. I recognise these difficulties. Notwithstanding all that, I deem it my duty to warn you in the strongest possible manner how dangerous would be from the view-point of our common cause further delay in the opening of the second front in France. This is the reason why the uncertainty of your statements concerning the contemplated Anglo-American offensive across the Channel arouses grave anxiety in me, about which I feel I cannot be silent.

* * * * *

At this time the Russian Government, doubtless as a result of their successful spring offensive against the Germans, had been sounding both the British and American Foreign Offices upon the post-war arrangements on Russia's western frontier. American opinion was sensitive to any suggestion of recognising the Russian position in the Baltic States, and the cause of Finland had considerable support in Washington. The Russians had refused an American offer of mediation between Finland and the Soviet Union with the object of drawing the Finns out of the war.

Premier Stalin to Premier Churchill 15 Mar. 43

On March 12 the American Ambassador, Admiral Standley, on behalf of the U.S.A. Government, conveyed to Mr. Molotov the following message:

"The Government of the U.S.A. offers its good offices as intermediary between the U.S.S.R. and Finland in order to explore the possibility of a separate peace."

On Mr. Molotov's question whether the American Government has information that Finland desires peace and what is her real position, Admiral Standley replied that he cannot say anything on the matter. As is well known, the Anglo-Soviet Treaty of May 26, 1942, stipulates that our countries cannot negotiate on the conclusion of a separate peace with Germany or her Allies otherwise than by mutual agreement. I consider this as a fundamental and unalterable principle. In view of this I felt it is my duty first to inform you about the American proposal and second to ask your opinion on the matter.

I have no reasons to believe that Finland really desires peace, that she has decided already to part with Germany and to offer acceptable conditions. It seems to me that Finland has not yet escaped from Hitler's claws, if she has this intention at all. The present Finnish Government, which concluded a peace treaty with the Soviet Union and then violated it and attacked the Soviet Union in alliance with Germany, is hardly able to break with Hitler.

Notwithstanding all that, in view of the proposal made by the Government of the U.S.A., I deemed it my duty to inform you of the above.

To this I sent the following answer:

Prime Minister to Premier Stalin 20 Mar. 43

You can best judge of how much military value it would be in the struggle against the Germans on your front to get Finland out of the war. I should suppose that it would have the effect of releasing more Soviet divisions than German divisions for use elsewhere. Further, the defection of Finland from the Axis might have considerable effect on Hitler's other satellites.

Generally speaking, I should have thought that the Finns would be anxious to withdraw from the war as soon as they are convinced that Germany must be defeated. If so, it seems to me that it might not be altogether premature for you to ask the United States Government whether they know or could find out, without disclosing your interest, what terms the Finns would be prepared to accept. But you will be the best judge of the right tactics.

* * * *

Our plans for Sicily strained our shipping resources to the point where it might be necessary to postpone the convoys to Russia. We consulted the Americans on this, through Mr. Eden who was still in Washington.

Mr. Eden to Prime Minister 19 Mar. 43

I saw the President this morning and gave him your message about Russian convoys. He agrees that in the light of enemy dispositions it is right to postpone the March convoy. He was doubtful however whether it would be wise now to decide on no further convoy until after Sicily. He felt that this would be a severe additional blow to Stalin, and that if the enemy concentrations were to disperse, for whatever reason, within the next few weeks, we might still be in a position to run a convoy. He will however think the whole matter over further and send you a personal message very shortly.

2. The President has had a message from Stalin similar to your rough one. This he had apparently anticipated.

This came the next day:

President Roosevelt to Former Naval Person   20 Mar. 43
Your message of March 18.

In the face of known German naval and Air Force concentration on route of March convoy there appears to be no military justification for its departure at scheduled time. . . . In another three or four weeks it may of course be necessary to break the news to Stalin that convoys to Russia must be interrupted until August or September in order to provide for the Sicily effort, but it seems to me now that a delay in giving him the bad news would be the wiser course. Incidentally, none of us can be positive about the situation four or five months hence.

* * * * *

A more agreeable note now crept into my correspondence with Stalin.

Premier Stalin to Premier Churchill   27 Mar. 43
I received your message on the main battle in Tunis. I wish British and American troops full and speedy success. I hope that you will be able now to break and defeat the enemy and completely drive him out of Tunis.

I hope also that the air offensive against Germany will go on inexorably increasing. I will be very grateful if you will send me your photographs of the destructions in Essen.

Premier Stalin to Premier Churchill   29 Mar. 43
I congratulate the British Air Force on the new big and successful bombing of Berlin.

I hope that the British armoured units will be able to use to the full the improvement in the Tunis situation and not give any respite to the enemy.

Yesterday, together with my colleagues, I have seen the film *Desert Victory*, which you have sent me. It makes a very strong impression. The film depicts magnificently how Britain is fighting, and stigmatises those scoundrels (there are such people also in our country) who are asserting that Britain is not fighting at all, but is merely an onlooker. Impatiently I will await a similar film on your victory in Tunis.

The film *Desert Victory* will be widely shown in all our armies at the front and among the widest masses of our population.

I thought this was the moment to tell him the bad news about the convoys.

Prime Minister to Premier Stalin   30 Mar. 43

The Germans have concentrated at Narvik a powerful battle fleet consisting of *Tirpitz, Scharnhorst, Lützow,* one six-inch cruiser, and eight destroyers. Thus danger to Russian convoys which I described in my message to you of July 17 last year has been revived in even more menacing form. I told you then that we did not think it right to risk our Home Fleet in the Barents Sea, where it could be brought under attack of German shore-based aircraft and U-boats without adequate protection against either, and I explained that if one or two of our most modern battleships were to be lost or even seriously damaged while *Tirpitz* and other large units of the German battle fleet remained in action the whole command of the Atlantic would be jeopardised, with dire consequences to our common cause.

2. President Roosevelt and I have therefore decided with the greatest reluctance that it is impossible to provide adequate protection for the next Russian convoy, and that without such protection there is not the slightest chance of any of the ships reaching you in the face of the known German preparations for their destruction. Orders have therefore been issued that sailing of March convoy is to be postponed.

3. It is a great disappointment to President Roosevelt and myself that it should be necessary to postpone this convoy. Had it not been for German concentration it had been our firm intention to send you a convoy of thirty ships each in March and again early in

May. At the same time we feel it only right to let you know at once that it will not be possible to continue convoys by Northern route after early May, since from that time onward every single escort vessel will be required to support our offensive operations in the Mediterranean, leaving only a minimum to safeguard our lifeline in the Atlantic. In the latter we have had grievous and almost unprecedented losses during the last three weeks. Assuming Sicily goes well, we should hope to resume the convoys in early September, provided that the disposition of German main units permits and that the situation in the North Atlantic is such as to enable us to provide the necessary escorts and covering force.

4. We are doing our utmost to increase the flow of supplies by the Southern route. The monthly figure has been more than doubled in the last six months. We have reason to hope that increase will progress and that figures for August will reach 240,000 tons. If this is achieved the monthly delivery will have increased eightfold in twelve months. Furthermore, the United States will materially increase shipments via Vladivostok. This will in some way offset both your disappointment and ours at the interruption to Northern convoys.

Premier Stalin to Prime Minister   2 Apr. 43

I received your message of March 30 conveying to me that necessity compels you and Mr. Roosevelt to stop convoys to the U.S.S.R. till September.

I understand this unexpected action as a catastrophic diminution of supplies of arms and military raw materials to the U.S.S.R. on the part of Great Britain and the United States of America, as transport via Pacific is limited by the tonnage and not reliable and the Southern route has a small transit capacity. In view of this both just mentioned routes cannot compensate for the discontinuation of transport via the Northern route.

You realise of course that the circumstances cannot fail to affect the position of the Soviet troops.

Prime Minister to Premier Stalin   6 Apr. 43

I acknowledge the force of all you say in your telegram about the convoys. I assure you that I shall do my utmost to make any improvement which is possible. I am deeply conscious of the giant burden borne by the Russian armies and their unequalled contribution to the common cause.

2. We sent 348 heavy bombers to Essen on Saturday, casting 900
tons of bombs in order to increase the damage to Krupp's, which
was again effectively hit, and to carry ruin into the southwestern
part of the city, which had previously suffered little. Last night
507 aircraft, all but 166 being heavies, carried 1400 tons to Kiel.
This is one of the heaviest discharges we have ever made. The
cloud layers were thicker than we expected, but we hope the
attack got home. The American daylight bombing with the Flying
Fortresses is becoming more effective. Yesterday they struck at the
Renault works near Paris, which had begun to spring to life again.
Besides the bombing which they do from great altitudes with re-
markably precision by daylight, they provoke the enemy fighters to
attacks in which many are destroyed by the heavy armament of
the Flying Fortresses. Four American and about thirty-three British
bombers were lost in these three enterprises. I must again emphasise
that our bombing of Germany will increase in scale month by
month, and that we are able to find the targets with much more
certainty.

3. This present week the general battle in Tunisia will begin,
and the British Eighth and First Armies and the American and
French forces will all engage according to plan. The enemy is preparing to retire into his final bridgehead. He has already begun
demolitions and the removal of coastal batteries from Sfax. Under
the pressure about to be renewed upon him he seems likely to retire,
perhaps rapidly, to a line he is fortifying from Enfidaville, in the
Gulf of Hammamet. This new position will run into the main
front he now holds in Northern Tunisia, facing west, and which
rests its northern flank on the Mediterranean about thirty miles
from Bizerta. At this northern flank also we are striking. I shall
keep you informed of how we get on, and whether we are able to
cut off any large body of the so-called "Rommel's Army" before
they reach the final bridgehead.

4. Hitler, with his usual obstinacy, is sending the Hermann
Goering and the 9th German Divisions into Tunisia, chiefly by
air transport, in which at least a hundred large machines are employed. The leading elements of both of these divisions have already arrived. Therefore we must expect a stubborn defence of
the Tunisian tip by about a quarter of a million men, less any they
lose on the way. Our forces have a good superiority both in numbers and equipment. We are bringing a very heavy constant air

attack to bear upon the ports, and we are making every preparation to prevent a Dunkirk escape. This is particularly important in the interests of the Sicilian operation. In about a month after we are masters at Bizerta and Tunis we hope to be able to pass store-ships through the Mediterranean, thus shortening the voyage to Egypt and the Persian Gulf.

My full explanations and accounts were not wholly unrewarded. The answer was more friendly than usual.

Premier Stalin to Premier Churchill   12 Apr. 43

The speedy development of the Anglo-American advance in Tunis constitutes an important success in the war against Hitler and Mussolini. I wish you to kill the enemy and capture as many prisoners and trophies as possible.

We are delighted that you are not giving respite to Hitler. To your strong and successful bombing of the big German cities we add now our air raids on the German industrial centres of East Prussia. Many thanks for the film depicting the results of the bombing of Essen. This film, as well as all the other films which you promise to send, will be widely shown to our Army and population.

The contemplated deliveries of fighters from the cancelled convoys are of great value to us. I am also very grateful for your offer to send us sixty Hurricanes armed with 40-mm. cannon. Such planes are very needed, especially against heavy tanks. I hope that your and Mr. Harriman's efforts to secure the despatch of planes to the U.S.S.R. will be crowned with a speedy success.

Our people highly appreciate the warm feelings and sympathy of the British people which have found expression in the creation of the Aid to Russia Fund mentioned by you.[1] Please convey to your wife, who is at the head of the fund, my thanks for her untiring activities in this sphere.

*   *   *   *   *

A breach now occurred between the Soviet Government and the Polish Government in exile in London. After the over-

[1] See Vol. III, pages 474–75.

running of Poland by the German and Russian armies, following the Ribbentrop-Molotov agreement of September, 1939, many thousands of Poles had given themselves up to the Russians, with whom Poland was not at war, and were interned. By further Nazi-Soviet agreements many of these were handed over to the Germans for forced labour purposes. Under the Geneva Convention prisoners of officer status cannot be so treated, and of the 14,500 Poles held by the Soviets in three camps in the Smolensk region 8000 were officers. A considerable number of these officers were members of the Polish intelligentsia, including university professors, engineers and leading citizens, who had been mobilized as reservists. Until the spring of 1940 there had been intermittent news of the existence of these prisoners. From April, 1940, silence descended upon the three camps. Not a single sign or trace of their occupants ever appeared for thirteen or fourteen months. They were certainly in Soviet power, but no letter, message, escapee, or scrap of information ever came from them.

When Hitler surprised the Russians by his invasion on June 22, 1941, the relations between Russia and Poland changed overnight. They became allies. General Anders and other Polish generals, who had hitherto been confined under rigorous conditions, including beatings, in Russian prisons, were now washed, clothed, released, welcomed, and given high commands in the Polish forces, which the Soviets were now raising to fight the German invaders. The Poles, who had long been anxious about the fate of the large group of officers in the three internment camps, asked for their release in order to join the new Polish Army, to which they have been invaluable. About four hundred officers were collected from other parts of Russia, but not one from the three camps now in German power could ever be found. No explanation could be offered to repeated Polish inquiries by their new comrades-in-arms. Polish leaders, who now had access to many Soviet authorities with whom they were working and who were helping them form their Army, were conscious on numerous occasions of embarrassment on the part of the Russian officials, but no news of the whereabouts of the 14,500 occupants of the three camps was ever forthcoming, and no survivor ever appeared. This naturally led to suspicion and friction between the Polish and the Soviet Governments.

The war rolled on. The Germans held the territory in which the camps had stood. Nearly another year passed.

Early in April, 1943, Sikorski came to luncheon at No. 10. He told me that he had proofs that the Soviet Government had murdered the 15,000 Polish officers and other prisoners in their hands, and that they had been buried in vast graves in the forests, mainly around Katyn. He had a wealth of evidence. I said, "If they are dead nothing you can do will bring them back." He said he could not hold his people, and that they had already released all their news to the press. Without informing the British Government of its intention, the Polish Cabinet in London issued a communiqué on April 17 stating that an approach had been made to the International Red Cross in Switzerland to send a delegation to Katyn to conduct an inquiry on the spot. On April 20 the Polish Ambassador in Russia was instructed by his Government to ask for the comments of the Russians upon the German story.

On April 13 the German wireless publicly charged the Soviet Government with the murder of 14,500 Poles in the three camps, and proposed to hold an international inquiry on the spot into their fate. We cannot wonder that the Polish Government was attracted by this plan, but the International Red Cross announced from Geneva that they could not undertake any inquiry into the German allegations unless a corresponding invitation to do so was received from the Soviet Government. The Germans therefore conducted their own investigations, and a committee of experts, drawn from the countries under German influence, produced a detailed report claiming that upwards of 10,000 bodies had been found in mass graves, and that the evidence of documents found on them and the age of the trees planted over the graves showed that the executions dated back to the spring of 1940, when the area was under Soviet control.

Eventually in September, 1943, the region of Katyn was
occupied by the Russians. After the recapture of Smolensk a
committee composed exclusively of Russians was appointed to
inquire about the fate of the Poles of Katyn. Their report,
issued in January, 1944, claims that the three camps were not
evacuated in time, owing to the rapidity of the German advance, and that the Polish prisoners fell into German hands
and were later slaughtered by them. This version, to be
believed, involves acceptance of the fact that nearly 15,000
Polish officers and men, of whom there was no record since the
spring of 1940, passed into German hands in July, 1941, and
were later destroyed by the Germans without one single person
escaping and reporting, either to the Russian authorities or
to a Polish Consul in Russia or to the Underground Movement
in Poland. When we remember the confusion caused by the
German advance, that the guards of the camps must have fled
as the invaders came nearer, and all the contacts afterwards
during the period of Russo-Polish co-operation, belief seems
an act of faith.

* * * * *

I made one of my rare visits to Chartwell to spend the night
at my cottage. The telephone announced that the Soviet Ambassador must see me at once and was on his way. Maisky
arrived in unusual perturbation. He brought me a message
from Stalin that after the hideous charges which the Polish
Government in London had published and sponsored against
Russia of the wholesale murder of the Polish officer prisoners
the agreement of 1941 would be immediately denounced. I
said I thought the Poles had been unwise to make or lend
themselves to such accounts, but that I earnestly hoped a
blunder of this kind would not entail a breach in their relations with the Soviets. I drafted a telegram to Stalin in this
sense. M. Maisky proceeded to argue the falsity of the accusation, and gave various reasons to prove the physical impossibility of the crime having been committed by Russia. I had
heard a lot about it from various sources, but I did not attempt

to discuss the facts. "We have got to beat Hitler," I said, "and this is no time for quarrels and charges." But nothing I could say or do prevented the rupture between the Russian and Polish Governments. Many inconveniences resulted from this. Anyhow, we had got a lot of the Polish fighting men and many of their women and children out of Russia. This beneficial process still went on fitfully and I continued the formation and equipment in Persia of three Polish divisions under General Anders.

In the trials of Germans at Nuremberg for war crimes the murder of the Poles at Katyn was mentioned in the indictment of Goering and others, who laid the White Book of the German investigation before the court. It was decided by the victorious Governments concerned that the issue should be avoided, and the crime of Katyn was never probed in detail. The Soviet Government did not take the opportunity of clearing themselves of the horrible and widely believed accusation against them, and of fastening the guilt conclusively upon the German Government, some of whose principal figures were in the dock on trial for their lives. In the final judgment of the International Tribunal at Nuremberg Katyn is not mentioned in the section dealing with the treatment of prisoners of war by Nazi Germany. Everyone is therefore entitled to form his own opinion, and there is certainly no lack of material in the many books that have been published by the Polish leaders still in exile from their country, and in particular those written by Mr. Mikolajczyk, the former Polish Prime Minister, who joined the first Polish Government after the war, and by General Anders.

19

Victory in Tunis

GENERAL ALEXANDER took command of the whole front in the last week of February. At the same time, in accordance with the Casablanca Agreement, Air Marshal Tedder assumed control of the Allied Air Forces. The battle in Tunisia was then at its height. General Eisenhower with supreme responsibility could not conduct operations of this

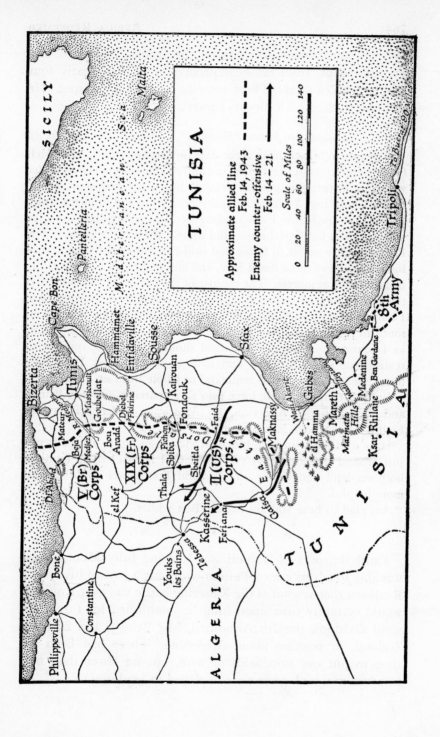

TUNISIA

Approximate allied line
Feb. 14, 1943
Enemy counter-offensive
Feb. 14 – 21

Scale of Miles

0   20   40   60   80   100   120   140

SICILY

Mediterranean   Sea

Malta

Pantelleria

Cape Bon.

Bizerta

Tunis

Mateur
Massicault
Goubellat
Djebel
R. Medjerda
Bou
Arada
Pichon
Sbiba
Thala
Sbeitla

V (Br)
Corps

XIX (Fr)
Corps

Fondouk
Fkrine
Kairouan

Hammamet
Enfidaville
Sousse

Sfax

II (US)
Corps

Faid
Maknassy
Gafsa
Wadi Akarit
Gabes

Kasserine
Feriana

Youks
les Bains

Tebessa

el Kef

Bone

Philippeville

Constantine

A L G E R I A

T U N I S I A

d'Hamma
Mareth
Matmata
Hills
Medenine
Ben Gardane
Ksar Rhilane

8th
Army

Tripoli
To Buerat 90 Miles

Dj Abiod
Beja
Medjez
Bou Arada

complex and convulsive character, by British, American, and French troops, from his headquarters at Algiers nearly four hundred miles away. There must be a man on the spot. He had now arrived with plenary powers.

General Alexander to Prime Minister   27 Feb. 43

Have just returned from three days on the American and French front lines. Regrouping, sorting out and reorganisation is now under way, but is being somewhat delayed by enemy action in north. Broadly speaking, Americans require experience and French require arms. For Americans I am sending best officers available to give instruction in battle technique and to help them train for war. For French I have wired to home and mid-East for essential arms and light equipment to be flown here, and am helping as far as possible from my own resources. The repulse of the enemy in the south and re-establishment of former positions have put heart into Americans. I have ordered vigorous but in meantime minor offensive action in south to regain initiative. I am frankly shocked at whole situation as I found it. Although Anderson should have been quicker to realise true state of affairs and to have started what I am now doing, he was only put in command of whole front on January 24.

I am regrouping whole force into three parts, as follows: British and French under Anderson, all Americans under Friedendall, Eighth Army under Montgomery.

Hate to disappoint you, but final victory in North Africa is not just around the corner. A very great deal is required to be done both on land and in the air. General Eisenhower could not be more helpful.

Am glad to hear you are better. Best wishes.

*   *   *   *   *

Until the port of Tripoli was working fully Montgomery was able to advance into Tunisia with only a part of his forces. Realising that as soon as the Kasserine battle was over Rommel would certainly turn upon him, he established his three forward divisions, the 7th Armoured, 51st British, and 2d New Zealand, in position about Medenine. There had been no time to put out minefields or wire, but no fewer than five hundred anti-tank guns were deployed in readiness.

Xth Corps has got back all its transport, and is now on the move forward from Benghazi. Leading [units] will be complete in Tripoli area by March 10, and others in succession. Whole Xth Corps will be concentrated up with me in forward area by March 19. I am taking the necessary steps to fight Rommel in my present positions, and see him off should he attempt any dirty work before I am ready to resume my own offensive against him. I intend to hold my present positions firm, as they are exactly what I require for the development of my own offensive against Mareth position in due course.

On March 6 Rommel made four major attacks, using all three of the German Panzer divisions. Every attack was beaten off with heavy loss. The enemy withdrew, leaving on the field fifty-two tanks destroyed by gunfire. We lost no tanks and only 130 killed and wounded. Nothing like this example of the power of massed anti-tank artillery had yet been seen against armour. This was probably Rommel's sharpest rebuff in all his African exploits. Moreover, it was his last action there. Shortly afterwards he was invalided to Germany, a sick man, and von Arnim succeeded him in command.

The Eighth Army now moved forward to close with the enemy's main position, the Mareth Line.[1] This was a highly organised twenty-mile-long defence system constructed by the French before the war to prevent Italian incursion into Tunisia. Now Italians were manning it against the British! At its seaward end the steep-sided Wadi Zigzaou was a formidable anti-tank obstacle immediately in front of the main defences; farther south, concrete pill-boxes, anti-tank ditches, and wire continued the front to the Matmata hills. There was no chance of an outflanking movement except by a long détour leading to the narrow defile between the Djebels Tebaga and Melab. The route had formerly been pronounced by the French as impossible for vehicles, but it had been reconnoitred in January by the Long Range Desert Group and declared feasible, if very difficult. Here was not the least valuable of the many services rendered throughout the African campaign

1 See map, "The Battle of Mareth," page 768.

by this hardy and highly mobile reconnaissance unit. Clearly
the enemy were not under any illusions, for they had fortified
the pass and occupied it with a German Panzer division and
Italian infantry. But in view of the frontal strength of the
Mareth position, held as it was by six divisions, two of them
German, with the 15th Panzer Division in reserve, Montgomery
decided to include in his plan a flanking column to break
through the pass and establish itself behind the main enemy
front.

A fortnight was needed for preparing a deliberate assault
against such strongly held defences. During that time the U.S.
IId Corps recaptured Gafsa and thrust eastwards. Although
they were unable to break into the coastal plain, they pinned
the 10th Panzer Division to this front throughout the Mareth
battle. On March 10 also General Leclerc's troops were severely
attacked by a mixed force of armoured cars and artillery, supported by air action. The French stood firm, and, helped by
the R.A.F., drove off the enemy with considerable loss.

The stage was thus set for the battle of the Mareth Line.
The operation was called "Pugilist." An intensive day bombing programme had been ordered to pave the way, but bad
weather prevented the bomber forces working till the 20th.
A preliminary attack by the 201st Guards Brigade on March
16 proved unsuccessful and costly. Montgomery pressed on
with the rest of his plan. On the night of the 19th he despatched on its long flank march a force under General
Freyberg, which included the 2d New Zealand Division, the 8th
Armoured Brigade, and a medium artillery regiment. By the
next evening, the 20th, they were approaching the defile.

General Alexander to Prime Minister   21 Mar. 43

"Zip" is timed by Eighth Army for tonight. The stage is set, and
you will receive confirmation when the curtain goes up. American
IId Corps has taken Gafsa, and their 1st Armoured Division is
moving on Maknassy. So far Germans have not reacted to this
threat, which was designed to draw them off from Eighth Army,
but tomorrow may tell us more. Montgomery will communicate
with you direct tomorrow.

General Alexander to Prime Minister   21 Mar. 43
    "Zip."

General Montgomery to Prime Minister   21 Mar. 43

"Pugilist" launched successfully yesterday. New Zealand Corps moved round enemy west flank, and today was fifteen miles south-west of El Hamma and is directed on Gabes. XXXth Corps attacked enemy east flank last night and established a bridgehead through the main obstacles and minefields of Mareth position, and this bridgehead is being widened and its success exploited. Enemy clearly intends to stand and fight, and I am preparing for a dog-fight battle in Mareth area, which may last several days. Action of New Zealand Corps in Gabes area may have a decisive effect on the battle.

Just before midnight the XXXth Corps delivered the main attack on the coastal sector of the Mareth defences. The 50th Division crossed the Wadi Zigzaou, and gained a footing beyond. The Wadi proved even more severe an obstacle than had been expected; neither tanks nor anti-tank guns could cross, despite the unsparing efforts of the engineers. All next day the division held its ground, but on the 22d a violent counter-attack by the 15th Panzer Division and German infantry forced them back. During the night of the 23d they were withdrawn across the Wadi.

The frontal attack having failed, Montgomery swiftly changed his plan. He gave the divisions confronting the Mareth Line a containing rôle and transferred the main weight to his left wing. The headquarters of the Xth Corps and the 1st Armoured Division were dispatched to join Freyberg at the defile by the same long and arduous route, while the 4th Indian Division opened up a way across the Matmata hills west of Medenine.

The problem of breaking through the defile to El Hamma was formidable, even with the strong reinforcements that Freyberg received. The enemy became aware of the danger, and reinforced this flank with the German 164th Infantry Brigade and part of the 15th Panzer Division. Only heavy

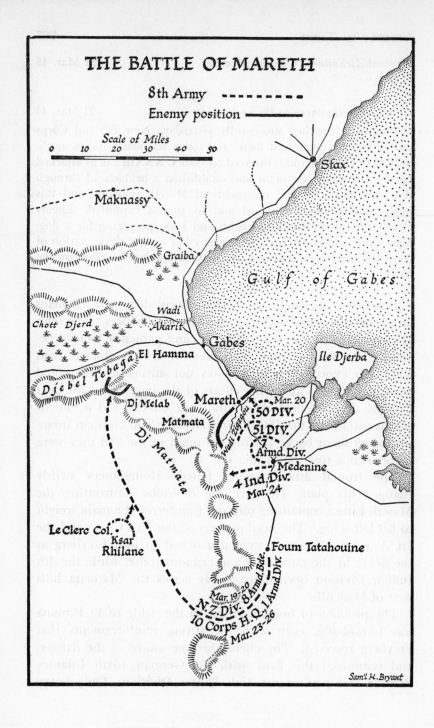

THE BATTLE OF MARETH

8th Army ----------
Enemy position ——————

Scale of Miles
0   10   20   30   40   50

Sfax

Maknassy

Graiba

Gulf of Gabes

Wadi
Akarit

Chott Djerd

Gabes

Ile Djerba

El Hamma

Djebel Tebaga

Dj Melab

Mareth   Mar. 20
50 DIV.
Matmata   51 DIV.

Dj Matmata   Armd.Div.

Medenine

4 Ind.Div.
Mar. 24

Le Clerc Col.
Ksar
Rhilane   Foum Tatahouine

Mar. 19-20   8Armd.Bde.
N.Z.Div.   1 Armd.Div.
10 Corps H.Q.
Mar. 23-26

Sam'l H. Bryant

pounding could force a passage, and in this the Western Desert Air Force, which had given unfailing support to the Eighth Army in all its battles, rose to a supreme endeavour. Thirty of its squadrons, eight of them American, inflicted a series of intense air bombardments on the defences of the pass. This culminated on the afternoon of March 26 in a two-and-a-half-hour continuous attack by relays of bombers and low-flying fighters. Sustained by this and a strong artillery barrage, the New Zealanders and the 8th Armoured Brigade broke into the enemy defences. They were followed by the 1st Armoured Division, which, when the moon rose, passed through them, and by dawn had nearly reached El Hamma. Caught between the New Zealanders in front and the Armoured Division behind them, the enemy fought desperately, but in vain. Their losses were crippling; 7,000 prisoners were taken. Thus was gained a fine victory, in which not only the quality of the troops but also the skill of their Commander was prominent.

General Montgomery to Prime Minister   28 Mar. 43

After seven days of continuous and heavy fighting Eighth Army has inflicted a severe defeat on enemy. Enemy resistance south of line El Hamma-Gabes is disintegrating. My troops are in possession of whole Mareth defences.

Faced with the danger of having his retreat cut off, the Italian General Messe, in command on this front, hastily withdrew his forces and formed front again ten miles north of Gabes, on the Wadi Akarit, which lies athwart a gap between the sea and marshes to the west. The Eighth Army closed on the enemy, but before it was ready to attack there were significant events farther north. At the end of March the British 46th Division in the coastal sector began an advance, and after several days of fighting regained all the ground previously lost. East of Beja the British 4th and 78th Divisions also attacked successfully. In a fortnight the whole position north of Medjez had been substantially restored to the line held, before the German offensive had forced it back. On March 31 the U.S. IId Corps renewed their thrust down the Gafsa-Gabes road, threatening the rear of the enemy on the Wadi Akarit. They did not succeed in breaking through, but the operation had the important result of drawing in the 21st Panzer Division to reinforce the 10th. Both of these divisions were thus fully occupied against the Americans while the assault upon the Wadi Akarit was taking place. At the same time the Tactical Air Force began a series of attacks against enemy landing-grounds. These were most successful, and indeed eventually drove the enemy Air Force out of Tunisia.

*   *   *   *   *

On April 5, General Alexander submitted his plan in full detail to General Eisenhower. By April 6 the Eighth Army was set for its new attack. The Wadi Akarit, itself a consider-able obstacle, was overlooked by hills to the north, and the whole formed a naturally strong defensive position. Mont-gomery made his characteristic use of the artillery. Before dawn the 51st and 50th British and 4th Indian Divisions, supported by massed artillery, were launched against fierce opposition. The enemy made determined counter-attacks, and it was not till nightfall that the battle was won.

General Montgomery to Prime Minister   6 Apr. 43

I delivered a heavy attack against enemy in Akarit position early this morning. I did two things not done by me before, in that I attacked centre of enemy position, and in the dark with no moon. Attack delivered by about three infantry divisions, supported by 450 guns, and enemy was surprised and overwhelmed and all objec-tives were captured. Through the hole thus made I am passing Xth Corps, consisting of New Zealand Division and one armoured divi-sion, and this movement has now just begun at the time of sending you this. The prisoners are estimated at two thousand after only six hours' fighting, and many more are flowing in.

I shall endeavour to fight the enemy to a standstill in this area and inflict damage on him here, so that he will have all the less troops and material to fight on rearward positions. Heavy fighting is going on, and when enemy recovers from his surprise he will probably fight desperately. But he cannot fight any longer on the

Akarit position, as I have driven a deep wedge into the centre of it, and the dominating key points are all in my possession.

My troops are in TREMENDOUS form and have fought splendidly. Will press on northwards when I have finished here.

The enemy were followed up next day on both the roads running northwards, and all available British and American aircraft punished their retreating columns. On April 7 a patrol of the 4th Indian Division met one from the U.S. IId Corps. The American greeting "Hello, Limey," [2] although not understood, was accepted with the utmost cordiality. The two armies which had started nearly two thousand miles apart were now at last joined together. The same day, in order to cut off the enemy's northward retreat, the IXth British Corps, with the British 6th Armoured Division, a brigade of the 46th Division, and the U.S. 34th Infantry Division, tried to break through the Fondouk Pass. Pichon was taken, but it was not till the 9th that the Armoured Division penetrated the defences, entering Kairouan on the 11th after a successful action against the 10th and 21st Panzer Divisions.

The enemy's withdrawal before the Eighth Army was skilfully conducted, though the bold action of our 6th Armoured Division doubtless accelerated its time-table. Sfax, important for its port facilities now that Tripoli was three hundred miles behind, was taken on April 10, and Sousse two days later. On April 13 contact was made with the enemy's final position on the mountains north of Enfidaville. The first probing attacks found them strongly held.

We had possession of the forward airfields and General Eisenhower could intensify the sea and air blockade of Tunisia. The enemy had increased their use of air transport as our sea blockade tightened; large convoys of transport aircraft, escorted by fighters, were arriving every day. Our own fighters, British and American, were given these tempting targets as a primary task. On April 10 and 11 seventy-one transport aircraft were claimed as destroyed. On the 18th a great convoy a

---

[2] A name for British sailors in vogue in the United States Navy, arising from the use of lime juice on British ships to prevent scurvy in bygone days.

hundred strong was set upon by our Spitfires and four squadrons of American Warhawks off Cape Bon. The convoy was
scattered in confusion; over fifty were brought down. Next day
South African Kittyhawks destroyed fifteen out of eighteen;
and finally on April 22 a further thirty, including many laden
with petrol, went flaming into the sea. This virtually ended
Hitler's obstinate attempt, which Germany could ill afford.
No more transport aircraft dared to fly by day. Their achievement had been great. In the four months December to March
they had ferried more than 40,000 men and 14,000 tons of
supplies to Africa.

Realising the strength of the Enfidaville position, Alexander
decided that the main attack on Tunis must come from the
west. The U.S. IId Corps, freed from the southern front, was
brought up during the first weeks of April and relieved the
British Vth Corps in the sector from Beja to the sea. The 1st
British Armoured Division was transferred from the Eighth to
the First Army. The Eighth Army, however, still had the task
of containing the enemy holding the Enfidaville front, and
while the main blow was being prepared it attacked on the
night of April 19 with three divisions, strongly supported by
artillery and the Air Force. In two days of heavy fighting
appreciable gains were made, but it was becoming clear that
further progress from this direction could be made only at the
cost of heavy casualties.

*　　*　　*　　*　　*

The main attack of the First Army began on April 22. On
the right, south of Goubellat, the IXth Corps advanced with
the 46th Infantry and the 1st and 6th Armoured Divisions;
north of them was the Vth Corps, the 1st, 4th, and 78th Divisions, moving astride the Medjerda River towards Massicault.
Five days of hard fighting failed to break the enemy's resistance,
but his losses were heavy, and important ground was gained
which was to prove of value a week later. South of the British
sector the French XIXth Corps occupied the Djebel Fkirine,
while in the north the U.S. IId Corps, attacking on the 23d,

made steady progress towards Mateur. Despite the physical difficulties of the ground the Americans kept up unremitting pressure, and gradually forced the Germans back.

General Alexander to Prime Minister   30 Apr. 43

I had a long conference with Montgomery today, and have decided that owing to the extreme difficulties of the ground and the fact that the enemy has concentrated a strong force of guns against Eighth Army in the coastal sector his operations towards Bou Ficha would have been very costly in casualties and were not certain of success. I have therefore cancelled his large-scale operations, and Eighth Army will undertake active local action, with the chief object of preventing the enemy transferring troops from their front to First Army front. 4th Indian Division, 7th Armoured Division, and 201st Guards Brigade are moving over to First Army, starting tonight. A very strong attack with all available air and artillery support will be launched by Vth Corps probably on May 4, on the axis Medjez-Tunis. IXth Corps, with two or three armoured divisions, to pass through Vth Corps, directed on Tunis. I have every hope that this attack will lead to decisive results.

The last two days have been days of continuous enemy counter-attacks on the front of the 4th and 1st Divisions, and also on IId U.S. Corps front. On Vth Corps front fighting has been particularly fierce and bitter. Localities have changed hands several times. Both 1st and 4th Divisions have fought very well, and our positions are in the main intact. The enemy's losses have been very heavy. He has used tanks in several of these counter-attacks, and about seven [of his] Mark VI's have been knocked out.

As an instance of the desperate nature of the enemy's resistance, fifty men of the Hermann Goering Division had just surrendered, when one of them persuaded them to take up arms again, and the whole party started fighting and had to be shot to a man.

General Crocker has been wounded, and Horrocks is taking over the command of IXth Corps and Freyberg the Xth Corps.

Prime Minister to Marshal Stalin   3 May 43

The battle in the Tunisian tip continues at a high pitch, and with considerable casualties on both sides. Since we entered Tunisia we have taken about 40,000 prisoners; in addition, the enemy have suffered 35,000 dead and wounded. The casualties in the First

Army have been about 23,000, and in the Eighth Army about
10,000. The total Allied casualties are about 50,000, of which two-
thirds are British. The battle will be maintained along the whole
front with the utmost intensity, and General Alexander is regrouping for a strong thrust very soon. The enemy have just under
200,000 encircled. They are still steadily reinforcing, but in the
last few days our Air, which is growing ever stronger and coming
closer, has cut into them well. So many destroyers and transports
have been sunk, including several carrying German reinforcements,
that all traffic was temporarily suspended. Unless it can be immediately reopened the supply situation of the enemy will be very
serious for him. Also, his chances of getting away by sea in any
numbers are not good. The peculiar mountainous character of the
country, with flat plains commanded by rugged, upstanding peaks,
each of which is a fortress, aids the enemy's defence and slows up
our advance. I hope however to have good news for you before the
end of this month. Meanwhile the whole campaign is most costly
to the enemy on account of his additional losses in transit.

*   *   *   *   *

It was clear that yet one more heavy punch would be needed
before the enemy would break. A final attack by the Eighth
Army on April 24 had proved that the Enfidaville position was
too strong to be overcome without heavy loss. As we have
seen, General Alexander transferred to the First Army three
of their veteran divisions who had fought in the Desert since
the earliest days. On May 6 the culminating attack was
launched.[3] The IXth Corps made the principal assault, on a
narrow front on either side of the Medjez-Tunis road. The
leading infantry, the 4th British and 4th Indian Divisions, were
closely followed by the 6th and 7th Armoured Divisions. On
their left the Vth Corps protected the flank of the advance.
The Allied air forces again put forth a supreme effort, with
twenty-five hundred sorties in the day. The Axis Air Force had
been gradually worn down over many weeks, and at this crisis
was able to make only sixty sorties in reply. The climax was at
hand. The relentless blockade by sea and air was fully estab-

[3] See map, "Tunis — The Last Phase," page 775.

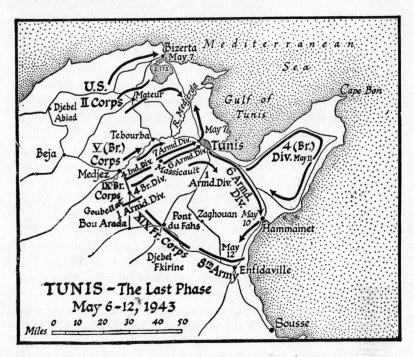

TUNIS - The Last Phase
May 6-12, 1943

lished. Enemy movement over the sea was at a standstill, their
air effort ended. To quote from a subsequent German report:

The Anglo-American air forces played a decisive part in the
enemy operational success which led to the destruction of the
German-Italian bridgehead in Tunisia. They took part in the
ground fighting to an extent never before attempted.

The IXth Corps made a clean break in the enemy front. The
two armoured divisions passed through the infantry and
reached Massicault, halfway to Tunis. Next day, May 7, they
pressed on and the 7th Armoured Division entered Tunis, and
then swerved north to join hands with the United States forces.
Resistance on the main American front had cracked at the
same time, and their 9th Infantry Division reached Bizerta.
Three German divisions were thus trapped between the Allied
troops, and surrendered on May 9.

General Alexander to Prime Minister   8 May 43

Things have gone even better than I could have hoped. So as
to give the Americans Bizerta for themselves, I had regrouped, and,
as you know, they entered it at the same hour as the First Army took
Tunis. I have sent a French regiment into Tunis to take over the
guards and to run up the Tricolour. We had a deception plan to
mislead the enemy into thinking the blow was in the south, and it
worked well, as they sent the majority of their tanks and of
their 88-mm. guns down opposite 1st British Armoured Division,
weakening the front facing IXth Corps. IXth Corps attacked with
a huge weight of arms and armour, supported by practically the
entire Air Force: it was a real thunderbolt. As a result IXth Corps
reached Tunis, a distance of thirty miles, in thirty-six hours.

The Axis front has completely collapsed and disintegrated. We
shall have to mop up pockets of Germans, but up to date probably
20,000 prisoners have been taken, besides many guns, lorries, and
dumps. Our casualties both in men and tanks are light. First Army
casualties are estimated at some 1200.

Coningham and I have just returned from Tunis, where we were
greeted enthusiastically by the population. We then went to IXth
Corps front, where 26th Armoured Brigade were attacking Ham-
man Lif. 1st Guards Brigade is clearing some high ground south
of that place. 1st British Armoured Division reached the road.
The French tanks are operating just west of Zaghouan.

Our main object now is to cut off as many enemy as possible
from gaining the Cape Bon peninsula. R.A.F. work has been quite
magnificent, and all troops are in terrific heart.

The 6th Armoured Division, followed by the 4th British
Division and with the 1st Armoured on their right, drove east,
through and beyond Tunis. They were held up by a hastily
organised resistance at a defile by the sea a few miles east of the
city, but their tanks charged through at nightfall on May 10
and reached Hammamet, on the east coast. Behind them the
4th Division swept round the Cape Bon peninsula, meeting no
opposition. All the remaining enemy were caught in the net
to the south.

General Alexander to Prime Minister   10 May 43

Coningham and I have just returned from motoring and flying

over area between Bizerta and Tunis, where ground is littered with
enemy vehicles, guns, and equipment of all sorts, some abandoned
and much destroyed. 50,000 prisoners already counted through
cages, and still coming in. Nine German generals so far. Advanced
elements of First Army reached Grombalia by 6 P.M. today. With
luck all Axis forces opposite Eighth Army will be completely surrounded.

Prime Minister to General Alexander 10 May 43

It has fallen to you to conduct series of battles which have ended
in destruction of the German and Italian power in Africa. All the
way from Alamein to Tunis in ceaseless fighting and marching of
last six months you and your brilliant lieutenant Montgomery
have added a glorious chapter to annals of British Commonwealth
and Empire. Your combinations in the final great battle will be
judged by history as a model of the military art. But more than this,
you have known how to inspire your soldiers with confidence and
ardour which overcame all obstacles and outlasted all fatigue and
hardship. They and their trusty United States and French Allied
soldiers and airmen together can now be told of the admiration and
gratitude with which the entire British nation and Empire regard
them and their famous deeds. The generous rivalry in arms of the
First and Eighth British Armies has achieved victory, full honour
for each and all.

General Alexander to Prime Minister 11 May 43

. . . I expect all organised resistance to collapse within the next
forty-eight hours, and final liquidation of whole Axis forces in the
next two or three days. I calculate that prisoners up to date exceed
100,000, but this is not yet confirmed, and they are still coming in.
Yesterday I saw a horse-drawn gig laden with Germans driving
themselves to the prisoners' cage. As they passed we could not help
laughing, and they laughed too. The whole affair was more like
Derby Day. The equipment of all sorts will take some time to
count up; some is destroyed, but a lot intact.

No one has got away except a mere handful by air.

We have recovered two thousand of our own prisoners, including
wounded. It is all very satisfying and augurs well for the future.

Prime Minister to General Eisenhower (Algiers) 11 May 43

Let me add my heartfelt congratulations to those which have

been sent to you by His Majesty and the War Cabinet on the
brilliant result of the North African campaign by the army under
your supreme direction.

The comradeship and conduct with which you have sustained
the troops engaged in the fierce and prolonged battle in Tunisia
and the perfect understanding and harmony preserved amidst the
shock of war between British and United States forces and with
our French Allies have proved solid foundation of victory.

The simultaneous advance of British and United States armies
side by side into Tunis and Bizerta is an augury full of hope for
the future of the world. Long may they march together, striking
down the tyrants and oppressors of mankind.

General Eisenhower to Prime Minister   11 May 43

Yesterday I wrote you a letter attempting to express in some
small degree the depth of my appreciation for the unwavering
support and the confidence that you have shown in me and in this
Allied force. Today your heart-warming telegram arrived, and I
regret that I have *no* words to tell you how pleased I am. I can
only say "Thank you," and assure you that this army will never
stop pounding until Hitlerism is abolished from the earth.

Prime Minister to General Giraud (*Algiers*)   12 May 43

It cheers all our hearts to see a line of French divisions advancing
triumphant against the common foe and leading German prisoners by the thousand to the rear. Accept my most hearty congratulations on the fighting spirit of the French Army under your
command, and the tenacity in defence and aggression in assault
which it has displayed in spite of being at a disadvantage in equipment. Every good wish.

*   *   *   *   *

Admiral Cunningham had made full preparation for the
final collapse, and on May 7 he ordered all available naval
forces to patrol the straits to prevent any Axis attempt to stage
a "Dunkirk" evacuation. The appropriate code-name of this
operation was "Retribution." On the 8th he signalled, "Sink,
burn, and destroy. Let nothing pass." But only a few barges
tried to escape, and nearly all were captured or sunk. Day and

night destroyers and coastal craft, together with the R.A.F., continued the ruthless work. In all, 897 men surrendered to the Navy, and only 653 are known to have escaped, mostly by air and at night. Our casualties were negligible.

It was not till I visited Algiers a month later that I was able to do justice to the share of all branches of the Navy in our success.

Prime Minister to Admiral Cunningham   11 June 43

The daring and devotion of our submarines succeeded in sinking forty-seven ships and our surface forces forty-two ships of an aggregate tonnage of 268,600. When to this is added sinkings by air, a grand total of one hundred and thirty-seven ships and 433,400 tons is reached. This was 32 per cent. of the estimated shipping initially available to the Axis at beginning of Tunisian campaign.

During the long struggle on the mainland the Navy and Air Force, working in closest co-operation, sank twenty-one destroyers or torpedo boats and many small craft, and prevented 35 per cent of enemy supply ships and transports from reaching Tunisia.

To the minesweepers fell the honour of reopening the Mediterranean by clearing the channels, six hundred miles long, between May 9 and 21.

The protection of our own convoys was carried to very highest point. Over the whole vast mass of shipping which entered Mediterranean between November 8, 1942, and May 8, 1943, losses were less than 2¼ per cent. . . .

The first through convoy to complete the Mediterranean passage since 1941 left Gibraltar on May 17, 1943, and reached Alexandria without loss on May 26. The reopening of this route to the Middle East reduced the length of the journey by nearly nine thousand miles, representing a saving of about forty-five days in the time spent by an average store ship on passage.

*   *   *   *   *

On May 12 I received the following telegram:

General Alexander to Prime Minister   12 May 43

The end is very near. Von Arnim has been captured, and

prisoners will most likely be over 150,000. All organised resistance has collapsed, and only pockets of enemy are still holding out. It appears that we have taken over 1000 guns, of which 180 are 88-mm., 250 tanks, and many thousands of motor vehicles, many of which are serviceable. German prisoners driving their own vehicles formed a dense column on the road from Grombalia to Medjez el Bab all day today.

My next telegram, denoting the formal end of the campaign, will follow, I hope, in a few hours.

That day the 6th Armoured Division joined hands with the Eighth Army. The encircling ring was closed. The enemy laid down their arms. In the words of Alexander's dispatch:

It was an astonishing sight to see long lines of Germans driving themselves in their own transport or in commandeered horse-carts westwards in search of prisoner-of-war cages.

At 2.15 P.M. on May 13 he signalled to me:

Sir:

It is my duty to report that the Tunisian campaign is over. All enemy resistance has ceased. We are masters of the North African shores.

* * * * *

No one could doubt the magnitude of the victory of Tunis. It held its own with Stalingrad. Nearly a quarter of a million prisoners were taken. Very heavy loss of life had been inflicted on the enemy. One third of their supply ships had been sunk. Africa was clear of our foes. One continent had been redeemed. In London there was, for the first time in the war, a real lifting of spirits. Parliament received the Ministers with regard and enthusiasm and recorded its thanks in the warmest terms to the commanders. I had asked that the bells of all the churches should be rung. I was sorry not to hear their chimes, but I had more important work to do on the other side of the Atlantic.

I was already at the White House when I received the following gracious message from the King:

His Majesty the King to Prime Minister   13 May 43

Now that the campaign in Africa has reached a glorious conclusion, I wish to tell you how profoundly I appreciate the fact that its initial conception and successful prosecution are largely due to your vision and to your unflinching determination in the face of early difficulties. The African campaign has immeasurably increased the debt that this country, and indeed all the United Nations, owe to you.

GEORGE R.I.

20

My Third Visit to Washington

Need for an Anglo-American Conference — Voyage in the "Queen Mary" — Our Preparatory Work for the "Trident" Conference — Our Disappointing Tale About Burma — My Paper on the Indian and Far Eastern Spheres — Importance of Using Surprise by Sea-Power — A Variety of Island Prizes — The Japanese at Full Spread — The Air Route from India to China — Our Arrival at Washington — President Roosevelt's Welcome — The Beginning of the "Trident" Conference, May 12 — My Opening Statement — Grasp the Fruits of Success — Turkey and the Balkans — Advantage of a Separate Peace with Italy — Need to Take the Weight off Russia — Our Armies Must Not Stand Idle — The Cross-Channel Invasion — Aid to China — The Sumatra Tip — The Long-Term Plan — The Ultimate Defeat of Japan — The President's Reply — A Week-End at Shangri-La — We Pass Through Frederick — "Barbara Frietchie" — I Get Full Marks for My Recitation — The President's Log Cabin Retreat — Proposed Meeting With Madame Chiang Kai-shek — I Address Congress for the Second Time, Wednesday, May 19 — A Milestone in the War — "One Continent Redeemed" — The Heavy Task Before Us — Dangers of a Dragged-Out War.

THE REASONS which led me to hasten to Washington, once the decision in Africa was certain, were serious. What should we do with our victory? Were its fruits to be gathered only in the Tunisian tip, or should we drive Italy out of the war and bring Turkey in on our side? These were fateful questions which could only be answered by a personal conference with the President. Second only to these were the plans for action in the Indian theatre. I was conscious of serious divergencies beneath the surface which, if not adjusted, would lead to grave difficulties and feeble action during the rest of the year. I was resolved to have a conference on the highest possible level.

On April 29 I telegraphed to President Roosevelt:

It seems to me most necessary that we should all settle together, now, first Sicily and then exploitation thereof, and secondly the future of the Burma campaign in the light of our experiences and shipping stringency. There are also a number of other burning questions which you and I could with advantage bring up to date. I think I could manage to be with you by Tuesday, May 11. Please say whether you would like this or whether you would prefer to send your people over here, which of course would be easier for us.

* * * * *

The doctors did not want me to fly at the great height required in a bomber, and the Northern route clipper seaplanes could not take off on account of late ice till after May 20. It was therefore decided to go by sea. We left London on the night of May 4, and went aboard the *Queen Mary* in the Clyde on the following day. The ship had been admirably fitted up to meet all our needs. The whole delegation was accommodated on the main deck, which was sealed off from the rest of the ship. Offices, conference rooms, and of course the Map Room, stood ready for immediate use. From the moment we got on board our work went forward ceaselessly.

All kinds of clever precautions had been taken to conceal the identity of the passengers in the *Queen Mary*. A number of notices had been put up in Dutch to suggest that Queen Wilhelmina and her suite were travelling to America in the ship. Ramps were ostentatiously built in the passages so that a wheel chair could traverse them smoothly. This was in order to start a rumour that the President of the United States and a considerable staff were to be brought to England on the return voyage. The more tales, the more safety. So effective were the cover plans that even some members of the Cabinet Office

staff, who had embarked in the *Queen Mary* for the Hot
Springs Food Conference, were dumbfounded to see us aboard
the ship. About five thousand German prisoners were already
on board. It had been suggested that they should be transferred to another ship, but I could not see what harm they
could do us, under due control and without weapons, and,
since the point was referred to me, had given instructions that
they should come along.

                    *   *   *   *   *

The conference, which I had christened "Trident," was to
last at least a fortnight, and was intended to cover every aspect
of the war. Our party had therefore to be a large one. The
"regulars" were in full force: the Chiefs of Staff, with a goodly
number of staff officers; Lord Leathers, with senior officials of
the Ministry of War Transport; and Ismay, with members of
my Defence Office. The Commanders-in-Chief in India, Field-
Marshal Wavell, Admiral Somerville, and Air Chief Marshal
Peirse, were also with us. I had summoned them because I was
sure that our American friends would be very anxious that we
should do everything possible — and even impossible — in the
way of immediate operations from India. The conference must
hear at first hand the views of the men who would have to do
whatever task was chosen.

There was much to be settled among ourselves before we
reached Washington, and now we were all under one deck.
The Joint Planning and Intelligence Staffs were in almost
continuous session. The Chiefs of Staff met daily, and sometimes twice a day. I adhered to my usual practice of giving
them my thoughts each morning in the shape of minutes and
directives, and I generally had a discussion with them each
afternoon or evening. These processes of probing, shifting,
and arguing continued throughout the voyage, and grave decisions were reached in measured steps.

We had to think about all the theatres at once. Upon the
operations in Europe, following the victory in Africa, we were
in complete agreement. It had been decided at Casablanca to

attack Sicily, and, as has been seen, all preparations were far advanced. The Chiefs of Staff were convinced that an attack upon the mainland of Italy should follow, or even overlap, the capture of Sicily. They proposed the seizure of a bridgehead on the toe of Italy, to be followed by a further assault on the heel as prelude to an advance on Bari and Naples. A paper setting out these views and the arguments which led up to them was prepared on board ship and handed to the American Chiefs of Staff as a basis for discussion on our arrival in Washington.

* * * * *

We anticipated more difficulties in reaching agreement with our American friends over the second great sphere of British military action, namely, the operations from India. At Casablanca it had been agreed to aim at the capture of Akyab before May, 1943,[1] in order by a limited advance from Assam to gain new starting-points for improving the air route and air lift to China. A provisional date of November 15, 1943, for an assault on Burma had also been fixed, subject to a review of forces available in July. All this had been set forth on paper, but we had little to show in fact. The advance on Akyab had failed, and its capture before the monsoon had now to be ruled out. The advance from Assam had not been undertaken because of administrative difficulties and the inability of the Chinese to advance to Yunnan during the spring. Some increase had been made in the air transport available for the China route, but the full development of the air route and the requirements for a land advance towards Central Burma had proved utterly beyond our resources. It therefore seemed clear beyond argument that the full "Anakim" operation could not be attempted in the winter of 1943–44.

I was sure that these conclusions would be very disappointing to the Americans. The President and his circle still cherished exaggerated ideas of the military power which China could exert if given sufficient arms and equipment. They also feared unduly the imminence of a Chinese collapse if support were

[1] Called Operation "Cannibal."

not forthcoming. I disliked thoroughly the idea of reconquering Burma by an advance along the miserable communications in Assam. I hated jungles — which go to the winner anyway — and thought in terms of air-power, sea-power, amphibious operations, and key points. It was however an essential to all our great business that our friends should not feel we had been slack in trying to fulfil the Casablanca plans and be convinced that we were ready to make the utmost exertions to meet their wishes. I therefore prepared in the early days of the voyage a very lengthy paper on the whole position in the Indian and Far Eastern spheres, and especially of those regions for which we bore the main responsibility.

4. "Anakim" [Burma] as planned is recognised by all of us to be physically impossible for 1943, and the Chiefs of Staff are rightly searching for variants or alternatives. On these a few general observations may be made.

5. Going into swampy jungles to fight the Japanese is like going into the water to fight a shark. It is better to entice him into a trap or catch him on a hook and then demolish with axes after hauling him out on to dry land. How then to deceive and entrap the shark?

6. The strategic virtues of "Torch" compelled or induced the enemy to fight in a theatre most costly to himself. It gained us important territories, bases, and a new French Army, ultimately perhaps eight or ten divisions. Its success opens the Mediterranean, thus freeing a vital part of our sea communications. Can we not seize in the A.B.D.A. area some strategic point or points which will force the Japanese to counter-attack under conditions detrimental to them and favourable to us? For this purpose the naval command of the Bay of Bengal must be secured. It will next be necessary to establish effective shore-based air command radiating from the key point capt red. Thus protected, comparatively small numbers of troops can maintain themselves, unless the enemy brings a disproportionate army to bear, in which case our people can either be reinforced or withdrawn, according to our general plans.

7. The surest way to make a successful landing is to go where you are not expected. It should be possible to carry up to 30,000 or 40,000 men across the Bay of Bengal, as required, to one or more points of the crescent from Moulmein to Timor. This crescent

would include: (i) the Andaman Islands; (ii) Mergui, with Bangkok as objective; (iii) the Kra Isthmus; (iv) assault of Northern Sumatra; (v) the southern tip of Sumatra; (vi) Java.

8. The method of landing should first of all have regard to the importance of getting ashore and establishing rapidly by a carefully prepared evolution a powerful air base. It is not always necessary to conquer in the first stage the real objective. This may be more surely achieved as a second step under the effective shore-based air cover. But in any case the landing, if likely to be opposed, can only be achieved by the provision of a large seaborne air force in carriers of all classes. This seaborne air cover can be withdrawn for use elsewhere once the shore-based air is established under improvised or permanent conditions. The seizure of even one key point intolerable to the enemy would impose upon him not only operations to recapture it, but a dispersion of his forces over the immense coastline exposed to the menace of sea-power. Nothing less than a definite attack on some point will enforce this dispersion. Otherwise the enemy rests at his ease, disposed to advantage in selected best defensive positions. He is content with the valuable property which he has seized, while we have to find a means to recapture it by the offensive. All the alternatives should be examined in a hopeful spirit, resolute to overcome the real difficulties and brush away the still more numerous imaginary difficulties which always weigh on action.

9. Once the Italian Fleet has been destroyed or neutralised and air control of our routes through and across the Mediterranean is established, powerful British naval forces will be available to reconstitute the Eastern Fleet in battleships, aircraft-carriers, and ancillary vessels. We must not exaggerate the Japanese strength. They cannot possibly be strong enough at all points to resist the concentrated impact of a seaborne air-sustained descent. Their own Air Force is dwindling steadily, and will be under great strain through the American and Australian campaign in the Pacific. It should be easy after one point has been attacked to compel still greater dispersion of enemy forces.

10. Our reports show only about 20,000 Japanese in Sumatra, which is six hundred miles long, and 40,000 in Java. The Japanese themselves conquered Sumatra and Java with comparatively small forces against much larger garrisons than they have themselves installed. Why should we assume that we are not capable of plan-

ning and executing operations of the same vigour, and with the same close combination of naval, army, and air forces? We have larger forces available; sea-power gives us almost unlimited choice of the point of attack, and we also ought to have learnt a lot from what has happened in the last fifteen months. Let us not rest content with the bleak and skinny programme set out. It could only be said of this that it is better than nothing and will serve to fill in time.

11. Notwithstanding the foregoing, we should be chary of committing ourselves in the forthcoming meeting to any particular plan. It is certain that prejudice will discredit every plan. Moreover, if we show ourselves unduly keen on any one plan others will be pressed as superior alternatives owing to the natural contrariness of allies. We should first confront our friends with the reasons which require modification of "Anakim." We should assert our earnest desire to maintain the operations in this theatre on the level of the priorities and status which they occupied at the Casablanca Conference. We should invite their views upon alternatives, and only become involved in detailed argument if and when the discussion reaches this stage. My own impression is that the Americans will require to be satisfied that the maximum action is taken in this theatre and that it is not being displaced in its importance in our minds, and that once reassured on these points they will be ready to consider variants and alternatives. It is for this moment that our studies must be ready.

12. I agree that the time and occasion have come to make a long-term plan for the defeat of Japan, and to interweave that plan as far as is humanly possible with the phases of the prime struggle against Hitler. . . .

15. The unsatisfactory course of the recent Burma campaign cannot be repeated on a far larger scale in 1943–44. Unless there is complete confidence in our ability to carry out the campaign as planned and in reasonable time, we must seek the only two other alternatives for action, namely, (a) a vast increase in the air route to China, and (b) an overseas expedition to one or more of the key points mentioned in paragraph 7.

There were no serious differences of view among ourselves, and a Chiefs of Staff statement was prepared for presentation in Washington.

*   *   *   *   *

Another burning question for us was how to obtain the use of the Portuguese Atlantic islands. We wanted facilities in the Azores for operating our long and very long range aircraft from Terceira and San Miguel Islands. We wanted to be allowed to refuel our naval escorts at either San Miguel or Fayal, and to have freedom to use the Cape Verde Islands for reconnaissance aircraft. All these facilities would give far better and wider air cover to our convoys, and consequently more scope for evasive routing. They would increase our carrying power by enabling us to come more directly through the middle of the Atlantic. They would give us the power to attack U-boats not only going to and from the Biscay bases, but also while they were resting, refuelling, and recharging their batteries in mid-ocean. We were to find the Americans even more ardent than ourselves on all these points.

*   *   *   *   *

On May 8 I cabled to Stalin:

I am in mid-Atlantic on my way to Washington to settle further exploitation in Europe after Sicily, and also to discourage undue bias towards the Pacific, and further to deal with the problem of the Indian Ocean and the offensive against Japan there.

I also telegraphed to the President, who had brushed aside my suggestion that I should stay at the Embassy:

10 May 43

Since yesterday we have been surrounded by the United States Navy, and we all greatly appreciate the high value you evidently set on our continued survival. I look forward to being at the White House tomorrow afternoon, and also going to Hyde Park with you at the week-end. The voyage has been so far most agreeable, and the staff have done vast amount of work.

On May 11 we arrived off Staten Island. Harry Hopkins was there to meet us, and we immediately entrained for Washington. The President was on the platform to greet me, and whisked me off to my old rooms at the White House. The next afternoon, May 12, at 2.30 P.M., we all met in his oval

study to survey and lay out our work at the conference. Here
is an extract from the agreed Anglo-American record of the
meetings. At first we were twelve.

British	*United States*
The PRIME MINISTER	The PRESIDENT.
Field-Marshal SIR JOHN DILL.	Admiral WM. D. LEAHY.
General SIR ALAN F. BROOKE.	General G. C. MARSHALL.
Admiral of the Fleet SIR DUDLEY	Admiral E. J. KING.
POUND.	Lieut.-General J. T. McNARNEY.
Air Chief Marshal SIR CHARLES	Mr. HARRY HOPKINS.
F. A. PORTAL.	
Lieut.-General SIR HASTINGS	
ISMAY.	

Secretaries
Brigadier-General J. R. DEANE.
Brigadier E. I. C. JACOB.

The President welcomed us. It was less than a year ago, he
said, since we had all met in the White House, and had set on
foot the moves leading up to "Torch." It was very appropriate
that we should meet again just as that operation was coming to
a triumphant conclusion. The meeting at Casablanca had set
on foot Operation "Husky," and he hoped that this would
meet with similar good fortune. He thought that the keynote
of our plans at the present time should be an intention to employ every resource of men and munitions against the enemy.
Nothing that could be brought to bear should be allowed to
stand idle.

He then asked me to open the discussion. According to the
records, I spoke as follows:

The Prime Minister recalled the striking change which had taken
place in the situation since he had last sat by the President's desk
and had heard the news of the fall of Tobruk. He could never
forget the manner in which the President had sustained him at that
time, and the Shermans which had been handed over so generously
had made their reputation in Africa. The British came to the
present meeting adhering to the Casablanca decisions. There might

have to be adjustments made necessary by our success, which also enabled us to take a longer forward view. "Torch" was over, Sicily was near, what should come next? We had been able by taking thought together to produce a succession of brilliant events which had altered the whole course of the war. We had the authority and prestige of victory. It was our duty to redouble our efforts and to grasp the fruits of our success. The only questions outstanding between the two Staffs were questions of emphasis and priority. He felt sure that these could be solved.

He did not propose to deal with the U-boat war and the aerial bombardment of Germany. There were no differences of opinion on these subjects. He would like to put forward for consideration a number of objectives, and questions which might focus subsequent study. The first objective was in the Mediterranean. The great prize there was to get Italy out of the war by whatever means might be the best. He recalled how in 1918, when Germany might have retreated to the Meuse or the Rhine and continued to fight the defection of Bulgaria brought the whole of the enemy structure crashing to the ground. The collapse of Italy would cause a chill of loneliness over the German people, and might be the beginning of their doom. But even if not immediately fatal to Germany, the effects of Italy coming out of the war would be very great, first of all on Turkey, who had always measured herself with Italy in the Mediterranean. The moment would come when a joint American-Russian-British request might be made to Turkey for permission to use bases in her territory from which to bomb Ploesti and clear the Aegean. Such a request could hardly fail to be successful if Italy were out of the war, and the moment were chosen when Germany could take no powerful action against Turkey. Another great effect of the elimination of Italy would be felt in the Balkans, where patriots of various nationalities were with difficulty held in check by large Axis forces, which included twenty-five or more Italian divisions. If these withdrew, the effect would be either that Germany would have to give up the Balkans or else that she would have to withdraw large forces from the Russian front to fill the gap. In no other way could relief be given to the Russian front on so large a scale this year. The third effect would be the elimination of the Italian Fleet. This would immediately release a considerable British squadron of battleships and aircraft-carriers to proceed either to the Bay of Bengal or the Pacific to fight Japan.

Certain questions presented themselves in relation to the Mediterranean. Need we invade the soil of Italy, or could we crush her by air attack? Would Germany defend Italy? Would Italy be an economic burden to us? He did not think so. Would arguments against a general conquest of Italy apply equally against a "toe and heel" operation to establish contact with Yugoslavia? Finally, there was a large political question for the British and United States Governments. What sort of life after the war should we be willing to accord to Italy if she placed herself unreservedly in our hands? Mr. Churchill said that if Italy made a separate peace we should have the use of Sardinia and the Dodecanese without having to fight for them.

The second objective was the taking of weight off Russia. He was much impressed by Stalin's attitude, in spite of the stopping of the Arctic convoys. For the first time, in his recent speech, Stalin had acknowledged the efforts and victories of his Allies. But we desired to undertake a full-scale invasion of the Continent from Russian front. We had destroyed the German army in Africa, but soon we would not be in contact with them anywhere. The Russian effort was prodigious, and placed us in their debt. The best way of taking the weight off the Russian front in 1943 would be to get, or knock, Italy out of the war, thus forcing the Germans to send a large number of troops to hold down the Balkans.

The third objective had already been mentioned by the President in his opening remarks. It was to apply our vast armies, air forces, and munitions to the enemy. All plans should be judged by this test. We had a large army and the Metropolitan Fighter Air Force in Great Britain. We had our finest and most experienced troops in the Mediterranean. The British alone had thirteen divisions in Northwest Africa. Supposing that Sicily was completed by the end of August, what should these troops do between that time and the date [in 1944], seven or eight months later, when the cross-Channel operation might first be mounted? They could not possibly stand idle, and so long a period of apparent inaction would have a serious effect on Russia, who was bearing such a disproportionate weight.

Mr. Churchill said that he could not pretend that the problem of landing on the Channel coast had been solved. The difficult beaches, with the great rise and fall of tide, the strength of the enemy's defences, the number of his reserves, and the ease of his

communications, all made the task one which must not be under-
rated. Much however would be learned from Sicily. He wished
to make it absolutely clear that His Majesty's Government earnestly
desired to undertake a full-scale invasion of the Continent from
the United Kingdom as soon as a plan offering reasonable prospects
of success could be made.

The fifth objective was aid to China. The difficulties of fighting
in Burma were apparent. The jungle prevented the use of our
modern weapons. The monsoon strictly limited the length of the
campaigning season, and there was no means of bringing sea-power
to bear. . . . If further study showed that it would be better to by-
pass Burma, he was anxious that another means should be found
of utilising the large forces standing in India. He thought that this
alternative might well be found in an operation against the tip of
Sumatra and the waist of Malaya at Penang. He was most anxious
that we should find in that theatre some means of making use of
those advantages which had been so valuable in "Torch." In that
operation sea-power had played its full part; complete surprise had
been possible; we had been able to seize a territory of importance
which not only brought in a new army on our side, but forced the
enemy to fight in a place most disadvantageous to him. These conditions might apply [elsewhere].

He felt that the time had now come to study the long-term plan
for the defeat of Japan. He would like once more to state the
British determination to carry the struggle home to Japan. The
only question was how best to do it. He thought that the United
States Chiefs of Staff should lead in a joint study, on the assumption that Germany would be out of the war in 1944, and that we
could concentrate on the great campaign against Japan in 1945. . . .

The President, in his reply, pointed out that the United
Nations were already producing more than both the Germans
and Japanese. It was therefore most important to keep the
large army and naval forces actively engaged. He was optimistic about Turkey. The entry of that country into the war
would provide an important base for air operations against the
German lines of communication to the Russian front. It was
particularly urgent to consider "Where do we go from Sicily?"
It was clearly necessary to keep employed the Anglo-American

forces of over twenty divisions in the Mediterranean area. The drain on Allied resources which might follow the occupation of Italy must be carefully considered in the light of any future operations in the Mediterranean. In any case, after the completion of "Husky" there would be a surplus of man-power. This should be used to build up "Bolero," and should start at once. He felt that everyone was agreed that there was no possibility of a cross-Channel enterprise this year, but the operation must be carried out on the largest scale in the spring of 1944.

In the Pacific area the President said that the Japanese were being steadily worn down. The Americans had landed in the Aleutians, and operations in the Solomons and in New Guinea were being carried out. It was particularly important to concentrate on the lengthy Japanese supply lines. Since the war started Japan had lost a million tons of shipping, and if this continued their field of operations would be restricted. They had suffered similar losses in the air. In order to keep up the offensive at sea it was important to establish air bases in China. The President said that the conference was not justified in ignoring the possibility of a Chinese collapse. Priority for aid to China in 1943 and 1944 must be considered. Regaining Burma would not be enough. China could only be helped immediately by air. To do this, airfields in Assam must be secured, regardless of the cost. The strengthening of the United States Air Force operating from Chinese bases would mean increased pressure against Japanese shipping. The President ended by saying that in order to relieve Russia we must engage the Germans. For this reason he questioned the occupation of Italy, which would release German troops to fight elsewhere. He thought the best way of forcing Germany to fight would be to launch an operation across the Channel.

I now replied that as we were agreed that the cross-Channel operation could not take place till 1944, it seemed imperative to use our great armies to attack Italy. I did not think that an occupation of all Italy would be necessary. If Italy collapsed, the United Nations would occupy the ports and airfields needed for further operations into the Balkans and Southern Europe. An Italian Government could control the country, subject to Allied supervision.

All these grave issues were now to be thrashed out by our combined Staffs and their experts.

*   *   *   *   *

For the week-end of May 15 the President proposed to take me, not to Hyde Park, but to Shangri-La, which was the name he gave the mountain refuge, about two thousand feet high, in the Catoctin Hills, in Maryland, where he sheltered, whenever the chance offered itself, from the stifling heat and buzz of Washington. We had a dispute about where we should sit in the car for this three-hour journey. Alike by his rank and from his infirmity there was only one place for the President. Mrs. Roosevelt wished to sit in one of the small front seats, and put me next to the President. I would not have this, and the British Empire went into action. After about three minutes' conflict of wills I won, and Mrs. Roosevelt took her proper place by her husband's side. Harry Hopkins filled the fourth seat, and we whirled off amid our cyclist escort. After about two hours we approached the town of Frederick. I had of course visited the famous battlefield of Gettysburg some years before, but I now made inquiries about Barbara Frietchie and her house. This moved Harry Hopkins to quote the famous lines

> " 'Shoot if you must this old grey head,
> But spare your country's flag,' she said."

When it was clear that no one else in the car could add to this quotation I started out:

> "Up from the meadows rich with corn,
> Clear in the cool September morn,
> The clustered spires of Frederick stand" . . .

and sailed steadily on:

> "Up rose old Barbara Frietchie then,
> Bowed with her threescore years and ten;

> Bravest of all in Frederick town,
> She took up the flag that the men hauled down.
>
> . . . .
>
> " 'Halt,' the dust brown ranks stood fast.
> 'Fire!' Out blazed the rifle-blast.
> It shivered the window with frame and sash,
> It rent the banner with many a gash.
> Quick as it fell from the broken staff,
> Dame Barbara seized the silken scarf.
> She leant full out of the window-sill,
> And shook it forth with a right good will.
> 'Shoot if you will this old grey head,
> But spare your country's flag' . . ."

At this point they all joined in the chorus:

> " . . . *she said.*"

I went on:

> "A shade of sadness, a touch of shame
> Over the face of the leader came,
> And a nobler nature within him stirred
> At the sight of this woman's deed and word.
> 'Who touches a hair of yon grey head

[he is said to have exclaimed, somewhat inconsistently with his previous instructions]

> 'Dies like a dog. March on,' he said.
>
> "So all day long through Frederick's street
> Sounded the tramp of marching feet,
> And all day long that free flag tossed
> Over the heads of the rebel host."

I got full marks for this from my highly select American audience, none of whom corrected my many misquotations, and I was encouraged to discuss at some length the characters of Stonewall Jackson and Robert E. Lee, two of the noblest men ever born on the American continent.

After a while silence and slumber descended upon the company, as we climbed with many a twist and turn up the spurs of the Alleghenies. Soon we arrived at Shangri-La, which was in principle a log cabin, with all modern improvements. In front was a fountain and pool of clear water, in which swam a number of large trout, newly caught in the neighbouring stream and awaiting the consummation of their existence.

The President had been looking forward to a few hours with his stamp collection. General "Pa" Watson, his personal aide, brought him several large albums and a number of envelopes full of specimens he had long desired. I watched him with much interest and in silence for perhaps half an hour as he stuck them in, each in its proper place, and so forgot the cares of State. But soon another car drove up to the door, and out stepped General Bedell Smith, quick-winged from Eisenhower's headquarters, with a budget of serious questions on which decisions were urgently required. Sadly F.D.R. left his stamp collection and addressed himself to his task. By the evening we were all tired out, and went to bed at ten.

*　　*　　*　　*　　*

On this week-end was discussed the question of my meeting Madame Chiang Kai-shek, who was making an extensive tour of the United States. She was at this time in New York, and intimated that she would be glad to receive me there. Amid the pressures under which we were working and in the few days that remained before I must leave I did not feel able to make so long a journey. The President therefore invited the lady to lunch with him to meet me at the White House. The invitation was refused with some hauteur. Madame was of the opinion that I should make the pilgrimage to New York. The President was somewhat vexed that she had not adopted his plan. It was my strong desire to preserve unity in the Grand Alliance, and I offered to go halfway if she would do the same. This offer was however considered facetious, so I never had the pleasure and advantage of meeting this lady until the Cairo Conference.

*　　*　　*　　*　　*

On Sunday the President wanted to fish in a stream which flowed through lovely woods. He was placed with great care by the side of a pool, and sought to entice the nimble and wily fish. I tried for some time myself at other spots. No fish were caught, but he seemed to enjoy it very much, and was in great spirits for the rest of the day. Evidently he had the first quality of an angler, which is not to measure the pleasure by the catch. On the Monday we had to leave this agreeable cool abode, and descended the Alleghenies for the really great heat of Washington. On the journey back through Frederick I asked to be shown Barbara Frietchie's house. I was surprised to see it was only one and a half storeys high. I had always pictured it as at least three, if not four, and I had considered exactly how far the heroic dame would have had to stand back from the sill to be safe from an upward volley from the street. It now appeared that the famous window, which I saw for the first time, was only about twelve feet from the ground, and it was clear that the Confederates must have taken great care to avoid doing her any harm. Thus the story ended well for both sides, and Harry Hopkins solemnly repeated:

> " 'Shoot if you must this old grey head,
>   But spare your country's flag,' she said."

In the regretted absence of Madame Chiang Kai-shek, the President and I lunched alone in his own room, and made the best of things.

*　　*　　*　　*　　*

I had undertaken, at the invitation of the Speaker of the House of Representatives, to address Congress on Wednesday, the 19th, at noon. It was seventeen months since I had last spoken to this august assembly. The speech, in which I tried to cover the whole field, is on record. It was also broadcast to the world. I shall quote only a brief extract.

In North Africa we builded better than we knew. The unexpected came to the aid of the design and multiplied the results.

For this we have to thank the military intuition of Corporal Hitler. We may notice, as I predicted in the House of Commons three months ago, the touch of the master-hand. The same insensate obstinacy which condemned Field-Marshal von Paulus and his army to destruction at Stalingrad has brought this new catastrophe upon our enemies in Tunisia. . . .

The African excursions of the two Dictators have cost their countries in killed and captured 950,000 soldiers. In addition nearly 2,400,000 gross tons of shipping have been sunk and nearly 8000 aircraft destroyed, both of these figures being exclusive of large numbers of ships and aircraft damaged. There have also been lost to the enemy 6200 guns, 2550 tanks, and 70,000 trucks. . . . Arrived at this milestone in the war, we can say, "One continent redeemed." . . .

I was driving the other day not far from the field of Gettysburg, which I knew well, like most of your battlefields. It was the decisive battle of the American Civil War. No one after Gettysburg doubted which way the dread balance of war would incline, yet far more blood was shed after the Union victory at Gettysburg than in all the fighting which went before. It behoves us therefore to search our hearts and brace our sinews and take the most earnest counsel one with another, in order that the favourable position which has already been reached both against Japan and against Hitler and Mussolini in Europe shall not be let slip.

This statement was well received by Congress, and the President, who had listened on the radio, seemed very pleased with me when I returned to the White House.

21

Problems of War and Peace

THE STAFFS engaged in perpetual discussion. Sometimes there were four meetings a day. At first the differences seemed insuperable and it looked like a hopeless breach. During this period leakages from high American officers were made to Democratic and Republican Senators, leading to a debate in the Senate. By patience and perseverance our difficulties were gradually overcome. In a speech to Congress on May 20 I tried to put the whole picture in true perspective and proportion so far as was possible in public. The fact that the President and I had been living side by side seeing each other at all hours, that we were known to be in close agreement, and that the President intended to decide himself on the ultimate issues — all this, together with the priceless work of Hopkins, exercised throughout a mollifying and also a dominating influence on the course of Staff discussions. After a serious crisis of opinions, side by side with the most agreeable personal relations between the professional men, an almost complete agreement was reached about invading Sicily.

There was profound dissatisfaction in Washington, which we all shared, at the lack of vim in the recent operations in Burma. I considered remodelling the commands by making Wavell Commander-in-Chief in India, with Auchinleck as his deputy and one of the best younger Corps Commanders as Commander-in-Chief of the East Asian front.

I was sure changes of this character were indispensable if we were to treat the problems of this theatre with the gravity they deserved.

* * * * *

A very stern mood developed in Washington about de Gaulle. Not a day passed that the President did not mention the subject to me. Although this was done in a most friendly and often jocular manner, I saw he felt very strongly indeed upon it. Almost every day he handed me one or more accusing documents against de Gaulle from the State Department or the American Secret Service. De Gaulle was alleged to have used British money to offer inducements to the sailors of the *Richelieu* to come over to him personally. Only politeness prevented our hosts from suggesting that our financial relations with the United States made it in a certain sense almost American money. I was at this time most indignant with de Gaulle. I felt that our continued support of him might lead to an estrangement between the British and United States Governments, and that no one would like this better than de Gaulle. I brought all this forcibly to the notice of my colleagues at home. It hung in the balance whether we should not break finally at this juncture with this most difficult man. However time and patience afforded tolerable solutions.

Another very difficult question arose about the Atlantic islands. The War Cabinet wished to invoke the ancient alliance and request the Portuguese Government to give us the facilities to which both the President and I, strongly pressed by the Combined Chiefs of Staff, attached the greatest importance. It was estimated by the experts that a million tons of shipping and many thousands of lives might be saved. I had a particular regard for the rights of Portugal, but felt we were fighting for her life and independence as well as our own. It was not until six months had passed and substantial loss had been suffered that we obtained the sorely needed relief. However, the result was achieved by long and friendly negotiation, aided by the general progress of our arms.

*   *   *   *   *

On May 22 I had an important conversation on the structure of a post-war settlement at luncheon at the British Embassy. I had asked the Ambassador to gather those whom he thought most necessary to a discussion of this immense theme. The Vice-President, Mr. Wallace, the Secretary of War, Mr. Stimson, the Secretary of the Interior, Mr. Ickes, the Chairman of the Foreign Relations Committee of the Senate, Senator Connally, and the Under-Secretary of State, Mr. Sumner Welles, were invited and apprised of the topic beforehand. The Embassy staff kept a full record of what passed and of the statement which I made at the formally expressed desire of our guests.

In the course of a general talk I said that the first preoccupation must be to prevent further aggression in the future by Germany or Japan. To this end I contemplated an association of the United States, Great Britain, and Russia. If the United States wished to include China in an association with the other three, I was perfectly willing that this should be done; but, however great the importance of China, she was not comparable to the others. On these Powers would rest the real responsibility for peace. They together, with certain other Powers, should form a Supreme World Council.

Subordinate to this World Council there should be three Regional Councils, one for Europe, one for the American Hemisphere, and one for the Pacific.

As for Europe, I thought that after the war it might consist of some twelve States or Confederations, which would form

the Regional European Council. It was important to re-create
a strong France, for the prospect of having no strong country
on the map between England and Russia was not attractive.
Moreover, I said that I could not easily foresee the United States
being able to keep large numbers of men indefinitely on guard
in Europe. Great Britain could not do so either. No doubt it
would be necessary for the United States to be associated in
some way in the policing of Europe, in which Great Britain
would obviously also have to take part.

I also hoped that in Southeastern Europe there might be
several confederations — a Danubian Federation based on
Vienna and doing something to fill the gap caused by the disappearance of the Austro-Hungarian Empire. Bavaria might
join this group. Then there should be a Balkan Federation.

I said that I would like to see Prussia divided from the rest
of Germany, forty million Prussians being a manageable European unit. Many people wished to carry the process of division
further and divide Prussia itself into component parts, but on
this I reserved judgment. Poland and Czechoslovakia should
stand together in friendly relations with Russia. This left the
Scandinavian countries and Turkey, which last might or might
not be willing, with Greece, to play some part in the Balkan
system.

Mr. Wallace asked about Belgium and Holland, suggesting
that they might join France. I said that they might form a
group of the Low Countries with Denmark. Mr. Wallace also
asked whether I contemplated the possibility of Switzerland
joining with France, but I said that Switzerland was a special
case.

Each of the dozen or so of the European countries should
appoint a representative to the European Regional Council,
thus creating a form of United States of Europe. I thought
Count Coudenhove-Kalergi's ideas on this subject had much to
recommend them.

Similarly, there might be a Regional Council for the Ameri-
cas, of which Canada would naturally be a member and would
represent the British Commonwealth. There should also be a

Regional Council for the Pacific, in which I supposed that Russia would participate. When the pressure on her western frontiers had been relieved Russia would turn her attention to the Far East. These Regional Councils should be subordinate to the World Council. The members of the World Council should sit on the Regional Councils in which they were directly interested, and I hoped that in addition to being represented on the American Regional Council and the Pacific Regional Council the United States would also be represented on the European Regional Council. However this might be, the last word would remain with the Supreme World Council, since any issues that the Regional Councils were unable to settle would automatically be of interest to the World Council.

Mr. Wallace thought that the other countries would not agree that the World Council should consist of the four major Powers alone. I agreed, and said that to the four Powers should be added others by election in rotation from the Regional Councils. The central idea of the structure was that of a three-legged stool — the World Council resting on three Regional Councils. But I attached great importance to the regional principle. It was only the countries whose interests were directly affected by a dispute who could be expected to apply themselves with sufficient vigour to secure a settlement. If countries remote from a dispute were among those called upon in the first instance to achieve a settlement, the result was likely to be merely vapid and academic discussion.

Mr. Wallace asked what in practice would be the procedure if, for example, there were a dispute between Peru and Ecuador. I answered that it would be dealt with in the first place by the American Regional Council, but always under the general overriding authority of the World Council. In such an instance the interests of countries outside the American Hemisphere would hardly be affected; but plainly a dispute which threatened the peace of the world might very well not be susceptible to being treated only on a regional basis and the Supreme World Council would quickly be brought in.

I was asked whether the association of nations which I contemplated would be confined to the United Nations, or include the neutrals. I replied that there was advantage in trying to induce those nations at present neutral to join the United Nations before the end of the war, and that we ought to use all possible persuasion and pressure to secure this when it could be done with safety to the nation concerned. An example was Turkey. My policy was to help Turkey to build up her own forces to the point where, at the right moment, she could and would effectively intervene. When the United Nations brought the guilty nations to the bar of justice, I could see little but an ineffective and inglorious rôle for Mr. de Valera and others who might remain neutral to the end.

We had much to learn, I said, from the experience of the League of Nations. It was wrong to say that the League had failed. It was rather the member States who had failed the League. Senator Connally agreed, and pointed to the achievements of the League in the years immediately after 1919. So did Mr. Stimson, who thought that if the original guarantee to France had not fallen through, subsequent French policy, and also the history of the League, would have been very different.

Force would clearly be required to see that peace was preserved. I suggested an agreement between the United Nations about the minimum and maximum armed forces which each would maintain. The forces of each country might be divided into two contingents, the one to form the national forces of that country, and the other to form its contingent to an international police force at the disposal of the Regional Councils under the direction of the Supreme World Council. Thus, if one country out of twelve in Europe threatened the peace, eleven contingents would be ready to deal with that country if necessary. The personnel of the international contingent provided by each country would be bound, if it were so decided by the World Council, to undertake operations against any country other than its own.

Mr. Wallace said that bases would be required for these contingents.

I said that there was something else in my mind which was

complementary to the ideas I had just expressed. The proposals for a world security organisation did not exclude special
friendships devoid of sinister purpose against others. Finally
I said I could see small hope for the world unless the United
States and the British Commonwealth worked together in
fraternal association. I believed that this could take a form
which would confer on each advantages without sacrifice. I
should like the citizens of each, without losing their present
nationality, to be able to come and settle and trade with freedom and equal rights in the territories of the other. There
might be a common passport or a special form of passport or
visa. There might even be some common form of citizenship,
under which citizens of the United States and of the British
Commonwealth might enjoy voting privileges after residential
qualification and be eligible for public office in the territories
of the other, subject, of course, to the laws and institutions
there prevailing.

Then there were bases. I had welcomed the destroyer bases
deal, not for the sake of the destroyers, useful as these were,
but because I felt it was to the advantage of both countries
that the United States should have the use of such bases in
British territory as she might find necessary to her own defence;
for a strong United States was a vital interest of the British
Commonwealth, and *vice versa*. I looked forward therefore
to an extension of the common use of bases for the common
defence of common interests. In the Pacific there were countless islands possessed by enemy Powers. There were also British
islands and harbours. If I had anything to do with the direction of public affairs after the war, I should certainly advocate
that the United States had the use of those that they might
require for bases.

*   *   *   *   *

All the American guests present said that they had been
thinking on more or less the lines which I had propounded,
and thought that it was not impossible that American opinion
would accept them or something like them. Lord Halifax asked

Mr. Welles whether he thought that the establishment of a Regional Council for Europe would have the effect of leading United States opinion to disinterest itself in European affairs. Mr. Welles was not afraid of this, having regard to the overriding responsibility of the Supreme World Council and the relation between it and the Regional Councils. Mr. Stimson said most emphatically that in his opinion there would be a tendency to relax after hostilities ceased, and a reluctance to embark upon new international experiments. He believed that it would be much easier to secure American agreement during the war; indeed, that it was a case of during the war or never. The others were disposed to agree, and we all felt that the best approach was to present such plans for the future as a continuation of our present co-operation, and to do so while the war was still proceeding.

I made two other suggestions, both of which carried warm assent. First, that after the war we should continue the practice of Combined Staff conversations, and, second, that we should by constant contact take whatever steps were necessary to ensure that the main lines of our foreign policy ran closely together.

Mr. Wallace said to the Ambassador as he left that it was the most encouraging conversation in which he had taken part for the last two years. I was of course careful to explain that I was expressing only personal views.

* * * * *

The Vice-President at luncheon with the President and me next day seemed a little anxious lest other countries should think that Britain and the United States were trying to boss the world. I made it perfectly clear that they ought not to put off necessary and rightful action by such suggestion. It was the essence of my idea that citizenship should be retained in the Anglo-American sphere even if this were wholly exceptional. The President liked the ventilation of these ideas, especially the military aspect. We both thought it essential that the institution of the Anglo-American Combined Staff should be continued for a good long time after the war —

at any rate, until we could all be sure that the world was safe.

* * * * *

On the main issues of war strategy we had six plenary meetings during "Trident," at which the President and I were present. The Combined Chiefs of Staff presented us each day with the questions on which they desired decisions as a result of their ceaseless labours. Thus all moved forward smoothly, and at the last meeting, on the morning of May 25, we were presented with their report. I had suggested a number of amendments, with which the Combined Chiefs of Staff declared themselves in agreement. The President and I then gave formal approval to the report, as amended, which follows:

OVER-ALL STRATEGIC CONCEPT FOR THE PROSECUTION OF THE WAR

1. In co-operation with Russia and other Allies to bring about, at the earliest possible date, the unconditional surrender of the Axis in Europe.

2. Simultaneously, in co-operation with other Pacific Powers concerned to maintain and extend unremitting pressure against Japan with the purpose of continually reducing her military power and attaining positions from which her ultimate surrender can be forced. The effect of any such extension on the over-all objective to be given consideration by the Combined Chiefs of Staff before action is taken.

3. Upon the defeat of the Axis in Europe, in co-operation with other Pacific Powers and, if possible, with Russia, to direct the full resources of the United States and Great Britain to bring about at the earliest possible date the unconditional surrender of Japan.

BASIC UNDERTAKINGS IN SUPPORT OF OVER-ALL STRATEGIC CONCEPT

Whatever operations are decided on in support of the over-all strategic concept, the following established undertakings will be a first charge against our resources, subject to review by the Combined Chiefs of Staff in keeping with the changing situation.

1. Maintain the security and war-making capacity of the Western Hemisphere and the British Isles.

2. Support the war-making capacity of our forces in all areas.

3. Maintain vital overseas lines of communication, with particular emphasis on the defeat of the U-boat menace.

4. Intensify the air offensive against the Axis Powers in Europe.

5. Concentrate maximum resources in a selected area as early as practicable for the purpose of conducting a decisive invasion of the Axis citadel.

6. Undertake such measures as may be necessary and practicable to aid the war effort of Russia.

7. Undertake such measures as may be necessary and practicable in order to aid the war effort of China as an effective Ally and as a base for operations against Japan.

8. To prepare the ground for the active or passive participation of Turkey in the war on the side of the Allies.

9. To prepare the French Forces in Africa to fulfil an active rôle in the war against the Axis Powers.

* * * * *

I was able to cable home that an agreement most satisfactory to our Chiefs of Staff was "being reached over the whole strategic field." This is a tribute to the authority of the President and to my close contact with him, the Staff differences of view at one time having been most serious. Moreover, we now hope to obtain a promise for the wartime transfer of twenty new American ships a month to our flag for ten months, thus affording full employment for our surplus seafaring crews. This could certainly not be arranged without the President overruling much opposition.

I was also able to send the following message to Sir John Anderson about the atomic bomb and Anglo-American research:

Prime Minister to Lord President 26 May 43

The President agreed that the exchange of information on tube alloys should be resumed and that the enterprise should be considered a joint one, to which both countries would contribute their best endeavours. I understood that his ruling would be based upon the fact that this weapon may well be developed in time for the present war and that it thus falls within the general agreement covering the interchange of research and invention secrets.

Lord Cherwell to be informed.

* * * * *

Although so much had gone well, I was extremely concerned that no definite recommendations had been made by the Combined Staffs to follow up the conquest of Sicily by the invasion of Italy. The best I had been able to get was the following resolution by the Combined Chiefs of Staff:

That the Allied Commander-in-Chief North Africa will be instructed, as a matter of urgency, to plan such operations in exploitation of "Husky" as are best calculated to eliminate Italy from the war and to contain the maximum number of German forces. Which of the various specific operations should be adopted, and thereafter mounted, is a decision which will be reserved to the Combined Chiefs of Staff.

I knew that the American Staff's mind had been turned to Sardinia. They thought that this should be the sole remaining objective for the mighty forces which were gathered in the Mediterranean during the whole of the rest of 1943. On every ground, military and political, I deplored this prospect. The Russians were fighting every day on their enormous front, and their blood flowed in a torrent. Were we then to keep over a million and a half fine troops, and all their terrific air and naval power, idle for nearly a year?

The President had not seemed ready to press his advisers to become more precise on the invasion of Italy, but as this was the main purpose for which I had crossed the Atlantic I could not let the matter rest. Hopkins said to me privately, "If you wish to carry your point you will have to stay here another week, and even then there is no certainty." I was deeply distressed at this, and on May 25 appealed personally to the President to let General Marshall come to Algiers with me. At the final conference therefore Mr. Roosevelt said the Prime Minister would shortly have an opportunity of talking to the Commanders-in-Chief in North Africa on "Post-Husky" policy, and had suggested that it would be of great value if General Marshall could go there too. He had accordingly spoken to General Marshall and asked whether he could defer his visit to the Southwest Pacific in order to fall in with the Prime Minister's request. General Marshall had said that he was perfectly willing to do this.

I then explained to the conference that I should feel awkward in discussing these matters with General Eisenhower without the presence of a United States representative on the highest level. If decisions were taken it might subsequently be thought that I had exerted an undue influence. It was accordingly a source of great gratification to me to hear that General Marshall would accompany me, and I was sure that it would now be possible to arrange everything satisfactorily in Algiers, and for a report to be sent back to the Combined Chiefs of Staff for their consideration.

*　　*　　*　　*　　*

It had been agreed that the President and I should draft the statement to be made to Russia about the conference. We made several drafts, which were typed at once and brought back. These were corrected again and again, until they were almost illegible with our scribbles. We were puzzling what to put in and what to leave out. Finally, at two o'clock in the morning, I said, much to the President's relief, "Let me take it away with me tomorrow. I will tidy it up and send it back to you from Botwood." He was content with this. I added, "It would be a good thing if Marshall came with me. There is plenty of room in the plane." We rose to go to bed, worn out by the ceaseless mental toil. At this moment General Marshall appeared. Although it had been decided that he should come to North Africa, he had not apparently expected to fly in the same plane with me or at exactly the same time. He had therefore come to say good-bye. But now the President said to him, "Why don't you go with Winston? You can talk over the Russian communiqué together." The General was surprised, but waved his hand agreeably and said, "I will be there."

22

Italy the Goal

*We Start for North Africa, May 26 — General Marshall and the
Russian Communiqué — A Long Hop to Gibraltar — The Fly-
ing-Boat Struck by Lightning — Arrival at "The Convent" —
Marshall Inspects the Gibraltar Defences — Evening Landing at
Algiers — Our Determination to Invade Sicily and Italy — Brit-
ish Strength in the Mediterranean — Conference with General
Eisenhower, May 29 — "Hobgoblin" — A Crucial Issue: The
Cross-Channel Assault — General Brooke and the Invasion of
Italy — Twenty-Seven Allied Divisions in the Mediterranean
Area — My "Background Notes" — Turkey and a Balkan Front
— An Impressive Statement by General Alexander — My Trip
to Carthage — Our Final Meeting, June 3 — Montgomery's Con-
fidence About the Attack on Sicily — We Part in Accord — A
Distressing Tragedy — The Hinge Turns.*

ARLY THE NEXT DAY, May 26, General Marshall, the
Chief of the Imperial General Staff, Ismay, and the rest
of my party took off from the Potomac River in the flying-boat.
President Roosevelt came to see us off.

As soon as we were in the air I addressed myself to the
Russian communiqué. As I found it very hard to make head
or tail of the bundle of drafts, with all our emendations in the
President's scrawls and mine, I sent it along to General Marshall, who two hours later presented me with a typed fair copy.
I was immensely impressed with this document, which exactly
expressed what the President and I wanted, and did so with
a clarity and comprehension not only of the military but of
the political issues involved. It excited my admiration.

Hitherto I had thought of Marshall as a rugged soldier and a magnificent organiser and builder of armies — the American Carnot. But now I saw that he was a statesman with a penetrating and commanding view of the whole scene. I was delighted with his draft, and also that the task was done. I wrote to the President that it could not be better, and asked him to send it off with any alterations he might wish, without any further reference to me. We landed to refuel at Botwood, in Newfoundland, and from there Marshall's draft and my letter were flown back to Washington. The President did not alter a word.

After an early dinner we took off again on our flight of three thousand miles across the ocean to Gibraltar. It looked a very long hop, but Commander Thompson, "Tommy," who kept me informed about the arrangements for my journey, explained that we should be nearly following the Great Circle, so apparently it was not so long as it looked. It was dark by the time we took off, and we were all ready for sleep. The large double bed in the bridal suite of the Boeing was most comfortable, and I slept soundly for a good many hours. All at once there was a sudden shock and bump. I awoke. Something had happened. There were no consequences, which are after all what is important in air journeys. Nevertheless, being thoroughly awake, I put on my zip suit and went forward down the long central gallery of our spacious machine, and climbed the staircase to the navigating controls. I sat in the co-pilot's seat. It was by now a lovely moonlight night. After a while I asked the pilot what caused the bump. "We were struck by lightning," he said, "but there's nothing wrong." This was good news. We had not caught fire or broken up in the air; there was no need to make a forced landing a thousand miles from anywhere. I had always wondered why aircraft did not mind being struck by lightning. To a groundsman it would seem quite a dangerous thing. Afterwards I learned that there had been a good deal of anxiety.

I looked down upon the calm ocean, seven thousand feet below; but an ocean always looks calm at that height. Almost

underneath us was what looked like a little tramp steamer.
I was conscious of a distinct sense of comfort from her presence.
Under this reassuring illusion I returned to my bed, and did
not wake until just before dawn.

I went forward again, as I love to see the daylight come.
When you are flying east at one hundred and sixty miles an
hour, you meet the sun very early and he rises quickly. I adhered to my rule in these long flights that meals should be regu-
lated by stomach-time. When one wakes up after daylight one
should breakfast; five hours after that, luncheon. Six hours
after luncheon, dinner. Thus one becomes independent of the
sun, which otherwise meddles too much in one's affairs and
upsets the routine of work. General Marshall and I had some
very agreeable talks. He questioned me closely on the difference between Impeachment, which is allowed by the United
States Constitution, and Attainder, which the British Parliament still preserve. I had no difficulty in convincing him of the
necessity of retaining this sovereign procedure. We both took
advantage of our leisure to clear away some accumulation of
papers. As we approached Gibraltar we looked around for our
escort. There was no escort. Everyone's attention was attracted
by an unknown aircraft which we thought at first was taking
an interest in us. As it came no closer we concluded it was
a Spaniard. But they all seemed quite concerned about it
till it disappeared. On alighting, at about 5 P.M., we were
met by the Governor. It was too late to continue our journey
to Algiers that night, and he conveyed us to the Convent,
where he resides, the nuns having been removed two centuries
ago.

There is a story attached to the name. Up till 1908 the
Governor's residence was always called the Convent. In that
year however King Edward VII's Private Secretary, Sir Henry
Ponsonby, wrote to the Governor and told him that the King
thought it advisable to change the name to "Government
House." The reason given was that during the King's visit to
Gibraltar in Sir George White's Governorship a paragraph
had appeared in the English newspapers to the effect that the

King had had luncheon at the Convent. Ten days afterwards His Majesty received a resolution passed by a Protestant association deploring the fact that the King should have thought it necessary not only to visit but even to have luncheon at a Roman Catholic institution. However, when King George VI visited North Africa in June, 1943, he expressed the wish that the Governor's residence should be renamed the Convent, so the Convent it still is.

We did not leave Gibraltar for Algiers until the following afternoon. There was therefore an opportunity to show General Marshall the Rock, and we all made a few hours' pilgrimage, and inspected the new distillery which assures the fortress a permanent supply of fresh water, and various important guns, some hospitals, and a large number of troops. I finally went below to see the Governor's special pet, the new Rock gallery, cut deep into the rock, with its battery of eight quick-firing guns commanding the isthmus and the neutral ground between Britain and Spain. An immense amount of work had been put into this, and it certainly seemed, as we walked along it, that whatever perils Gibraltar might have to fear, attack from the mainland was no longer one of them. The Governor's pride in his achievement was shared by his British visitors. It was not until we said good-bye upon the flying-boat that General Marshall somewhat hesitatingly observed, "I admired your gallery, but we had one like it at Corregidor. The Japanese fired their artillery at the rock several hundred feet above it, and in two or three days blocked it off with an immense bank of rubble." I was grateful to him for his warning, but the Governor seemed thunderstruck. All the smiles vanished from his face.

We flew off in the early afternoon with a dozen Beaufighters circling far above us, and in the evening light reached the Algiers airfield, where Generals Eisenhower and Bedell Smith, Admiral Andrew Cunningham, General Alexander, and other friends were waiting for us. I motored straight to Admiral Cunningham's villa, next door to General Eisenhower, which he placed at my disposal.

*   *   *   *   *

I have no more pleasant memories of the war than the eight days in Algiers and Tunis. I telegraphed to Eden to come out and join me so as to make sure we saw eye to eye on the meeting we had arranged between Giraud and de Gaulle, and all our other business.

Prime Minister to Foreign Secretary   29 May 43

If House of Commons business allows I should be very glad if you would consider joining me here for a few days. Can make you very comfortable. There are a lot of things going on. If you can, send simply the word "Porcupine" and day and hour of arrival.

I explained to the Cabinet why his presence was particularly required.

Prime Minister to Deputy Prime Minister and
Dominions Secretary   29 May 43

. . . It seems to me important that Eden should come here for a few days. He is much better fitted than I am to be best man at the Giraud–de Gaulle wedding. He ought to be conscious of the atmosphere and in touch with the actors in what may easily be a serious drama. General Georges has just visited me. He is in great form and working closely with Giraud.

I propose to stay here or hereabouts till about the 6th, as I need some rest in this sunshine after the hustle of Washington. Opinion here must be allowed to form itself naturally upon the important military issues now open. With a little patience, we British, being all agreed, will probably obtain the desired solutions, as we did at Washington.

I was determined to obtain before leaving Africa the decision to invade Italy should Sicily be taken. General Brooke and I imparted our views to General Alexander, Admiral Andrew Cunningham, and Air Marshal Tedder, and later to General Montgomery. All these leading figures in the recent battles were inclined to action on the greatest scale, and saw in the conquest of Italy the natural fruition of our whole series of victories from Alamein onwards. We had however to procure the agreement of our great Ally. General Eisenhower was very reserved. He listened to all our arguments, and I am sure agreed with their purpose. But Marshall remained up till almost the last moment silent or cryptic.

The circumstances of our meeting were favourable to the British. We had three times as many troops, four times as many warships, and almost as many airplanes available for actual operations as the Americans. We had since Alamein, not to speak of the earlier years, lost in the Mediterranean eight times as many men and three times as many ships as our Allies. But what ensured for these potent facts the fairest and most attentive consideration with the American leaders was that notwithstanding our immense preponderance of strength, we had continued to accept General Eisenhower's Supreme Command and to preserve for the whole campaign the character of a United States operation. The American chiefs do not like to be outdone in generosity. No people respond more spontaneously to fair play. If you treat Americans well they always want to treat you better. Nevertheless I consider that the argument which convinced the Americans was on its merits overwhelming.

*　　*　　*　　*　　*

We held our first meeting at General Eisenhower's villa in Algiers at 5 o'clock on May 29. General Eisenhower, as our host, presided, and had with him Marshall and Bedell Smith, as his two principals. I sat opposite to him, with Brooke, Alexander, Cunningham, Tedder, Ismay, and some others.

The first topic was "Hobgoblin." General Eisenhower explained that this was the code-name for the island of Pantelleria. Its capture was proposed for June 11. The military advantages were obvious from a glance at the map. The possession of the airfield was judged almost essential for the southern assault on Sicily. There was no reason to suppose that this attack would prejudice surprise, since the operation was also a necessary step in clearing the Sicilian Narrows. Admiral Andrew Cunningham stated that his present plan was to support the aerial bombardment with six-inch-gun cruisers, but he was ready to bring in a fourteen-inch battleship if this appeared desirable. I said that "the operation would provide a very useful experiment as to the extent to which coast defences could be neutralised by air attack. There was a school of thought in the United Kingdom which thought that air forces could knock out coast defences sufficiently to admit practically unopposed landings." Brooke observed that the difficulty lay in the fact that there was a time-lag between the end of the aerial bombardment and the arrival of the assaulting troops, which gave the enemy time to recover. The Admiral said that eight destroyers would go right in with the landing-craft and cover the landings at point-blank range. I was also assured that nineteen Sherman tanks were included in the assaulting forces. The Italian strength was thought to be about ten thousand men, including coast defence troops, together with about a hundred tanks.

General Eisenhower, at my request, gave a brief description of the plan for invading Sicily, for which all the resources seemed to be coming forward punctually and in adequate numbers. We then came to the crucial issue. General Eisenhower told us he had had a long talk with Sir Alan Brooke, who had emphasised that the Russian Army was the only land force that could produce decisive results [in 1943]. The efforts of our armies should therefore be directed towards diverting the Germans from the Russian front in order to enable the Russian armies to inflict decisive defeat upon them. General Eisenhower, speaking of 1944, said that he himself thought that if we had the command of the air an Anglo-American force of, say, fifty divisions would probably be able to hold a force of seventy-five divisions on the Continent. If we were going to knock out Italy we ought to do so immediately after Sicily and with all the means at our disposal. This would give a good indication of the type of resistance likely to be encountered on the mainland of Italy itself. If capturing Sicily proved to be easy, we ought to go directly into Italy. This would yield far greater prizes than any attack on islands.

I then said on the major question that it was true that there was no chance of our putting into Europe an Anglo-American army in any way comparable in size to that of the Russians, who were now holding two hundred eighteen German divisions on their front. By May 1, 1944, however we should have an expeditionary force of twenty-nine divisions in the United Kingdom, seven of which would have come from North Africa. The United Kingdom must be the assembly-point of the largest force which we could accumulate. It was also necessary to have plans ready to cross the Channel in force at any time in case the Germans were to crack. As General Marshall had frequently pointed out, Northern France was the only theatre in which the vast British Metropolitan and United States Air Forces in the United Kingdom could be brought into full play. I emphasised that both the British people and the British Army were anxious to fight across the Channel.

General Marshall said that a definite date for the cross-Channel operation had been settled by the Combined Chiefs of Staff and that five divisions would be used in the assault phase. General Eisenhower had asked for information as to when he should submit his (Mediterranean) plan for knocking Italy out of the war. The United States Chiefs of Staff felt that no decision could be made until the result of the attack on Sicily and the situation in Russia were known. The logical approach would be to set up two forces, each with its own staff, in separate places. One force would train for an operation against Sardinia and Corsica, and the other for an operation on the mainland of Italy. When the situation was sufficiently clear to enable a choice to be made, the necessary air forces, landing-craft, etc., would be made over to the force charged with implementing the selected plan. Eisenhower said at once that if Sicily was polished off easily he would be willing to go straight to Italy. General Alexander agreed.

The C.I.G.S. then made his general statement. A hard struggle between the Russians and the Germans was imminent, and we should do all in our power to help the former and disperse the latter. The Germans were threatened at many points. We had already made them disperse their forces by our pres-

ence in North Africa and the skilful use of cover plans. Taking
Sicily would be another step in the right direction. The Germans were faced with operations in Russia, with possible
trouble in the Balkans, and with dangers in Italy, France, and
Norway. Their forces were already widely stretched, and they
could not further reduce them either in Russia or in France.
The place where they could most conveniently do this was
Italy. If the foot of Italy were found to be packed with troops
we should try elsewhere. If Italy were knocked out of the war
Germany would have to replace the twenty-six Italian divisions
in the Balkans. They would also have to reinforce the Brenner
Pass, along the Riviera, and on the Spanish and Italian frontiers. This dispersal was just what we needed for a cross-
Channel operation, and we should do everything in our power
to increase it. The defences on the coast of France would
present no difficulty unless they were held by determined men
and the Germans had mobile reserves with which to counter-
attack.

Eisenhower then declared that the discussion had seemed to
simplify his problem. If Sicily were to succeed, say within a
week, he would at once cross the straits and establish a bridgehead. The coast defences of southern Italy would probably
be easier to crack than those of Sicily.

I expressed a personal view that Sicily would be finished by
August 15. General Marshall thought we ought to have a good
idea of this by the end of July. I said that if we were masters
of Sicily by August, and the strain had not been too heavy,
we should at once go for the toe of Italy, provided that not
too many German divisions had been moved there. The
Balkans represented a greater danger to Germany than the loss
of Italy, as Turkey might react to our advantage.

Brooke raised the possibility of a crack-up in Italy during
the Sicily fighting. In that case we ought to have a scheme of
action, and he felt that General Eisenhower should give some
thought to the consideration of armistice terms and how far
up into Italy we should go. This was getting on very fast.
Surveying the forces at our disposal, I said that, apart from the

British Army, there were nine United States divisions in North
Africa, including an airborne division. Seven divisions, including some British and United States, would begin to leave
around November 1. There were two and a half well-armed
Polish divisions in Persia, and they wished to take part in any
move directed against Italy. The New Zealand Parliament had
agreed that their division should be available by September,
and that an armoured brigade would be ready by October.
The Poles and the New Zealanders would thus provide four
divisions.

The Chief of the Imperial General Staff thereupon set out
our whole Mediterranean strength, which would amount to
twenty-seven British and British-controlled divisions, nine
United States, and four French divisions. Allowing for casualties, the total would be equivalent to thirty-six. Deducting the
seven divisions to be sent home for the cross-Channel operation
and two to cover British commitments to Turkey, there would
thus be twenty-seven Allied divisions available in the Mediterranean area. I added at this point that the strength of one
of our divisions was almost double that of a German division,
which was little more than a glorified brigade group. With
such forces in our hands it would be bad indeed if nothing
happened between August or September and the following
May.

*   *   *   *   *

Although much lay in the balance, I was well satisfied with
this opening discussion. The desire of all the leaders to go
forward on the boldest lines was clear, and I felt myself that
the reservations made on account of the unknowable would
be settled by events in accordance with my hopes. I now prepared what I called "Background Notes," setting forth the
whole case for the attack on Italy, together with tables of the
forces available. I circulated this document to the principals
before we met again on Monday, May 31.

I set forth in detail the divisions or their equivalent in the
Mediterranean theatre, showing a total of 9 American, 3⅓

French, and 27⅔ British or British-controlled. From this 7 were to be sent home for "Bolero," of which 3 were British. Of the remaining 24⅔ British only 11⅓ had so far been placed under General Eisenhower or earmarked for Sicily. With Brooke's assent I now offered to transfer to General Eisenhower 8⅔ additional British and British-controlled divisions, making a total British contribution of 20 divisions, compared wth 12⅓ from all other sources. On this basis I proceeded:

. . . His Majesty's Government feel most strongly that this great force, which comprises their finest and most experienced divisions and the main part of their army, should not in any circumstances remain idle. Such an attitude could not be justified to the British nation or to our Russian allies. We hold it our duty to engage the enemy as continuously and intensely as possible, and to draw off as many hostile divisions as possible from the front of our Russian allies. In this way, among others, the most favourable conditions will be established for the launching of our cross-Channel expedition in 1944.

3. Compelling or inducing Italy to quit the war is the only objective in the Mediterranean worthy of the famous campaign already begun and adequate to the Allied forces available and already in the Mediterranean basin. For this purpose the taking of Sicily is an indispensable preliminary, and the invasion of the mainland of Italy and the capture of Rome are the evident steps. In this way the greatest service can be rendered to the Allied cause and the general progress of the war, both here and in the Channel theatre.

4. We cannot tell at present what degree of resistance the enemy will oppose to our action. Germany may make the strongest effort to defend Sicily and Italy. We are told one division a week could be transported to Sicily or the southern part of Italy. It is desirable that this possibility should be reviewed in the light of the latest information, and stated in precise terms — i.e., the strength, gross and net, of the German divisions, the number of guns, tanks, and vehicles accompanying them, the areas from which they would most likely be drawn during the next twelve weeks, and whether they will come by rail, march, or sea. There are no signs at present of any movement of this character or on this scale. In order to have six divisions in Sicily before the operation, the enemy decisions and

preparations must already have been made and their movement should already be apparent. Moreover, if these six divisions are to move to Sicily the southern parts of Italy must remain denuded. It is asked that the most searching re-examination of the German movements and capacity to move in the direction mentioned should be made by the Staffs.

5. If the Germans decide to move forces of the order of between six and twelve divisions into Sicily and Italy we shall certainly have achieved part of our task in drawing, directly or indirectly, forces off our Russian allies. If they do not do so, but only send one or two divisions to stimulate Italian effort, the tasks mentioned in paragraph 3 should not be beyond our strength in the next three or four months. If, on the other hand, the Germans elect to fight a major battle for Sicily or for the Italian toe, or both, our armies will be fully engaged and we shall bring about that intensity of air fighting which from our growing relative strength is so greatly to our advantage. If after we have established ourselves in the southern parts of Italy she still continues to fight and the Germans send belated reinforcements on a large scale we might have to withdraw towards the tip, forcing them to attack successive prepared positions at heavy cost, with all the advantages of a procured diversion and of the air battle aforesaid. There would be no reason to regard this as a disaster. As long as we are fighting heavily with the Germans or even with the Italians we shall be playing our part.

I then set out the believed distribution of the Italian Army, amounting to fifty-eight field and fourteen coastal divisions.

6. It will be seen that there are only eleven Italian divisions in the mainland of Italy, about four in Sicily, and five along the Riviera, and that no fewer than twenty-eight are tied up in Yugoslavia, Albania, and Greece. To these twenty-eight must be added eight Rumanian and eleven German divisions, making a total of forty-seven held in the Balkan peninsula by the guerilla activities of the Serbian Michailovitch, the Croatian partisans, the general disorders in Greece, and the unrest in these enslaved countries.

7. Should Italy be made to quit the war the following practical advantages would be gained by us. The Germans would be forced to provide troops to occupy the Riviera, to maintain a new front along the Po or on the Brenner, and above all to fill the void in the Balkans caused by the demobilisation and withdrawal of Italian

divisions. Up to the present the guerrillas, etc., have only been nourished by parachute packets dropped from less than a dozen airplanes. Nevertheless, they are accomplishing the prodigious feat of immobilising forty-seven enemy divisions. The occupation of the southern parts of Italy, or even merely of the whole of the toe or heel, would give us access to the Adriatic and the power to send shiploads of munitions to Adriatic ports, and also agents and possibly small Commando bands. We should not have the troops to engage in any serious operations there, and His Majesty's Government do not contemplate or desire the provision of any organised armed force for the Balkan theatre, either this year or in any period with which we are now concerned. Nevertheless, the aiding, within the limits proposed, of the patriot bands in Yugoslavia, the fomenting of revolt in Greece and Albania, are measures of high importance, all of which, together with our main operations, will influence the action of Turkey. In this way the utmost aid in our power will be given to Russia and also to "Bolero." It is only if and when these prospects are decisively closed to us that we should consider secondary or minor alternatives for Mediterranean action.

8. All attempts to forecast the German action in the Mediterranean are of course highly speculative. Importance should however be attached to the painful impression certainly sustained by the German High Command of the complete destruction of an army of over a quarter of a million men. In the light of this event it may be doubtful whether they would court the repetition in Sicily of a similar disaster though on a smaller scale. Our situation has vastly improved: first, by the inspiring of the Allied armies through their recent victories; secondly, by the fact that only a few hundred of the enemy escaped from Tunisia to Sicily; thirdly, by the psychological effects produced on Spain and Portugal, on Metropolitan France, in Italy and in Turkey, and indeed throughout the whole area of the war. The German position has proportionately deteriorated. The series of immense battles impending on the Russian front must absorb their main strength. If the Germans do not attack, the Russians certainly will, and may indeed even forestall their enemy. We cannot foretell the results of these battles, but there is no reason to suppose that the conditions are not more favourable to the Russians than they were at this time last year. It must therefore be considered unlikely (a) that the Germans will attempt to fight a major battle in Sicily, or (b) that they will send

strong forces into the leg of Italy. They would be wiser to fight only delaying actions, stimulating the Italians in these regions and retiring to the line of the Po, reserving their strength to hold the Riviera and the Balkans, which [latter] are of value as a supply area. If the battle goes against them in Russia and if our action upon or in Italy is also successful the Germans may be forced by events to withdraw to the Alps and the Danube, as well as to make further withdrawal on the Russian front and possibly to evacuate Norway. All these results may be achieved within the present year by bold and vigorous use of the forces at our disposal. No other action of the first magnitude is open to us this year in Europe.

* * * * *

We met again at Eisenhower's villa on the afternoon of May 31. Mr. Eden arrived in time to be present. I tried to clinch matters, and, after referring to the paper I had circulated, said that my heart lay in an invasion of Southern Italy, but the fortunes of battle might necessitate a different course. At any rate, the alternative between Southern Italy and Sardinia involved the difference between a glorious campaign and a mere convenience. General Marshall was in no way hostile to these ideas, but he did not wish for a clear-cut decision to be taken at this moment.

He said that it would be better to decide what to do after we had started the attack on Sicily. He felt it would be necessary to know something of the German reactions in order to determine whether there would be real resistance in southern Italy: whether the Germans would withdraw to the Po, and, for example, whether they could organise and handle the Italians with any finesse; what preparations had been made in Sardinia, Corsica, or in the Balkans; what readjustments they would make on the Russian front. All these things would be factors in deciding our "Post-Husky" plans. There were two or three different ways in which Italy might fall; and a great deal could happen between now and July. He, General Eisenhower, and the Combined Chiefs of Staff were fully aware of my feelings about invading Italy, but their only desire was to select the "Post-Husky" alternative, which would give the best results.

I said that the conclusions of the minutes of the last meeting did not represent my whole feeling. I very passionately wanted to see Italy out of the way and Rome in our possession, and I offered to send the eight additional British divisions from other parts of the Middle East if these were needed. There was a considerable discussion about these reinforcements and the shipping required to move them. I said it would be hard for me to ask the British people to cut their rations again, but I would gladly do so rather than throw away a campaign which had possibilities of great success. I could not endure to see a great army stand idle when it might be engaged in striking Italy out of the war. Parliament and the people would become impatient if the Army were not active, and I was willing to take almost desperate steps in order to prevent such a calamity.

General Marshall replied that he was not arguing against the broad commitment made in Washington to aim at the fall of Italy. He only wished to emphasise that we must exercise great discretion in choosing what to do after the conquest of Sicily.

* * * * *

An accident now occurred which, as it relates to matters which have become the subject of misunderstandings and controversy after the war, must be related. Mr. Eden, at my request, commented on the Turkish situation, and said that knocking Italy out of the war would go a long way towards bringing the Turks in. They would become much more friendly "when our troops had reached the Balkan area." Eden and I were in full agreement on the war policy, but I feared that the turn of his phrase might mislead our American friends. The record states, "The Prime Minister intervened to observe emphatically that he was not advocating sending an army into the Balkans now or in the near future." Mr. Eden agreed that it would not be necessary to put an army into the Balkans, since the Turks would begin to show favourable reactions as soon as we were able to constitute an immediate threat to the Balkans.

Before we separated I asked General Alexander to give his view. He did so in an extremely impressive speech.

He said that he was optimistic. The fighting value of our troops and equipment was excellent and so were our chances of success, although it might take a fortnight of very bitter fighting. Once we joined battle, the slogging generally lasted from ten days to a fortnight, or even three weeks. Then the end came quickly. The most important points in Sicily were the airfields in the southeast corner of the island, and the ports. Once we had a firm grip on these we could ignore the remainder of the island for the time being. It should be possible to cross the Straits of Messina and secure a foothold on the opposite shore, which was the very windpipe of Sicily. He repeated his statement made at the meeting of May 29 that securing a bridgehead on the Italian mainland should be considered as a part of the plan. It would be impossible for us to win a great victory unless we could exploit it by moving ahead, preferably up into Italy. All this however would be clarified as the Sicily operation moved along. It was not impossible, although it seemed unlikely, that the toe of Italy would be so strongly held as to require a complete re-staging of our operations and we should be ready to keep moving with no stop at all once the attack on Sicily was started. "Modern warfare allowed us to forge ahead very rapidly, with radio controlling troops at a great distance and with air providing protection and support over a great area. The going might become more difficult as we moved up the Italian mainland, but this was no argument against going as far as we could on the momentum of the 'Husky' drive." He stated that none of the possibilities he had discussed could be accurately foreseen. In war the incredible often occurred. A few months before it would have been impossible for him to believe what had actually happened to Rommel and his Afrika Corps. A few weeks since, he would have found it difficult to believe that three hundred thousand Germans would collapse in a week. The enemy air forces had been swept out of the skies so completely that we could have a parade, if we chose, of all our North Africa forces on one field in Tunisia without any danger from enemy aircraft.

He was at once supported by Admiral Cunningham, who said that if all went well with "Husky" we should go directly across the Straits. Eisenhower concluded the meeting by expressing appreciation of the journey which Mr. Churchill and General Marshall had made to clarify for him what the Combined Chiefs of Staff had done. He understood it was his responsibility to get information regarding the early phases of "Husky" and forward them to the Combined Chiefs of Staff in time for them to decide on the plan which would follow, without a break or a stop. He would send not only information but also strong recommendations, based upon the conditions of the moment. He hoped that his three top commanders (Alexander, Cunningham, and Tedder) would have an opportunity to comment more formally on these matters, although he agreed completely with what they had said thus far.

*   *   *   *   *

On the two following days we travelled by plane and car to some beautiful places rendered historic by the battles of a month before. General Marshall went on a brief American tour of his own, and then travelled with General Alexander and myself, meeting all the commanders and seeing stirring sights of troops. The sense of victory was in the air. The whole of North Africa was cleared of the enemy. A quarter of a million prisoners were cooped in our cages. Everyone was very proud and delighted. There is no doubt that people like winning very much. I addressed many thousand soldiers at Carthage in the ruins of an immense amphitheatre. Certainly the hour and setting lent itself to oratory. I have no idea what I said, but the whole audience clapped and cheered as doubtless their predecessors of two thousand years ago had done as they watched gladiatorial combat.

*   *   *   *   *

Our last meeting, on June 3, was largely concerned with the question of bombing the marshalling yards of Rome, and there was agreement that they were an important and necessary

military objective, and that there was no valid reason for re-
fraining from bombing this target, provided the attacks were
made by day and due care was taken to prevent damage elsewhere. General Marshall and I undertook to seek authority
from our respective Governments authorising such action.

I now asked General Montgomery, who had joined us at this
meeting, to say what he thought about the plan of invading
Sicily, with the execution of which he had been entrusted.
Montgomery said that all his commanders had complete confidence in the present plan, and that the troops would be filled
with enthusiasm when they stepped ashore. Some administrative risks were involved, but they had been gone into very
carefully and he felt that they were justified. He pointed out
that although he had two airborne divisions he had only
enough air transport for one. In the early stages he would be
able to employ only about one-third of his airborne strength;
the remainder should be brought in on D + 2 or D + 3. With
one hundred forty more aircraft he could employ another airborne brigade at the very first. However, he understood that
these were not available and the limitation was accepted. His
officers were completely happy about the whole thing. As
regards "Post-Husky," he felt it important that we should
decide in what direction we wanted to go, and use our military
strength to make the battle move that way.

I felt that great advances had been made in our discussions
and that everybody wanted to go for Italy, I therefore, in
summing up, stated the conclusions in a most moderate form
and paid my tribute to General Eisenhower. I said I would
take home the feeling of confidence and comradeship which
characterised action in this theatre. I had never received so
strong an impression of co-operation and control as during my
visit. It would be impossible to embark on an undertaking
under better augury. I said that I should not like to go away
without reaffirming my full confidence in General Eisenhower,
and without expressing my admiration of the manner in which
he had handled his many great problems.

General Eisenhower replied that any praise which might be

given belonged to the officers round the table, and stated that while there might be differences of opinion and discussion in his headquarters, these were never based upon national lines. General Marshall and General Brooke warmly concurred, and we all parted on the best of terms.

* * * * *

Eden and I flew home together by Gibraltar. As my presence in North Africa had been fully reported, the Germans were exceptionally vigilant, and this led to a tragedy which much distressed me. The regular commercial aircraft was about to start from the Lisbon airfield when a thickset man smoking a cigar walked up and was thought to be a passenger on it. The German agents therefore signalled that I was on board. Although these passenger planes had plied unmolested for many months between Portugal and England a German war plane was instantly ordered out, and the defenceless aircraft was ruthlessly shot down. Thirteen passengers perished, and among them the well-known British film actor, Leslie Howard, whose grace and gifts are still preserved for us by the records of the many delightful films in which he took part. The brutality of the Germans was only matched by the stupidity of their agents. It is difficult to understand how anyone could imagine that with all the resources of Great Britain at my disposal I should have booked a passage in an unarmed and unescorted plane from Lisbon and flown home in broad daylight. We of course made a wide loop out by night from Gibraltar into the ocean, and arrived home without incident. It was a painful shock to me to learn what had happened to others in the inscrutable workings of fate.

* * * * *

Here then we end this volume which describes the turning-point of the Second World War. The entry of the United States into the struggle after the Japanese assault on Pearl Harbour had made it certain that the cause of Freedom would not be cast away. But between survival and victory there are many stages. Over two years of intense and bloody fighting lay before us all. Henceforward however the danger was not Destruction but Stalemate. The Americans' armies had to mature and their vast construction of shipping to become effective before the full power of the Great Republic would be hurled into the struggle. But further success lay right before us and the fall or rather liberation of Italy was near. Hitler had still to pay the full penalty of his fatal error in trying to conquer Russia by invasion. He had still to squander the immense remaining strength of Germany in many theatres not vital to the main result. Soon the German nation was to be alone in Europe, surrounded by an infuriated world in arms. The leaders of Japan were already conscious that their onslaught had passed its zenith. Together, soon Great Britain and the United States would have the mastery of the Oceans and the Air. The hinge had turned.

END OF BOOK TWO

★

Appendices

★

Contents

APPENDICES TO BOOK ONE

APPENDICES TO BOOK TWO

★

Book one

Appendix A, Book One

LIST OF ABBREVIATIONS

A.A. GUNS	Anti-aircraft guns, or ack-ack guns
A.D.G.B.	Air defence of Great Britain
A.F.V.s	Armoured fighting vehicles
A.G.R.M.	Adjutant-General Royal Marines
A.R.P.	Air raid precautions
A.T. RIFLES	Anti-tank rifles
A.T.S.	(Women's) Auxiliary Territorial Service
C.A.S.	Chief of the Air Staff
C.I.G.S.	Chief of the Imperial General Staff
C. -in-C.	Commander-in-Chief
CONTROLLER	Third Sea Lord and Chief of Material
C.O.S.	Chiefs of Staff
D.N.C.	Director of Naval Construction
F.O.	Foreign Office
G.H.Q.	General Headquarters
G.O.C.	General Officer Commanding
H.F.	Home Forces
H.M.G.	His Majesty's Government
M.A.P.	Ministry of Aircraft Production
M.E.W.	Ministry of Economic Warfare
M.O.I.	Ministry of Information
M. OF L.	Ministry of Labour
M. OF S.	Ministry of Supply
P.M.	Prime Minister
U.P.	Unrotated projectiles — i.e., code-name for rockets
V.C.A.S.	Vice-Chief of the Air Staff
V.C.I.G.S.	Vice-Chief of the Imperial General Staff
V.C.N.S.	Vice-Chief of the Naval Staff
W.A.A.F.	Women's Auxiliary Air Force
W.R.N.S.	Women's Royal Naval Service ("Wrens")

839

Appendix B, Book One

LIST OF CODE-NAMES

ACROBAT: Advance from Cyrenaica into Tripolitania.

ADMIRAL Q: President Roosevelt.

ANAKIM: Recapture of Burma.

ASPIDISTRA: Secret wireless station in United Kingdom.

ATTILA: German code-word for occupation of free zone of France.

BACKBONE: Plan for operation against Spanish Morocco.

BOLERO: Administrative preparations for main invasion of France (afterwards the foundation of OVERLORD).

BONUS: Operation against Madagascar (later called IRONCLAD).

BRIMSTONE: Capture of Sardinia.

CANNIBAL: Capture of Akyab.

COLONEL WARDEN: The Prime Minister.

CORKSCREW: Capture of Pantelleria.

CRUSADER: Operations in the Western Desert.

FIREBRAND: Capture of Corsica.

GEE: A radar aid to bomber navigation.

GYMNAST: Plan for operations in French North Africa (later called TORCH).

HABBAKUK: Floating seadrome made of ice.

HERCULES: Enemy code-name for operations against Malta.

HOBGOBLIN: Operation for capture of island of Pantelleria.

HUSKY: Capture of Sicily.

IMPERATOR: Plan for raid on French coast, 1942.

IRONCLAD: Operations against Madagascar.

JUBILEE: Raid on Dieppe, 1942.

JUPITER: Operations in Northern Norway.

KINGPIN: General Giraud.

LIFEBELT: Operations against Portuguese Atlantic islands.

LIGHTFOOT: Operations by the Eighth Army in the Western Desert in October, 1942: Alamein.

MAGNET: Transportation of American troops to Northern Ireland.

OVERLORD: The liberation of France in 1944.

PEDESTAL: Convoy to Malta, August 1942.

PUGILIST: Offensive in Western Desert against Mareth Line.

RETRIBUTION: Naval operations against German evacuation of Tunis.

ROUND-UP: Plan for the liberation of France in 1943.

SLEDGEHAMMER: Plan for attack on Brest or Cherbourg in 1942.

SUPERCHARGE: Operations by the Eighth Army in the Western Desert in November 1942.

SYMBOL: Casablanca Conference, January 1943.

TORCH: Allied invasion of French North Africa.

TRIDENT: Washington Conference, May 1943.

TUBE ALLOYS: Atom bomb research.

UPKEEP: Special aircraft weapon.

VELVET: Allied air assistance to Russian southern flank.

VIGOROUS: Eastern Mediterranean convoy, 1942.

VULCAN: Allied operations for capture of Tunisia.

WATCHTOWER: American operations in Solomon Islands.

WINDOW: The use of tinfoil strips to confuse German radar.

Appendix C, Book One

PRIME MINISTER'S PERSONAL MINUTES

January — June, 1942

JANUARY

Prime Minister to General Ismay, for C.O.S. Committee   18 Jan. 42

Please report what is being done to emulate the exploits of the Italians in Alexandria harbour and similar methods of this kind. At the beginning of the war Colonel Jefferis had a number of bright ideas on this subject, which received very little encouragement. Is there any reason why we should be incapable of the same kind of scientific aggressive action that the Italians have shown? One would have thought we should have been in the lead.

Please state the exact position.

Prime Minister to Secretary of State for Air   18 Jan. 42

I hear you are in default of 45 aircraft for December for Russia, and that this will not be rectified until January 25, and that the January quota will not be cleared until February.

It seems a very great pity to fall short in Russian deliveries by these comparatively small quantities, which cannot affect your main problem here.

I must emphasise that exact and punctual deliveries to Russia are of the utmost importance, as this is all we can do to help them.

NOTE FOR AIR MINISTRY AND WAR OFFICE

DEFENCE OF AERODROMES

22 Jan. 42

It is important that the arrangements should be simple and easy to understand. The first object is the local defence of the aerodrome, which requires unity of command both in the preparation and the event.

2. This immediate local defence falls to the R.A.F., because they have

the bulk of the people on the spot. It is also most important to release as many as possible of the young soldiers' battalions and other military personnel for the mobile field army from this static defence.

3. In order to take over all existing aerodromes, the R.A.F. will require an additional 13,000 men over and above the 66,000 R.A.F. ground personnel already serving. This additional 13,000 will not however constitute an additional burden on the country's man-power since they will be deducted from the ceiling allotted to the Army for aerodrome defence.

4. Nothing in the above conflicts with the general responsibility of the War Office for attacking any invader or intruder wherever found, and especially acting promptly in the defence and relief of airfields. The Commander-in-Chief Home Forces will make all arrangements necessary for this purpose, and he will concert the operations of Home Forces so far as may be necessary with the airfield defence personnel. He will assist the Air Force stations by advising on their plans of local defence, and will possess independent right of inspection [with liberty] to report to the War Office for transmission to the Air Ministry upon the standards of efficiency obtained.

Prime Minister to General Ismay, for C.O.S. Committee   23 Jan. 42

This [report about deficiencies in supplies to Russia] is very serious. If the figures are true they amount to a breach of faith. Pray let me have the explanation and the correct figures, together also with the amounts which have been sent. Any short-fall on the part of the Service departments will be in direct disobedience of the Cabinet instruction.

Prime Minister to C.I.G.S. and Director of Military Intelligence   23 Jan. 42

I understood some time ago that the Turks had moved the bulk of their forces from Thrace to the Asiatic shore, and this was certainly the advice given them by Sir John Dill. I spoke to the President of the United States in this sense. But now it seems that either I was misinformed or there has been a change in dispositions.

Let me know how the matter stands, as I must put myself right with the President.

Prime Minister to Secretary of State for Air   23 Jan. 42

The vanguard of the American troops, numbering over 4000 men, arrives at Belfast on Sunday evening or Monday morning. I am inviting the American Ambassador to meet them there, together with the Governor-General and the Prime Minister of Northern Ireland. I should also like one of the Service Ministers to meet these troops on their arrival, and I should be obliged if you would undertake this journey. Perhaps you will get in touch with the Home Secretary in order to concert arrangements.

Prime Minister to C.A.S.   24 Jan. 42

This [aircraft wastage] is a frightful total, in a week while so little has been going on. I must request you to make me proposals for effecting a substantial reduction. I hope you will be able to reassure me that this is possible.

Meanwhile please let me have the figures for operational losses at the hands of the enemy, and the rest separately.

Prime Minister to M.A.P.   24 Jan. 42

Pray let me have the reasons for this extremely bad week, which is not a holiday week. All your figures for January are most disappointing, and far below target.

Prime Minister to C.A.S.   25 Jan. 42

I am of opinion that another four squadrons of Hurricanes will have to be found for the second trip of the *Indomitable* to the Malay peninsula. These must come from the Middle East, and must be replaced as soon as possible by fighter aircraft flown to Malta.

2. The report [from Air-Marshal Tedder] shows that there is difficulty in fuelling and servicing in the East the aircraft already on the spot. The report I received yesterday about the Takoradi route shows a substantial congestion of Hurricanes and Blenheims at Takoradi. There is at present no immediate hurry, because *Indomitable* has not yet flown off her first party, but a decision will have to be taken this week by the Defence Committee, and a time-table should be worked out.

Prime Minister to First Lord   27 Jan. 42

Is it really necessary to describe the *Tirpitz* as the *Admiral von Tirpitz* in every signal?

This must cause a considerable waste of time for signalmen, cipher staff, and typists. Surely *Tirpitz* is good enough for the beast.

Prime Minister to General Ismay, for Chief of Staff Committee 30 Jan. 42

Consider whether the West African Brigade, now brought back to its home station from East Africa, should not be got ready to reinforce General Wavell's command in the Far East.

Let me have the quickest possible time-table, observing it is halfway already.

Prime Minister to General Ismay   30 Jan. 42

Let me have a table showing location of every Indian division, including divisions in training, together with approximate strength in men and guns.

Prime Minister to Secretary of State for War and Minister   30 Jan. 42
of Information

I am concerned about the fullness of the information given in the newspapers of the Singapore position. For instance, why is it necessary to state that a mile has been evacuated for defensive purposes on the north side of the island? Considering that the siege is now entering on its vital phase, we cannot afford to have our point of view about it so candidly disclosed. Sir John Wardlaw-Milne's statement in the House of Commons should be examined by the Staffs. I asked General Wavell some time ago to have a stricter censorship on Singapore. What has been done about this? They seem to give everything away about themselves in the blandest manner. After all, they are defending a fortress and not conducting a Buchmanite revival.

Prime Minister to C.A.S.   31 Jan. 42

Please observe that, out of 1550 serviceable aircraft, Fighter Command has managed to smash up 126, or one aircraft in twelve, during a week in which there has been hardly any fighting. Let me know how many sorties there have been against the enemy. Let me have also a detailed analysis of the accidents during the week in question in Fighter Command, showing at least a dozen classes of cause.

Fancy all this wanton waste happening at a time when we have got so few in the kitty and ought to be fattening up for the spring fighting.

FEBRUARY

Prime Minister to C.I.G.S.   22 Feb. 42

Now that Mr. Lyttelton, the Minister of State, is leaving Cairo, I contemplate somewhat different arrangements, namely: (*a*) General Auchinleck to be Supreme Commander over the three Services in his command, Navy, Army, and Air. (*b*) A resident Cabinet Minister in Cairo, who would do all the work which Mr. Lyttelton relieved him of, and in addition play a larger part in securing the proper handling of the rearward services.

2. It seems essential to find out why our forward servicing is so inferior to that of the enemy, and why such a small proportion of our tanks can be maintained in action.

3. Let me know your personal views in the next days.

Prime Minister to Secretary of State for Air and C.A.S.   26 Feb. 42

It is thought in many quarters that the air news and propaganda defeats itself by the excessive recording of ordinary routine fighting. Many people turn off the wireless when the air news is reached. There is perhaps an inevitable sameness about it, and one cannot see the wood for the trees.

It is a pity, because fine exploits and exceptional occurrences do not always receive the distinction and attention which they deserve.

2. You would be well advised to adopt a much more highly selective process not only in the communiqués and on the broadcast, but in the reports made to the Cabinet. It has never been thought necessary to give an exact list of ordinary trench raids or skirmishes on the fronts of large armies. Fighting of a normal character in the different theatres should surely be summarised once a week — e.g., Malta has had a hard week (or a busy week) in the air, so many sorties have been made, and so many enemy shot down, etc., instead of a daily laborious catalogue. If this were done, any event like twenty or thirty enemy aircraft being bowled over would make the right impression on the public. As it is, the Air Ministry's fine tale runs the risk of becoming a bore instead of an inspiration. Monotonous repetition should at all costs be avoided.

Prime Minister to Secretary of State for Air   28 Feb. 42

I have had prepared for me the following table showing the numbers of aircraft wrecked or damaged by enemy action and in flying accidents in 1941:

	Enemy Action. Operational Machines	Flying Accidents	
		Operational Machines	Trainers
Wrecked beyond repair............	1,900	2,500	1,100
Repairable —			
Only at contractor's works.......	300	2,900	1,500
By working party from contractor's			
works......................		3,300	1,300
By ground staff of unit..........		1,800	1,900

It is true that nearly all the damaged airplanes are repaired and ultimately come back to service, but this all means many man-hours of skilled labour. Even without exact figures there seems to be little doubt that by far the greater part of the efforts of M.A.P. are squandered in making or repairing machines which are destroyed or damaged, not by enemy action, but in flying accidents.

Pray let me know what steps you propose to take to remedy this very unsatisfactory position.

MARCH

Prime Minister to General Ismay, for C.O.S. Committee   2 Mar. 42

I am increasingly impressed with the disadvantages of the present system of having Naval, Army, and Air Force officers equally represented at all points and on all combined subjects, whether in committees or in commands. This has resulted in a paralysis of the offensive spirit, due to the fact that the officers of the three Services together nearly always, except in the higher ranks, present the sum of their fears and difficulties.

2. It seems to me that we should move in the direction of appointing Supreme Commanders in particular areas and for special tasks. The Task Commander should be the new feature, who might sometimes be an admiral, a general, or an airman. This would also be true of the staff work and joint planning. When any plan is to be studied an officer of one or other of the three Services should be told to make a plan and the others to help him. Which Service is selected depends upon (*a*) the nature of the operation and which Service is predominant, and (*b*) the personality concerned.

3. I shall be obliged if you will give these matters your careful consideration.

Prime Minister to Dominions Secretary   4 Mar. 42

(Lord Privy Seal to see.)

I do not see much use in pumping all this pessimism [appreciation of situation in the Far East] throughout the Empire. It is the fashion here; but it will do great harm wherever else it goes. Has it gone? Altogether there is too much talk. A very different picture and mood may be with us in a couple of months.

Prime Minister to Colonel Jacob   5 Mar. 42

Surely there must be many air groundsmen in the Far East whose squadrons have been destroyed? Have these been taken into account in the new lay-out? The Air Force are taking up almost the convoy-space of a fighting division for their ground personnel.

Prime Minister to C.I.G.S.   5 Mar. 42

What is the meaning of the expression "Failed to silence machine-gun posts"? It seems an odd description of an action. Evidently what happened was only a skirmish. Surely the way to silence machine-gun posts is to bring up some guns and shell them.

Prime Minister to Lord Privy Seal   8 Mar. 42

I held last year a number of "Tank Parliaments," at which all the Divisional Commanders were present. They seemed a very fine lot. But of course the experiences we have gained at the front should make continual changes.

I am not at all sure that speed is the supreme requirement of tanks, certainly not of all tanks. Armour and gun-power decide the matter whenever tank meets tank. Anti-tank weapons are advancing fast in power, and thin-skinned animals will run ever-increasing risks.

Prime Minister to Lord Cherwell   10 Mar. 42

I agree with the general outline of your minute [about further restriction of civil consumption]. In particular I am opposed to the heavy taxation of entertainments. It would be well worth while rationing bread moderately in order to bring in the more nourishing Lend-Lease foods. It would be better to ration than to let the stocks run down. Bread is scandalously wasted now and often fed to pigs and chickens. The great thing is to keep the price down, so that the poorest can buy their full ration.

I deprecate the policy of "misery first," which is too often inculcated by people who are glad to see war-weariness spread as a prelude to surrender.

The value of all the various self-strafing proposals should be estimated in tonnage of imports. If there is a heavy economy to be achieved on any article, let us effect it; but it would be unwise to embark upon a lot of fussy restrictions in order to give, or try to give, satisfaction to the Fleet Street journalists who are exempted from military service, have no burden of responsibility to bear, and live in the restaurants of the Strand.

You should draft something for me couched in more decorous form.

Prime Minister to Chief of the Air Staff   13 Mar. 42

What is the position about dive-bombers for the Army? Surely it is more than a year ago that they were ordered by Lord Beaverbrook. Let me have the dates, also dates of the discussions on the Defence Committee. Where are they now? How many have been delivered? What is the forecast of deliveries for the next three months? What is thought of them from an air point of view?

Prime Minister to First Sea Lord   13 Mar. 42

I noticed that when *Tirpitz* was attacked unsuccessfully by our torpedo aircraft she turned away behind a smoke-screen. Why was this manoeuvre not open to Admiral Phillips? Had he the means of making smoke? Could not his destroyers have put up a smoke-screen? or were they afraid of spoiling the shooting of his A.A. guns?

Prime Minister to Secretary of State for War, Lord Leathers, and Lord Cherwell   13 Mar. 42

Pray meet together as early as convenient and discuss the points raised in this file.[1] Is it really true that the War Office have been guilty of sending two Australian divisions to Australia without any question of

1 About dismantling lorries in order to save shipping space.

combat landings, yet with all their vehicles unbroken down? How much
shipping will be wasted on this? Pray advise me what directions should
be given for our general policy in the future.

Prime Minister to Minister of Information   22 Mar. 42

It should surely be possible to point out to the newspaper proprietors or to
the editors that before articles are printed advocating specific operations
or drawing attention to the dangers attaching to particular places the
Military Adviser to the Ministry of Information should be consulted.
General Lawson is fully capable of giving guidance. For instance, suppose it were desirable for us to occupy Bear Island or Spitzbergen, articles
advocating this would make the operation far more dangerous to our
troops. Or, alternatively, articles pointing out that Thursday Island or
Christmas Island was a very important strategic point and that strenuous
efforts should be made to retain it, or that great alarm prevailed in the
local population, or that special measures had been taken to enforce a
blackout, would tend to concentrate the enemy's attention upon these
places and increase the danger. It is not intended that the rule should
be hard and fast, so as to paralyse speculation, but reasonable consultation beforehand is most desirable. No other country tells the enemy
all they are likely to do beforehand, or where they feel most vulnerable.

A much larger case is that of the invasion of the Continent. An
agitation in the British press to invade the Continent, maintained
throughout the spring, would certainly lead to the loss of many British
lives through the improved preparations and fortifications made against
it, should such an operation ever be undertaken. I realise this is hard
upon the press. It is also hard upon the men who would be killed, and
their dependents, should action be taken. Surely points like this can be
put with your authority and influence to the proprietors and editors.

When operations are intended or in progress surmise is just as bad as
leakage. The enemy does not know that it is not leakage. Promising
operations may actually have to be abandoned because of press discussion
about them. I regard all this as most serious if we are to embark upon a
period of offensive operations. I get little comfort from the theory that
so much is written that the significance cancels itself out. The enemy is
very intelligent, and these newspapers reach him in a few days via Lisbon.
All is carefully sifted and collated with other knowledge.

Prime Minister to General Ismay   29 Mar. 42

You should write to Lord Hankey as follows:

"In view of the statements which you made in the House of Lords
about late sittings on defence matters, the Prime Minister had the question examined.

"In the last six months the total is 19, or about 3 a month. At least 50 per cent of these meetings ended before midnight.

Prime Minister to C.I.G.S. and Commander-in-Chief   30 Mar. 42
Home Forces

If we are to believe the latest estimates of the Combined Intelligence Centre [about the number of tank landing-craft in the possession of the Germans], all the stories about 800 specially constructed vessels and the deductions founded upon them as to the scale of invasion are obsolete. I was always sceptical about these 800 vessels, and have repeatedly questioned the trustworthiness of the rumours.

I hope all our calculations are kept up to date.

APRIL

Prime Minister to First Lord   2 Apr. 42

New Construction Programme. Let me have the details of the 2250-ton destroyers which you propose to build. I do not understand how they will be a screen against torpedo-carrying aircraft comparable to that which could be afforded by fighter aircraft working from carriers. Does all this arise out of the *Prince of Wales–Repulse* disaster? How far away from the battle fleet to be protected are the screening destroyers to lie? Let me have the argument set forth.

2. I am naturally prejudiced against destroyers which take 21 months to build, at a time when the multiplication of U-boats requires above all things numbers and speed of construction. On general grounds, an unarmoured vessel of 2250 tons — i.e., practically a *Scout* class cruiser — is a divergence from sound principles of naval construction. You make a ship which is neither a cruiser nor a destroyer, which is hunted by U-boats rather than being their hunter, and which exposes, I imagine, 180 officers and men, without the slightest armour protection, to destruction at the hands of any light cruiser.

3. If these two flotillas of very large destroyers were converted into more destroyers of the class capable of being completed in a year, how many of them could we get?

4. It is a great mistake to blur types. The Navy successfully resisted the temptation to multiply the old *Swift*.

5. The fact that you have to construct these immensely powerful and costly (to the war effort) destroyers to protect the battle fleet is another point telling against the whole conception of the battleship.

Prime Minister to Minister of Production, Minister of Supply,   3 Apr. 42
and General Ismay, for C.O.S. Committee

Churchill tanks. Our policy must be reviewed. There are 1185 tanks delivered, of which about 900 are in the hands of troops. In the next six months we can either make 1000 new ones, with all the improvements up to date, and all mounting the 6-pounder gun, or make 500 new ones and rework 500 of the 1185. The pros and cons of this have to be very carefully weighed.

2. In any competitive peacetime business no one would worry about the 1185, but would pass rapidly on to new improved production. If we do this, we get the 1000 new, plus the 1185. All the new have the 6-pounder; all the 1185 have the 2-pounder. Total 2185. If we rework the 1185 to the detriment of new production, we get 500 new, 500 reworked, and 685 of the original unimproved. Total 1685.

3. By this second method we lose 500 tanks, and we have to throw away 500 2-pounder turrets for which no use is at present proposed. This seems a dead loss. Decision turns upon the quality of the 1185. What exactly is their unimproved value? They cannot be called useless. There is only one under repair for every two in service with troops. This is about the same proportion as the Matildas, and compares as 2 to 1 *versus* 3 to 1 with the various cruiser types. Is it not better to have the 1000 new 6-pounder Churchills and make the best we can of the 1185? I am going to inquire myself into the possible uses of the 1185. Two or three hundred of the worst could very likely be used for defence of aerodromes. The rest could be reworked gradually *without prejudice to new production*.

4. Meanwhile care might be taken in handling the rest of the 1185. Some could be used for training. The Canadian Anti-tank Brigade speak well of them, and say that in the hands of tractor-practised drivers breakdowns are greatly reduced. Can we not, by bonuses, etc., and greater practice, induce similar proficiency in the British drivers? The Commanding Officers must be asked about this. Another question to put to them is whether the breakdowns in Churchills choke the field repair shops unduly. If this is so, some of them might be laid up temporarily as new 6-pounder Churchills arrive. The full equipment of the armoured units might be delayed accordingly, having regard to the receding of immediate invasion danger. Arrangements can be made to make sure that none of the 1185 are employed outside this country.

5. Reflecting on the whole matter, the argument for leaving the 1185 unimproved and making the best of them and their 2-pounder guns, and going ahead full speed on the new type, seems overwhelming. Pray let this be considered by the Ministry of Supply and the General Staff before the conference on Monday at Eastbourne.

Prime Minister to C.A.S. 4 Apr. 42

Have you seen the figures which Sir Arthur Street has sent me about the relative aircraft production, actual and prospective, of the two sides

in this war? If these are true — and he vouches for them, on the authority
of the Air Staff — it looks as if the surplus of pilots will soon be reversed.
The figures certainly justify you in forming new squadrons, not only to
replace those sent abroad, but additional.

2. The extreme importance of pressing the enemy in the next six
months and forcing him to use up his dwindling air-power is obvious.
Could you let me have some figures to show the estimated wastage on
both sides? The Axis must be more fully deployed and engaged than the
Allies because so great a part of the British and American air forces cannot be applied to the fighting front, whereas Germany is fighting in
Russia, before Malta, and in Libya; and Japan [is fighting] on all fronts
simultaneously. Our interest is to engage wherever and whenever possible.
Our problem will be to apply the broadest superficies of attack. Here
again transportation rears its ugly head.

3. Let me know what you feel about [the safety of] the great numbers
of pilots massed together in the Bournemouth hotel. All these men will
be wanted quite soon if American production opens out as promised.

Prime Minister to Secretary of State for War   4 Apr. 42

If you are to get any effective reduction [in vehicles] you must aim at
a cut of, say, 35 per cent, and then see how near you can get to it. You
will have to fight every inch of the way. I shall be glad to see an interim
report in a week's time.

2. It would be wise to issue a definite order that no transport is to be
packed on board ship un-broken-down, without special authorisation
from C.O.S. Committee, such authorisation to be given only when it is
needed for expected combat-landings. A great waste of shipping has been
incurred in carting all the lorries of the Australians from the Middle East
to Australia with their wheels on.

Prime Minister to General Ismay, for C.O.S. Committee   7 Apr. 42

The requirements of the General Staff for the Army appear to be out
of all proportion to existing or prospective resources, and if satisfied
would be destructive of the principle of an independent Royal Air Force.
In this respect it would appear that the Air Ministry's view requires
careful consideration and comment by the General Staff with a view to
accepting fair points and minimising differences.

2. There would be enormous dangers in tethering an immense proportion of our Air Force to Army units, most of which will be waiting
about for months, and perhaps years, without becoming engaged with the
enemy.

3. The General Staff request for 2484 specially designed transport aircraft seems to be beyond all immediate possibilities. I am however most
anxious to increase the airborne forces to the utmost limit as soon as

possible. A scheme should be prepared for converting all bombers as they fall obsolete to troop-carrying purposes, either parachute or ordinary. It should not make great demands upon production to fit new compartments to existing machines, but a special Conversion Branch should be set up and a good plan made.

4. I am sceptical of the Ministry of Aircraft Production assertion that it would be "at least four years before a new machine could be made available in quantity for transport purposes." Considering how very low and simple is the standard of performance required, all the elements of this problem must be known. A variety of patterns might be adopted to work in discarded engines and other material. It is only necessary to make flying buses, and uniformity is not essential as long as safety is secured. As a long-term project the United States might be willing to make and share a class of specially designed transport aircraft. What are they doing about it now?

5. Meanwhile I hope proposals may be made here for increasing the airborne transportation programme. It is not necessary to have these worked out as if we were making a lady's dressing-case. The existing proposals of the Air Ministry are exactly fitted to the tactical units they are to carry. The additions which we must make should consist, in the first instance at any rate, of anything that can be improvised to carry men or stores. Let me see the establishments proposed for an air borne division. I trust simplicity and avoidance of fancy frillings will be sedulously sought for. A note on what the Germans do would be very helpful.

Prime Minister to Lord President   11 Apr. 42

There is general agreement about the proposals in your paper about coal, except for the transfer of 7,000 trained soldiers from the Field Army to the pits. These 7,000 men, if they produce the same as the average mine-workers, might hew 2 million tons of coal in a year. The effect of such a dislocation in the Army at this critical time is so serious that I hope all other alternatives to find these 2 million tons will be exhausted. There are many alternatives, it seems to me, at first sight, which are less injurious to our general war effort: (*a*) Drawing from the coal reserve of 12 million tons. (*b*) Economies might be effected by a system of allocating coal to various users, such as obtains in other raw materials. (*c*) Further economies in the war production departments. (*d*) Reduction in industrial users than munitions. (*e*) A possible reduction in the export programme. (*f*) Monetary rewards to miners for surrender of a portion of their customary coal allowance. (*g*) Directing a large number of untrained youths of 18–19 years into the pits. (*h*) Persuading or allowing a proportion of ageing men to work for another year. (*i*) Possible expansion in outcrop working. (*j*) Getting miners to work an extra 15 minutes a week.

With all these possibilities in view, each of which might mean nearly a million tons a year, there should be no difficulty in finding the two million tons, thus avoiding the injury to the Army.

2. Further help will be given by all your long-term projects, including the financial point about relating excess profits tax to tons mined.

3. Meanwhile the War Office are to specify how many miners they have in the Metropolitan Field Force, what proportion are face-workers, and how many of them are with the fighting formations — that is to say, excluding transport, R.A.S.C., R.A.O.C.,[2] and other ancillary services. The War Office will of course find the 5000 men out of the 12,000 asked for, which are to be given from A.D.G.B. and other Field Force branches.

4. I hope all these possibilities will enable us to round the corner without taking the very grave step at this juncture which would derange the solidity of the Army.

Prime Minister to First Sea Lord   12 Apr. 42

Can you give me details of the method of supplying Malta by submarine? I understand that removal of certain batteries greatly increases the carrying capacity of the submarine, and I would like to inform the United States authorities of these details for use in supplying Corregidor.

Prime Minister to First Sea Lord   14 Apr. 42

Give me the latest dates for completion of repairs to *Nelson* and refit of *Rodney*. Has work been proceeding night and day on these two ships and the two *Ansons,* as ordered by the War Cabinet four months ago?

2. You surely do not propose to send *King George V* for refit in the present stringency?

3. What are the defects in *Malaya* to which Admiral Somerville takes exception? What is her speed, and in what respect is her radius less than *Valiant*? Are her guns cocked up?

4. Admiral Cunningham told me that the *Valiant* crew were in perfect order, and he could not understand why they should require a lengthy period of working up. He seemed very much surprised when I told him you did not think they would be ready till the end of June.

Prime Minister to Foreign Secretary and General Ismay,   19 Apr. 42
for C.O.S. Committee

A large number of German and Italian prisoners of war are at present in Egypt, and substantial numbers in India. Those in Egypt are a burden on the Army and a danger to internal security. In particular there are 8000 Germans, and large numbers of troops are required to guard them.

2. Mr. Hopkins suggested that the United States might gladly take these prisoners if asked. A start should certainly be made on the 8000

[2] Royal Army Service Corps and Royal Army Ordnance Corps.

Germans. There are many American ships returning empty from the Red Sea ports which might well carry them. No special escort would be necessary.

3. Pray let this matter be examined and proposals made for action. General Auchinleck should be consulted.

Prime Minister to General Ismay   25 Apr. 42

Let me know exactly what improvements have been made in the garrison, air force, and defences of Ceylon since the Japanese attack at the beginning of April. What reinforcements have already reached Colombo, what are on the way, and what will be there by (*a*) the end of May? (*b*) the end of June? Let me have a special report on the air and other forces to be used in holding Madagascar, if captured. Madagascar should have precedence over Kilindini, though not over Colombo. But C.O.S. Committee should check this opinion.

Prime Minister to General Ismay   26 Apr. 42

I am astounded to see the numbers of copies that were struck off of this "All Most Secret and Personal" telegram. Who is the officer responsible for this? Show me the rules governing such distributions. I intend to bring the matter before the Cabinet.

Prime Minister to Chief of the Air Staff   27 Apr. 42

Please make me proposals for increasing the number of discarded bombers which can be placed rapidly at the disposal of the Airborne Corps. At least 100 should be found within the next three months. We cannot go on with 10,000 keen men and only 32 aircraft at their disposal.

Prime Minister to Secretary of State for War   28 Apr. 42

I have carefully studied the new organisation of the armoured divisions, and of the infantry divisions which is now proposed, and I need scarcely say, in view of opinions I have expressed from time to time, how cordially I agree with it. The intimate, harmonious mingling of armoured forces and infantry is essential if the infantry is to regain its rights as the leading arm upon the battlefield. The emphasis placed upon artillery by the Germans in armoured divisions also seems to me wise. In short, it seems that both armoured and artillery divisions will be the gainer by the changes. I cannot believe that any general, having the choice between an existing infantry division and a new division with its armoured element, would hesitate to choose the new one. The armoured divisions also can easily be grouped together when it is desirable to use mass formations of armoured troops in the same way as cavalry brigades and divisions have been used in the past to form a cavalry corps. Such an organisation would rise naturally out of the tactical requirements of a particular operation or a particular theatre, and need not have a permanent cadre or fixed establishment prescribed beforehand.

2. Let me see the strengths and composition of the Home Field Army before and after the reorganisation under the following heads:

(1) Infantry battalions.

(2) Number of guns in the field artillery (including howitzers).

(3) Flak and anti-tank units.

(4) Machine-guns of all kinds.

(5) Armoured fighting vehicles of all types.

(6) Non-fighting vehicles of all types.

(7) Staffs of all kinds.

(8) Numbers of supply, transport, and administrative services of all kinds.

(9) And the total of officers and men of all ranks.

3. In comparing these new tables with those of the German system, it would be worth while to test our new organisation by comparing the percentage of staffs, divisional and brigade, with the numbers of men in the division. This might also be applied to signals, postal units, etc. It does not follow that the Germans are right, but I think it will be found that they serve more fighting men with fewer overheads.

MAY

Prime Minister to Minister of Production   1 May 42

I note from [the Monthly Progress Report for March] that the output of aircraft is still far below programme. Heavy bombers are one-fifth down, light bombers nearly one-half. This is most disappointing in a long month after we had been promised that these were truly realistic forecasts. I hope you will be able to find out what is the real limiting factor, so that it can be put right.

Neither the programme of labour requirements, which has been outstanding for a long time, and which you asked for at your last meeting, nor the report on specialised machine tools, with a statement about double-shifting and the types in short supply, has yet been presented.

Can we rely absolutely upon sufficient allocations of magnesium from America in the second half of this year? According to [this report], our supplies will only be 10,600 tons, as against requirements of 14,900 tons.

I observe that air-screws are not mentioned in this monthly report. Last autumn the position was held to be disquieting, and now it appears that the difficulties have not been overcome. This is a most serious matter, and every effort must be made to put it right immediately.

Prime Minister to Chief of the Air Staff   1 May 42

Let me have by tomorrow the proposed policy for bombing during

May, together with a list of the principal objectives at which it is desired
to strike. I realise of course that the weather governs our actions from
day to day, but give me the plan apart from weather.

2. You have no doubt seen General Dobbie's appeal for an intervention
by Bomber Command in Sicily. It might be that this would be necessary
in order to keep down the attack just before a wave of Spitfires was
landed [by us]. How would you do it? Could the Wellingtons fly from
England to bomb Sicily, land on the possibly cratered airfields of Malta,
and return home the next night, dropping another load of bombs? If
not Wellingtons, what aircraft would you use? It is quite understood this
would be very costly if it had to be done. Pray let me have the best plan
possible.

3. Will a P.R.U.[3] be sent over *Tirpitz* today? This might reveal tugs
in position round her. It is most important to get information.

Prime Minister to First Lord and First Sea Lord   4 May 42

It is probable that we shall not have the use of *King George V* for at
least three months, after which I suppose a long period of working-up
will be required. Pray examine therefore the following plan to tide us
over this most critical interlude.

2. Let the whole of the *King George V* crew go on leave simultaneously
for a fortnight, or whatever is the proper period. Meanwhile let the
Anson's crew be transferred to *King George V,* and the *King George V*
men go as a complete, integral, highly trained unit to the *Anson,* which is
an identical ship in almost every respect. Thus the working up of the
Anson would consist almost entirely of testing her material qualities.
This change ought to save at least a month's or six weeks' delay in the
ship being ready for battle.

Prime Minister to General Ismay   6 May 42

This is very unsatisfactory. The whole object was to give the Middle
East a supply [of puff-balls] [4] in time for any battle they might fight.
Now we have just enough in both places not to be an important feature
in any operations that may occur. I made some efforts to get these out to
Middle East before the November battle, and even so it has not been
possible to bring them into action in any appreciable numbers.

Prime Minister to First Lord and First Sea Lord   6 May 42

I should be glad if you would send the following:

"Prime Minister to Commander-in-Chief, Eastern Fleet

"Should be glad if you would address yourself particularly to (*a*) im-

3 A Photographic Reconnaissance Unit of the R.A.F.
4 Aerial anti-tank bombs invented by Colonel Jefferis.

proved reciprocal defence by three carriers in company as compared with one alone; (b) special dangers of an attack by enemy aircraft before dawn and how best to meet them; and (c) what would be the best proportion of fighters and torpedo planes for each aircraft-carrier to carry, and what your three carriers would have available for the occasion.

"2. We shall know several important things by June 1 now hidden, and we must then survey the whole scene and count the cost and risk either way.

"3. All good wishes."

Prime Minister to Minister of Production　　　　　　　8 May 42

Please see attached [minute about agricultural caterpillar tractors from United States] from the Minister of Agriculture. There is a considerable argument that if we are to have three-quarters of a million American troops here next year we shall require [to grow] more food, especially as the stringency on the Atlantic is increasing. These heavy caterpillar tractors will yield a direct result, but I have not yet been informed how large in tonnage is the estimated food yield.

Will you see the Minister of Agriculture, and also consider how this could be fitted in with our other American requirements?

I should be ready to send a telegram to Hopkins if all is tidied up.

Prime Minister to Minister of Aircraft Production　　　　8 May 42

Thank you very much for your minute [about production of aircraft in April]. By the annexed table you will see that our output of heavy bombers seems to be about a month behind what was promised. So far from the target having been pushed "rather higher than was likely to be achieved," the targets we are now working to represent three or four writings down, including one quite recent. I am glad of the improvement, but the need is more urgent than ever.

Aircraft Production

		Actual	Programme
1941	December	55	79
1942	January	81	91
	February	81	103
	March	104	130
	April	127	149

Prime Minister to Secretary of State for War, C.I.G.S.,　　8 May 42
and Minister of Production

It seems very important to raise the figure of 60 rounds practice ammunition per rifle to 100 at the earliest. This should be possible by the middle of June. The position at the present moment is serious, and every effort should be made to relieve it.

2. What arrangements are made now for practice? How much ammunition have the Home Guard been allowed to fire? It is more important to build up the reserve than to train them under present hard conditions. Let me know what has been done, and what is proposed in the future as things improve.

3. 1,700,000 is the figure given for men in the Home Guard. My latest figure is 1,450,000, of which only 840,000 have rifles. Of course those with rifles are relieved by those without, and they all ought to be trained, but surely the emphasis should be on getting a number trained in shooting equal to the rifles issued. Let me know what is the plan about this.

4. I still think that, in view of the immense quantities of .30 ammunition now being produced in America — 319,000,000 rounds in March, for instance — we ought to try to get another 100,000,000 over to improve holdings of the Home Guard and for practice. I should be willing to make an effort for this.

5. Let me have a return showing the equipment of the Home Guard, including rifles, American machine-guns, and tommy guns, and also the British weapons of this kind which they may have. I suppose a machine-gun accounts for two or three men to only one with a rifle? Also, how many sporting and shot-guns are available with the Home Guard? How many are there without firearms of any kind? We cannot afford to let the whole of this vital factor in our defence fall into twilight because for the moment invasion is not obviously threatened.

Prime Minister to Secretary of State for War   10 May 42

The greatest problem in A.A. Command today seems to be personnel. It appears indefensible to maintain 280,000 men waiting for an attack that may never develop, if other means can be found to man the weapons. I realise that the Home Guard can never man weapons required in working hours. Light A.A. regiments must therefore be manned by whole-time soldiers. I am sure however that rocket batteries and heavy A.A. searchlights, in varying proportions, could be manned, wholly or in part, by Home Guard and A.T.S. How is the scheme of mixed batteries getting on? I am told women are not volunteering in sufficient numbers.

2. General Pile should be asked to state a ceiling for Home Guard and A.T.S., and to estimate how many men he could release for use with the Field Army if this ceiling were reached. Ways and means can then be examined for making this exchange. He has been most helpful in releasing and diluting.

Prime Minister to First Lord, First Sea Lord,   12 May 42
and Fifth Sea Lord

The immediate need is to give Admiral Somerville the largest number
of Martletts and Sea Hurricanes in the very shortest time, and let him
use them as he thinks best. Please let me know what can be done, with
dates.

Prime Minister to Foreign Secretary   13 May 42

The following seems to me to be the policy of munitions to Turkey:
Nothing much can be done this summer or before the Russian campaign
decides itself more clearly. Nor do we ask anything more of the Turks
than to keep intruders out. But as soon as the Russian front shuts down
with the winter an effort should be made, for which preparations must
be begun forthwith, to give them a substantial packet of tanks, anti-tank
guns, and flak. By that time there should be an immense flow of munitions in the United States and our own output running higher. The
figures mentioned in America are enormous, and there should be no
difficulty in sparing 1000 tanks and 1000 anti-tank and A.A. guns. No
doubt older marks might form the bulk.

2. If a plan is prepared on this sort of scale, and deliveries begin in
November, the promise will make the Turks stand during the summer
neutral, and the arrival of these weapons, which they can train upon
during the winter, may make them our allies in the spring.

3. If you think well of this, let us take it up with Production here and
in the United States.

Prime Minister to Minister of Aircraft Production   13 May 42

Your latest return shows that you have 1797 "in preparation." These
are presumably in addition to the 649 ready, and ready within four days.
The shortage of aircraft at the present moment is acute. Now is the
time for you to bring forward this reserve of 1797, which are presumably
defective in this or that spare part.

Lord Beaverbrook in 1940 gained great advantages for us by a searching analysis and scrutiny of the machines in the Air Supply Units. What
we want now is *more aircraft in the front line*. Get at it and bite at it.

2. Give me therefore the following reports: (*a*) The corresponding
figures to 649 and 1797, week by week, for the last two years, and (*b*)
make me a proposal to bring forward into the squadrons 500 of the 1797
by July 15. It may well be that there are some additional spare parts
with the R.A.F. at home, surplus to immediate requirements, which would
make some of these machines alive. I am told the Beaufighters in particular could be brought forward, and are urgently needed. There are 280
of these on your hands. Let me have a separate return, showing what is
holding back the 100 most promising Beaufighters.

3. I presume you have an exact record of each of these types of machines, and can say exactly what is needed to bring any one of them forward to the fighting line. If so, let me see it. If not, you ought to have. You need not give any explanation about the 363 Wellingtons; I am already aware of it.

Prime Minister to Foreign Secretary   15 May 42

There is no need to unsay anything we have said, but the fact remains that should Turkey be attacked in the summer or autumn of 1942 there are practically no forces that we could send to her aid, and even if we had large forces the communications from Syria do not lend themselves to their movement. Something no doubt will be done under the pressure of the event.

2. We have made certain promises of minor allocations of munitions during the summer and autumn. These should be kept so far as is physically possible.

3. My idea was to make a large, simple offer to the Turks, operative from November on. I should not propose to work the policy I have set out through the Joint Assignments Board, but to persuade the President to join with me in making a promise to Turkey which, if they and others survive the summer, would give them effective hope of being in a strong position by the spring of 1943. Something on the lines I have suggested might play a very important part in encouraging Turkey through these anxious months and in enabling her to participate in the 1943 campaign, should our affairs in these regions prosper.

Prime Minister to Foreign Secretary and Minister   17 May 42
of War Transport

Have we thanked the Americans properly for the allocation of 70 tankers? This seems to me to have been a very open-handed action on their part, considering the losses they have suffered. No doubt thanks are conveyed departmentally, but should I not make some reference to this in one of my telegrams to the President? If so, let me have the materials.

Prime Minister to First Lord and First Sea Lord   17 May 42

Dr. Evatt has made me the strongest appeals about an aircraft-carrier. We had of course promised them the *Hermes* but she was sunk on our business before being sent to them. You now tell me that they had said they did not want her. Have you seen however the long telegram which Dr. Evatt has received from Mr. Curtin, in which the need of two aircraft-carriers is stressed? I carefully avoided making the slightest promise, but I have been wondering whether the *Furious* could be spared. Will you let me know what are your plans for her?

2. Why should the *Victorious* require a refit now? How long has she been with the Fleet? I should have thought less than a year. What is the nature of the defects which require her withdrawal at this critical juncture? I recognise the fact that the Americans have withdrawn *Wasp* and that this makes our position more difficult, and of course *Wasp* is a reinforcement for the Pacific. We have to consider our permanent relationship with Australia, and it seems very detrimental to the future of the Empire for us not to be represented in any way in her defence.

Prime Minister to First Lord and First Sea Lord   17 May 42

What actually has happened in the Caribbean Sea? Did the convoy system come into operation on the 15th as promised?

Prime Minister to General Ismay   18 May 42

A squadron of fighters — i.e., 16 — should be provided. They can be of the older types. A large allocation of 3.7-inch and Bofors A.A. guns is required. Surely we have some light tanks of the original marks. These would play their part in the primitive warfare of [Central] Africa. Please report what is available. There was certainly no lack of anti-tank rifles some time ago, ammunition being the shortage. Surely something better can be done than 60?

2. On the other hand, I would not give these weapons without obtaining from the Belgians a clear indication of the forces they would raise. My son, who stayed a week at Leopoldville, has written me a letter, an extract from which I append. There seems to be great force in getting some Belgian officers out to the Congo. At least four brigade groups should be raised in the Congo. They would be available for service on the west or east coasts of Africa, in Madagascar, or even farther east should the war move that way.

Extract from letter to the Prime Minister from Mr. Randolph Churchill, dated April 28, 1942

"All the Belgians who are keenest on the war are puzzled why all the Belgian troops are kept in England. They say that with a few hundred officers they could raise a considerable native force. And they are also very short of white personnel both for administration and the expansion of war industries. They think that the Belgian Government are trying to build up a large force in England for purely prestige purposes. So much so that any young Belgian in the Congo who volunteers to fight is promptly shipped off to England."

THE AUTUMN CAMPAIGN OF 1942 IN THE INDIAN OCEAN

Prime Minister to General Ismay, for C.O.S. Committee   18 May 42

We should aim at assembling the Eastern Fleet at Kilindini by July 7

at the latest, and at basing this fleet on Colombo or/and Trincomalee by
July 15. All arrangements, including A.A., fighter and torpedo aircraft,
moorings, etc., for the protection and accommodation of the fleet at either
of these stations, should be pressed forward with the utmost urgency.

2. The movement of the four modernised ships and the three carriers
to Ceylon harbours should not be prevented for the sake of including
the four "Rs." Otherwise we shall see another case of their low fighting
quality and obsolete character becoming an actual hindrance rather than
a help to our operations. Based upon Diego Suarez, they can, at this
great distance from the enemy and with strong naval forces established in
Ceylon, afford protection to the convoy route. When the accommodation
in Ceylon is prepared for their reception they may, if desired, move there.

3. We must resist the temptation to disperse our anti-aircraft resources
between Colombo and Trincomalee. Whatever is necessary should be
given to one port, and the other should make shift with what is left
pending further improvement. We must make up our mind which. Until
we have one invincibly defended base in Ceylon we cannot provide for
Addu Atoll. Remember the Scotch saying, "Ain guid house, and that weel
plenished."

4. As between Kilindini and Diego Suarez, the priority for A.A. defences
should go to Diego Suarez, which should be developed as a stronghold
against all forms of attack, *and advertised as such to an even greater
extent.* As it is highly improbable that any attack will be made upon it
or upon any part of Madagascar by the Japanese, the forces and resources
employed there must remain, as proposed by the Chiefs of Staff Committee, on an altogether secondary level.

5. The task of Commander-in-Chief Eastern Fleet, "to deter the Japanese from operating in the Bay of Bengal except by a superior force," is
admirably defined in Admiralty [instructions]. Let us stick to this, *and
make other ideas conform to it.*

6. The probability of the Japanese sending into the Indian Ocean a
fleet superior to the Eastern Fleet (less the four "Rs") appears small.
Their narrowly measured resources in capital ships and regular aircraft-
carriers enforce upon them extreme care. It does not seem that they would
be anxious to seek a battle with so substantial a force as the Eastern Fleet
(even less the four "Rs"), provided — and provided only — (*a*) that our
aircraft-carriers have their full equipment of Martletts or other fast fighters,
and (*b*) that we keep as much as possible within the range of our shore-
based torpedo aircraft. If the losses in a fleet action were anything like
equal, the result to Japan would be irreparable disaster. Nothing in the
Japanese strategy has hitherto shown them willing to risk any part of
their battle fleet. Their incursion into the Bay of Bengal was very carefully conducted. Their abandonment of their expedition after the action
in the Coral Sea shows the stringency of the aircraft-carrier problem with

them. Therefore we need not expect them to seek a trial of strength in the Indian Ocean except with a detachment only of their fleet. To send the main fleet would be for them a most adventurous decision.

7. Every effort should be made to reach the full quota of shore-based aircraft (reconnaissance, bomber, and torpedo) required to give protection to the Eastern Fleet when operating in the Bay of Bengal, and to dominate the shore-based aircraft of the enemy which he must be expected to be building up on the territories he has conquered in that region. The combination of sea- and air-power which we should seek to establish there by the end of September should· be sufficient not only to prevent seaborne invasions of India, but also to enable us to take oversea action of our own. In this theatre, as in others, it pays us to force the air fighting and to lose machine for machine.

8. All military reinforcements to India are of course dependent upon the fortunes of war in Libya, in the Caucasus, and in Australia. Assuming however that the course of events is not unfavourable to us, we should be able to send the 8th Armoured Division and at least one British infantry division, besides the 2nd and 5th Divisions, to arrive in India by the end of September. This would give General Wavell the 70th, 2nd, 5th, 45th, and 8th (Armoured) Divisions, together with the British-Indian Army and garrisons of, say, four divisions. Total, nine divisions. In October therefore conditions should permit his assumption of a general offensive against the Japanese in Burma.

9. It is absolutely necessary that this offensive should be planned from now on, and every effort made, subject to events, to carry it into effect. Landing-craft must be prepared locally and a proportion sent from home. British and American air reinforcements must be gathered to the utmost limit permissible by other needs. The attack upon the Japanese lines of communication might be vital in the continued resistance of China. We ought also to hold out the prospect to Chiang Kai-shek, under all necessary reservations, of such an attack, in order to keep him fighting. Everything goes to show the correctness of the judgment we formed that the drive against Chungking is the first Japanese objective, apart of course from Russia, which depends upon how the battle in the West develops. A general amphibious British air and land offensive from Moulmein to Assam must be the aim we set before ourselves for the autumn and winter of 1942.

Prime Minister to Foreign Secretary   19 May 42

The telegrams seem to be growing longer and longer. For a while, after you issued some warning, there was an improvement. The waste of time and energy involved in these long codings and decodings is most serious. I quite understand they all want to help the war by increasing their output. In fact, they clog and hamper.

Prime Minister to Foreign Secretary   19 May 42

I quite understand the French resisting when we attacked them at
Oran, Dakar, Syria, and Madagascar, under the present unhappy conditions. But this wanton attack [5] by them on our aircraft so far out at sea
seems to stand on a different footing. We have never accepted their 20-
mile notification, and anyhow this was probably outside that limit. Can
we not do something about it?

Prime Minister to Lord Cherwell   22 May 42

Let me have the totals in the weekly returns which have been made
for me for the last few months of wastage in the Metropolitan Air Force
set in a column side by side with the weekly subscription of new and
repaired aircraft. Then in a third column show, if known, the exports of
aircraft to Russia and the East, including all abroad; and finally, deducting wastage and export from the total contribution (new and repaired),
let me see the balance credit remaining in this country, if any.

Prime Minister to Minister of Production and   25 May 42
Minister of Works and Buildings

When driving through South London today I noticed a great many
private houses damaged by air raids which appear structurally all right,
but are nevertheless unrepaired and uninhabitable. In view of certain
accessions of population which we are to receive from abroad, we shall
surely need every habitable dwelling-house, and it would seem that some
relief might be had from a vigorous policy in this direction.

Please let me have a report upon the numbers of houses in this condition, and whether you think a useful policy could be developed, with
resultant economy of labour and material.

Prime Minister to Minister of Economic Warfare   27 May 42

I commend to your notice a recent book by John Steinbeck, *The Moon
is Down,* published this year by the Viking Press, of New York.

In addition to being a well-written story, it stresses, I think quite rightly,
the importance of providing the conquered nations with simple weapons,
such as sticks of dynamite, which could be easily concealed and are easy
in operation.

Prime Minister to Secretary of State for War and C.I.G.S.   27 May 42

A company of a Young Soldiers Battalion of corps troops, Buffs, were
detailed for my protection when I visited Chartwell this week-end. I
naturally inspected it, and asked questions about its equipment. I was

[5] By a French fighter aircraft on a Catalina on anti-submarine patrol from
Gibraltar.

told that they were short of Bren gun carriers and very short of Bren guns. The output of Bren guns and Bren gun carriers has been very good for some time. I was not aware that there was any deficiency in these two items.

2. I also noticed there were in the battalion two different marks of Lee-Metford rifles. Even some platoons were half and half. The sighting of these rifles is different, although of course they take the same ammunition. Could you let me have a note on this, stating whether any other units are in a similar condition?

3. I request that no trouble should be caused to the company or the battalion, as I am responsible for asking the questions, which it was the duty of those concerned to answer.

JUNE

Prime Minister to General Ismay, for C.O.S. Committee   1 June 42

Your last paragraph really does not bear on the question of the Western theatre *versus* the attack on Japan. I have never suggested sending any further troops to the East than those now on the sea or under orders. The most that would be asked would be aviation, certain landing-craft, and any special tackle that may be required. Should we gain success in Libya we must review the whole position, and by then I hope General Wavell will have let us know his views, what he would like to do and what he wants to do it with. There is no need to take any decision about the 8th Armoured and 44th Infantry Divisions until we see what the situation is as they round the Cape. Neither are we committed to any attack on the Japanese communications through Burma this year. But, having regard to the immense disaster which the falling out of China would spell, it seems only prudent to get everything moving to the aid of the Chinese, subject to the progress of the war. Of course, if the Russian southern front crumbles there could be no question of our pushing hard in the Far East. In any case, I repeat, it is only the use of the troops now assigned to the Eastern theatre that would be involved.

2. We must not acquiesce too easily in the many delays which hamper the assembly of the Eastern Fleet. There is a good deal in Admiral Somerville's telegrams which favours the idea of his playing a passive rôle, avoiding "frittering away" his strength in the Bay of Bengal, etc. . . . His duty, once his fleet is assembled and based on Ceylonese harbours, is to prevent any seaborne invasion of Eastern India unless escorted by markedly superior Japanese strength. Also, when our shore-based air is established on the east coast of India in adequate strength he may have to escort an amphibious expedition of our own. I entirely agree that the air will be the key to movement here. Let us therefore wait (*a*) the results of the battle in Libya, and (*b*) Wavell's ideas.

3. As they advance, the Japanese will be spread about enormous areas of wild country in Burma and South China, and will be in contact with the Chinese. The Japanese have only five or six divisions in these regions, and their supply problem will become one of great difficulty, ragamuffins though they be. We cannot afford to have idle troops or idle aircraft anywhere, and as the summer advances we may be able to re-establish ourselves at Akyab and make them wear out their Air Force by fighting at continually closer quarters. No one can tell whether the conditions which would render an amphibious stroke possible will establish themselves, but it would be most improvident not to have everything ready so as to take advantage of such a situation should it arise. We shall know a lot by August that we do not know now.

Prime Minister to Director of Military Intelligence　　2 June 42

Let me have a report, on not more than two pages, about the patriotic activities in Yugoslavia, and the relative position of the German and Italian invaders.

Prime Minister to Chief of the Air Staff　　2 June 42

I presume General Pile and all others concerned have been keyed up to expect a German retaliation for our [thousand bomber] raids.

Prime Minister to Minister of Labour　　2 June 42
(Copies to Minister of Production and
　　Lord President of the Council.)
Thank you for your note of May 14 [comparing the manpower position today with pre-war].

I agree that we have done well to draft two million people into the Forces, Civil Defence, industry, and services, especially when it is remembered that the unemployed have also been absorbed, and that so many have been transferred from civil employment to the Forces and other Government work.

We are rapidly approaching the limits of man-power which can be devoted directly to the war. It will be for the Minister of Production and the supply departments to endeavour to increase the efficiency of management, and to achieve the best distribution of effort in the Government sector, as between constructional and production work, and as between the three Services and the various weapons. This may have to be modified in some degree by the American entry into the war.

Prime Minister to General Ismay, for C.O.S. Committee　　3 June 42

This [telegram from Commanders-in-Chief Middle East] is a good example of how resources can be frittered away and dispersed in an

unending process of passive defence. It is no use being afraid of getting
into trouble because an enemy raiding party turns up at some unguarded
spot. The defence of all these places can only be maintained by naval
power based on Ceylon harbours, with adequate seaborne air and shore-
based air protection. In case anything slips through the naval defence, a
mobile force with amphibious equipment should be prepared, organised,
and kept in the Egyptian theatre. This force, which might be a suitably
equipped brigade group, would proceed to the attack of the raiders after
their descent had been made and inflict a salutary punishment upon
them. But while this force is organised on paper, and even sometimes,
if occasion serves, exercises as a tactical unit, it must of course not be
earmarked from existing resources in the Middle East, and should take
part in all the fighting whenever it is needed. This seems to me a good
opportunity for impressing upon these Commanders-in-Chief the fallacy
of trying to be safe everywhere. There are not enough troops in the
world to meet this kind of demand.

Prime Minister to General Ismay, for C.O.S. Committee   3 June 42

I have heard nothing of the Royal Marine Division since the Royal
Marine brigades went with the Dakar expedition. What are the plans
for its employment? Is it to be used in "Sledgehammer" or "Round-up"?
If not, might we not offer it to General Wavell? There should be good
opportunities for well-trained, lightly equipped amphibious troops in his
area in the near future.

2. Let me have a report about this.

Prime Minister to Dominions Secretary   6 June 42

The situation has changed very much in our favour since this question
[of supplies for Southern Ireland] was last considered. Very large United
States forces are coming into Ireland. The Germans are deeply involved
on the Eastern front. It is *we* who are making preparations now to invade
the Continent. There is therefore very little likelihood of the weapons
which it is now proposed to give to Southern Ireland being used against
anybody but ourselves, in case we have need of these bases.

I cannot consider the matter as in any way urgent. I hope therefore
that it may be reconsidered when we see how the fighting goes in Russia.

*Prime Minister to Secretary of State for War, Secretary of State
for Air, and Minister of Works and Buildings*   11 June 42

It is, as you know, the policy of the Government to refrain from
rationing domestic fuel, if by other means the production and consumption of coal can be brought into equilibrium.

As part of the measures for bridging the gap between production and
consumption, the War Cabinet have directed the new Ministry of Fuel

and Power to see that full use is made of existing stocks of coal held at
the collieries. Some of this is inferior coal, and the Ministry will have
to insist that industrial undertakings and other large consumers shall
take some coal of a poorer quality than that which they are accustomed
to use.

The new Ministry will need the fullest co-operation from all Government departments who are large users of coal, and I should be glad if
you would make it clear to all concerned in your department that they
must support the Ministry by accepting their share of this low-quality
coal.

Prime Minister to First Lord   11 June 42

The Horse Guards Parade has now been disfigured for many months
by untidy dumps of material for your new construction at the Admiralty.

I hope the time has now come when it will be possible to remove all
these obstructions, and I trust that this work may be taken in hand with
the least possible delay.

Pray let me know what is proposed, and how soon the Admiralty side
of the Parade will be completely cleared.

Prime Minister to General Ismay   12 June 42

Let me have a list of all tanks landing at or approaching Suez during
June and July, specifying types.

Prime Minister to First Sea Lord   14 June 42

Let me have a report about the sinkings in the Mozambique Channel.
Where are the Japanese submarines or U-boats based, and what measures
are you proposing?

Prime Minister to Lord President of the Council   14 June 42

Your minute [about the repair of damaged houses] does not altogether meet the need as I see it. If by the expenditure of fifteen or sixteen
million pounds we can get 158,000 new serviceable houses we shall be in a
far better position to cope with the great influx that is to be expected from
the United States, and it would be very cheap in money and labour at the
price. I am astonished that more has not been done already.

2. The return of Government departments to London should also be
emphasised. To what extent are evacuated children coming back? They
are in no more danger in London, where the defences are so strong, than
in the country.

Prime Minister to First Lord, First Sea Lord, and   15 June 42
General Ismay

It will be necessary to repeat the Thousand [Bomber] Operation in the
June moon. On the coming occasions it will be necessary that Coastal

Command should participate, and I must ask definitely for compliance with this request.

Pray inform me what will be done.

Prime Minister to Chief of the Air Staff   15 June 42

In conversation with Air Marshal Harris, on Saturday last, I learned with pleasure that he is keen upon using the June moon for another edition of "Arabian Nights." I hope you will approve of this, unless there is some very serious reason to the contrary.

Meanwhile I have asked the Admiralty to make sure that they do not prevent Coastal Command from playing its part. I understand Joubert had 250 machines ready, but that the Admiralty stopped their use.

Pray let me know if I can assist you.

Prime Minister to General Ismay, for C.O.S. Committee   16 June 42

All this shows quite clearly the need for getting busy on the Burma plan. It seems to me that the Joint Intelligence Staff might well be asked to make a plan of their own, or possibly even confer with the Joint Planners, impressing upon them the need of action. I have repeatedly stated that the danger of the collapse for Chiang Kai-shek is one of the greatest we have to face at the present time.

Prime Minister to Minister of Aircraft Production   27 June 42

I heard suggestions in the United States that the range of fighter aircraft could be increased by building auxiliary fuel tanks into the wings, or using the wings as fuel tanks. Pray let me have by Monday a report on this proposal, setting out the possibilities and any development that has been undertaken here.

Appendix D, Book One

SINGAPORE DEFENCES

MEMORANDUM BY GENERAL POWNALL

IN 1921 it was decided to build a naval base at Singapore, and all subsequent defence arrangements hinged on its protection against attack by sea, air, or land. The base itself was to be located on the north shore of Singapore Island, facing out on to the Johore Strait, which was the naval anchorage.

At that time, and for many years to come, it was considered that the security of the base depended ultimately on the ability of the British Fleet to control the sea approaches to Singapore. As soon as it arrived it would deal with any Japanese sea forces in the vicinity and cut the communications of any land or air forces that might have installed themselves in the neighbourhood. It was the duty of the land and air forces of the garrison to hold off the enemy forces until the British came. This period, "the period before relief," was first estimated at seventy days, it being assumed that the enemy forces started from Japan, since at the time Japan had not begun to expand into China and beyond. With such a relatively short time available to them before the arrival of our Fleet, the most likely form of Japanese attack was held to be a *coup de main* direct on the island. Defences were planned accordingly and only a comparatively small garrison was needed.

The international situation in the nineteen-twenties did not necessitate costly outlay on modernising the defences, and it was not until 1933, after Japan had withdrawn from the League of Nations, that the Cabinet decided to take active steps.

By now developments in air-power greatly affected the defence problem. Singapore was exposed to carrier-borne attacks and to shore-based aircraft from ever-increasing ranges. Our own aircraft, too, could reconnoitre and strike further afield. Hitherto the only R.A.F. aerodrome had been on Singapore Island. Two more aerodromes were constructed there, and work began on others on the east coast, eventually as far north as the frontier of Siam. This was a new commitment for the Army. Not only had the Army to protect these aerodromes for our own use, but it also had to ensure that the enemy was denied the use of them for launching attacks on the naval base. In this connection there was friction between the authorities, due to a tendency to site airfields from the point of view of operational flying and with little regard to their ground defence. In any case, it was obviously not only wasteful but positively dangerous to make new airfields unless there was a reasonable certainty of a strong and efficient air force to use them and to co-operate in the defence as a whole.

In 1937 the general position was again fully reviewed, and an assessment made of defence requirements based on two main assumptions: (a) that any threat to our interests would be seaborne; (b) that we should be able to send to the Far East within three months a fleet of sufficient strength to protect the Dominions and India and give cover to our communications in the Indian Ocean.

In essence there was little change between the view taken in 1937 and that of 1921, but in 1939 the "period before relief" was raised to one hundred and eighty days, authority was given for reserves to be accumulated on the extended scale, and a reinforcing infantry brigade was sent from India.

The consequences of the first year of the war completely altered the outlook. Principal among these were the Japanese advance into Southern China and Hainan; the situation in Indo-China resulting from the French collapse; the increased range of aircraft; above all, the necessity for retaining in European waters a fleet of sufficient strength to match both the German and Italian Fleets, so making it impossible for us to send to the Far East an adequate naval force should the need for it arise.

In August, 1940, the Chiefs of Staff reviewed the position. Their main conclusions were: (a) Until Germany and Italy were defeated, or drastically reduced in naval strength, we were faced with the problem of defending our Far Eastern interests without an adequate fleet. Our object must be to limit the extent of inevitable damage, and at least to retain a footing from which we could eventually retrieve the position when stronger forces became available. (b) It was no longer sufficient to concentrate upon the defence of Singapore Island; it was now necessary to hold the whole of Malaya. This involved an increase in the existing army and air forces. (c) In the absence of a fleet our policy should be to rely primarily on air-power. The necessary air forces could not be provided for some time; until then substantial additional land forces were needed. (d) Our naval building programmes have never allowed for a war in which we alone fought Germany, Italy, and Japan. The best hope of being able to supply naval forces in the Far East lay in the possibility of early and successful action against Italian naval forces in the Mediterranean.

In August, 1940, the *air force* in Malaya numbered eighty-four first-line aircraft. The Chiefs of Staff considered, subject to the views of local commanders, that 336 *first-line aircraft* were required in the Far East (including fifty-four aircraft for trade protection in the Indian Ocean) to meet the new responsibilities placed upon the Royal Air Force.[1]

A conference assembled at Singapore in October 1940 recommended that the figure of 336 should be raised to 582. The Air Ministry considered this far beyond the bounds of practical possibility; the Chiefs of Staff agreed that 582 was an ideal, but considered that 366 should give a fair degree of security.

On December 7, 1941, the strength of the R.A.F. in Malaya was 158 aircraft (of which twenty-four were obsolete Vildebeestes). Authorised reserves for this first-line strength were 157; actual reserves held were eighty-eight.

In August, 1940, the *Army garrison* in Malaya, apart from coast defence, A.A., and auxiliary troops, consisted of *nine battalions* and one mountain artillery brigade.[1]

The Chiefs of Staff further recommended that *when the Royal Air Force had reached the figure they advised* (336) the minimum garrison should be six brigades (*eighteen battalions*), with ancillary troops. In January 1941, on the advice of G.O.C. Malaya, this was raised by the Chiefs of Staff to *twenty-six battalions*. But until the Air Force was able adequately to undertake its responsibilities they considered the garrison should be increased by the equivalent of three divisions; total garrison would thus be nine plus twenty-seven equals *thirty-six battalions*, with ancillary troops.

In August, 1941, General Percival put forward a new proposal in which the battalion strength amounted to forty-eight. This was accepted by the Chiefs of Staff, but it was recognised that it could not be met in the foreseeable future.

On December 7, 1941, the Army strength in Malaya (apart from coast defence and A.A.) was: [2]

> 32 battalions
> 7 field artillery regiments
> 1 mountain artillery regiment
> 2 anti-tank artillery regiments

The above numbered 76,300 men (there were no tank units).

Although the War Office, but not General Percival's, target was thus nearly achieved, some of the troops recently arrived from India were raw and their fighting quality was low. Three of the artillery regiments arrived less than a month before the outbreak of hostilities, and had had little opportunity to train with other arms in the peculiarities of jungle warfare.

[1] See Table A, page 874.
[2] This does not include local volunteer troops and Indian State forces, sixteen battalions in all. These were outside the calculations here summarised and kept apart from the argument. They were used almost entirely for static guards, internal security, etc., and did not form part of battle formations.

TABLE A

FORCES FOR DEFENCE OF MALAYA

ROYAL AIR FORCE

(Far East, excluding Burma)

Strength August, 1940	Scale approved by C.O.S. August, 1940	Recommended by C.-in-C.'s	Strength Dec. 7, 1941
Malaya 84	Malaya 282 Indian Ocean 54 Total 336	Total 582	Malaya 158

ARMY

(Malaya; Regular battalions only)

Strength August, 1940	Scale accepted by C.O.S. when R.A.F. reached approved scale	Scale accepted by C.O.S. until R.A.F. reached approved scale	Recommended by General Percival until R.A.F. reached approved scale	Strength Dec. 7, 1941
9	18 (Aug., 1940) 26 (Jan., 1941)	36	48	32

ROYAL NAVY

Naval Forces based on Singapore, December 7, 1941

FLEET UNITS

Eastern Fleet		China Command	
Capital ships	2	Light cruisers	3
Destroyers	5	Destroyers	4
		River gunboats	3
		Minesweepers (R.A.N.)	4

LOCAL DEFENCE FORCES

(Converted merchant vessels manned by locally organised volunteers)

Auxiliary patrol and anti-submarine vessels	18
Auxiliary minesweepers	17
Naval armed launches	12

Appendix E, Book One

MINISTERIAL APPOINTMENTS FOR THE YEAR 1942
(Members of the War Cabinet are shown in italics)

Prime Minister and First Lord of the Treasury, Minister of Defence — *Mr. Winston S. Churchill*

Admiralty, First Lord of the — Mr. A. V. Alexander

Agriculture and Fisheries, Minister of — Mr. R. S. Hudson

Air, Secretary of State for — Sir Archibald Sinclair

Aircraft Production, Minister of —
(a) Colonel J. T. C. Moore-Brabazon
(b) Colonel J. J. Llewellin (appointed February 22)
(c) Sir Stafford Cripps (appointed November 22)

Burma, Secretary of State for — Mr. L. S. Amery

Chancellor of the Duchy of Lancaster — Mr. A. Duff Cooper

Chancellor of the Exchequer — Sir Kingsley Wood (ceased to be member of War Cabinet February 19)

Colonies, Secretary of State for the —
(a) Lord Moyne
(b) Viscount Cranborne (appointed February 22)
(c) Colonel Oliver Stanley (appointed November 22)

Dominions Affairs, Secretary of State for —
(a) Viscount Cranborne
(b) *Mr. Clement Attlee* (appointed February 19; also appointed Deputy Prime Minister on this date)

Economic Warfare, Minister of —
(a) Mr. Hugh Dalton
(b) Viscount Wolmer (later succeeded to title of Earl of Selborne; appointed February 22)

Education, President of the Board of — Mr. R. A. Butler

Food, Minister of — Lord Woolton

Foreign Affairs, Secretary of State for — *Mr. Anthony Eden*

Fuel and Power, Minister of — Major G. Lloyd George (appointed June 3)
(The Ministry of Fuel and Power was created on June 3, 1942. It absorbed the former Mines and Petroleum Departments of the Board of Trade, and took over such responsibilities for gas and electricity as were formerly assigned to the Board.)

Health, Minister of — Mr. Ernest Brown

Home Department, Secretary of State for the; and Home Security, Minister of — *Mr. Herbert Morrison* (entered the War Cabinet November 22, 1942)

India, Secretary of State for	Mr. L. S. Amery
Information, Minister of	Mr. Brendan Bracken
Labour and National Service, Minister of	*Mr. Ernest Bevin*
Law Officers:	
Attorney-General	Sir Donald Somervell
Lord Advocate	Mr. J. S. C. Reid
Solicitor-General	(a) Sir William Jowitt
	(b) Sir David Maxwell **Fyfe** (appointed March 4)
Solicitor-General for Scotland	Sir David King Murray
Lord Chancellor	Viscount Simon
Lord President of the Council	*Sir John Anderson*
Lord Privy Seal	(a) *Mr. Clement Attlee*
	(b) *Sir Stafford Cripps* (appointed February 19)
	(c) Viscount Cranborne (appointed November 22)
Minister without Portfolio	(a) *Mr. Arthur Greenwood* (resigned February 19)
	(From February 19 to December 30 there was no Minister without Portfolio. The duties in regard to post-war reconstruction problems hitherto performed by Mr. Greenwood being assumed by the Paymaster-General.)
	(b) *Sir William Jowitt* (appointed December 30)
	(Following his appointment as Minister without Portfolio, Sir William Jowitt continued to carry out the duties in regard to post-war reconstruction problems hitherto performed by him as Paymaster-General.)
Paymaster-General	(a) Lord Hankey
	(b) Sir William Jowitt (appointed March 4)
	(See note under Minister without Portfolio.)
	(c) Lord Cherwell (appointed December 20)
Pensions, Minister of	Sir Walter Womersley
Postmaster-General	Mr. W. S. Morrison
Production, Minister of	(a) Lord Beaverbrook (appointed February 4)
	(Lord Beaverbrook was appointed "Minister of War Production." When he relinquished this appointment the title was changed to "Minister of Production.")
	(b) *Mr. Oliver Lyttelton* (appointed February 19)
Scotland, Secretary of State for	Mr. Thomas Johnston
Supply, Minister of	(a) Lord Beaverbrook
	(b) Sir Andrew Duncan (appointed February 4)

Trade, President of the Board of	(a) Sir Andrew Duncan
	(b) Colonel J. J. Llewellin (appointed February 4)
	(c) Mr. Hugh Dalton (appointed February 22)
War, Secretary of State for	(a) Captain H. D. R. Margesson
	(b) Sir James Grigg (appointed February 22)
War Transport, Minister of	Lord Leathers
Works and Planning, Minister of	(a) Lord Reith
	(b) Lord Portal (appointed February 22)
	(The duties in regard to town and country planning hitherto carried out by the Minister of Health were transferred to the Minister of Works and Buildings on February 11. The title of that office was then changed to "Minister of Works and Planning.")
Ministers Overseas:	(a) *Mr. Oliver Lyttelton*
Middle East, Minister of State in the	(b) *Mr. R. G. Casey* (appointed March 18)
	(This office was vacant between the appointment of Mr. Oliver Lyttelton as Minister of Production on February 19 and the appointment of Mr. R. G. Casey on March 18.)
Washington, Minister Resident for Supply in	Colonel J. J. Llewellin (appointed November 22)
	(The office of Minister Resident for Supply in Washington was created on November 22, 1942. It lapsed with the change of Government on May 26, 1945.)
Allied Force Headquarters, Mediterranean Command, Minister Resident at	Mr. Harold Macmillan (appointed December 30, 1942)
	(The office of Minister Resident at Allied Headquarters in Northwest Africa was created on December 30, 1942. It lapsed with the change of Government on May 26, 1945.)
West Africa, Minister Resident in	Viscount Swinton (appointed June 8)
	(The office of Minister Resident in West Africa was created on June 8, 1942. It lapsed with the change of Government on July 27, 1945.)
Middle East, Deputy Minister of State Resident in the	Lord Moyne (appointed August 28)
	(The office of Deputy Minister of State (in the Middle East) was created on August 28, 1942. On the appointment of Mr. R. K. Law as Minister of State on September 25, 1943, the title of the office was changed to "Deputy Minister of State Resident in the Middle East." On the appointment of Lord Moyne as Minister Resident in the Middle East in January 29, 1944, the office lapsed.)

House of Lords, Leader of the

House of Commons, Leader of the

(*a*) Lord Moyne
(*b*) Viscount Cranborne (appointed February 22)
(*a*) Mr. Winston S. Churchill
(*b*) Sir Stafford Cripps (appointed February 19)
(*c*) Mr. Anthony Eden (appointed November 22)

Appendix F, Book One

SHIPPING LOSSES FOR 1942

Monthly Totals of Shipping Losses, British, Allied, and Neutral, by Enemy Action in 1942

Month	British		Allied		Neutral		Total	
	No. of Ships	Gross Tons	No. of Ships	Gross Tons	No. of Ships	Gross Tons	No. of Ships	Gross Tons
January.........	38	147,920	56	253,323	3	14,498	97	415,741
February.......	60	314,184	63	302,125	7	36,207	130	652,516
March.........	67	250,679	150	517,372	8	26,638	225	794,689
April..........	52	292,882	72	364,842	3	9,090	127	666,814
May...........	58	258,273	84	410,005	7	36,395	149	704,673
June..........	50	233,740	108	560,714	12	29,202	170	823,656
July..........	43	232,718	74	350,473	10	30,450	127	613,641
August........	58	344,763	53	281,262	13	39,608	124	665,633
September.....	50	274,952	55	275,786	9	16,589	114	567,327
October.......	59	404,406	40	224,537	1	3,777	100	632,720
November.....	76	474,606	59	338,261	—	—	135	812,867
December.....	45	225,307	24	113,074	3	9,247	72	347,628
Totals.......	656	3,454,430	838	3,991,774	76	251,701	1,570	7,697,905

★

Book two

Appendix A, Book Two

PRIME MINISTER'S PERSONAL MINUTES
July 1942 — May 1943

JULY

Prime Minister to First Lord   6 July 42
(Copy to Minister of Works and Planning)

The Horse Guards Parade is not Admiralty Property, and you should have obtained permission from the Cabinet before erecting the bicycle sheds which cover so large a space.

2. As to the buildings used for the construction of the Admiralty fortress that you wish to keep, you should ask the Minister of Works and Planning to prepare a plan, and make your case and bring it before the War Cabinet.

Prime Minister to Foreign Secretary   6 July 42
(Copy to Major Morton)

I will most certainly do everything to help Blum if he desires to escape. I hope however that Mandel, and Reynaud if he wishes, will also be assisted. I consider we have obligations towards these men.

Prime Minister to Minister of War Transport   7 July 42

Make sure that the Red Cross supplies to Russia are always distributed in at least six ships of any one convoy, and arrange with the Red Cross to facilitate this, while also taking care that the components of any one article are not separated. Report what action has been taken before the next convoy sails.

Prime Minister to Minister of Supply   8 July 42

The King told me yesterday that there was a shortage of silk for V.C.s and other decorations. I could not believe that this minute requirement could not be met, and I consider it should have super-priority. Please let me know.

Prime Minister to Secretary of State for War and Minister   10 July 42
of War Transport

I see that a beginning has been made in boxing vehicles shipped abroad from this country, and that during May 1126 (not 1453 as originally stated) out of 7517 were boxed. I trust the proportion will show a steady rise, and that every effort is being made to improve the methods of packing and to devise means to crate the vehicles still outstanding.

2. Well over 1000 vehicles, which could have been packed in this way were not boxed, on the ground that they were required for operations on arrival. Having regard to the immense importance of freeing shipping for imports, this argument can only be accepted in really urgent cases. Over 850 small vehicles were not boxed because we are told that it would save no appreciable amount of shipping space. But every little helps.

3. When we remember that boxing 15 per cent of the vehicles has in one month saved about 80,000 tons of imports — as much as the quantity saved monthly by raising the milling ratio, clothes and soap rationing, and abolishing the basic petrol, all put together — the importance of carrying this policy to the limit of refinement both here and in America is evident.

4. I trust your departments will co-operate in pursuing the matter vigorously.

Prime Minister to C.A.S.   11 July 42

It is vital that the use of Benghazi and Tobruk as supply ports should be denied to the enemy. They must be subjected to heavy and continuous bombing on the largest scale. Please let me know the resources Tedder will have available, and the use he intends to make of them. He should be informed of the great importance we attach to the destruction of these ports.

Prime Minister to Chancellor of the Exchequer   13 July 42

Pray let me have the following information. What is the difference in the yearly pay of a British soldier anywhere and an American soldier quartered in this country? You should take allowances into consideration and give me a simple block figure.

What would be the cost to the Exchequer of advancing the British pay (taking allowances, etc., into consideration) halfway up to the American level, on condition that the Americans reduced theirs to meet us and paid the surplus to their troops as a nest-egg in the United States?

I am deeply concerned about the troubles that will arise here and the tremendous demand that may be made upon you to equalise upwards. I therefore wish to explore the possibilities of equalising downwards. There is no need for you to argue the matter at this stage, because anyone can see the disadvantages. But let me know the figures. They may indeed be staggering.

Prime Minister to Minister of Food   16 July 42

Complaints reach me about your new plans for poultry rationing as they affect country-folk. The hen has been part and parcel of the country cottager's life since history began. Townsfolk can eke out their rations by a bought meal. What is the need for this tremendous reduction to one hen per person? Anyhow, the Cabinet ought to have been informed.

Prime Minister to General Ismay, for C.O.S. Committee   18 July 42

Before I could agree to converting the two South African divisions to armour I should like to know how the tank position stands. We ought not, in this phase of the war, to accumulate large reserves of tanks behind the armoured formations in Great Britain. Invasion is unlikely, and these reserves can be accumulated in time for any offensive by us in 1943. The 300 Sherman tanks are a windfall, and the decision not to send P.Q.18 and possibly to suspend sendings to Russia during the daylight period certainly give us at least another 250 tanks. Moreover, tank production is expanding. There should be very large numbers of tanks available in 1943. I consider therefore that no case has been shown for not providing the tanks as promised for both South African divisions.

First however let me know what scale these divisions are to be upon. Are they to be on the new scale of the armoured brigade and one motorised brigade, in which case they only require 200 tanks apiece; or are they on the old 350 scale? I imagine the former as being correct, and if so there are only 400 tanks to be found altogether.

I recognise the force of the argument that we cannot withdraw the South African divisions for training in a different rôle at the present time; but the course of the battle and the arrival of other reinforcements may render this possible in, say, a couple of months. I should hope therefore that the promised dates and programme could be maintained.

A REVIEW OF THE WAR POSITION

MEMORANDUM BY THE PRIME MINISTER

21 July 42

The time has come to review the whole field of the war and place its salient features in their true proportion.

2. The first is the immense power of the German military machine. Because the German armies have been so long busy in Russia, we are apt to forget this terrible engine. When we feel what a couple of Panzer divisions and the 90th German Light Division can do in North Africa

against our greatly superior numbers and resources, we have no excuse for underrating German military power in 1943 and 1944. It will always be possible for them to set up a holding front against Russia and bring back fifty or sixty, or even more, divisions to the West. They could make the transference with very great rapidity across the main railway lines of Europe. We have no right to count upon a collapse of German military power on the European Continent. In the event of the overthrow of the Nazi régime, it is almost certain that the power would pass to the Chiefs of the German Army, who are by no means ready to accept the kind of terms which Britain and the United States deem essential to future world security.

3. The second main fact is seaborne tonnage. We can only get through this year by running down our stocks heavily. At the cost of much internal friction and disturbance, we may, by "tightening the belt," save perhaps a million tons. Whether this should be done as a moral exercise, should be carefully weighed. It can however have no appreciable effect upon the problem of maintaining our war effort at home and abroad. There is no reason to assume that we cannot get through the present year or that the tonnage position in 1943 will not steadily improve as a result of the prodigious American shipbuilding. But we must be careful not to let our position deteriorate to an unmanageable degree before we have a clear understanding with the United States as to the future. With this object we must now in the next few weeks come to a solemn compact, almost a treaty, with the United States about the share of their new building we are to get in 1943 and 1944. Up till the time when the United States entered the war, we had pretty well recouped ourselves for our losses by acquiring control of the shipping of Continental States as they were successively subjugated by the enemy. No more windfalls can be expected from this source. We can only expand our own building sensibly at dire expense to our war effort. Nothing we can do can change our minimum import requirements appreciably. The tonnage needed to guarantee these must be a first charge. We ought therefore to ask the United States to deliver to us during 1943 sufficient tonnage to occupy fully our available merchant crews. As it would be foolish to have large numbers of British life-trained merchant seamen and officers standing idle without ships while in the United States crews will have to be trained specially, our desire should not be deemed unreasonable.

4. On no account must we run our stocks down to a dangerous level for the sake of getting through 1942, without knowing where we stand in 1943. And the minimum stocks needed must not be written down unduly. Serious bombing of our ports might well hamstring our intake for considerable periods when we should be lost without something in the larder. Moreover, we should not start on the basis that the British should make a greater sacrifice of their pre-war standard of living than

the American people. We should point out that any further curtailment of imports taking 1942 and 1943 together can only be made through a definite curtailment of our munitions output. Already nearly three-quarters of British and British-controlled shipping is primarily employed on the war effort, and only one-quarter is exclusively engaged in feeding and supplying this island.

5. It might be true to say that the issue of the war depends on whether Hitler's U-boat attack on Allied tonnage, or the increase and application of Allied air power, reach their full fruition first. The growth of U-boat warfare and its spread to the most distant waters, as well as improvements in U-boat design, in a formidable degree must be expected. Against this may be set the increase of Allied anti-submarine craft and improvement in methods. But here is a struggle in itself.

6. On the other hand, we Allies have the air power. In the days when we were fighting alone, we answered the question: "How are you going to win the war?" by saying: "We will shatter Germany by bombing." Since then the enormous injuries inflicted on the German Army and manpower by the Russians, and the accession of the manpower and munitions of the United States, have rendered other possibilities open. We look forward to mass invasion of the Continent by liberating armies, and general revolt of the populations against the Hitler tyranny. All the same, it would be a mistake to cast aside our original thought which, it may be mentioned, is also strong in American minds, namely, that the severe, ruthless bombing of Germany on an ever-increasing scale will not only cripple her war effort, including U-boat and aircraft production, but will also create conditions intolerable to the mass of the German population.

7. It is at this point that we must observe with sorrow and alarm the woeful shrinkage of our plans for bomber expansion. The needs of the Navy and of the Middle East and India, the short-fall of our British production programmes, the natural wish of the Americans to fly their own bombers against the enemy, and the inevitable delay in these machines coming into action, all these falling exclusively upon Bomber Command, have prevented so far the fruition of our hopes for this summer and autumn. We must regard the bomber offensive against Germany at least as a feature in breaking her war-will second only to the largest military operations which can be conducted on the Continent until that war-will is broken. Renewed, intense efforts should be made by the Allies to develop during the winter and onwards ever-growing, ever more accurate and ever more far-ranging bomber attacks on Germany. In this way alone can we prepare the conditions which will be favourable to the major military operations on which we are resolved. Provision must be made to ensure that the bombing of Germany is not interrupted, except perhaps temporarily, by the need of supporting military operations.

Having regard to the fact that Allied aircraft construction already out-numbers Axis aircraft construction by between two and three to one, these requirements should not be unattainable.

8. Although no expansion of A.R.P. services can be accepted and, on the contrary, judicious pruning must still continue, we should be unwise to assume that heavy bombing attacks on Great Britain will not be re-newed. At present over half of the German bomber strength is occupied against Russia. By a transference to the West, the Germans could assemble during the next few months an equality in bomber aircraft for our account. We have developed an elaborate, and indeed wonderful system of scientific defence which has enabled us to await a renewal of the former "blitz" with confidence. If anything should go wrong with this scientific system of defence, even though the enemy were similarly affected, then the reciprocal bombing of both countries would be conducted on very much the conditions of the winter of 1940–41. Should this develop, our advantage over Germany would have to be expressed by the ever-increasing numerical superiority of our bomber aircraft and the bomb-content capable of being discharged by us.

Prime Minister to General Ismay, for C.O.S. Committee   22 July 42

Special authority must be obtained from the C.O.S. Committee in respect of any mechanical vehicles shipped without being boxed. It may be convenient for the C.O.S. Committee to devolve this work either upon the Vice-Chiefs' Committee or to any one of the Vice-Chiefs of Staff selected for the purpose.

It is essential that, except where actual combat landings are to be prepared for, all mechanical transport should be boxed. The saving in shipping space achievable far exceeds the results of many galling restrictions on the life and food of the country.

I must ask for active and continuous help in this matter.

Prime Minister to Sir Edward Bridges   25 July 42

Will you please set out clearly the existing organisation of Scientific Research, departmental and extra-departmental, giving some idea of the numbers of scientists employed by the great Service departments and the committees on invention and research?

Prime Minister to First Sea Lord   25 July 42

It was never intended to keep anti-submarine craft idle in a pool, but only to treat the whole onflow of new construction as available for direction either to British or to American hands, the decision being taken on a forecast of the strategic situation at the time when the question of gun armament and other fittings had to be settled. Our use of the word "pool" is perhaps unfortunate.

Pray let me have a draft for the President, clearing the matter up.
I was not aware there was shortage of equipment.

Prime Minister to General Ismay, for C.O.S. Committee   26 July 42

In view of "Torch," "Anakim" may be affected. I consider it of great importance that "Anakim" should not be turned down or hamstrung. Pray let me know what can be done to save the position; otherwise General Wavell's preparations will come to a standstill. Only the very gravest reasons should prevent General Wavell having the "Ironclad" outfit of landing-craft. Let me know what these reasons are.

Prime Minister to Minister of Production, Secretary of State   27 July 42
for War, C.I.G.S., Minister of Supply, and Sir Edward Bridges

We have at present made or are completing about 20,000 2.4-pounder tank and anti-tank guns. It is proposed in the next twelve months to make 20,000 more. This weapon is already out of date, and we shall be justly censured if we commit ourselves to a further enormous production of it. I understand that it is proposed to make a wide distribution to the infantry, so that every battalion may feel it can face enemy tanks. But the 2-pounder is not the weapon that we should make for this, as it cannot stop a tank except under the most favourable conditions. The bombard or the Jefferis rifle rocket gives better results and is much easier to make. Even the 6-pounder is now falling behind. In all these circumstances we must this week review the 2.4-pounder programme at a Defence (Supply) Committee, which I can preside over at 11.30 on Thursday morning, July 30. We might also then consider the tank supply position, including the progress made in improving the Churchills.

Prime Minister to D.M.I.   27 July 42

I see that our Grant strength in the Middle East is now 61, whereas before the recent attack it was 91. During the interval a number of Grants have arrived. How many Grants have we lost in the battle, and what were the total tank losses?

Prime Minister to Minister of Production   28 July 42

I do not know whether you realise the extreme gravity of the incendiary bomb position. The shortage is so acute that it is forcing the R.A.F. to restrict the scale of fire-raising attacks planned for the next few months.

Are we going to get our fair share of the magnesium available from America this year? In your minute of May 5 you told me you would take this matter up on the highest level if satisfactory assurances could not be obtained.

Is the development of substitutes for the use of magnesium going ahead at full speed?

Pray let me know what supplies the R.A.F. can expect in the coming autumn and winter.

Prime Minister to First Lord   29 July 42
(Copy to Minister of War Transport)

The recent statement in America that our shipping losses in the week beginning July 12 had been the worst since the outbreak of war was most unfortunate. It can only be understood if the American authorities work on a notification basis, and by some mischance were notified in this one week of losses which had actually occurred in the course of several weeks. Such a procedure naturally gives no true picture of the course of the war at sea.

We should try to work out with the Americans a common policy about publication of shipping losses. Perhaps you would take up with their authorities, if you have not already done so, the question whether any ïgures at all should be made public, and if so what they should cover.

Pray let me know the result.

Prime Minister to President Roosevelt   9 Aug. 42

I hope you will let me see beforehand the text of any message you are thinking of sending me upon the anniversary of the Atlantic Charter on August 14. We considered the wording of that famous document line by line together and I should not be able, without mature consideration, to give it a wider interpretation than was agreed between us at the time. Its proposed application to Asia and Africa requires much thought. Grave embarrassment would be caused to the defence of India at the present time by such a statement as the Office of War Information has been forecasting. Here in the Middle East the Arabs might claim by majority they could expel the Jews from Palestine, or at any rate forbid all further immigration. I am strongly wedded to the Zionist policy, of which I was one of the authors. This is only one of the many unforeseen cases which will arise from new and further declarations.

2. Would it not be sufficient to dwell on the progress made in this memorable year, to the growth of the United Nations, to the continued magnificent resistance of Russia to aggression, to the success of the arms of the United States in the Pacific and to the growth of our combined air power? Finally, we could reaffirm our principles and point to the hope of a happier world after some preliminary intervening unpleasantness has been satisfactorily got over. I am sure you will consider my difficulties with the kindness you always show to me.

Prime Minister to First Sea Lord   9 Aug. 42

I am deeply disappointed that Shermans cannot arrive before September 5. All yesterday I was inspecting four splendid brigades of armoured troops who only await these weapons to become the most formidable armoured force in Africa. I am giving considerable attention to the synchronisation of the equipment of these brigades and to the acceleration of their training, but I do not see how they can come into action, except in emergency, before the third week in September. I had always counted on the Shermans arriving September 1. This would be 45 days from sailing.

2. In view of the immense importance of beating Rommel as a prelude to "Torch," I beg you will make a renewed effort to regain the lost five days, all of which can be used. Pray cable what is present speed of convoy, and what you can do.

3. 51st Division was promised for August 13. Where is it and will date be kept?

Prime Minister to Secretary of State for Air and C.A.S.   9 Aug. 42

I am most impressed with all that Tedder and Coningham have told me of the extreme importance of having out here a proportion, if only a small one, of the very latest types of fighter aircraft. Coningham declares he could make them desert-worthy himself. The fact that these machines are in the air keeps the enemy always wondering when he will meet them, the quality of our leadership in design makes the value out of all proportion to the number sent. Please make me proposals.

TANK NOMENCLATURE

Prime Minister to General Ismay and others concerned   28 Aug. 42

Confusion will be caused if we start calling the Sherman M.3, as the best class of German tank is similarly named. The following names in particular are to be taken into universal and permanent use: Sherman, Grant, Lee, Stuart. It is not necessary to add the prefix "General," as this only causes confusion with live generals.

2. Let me have a list of the existing official nomenclature of all British and American tanks, and similarly of all German tanks we have encountered. I will then see what amendments are required.

FIGHTER AIRCRAFT FOR THE FLEET AIR ARM

Prime Minister to General Ismay and Sir Edward Bridges   28 Aug. 42

There can be no question of taking machines which will be used in action by the R.A.F. in order to build up inordinate reserves for the Admiralty. The Admiralty always want not only to win the game, but to go to bed with the ace. This tendency must be strongly resisted. The deficit is very small, and only occurs on reserves which have already been expanded far above the R.A.F. reserves, and which include reserves for reserves.

A Defence Committee meeting can be held on Monday night, and this can come high on the agenda. I have asked Lord Cherwell to prepare a paper, which I will circulate.

Prime Minister to General Ismay, for C.O.S. Committee   28 Aug. 42

I am much concerned about the account of the Turkish position given me by the Turkish Ambassador, whom I saw this morning at the request of the Cabinet.

2. We should now prepare a scheme, on the assumption of definite success in the Western Desert by the middle of October, of sending more war material to Turkey. It ought to be possible to spare 200 tanks of the Valentine or other older type. These would be replaced in Egypt by the improved tanks now approaching in a regular stream. Similarly, 300 2.4 two-pounder anti-tank guns should be made available, and 100 Bofors. If these were earmarked and prepared ready to move forward into Turkey the moment a favourable decision has been reached, they would be in Turkish hands by the end of October. This might make all the difference to the Turkish will-power to resist in a situation where the Russians may have lost the naval command of the Black Sea and where Turkey may be subjected to very severe Axis pressure.

3. What is the objection to giving the Turks some Radar installations? The Germans surely know the secret, or have other equally satisfactory variants of their own.

4. We must proceed on the basis, which personally I adopt, that we trust Turkey. The whole Nile position would be greatly embarrassed if Turkey were forced to succumb.

5. Let me have a plan worked out on these lines for discussion.

Prime Minister to Minister of Aircraft Production   30 Aug. 42

I observe from your Progress Report for July that heavy-bomber production has fallen considerably behind the programme. In December 1941 we were promised a July production of 267 heavy bombers. In the programme of July 1 we were promised 229. Actually, we have received 179 — barely two-thirds of the December programme, or four-fifths of the July programme. I am especially concerned that the largest drop is in Stirlings, of which only 44 were produced out of a promised 79.

Pray let me know what steps you are taking to rectify the position.

Prime Minister to Secretary of State for War   30 Aug. 42

It is natural that there should be some resentment in the Army at the undue emphasis laid upon the work of the Commandos by the press. Your press officers should point out to the newspapers the ill-effects which are caused by, for instance, referring to the raid on Dieppe, in which numerous battalions of Canadian troops took part, as "a Commando raid." This is neither fair to the troops nor to the Commandos.

2. At the same time it must be most clearly understood that the policy of His Majesty's Government is to maintain and develop the Commando organisation with the utmost energy and to make sure that the wastage and losses are replaced with good quality men. There can be no question of going back on the decisions taken in favour of the Commando system for a portion of our troops. My previous minutes on this subject, dating from more than two years ago, should be read by you if you have not already seen them. I should not be able to agree to any curtailment of their functions or their importance. Please report to me.

Prime Minister to Secretary of State for the Colonies   31 Aug. 42

Am I not right in thinking that the only attack against the Bahamas possible is by a party landed from a U-boat? If so, Government House seems to be the obvious quarry. A U-boat would not have the facilities for finding out where the Duke of Windsor was if he were not there or were moving about. The right rule is, one may always take a chance but not offer a "sitter." I am therefore in favour of putting an electrified fence round Government House and the other places mentioned, but not interfering with H.R.H.'s liberty of movement otherwise than by informing him of the dangers. It is essential that the seat of government should be protected against a U-boat raiding force, and for this purpose additional platoons should be sent.

SEPTEMBER

Prime Minister to Minister of Information   2 Sept. 42

What are the arrangements for controlling broadcasts by British Service officers in the overseas Empire, such as that referred to in the attached extract about a broadcast by General Wavell? In the United Kingdom a speech by a Minister not in the War Cabinet on such a topic would not be broadcast without reference to me, and I cannot agree to any lesser control outside this country. Pray make yourself responsible for ensuring, in consultation with the Secretaries of State concerned, that no permission is given for such broadcasts, save in accordance with arrangements approved by you. Any proposals for broadcasts by officers of the highest rank should be referred to me personally.

Prime Minister to Minister of Production   2 Sept. 42

All their forecasts have been several times written down, and all their performances fall short of their reduced forecasts. The falling off in the heavy bombers is particularly serious. There is no justification for blaming holidays, as it is known beforehand that holidays will be taken in certain months.

The non-expansion of M.A.P. output is really very grave. What action do you propose?

Prime Minister to Minister of Information   4 Sept. 42

This telegram from Canada reporting that a British United Press message from London was published in the *Ottawa Journal* to the effect that relations between the United States and Vichy might soon be broken off, and that this rumour was coupled by a growing conviction in Great Britain that the Axis must be cleared out of North Africa by the British with the aid of the United States, is a very serious matter. Mr. Duff Cooper should also be asked to report. Who are the censors who let this through? While making these most searching and urgent inquiries, it is important not to raise a hullabaloo, which would only emphasise the significance of the disclosure.

It also should be asked what he means by the expression "some diplomatic quarters." I regard the matter as most urgent and important, and indeed the gravest one which I have ever referred to you.

Prime Minister to Secretary of State for War   4 Sept. 42

I see nothing in these reports [of the Medical Board report on General Hobart] which would justify removing this officer from the command of his division on its proceeding on active service.

General Hobart bears a very high reputation, not only in the Service, but in wide circles outside. He is a man of quite exceptional mental attainments, with great strength of character, and although he does not work easily with others it is a great pity we have not more of his like in the Service. I have been shocked at the persecution to which he has been subjected.

I am quite sure that if, when I had him transferred from a corporal in the Home Guard to the command of one of the new armoured divisions, I had instead insisted upon his controlling the whole of the tank developments, with a seat on the Army Council, many of the grievous errors from which we have suffered would not have been committed. The High Commands of the Army are not a club. It is my duty and that of His Majesty's Government to make sure that exceptionally able men, even though not popular with their military contemporaries, should not be prevented from giving their services to the Crown.

Prime Minister to Minister of Production   5 Sept. 42

I attach the greatest importance to this subject. We have made 20,000

2.4-pounder anti-tank guns. We are making another 11,000 for issue to
infantry. At present these guns are smirched in reputation. It is of the
utmost consequence that confidence should be restored. It can only be
restored through the success and issue of the new ammunition. Pray give
this your most earnest attention, and report to me what you think can
be done.

Prime Minister to First Sea Lord and Chief of Air Staff   6 Sept. 42

This [sailing of an enemy convoy from Italy to North Africa] is
evidently an occasion for a supreme effort, even at the risk of great
sacrifices by the Navy and Air Force. Pray inform me tonight what action
you are taking.[1]

Prime Minister to Lord President of the Council   6 Sept. 42

Thank you very much for the trouble you have taken. The fact remains
that the Metropolitan Water Board are giving better treatment to a
conscientious objector than to a young man who volunteered for the
Army. This is a disgrace to any body of Englishmen, and is on a par
with the same miserable sentiments which degraded our country before
the war and played a recognisable part in bringing these miseries upon
the world.

Your remark about "stealing a march on their colleagues," to be just,
requires amplification as follows: "stealing a march *towards the enemy*
on their colleagues."

As soon as I have got through with my speech I will take the matter
up myself in writing with the Board, and unless I get satisfaction I shall
publish the correspondence.

Prime Minister to Chief of the Air Staff   10 Sept. 42

Air Marshal Harris spoke to me the other night about the large number
of bomber crews sent to the Middle East which were not returned to this
country after having delivered the machines.

In view of the great importance of increasing the strength of Bomber
Command at home, please look into this and draft something to Tedder.

Prime Minister to Admiral Moore   10 Sept. 42

I wish you to look in great detail into the 8-day boiler-cleaning and
repair period. How many destroyers are involved? How many men in
each destroyer are boiler-cleaning? What is the total number of men in
all the destroyers involved who would be boiler-cleaning? Is this special

[1] This convoy of four merchant ships with strong naval and air escorts was
heavily attacked by the R.A.F. on September 6 and again on September 7. Three
ships and a destroyer were sunk or damaged.

work for engineers, or can it be done by able seamen? Are there any other boiler-cleaners available in the Navy? Supposing that, say, 50 men in each destroyer are boiler-cleaning and 20 destroyers are involved, this would be 1000 men. Surely the depots, damaged ships refitting, etc., could provide 1000 men, and these men be brought by special trains to the harbours, so that the moment the destroyers came in the weary crews could walk off to their leave and rest, and the boiler-cleaning be done by special men. This should be under a small skeleton staff from the destroyers, to make sure that all is correctly done. An arrangement like this should save three days extra for rest, leaving five days for boiler-cleaning. Therefore, on two 8-day periods there should be 6 days' saving.

2. It is admitted that three days can be saved on the slow convoy by going the nearer route. Let me have the speed of advance each day for these convoys by each of the routes, showing how many days you have got in the totals for accidents of weather. I appreciate the point about being able to take a short cut, and having that up your sleeve.

3. I cannot believe that we are unable to scrape two days off the ten days allowed for loadings. This gives a total of eleven days, which should make it possible to run P.Q. 19 and yet do "Torch" on November 4, which is the earliest date that the United States contingent sailing on October 20 can arrive. As for other reasons I should be content with November 8 as the firm, final date, there are four days to veer and haul upon.

Prime Minister to Minister of Production 13 Sept. 42

The forecast of production of tanks in this country is very poor. Even the fourth quarter of 1943 does not achieve 1000 a month. Pray let me have the corresponding table showing what we may expect to get from the United States in the same period. I am very anxious to make the locomotives [2] over here and save the shipping, but the loss of 900 Centaurs is very serious.

2. It may be you have already acted on the decision to make the locomotives. In this case of course I accept it, but I should like to know the figures all the same.

Prime Minister to Secretary of State for Air 13 Sept. 42

Many thanks for your paper on the expansion of Bomber Command. I am glad to see the great efforts which you and the Air Staff are making to improve the position. Will you please let me have your programme of expansion by squadrons?

2. Will you also let me know — (a) How many bombers we have sent to the Middle East since May 1, 1942, and (b) How many crews of these

2 For "Bolero" and "Round-up."

bombers have been returned? Tedder has got into the habit of keeping all, or nearly all, of the crews used for ferry purposes. This cannot be allowed. I had thought of sending him a telegram myself, but I await your reply to this.

Prime Minister to C.I.G.S.   13 Sept. 42

You will see on other papers that General Alexander says that the date of "Lightfoot" will be delayed by the late battle. On the other hand, the enemy has been seriously weakened by that battle. If "Lightfoot" is to straggle over into October we must be careful not to ask Malta to do too much meanwhile, and General Alexander should be made aware of the fact that Malta cannot be run to a standstill [in petrol].

Prime Minister to Secretary of State for Air and C.A.S.   17 Sept. 42

It is necessary that the Bomber Command at home should be raised from 32 operating squadrons, which it now has, to 50 squadrons, fully operative, by the end of the year. The expansion should be progressive. No American squadrons should be counted. Let me have the best plan that you can make for achieving this prime military object. For this purpose you should bring under new and close scrutiny all the following spheres, so as to obtain —

	Squadrons
From the Coastal Command	2
From the Airborne Division	1
By restricting the flow of heavy bombers to the Middle East and India	2
By improving the working-up arrangements of the Bomber Command itself so as to make operational additional	2
By present promised increase from M.A.P.	9
By further exertions of M.A.P. additional	2
Total	18

2. You should of course vary these apportionments if the same results can be produced more conveniently. When the resulting plan has been shaped I will bring it before the War Cabinet and ask for discussion and approval. It will then become binding, and will have, within the above limits and for the above period, priority over every other competing claim.

Prime Minister to Brigadier Hollis   18 Sept. 42

I shall be glad to receive a report on the Churchill tanks from the two or three divisions which have most of them.

Do not let it be known that the report is for me, as I simply want to know how the tank is viewed by the troops.

Prime Minister to Brigadier Hollis, for C.O.S. Committee   18 Sept. 42
and Commander-in-Chief, Home Forces

This [58th County of London (Civil Service) Battalion of the Home Guard] is a very fine battalion, 1290 strong, of high personnel, posted in the very heart of our defences. It is most disconcerting that it should only have 546 Sten guns and no rifles at all, except seventy-two .300s and 370 .303s, which "have been lent by private arrangement by the Admiralty and the War Office." This lack of arms and mixture of arms and ammunition is most disquieting.

What is the reason also for the War Office Company being detached from the London District Command and placed personally under the C.I.G.S.?

2. This sample of the Home Guard makes me curious about the equipment of the rest. Over 800,000 .300 rifles were sent to us from the United States in July 1940. How have they been distributed? How many .303 rifles are in the possession of the Home Guard? In how many battalions are there two kinds of rifles with different ammunition? What other weapons have the Home Guard got? How many men are there in the Home Guard for whom no weapons are yet available?

Prime Minister to Chief of the Air Staff   19 Sept. 42

The point you make must be put to the Minister Resident, and we must have time to consider his reply before any further white personnel can be sent [for aerodrome defence in West Africa]. I had no idea you had created a private army of 80,000 men and were looking for custom. You really must aim at reducing this private army by at least 30,000 men.

Prime Minister to Minister of Information   19 Sept. 42
(or Director-General) and Brigadier Hollis

No speculation upon future operations is to be allowed to pass the censors. In any case of doubt the message is to be held up until it has received the personal sanction of the Minister himself. I should be glad if the Minister would again see the newspaper proprietors and impress upon them the dangers of speculative articles upon future operations. It should be a point of honour to exclude them. You need not be too much afraid of seeming to confirm the rumours that have been circulated. The offence is equally heinous whether the rumours are true or false.

Had such a message as that quoted been sent, I am of opinion that the sender should be arrested under the Official Secrets Act or 18B, or other emergency power, and kept in complete seclusion for a considerable time. Let me know what powers are possessed.

The whole matter should be brought before the War Cabinet on Monday.[3]

Prime Minister to Minister of Labour 20 Sept. 42

I have been informed that the first pick of the intake of Service recruits is taken for the Royal Air Force Regiment. Is there any truth in this suggestion?

Prime Minister to Secretary of State for Air 20 Sept. 42

Omitting the light squadrons, give me the numbers that will be operationally fit on each of the dates mentioned. . . .

The fact that out of 316 bombers only 6 crews have returned to this country is really quite scandalous. You are getting a mass of sediment in the Middle East and are hampering your own development at home. Let me have a table showing the strength in squadrons, men and machines, of the R.A.F. in the Middle East on September 1, 1941, and on September 1, 1942.[4]

Prime Minister to Minister of Production 20 Sept. 42

I have to-day read the report of the Select Committee on National Expenditure about tanks and guns. It is a masterly indictment which reflects on all who have been concerned at the War Office and the Ministry of Supply. It also reflects upon me as head of the Government, and upon the whole organisation.

So far only a formal acknowledgment has been sent to Sir John Wardlaw-Milne and his committee. A very much more detailed and reasoned reply must be prepared, and should be in the hands of the committee before Parliament meets on September 29. Let me know therefore before Wednesday next what you have done and are going to do in this field, and how far you are able to meet the criticisms of the committee. Give me also the materials on which I can base a reply to the committee, who have certainly rendered a high service in bringing this tangle of inefficiency and incompetence to my notice. It is now more than a fortnight since this report was put in your hands and those of the Ministry of Supply.

I must regard this matter as most serious, and one which requires immediate proposals for action from yourself, the Secretary of State for War, and the Minister of Supply, so that at any rate the future may be safeguarded.

PROHIBITION OF THE MANUFACTURE AND SALE OF ICE CREAM

Prime Minister to Minister of Food 22 Sept. 42

Without definite information as to the saving in transport and man-

[3] See minute of September 4, page 894.
[4] See minute of September 13, pages 896–97.

power, I cannot judge whether the destruction of this amenity was worth while.

I suppose the large numbers of American troops in this country will have their own arrangements made for them. They are great addicts of ice-cream, which is said to be a rival to alcoholic drinks.

The step should not have been taken without the Cabinet having an opportunity to express an opinion.

BOXING OF LORRIES

Prime Minister to Secretary of State for War and others   23 Sept. 42

The August figures show a welcome improvement, and I am glad to see that the bulk of the so-called "non-technical" War Office vehicles are being boxed. I trust that every effort will now be made to ship in boxes the largest possible proportion of "technical" vehicles, cars and R.A.F. vehicles, and to improve existing methods of boxing.

Prime Minister to Minister of Labour   23 Sept. 42

It would certainly be wrong for the Air Ministry to take Grade I men for the R.A.F. Regiment, which is for sedentary duties around airfields. Especially would this be so if they had the power to divert these men from the Field Army, who have to fight everywhere under all conditions.

I am going to make a searching examination of the R.A.F. Regiment, which is no less than 80,000 strong. I am asking that at least 30,000 should be transferred to the Army.[5]

*Prime Minister to Lord President and Minister of Fuel   24 Sept. 42
and Power*

I understand that the question of releasing more miners from the Army is again being considered. We cannot break up the Army at the present time, and I trust that all other methods of increasing output will be vigorously pursued.

What progress has been made in transferring miners to the more efficient pits? Last May we were told that by moving a comparatively small number a large increase in output could be obtained.

What has been done to increase the intake of boys and youths, and to check the outflow of middle-aged men from the industry?

Has our wage policy been effective in increasing output?

What progress has been made in developing the working of outcrop coal? Great claims have recently been voiced in the Press.

What arrangements have been made with the consuming departments for reduced allocations of industrial coal?

[5] See minute of September 20, page 899.

I hope it will be possible, by pressing forward such measures energetically, to bridge the gap which remains.

Prime Minister to Minister of Labour   24 Sept. 42

I have read with great interest your note describing what has been achieved in the man-power field during the year ended last June.

I see that you drafted nearly a million men and women into the Services, thereby fulfilling the great bulk of their requirements, and at the same time added 800,000 to the labour force on munitions.

I congratulate you on this great performance.

Prime Minister to Sir Edward Bridges   25 Sept. 42

The following notice should be issued:

Ministers should be chary of being drawn into discussions on official matters with the Ambassadors of foreign Powers. Should such occasions arise, they should furnish a report of what passed to the Foreign Secretary, who otherwise may find himself holding different language in his formal interviews.

Prime Minister to General Ismay   25 Sept. 42

Let me have a report on the strength of the Commandos in the United Kingdom and on the process of recruitment. Are they getting good quality men and in sufficient numbers?

Prime Minister to C.A.S.   25 Sept. 42

It may be necessary at some moment or other in "Torch" or its preliminaries to threaten Vichy with severe and immediate bombing. Let me know what could be done during November, assuming it was considered necessary.

Prime Minister to First Lord and First Sea Lord   25 Sept. 42

I trust that not only *Renown,* but also one of the *King George Vs* will be assigned to "Torch." It is most necessary to overawe the enemy by superior strength, and especially to deter the Vichy French. With three *King George Vs* at Scapa you have ample margin.

Prime Minister to General Ismay, for C.O.S. Committee   25 Sept. 42
and Minister of Production

It seems to me that we ought to have three or four miles of this pier tackle [for use on flat beaches]. It could of course be used in many places in short sections. Pray do not lightly turn this aside. We must however know what we should have to give up.

Prime Minister to Lord President of the Council   26 Sept. 42

In trying to effect economy of fuel or labour on the home front I hope you will bear in mind that these may react upon the efficiency of the workers. For instance, fewer bus services mean longer journeys, and workers arrive tired at their offices or plants. A businessman could of course clean his own room and arrive an hour late at an important job, and so forth. I do not wish to dogmatise, but hope this point is being borne in mind.

Prime Minister to Lord Privy Seal   26 Sept. 42

It would be a good thing to hear what the Commander-in-Chief Bomber Command thinks about the publication of aircraft losses. This we must have before the Cabinet decision is reopened. Personally, I think it very foolish to give this information to the enemy, and without a statement of the numbers taking part in the raid it is most misleading and needlessly distressing. I should have no difficulty in explaining the matter to the House.

Prime Minister to Mr. Geoffrey Lloyd   26 Sept. 42

It is of great importance to find means to dissipate fog at aerodromes so that aircraft can land safely. Let full experiments to this end be put in hand by the Petroleum Warfare Department with all expedition. They should be given every support.

Prime Minister to First Lord and First Sea Lord   27 Sept. 42

The report of 650 survivors being brought in from the *Laconia* and another ship shows that a very serious tragedy has taken place. Is it known what proportion of the rescued are Italian prisoners of war and what proportion are British personnel? There were nearly 3000 people to be accounted for, so over 2000 must have lost their lives.

Prime Minister to Secretary of State for War and C.I.G.S.   28 Sept. 42

I am not prepared to approve reserves of tanks of 90 per cent being assigned to some armoured divisions, while others have no tanks at all. When an army is expanding its armoured forces, as we are doing, every effort should be made to give priority to the initial equipment of all units, and it is only after these needs have been satisfied that the reserves can be built up. Of course where the forces are in contact with the enemy a large proportion of spare tanks must be provided.

2. In the Middle East all the Shermans should be put in the front line, the reserves being found by Grants. In any particular theatre where a large number of one mark of tank is used by several units it would be well to make a general pool rather than to assign a fixed reserve to each

unit. This applies particularly at home, where we have very large numbers of Churchills, of Crusaders, and of Valentines. Here in this small island, where the units lie close to their large workshops, a very much lower standard of reserves is possible than in the Middle East or India. We cannot afford to have tanks standing idle on the one hand and formations left unequipped on the other.

3. I should be glad to have a statement of all the armoured units at home and abroad, formed and in formation, with their initial equipment, and the actual numbers of tanks they have got, either with the units or in reserve.

Prime Minister to First Lord and First Sea Lord   28 Sept. 42

Pray consider in what way the ships of P.Q.19 can best be used to make the enemy believe we intend to run another convoy. It will be a great advantage to us, and indeed a help to "Torch," if the Germans are induced to keep their submarines, aircraft, and surface vessels in the North this winter, doing nothing. Everything should therefore be done to favour the idea of an October convoy.

Prime Minister to Chief of the Air Staff   28 Sept. 42

Everything shows the increasing dependence of the enemy on Tobruk as against Benghazi. It seems to me astonishing that the whole of the air forces which we and the Americans have in Egypt are not able to bring the work of this port, which lies so near them, to an end.

Prime Minister to C.A.S.   29 Sept. 42

What has happened to the three squadrons of Spitfires which we gave to Mr. Evatt? Are they in action yet?

Prime Minister to General Ismay, for C.O.S. Committee   30 Sept. 42

So far as can be ascertained, it is far more expensive in man-hours to bring down an enemy aircraft by fire from the ground than by fighters from the air. It is true that there is some danger of interference with our present radio methods, which would probably render it inexpedient to reduce our flak this winter. But next year, when we hope these dangers will be overcome, and when there should be more fighters available, it might be possible to rely on aircraft in greater measure. Anti-aircraft guns will of course always be useful, and indeed necessary, for the defence of small important targets, but in view of the looming man-power stringency the possibility of further reducing A.A. Command in 1943 should be explored.

Prime Minister to C.I.G.S. and C.A.S.   30 Sept. 42

I am told that the Whitley aircraft which I saw when I visited the

Airborne Division at Netheravon is unsuitable for tugging gliders, and therefore that the commander of the Airborne Division has literally no airplanes suitable for this purpose.

Pray let me know the position and what is being done about it.

OCTOBER

Prime Minister to Foreign Secretary   2 Oct. 42

Your minute about "Aspidistra." [6]

1. Let me have a short description of what it can actually do, and also a good plan for using it during "Torch." My idea was, that the President should let us have some records which could be let off at appropriate moments as General Eisenhower thought fit. In addition, I would, once the show was well started, have a go in French or English, as the case might be, to France.

2. Pray let me have the draft of the telegram I could send to the President asking for the extra valves.

Prime Minister to General Ismay, for C.O.S. Committee   4 Oct. 42

I presume plans are in hand for accompanying "Torch" with large-scale air diversions to tie the German Air Force to the French coast?

2. Would it not be well to have a certain number of American ships, not necessarily very powerful ones, showing the American flag in the British squadrons which might have to deal with a sortie of the Vichy fleet from Toulon?

3. What is the truth of the newspaper rumours about French submarines being sent to Dakar?

Prime Minister to C.I.G.S.   4 Oct. 42

This tells me very little about German tanks. Please let me have the weight and speed of each of these tanks, and the weight of the projectile fired by their gun. Also let me have the name of the tank in British possession most nearly equal to each of these tanks.

Prime Minister to General Ismay, for C.O.S. Committee   7 Oct. 42

Naturally I am very much in favour of the development of an amphibious striking force in the Middle East. I greatly regretted the manner in which the three Commandos we sent out with assault ships were frittered away, and also that our fine Marine party was put to no good use. I have always believed that operations of this character, whether against the Island or in the rear of the enemy's position, ought to play

6 A special wireless transmitter for radiating messages to enemy-occupied countries.

an important part in the campaign. It seems all the more necessary that they should do so now that larger prospects are open.

2. The only thing that worries me is, what about Wavell's Akyab, etc.? It would be a fine piece of work if we could manage to concentrate the Mobile Naval Base Defence Organisation without paralysing Wavell. Perhaps you will let me have a report.

Prime Minister to Secretary of State for War and Secretary   7 Oct. 42
of State for Air

Whenever our Army is established on land and is conducting operations against the enemy the system of organisation and employment of the Royal Air Force should conform to that which has proved so successful in the Western Desert. The characteristics of this system are that the whole Air Force will be under the command of one Air Officer Commanding-in-Chief, whose relationship to the Army Commander-in-Chief will be that laid down in paragraphs 4 and 5 of my directive of October 7, 1941. This fact must be the starting-point in our investigation of the part to be played by the Royal Air Force in Continental operations based on the United Kingdom. I should like to see, set out in simple terms, the application of the Western Desert system to France. Let this statement be prepared and agreed by the time I return from the North.

2. Working backwards from the result which we must achieve in France, we can then determine how the awkward second phase, involving the spring across the Channel, can be best managed. Finally, we can see what arrangements should be made for the preparatory training period, so that there will be no break in the continuity throughout the three phases.

3. In the meanwhile, so that there may be no delay, and without prejudice to any final decision, the twelve Army Support Squadrons should begin forming in Army Co-operation Command as agreed upon between C.I.G.S. and C.A.S.

Prime Minister to Sir Edward Bridges   8 Oct. 42

For your private information, I rate the capacity of a man to give a useful opinion on any question connected with war in accordance with the following three conditions:

First, courage and ability. Second, real experience of the fire. Third, peacetime Staff studies and routine promotion.

Prime Minister to Foreign Secretary   8 Oct. 42

In my opinion this is not the way this matter should have been handled. In the picture I make to myself of the Turk, comradeship, generosity, the impression of power and resources, are what will count. I had never meant to mix this gift up with any bargain about chrome, about which they are obviously in great difficulties. When the Ambassador speaks about taking advantage to "rub it in" he utterly misconceives the gesture. I took great trouble to get these tanks, etc. I am after the Turk; I am not after your chrome. I particularly asked that the two ideas should be kept quite separate.

I am very sorry about this. Do please see if you can get the issues on a right footing. We offer this hard-bought gift to Inönü. All that happens is, he is "rather discomposed." I should like to send the following telegram to Inönü:

"The gift of arms from Britain to Turkey reported to you by the Ambassador on October 1 is meant by me as a token of comradeship and comprehension, and it is independent of every other consideration or matter in negotiation between our Governments."

Prime Minister to First Lord and First Sea Lord   8 Oct. 42

I am disquieted to learn that the German E-boats are getting the upper hand again, and that they are becoming a serious danger to East Coast shipping by laying mines. I had the impression that you had overtaken the mosquito fleet menace. Pray let me have a statement showing the position, and also what measures you will take. We cannot possibly allow ourselves to be outmatched in mosquito warfare.

Prime Minister to Secretary of State for Air and   8 Oct. 42
Minister of Labour

I cannot agree that men under twenty-five should be employed on these highly localised duties. No more should be recruited at present [into the R.A.F. Regiment]. With regard to those now there, I am not certain under what tenure they are serving. Have we the power to transfer them to Army units? Please advise me. The transference should be made gradually, so as to avoid any shock to the formations. A period of four months would not be excessive for this.

2. The replacement of the under-twenty-fives would of course come from the older categories called up, and these should be supplied sufficiently to maintain the approved strength of the Royal Air Force Regiment. I shall be content if the total strength is allowed to run down from 79,000 to, say, 70,000.

3. Is it not very absurd that the officers of this ground service should be called pilot officers, flight-lieutenants, etc., when they have never flown and are never going to fly? No one ought to be called a pilot officer who has not flown or does not fly. Most people would be ashamed to call themselves pilots of the Royal Air Force when in fact they are never going to get off the ground. I wonder the pilots themselves do not feel rather scornful about this multiplication of borrowed plumes.

Prime Minister to Foreign Secretary   12 Oct. 42

I do not feel safe with the present free use of the radio telephone either to United States or to Russia. I agree that technical arrangements for the Russian line should be made. In both cases however no subordinate persons should be allowed to use this telephone unless they obtain beforehand in each case written permission from the Postmaster-General, who will ascertain from them that they are fully aware of the dangers inherent in such communication. There is no reason why they should not telegraph whenever possible. A certain number of people of high rank might be given a general permit.

Pray let me have some scheme of this kind before we go any further.

Prime Minister to Secretary of State for Air and   14 Oct. 42
Chief of the Air Staff

This return of Middle East air reinforcements is really very bad indeed, and must be regarded as a lamentable breakdown in Air Force arrangements. No explanation can justify the congestion of 98 Hurricanes, 61 Beaufighters, 36 Spitfires, and 37 Kittyhawks at Takoradi when every one of these machines is urgently needed in Egypt.

I must ask that an immediate remedy should be applied.

Prime Minister to Foreign Secretary   14 Oct. 42

Pray consider the following:

The Madagascar situation should be handled in the following method and timing. There would be no objection to telling Dejean about the middle of next week that we should be glad to see Le Gentilhomme become Governor of Madagascar as de Gaulle's lieutenant and as representing Fighting France. We do not want to have more trouble than is necessary in Madagascar, and it would be best to begin by spreading reports there about Le Gentilhomme returning as Governor, and indicating that this would be very agreeable to the British. Then a little later, if all went well, Le Gentilhomme could go out and be installed as Governor without, in the first instance, setting up a new administration. Once he was installed we would transfer to him power, in such a way as to cause the fewest possible resignations of necessary French administrative officials. It would be for General de Gaulle to announce, with our approval, that he had appointed Le Gentilhomme as Governor, and this might be done about the middle of November. . . .

It should be made clear to de Gaulle that he, Le Gentilhomme, was *persona grata* to us, and that we could not have someone appointed whom we did not trust and like.

Prime Minister to Secretary of State for War   14 Oct. 42

It occurs to me that the Lovat Scouts, by reason of their origin, traditions, and composition, might with advantage be added to the existing Commandos, to take the place of the three Commandos which were sent out to the Middle East in 1940 and there disbanded. Pray put me up proposals. The Chief of Combined Operations will of course have to be consulted. I have not mentioned the matter to him.

Prime Minister to First Sea Lord 15 Oct. 42

See Admiral Harwood's telegram about the French fleet in Alexandria. We want to get them on our side as "Lightfoot" and "Torch" develop. Superior force is a powerful persuader. Pray consider urgently sending *Warspite* or *Valiant* from Kilindini to arrive at Alexandria a few days before "Torch," or in whatever is the best timing. Harwood could send a few destroyers from his scanty stock to pick her up in the Red Sea, if possible in the Gulf of Aden. She is a fast ship and could look after herself up to there. I hate to see ships standing idle at a crisis. According to my ideas the whole lot should go, including the carrier. The appearance of this fleet at Alexandria would start up all these ideas about Crete and Italy which are helpful to "Torch." How many destroyers has Harwood got, and how far south could they get in time?

Prime Minister to Secretary of State for War 15 Oct. 42

It has been reported to me by an officer now serving with the Royal Air Force Regiment in Ireland that American officers are never invited to British officers' messes, either Army or R.A.F., and that the Americans are, generally speaking, left to fend for themselves. This is a grave reflection on our comradeship and common courtesy.

Pray let me have a report.

NOVEMBER

Prime Minister to C.C.O. and Brigadier Jacob 1 Nov. 42

We must be careful not to make heavy weather over the manning of landing-craft. No doubt there must be a nucleus of skilled personnel to handle them and keep the engines in order. They do not have to be kept up however like a fleet or flotilla, as they are only needed for a special operation, and, if all goes well, only for the preliminary stages of that. If it were decided that the time had come for such an operation, both the Fleet and the Army would have to provide men specially for the month or three weeks concerned. We could not possibly afford to tie up a large mass of men indefinitely waiting for the chance of a big cross-Channel operation. First let us get the craft, and meanwhile make a scheme to put them into skeleton preparation capable of being brought up to fuller strength as the moment comes nearer. In trying to be perfect you will spoil the whole thing.

Prime Minister to First Lord 5 Nov. 42

Let me see the list of the submarines that will come into service by December 31, 1943, in their classes, and also those at present in service with no names.

2. I have no doubt whatever that names should be given, and I will myself make some suggestions which may stimulate others.

Prime Minister to General Ismay, for C.O.S. Committee 12 Nov. 42

I am disquieted by these notes [about tugs for gliders], which Lord Cherwell, at my request, has put before me. You may remember that the Lord Privy Seal recently raised the question of the excessive construction of gliders. As you know, I think they will play their part when demoralisation sets in; but I am worried by the difficulty of storing these wooden machines and the very heavy drain upon the bomber offensive. It is all a question of balance and emphasis.

2. I am sure it requires review. I do not want the Chiefs of Staff in this operational crisis to be unduly burdened with this. It would be better that the Vice-Chiefs should give it a special examination, which of course should not take more than two sittings. Their report would give us something to work upon. We might look very foolish if we had a lot of these things standing out in the rain and spoiling when no opportunity for their offensive use occurred. My feeling is at present that the "Horsa" programme should be curtailed.

Prime Minister to Chiefs of Staff Committee 12 Nov. 42

We cannot divest ourselves of responsibility for the convoy from the East to Malta. If it is to sail on the 15th, what arrangements are made to protect it against surface attack by the Italian Fleet? Is it to approach Malta in darkness or in daylight? What protection would it have against bombers from Crete, and generally until it gets under the Malta air umbrella? This is no time to throw away four fast heavily laden ships. Will the airfield at Derna be working by the time the convoy gets there? If it is not, we ought to wait a few more days till it is. The prospects in Cyrenaica are now so good that there is no need for forlorn, desperate adventures. Admiral Harwood should submit his scheme, showing exactly his daylight and darkness passage, and how he plans to get through.

2. It is of course of the utmost importance that Lord Gort should intervene by air in Tunis. But I do not think we ought simply to leave the responsibility of using up his petrol to him. What view do the Chiefs of Staff take about the amount he should keep in hand?

3. It would seem that everything should be calculated from the date when the Derna airfield is effectively occupied.

Prime Minister to General Ismay   13 Nov. 42

I saw the Jefferis gun last week. It appeared to be a powerful weapon, which would enable infantry to face tank attack.

How many have been ordered?

When will they be delivered?

How is it proposed to distribute them?

I should hope that the Middle East and India would receive their quota at a very early date.

Pray let me have a report.

Prime Minister to Secretary of State for War   21 Nov. 42

I was shocked to hear yesterday, when visiting the 53d Division, that an Army Council instruction had been issued three days ago ordering the immediate removal of all regimental shoulder-badges. Both the General commanding the division and the Commander-in-Chief Home Forces expressed to me their surprise and regret. There is no doubt that it will be extremely unpopular and tend to destroy that regimental *esprit de corps* upon which all armies worthy of the name are founded. I was also told that the Army Council instruction was accompanied by a notification that no discussion of it was to be allowed. Who is responsible for this?

I hope you will give directions to cancel the instruction before great harm is done.

Prime Minister to Minister of Food   21 Nov. 42

I hope it is not true that we are enforcing a whole set of vexatious regulations of this kind [about the ban on the exchange of rationed food]. It is absolutely contrary to logic and good sense that a person may not give away or exchange his rations with some one who at the moment he feels has a greater need. It strikes at neighbourliness and friendship. I should be so sorry to see the great work you have done spoilt by allowing these officials, whose interests are so deeply involved in magnifying their functions and their numbers, to lead you to strike a false note.

The matter must be brought before the Cabinet next week, unless you can reassure me.

Prime Minister to C.I.G.S.   25 Nov. 42

With regard to the rearmament of the French in Northwest Africa as may be expedient, could we not send some of the "seventy-fives" and ammunition, which are now almost entirely superseded by our own guns? These would be very welcome to the French. Perhaps 20 batteries could be sent quite soon, if General Eisenhower approves.

Prime Minister to C.I.G.S.   25 Nov. 42

Are we not dispersing the Desert Army rather rapidly? If 9th Australian and 2d New Zealand Divisions leave and now two South Africans, and then there is to be cannibalisation, what is going to be left? It seems to me that we have got to think of the whole picture in relation to the next six months. Please report. I am disquieted.

Prime Minister to Minister of War Transport   28 Nov. 42

Pray convey to all those in your department who have contributed to the success of "Torch" my warm congratulations and thanks for the part they played in the preparation and movement of this great armada. It owed much to their skill, industry, and reticence, and they share in the honour of a great achievement.

December

Prime Minister to C.I.G.S.   1 Dec. 42

The rôle of the Tenth Army is dependent upon the Russian defence of the Caucasus. Since we formed it in August, a vast favourable change has taken place, and it may be that before the end of the year all danger to Persia and Iraq will have rolled far to the westward.

2. Our policy towards Turkey may require that a large portion of the Tenth Army should be available to help the Turks. In view of the victories gained by the Allies both to the north and south of Turkey, the idea of Turkey opening a path voluntarily to the Germans need no longer be entertained.

3. Will you let me have a report showing how you could move four to six divisions of the Tenth Army westward into Syria and Turkey? Could they be maintained in Syria, or how many of them? How fast could they move into Turkey by rail if desired? Let a scheme be worked out having as its target date six divisions in Western Turkey by May 1. It is not necessary to go into this in undue detail.

Prime Minister to President of the Board of Trade   4 Dec. 42

I am told that the whole of the Army have been made to strip off their regimental badges, at great detriment to *esprit de corps*. As many of the soldiers paid for these badges themselves there has been a lot of distress caused. The War Office stated the Board of Trade have informed them that the amount of material and labour used to make these badges (most of which are already in existence) is more than we can afford in the present stringency.

Will you let me know exactly what the burden is? It must be taken into account that a great deal can be done by regimental and local arrangements. It would seem to me this was a very small proportion of the Army clothing. Let me know exactly what the Board of Trade said to the War Office which led them to this step.

Prime Minister to General Ismay, for C.O.S. Committee   6 Dec. 42

This [telegram about the lessons to be learned from the Dieppe raid in connection with landing ships and craft] is of course sound so far as concerns the landing ships and craft required for the actual spearhead of assault. If it is attempted to apply these high-grade conditions to all movements from one shore to the other the only result will be to render operations of this character utterly impossible. The maxim "Nothing avails but perfection" may be spelt shorter, "Paralysis."

Prime Minister to First Sea Lord   6 Dec. 42

Apparently, from the attached telegram, Admiral Harwood is going to use *Orion* and seven destroyers to convoy back empty merchant ships from Malta to Alexandria, after which the escort will return to Malta. But this is the week of all others when the Malta surface force (Force K) must strike upon the communications of the Axis forces in Tunis. A week or ten days later will be too late. Infinite harm will be done and the whole battle compromised.

2. This also is the time for Admiral Cunningham to use his cruisers and destroyers, even at heavy risk, against enemy convoys. These vessels could never play so useful a part as in stopping the reinforcements of the enemy during the battle. The first duty of the Navy for the next ten days is to stop the reinforcements to Tunisia. This duty should be discharged even at a heavy cost.

Prime Minister to General Ismay, for C.O.S. Committee.   7 Dec. 42

I attach the greatest importance to the prompt examination of these ideas [about "Habbakuk"],[7] and every facility should be given to the Chief of Combined Operations for developing them. He will report to me weekly on the setting up of the organisation and the preliminary work.

2. I do not of course know anything about the physical properties of a lozenge of ice 5000 feet by 2000 feet by 100 feet, or how it resists particular stresses, or what would happen to an iceberg of this size in rough Atlantic weather, or how soon it would melt in different waters at different periods of the year. The advantages of a floating island or islands, even if only used as refuelling depots for aircraft, are so dazzling that they do not at the moment need to be discussed. There would be no difficulty in finding a place to put such a "stepping-stone" in any of the plans of war now under consideration.

3. The scheme is only possible if we make nature do nearly all the work for us and use as our materials sea-water and low temperature. The

[7] The proposal to use artificial icebergs as staging-points for aircraft in the Atlantic.

scheme will be destroyed if it involves the movement of very large numbers of men and a heavy tonnage of steel or concrete to the remote recesses of the Arctic night.

4. Something like the following procedure suggests itself to me. Go to an icefield in the far north which is six or seven feet thick but capable of being approached by ice-breakers; cut out the pattern of the ice-ship on the surface; bring the right number of pumping appliances to the different sides of the ice-deck; spray salt water on continually so as to increase the thickness and smooth the surface. As this process goes on the berg will sink lower in the water. There is no reason why at the intermediate stages a trellis-work of steel cables should not be laid to increase the rate of sinking and give stability. The increasing weight and depth of the berg will help to detach the structure from the surrounding ice-deck. It would seem that at least 100 feet in depth should be secured. The necessary provision for oil fuel storage and motive power can be left at the proper stages. At the same time, somewhere on land the outfit of huts, workshops, and so forth will be made. When the berg begins to move southward, so that it is clear of the ice floes, vessels can come alongside and put all the equipment, including ample flak, on board.

Prime Minister to Minister of Aircraft Production   12 Dec. 42
  (*Sir Stafford Cripps*)

I have given careful consideration to your minute of November 30 about the control of anti-U-boat operations.

I do not think the plan you propose of having an officer of very high naval rank in sole charge of these operations under the First Sea Lord is sound. The sea war is all one. The Admiralty and the Naval Staff have been carefully organised and shaped through years of thought and practice to deal with it as a whole. To try to take out one particular aspect of the sea war and place it under a separate authority for all purposes would, I am sure, cause an immense amount of friction and confusion.

Anti-U-boat warfare affects every command afloat and ashore and almost every branch of the Admiralty. Such an organism as you propose would cut across all existing arrangements and disturb all existing loyalties. New frontiers would be established within the Admiralty itself on which at a hundred points new bickerings would proceed. It is always tempting in times of stress to set up a local dictatorship, but it is very easy thereby to rupture the constitution. In trying to lay a desirable emphasis on the anti-U-boat warfare you might well find that you had cast a spanner into the fast-running machinery by which our naval defence has been so well conducted.

In our difficulties in the Atlantic I do not think the Americans and Canadians would pay more heed to such an officer as Admiral Somerville, whom you suggest, than they do at present to Sir Dudley Pound. Indeed, I think there would be a loss of influence.

It is essential of course at all times to watch carefully the working of the machine and the efficiency of the liaison arrangements between the air and sea forces, and to make such changes in personnel, methods, and devices as are required. It is with this end in view that I set up the Anti-U-boat Committee, in which these matters may be discussed and action taken above the departmental level.

Prime Minister to Foreign Secretary   13 Dec. 42

Of course it would be a very good thing to have an Austrian unit if it could be managed without too much trouble. I am extremely interested in Austria, and hope that Vienna may become the capital of a great Confederation of the Danube. It is perfectly true that Europe left Austria to her fate in a pusillanimous manner in 1938. The separation of the Austrians and Southern Germans from the Prussians is essential to the harmonious reconstitution of Europe.

Prime Minister to C.I.G.S., and to General Ismay for   13 Dec. 42
C.O.S. Committee

Out of over 34,000 men in these two "Torch" convoys assigned to the Eastern Task Force, which is the only one engaged or likely to be engaged, there are less than 9000 fighting troops, including both a new unit and reinforcements. This is the crisis period of the Tunisian battle. I doubt very much whether we and the Americans have yet brought more than 15,000 actual fighting men into contact with the enemy out of, perhaps, a quarter of a million landing or about to land.

2. [Convoy] K.M.S.5 has passed out of our control. Is it not possible and would it not be well to find two or three more ships and get a brigade group of the 46th Division out with the Christmas convoy? Ought we not to include another two or three thousand reinforcements as well? When there are two or three hundred thousand men in or approaching the theatre it seems an awful pity to stake the fortunes of battle on the very small spearhead at present available for the Eastern Task Force. Observe, I am not proposing to cut the enormous non-combatant tail which fills up K.M.S.5 and K.M.S.6, but only to make sure there are some teeth to bite the enemy with. It is the teeth that we always run short of, and however good the Supply, the Signals, the Pioneers, the R.E., and the hospitals are, there must always somewhere up in front be a certain number of people who actually are engaged on trying to kill the enemy with the weapons which they hold.

Prime Minister to First Sea Lord   14 Dec. 42

How do we stand now about the Russian convoys after the one to be run in two portions late this month? I am expecting that convoys should be planned, in one or two portions as convenient, at least for January, February, and March, between thirty and forty ships going in each.

2. The threatened delay in "Brimstone," "Husky," etc., should ease the position as far as the Russian convoys are concerned. Also it is to be noted that a decision in favour of "Round-up" instead of "Brimstone," etc., operative as it would be only in August, would assist and prolong the running of the P.Q. convoys. I am, as you know, at present thinking along both lines, "Brimstone" and "Round-up," but it will almost certainly be necessary to choose. Personally, I should only choose "Brimstone," etc., if I were satisfied after intense efforts that "Round-up" was impossible in 1943.

Prime Minister to Secretary of State for War   14 Dec. 42

Let me have a report showing the shortage of officers in the Home Army, especially in the battalions, batteries, and armoured units. I am told that a very large proportion of candidates have been rejected by the Selection Boards, returning to the ranks with a sense of disappointment. I am of opinion that the Commanding Officer of a battalion or tank unit is the best judge, and that if he is not a good judge he is scarcely fit for his position. In these circumstances, having regard to the shortage, it would seem advisable that all recommendations emanating from Commanding Officers through the brigades should be endorsed by the War Office, unless some special reason can be adduced to the contrary.

2. Let me also have figures showing (a) the number of officers of each rank on the establishment of the Home Army, and (b) the number of those in Great Britain not included in the Home Army. Let me also have the number of commissions granted in 1942 in the United Kingdom, irrespective of where these officers have been sent.

Prime Minister to Secretary of State for War   16 Dec. 42

Pray send round samples of the printed and embroidered slip-on regimental flashes to which you refer in the first paragraph of your minute of December 14.

2. Let me have the text of the original instruction issued by your predecessor, together with the War Office files upon which he took this decision.

3. What is General Paget's explanation of the non-enforcement of this instruction until the sending out of the order by him in July 1942?

4. What were the circumstances which led to the issue of the Army Council instruction of last month? Pray let me see the War Office files on this subject. Was General Paget consulted before this instruction was issued?

5. It was of course from General Paget, when I inspected the 53d

Division, that I learnt of the distress [caused] to the troops by the enforcement of the order, and he certainly expressed himself in a manner which led me to believe that he greatly regretted it.

6. It seems to me that if the Commander-in-Chief condoned over a great many months the numerous breaches of this order which you mention it was hard on units concerned to enforce so sudden a change of policy. . . .

8. I should be glad if you would also explain to me why the Guards are to be specially favoured in this matter. Has a special permission been granted to them, and, if so, on what grounds? I should have thought that line regiments, and especially national regiments like the Welsh or the Scots, were even more anxious for the support to *esprit de corps* and the expression of individuality which the enjoyment of distinctive badges confers.

9. I can quite see that the difficulty is one into which you have got yourself by making the enforcement of this wrong principle a matter of prestige, and I should be willing to allow a longer interval to elapse before the general mounting of badges is authorised.

Prime Minister to Chancellor of the Exchequer, Foreign   17 Dec. 42
Secretary, Paymaster-General, President of the Board of
Trade
(Copy to the Lord President of the Council)

I hope that in studying the various proposals for social reform, land development, etc., you are giving full consideration to our post-war financial position. The implications of these schemes must be related to the cost of the armed forces which it will be necessary to maintain, and to the prospects of restoring our export trade. Nothing would be more dangerous than for people to feel cheated because they had been led to expect attractive schemes which turn out to be economically impossible.

What progress has been made in the talks with the Americans? The vital question of the rapid restoration of our export trade must depend on the result of these conversations, and no doubt you are examining all possible markets. This work will be of value whatever international trading arrangements are agreed upon. Pray consider these matters at your convenience.

Prime Minister to General Ismay and Brigadier Jacob,   18 Dec. 42
for C.O.S. Committee

Considering how few of our armoured divisions are going to be in action, we ought not to send 2-pounder Crusaders [with the next armoured division going to North Africa]. It is only laying ourselves open to the kind of criticism we had in the Gazala battle to put these under-gunned tanks on to the backs of our harassed shipping. It is only worth while sending the best. There seems to be time enough to make a change. Pray let me have a plan to replace the 2-pounders by 6-pounders.

Prime Minister to General Ismay and Brigadier Jacob   19 Dec. 42

I see that 150,000 new .303 rifles and 332,000 Sten guns were manu-factured in October and November. Pray let me know how these weapons have been distributed.

2. How many of the Home Guard have at present individual firearms, and how many have not?

3. The Middle East should be asked to supply the best information possible of all undamaged or repairable weapons, including rifles, mortars, guns, lorries, tanks, aircraft, etc., taken in Cyrenaica — i.e., up till the period before the fighting west of Agheila.

Prime Minister to Brigadier Jacob   19 Dec. 42

The hundred and twenty 75-mm. guns and equipment should go at the same time as the two hundred 2-pounders and thirty-two Bofors. I attach great importance to building up a good French army in Morocco under Giraud as fast as possible, and thus render it unnecessary for British and American troops to squat there all the summer. Let all preparations proceed.

Prime Minister to First Lord and First Sea Lord   19 Dec. 42

Many thousands of British soldiers have been three and four years in the Middle East and in India who would no doubt very much like to come home and be given leave before resuming their duties. I do not know why special favour should be shown to the Navy. Many of the soldiers have in fact probably been more often in action. How much petrol will be used in bringing the *Valiant* home and sending her back merely for the purpose of giving leave? Have we a right to make this movement?

2. It certainly would be a very sensible thing to bring the old Rs back and lay them up in some safe harbour, using the crews to man new vessels. They are only coffin ships, and a cause of grievous anxiety the moment any modern enemy vessel appears. If these ships are brought home one by one the crews who have been shipwrecked or have been out a particularly long time could be given passages in them.

3. I am certainly very glad that *Anson* or *Howe* should play a part in the Mediterranean.

Prime Minister to Foreign Secretary and Chief Whip   19 Dec. 42

As an old member of the House of Commons I take quite a different view [of the proposal that Ministers should condense their answers to oral questions in the House of Commons and the statements made at the end of Questions in order to avoid encroaching upon the time available for debates or public business]. It is the interest and privilege of the House to receive full statements on public affairs from the Executive. No band of Members has any right to stand between the House and this great advantage. In time of war it is more important than in time of peace. The House would be ill served and would rightly take offence if statements, instead of being made to Parliament at the end of Questions, were handed to the Press, as would otherwise be inevitable. I am sure myself that the present demand would not represent the wish of the House if they considered the matter fully, and I think the case should be put before them so that other opinions may be expressed besides those yet obtained or audible. The fact that the House is nearly always filled during such a statement and empties at its close is a very fair indication of what the ordinary silent Member feels. It is of course understood that Ministerial statements should be confined to imparting information.

2. On the other hand, Ministers should certainly not read long answers during Question time, as this is very unfair on Members whose later questions may be shut out. Question time is one of the most lively and vital features of Parliamentary life. I wish this matter to be discussed by the Cabinet before anything like this is put out.

Prime Minister to Lord President of the Council   19 Dec. 42

On August 4, 1942, the War Cabinet set up a Ministerial committee, consisting of the then Lord Privy Seal, Sir Stafford Cripps (in the chair) and the three Service Ministers, to supervise the work of an expert committee on the use made of psychologists and psychiatrists in the Fighting Services.

Sir Stafford Cripps has suggested that it might now be more appropriate that some other Minister should take over the chairmanship of the body. I agree with this view, and would be grateful if you would undertake this duty.

I am sure it would be sensible to restrict as much as possible the work of these gentlemen, who are capable of doing an immense amount of harm with what may very easily degenerate into charlatanry. The tightest hand should be kept over them, and they should not be allowed to quarter themselves in large numbers upon the Fighting Services at the public expense. There are no doubt easily recognisable cases which may benefit from treatment of this kind, but it is very wrong to disturb large numbers of healthy, normal men and women by asking the kind of odd questions in which the psychiatrists specialise. There are quite enough hangers-on and camp-followers already.

Prime Minister to First Sea Lord   19 Dec. 42

I am still grieved to see our submarines described as "P.212," etc., in the daily returns. I thought you told me that you would give them names. It is in accordance with the tradition of the Service and with the feelings of the officers and men who risk their lives in these vessels. Not even to give them a name is derogatory to their devotion and sacrifice.

Prime Minister to General Ismay, for C.O.S. Committee   21 Dec. 42

I regard the equipment of the Polish Corps as of first importance and urgency in view of the cannibalisation of British divisions and the withdrawal of the Australians and South Africans from the Eighth Army. Let a scheme be prepared showing dates by which the various divisions can be equipped with rifles, 25-pounders, anti-tank and anti-aircraft mortars and machine guns, and Bren-gun carriers; also tanks. It is not necessary to adhere exactly to the British standards. These can be attained later. Let me have the earliest dates when these fine troops will have the minimum equipment to acquire substantial fighting value. Let me have forecast for January 31, February 28, March 31.

11TH ARMOURED DIVISION

Prime Minister to Secretary of State for War and C.I.G.S   23 Dec. 42

General Anderson is complaining that his tanks are ineffective compared to the Germans'. It is the same story we had a year ago in the Gazala battle. You now say that the layout in your paper attached is the best possible. It means that eighty-nine obsolete 2-pounder tanks are to go into action with the 11th Division, and only eighty 6-pounders. I am not at all convinced that this is right. The armoured divisions have already been reduced to a single brigade of tanks. Now this brigade of tanks is to be further more than halved to accommodate the organisation of command. Thus a British armoured division to go into action in February is only to have eighty effectively gunned tanks. This is an altogether inadmissible diminution of striking power, and I wish the matter to be reviewed. I shall be very glad to see you both at 12 noon tomorrow with any officers you may wish to bring.

Prime Minister to Secretary of State for War and C.I.G.S.   26 Dec. 42

The Tunisian tip, in which this division will operate with other troops, is about thirty-five miles deep by fifty-five miles broad. It therefore bears no resemblance to the vast distances of the Western Desert. On the other hand [the division] may have to face permanent fortifications at Bizerta and strong field positions around Tunis. It may be needed to support an infantry break-through. For all these purposes heavy weapons and thick armour are required. No question is raised of standard establishments, but of creating a particular instrument for a special task.

2. I am glad you are able to add thirty-six 6-pounder tanks by increasing the tank troops [in each squadron] from three to four. I wish you to consider urgently whether we cannot add a fourth regiment of 6-pounder tanks as a self-contained unit of the divisional reserve. Best of all would be if this unit could have Churchills, because in punching through the defences of Bizerta or Tunis and in street fighting this tank alone has the necessary armour. Lord Leathers informs me that the addition to the convoy would not be more than two or at the most three ships. We thus increase the punch enormously. However, perhaps the landing facilities at Algiers, and still more at Bone, could not handle 40-ton tanks. Nevertheless, this would be the tool for the job. The additional regiment, apart from its special workshops and spare parts, would not require any additional overheads in the divisional organisation.

3. In anti-tank and flak units this division must be regarded as exceptional. In view of the importance of its mission, other units in the Home Army may be drawn upon temporarily. The Divisional Commander has shown me, at my request, the letter which he has already written to the War Office. I certainly think that all his anti-tank weapons should at least be 6-pounders, and I hope it may be possible to add a dozen 17-pounders in view of the fact that the delay will certainly bring more German "Tigers" to the scene.

4. Considering the vitally important part that this division may be called upon to play in February, or at the latest March, it is necessary to give it an altogether special outfit. This should certainly include the support company of mortars. Pray let me have a scheme for effecting the above, or as much of it as is practicable. There must be no retardation in the sailing date of this division in consequence of any of the above changes without my being duly informed.

5. Besides all this, I should be willing to ask the President to send two or three hundred Shermans out to Algeria so that our 6th Armoured Division could work into these regiment by regiment as the withdrawals from the front line rendered possible. We cannot go on with these Gazala defeat outfits without exposing ourselves to very grave Parliamentary censure.

SICKNESS

Prime Minister to Lord President   26 Dec. 42

According to the figures supplied by the Health Insurance Approved Societies to the Government actuary, the average number of people away from work owing to minor illness has increased in the last year by more than a quarter. If this applies to the whole working population it is equivalent to having 80,000 fewer people working than would normally be the case. It may well be that such absenteeism is due, in part at any rate, to causes other than deterioration of health, but such a notable increase may be an indication of the danger of imposing more and more hardships on the civil population.

Prime Minister to Minister of War Transport 26 Dec. 42

Prospective imports into the United Kingdom in the first half of next year are so low that we must take immediate definite steps to increase them. In view of the improved strategic situation in the Middle East it would seem possible to fix a definite ceiling to the number of ships made available monthly to the War Office and Air Ministry for servicing the Eastern theatres from the United Kingdom and United States.

Pray let me know how much imports to this country could be increased if the Service departments were rationed to the use of (a) fifty ships a month, (b) forty ships a month, for the Eastern theatres.

Prime Minister to General Ismay 27 Dec. 42

The German divisions are estimated by the Joint Intelligence Committee's paper about the Order of Battle and Distribution of the German Army as 320 divisions, but on other papers I have seen a J.I.C. estimate of 300 divisions. Will you have this discrepancy probed?

2. The J.I.C. paper about German strategy in 1943 gives a number of 6,250,000 men. This makes a German gross division 20,000, as opposed to our 41,000. If their proportion of corps, army, and L. of C. troops is the same as ours, this would make the division proper consist of less than 10,000 men. Alternatively, it shows very excessive War Office tail. What do they say about this? I will keep the report.

Prime Minister to First Lord 27 Dec. 42

These names for submarines are certainly much better than the numbers. Please see my suggestions. I have no doubt a little more thought, prompted by the dictionary, would make other improvements possible.

Now do please get on with it, and let them be given their names in the next fortnight.

Prime Minister to Secretary of State for War, Minister 31 Dec. 42
of War Transport, and C.I.G.S.

I am not satisfied with the dates given for sending the brigade of Churchill tanks to Tunis. A strenuous effort must be made with full battle urgency to have this brigade embarked complete in the convoy which leaves about January 17. If the Ministry of War Transport can produce the ships, a very grave responsibility will fall upon the War Office if they are not able to load this brigade, which has already once been mobilised, in time.

Prime Minister to Secretary of State for War   31 Dec. 42

No doubt it is more economical to reject the candidates before they have been to the Officer Cadet Training Units than after training has been wasted upon them. The question was however brought to my notice on the grounds that the combatant units of the Home Army were seriously short of officers and that the supply was not keeping pace with the demand.

2. It is clear from your table that there is a deficiency of over 2000 officers, of whom nearly 700 are in the infantry alone. How and when do you propose that this deficiency should be made up? I notice that of the officers in Great Britain no fewer than 40,979 out of 87,633 are not included in the Field Army at home, or in Air Defence Great Britain, or in the First Army elements still at home. Surely out of this mass of 40,979, the greater part unconnected with fighting troops, you could find the necessary 2000 to fill up the Field Army. Let me have an analysis of the employments to which the majors, captains, and subalterns, in column 4, "All Others at Home," are put. I may add that this figure of 40,979 officers engaged on non-fighting duties contrasts very pointedly with a shortage of 2000 for the fighting units.[8]

Prime Minister to Chancellor of the Exchequer   31 Dec. 42

I consider the case of Under-Secretaries of £1500 salary and less is painful, and I should like it mitigated if you can find a way. One idea would be to count the first £600 of their salary as if it was their salary as M.P.s, letting the Ministerial salary overlap the Parliamentary. We have a large number of Under-Secretaries who are Labour Members, and I think they are feeling the pinch very severely — in fact, they are worse off than they were out of office, and are thus giving their services for less than nothing. This is not right.

I should even be prepared to treat the first £600 of all Ministers' salaries as if it was the £600 they get as M.P.'s, letting the rest overlap, even above the £1500. I should think the House would be quite willing to entertain this, especially as it affects the poorer men of the Labour Party. It must be remembered that the constituency and other expenses continue. Perhaps you could think of some other way. Pray let me have your views.

JANUARY

Prime Minister to General Ismay   1 Jan. 43

Why do the Canadian Corps require 13,000 more rifles? Have they increased their strength? What has been the wastage? Why do the Middle

8 See minute of December 14, page 915.

East require 63,500 rifles, in view of the fact that two divisions are being cannibalised? What is the reserve of rifles in the Middle East? What have been the losses of British rifles in the recent fighting? How many rifles have the Polish Corps got at the present time? Why have 18,000 rifles to go to East Africa, a theatre where, on the whole, there is a reduction of forces? What is the policy about reducing the Home Guard in accordance with the discussions in the Cabinet?

Prime Minister to First Lord of the Admiralty   1 Jan. 43

My warm congratulations on the fine output of merchant tonnage last year, a result of which all concerned may indeed be proud.

Prime Minister to Foreign Secretary   2 Jan. 43

You should surely explain that, under our present Constitution and wartime procedure, we have been ceaselessly exposed to the "emotional views of little men on political matters," and to check this entirely would involve His Majesty's Government in a direct attack on the freedom of Parliament and press. There is a deep loathing in this country, particularly strong among the working classes, against what are thought to be intrigues with Darlan and Vichy, which are held to be contrary to the broad, simple loyalties which unite the masses throughout the world against the common foe. It took the Prime Minister all his time and all his influence to smooth things out with the House of Commons in Secret Session. You should warn Hull that there is almost a passion on this subject, and one which, if it broke loose, would certainly cause differences of opinion and controversy in the United States.

2. We have done our very best to help in the Darlan business, and continue to do so in regard to the Vichy contacts still being preserved. But the general feeling is that a brilliant military episode has been tarnished and tainted. The danger of the situation is fully recognised here. The Prime Minister can no more embark on an effective policy of muzzling the press and Parliament than the State Department could gag Americans when they say things which give profound offence here. The remedy is to amend the policy and reach sound ground in this French quagmire.

Prime Minister to General Ismay, for C.O.S. Committee   4 Jan. 43

It is important to make the best possible estimate of the German and Italian strength in Tunisia as on March 1.

2. In two months since the landing the Axis have built up about 29,000 Germans and 14,000 Italians, making a total of 43,000. Since about 1500 of these were Italians who crossed over from Tripolitania, the rate of build-up does not exceed 700 a day. There are no grounds for assuming

a future rate of build-up of more than a thousand a day. We may therefore assume a maximum of 100,000 men by March 1. In the present
43,000 are included 3000 or 4000 air personnel and a proportion of the
supply troops of the 90th German Army Corps, together with the Staffs,
flak, etc. In order to maintain four divisions of our First Army a total
of 211,000 men is said to be required. Assuming that the Germans and
Italians work on a similar basis, and making some allowance for their
shorter lines of communication, it is unlikely that they could form and
maintain from Tunisian resources more than two, or at the outside three,
German divisions and two weak Italian divisions, which are no stronger
than brigade groups. An equivalent of four divisions might well be found
correct.

3. This force cannot have normal mobility. The 43,000 now there are
desperately short of artillery and of transport, reinforcement by air or
destroyer not allowing vehicles to be brought in. A careful check must
be kept of the ships entering Bizerta and Tunis, about one-third of which
we sink. The attempt to supply Rommel's army from Sousse, Sfax, and
Gabes does not seem likely to succeed in the teeth of our heavy air attack.
To sum up, we might count on the equivalent of four divisions lightly
equipped with artillery and so ill-supplied with transport as to be incapable of far-ranging operations.

4. It seems probable that Rommel's army will try to retreat upon
Tunisia, closely followed by Generals Alexander and Montgomery. It
must not be taken for granted that Rommel will escape heavy mauling
in the various battles he is to fight and in the defence of Tripoli. Should
we capture Tripoli at the beginning of February, he will then have to
retire first to the frontier and then into Tunisia. It is assumed too readily
that this is a feasible operation, and a report on the communications
should be furnished. Moreover, the route may be cut by the operations
of the Eastern Task Force, and will certainly be seriously hampered by
our air attack. However, assuming that Rommel is able to make his way
into Tunisia with the main part of his forces, let us see what these
amount to.

5. We know that the German ration strength in the middle of
December was about 70,000, but the great bulk of these are air force
ground personnel, supply and administrative services, which have grown
up in two years of this desert war. The strength of the German divisions,
namely, the 15th and 21st Panzers, the 164th Motorised, and the Brigade
Ramcke, is less than a third, or even a quarter, of their strength at the
Battle of Alamein. It is very unlikely that Rommel has with him at the
front more than 22,000 Germans in the above fighting formations.

6. The Italians must also be considered to have about 70,000 men in
Tripolitania. For these however very little or no transport is available.
The two corps, XXth and XXIst, which they have at the front are an

encumbrance and an anxiety to Rommel, and may conceivably be cut off and mopped up by our attack. The combined strength of both Italian units at present in the line with Rommel does not exceed 22,000 men. There is of course the accumulation of the supply services, air groundsmen, and the like, strewed along the road to Tripoli, but the fighting value of these is so low as to be negligible. Even before the Battle of Alamein the Italian divisions had little more than the strength which we assign to brigade groups.

7. Assuming therefore that Rommel is not reinforced from across the Mediterranean and that he makes his way without serious mauling into Tunisia by March 1, the maximum forces which he can bring will not exceed the equivalent of one Panzer and one motorised German division and two weak Italian divisions.

8. It would seem safe therefore from all the above to conclude that the total enemy forces in Tunisia on March 1 will not exceed 200,000 ration strength, of which 120,000 will represent the fighting strength, or four or five German divisions, two of which will be Panzer, and the equivalent of two or three full-strength Italian divisions, although these may be called by higher denominations; grand total, six or seven divisions, the whole ill-equipped with transport and artillery.

Prime Minister to Secretary of State for Air   4 Jan. 43

The failure to carry out the bomber expansion programme is a disappointment to me, and I think I should have been warned beforehand.

2. I note that the Americans have not yet succeeded in dropping a single bomb on Germany.

Prime Minister to Secretary of State for War, and C.I.G.S.   4 Jan. 43

I had a long conference yesterday with Generals Weeks and Galloway, who gave me a number of returns which I am now examining.

2. I notice in the establishment of the First Army that out of 211,000 men only 27,000 are infantry. The latest returns from Northwest Africa show that 51 per cent of the casualties have fallen on this eighth part of the Army. Apparently it is seven times more dangerous to belong to the infantry than to the rest of the Army, including artillery, armour and other fighting units. When we remember what duties are thrown upon the infantry in Northwest Africa — to hold with perhaps 15,000 effectives out of 22,800 disembarked a sixty-mile front, to do all the storming or hand-to-hand fighting that may arise, as well as providing the outpost line and many other duties — it would seem that the infantry component of the Army should be strengthened proportionately.

3. I understand, on the other hand, that it is now proposed to reduce battalions from four to three companies and to strengthen these companies. It would seem better to retain the four companies and raise each

one of them to the strength purposed for the three companies. I also consider it would be well to add a hundred men to the strength of each of the infantry battalions. I am well aware of, and I sympathise with, the modern tendency which has led the great development of specialist arms of all kinds. It would seem that this tendency has been carried too far when the infantry, who bear the brunt of the fighting, are reduced to such extremely small proportions. We have certainly gone a long way from the days when the maxim held, "The Infantry is the Army, and uses the other arms as its assistants." It is a question of emphasis and proportion. The figures for the First Army show 4200 officers and men on the various headquarters staffs to 27,000 infantry, or one [on] headquarters staff to every six infantry soldiers.

4. In view of the advance made by the Eighth Army and the possibility of its entering Tunisia, we do not need any longer to consider sending more than four divisions in all to Tunisia. It would be well if the two infantry divisions had a somewhat larger proportion of infantry, and above all it is important that infantry drafts are lavishly supplied.

5. The proportion of infantry to other arms requires to be carefully reviewed in connection with the preparation of the force for "Round-up." About twenty good colonels commanding battalions should be asked individually to express their views on battalion strength and organisation.

Prime Minister to General Ismay, for C.O.S. Committee,   5 Jan. 43
Defence Committee, and Minister of War Transport

Grave anxiety must be felt about our import programme for the first six months of 1943. The imports for the five months ending March 31 are likely to be only on the 17,000,000-ton scale. Those for December so far reported conformed only to 13,000,000-ton total. The American promise of 300,000 tons a month, beginning in December, would have produced on present lines only 50,000 tons to the end of January. Stocks not only of food but of raw materials are becoming seriously depleted. A breakdown in raw materials would lead to widespread cessation of work in the munitions industries, and would be discreditable in the last degree to His Majesty's Government. There is still time to take the necessary measures.

2. A restriction on the shipments to the Middle East and India from the United Kingdom and from the United States to not more than forty ships a month, if enforced from January to June 1943, inclusive, would improve the imports by 33,000,000 tons, thus avoiding the threatened breakdown and not making us live from hand to mouth, absolutely dependent on the fulfillment of American promises, in the last six months of the year. I wish this proposal to be examined forthwith by all departments concerned.

3. Account must be taken of the complete change in conditions in the

Middle East since August. The decisive victories in the Western Desert and the immense come-back of the Russians in South Russia and the Caucasus have removed for an indefinite period the principal dangers which we then faced. Rommel's army has been destroyed, and there will soon be no enemy within 1000 miles of Cairo, except for garrisons in the Balkans and the islands. The need which called the Tenth Army into being for the defence of Persia and Iraq has diminished and taken quite a different form. This army can now be considered available in whole or in part for action in the Eastern Mediterranean or in Turkey. The Eighth Army and the British troops in Egypt have undergone the following reductions: the Australian Division has gone, leaving its equipment behind; the 44th British Infantry and 8th British Armoured Divisions have been suppressed and their personnel carried to maintain the remaining formations. All stocks and equipment must be examined in the light of these facts.

4. There are at least three divisions' worth of equipment going spare. 91,000 men have been found from the rear services and from the above divisions to reduce the previous requirements of reinforcements. There are 400,000 tons of ammunition alone in the Middle East, and 220,000 tons in India or on the way there. Only 25,000 tons were fired in the first month of the campaign that began at the Battle of Alamein. Generally speaking, the Eighth, Ninth, and Tenth Armies and India must live on their tail, on their stocks, and on their share of the forty ships per month. A scheme must be prepared showing how this could be achieved and what, if any, further contraction it would entail. In addition however the equipment of the two and one-half Polish divisions must proceed with high priority, these troops being the only new reinforcements we can provide for the Eastern theatres in the next six months, when the position must be again reviewed.

5. It is for consideration whether the 4th and 5th Indian Divisions in the Eighth Army should not be exchanged for the 56th and 5th British Infantry Divisions in the Tenth Army. Pray let this be examined, both as respects exchanging two divisions or one.

Prime Minister to Home Secretary 7 Jan. 43

Many thanks for showing me your notes for your speech on colonial policy. I have scribbled a few comments as I read them.

I should have thought you could have a more confident ring. The influence of the House of Commons upon colonial development for at least a hundred years has built up moral standards in regard to native populations which have set an example to the world. In fact, our problem with the Boers was originally due to our insistence on the proper treatment of the Kaffirs, and at this moment we withhold native territories from their control. We have forbidden the commercial exploitation of India, perhaps to the detriment of its people.

The idea that all service is valueless unless disinterested is a fallacy. Mutually advantageous exchange of goods and services between communities is the foundation alike of the prosperity and peace of the world. The Little Englanders of Victorian days argued that all colonial possessions were mere burdens and responsibilities, and I believe it was Disraeli who in early youth spoke of them as "dropping off like ripe plums" when the time came.

If it were established that we were never to have any advantage from our colonies except that of pure philanthropy, a good many people would argue that we had better spend our money on improving the health and social services of our workers at home. Considering that for seventy or eighty years we kept our colonies absolutely open to the trade of the whole world without claiming the slightest preference or imposing any taxation except for revenue, and that it was the Americans, by their high tariff policy, who led the world astray, it is pretty good cheek of them now coming to school-marm us into proper behaviour. However, I am not suggesting you should use that particular sentence.

Prime Minister to Secretary of State for Air and Chief   7 Jan. 43
of the Air Staff

Considering that Bomber Command have done hardly any flying in the last month worth speaking of, it is astonishing that only 547 aircraft should be serviceable and fit for operations out of an establishment of 808. And why are only 557 crews available out of 1010 establishment and 909 effective strength?

I quite understand not going out in impossible weather, but then the result should be a strong accumulation, whereas an increasingly low standard of readiness prevails.

Prime Minister to Sir Edward Bridges   9 Jan. 43

The following formula should be examined by an inter-Service committee of the various research departments, who should say how far it would assist their work or what modifications are suggested.

Although no one can tell when the war against Hitler will end, a reasonable assumption at this date would be before the end of 1944. The date should be reviewed every three months. However, the war against Japan may well continue to the end of 1946, and may require quite a large effort from the three leading United Nations and China. Research therefore should aim primarily at what can be brought into action before the end of 1944. At the same time studies which do not seriously burden the next two years should be undertaken although they cannot reach fruition before the end of 1946. As a rough-and-ready rule, nine-tenths

of the effort should be concerned with the next two years and one-tenth
with what happens afterwards. Guidance should be sought in doubtful
cases on their individual merits.

Prime Minister to Foreign Secretary, First Lord,   9 Jan. 43
and First Sea Lord

Monsieur Maisky is not telling the truth when he says I promised Stalin
convoys of 30 ships in January and February. The only promise I have
made is contained in my telegram of December 29, paragraph 3, which
was agreed to by the Admiralty. I now understand that 20 ships only
are to go on January 17, and 30 on February 11. I think it a great pity the
Admiralty could not take the whole 30 as promised. On the other hand,
they have undertaken the February convoy.

Maisky should be told that I am getting to the end of my tether with
these repeated Russian naggings, and that it is not the slightest use trying
to knock me about any more. Our escorts all over the world are so
attenuated that losses out of all proportion are falling upon the British
Mercantile Marine. Only this morning news has come in of six out of
nine great tankers being sunk, full of oil and greatly needed, because we
can only provide an escort of one destroyer and a few corvettes for this
vital convoy. The Admiralty have definitely stated that if the Americans
do not lend us more destroyers, nothing can go after the February W.S.
convoy until the middle of March, a 36-day cycle only being possible to us.

Prime Minister to First Lord and Minister of War Transport   9 Jan. 43

Let me have the fullest possible details of the number of miscellaneous
special small craft, such as dredgers, tugs, salvage vessels, cable ships, etc.,
the provision of which cannot be postponed. All experience shows how
dockyard admirals send in demands which accumulate, and the result is
large contraction from fighting programmes in order to supply all sorts
of minor comforts and gadgets.

This programme must be severely scrutinised before I can agree to the
deprivation of the merchant shipbuilding tonnage proposed.

Prime Minister to Secretary of State for War   9 Jan. 43

I am glad you are training soldiers to use the P.I.A.T. I understand
that the fuzes are now clear and that the way is open to try out the gun.

2. I should have thought that production of the anti-tank rifle and its
ammunition could be stopped if it is to be replaced by the P.I.A.T.
The existing stocks of 42,000 rifles and 10 million rounds of ammunition
should be ample for use in the S.W. Pacific and by reconnaissance units.
Surely it is not worth while to continue ammunition production at peak
rate in these circumstances?

3. Why should the name "Jefferis shoulder gun" be changed to P.I.A.T.? Nobody objected to the Boys rifle, although it had rather an odd ring.

Prime Minister to General Ismay   11 Jan. 43

Make sure that General Catroux has a talk with the Joint Planners or Joint Intelligence Committee about the terrain and defences of the Mareth, on the southern frontiers of Tunisia. The General knows all about this line, having commanded there, and very expert information should be forthcoming from him. The largest scale maps should be available, and a report should be made which I can forward to Generals Alexander and Montgomery.

Prime Minister to Minister of Agriculture and Fisheries   12 Jan. 43

Please make me a plan to have more eggs. I am told that 67,000 tons of oats or barley out of the millions of tons produced on the farms would suffice to restore the ration of all the garden hens, and this would make a large difference to the number of eggs produced. When you have done so well in other directions it seems a pity to have this large and obvious failure.

Prime Minister to General Ismay, for C.O.S. Committee   19 Jan. 43

Measures should be taken immediately to bring some long-range 9.2 mobile equipments in order to command from a very long range the airfields in Bizerta and Tunis. I do not know whether this has been done yet, but there should just be time. The omission would be disastrous.

Prime Minister to C.I.G.S.   21 Jan. 43

The War Cabinet are in entire accord with the following proposals:

(a) That a Press Conference be held at the end of this meeting at which the President and I will answer questions, the release of any news being held up until the President has left the African shores.

(b) That General Alexander should be appointed General Eisenhower's Deputy Commander-in-Chief for the whole of North Africa.

(c) That the command of any "Sledgehammer" or "Round-up" which may be undertaken in 1943 should be British.

(d) That both in munitions and diplomacy the United Kingdom plays the hand in Turkey, while the United States plays the hand in China and French North Africa.

(e) General Maitland Wilson to succeed General Alexander in the Middle East Command, which will again resume full control of the Persia-Iraq Command (an arrangement which cannot present much difficulty, but which I propose to explore on the spot).

FEBRUARY

Prime Minister to Chief of the Air Staff   9 Feb. 43

It would be more useful for me to see the aircraft before it was finally completed, so that I could make any suggestions for minor improvements. Therefore I hope it will come to Northolt next week, with someone who can explain it to me.

2. I am not contemplating any further journeys in the immediate future. Of course it would be a wonderful thing if there could be a pressure chamber fitted, so that an old person like me could make a direct flight to Russia.

Prime Minister to General Ismay, for C.O.S. Committee   10 Feb. 43

How is it that, out of 75,400 Axis troops under Von Arnim, as many as 62,100 are combatants, 10,100 are services, and 3200 are German air forces? How is it that there are seven German combatants to one non-combatant, whereas with us it is pretty well the other way round?

Prime Minister to Foreign Secretary, and to General Ismay,   10 Feb. 43
for C.O.S. Committee

I am thinking about the possibility of another conference in about six or seven months, to which I hope it may be possible to persuade Stalin to come. Cyprus struck me as being very suitable for this purpose. A Budolo ship could of course lie off in one of the ports for communications. A moderate expense in order to make temporary villas would be justifiable. Look what a short distance it is for Stalin.

If you think well of this, please discuss it with the Colonial Secretary, and let me have some idea of the ways and means.

Prime Minister to Major Morton   12 Feb. 43

Please show Lord Selborne the report I had from the S.O.E.[9] section dealing with Yugoslavia. I agree with this report in general terms. I consider it is a matter of the greatest importance to establish the desired closer contacts with the Yugoslav leaders. The number of enemy divisions being contained in these regions is most remarkable.

2. I appealed strongly to General Arnold, as he passed through Cairo, to give us eight more Liberators fitted for discharging paracargoes [cargoes dropped by parachutes] or agents. He was going off the next morning, but gave instructions to General Spaatz. I believe a meeting was held with the S.O.E. people on the subject. I also spoke to General Eisenhower in favour of eight additional aircraft.

3. Pray let me know how the matter stands, and whether there is any-

9 Special Operations Executive.

thing more we can do. If you show me where it is being held up I can probably get the block removed.

Prime Minister to Secretary of State for Foreign Affairs   13 Feb. 43

I am entirely in agreement with your view [about various Anti-Fascist elements in Italy]. There can be no harm in hearing what they have to say, as long as we do not make any commitments. I hope you will bring the matter up again in Cabinet. At any rate, I must inform the President. I have not the slightest doubt that should "Husky" succeed in its early stages the United States will insist, if the opportunity is forthcoming, upon an agreement being made which will put Italy out of the war. I shall support such a movement to the utmost. I am not going to take the responsibility of carrying on this war a day longer than is necessary to achieve full victory.

Prime Minister to Chief of Combined Operations, Paymaster-   16 Feb. 43
General, First Sea Lord, Chief of the Air Staff, and C.-in-C.
Bomber Command

Have you given up all plans of doing anything to *Tirpitz* while she is at Trondheim? We heard a lot of talk about it five months ago, which all petered out. At least four or five plans were under consideration. It seems very discreditable that the Italians should show themselves so much better in attacking ships in harbour than we do.

What has happened to the chariots and to the diving-mines?

I should be much obliged if you would take stock of the position, if possible together, and thereafter give me a report. It is a terrible thing that this prize should be waiting, and no one able to think of a way of winning it.

Prime Minister to General Ismay, for C.O.S. Committee   17 Feb. 43

The Prime Minister desires to express his sincere thanks to the Chiefs of Staff and to the Chief of Combined Operations for the extremely tenacious and persevering efforts they have made to accelerate "Husky." He has approved the consequential telegram, and is drawing the President's personal attention to it.

Prime Minister to General Ismay, for C.O.S. Committee   19 Feb. 43

In view of the delaying attitude adopted by certain Americans towards "Husky," I wish a small Joint Planners' sub-committee and the Chief of Combined Operations department to work out a study of our doing it all alone by ourselves in June, and taking nothing from the United States except landing-craft, escorts, etc. We have four divisions in Tunisia and two on the way or under orders — total six. The Eighth Army can

operate from Tripoli with six. For "Husky" two British divisions from
Persia will be thrown in, making a total of fourteen divisions for an
operation for which requirements were set at nine and a half.

2. There would be great advantages in having it all done by British
troops, with the Americans giving us a hand at the landings, with the air
force, etc. The Americans could then come into the ports we had taken
and go into action without having to go through the training for assault
landings. Anyhow, let us see how this would work out. It would at least
be a spur, in fact a tremendous spur, if we can make the offer.

Prime Minister to General Ismay, Sir Edward Bridges,　　26 Feb. 43
and others concerned

Please note how carefully the orders which I asked General Eisenhower
to give about printing the names of the American aircraft after their
numbers are being carried out by the American Command. Make absolutely sure that we conform. All cases of disobedience to this instruction
should be reported to me, and the offending document sent forward with
the statement of the department or branch responsible for its issue.

Prime Minister to Minister of Works　　　　　　　　27 Feb. 43

Pray accept my warm congratulations on the impressive White Paper
you have just issued about training for the building industry. Building
will certainly be one of the more important and urgent post-war tasks,
affecting practically the whole population in one way or another. I am
glad that you are taking timely steps to plan for it, and are planning
with courage and wide vision. I wish your scheme every success.

I am sending a similar minute to the Minister of Labour and National
Service.

Prime Minister to Home Secretary　　　　　　　　28 Feb. 43

Some time ago I was agreeably surprised by the return you gave me of
the prison population, which had gone up so little in spite of the vast
multiplication of war-time offences. I should be obliged if you would let
me have a fresh return, showing up to date the contrast between now
and the last pre-war year.

Prime Minister to Minister of Agriculture　　　　　　28 Feb. 43

I am not satisfied that it would be a costly business to give the country
more eggs. And it is disturbing to learn that the new cropping programme may lead to a further cut in the present niggardly supply.[10]

The picture you sent me shows that it is more economical to import
dried eggs than the feeding-stuffs required to produce fresh eggs in this

10 See minute of January 12, page 930.

country. The picture is impressive, but would have been more relevant if I had suggested increasing the production of eggs by importing extra cereals.

What I had in mind was the possibility of diverting a few hundred thousand tons out of our millions of tons of feeding-stuffs to hens at the expense of beef cattle. According to my information, this need not involve an undue decline in the output of beef. Moreover, I am told that hens are better converters of protein from a mixed diet than are cattle.

Indeed, there is some reason to believe that no appreciable loss need be incurred. If cereals were taken from the farms, this would merely mean that fewer cattle would be fattened during the winter and more fattened on grass during the summer. The timing of our slaughterings of home-produced cattle would be slightly altered, but the effect would be evened out by a slight alteration in the timing of our import programme or by our releases from stock. I am concerned by the moral as well as the nutritional effects of the drastic reductions we have already made in the supply of shell eggs.

I am greatly distressed that the most remarkable work you have done, to which I took occasion to have official tribute paid, should be marred, even to a partial extent, by failure in this very noticeable field. I wish I could persuade you to try to overcome the difficulties instead of merely entrenching yourself behind them. If you would like to come and talk to me, please do so.

MARCH

Prime Minister to C.I.G.S. and to Director   1 Mar. 43
of Military Intelligence

I have called for the attached comments by the Paymaster-General (Lord Cherwell) about the estimated strength of the German Army. We all seem to be in pretty fair agreement, but I should like to know whether you have any further remarks to make.

2. These data are of great importance, and we should now see how they square with the United States opinion. We should also tell the Russians the views we have formed.

3. The word "division" is becoming a stumbling-block and is no longer any form of yard-stick for measuring between the different countries. It seems to me that it will be necessary to state numbers of men, combatant and gross, as well as divisions.

Prime Minister to Secretary of State for War   2 Mar. 43

I agree with the Deputy Prime Minister's minute about the expenses of military funerals, and I think you should welcome the opportunity of

placing all military funerals, whether of soldiers or of officers, on a satisfactory dignified and honourable basis.

Pray let me have amended proposals more in harmony with the spirit
of the times. I will assist you with the Treasury.

Prime Minister to General Ismay, for C.O.S. Committee   3 Mar. 43

Pray proceed as you propose, but it should be clearly understood that
the military authorities for their part must also pull in their horns. All
our operations are being spoiled by overloading and playing for safety
as a certainty. The "Anakim" demands are altogether excessive. An
operation of war cannot be thought out like building a bridge; certainty
is not demanded, and genius, improvisation, and energy of mind must
have their parts. I am far from satisfied with the way the Indian campaign is being conducted. The fatal lassitude of the Orient steals over
all these commanders. Similarly, "Husky" is being run on the basis of
altogether excessive demands.

Commanders should be made to feel that they have to make some
personal contribution to victory if they are to get any honour out of it.
Everywhere the British and Americans are overloading their operational
plans with so many factors of safety that they are ceasing to be capable
of making any form of aggressive war. For six or eight months to come
Great Britain and the United States will be playing about with half a
dozen German divisions. That is the position to which we are reduced,
and which you should labour sedulously to correct.

Prime Minister to Minister of War Transport   3 Mar. 43

This note from your office about the ban on the transport of flowers
by rail certainly does not give me what I want. I asked that some effort
should be made to ease up this war on the flowers, in which your department is showing an undue relish. What is the difference now, and what
was done last year?

Prime Minister to General Ismay, for C.O.S. Committee   4 Mar. 43

I feel so very conscious of the poor contribution the British and
American Armies are making in only engaging perhaps a dozen German
divisions during the greater part of this year while Stalin is facing 185,
that I should not be prepared myself to court the certain rebuff which
would attend a request for information as to his plans.

Prime Minister to Minister of Production   4 Mar. 43

I am glad you have been able to reduce consumption of raw materials
by 200,000 tons a month during the first six months of 1943 without
serious consequences to the war effort. There has been a great short-fall

in United States help in the first three months, and the resulting serious fall in our stocks makes it essential to reduce our consumption within the narrowest possible limits. I hope therefore that you will press on with the investigation you promise as to the feasibility of increasing these cuts. Pray let me have a report.

Prime Minister to First Lord and First Sea Lord   5 Mar. 43

I am shocked at the renewed disaster to the convoy off the Cape. I thought you had made arrangements for this area and that all had been carefully studied. We have now lost 40,000 tons of shipping. We simply cannot afford losses of this kind on this route. I understood that fifteen or sixteen corvettes and mine-sweeping trawlers had come from Canada. Where are the destroyers which belong to the Eastern Fleet? Are they all sharing the idleness of that fleet? This is a very serious disaster.

THE FUTURE OF THE HOME GUARD

Prime Minister to Secretary of State for War, Lord President,   5 Mar. 43
Minister of Labour, and Home Secretary

My colleagues must not underrate the very serious burden involved in keeping 1,800,000 men under an obligation to do forty-eight hours a month drill and sentry duty lest they and the Army should think the danger of invasion has dwindled and lose keenness. Whatever anyone may say, this extra duty is bound to reduce a man's output. Forty-eight hours a month for 1,800,000 men is equivalent to 350,000 full-time workers.

2. In these circumstances the Commanders should be instructed not to insist on too many exhausting exercises and to release men in large numbers who have reached a reasonable degree of proficiency, especially if they are engaged on agricultural or industrial work. The intensity can easily be increased should the strategic situation change.

Prime Minister to Minister of War Transport   5 Mar. 43

Thank you so much for helping about the flowers.

SMOKE-SCREENS

Prime Minister to Secretary of State for War, Secretary   6 Mar. 43
of State for Air, and Minister of Home Security

I am told by the Minister of Home Security that there is some talk of reducing smoke-screens in this country in order to save man-power. So long as we maintain a large force in A.D.G.B. for protection against the night bomber, it seems a pity to reduce this comparatively economical form of defence.

I should have thought that, as all the installation is available, it is possible to run smoke-screens without much cost in manpower. At present, according to War Office returns, 9000 men are employed full time. I understand that smoke-screens operate on the average only about six nights a month. Surely it should be possible for all but a nucleus of the men engaged on this work to combine it with other duties, rather than having thousands set aside for this purpose alone. Pray let me have proposals.

TRANSPORT OF FLOWERS

Prime Minister to Lord President   6 Mar. 43

I am distressed that your Committee should not have seen their way to agree to any relaxation of the ban on the transport of flowers by train. I recognise that in present circumstances the provision of special trains for flowers cannot be justified; but surely some halfway house can be found between the provision of special facilities and the complete abolition of the traffic.

I should be glad if your Committee would give immediate consideration to an arrangement whereby such limited transport capacity as can properly be made available for flowers, without damage to essential war purposes, and having regard to the hardships and restrictions imposed on the travelling public, can be fairly distributed between the growers. In this way a legitimate outlet would be provided for as high a proportion of the flowers as can be carried to our big cities, and the temptations to a black market diminished.

I trust that this may be considered in conjunction with such other mitigations as the milder winter has rendered possible in our transport situation.

Prime Minister to First Sea Lord   7 Mar. 43

You very kindly last time arranged to take some of the Red Cross stores in the destroyers to Murmansk. How did this work? Did it cause trouble or risk? Could it be repeated?

Prime Minister to General Ismay, for C.O.S. Committee,   10 Mar. 43
to Chief of Combined Operations, and to Director
of Transportation

This matter is being much neglected [piers for use on flat beaches]. Dilatory experiments with varying types and patterns have resulted in our having nothing. It is now nearly six months since I urged the construction of several miles of piers. Was Brigadier Jefferis consulted? If the conditions for "Husky" are much easier than in the Channel, what proposals have you got for them? I was hoping to reduce the strain on landing-craft by the rapid building of these piers. I am very much disappointed.

Let me have now plans for having four miles of piers ready to take part in "Husky," without prejudice to what will have to be done for a "Sledgehammer" operation.

Prime Minister to First Lord   10 Mar. 43

I was naturally distressed at this renewed disastrous outbreak of sinkings off the Cape.[11] I am sure the Admiralty, as ever, are doing their best.

I am hoping the Mediterranean will be open by the end of May for all except troop-carriers, and that the traffic round the Cape will be cut to the smallest proportions.

Prime Minister to Secretary of State for Air   13 Mar. 43
and Chief of the Air Staff

I arranged with General Eisenhower at Algiers that the code numbers of American aircraft should always be followed by their names, the idea being that the names would eventually in practical working supersede the inconvenient code numbers, which are difficult to remember and confusing when mixed up with other figures in a telegram. General Eisenhower immediately issued orders to this effect, and you will see how strictly they are being fulfilled in all American communications.

I have also asked that a similar practice should be followed here. Pray note these two omissions, and take steps to prevent any such recurrence. Meanwhile kindly inform me what are B.25s and what are P.40s.

Prime Minister to Secretary of State for War   13 Mar. 43

Lord Horder spoke to me the other day about the work of the psychiatrists. I asked how many there are, and how much money is involved in their maintenance in the Army. Lord Horder informed me that when the present Adjutant-General held the Northern Command there were many more cases of discharge for physical neurosis than in any other part of the Army. He also stated that the Adjutant-General, I think when holding the Northern Command, desired that each recruit should be asked "with what degree of willingness he had entered the Service." Is it possible that this is true? Considering that we have compulsory service, anything more subversive to morale could hardly be imagined.

Prime Minister to Secretary of State for War   13 Mar. 43

I am prepared in principle to accept your proposals about regimental designations, and orders should be given at once so that they may be issued at the earliest possible moment. It is not necessary to wait until all

11 See minute of March 5, page 936.

are made before any are issued. The combatant infantry units should have precedence.

Prime Minister to Secretary of State for Air   15 Mar. 43
and Chief of the Air Staff

This week a record number, viz., ninety-five, of heavy bombers, Stirlings, Halifaxes, and Lancasters, were delivered by M.A.P. Would you please let me know exactly what will happen to these ninety-five aircraft? Where will they be sent?

In taking a concrete example like this one may be able to find out why it is that a more rapid increase in our Bombing Squadrons does not follow from the output.

Prime Minister to General Ismay, for C.O.S. Committee,   16 Mar. 43
and to Sir Orme Sargent

The sinkings in the South Atlantic bring the question of the Azores again to the fore. You know how keen the President is on establishing Allied control there. It seems hardly likely that at this moment such an event would bring the Germans down on Spain. Now that Mr. Eden is in Washington is the moment for this matter to be discussed over there.

Prime Minister to General Ismay, for C.O.S. Committee   22 Mar. 43

I am thinking of asking the President to send General Marshall out to North Africa, and, if the President agreed, I should propose myself to go with the C.I.G.S., when he has recovered. It may be that this journey should be put off till Bizerta is taken, which I still hope may be well before the end of April.

Further to General Eisenhower's telegram and General Alexander's comments, it would, I think, be most unfortunate to mix British and American troops. It is far better to assign them different spheres, and then there can be no recriminations so long as the Supreme Command is held by an American general. This follows the general principle that "relations are better apart."

I have no doubt myself that I could persuade the New Zealand Government to allow the New Zealand Division to take part in "Husky." What have we told them about "Husky"? I should be ready to send a telegram to Mr. Fraser on the subject if one were drafted for me.

Prime Minister to Home Secretary   22 Mar. 43

Two years ago I asked you about the Prince of Pless, whom you have in Brixton Gaol. He has now been there for three years in all. He is legally by nationality a Pole. His mother was an Englishwoman. I understand he has not been guilty of any subversive activity. I should be glad if you would let me see the whole dossier about him. We can then have a talk.

Prime Minister to Minister of Agriculture and Fisheries   22 Mar. 43

I thought it was understood between us that you and the Paymaster-General would endeavour to reach agreement upon the figures connected with poultry and eggs, or would at any rate bring out clearly the points of difference. However, I have heard no more of the matter, which in due course I intend to bring before the Cabinet, as I hold a very strong view on this subject. Pray therefore let me have during the course of the present week the result of your conversations.

2. I should be glad also if you and the Minister of Food would make me a report on the following suggestion. Suppose we allowed a proportion of the bread, not exceeding 10 per cent to be white bread diluted with not more than 5 per cent of potato flour, how much would be the loss entailed to tonnage savings, and how much of the husks and other tailings now incorporated in our bread would be available for poultry-feeding? I was very sorry that the experiment of using potato flour in bread was abandoned. Certainly the loaf up to 5 per cent seemed far more palatable than those now sold for universal consumption. I should be glad if this matter could be studied in precise detail.

3. Much of the little poultry which is still kept in the country is fed on bread, which is still unrationed. At first sight this would seem an uneconomic process, and I should have thought that it would be better to make a further contribution to feeding-stuffs for the poultry rather than to keep them going with the most expensive form of food, namely, that which has already been prepared for human consumption.

Prime Minister to Minister of Production and Minister   22 Mar. 43
of Works

Pray let me know how you are getting on with the reconditioning of blitzed houses.

Prime Minister to Sir Alexander Cadogan   22 Mar. 43

China is not a World Power equal to Britain, the United States, or Russia, and I am reluctant to subscribe to such statements. The Foreign Secretary will no doubt let us know if he finds any difficulty over there. I do not therefore think it necessary to send this telegram. My speech is perfectly clear, and I do not wish to attempt any explanation of it.

Prime Minister to General Ismay for C.O.S. Committee   25 Mar. 43

The change in the moon dates for "Husky" alters the picture. The delay till July 10 is only a fortnight, and not a month. Provided a good explanation is given of the reasons for the new moon period being chosen, we might have to accept this. Incidentally, if July 10 were taken it gives more chance of running another J.W. convoy, and the date May 7, now fixed as the latest, would be extended to May 22.

No action is required at the moment, except to await Eisenhower's explanation of the change of moon dates.

Prime Minister to Chancellor of the Exchequer   27 Mar. 43

Pray let me know what would be the loss to the revenue if there were to be enforced on the present basis an overriding provision that, whatever the rate of income and super-tax might be, there should always be left five shillings in the pound to the taxpayer. I am only asking this for information, and with no idea of action during the war.

2. What exactly is the position about the Service nest-eggs? I saw a statement the other day in one of the newspapers that it only amounted to £11 4s. But I understood from you that your plan secured them a fair equivalent of the nest-eggs of the higher-paid munitions workers.

APRIL

Prime Minister to Chancellor of the Exchequer   1 Apr. 43

£15,000,000 is an extraordinarily low figure. I had thought it might be about £100,000,000.

2. I am horrified to know that the nest-egg to be given to the troops, parallel to that given to munitions workers, now only amounts to £11 7s. 6d., and is accumulating only at this low rate. I consider myself pledged to the Services that they shall receive, in one form or another, a sum equal to the average nest-eggs of the income-tax-paying munitions workers. I had no idea that this promise of yours, about which I have spoken several times in public, had been whittled away to this paltry sum, and I am quite unable to associate myself with it.

Prime Minister to Minister of Aircraft Production   1 Apr. 43

Thank you for sending me advance figures of aircraft production in March. I congratulate you warmly on the excess production over the programme. The increase in the "heavies" is particularly satisfactory.

Prime Minister to General Ismay, for C.O.S. Committee   2 Apr. 43

Assuming, first, that "Vulcan" [capture of Tunisia] is finished by the end of April, or at worst by May 15, and that no large formed body of German or Italian troops escapes; secondly, that "Husky" takes place on July 10; thirdly, that there are not more than five Italian divisions, aggregating not more than 50,000 combatants, and not more than two German divisions, aggregating 20,000 combatants, total 70,000 combatants, in "Husky"-land, and furthermore that we place seven or eight British and American divisions ashore, at a combatant strength of 15,000 each, total 105,000, and reinforce by another 30,000 British, grand total 135,000;

and, fourthly, that we win the intense battles which the landing involves; how long is the subjugation of the armed forces of the enemy in "Husky"-land estimated to take?

2. In an operation of this kind everything depends upon the initial battle, lasting, say, a week, after which one might reasonably expect that the bulk of the enemy forces would be destroyed, captured, or driven into the mountains. The distances are not great and the resources of the country are small, and once we have the ports and the airfields we should be effectively the masters of "Husky"-land, and be able to disperse by air-power, and sea-power covered by air-power, all attempts by the enemy to reconquer it.

3. Hitherto the capture of "Husky"-land has been regarded as an end in itself; but no one could rest content with such a modest and even petty objective for our armies in the campaign of 1943. "Husky"-land is only a stepping-stone, and we must now begin to study how to exploit this local success. What has been done about this? Every reasonable alternative should be explored. Now that "Anakim" has receded owing to the shipping shortage, Mediterranean operations gain more prominence. If we take the end of July as the date by which we are established in "Husky"-land, what other operations are open? Of course our choice must depend upon what the enemy do. If large German forces are brought down into Italy and Italian morale and will to fight is thereby enhanced, the scale required for the taking of Rome and Naples might be beyond our power. In that case we must be ready with our plans in the Eastern Mediterranean, and put it hard across Turkey to come in with us. We must be ready for an attack on the Dodecanese, and for supporting Turkey if she gets into trouble.

4. If however the Germans do not come, and the Italians crumple, there is no limit to the amount of Italian territory we may overrun. Italy may be forced out of the war. We may become possessed of Sardinia without fighting. Corsica may be liberated. All our available forces, including divisions in Africa not involved in "Husky," will have to be moved northwards into Italy till they come into contact with the Germans on the Brenner or along the French Riviera. How far have these possibilities been studied?

5. Even if Italy remains in the war with a certain amount of German help, we ought, the moment we are masters of "Husky"-land, to try to get a footing both on the toe and heel of Italy. The possession of Taranto as well as of the isthmus governing the toe would confer great advantages upon us. The Italian Fleet would have to decide on which side of Italy it would take refuge. We cannot tell what its position or condition will be as a result of the "Husky" operation. If it has not retreated up the Adriatic before we are masters of "Husky"-land, with our Air Force established there, it will not be able to do so, and will have to content

itself with Spezia and Genoa. In any case, it must be considered a most important objective to get a footing on the Dalmatian coast, so that we can foment the insurgents of Albania and Yugoslavia by weapons, supplies, and possibly Commandos. I believe that, in spite of his present naturally foxy attitude, Mihailovic will throw his whole weight against the Italians the moment we are able to give him any effective help. Evidently great possibilities are open in this theatre.

6. The object of this paper is to request with the utmost urgency the close study of these problems, and to obtain from the Chiefs of Staff their view of what can be done and what it is best to do. I hope this work may be pressed forward with the greatest speed, because the mere capture of "Husky"-land will be a paltry and unworthy result for the campaign of 1943.

Prime Minister to General Ismay, for C.O.S. Committee   2 Apr. 43

It now becomes a matter of capital importance to prevent any large escape of the enemy from the Tunisian tip by sea. No doubt this is engaging the attention of the North African High Command in all its branches. But that is not enough. Occupied from day to day with the conduct of the battle, they may well relegate this vital business to a secondary position in their thoughts. A special study should be made here of all the possibilities open to the enemy and of all the means we can take to frustrate them. This should be ready early next week, and the C.O.S. Committee should consider whether, and in what form, our conclusions should be conveyed to General Eisenhower. I am inclined to think that it might be best to have a formal communication made through the Combined Chiefs of Staffs. However, I await the opinion of the C.O.S. Committee.

Prime Minister to Secretary of State for War   4 Apr. 43

As the war lengthens and the imminence of invasion fades the strain on the Home Guard becomes increasingly severe. Are we making enough of them? Ought there not to be a Home Guard Week or a Home Guard Day? Ought they not to receive public recognition in some way or other, and be made to feel that the nation realises all it owes to these devoted men, who are our standby against seaborne invasion and descents from the air by paratroops? I commend this to you.

2. Another practical way of encouraging them is to give them more ammunition for practice. They take the greatest interest in the practices, and regard them as the measure of the real usefulness of their services. The ammunition shortage period is over. Let me know what are the reserves of .300. They should by now be very big, as the American supply is enormous. In fact, I have not looked at my ammunition returns for

some months on account of the greatly eased situation. I await your proposals for, say, doubling the practice ammunition.

3. I hope that you will think of other ways of helping the Home Guard. They require to be nursed and encouraged at this stage in their life.

Prime Minister to Sir Alexander Cadogan   4 Apr. 43

Talk about a second front cannot be entirely prevented, and in any case is not harmful. On the contrary, if German troops are kept in the West some of the weight is taken off Russia and cover is provided for "Husky."

2. The populations of Europe should receive instructions, through any channels open to us, not to move until they are directed to do so by us, but to make the utmost preparations they can in secret.

Prime Minister to Chancellor of the Exchequer   6 Apr. 43

This nest-egg for the forces must be discussed again by the Cabinet. Meanwhile will you kindly let me know what is the average nest-egg accumulated up to the end of the financial year 1942–43 by the wage-earning income-taxpayers.

Prime Minister to C.I.G.S.   6 Apr. 43

Let me have the details of the calculations which give the Axis forces in Tunisia as 141 battalions. For instance, how many battalions are assigned to the Centauro Division? It certainly seems odd that with 225,000 men they should have almost an equal number of battalions with us, who have very nearly three times that number.

Prime Minister to Lord President, Minister of Town and   6 Apr. 43
Country Planning, Minister Without Portfolio, Chancellor of the Exchequer, and others concerned in the preparation of the Town and Country Planning Bill

From the discussion we had this morning I derived the conviction that the Ministry of Town and Country Planning must have statutory power *now* to compel recalcitrant, obstructive, or merely incompetent county authorities to do what is necessary in the larger interest. Pray let a clause be drafted giving this power, and let this be examined by the same Ministers who have prepared the Bill. The matter can then, in the event of any disagreement, be referred again to the War Cabinet on Friday.

Prime Minister to General Ismay, for C.O.S. Committee   8 Apr. 43

This campaign [in Burma] goes from bad to worse, and we are being completely outfought and out-manoeuvred by the Japanese. Luckily, the small scale of the operations and the attraction of other events has prevented public opinion being directed upon this lamentable scene. We cannot however count on a continuance of this.

When does General Wavell reach this country?

Prime Minister to Foreign Secretary   9 Apr. 43

I think you should see Maisky and tell him that if this sort of poison is to be served out by the Tass Agency from London to Algiers we shall have to ask their correspondents to leave these countries. The Minister of Information tells me it is within our power to close all facilities at a moment's notice. It is intolerable that the Russians should be put wrong in this way, when we are trying our best. Goebbels could not be more malicious. Would you like me to see Maisky before I leave for the country today?

Prime Minister to Secretary of State for War   9 Apr. 43

I should like to spend a morning or afternoon with a typical standard infantry battalion, in order to ascertain exactly the employment of every man in it. Let one be chosen within reasonable distance, and let it be placed at my disposal to check up with their establishment. I want to see for myself exactly how many men are employed on the machine-guns, mortars, anti-tank, signals, kitchens, clerical duties, etc.

They must on no account be warned beforehand, nor must any changes be made in preparation. I am assuming an effective strength of, say, 770.

I could do this one afternoon next week. I should be very glad if you could come with me.

Prime Minister to Secretary of State for Air and Chief of the   10 Apr. 43
Air Staff

These are impressive photographs,[12] given to me by Mr. Geoffrey Lloyd. I should have thought it would be well to have half a dozen installations at different parts of the country, so as to avoid a disaster if a sudden fog comes down upon our returning bombers. Also this would give greater freedom to act on doubtful nights. Will you consult the Chief Bomber, and let me know what he thinks.

2. How are you getting on with your infra-red approach methods?

Prime Minister to Secretary of State for War   10 Apr. 43

I am glad about the ammunition, but I really do not think the rest is good enough. Considering that we may shortly be sending away many of our best divisions, the Home Guard have a vital part to play, and now is the time to give them encouragement and publicity. Every effort must

---

[12] Showing effect before and after lighting the anti-fog device.

be made to make them feel the high importance of their task and how much their work is appreciated. Parades with weapons should be held everywhere, and be inspected by the leading personalities available in each district. Military bands should be lent.

I wonder that you do not throw yourself with delight into a feature of this kind, which would show the style and imagination of your administration of the War Office.

I never used the word "mammoth" about a parade in Hyde Park, and there is no need to use a term of prejudice like that.

2. The Minister of Information should be consulted so as to arrange for the widest publicity in the Press for Home Guard Week or Home Guard Celebration Day. I will certainly send a message, or even, if desired, speak a few sentences over the radio.

3. I am anxious that the enemy should have a vivid impression of the strength of our Home Guard. This will no doubt be conveyed to him by photographs of reviews, and will act as a deterrent on paratroop descents or overseas raids.

4. I send you attached some correspondence which has come into my hands. I take full responsibility for the fact that it is communicated to me at my request. Therefore no measures are to be taken against those concerned or mentioned. How is it we are now taking rifles away from the Home Guard? Now that we are making about 70,000 a month there can be no excuse for depriving men of their weapons.

5. I propose to bring up the general question of the Home Guard at the Cabinet on Monday, and have instructed Sir Edward Bridges to put it on the agenda.

See minute of April 4, pages 943–44.

JEFFERIS SHOULDER GUN

Prime Minister to Secretary of State for War   11 Apr. 43

I am informed that the statement that the P.I.A.T. gun [13] is "a weapon developed by Imperial Chemical Industries which incorporates points of design derived both from the Jefferis shoulder gun and from a similar weapon invented by Lieutenant-Colonel Blacker" is quite incorrect. The principle of absorbing recoil dynamically is of course not new, but Brigadier Jefferis was the first man to make a workable weapon with which a 3-pound projectile could be fired from the shoulder to anything like the distance now achieved. Moreover, the design of the ammunition, which has a far greater penetration than any previous type, was entirely due to his work.

The bombard, which was largely due to Jefferis, was assiduously called the Blacker bombard, though I believe it has now been rechristened. It

[13] See minute of January 9, pages 929–30.

seems therefore a little hard to grudge having Jefferis' name attached to the shoulder gun, especially as everyone speaks of Mills grenades, Stokes guns, Hawkins mines, Kerrison predictors, Northover projectors, etc.

* * * * *

On October 18, 1942, four men from S.O.E. were dropped near the German heavy-water factory at Vermork in Norway. The fighting party flew in next day but their gliders crashed in bad weather and all of them were killed either on landing or later by the Germans.

Six Norwegians were then dropped on February 16, 1943. A week later they found the four men who had survived the first attempt although the weather was very cold and they were half-starved. After a long ski-journey and a rock climb, they crossed a half-frozen torrent and attacked the factory on February 27/28. The German guards did not expect them to come from this direction because the route was so difficult. They were in their hut when the explosions began and did not at first realise what was happening. This gave the party time to escape. Five of them got back safely to Sweden and one stayed in Norway with his wireless set. All of them continued with other activities in Norway and all survived the war. A year's production of "heavy water" [14] had been destroyed.

Prime Minister to Lord Selborne   14 Apr. 43

What rewards are to be given to these heroic men?

* * * * *

Prime Minister to General Ismay, for C.O.S. Committee   14 Apr. 43

I see no reason why the church bells should not ring on Sundays in the ordinary manner to summon worshippers to church. I recommend that this permission be given in time for the Easter celebrations this year.

2. Invasion has become far less likely than in 1940, owing to our great preponderance in the air and the large Army and Home Guard we have well armed at home. Should it occur, it will take one of two forms: (*a*) a seaborne expedition, which if large will certainly attract our prior attention, and if small will be engaged by our coast defences; or (*b*) parachute descents inland.

The scale of a parachute invasion cannot in the circumstances of 1943 or 1944 be very large, on account of the stringency of the enemy's aircraft supply. In any case, the transport aircraft would be picked up by our radiolocation apparatus and engaged by night or day by our fighting aircraft. The certainty of this might indeed prove an effective deterrent on such enterprises. The risk therefore cannot be considered as very serious.

3. Attention is directed to the statement of the Chiefs of Staff that

[14] See Book I, Chapter 22, "My Second Visit to Washington."

there will be no invasion this year, and to my covering minute to the War Cabinet that minor raids, both seaborne and airborne, cannot be excluded.

4. Should a minor raid occur, any persons in the vicinity who may happen to notice it will inform His Majesty's nearest armed forces, who, after having reported the occurrence by telephone or dispatch-rider to superior authority, will take the best steps open to engage the enemy by fire. It is difficult to see how the ringing of the church bells in any particular parish would expedite the above process. Nothing could prevent the state of affairs from becoming rapidly known in the district, when all members of the various services would proceed to execute their prepared and approved plans. There is in my opinion no danger that the announcement that ringing the church bells will no longer play a part in our precautions against invasion would discourage our Home Guard or induce a degree of slothful inertia among the Regular forces.

* * * * *

Prime Minister to General Ismay 15 Apr. 43

I was shown a sketch the other day of a ship with a landing-bridge which Brigadier Jefferis suggested could be used for landing tanks on low cliffs apt to be weakly defended. This proposal seems very attractive, and I hope it is being followed up energetically.

Prime Minister to Secretary of State for War, C.I.G.S., and 15 Apr. 43
C.O.S. Committee

As practically all our landing-craft are being sent to "Husky," and as hardly any American troops will arrive this year and be trained before the weather breaks, we must recognise the fact that no important cross-Channel enterprise is possible this year. This is the fact which dominates action.

2. It is nevertheless highly important that this fact should not become widely known, and that powerful camouflage and cover operations should continue in order to pin the enemy to the French coast and not to discourage our Russian Allies. Therefore no sudden or violent stop should be put upon the "Bolero" preparations.

3. On the other hand, we must not use money and effort unduly for projects which are now impossible in 1943, and about which there is no fixed plan for 1944. The tempo of "Bolero" should be altered, but it should not be closed down. We should aim at a steady building up of American forces in this country for an overseas campaign in 1944. A precise plan should be made to slow down "Bolero" in such a way as to ensure steady progress for a target date not in 1943 but in 1944.

4. This principle also applies to the subdivision of the Home Com-

mands necessary to liberate an expeditionary force. The matter is clearly not so urgent as it was. Nevertheless it would be prudent to have at least one army in hand freed for overseas action, and this should be begun before the autumn. I presume this army would be called the Second Army, and would consist of six divisions. It is quite possible that this army might have to go to the Mediterranean. Alternatively, it may be thought better to carry out the whole plan of disentangling the Commands simultaneously and not to begin the change so soon.

5. Whatever happens, the impression must be steadily given that the American troops are continuing to arrive in large numbers, and nothing must be said or done which appears inconsistent with this conception.

Prime Minister to Minister of Information   16 Apr. 43

The old German film *Baptism of Fire,* which was produced at the beginning of 1940 and which deals with the destruction of Warsaw, was intended to terrorise neutral nations by showing the great power of the German Air Force. This film, considerably shortened and with an English commentary, would in my opinion be very good propaganda. It would show how ruthless the Germans were, and how they were prepared to use the weapon of the air to subjugate all other countries.

Pray consider whether it should not be resuscitated, with some examples of what they are getting now. A very good title would be *The Biter Bit.*

Prime Minister to Secretary of State for War and C.I.G.S.   17 Apr. 43

I am not satisfied about the position of General Freyberg. The services and experience of this officer are so outstanding that he should be promoted to the command of a corps. I cannot agree with the judgments which say, "He is the finest Divisional Commander in the world, but that is the measure of his ability." A man who wins such a position for himself has a right to be tried in the higher command, and the country has a right that a trial should be made of his services.

2. I shall be glad to know what happened when the Xth Corps was added to the New Zealand groups in the flanking movement to El Hamma. Did it pass under Freyberg's command, or did the Xth Corps Commander supersede him? In any case, Freyberg, as Commander of the New Zealand Corps, wrote a dispatch to the New Zealand Government in which he mentioned a large number of other units which were under his command. It therefore looks as if he were in effective command of the whole of this turning movement. If so, he has proved his quality in a sphere much larger than that of a division. I could not help wondering why it was, considering the vital importance of the turning movement, it was left for me to mention his name in the account I gave to the House of Commons.

3. You will have also in your mind the representations made by the New Zealand Government and by Mr. Jones, the Minister of Defence.

Apart from Freyberg's position, to keep him at the head of the New Zealanders when normally he should have received promotion is to bar promotion in that division. Considering the work they have done, there must be brigadiers fit to take command. I should like to be able to tell Mr. Fraser that if the New Zealand Division remains with us we hope that Freyberg will command the XXXth Corps.

Prime Minister to Secretary of State for War   17 Apr. 43

Thank you very much for the effective manner in which you have implemented the Cabinet conclusions about the Home Guard celebrations. You should print and circulate to the Cabinet as early as possible.

Prime Minister to Secretary of State for War   17 Apr. 43

Pray see the attached poster distributed by the Army Bureau of Current Affairs, and the comment which Mr. Bevin made upon it. The poster is a disgraceful libel on the conditions prevailing in Great Britain before the war. With all our shortcomings, conditions in this country were a model to Europe and to many parts of the United States. It is a very wrong thing that the War Office should be responsible for such exaggerated and distorted propaganda. The soldiers know their homes are not like that. As Secretary of State, a political matter of this kind should receive your personal attention. I shall be glad if you will give me an explanation, and of course withdraw the poster forthwith.

2. Generally speaking, it may be necessary to have a Cabinet inquiry into A.B.C.A. Meanwhile let me have a table of the numbers of officers and other personnel employed upon it, and their salaries, together with the total of any other moneys involved.

Prime Minister to Minister of Labour   17 Apr. 43

I entirely agree with your comment on the poster distributed by A.B.C.A. and I have drawn the attention of the Secretary of State for War to it.

THE EQUIPMENT OF THE WEST AFRICAN DIVISION

Prime Minister to C.I.G.S. and Brigadier Jacob   17 Apr. 43

It seems a very questionable policy to have a division of over 22,000 men with only twelve 3.7-inch howitzers for its field artillery. If it is decided that it is only to have mountain or pack artillery, it should nevertheless have its full complement. The employment of a division like this as a tactical unit covering a sector of a front would be impossible unless it was equipped with artillery or unless artillery was supplied from some other source. Infantry without artillery are like cavalrymen without horses, or, now, tanks. Infantry and artillery tactics are interwoven and part of one conception. Of course a very strong development of mortars or short-range artillery might be some substitute.

I am very anxious that if the West African troops go into action they should make a name for themselves.

Prime Minister to General Ismay, for C.O.S. Committee   17 Apr. 43

A German collapse being extremely unlikely and not to be counted upon this year, and neither American reinforcements nor landing-craft being available, we cannot do "Sledgehammer" in 1943. General Morgan should therefore be charged with: (a) Preparation, in concert with Fighter Command and the Chief of Combined Operations, for an amphibious feint, with the object of bringing on an air battle and making the strength of the Metropolitan Air Force count in the general process of air attrition. (b) Camouflage and pretence on the most elaborate scale to help (a) above, and to pin the enemy in the West by keeping alive the expectation of invasion. (c) The gradual building up of "Bolero" and long-term study for "Round-up" in 1944. (d) Month-to-month arrangements in case of a German collapse.

2. General Morgan's organisation does not require to be very large or numerous. There should be large reductions in staff appointments through its replacing the special Planning Staffs of the Commanders-in-Chief located at Norfolk House. I shall be glad to know the extent of the saving in staff officers.

3. "Jupiter" must again be considered as a possibility for January, 1944, or whatever is the best winter month. During the illness of C.C.O., I require weekly reports on "Habbakuk," also a further report on the snow-ploughs force and equipment. How is this getting on?

4. Neither can we exclude the possibility of a German incursion into the Spanish peninsula, and plans should be brought up to date for Anglo-American intervention there on the assumption, now almost certain, that the Spaniards and Portuguese will resist the Germans.

5. The rearrangements of the forces in Great Britain should be adapted to the above purposes rather than to a "Sledgehammer" or "Round-up." We ought to hold the Second Army of, say, six divisions ready for "Jupiter," for the Spanish peninsula, or for further exploitation of "Husky." I should be glad to receive your considered opinion whether it is necessary to proceed to the maximum with the rearrangement of the Home Army during the present year. We must not unduly or prematurely disturb our arrangements for defence against invasion. Whatever is decided, there must be a reduction rather than an increase in the number of staff appointments.

6. The whole of the above should be wrapped up in a vast scheme of cover and camouflage. If it gets about, as I fear it must, that any "Sledgehammer" is off for this year, it should be insinuated that this is part of

our cover, and that the real preparations are going forward. Very large preparations should be made at the embarkation ports, and the assembly of the greatest amount of barges and invasion craft should be made, culminating in July and August. The preparations of the Second Army should be directly related to "Sledgehammer." All this will make a good setting for the feint to provoke an air battle described in paragraph 1 (a).

7. It would perhaps be convenient if the Chiefs of Staff would shape and build the above notes into a report of their proposals, for which Cabinet approval should be obtained.

Prime Minister to Lord Privy Seal and Secretary of State   18 Apr. 43
for the Colonies

Please see the attached letter from Dr. Weizmann [about the Jewish problem]. I cannot agree that the White Paper of 1939 is "the firmly established policy" of His Majesty's present Government. I have always regarded it as a gross breach of faith committed by the Chamberlain Government in respect of obligations to which I was personally a party. Our position is that we have carried on for the time being in the exigencies of war the policy of our predecessors and have made no new pronouncement upon the subject. My position remains strictly that set forth in the speech I made in the House of Commons in the debate on the White Paper. I am sure the majority of the present War Cabinet would never agree to any positive endorsement of the White Paper. It runs until it is superseded.

Prime Minister to Minister of Agriculture and   19 Apr. 43
Minister of Food

I understand you have discontinued the small sugar ration which was allowed to bees, and which in the spring months is most important to their work throughout the whole year.

Pray let me know what was the amount previously allotted. What is the amount of sugar still issued to professional bee-keepers, and what is the saving in starving the bees of private owners?

CHURCH BELLS

Prime Minister to Sir E. Bridges, for all concerned   20 Apr. 43

The ringing of the bells to summon worshippers as described in my answer in Parliament today does not mean that the bells should be rung at odd times for weddings or funerals. This may come in a few months, but not yet. Although the ringing of the bells will no longer have the significance of invasion, this idea has been so sedulously inculcated that unexpected ringing at unusual times might cause alarm. I presume the existing powers can be modified accordingly, as the greater includes the less. If need be a special regulation can be made.

TANK SUPPLY POLICY

Part I

Prime Minister to Sir Edward Bridges, and to   **23 Apr. 43**
Brigadier Jacob for Defence Committee (Supply) and others

Practically the whole of the tank production and arrivals for 1943 are beyond our control, and we should approve the figures set out.

2. It seems however of the highest importance to have some thicker armour on a proportion of our tanks. At least 200 and preferably 400 Churchills should be fitted with the heaviest armour possible, at a sacrifice of speed down to eight or even six miles an hour or less. Let me have a definite programme for conversions of this kind, showing what is achieved, what must be paid in speed, how many will be treated, and when they will be finished. At least a hundred should be pushed forward as an emergency job.

3. We shall, I am sure, be exposed to criticism if we are found with a great mass of thin-skinned tanks of medium size, none of which can stand up to the German guns of 1943, still less to those of 1944. The idea of having a spear-point or battering-ram of heavily armoured vehicles to break the enemy's front and make a hole through which the lighter vehicles can be pushed has a very high military significance. A certain number of such vehicles should be attached to armies, and possibly even to corps, in each theatre. The wart-hog must play his part as well as the gazelle.

4. The experimental development of a heavy tank — 60, 70, or 80 tons — cannot be laid aside. Occasions will almost certainly arise when it would be a solution of particular problems. We shall be much to blame if the necessity appears and we are found to have fallen behind the enemy. Pray let me have a report on the Stern tank or any alternative that can be devised. What has happened to the amphibious tank? Surely a float or galosh can be made to take a tank of the larger size across the Channel under good conditions once a beach landing has been secured.

Part II

5. I was not convinced in favour of the widespread adoption of the 75-mm. gun, and a further meeting of the Defence Committee on this subject must take place before any decision is taken. For us this gun, which is the same as that mounted in the Shermans, is a new weapon. I understand that preparations for manufacture have already started. Report to what point they have reached. What arrangements are made for the ammunition on the scale of tank armament proposed? What amounts can be manufactured in the United Kingdom in 1943 and 1944? Are we to rely entirely upon supplies from America? Is it true that they **are**

turning from the 75-mm. medium velocity gun to the 76-mm. high velocity gun? If so, will they not regard this class of ammunition as obsolescent?

6. The 95-mm. tank howitzer, on the other hand, is already in production here. A detailed statement should be prepared, on one sheet of paper, showing the nature and qualities of both the 75-mm. (Sherman type) and the 95-mm. (British type). Also, an estimate should be prepared by the Ministry of Supply showing the relative deliveries of these weapons and their ammunition which would become effective in 1943 and 1944 if decisions were taken before the end of the month. These tables should be got ready for an early meeting of the Defence Committee.

7. Reports from the Middle East Army are of great interest so far as tactical operations in the Desert are concerned, and also generally. It must be remembered however that they have not seen the alternatives to the 75-mm. gun. They have only very recently had any H.E. ammunition for the 6-pounder. They have never seen the 95-mm. tank howitzer. We must be sure that this question is studied in all its bearings, or we may find ourselves lumbered up with obsolescent patterns, and thus be held most blameworthy.

Prime Minister to First Sea Lord   23 Apr. 43

What has happened to our aircraft-carrier that went to the American Fleet in the Pacific? Have we had any reports from her?

Pensions for Widows of Soldiers killed while on Leave

Prime Minister to Minister of Pensions   23 Apr. 43

How much would it cost to meet the point fully? My own feeling is that we should see the widow through, unless it is proved the accident was due to the man's misconduct. After all, a certain amount of leave, although not in any contract of service, is a recognised part of a soldier's life.

Probably the sum is petty when the ordinary widows' pensions have been taken into account, but these irritating distinctions do great harm, and I am sure expose you to many worries.

Prime Minister to C.I.G.S.   24 Apr. 43

Appointment of General Freyberg to the next vacant corps.
I am very glad, and think it only an act of justice.

Prime Minister to Secretary of State for War and   25 Apr. 43
Minister of Works

I am informed that arrangements had been made for weekly and week-end courses to be given in Balliol College, Oxford, for Dominions and American troops, where the university atmosphere would be particularly valuable in giving these troops from overseas a further insight into English life and history. I understand that this proposal is in jeopardy because the War Office are proposing to take over Balliol College for a senior officers' course.

I am sure that Balliol College would be of more value in the former rôle, and I can hardly believe that no alternative accommodation for the War Office could be found. Let me have a report on some of the alternatives.

MAY

Prime Minister to Chief of the Air Staff 1 May 43

I asked Monsieur Maisky last week to explain to me why the Russians had not accepted our twenty squadrons, with their personnel, as proposed in "Velvet." He replied that they understood about 25,000 men would be required to maintain these squadrons on the British and American scales, and this seemed too great a strain upon their resources in proportion to the fighting assistance that would be obtained. Even at the figure now given me by the Air Ministry of, say 20,000, it would be 1000 men per squadron, of which 11,750 would be British.

Please let me have a full explanation of why it is necessary that 11,750 British personnel should be required to man fourteen squadrons. Who made this calculation, and who approved it? How does it compare with air establishments in other quarters?

Prime Minister to Sir Edward Bridges and General Ismay 2 May 43

It is time to have another tone-up of security arrangements. Please draft me a circular for the more secret circles of all Government departments, dealing with the following points:

(*a*) Experience has shown that danger of leakage occurs through a habit of having secret papers placed in "In" or "Out" trays on the desks of important officers and in the rooms of private secretaries to Ministers. Every person to whom secret papers are sent should always have on his table a flat box with a snap-lock, and should make a practice of snapping it down himself at any moment when the paper is not in use.

(*b*) The practice of carrying secret documents in the pocket should be forbidden. A larger number of boxes with snap-locks should be brought into use.

(*c*) All existing boxes used for secret papers should be fitted as quickly as possible with snap-locks. A programme for doing this should be prepared.

2. Side by side with this you should make a further pruning of the number of people included in each particular secret circulation. Let me have a plan aiming at 25 per cent reduction.

3. How is your plan to cut down the number of committees, in response to a minute which I sent out about three months ago, getting on? We must have a good tightening up and pruning all round.

Prime Minister to First Lord, First Sea Lord,   2 May 43
and General Ismay

The activities of the motor torpedo-boats from Malta and Sousse are becoming extremely important. Can we not strengthen them? What is there at Malta? What is there in Alexandria? Are there any more suitable vessels that can be sent to Malta, Tripoli, or Sousse? I presume all this can be settled by Cunningham without further reference here. Let me know what he is doing.

I should be willing to send a message to the M.T.B.s, who seem to be putting up an extremely sporting fight.

2. There is a question whether all these fast small craft should not have a name. I have thought of them as the "Mosquito Fleet," but would it not be more dignified to call them the "Hornet Fleet"? Or, again, perhaps the "Shark Fleet" — "Sharks" for short.

FIRST ARMY BATTLE CASUALTIES

Prime Minister to C.I.G.S.   3 May 43

You should notice that 75 per cent of the latest losses fall on the Foot Guards and the rifle-armed infantry, while practically no loss is inflicted on the administrative services.

Taking the longer period, there is nearly 64 per cent in the Foot Guards and rifle-armed infantry. All the [other] categories together only make up 1443 officers and men.

If you contrast these figures and proportions with the reinforcements by units which have been sent during April and are to be sent during May, the extraordinary disparity becomes manifest.

Who is responsible for making out these drafts, and what instructions have been given him?

The picture unfolded at present is that the fighting troops are not being replaced effectively, although masses of drafts are sent to the technical and administrative services, who were originally on the most lavish scale, and who have since hardly suffered at all by the fire of the enemy. The first duty of the War Office is to keep up the rifle infantry strength.

Prime Minister to Minister of Aircraft Production   4 May 43

I was surprised to learn that the Secretary of State for Air was not invited to attend the display of aircraft which you gave me a fortnight ago. I only heard of this indirectly, as he himself made no comment upon it. Of course he has long known all about the "Squirt" [jet plane]. It would not be proper constitutionally for the Chief of the Air Staff to be invited to such a demonstration without his Secretary of State being invited too. The C.A.S. of course told him beforehand, as they work in the closest confidence. The First Lord should also have been invited, if the First Sea Lord was.

Prime Minister to Minister of Production   5 May 43

In considering the allocation of building labour please bear in mind that it is most important to complete the airfields required for the American Air Force.

Prime Minister to General Ismay   11 May 43

Have the Secretary of State for War's proposals been agreed to by the C.I.G.S.? If so, I am disposed to tell the Secretary of State for War by telegraph that he should go ahead with this organisation, aiming at an increase of 72 men instead of 36 in the rifle strength of the infantry battalions.

Prime Minister (Washington) to General Ismay,   12 May 43
for C.O.S. Committee, and to Lord Leathers

What is being done to start the trans-Mediterranean convoy? When does it leave England? Admiral Cunningham asked for a fortnight after the fall of Bizerta. Therefore by the end of May the convoy should be passing Gibraltar. What is the earliest date it can start from England? Have the ships been already loaded with the special cargo? I have promised the Red Cross Aid for Russia Fund 1000 tons for high-grade medical stores. Are all the aeroplanes ready boxed and loaded? What about the Turkish consignment? I wish to send a telegram to England today speeding all this up. We must not lose an hour of the windfall of time which has come to us.

Prime Minister to General Ismay, for Chiefs   21 May 43
of Staff Committee

I should be prepared to go further as follows:

"Statements will be made in public (possibly by the President and the Prime Minister) making it perfectly clear that the Italian people would have a free and independent life as one of the historic nations of Europe. We wish to see Italy freed from its Fascist tyranny, to resume its place, under a democratic system, as a member of the European family. In these months Italy has a last chance of avoiding the further tribulations which will otherwise fall upon her."

The Army propaganda should work in harmony with this theme.

Appendix B, Book Two

PROMISES ABOUT POST-WAR CONDITIONS

Note by the Prime Minister

12 Jan. 43

A dangerous optimism is growing up about the conditions it will be possible to establish here after the war. Unemployment and low wages are to be abolished, education greatly improved and prolonged; great developments in housing and health will be undertaken; agriculture is to be maintained at least at its new high level. At the same time the cost of living is not to be raised. The Beveridge plan of social insurance, or something like it, is to abolish want. The money which the wage-earning classes have saved during the war in nest-eggs or accumulated by War Savings Certificates must not lose its value.

2. Our foreign investments have almost disappeared. The United States will be a strong competitor with British shipping. We shall have great difficulties in placing our necessary exports profitably. Meanwhile, in order to help Europe, we are to subject ourselves to a prolonged period of rationing and distribute a large part of our existing stocks. We are to develop the tropical Colonies and raise the condition of their inhabitants. We must clearly keep a large Air Force and Navy, so as not to be set upon again by the Germans, and large military forces will be needed to garrison the enemy countries and make sure they do not begin again to rearm for revenge.

3. The question steals across the mind whether we are not committing our forty-five million people to tasks beyond their compass, and laying on them burdens beyond their capacity to bear. While not disheartening our people by dwelling on the dark side of things, Ministers should, in my view, be careful not to raise false hopes, as was done last time by speeches about "homes for heroes," etc. The broad masses of the people face the hardships of life undaunted, but they are liable to get very angry if they feel they have been gulled or cheated. If, for instance, we raise the old age pensions to £2 and other insurance benefits proportionately, and then, owing to a decline in the purchasing power of money, they find that the £2 buys no more than the 10s. formerly did, or that their nest-egg or War Savings Certificates only in fact yield a quarter of the sweat and

effort which their accumulation entailed, they will feel a sense of griev-
ance quite different from the pangs endured by mankind in its inevitable
struggle for existence. It is because I do not wish to deceive the people
by false hopes and airy visions of Utopia and Eldorado that I have
refrained so far from making promises about the future.

4. We must all do our best, and we shall do it much better if we are
not hampered by a cloud of pledges and promises which arise out of the
hopeful and genial side of man's nature and are not brought into relation
with the hard facts of life.

THE BEVERIDGE REPORT

NOTE BY THE PRIME MINISTER

14 Feb. 43

I think we should handle this matter in the following way, which I
gather from the reports I have seen is very much what my colleagues
desire.

1. This approach to social security, bringing the magic of averages
nearer to the rescue of the millions, constitutes an essential part of any
post-war scheme of national betterment.

2. There may be portions of it which would probably not be found
workable or acceptable, and these we have indicated in the speeches made
in this debate. It is desirable however that should the measure be produced it should be an integral conception and not merely what is left
after the critics have pulled out certain weak points.

3. There should be a body — if necessary a Commission — set up to
work from now till the end of the war, polishing, reshaping, and preparing for the necessary legislation.

4. We cannot however initiate the legislation now or commit ourselves
to the expenditure involved. That can only be done by a responsible
Government and a House of Commons refreshed by contact with the people.
We do not know what conditions will be at the end of the war, or how
the expenditure on social insurance will fit in with other social expenditure desired, or how this group of betterment expenditure can be reconciled with the need for maintaining strong naval and air forces and a
certain military force for a considerable time. We do not know what
Government is going to be in power after the war, or what Prime Minister.
We should get everything ready for them, and leave them a free hand to
take up or reject a scheme which will be perfect in itself.

5. We must not forget that we are a Parliament in the eighth year,

and we have been justified in prolonging our existence only by the physical fact of the war situation and for the purposes of the war. We have no right whatever to tie the hands of future Parliaments in regard to social matters which are their proper province. I could not as Prime Minister be responsible at this stage for binding my successor, whoever he may be, without knowledge of the conditions under which he will undertake his responsibilities.

Appendix C, Book Two

MINISTERIAL APPOINTMENTS FOR THE YEAR 1943

(Members of the War Cabinet are shown in italics.)

Prime Minister and First Lord of the Treasury, Minister of Defence	*Mr. Winston S. Churchill*
Admiralty, First Lord of the	Mr. A. V. Alexander
Agriculture and Fisheries, Minister of	Mr. R. S. Hudson
Air, Secretary of State for	Sir Archibald Sinclair
Aircraft Production, Minister of	Sir Stafford Cripps
Burma, Secretary of State for	Mr. L. S. Amery
Chancellor of the Duchy of Lancaster	(a) Mr. A. Duff Cooper
	(b) Mr. Ernest Brown (appointed November 17)
Chancellor of the Exchequer	(a) Sir Kingsley Wood
	(b) *Sir John Anderson* (appointed September 28)
Colonies, Secretary of State for the	Colonel Oliver Stanley
Dominions Affairs, Secretary of State for	(a) *Mr. Clement Attlee* (also Deputy Prime Minister)
	(b) Viscount Cranborne (appointed September 28)
Economic Warfare, Minister of	Earl of Selborne
Education, President of the Board of	Mr. R. A. Butler
Food, Minister of	(a) Lord Woolton
	(b) Colonel J. J. Llewellin (appointed November 12)
Foreign Affairs, Secretary of State for	*Mr. Anthony Eden*
Fuel and Power, Minister of	Major G. Lloyd George
Health, Minister of	(a) Mr. Ernest Brown
	(b) Mr. H. U. Willink (appointed November 17)
Home Department, Secretary of State for the, and Home Security, Minister of	*Mr. Herbert Morrison*
India, Secretary of State for	Mr. L. S. Amery
Information, Minister of	Mr. Brendan Bracken
Labour and National Service, Minister of	*Mr. Ernest Bevin*
Law Officers:	
Attorney-General	Sir Donald Somervell
Lord Advocate	Mr. J. S. C. Reid
Solicitor-General	Sir David Maxwell-Fyfe
Solicitor-General for Scotland	Sir David King Murray
Lord Chancellor	Viscount Simon

961

Lord President of the Council	(a) *Sir John Anderson* (b) *Mr. Clement Attlee* (appointed September 28) (Also Deputy Prime Minister)
Lord Privy Seal	(a) Viscount Cranborne (b) Lord Beaverbrook (appointed September 28)
Minister of State	Mr. R. K. Law (appointed September 25) (Lord Beaverbrook ceased to be Minister of State on June 29, 1941. Mr. Oliver Lyttelton was appointed Minister of State (in the Middle East) on July 1, 1941, and was succeeded in that office by Mr. R. G. Casey. On the appointment of Mr. R. K. Law as Minister of State on September 25, 1943, the title of the Middle East office was changed to "Minister of State Resident in the Middle East.")
Minister without Portfolio	Sir William Jowitt (Following his appointment as Minister without Portfolio on December 30, 1942, Sir William Jowitt continued to carry out the duties in regard to post-war reconstruction problems hitherto performed by him as Paymaster-General. He then assisted the Minister of Reconstruction as from November 12, 1943, when that office was created, until he (Sir William Jowitt) was appointed Minister of National Insurance on November 18, 1944, when the office of Minister without Portfolio lapsed.)
Paymaster-General	(a) Sir William Jowitt (b) Lord Cherwell (appointed December 20, 1942)
Pensions, Minister of	Sir Walter Womersley
Postmaster-General	(a) Mr. W. S. Morrison (b) Captain H. F. C. Crookshank (appointed February 6)
Production, Minister of	*Mr. Oliver Lyttelton*
Reconstruction, Minister of	*Lord Woolton* (appointed November 12) (The office of Minister of Reconstruction was created on November 12, 1943.)
Scotland, Secretary of State for	Mr. Thomas Johnston
Supply, Minister of	Sir Andrew Duncan
Town and Country Planning, Minister of	Mr. W. S. Morrison (appointed February 5) (The office of Minister of Town and Country Planning was created on February 5, 1943. The Minister assumed the duties in regard to town and country planning hitherto carried out by the Minister of Works and Planning.)

Trade, President of the Board of
War, Secretary of State for
War Transport, Minister of
Works, Minister of

Mr. Hugh Dalton
Sir James Grigg
Lord Leathers
Lord Portal
(Following the transfer of duties in re-
gard to town and country planning to
the Minister of Town and Country
Planning on February 5, 1943, the title
was changed from "Minister of Works
and Planning" back to "Minister of
Works.")

Ministers Overseas:
Middle East, Minister of State Resident in the

Mr. R. G. Casey (until December 23)
(On the appointment of Mr. R. K. Law
as "Minister of State" on September 25,
1943, the title of the office was changed
to "Minister of State Resident in the
Middle East.")

Washington, Minister Resident for
Supply in

(a) Colonel J. J. Llewellin
(b) Mr. Ben Smith (appointed November 12)

Allied Force Headquarters, Mediterranean Command, Minister Resident at

Mr. Harold Macmillan (appointed December 30, 1942)

West Africa, Minister Resident in
Middle East, Deputy Minister of
State Resident in the

Viscount Swinton

Lord Moyne
(The office of Deputy Minister of State
(in the Middle East) was created on
August 28, 1942. On the appointment
of Mr. R. K. Law as Minister of State
on September 25, 1943, the title of the
office was changed to "Deputy Minister
of State Resident in the Middle East.")

House of Lords, Leader of the
House of Commons, Leader of the

Viscount Cranborne
Mr. Anthony Eden

Appendix D, Book Two

LIST OF SOME OF THE SENIOR OFFICERS OF THE BRITISH AND UNITED STATES FORCES HOLDING HIGH APPOINTMENTS, 1942–43

(The ranks and appointments given are those appropriate to the period covered by this volume.)

ROYAL NAVY

Admiral of the Fleet Sir A. B. Cunningham	C.-in-C. Mediterranean; Head of British Admiralty Delegation, Washington
Admiral Sir B. A. Fraser	C.-in-C. Home Fleet
Admiral Sir H. Harwood	C.-in-C. Mediterranean; C.-in-C. Levant
Admiral Sir M. Horton	C.-in-C. Western Approaches
Admiral Sir G. Layton	C.-in-C. Eastern Fleet; C.-in-C. Ceylon
Vice-Admiral Sir H. Moore	Vice-Chief of the Naval Staff
Vice-Admiral Lord Louis Mountbatten	Chief of Combined Operations
Admiral Sir P. Noble	C.-in-C. Western Approaches; Head of British Admiralty Delegation, Washington
Admiral of the Fleet Sir D. Pound	First Sea Lord and Chief of the Naval Staff
Admiral Sir J. Somerville	C.-in-C. Eastern Fleet
Vice-Admiral Sir E. N. Syfret	Flag Officer Commanding Force H
Admiral Sir J. Tovey	C.-in-C. Home Fleet

ROYAL AUSTRALIAN NAVY

Admiral Sir G. C. C. Royle	First Naval Member Australian Naval Board

ROYAL CANADIAN NAVY

Vice-Admiral P. W. Nelles, R.C.N.	Chief of Naval Staff

UNITED STATES NAVY

Admiral W. F. Halsey	Commander United States Naval Forces, South Pacific
Vice-Admiral H. K. Hewitt	Commander United States Naval Forces, Mediterranean
Admiral R. E. Ingersoll	C.-in-C. Atlantic Fleet
Fleet Admiral E. J. King	C.-in-C. United States Fleet and Chief of Naval Operations

Admiral C. W. Nimitz	C.-in-C. Pacific Fleet
Admiral R. A. Spruance	Chief of Staff to C.-in-C. Pacific
Admiral H. R. Stark	Commander United States Naval Forces in Europe

BRITISH AND DOMINIONS ARMIES

General Sir H. R. Alexander	G.O.C. Burma; C.-in-C. Middle East; Deputy C.-in-C. North African Theatre of Operations
Lieut.-General Sir K. A. N. Anderson	G.O.C. First Army
General Sir C. J. E. Auchinleck	C.-in-C. Middle East
General Sir T. A. Blamey	G.O.C. Australian Imperial Forces, Middle East
General Sir A. F. Brooke	Chief of the Imperial General Staff
Field-Marshal Sir J. G. Dill	Head of British Joint Staff Mission, Washington
Lieut.-General Sir W. G. S. Dobbie	Governor of Malta
Major-General B. C. Freyberg	Commander 2nd New Zealand Division
Field-Marshal Viscount Gort	Governor of Gibraltar; Governor of Malta
General Sir A. F. Hartley	C.-in-C. India; Deputy C.-in-C. India
Lieut.-General Sir T. H. Hutton	G.O.C. Burma
Lieut.-General Sir H. L. Ismay	Chief Staff Officer to the Minister of Defence
General A. G. L. McNaughton	Commander Canadian Corps, Home Forces
General Sir B. L. Montgomery	G.O.C. Eighth Army
Lieut.-General Sir A. E. Nye	Vice-Chief of the Imperial General Staff
Lieut.-General A. E. Percival	G.O.C. Malaya
Lieut.-General Sir W. Platt	G.O.C.-in-C. East Africa
Lieut.-General Sir H. R. Pownall	C.-in-C. Far East; Chief of Staff A.B.D.A. Command; G.O.C. Ceylon; C.-in-C. Persia and Iraq
Lieut.-General N. M. Ritchie	G.O.C. Eighth Army
General Sir A. P. Wavell	Supreme Commander A.B.D.A. Command; C.-in-C. India
General Sir H. M. Wilson	C.-in-C. Persia and Iraq; C.-in-C. Middle East

UNITED STATES ARMY

Lieut.-General M. W. Clark	Commanding General U.S. Fifth Army
General D. D. Eisenhower	Allied C.-in-C. North African Theatre of Operations
General D. MacArthur	C.-in-C. Philippines; Supreme Commander S.W. Pacific
General G. C. Marshall	Chief of Staff U.S. Army
Lieut.-General G. S. Patton	Commanding General U.S. Seventh Army
Major-General Bedell Smith	Chief of Staff North African Theatre of Operations

ROYAL AIR FORCE

Air Vice-Marshal A. Coningham	A.O.C. Western Desert
Air Chief Marshal Sir S. Douglas	A.O.C.-in-C. Fighter Command
Air Marshal Sir A. T. Harris	A.O.C.-in-C. Bomber Command
Air Chief Marshal Sir P. Joubert de la Ferté	A.O.C.-in-C. Coastal Command
Air Marshal Sir T. Leigh Mallory	A.O.C.-in-C. Fighter Command
Air Vice-Marshal H. P. Lloyd	A.O.C. Malta
Air Chief Marshal Sir R. E. C. Peirse	A.O.C.-in-C. A.B.D.A. Command; A.O.C.-in-C. India
Air Chief Marshal Sir C. F. A. Portal	Chief of the Air Staff
Air Marshal Sir J. C. Slessor	A.O.C.-in-C. Coastal Command
Air Marshal Sir A. W. Tedder	A.O.C.-in-C. Mediterranean

UNITED STATES ARMY AIR FORCE

General H. H. Arnold	Chief of the Army Air Force
General I. A. Eaker	Commanding General U.S. VIII Bomber Command
General C. A. Spaatz	Commanding General U.S. VIII Army Air Force; Commanding General N.W. African Air Force

INDEX